INTELLIGENT SYSTEMS IN DESIGN AND MANUFACTURING

ASME PRESS SERIES ON INTERNATIONAL ADVANCES IN DESIGN PRODUCTIVITY

Editor:

K. M. Ragsdell, University of Missouri – Rolla, Rolla, Missouri, U.S.A.

Advisory Board:

Don P. Clausing, Massachusetts Institute of Technology,
Cambridge, Massachusetts, U.S.A.

Stuart Pugh, University of Strathclyde, Glasgow, Scotland

Genichi Taguchi, Ohken Associates, Tokyo, Japan

Other Books in the Series:

Total Quality Development, by Don P. Clausing, 1994

Taguchi on Robust Technology Development, by Genichi Taguchi,
translated by S.-C. Tsai, 1993

Intelligent Engineering Systems Through Artificial Neural Networks, Volume 3,
edited by Cihan H. Dagli, Laura I. Burke, Benito R. Fernández, and Joydeep Ghosh, 1993

Intelligent Engineering Systems Through Artificial Neural Networks, Volume 2,
edited by Cihan H. Dagli, Laura I. Burke, and Yung C. Shin, 1992

Intelligent Engineering Systems Through Artificial Neural Networks, Volume 1,
edited by Cihan H. Dagli, Soundar R. T. Kumara, and Yung C. Shin, 1991

ASME PRESS SERIES ON
INTERNATIONAL ADVANCES IN DESIGN PRODUCTIVITY

INTELLIGENT SYSTEMS IN DESIGN AND MANUFACTURING

EDITED BY

Cihan H. Dagli
Department of Engineering Management
University of Missouri – Rolla
Rolla, Missouri

Andrew Kusiak
Department of Industrial and Management Engineering
University of Iowa
Iowa City, Iowa

ASME PRESS
New York, 1994

Library of Congress Cataloging-in-Publication Data

Intelligent systems in design and manufacturing / editors, Cihan H.
Dagli, Andrew Kusiak.
    p. cm.
Includes bibliographical references and index.
ISBN 0-7918-0034-2
1. Engineering design — Data processing.   2. Computer-aided design.
3. CAD/CAM systems.   4. Manufacturing processes — Data processing.
5. Intelligent control systems.   I. Dagli, Cihan H., 1949– .
II. Kusiak, Andrew

TA174.I4688   1994
620'.0042'0285 — dc20   94-11140
                                                          CIP

Table of Contents

Foreword

Professors Cihan Dagli and Andrew Kusiak have produced a book, *Intelligent Systems in Design and Manufacturing*, which should be on the required reading list for all serious students of modern design. Over time we have learned the importance of the design phase of the product development process. The "80–20 rule" tells us that 80% of the cost of a product is the result of decisions made in the first 20% of the product development process. Clearly our products and services cannot be better than our designs.

The editors have organized the book into three sections:

(1) Part I—Engineering Design: Basic Concepts and Tools
(2) Part II—Concurrent Engineering: Use of Intelligent Systems
(3) Part III—Design in Manufacturing

in which there are seventeen chapters contributed by the leading experts in the field delimiting modern issues in design and manufacturing.

The content of the individual chapters of this book is sufficient to justify careful reading. On the other hand, the concatenation of the chapters and the development of the major themes sets the book apart as a significant contribution to the field.

Ken Ragsdell
University of Missouri—Rolla

Preface

Becoming and remaining competitive in global markets today depends on a number of abilities: to respond quickly to market changes, to have short product life cycles, to get the first product right, and to maintain large product variety. Methods used for product design have a definite impact on these attributes as the final design makes up sixty to eighty-five percent of the total manufacturing cost. This book introduces the reader to various problems in engineering design and basic tools for the improvement of design processes, stresses the need for intelligent systems, demonstrates their performance in design and manufacturing using practical examples, and examines the basic tools for building such systems.

Since design problems are complex and not well understood, it is not to be expected that they can be solved with one set of tools. Many aspects of design problems are of a qualitative nature, and thus a knowledge-based approach is well-crafted for solving them. Therefore, a knowledge-based approach, neural networks, and other artificial intelligence tools are emphasized throughout the book. The material covered in this book fills the gap between the two more direct approaches visible in engineering design literature: the first based on design experience, and the other stems from optimization. The carefully selected chapters show specific design problems, discuss their features, and point out rational ways of solving the problems. The content of the book and the level of material presentation is appropriate to practicing design and manufacturing engineers, systems engineers, analysts, managers, and students. A reader will not only be able to understand the major issues in engineering design and their impact on manufacturing, but also will get an appropriate assessment of suitable tools and techniques.

It would not be possible to compile this volume without the efforts of many people. First of all, we would like to thank the authors for their contributions and patience during the initial stages of the project. Second, we would like to thank Susan Pearson for her tireless and dedicated efforts in preparing the first draft of the manuscript. Third, our sincere thanks to Janet Weinrib of ASME Press for valuable discussion and collaborations, along with Ellen R. Kadin of ASME Press for her editorial assistance. Last, but more important, we would like to thank our families for their support and understanding throughout the preparation of this book.

Cihan H. Dagli
University of Missouri—Rolla

Andrew Kusiak
University of Iowa

PART I

Engineering Design:
Basic Concepts and Tools

Engineering design is essentially the process of converting the desires and needs of the customer into detailed specifications for a useable end product. It is a highly knowledge intensive and time-consuming activity which requires a great many decisions and judgements on the part of the human designer. It is also an imprecise art, since each designer differs in background, experience, preferences, and formal training. The more knowledge and experience the designers have, the better the chances for generating creative designs. Final product design impacts sixty to eighty-five percent of the total manufacturing cost. Hence, thorough analysis of design alternatives is essential prior to the finalization of the product design process. This is not an easy task as the number of possible design solutions increases exponentially as new functional requirements and manufacturing constraints are introduced. The NP-complete (non polynomial in time) characteristic of the design problem necessitates different search strategies in selecting the final design creating a wide variety of approaches adopted by researchers. How does an artifact get designed? How do fuzzy mental images and abstract concepts get converted to the crisp design: The process is not well understood at this time. Each researcher approaches the problem in a different way in an effort to generate the best design to satisfy functional requirements.

Coyne defines design as a purposeful activity which involves a conscious effort to arrive at a state of affairs in which certain characteristics are evident. Suh defines design as three distinct aspects of engineering and scientific endeavor: problem definition from fuzzy sets of facts and myths into a coherent state of the question, creative and analytical process of devising a proposed physical embodiment of solutions, and ultimate check of the fidelity of the design product to the original perceived needs. The main source of confusion about "engineering design" is that it lacks the sufficient scientific foundations. Dixon argues that without an adequate base of scientific principles, engineering design education and practice are guided too much by the specialized empiricism, intuition and experience. Simon argues that the science of design is possible, and that it will be possible to talk in terms of well-established theories and practices in the future. Some researchers conclude design is at a "pre-science" phase, and that it must go through several phases before it constitutes a "mature" science, is that state of a discipline in which there is a coherent tradition of scientific research and practice, embodying law, theory, application and instrumentation.

Coyne contends that in order to achieve the kind of maturity required, there is a need to borrow the methodologies from other disciplines that have reached "full-fledged" science. One can define, study, and understand the design activity by borrowing from other disciplines such as artificial intelligence and problem solving, namely; space search techniques, expert systems, artificial neural networks, fuzzy logic, genetic algorithms, and object-oriented methodology.

Literature on design clearly states there is no single model that can provide a perfect or at least a satisfactory definition of the design process. One must look at the design from various angles in order to grasp a better understanding of the process. Approaches proposed by Suh, Tomiyama, and Yoshikawa represent the general framework adopted by the researchers for the solution of the design problem.

Suh defines design as the culmination of synthesized solutions in the form of product, software, processes, or system by the appropriate selection of design parameters that satisfy perceived needs through the mapping from functional requirements in the function domain to design parameters in the structure domain. This mapping process is not unique, and more than one design may result from the generation of design parameters that satisfy the functional requirements. Therefore, there can be an infinite number of feasible design solutions and mapping techniques. Suh's design axioms provide the principles the mapping technique must satisfy in regard to input requirements in order to produce a good design and provide a framework for comparing and selecting designs. The axioms are independence and information. The independence axiom states that in an acceptable design, the design parameters and the functional requirements are related in such a way that specified design parameters can be adjusted to satisfy its corresponding functional requirements without affecting other functional requirements. The information axiom states that the best design is a functionally uncoupled design that has minimum information content.

Tomiyama and Yoshikawa have developed the general design theory, and its major achievements are the mathematical formulation of the design process and the justification of the knowledge representation techniques. General design theory, according to Tomiyama, is a descriptive model that tries to explain how design is conceptually performed in terms of knowledge manipulation. In general design theory, a design process is regarded as a mapping from the functional space onto the attribute space, both of which are defined on an entity concept set. Tomiyama argues that from this formulation, based on an axiomatic set theory, one can mathematically derive an interesting theory that can well explain a design process. They have developed the design theory under two circumstances: design under the ideal knowledge and design under the real knowledge. Under the ideal knowledge, design can be viewed as a mapping process from the functional space onto the attribute space. Three axioms under the ideal knowledge are the axiom of recognition: any entity can be recognized or described by attributes and/or other abstract concepts; the axiom of correspondence: the entity set and the set of the entity concept have one-to-one correspondence; and the axiom of operation: the set of abstract concept is topology of the set of entity concept. The real knowledge, unlike the ideal knowledge, is fuzzy, and one must take into account the following characteristics: design is not a simple mapping process, but a stepwise refinement process; the concept of function is difficult to prescribe and behavior must be used instead of function; and, finally, ideal knowledge does not take the physical constraints into consideration. The cognitive model of the design process can be derived from the results of the design experiment.

Many researchers have been trying to develop a scientific theory or at least a model of design. Their perspectives and views on the nature of design can be visualized as a feed-back loop of synthesis, evaluation, and analysis. The general model of the design process is inherently iterative and requires refinements and improvements until requirements are satisfied. These issues are examined in the first part of the book. Chapters 1 through 8 introduce the problem of engineering design and the basic tools of the design process. The design problem, conceptual and detailed design, and the hierarchical approach to design and design axioms are described. Generic steps of design, namely identifying needs, setting strategies, establishing design concepts, selecting feasible alternatives, selecting and specifying parameters of design, evaluation, and implementation are examined.

In Chapter 1, basic design concepts and axioms are discussed. After introducing the problem of engineering design, various classifications of design process are discussed and design models proposed in literature are surveyed. The use of the quality function deployment method for capturing fuzzy functional requirements of design is examined and the procedure to integrate quality into the design process is covered. General descriptions of design theories and axioms summarized in this chapter provide sufficient background to the computational models of conceptual and routine design models discussed in Chapters 3 and 4 and the basic motivation behind manufacturing feature identification and reasoning with symbolic descriptions. These aspects of design are discussed in detail in Chapters 5 through 8.

Chapter 2 examines the use of conceptual design models in early stages of the design process for reducing the search space of feasible design solutions. This approach is commonly used by designers. Once a conceptual design is selected, the later stages of design are more routine as the design space gets progressively narrower downstream. This activity is more intuitive rather than scientific. Communication between designers at this stage is very limited due to lack of appropriate language and an organized modeling effort.

Development of computational models for generating conceptual design models are explained in detail using time-measuring devices and hydraulic systems as examples. Language of conceptual design is developed through concepts as "functional configurations," "functional analysis," "design space discretization," and "computational schemes for configuration design."

These concepts are further investigated in Chapter 3 in defining the language of the conceptual design models. The conceptual design model is represented in terms of the relationships between function, structure, and behavior, with an attempt to delineate them in the process. Design is considered as a process of evolution, starting by identifying, refining, and transforming the basic functional requirements to structural descriptions that would ultimately define a physical device. In conceptual design model development, design is perceived as being guided by the functional specifications and constraints that would lead to the systems of the structure. Design language that could be used for this process for representing functional, structural, and behavioral abstractions are explained in this chapter.

Once a conceptual design selected the task of converting the solution, configuration into the final design is much simpler and does not require any abstract discription of concepts and structures. These tasks, identified as routine design, lend themselves well to the methods of artificial intelligence. In Chapter 4, computational models of routine design are explained in the context of an Intelligent Design System (IDS).

Computational models of routine design, namely Intelligent Computer Aided Design, Design Refinement, Constraint Programming, and Case-Based Reasoning in Design, are discussed as models to automate the routine design process. The use of artificial intelligence techniques in this area is demonstrated with routine design automation examples through IDS.

Chapters 5 through 8 provide details of the process of routine design automation. Theoretical framework for an intelligent CAD system, reasoning about symbolic description of parts and processes, and manufacturing feature recognition using artificial neural networks to enhance design automation are covered.

In Chapter 5, a unifying framework to describe and use design knowledge is provided through a IIICAD (Intelligent, Integrated, and Interactive CAD) which employs Artificial Intelligence techniques and knowledge engineering tools. The system clarifies, on an abstract level, what the design process is in relation to the design object. No distinction is drawn between the parts of the process carried out by the designer and by the assisting program. System automatically identifies the parts of the process and the objects best suited for computer representation.

Reasoning about symbolic descriptions of mechanical parts is further examined in Chapter 6. An approach is presented for representing geometric objects characterized by the use of symbolic rather than numeric values and the use of constraints. The performance of the algorithms developed are demonstrated with several examples by manipulating objects described symbolically.

These routine design automation concepts are examined further in Chapter 7. An overview of some issues of process descriptions, along with a proposal for a formal methodology—IDEF3—for capturing such descriptions are preserved.

Chapter 8 examines the use of artificial neural networks technology in manufacturing feature identification for routine design automation and provides a bridge between this technology and knowledge-based systems.

The need for neural network pattern recognition is introduced after highlighting some of the limitations to expert systems for feature identification. Various artificial neural network paradigms are described, with emphasis on the multilayered perceptions trained with backpropagation. Neural network-based feature design systems are described and current problems with neural networks are presented, along with the outlook for composite intelligent systems for design automation.

Chapter 1

Design Science

Ali Bahrami
Computer Information Systems
Department of Economics and Management
Rhode Island College
Providence, Rhode Island

Cihan H. Dagli
Department of Engineering Management
University of Missouri-Rolla
Rolla, Missouri

1.1 INTRODUCTION

Design is a process of developing plans or schemes of action; more particularly, a design may be the developed plan or scheme, whether kept in mind or set forth as a drawing or model.... Design in the fine arts is often considered to be the creative process per se, while in engineering, on the contrary, it may mean a concise record of embodiment of appropriate concepts and experiences. In architecture and product design the artistic and engineering aspects of design tend to merge; that is, an architect, craftsman, or graphic or industrial designer cannot design according to formulas alone, nor as freely as can a painter, poet, or musician. (Britannica, 1986)

How does a design come into being? How does a designer translate ideas from fuzzy mental images and abstract concepts to the crisp design? Tyng writes about Louis Kahn, the famous architect:

Kahn tended to synthesize elements from variety of sources into cohesive whole rather than to focus on a detail of a particular problem. He would have failed a trivia quiz, because facts were to him needless clutter that he impatiently pushed aside to delve straight to the essence of the matter. When Kahn spoke of felling (in design), he was referring to his preferred mode of functioning. Kahn believed that the creative mind intuitively understood the design process as a whole but required the help of rational thought to direct the process by separating it into steps. Thinking acts as a tool with which to articulate feeling (functioning) into expressive shape. (1984)

Kahn viewed design as a process by which the transcendent forms of thinking and feeling produce the realization of form. To Kahn, *form* meant the essence created by a certain relationship of elements in a whole. The form of chair, for instance, is a piece of furniture designed to accommodate one sitting person. It consists of a seat, a backrest, and a support system that elevates it from the floor. Despite whether the chair is made of plastic, wood, or metal, it is recognizable as a chair as long as the seat, backrest, and legs remain in a certain relationship to one another (Tyng, 1984).

Design or problem solving is a natural human activity. We have been acting as designers (sometimes unconsciously) throughout our lives. Design begins with the acknowledgment of needs and dissatisfaction with the current state of affairs and realization that some action must take place in order to correct the problem. When a small child moves a stool to an appropriate location so that she can use it to get to her toy, she has acted as the designer of a rudimentary design by positioning the stool so that she can satisfy her need of playing with the toy.

Design is a purposeful activity; it involves a conscious effort to arrive at a state of affairs in which certain characteristics are evident (Coyne *et al.*, 1990). Suh (1990) defines design as consisting of four distinct aspects of engineering and scientific endeavor (Fig. 1.1):

(1) Problem definition from fuzzy sets of facts and myths into a coherent statement of the question
(2) Creative process of devising a proposed physical embodiment of solutions
(3) Analytical process of devising a proposed physical embodiment of solutions
(4) Ultimate check of the fidelity of the design product to the original perceived needs

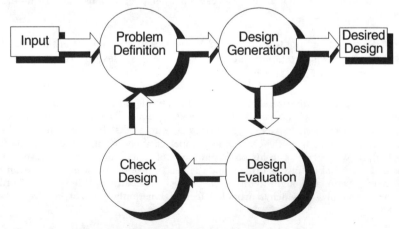

FIG. 1.1. Design as four distinct aspects of engineering and scientific endeavor.

Every field of engineering involves and depends on the design or synthesis process, which allows fulfillment of needs through the creation of physical and informational structures, including machines, software, and organizations (Suh, 1990).

1.2 SCIENTIFIC VIEWS OF DESIGN ACTIVITY

Although design is a natural human activity, and we all live in a man-made environment and use the products of human creativity, we cannot fully describe or understand the process that produces the design.

> Design is a word used loosely in all the arts, and particularly in their instruction, to mean composition, style, or decoration. Composition is the framework of relationships in a thing, considered analytically in isolation from the parts and from the whole; this is the meaning of phrases like—the design of Raphael's "Sistine Madonna"—Neoclassical design means the Neoclassical style of design. An all-over design is a regularly repeated decoration covering an expanse. Such loose, localized uses of the word are usually comprehensible in context but may confuse the readers or listeners who correctly suspect that design in aeronautics, for example is another thing. (Britannica, 1986)

The main source of the confusion about design is that "engineering design" lacks sufficient scientific foundations. Dixon argued that without an adequate base of scientific principles, engineering design education and practice are guided too much by specialized empiricism, intuition, and experience:

> Design is not an easy subject to research. It is quite different from domains like physics, chemistry, or biology where theories and hypotheses can be tested by laboratory or controlled field experiments. Because of the involvement of people and organizations, design is in part like cognitive psychology or sociology in terms of research. However, in addition to people and organizations, design also involves the natural physical world and in-progress design (that is, the to-be-manufactured-sold-and-used physical artifact of system). Thus design is extremely complex. Moreover design is a process, and processes are not the usual subject of theoretical formulations. (1987)

Simon (1969) has argued that a science of design is possible and that some day we will be able to talk in terms of well-established theories and practices. He concluded that design is at a pre-science phase and it must go through several phases before it constitutes a mature science, which is that state of a discipline in which there is a coherent tradition of scientific research and practice, embodying law, theory, application, and instrumentation (Kuhn, 1970). Coyne et al. (1990) argued that in order to achieve this kind of maturity, we must borrow the methodologies from other disciplines that have reached the status of "full-fledged" science. Basically there are two major approaches to increasing our understanding in a discipline that lacks scientific theories: these are case studies and models. The case studies approach was prevalent in such disciplines as early psychology, prior to the establishment of appropriate experimental methods. This technique is also the predominant approach in engineering design, which lacks the solid foundation of scientific theories and relies mostly on interpretation. The second approach is to use a model to define and understand the design process. Although models are less ambitious than theories, and unlike the theories that attempt to explain observed phenomena and predict behaviors that are somehow connected, models are content with the given explanation and prediction of phenomena (Coyne *et al.*, 1990). However, in most cases the mathematical relationships between the components are required in order to build a useful model. A designer may be able to describe how an artifact is designed, but it would be difficult to translate the designer's behavior into a mathematical model unless scientific theories can be developed for it. Coyne *et al.* (1990) have written that "In modeling design we do not attempt to say what design is or how human designers do what they do, but rather provide models by which we can explain and perhaps even replicate certain aspect of design behavior." A model does not constitute a theory; theory emerges when there is a testable explanation of why the model behaves as it does (Dixon, 1987).

Three types of models that can be used in the design process are perspective, cognitive, and computational (Dixon, 1987). A *perspective model* stipulates how something should be done. A perspective model of design concerns improving the design by advocating how design should be done under certain circumstances. A *cognitive model* represents how people perform some mental task or activity and the interrelationships of human designers with computerized tools such as computer aided drafting systems. Finally, a *computational model* delineates the methods by which a computer can perform a task by computing the variables that are presented in the model (Dixon, 1987).

By borrowing from other disciplines such as artificial intelligence and problem solving, i.e., space search techniques, expert systems and neural networks, logic in general and fuzzy logic in particular, object-oriented methodology, database, and language theory, one can define, study and understand the design activity. Coyne *et al.* (1990) elegantly summarized the definition of science and design:

> Science attempts to formulate knowledge by deriving relationships between observed phenomena. Design, on the other hand, begins with intentions and uses the available knowledge to arrive at an entity possessing attributes that will meet the original intentions. The role of the design is to produce form or more correctly, a description of forma using knowledge to transform a formless description into a definite, specific description. Moreover, design is a pragmatic discipline, concerned with providing a solution within the capacity of the knowledge available to the designer. This design may not be "correct" or "ideal" and may represent a compromise, but it will meet the given intentions to some degree. (1990)

1.3   DESIGN CATEGORIES

Duvvuru *et al.* (1989) have classified the design process into four categories: creative design, innovative design, redesign, and routine design. These classifications of design are process dependent and product independent. The descriptions of these design classes that have been defined by Duvvuru *et al.* (1989) can be summarized as follows:

(1) *Creative Design. A priori* plan for the solution of the problem does not exist. Design is an abstract decomposition of the problem into a set of levels that represent choices for the components of the problem. The key element in this design type is the transformation from the subconscious to the conscious.

(2) *Innovative Design.* The decomposition of the problem is known, but the alternatives for each of its subparts do not exist and must be synthesized. Design might be an original or unique combination of existing components. Duvvuru *et al.* argue that a certain amount of creativity comes into play in the innovative design process.

(3) *Redesign.* An existing design is modified to meet required changes in the original functional requirements.

(4) *Routine Design. A priori* plan of the solution exists. The subparts and alternatives are known in advance, perhaps as a result of either a creative or innovative design process. Routine design involves finding the appropriate alternatives for each subpart that satisfy the given constraints.

Duvvuru *et al.* explain that at the creative end of the spectrum, the design process might be fuzzy, spontaneous, chaotic, and imaginative. At the other end of the spectrum, namely the routine design, design is precise, crisp, predetermined, systematic, and mathematical (Fig. 1.2). These points are discussed in detail in Chapters 2 and 4 in reference to computational models for conceptual and routine design, respectively.

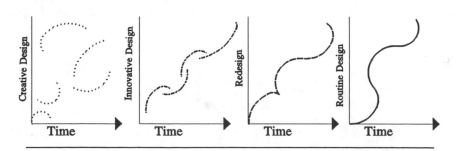

Creative Design   Innovative Design   Redesign   Routine Design

Fig. 1.2. At the creative end of the spectrum, design is very fuzzy. As it moves to routine design, it gets precise, crisp, and predetermined.

1.4 SURVEY OF DESIGN MODELS

There is no single model that can provide a perfect or at least a satisfactory definition of the design process. One must look at the design from various angles to grasp a better understanding of the process. Many researchers have been trying to develop a scientific theory and model of design. Their perspectives on design are summarized in the following sections. The models presented basically describe the same phenomena; therefore, they may overlap in more ways than one.

General Model of Design

The general model of design can be visualized as a feedback loop of synthesis and analysis (Fig. 1.3). The general model of the design process is inherently iterative; the designer repeatedly goes back to refine and improve the design until it satisfies the requirements (Serbanati, 1987). Design is initiated by specifying and analyzing a given problem. The first step in most cases consists of decomposing the problem into subproblems. The designer must then search for the practical solutions. In some cases, this requires ingenuity which may result in a new and original design. In other cases, the designer may recall the design solutions that have been employed in previous problems of a similar nature and apply one of those solutions (Anderson, 1977).

Three basic phases of design described by Coyne *et al.* (1990), Markus *et al.* (1972), Asimow (1962), and Luckman (1967) are analysis, synthesis, and evaluation. *Analysis* is concerned with defining and understanding the "WHAT's" that must be translated by the designer into an explicit statement of functional requirements (goals). *Synthesis* involves finding the feasible solutions among the alternatives. Finally, the *evaluation* phase is concerned with assessing the validity of the solutions relative to the original functional requirements (Coyne *et al.*, 1990). Analysis and synthesis are on the forward path of the design loop, and on the backward path, the designer verifies his assumption through the evaluation process (Serbanati, 1987; Fig. 1.4). A cycle is iterated so that the solution

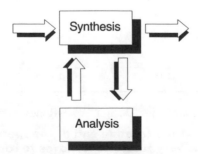

FIG. 1.3. General model of design process.

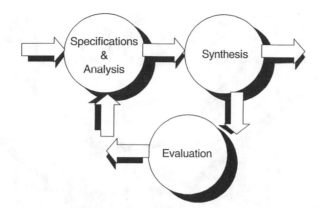

FIG. 1.4. Three basic phases of design process.

is revised and improved by reexamining the analysis. Coyne *et al.* (1990) argued that these three phases of design form the basis of the framework for planning, organizing, and evolving design activity.

The general model of design coincides with many other types of design methods, theories, and axioms that are described in the following sections. Other names for these phases of design are divergence, transformation, and convergence (Jones, 1970). Divergence is the process of decomposing the problem into subproblems and defining the boundaries of a space in which a thriving search for the solution can take place, transformation concerns combining the parts and generating a new form, and convergence is investigating the fidelity of the new arrangement of the parts.

Figure 1.5 depicts a more comprehensive version of the general model of design process. This version of the model consists of the following tasks: need assessment, analysis, decomposition, synthesis, integration, and evaluation. The first task is concerned with the assessment of the needs and requirements which are usually fuzzy in nature. Analysis involves the specification, identification, and preparation of the problem to produce an explicit statement of goals. Decomposition involves breaking the problem into parts and defining the boundaries of a space in which a fruitful search for the solution can take place. Synthesis is concerned with discovering the consequences of putting the new arrangement into practice (Coyne *et al.* 1990). Task evaluation is judging the validity of the solutions relative to the goals and selecting among alternatives. The inner cycle implies that the outcome of the integration phase is revised and improved by reexamining the analysis. The outer cycle demonstrates that an evaluation of the the solution might revise the perceived needs.

The general model of design is also known as *goal decomposition* (Alexander, 1964). Suh (1990) describes this process as a decomposition of the design process that can be summarized as follows. After stating the first-level functional requirements (FRs), the designer must systematically try to satisfy the FRs by decomposing these first-level FRs further into lower-level FRs. The designer must switch

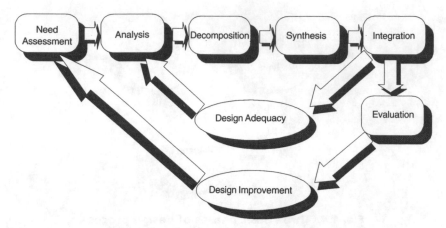

FIG. 1.5. Comprehensive version of general model of the design.

to the physical domain from the functional domain, and vice versa in order to be able to proceed with the design process. This process requires that the designer go back and forth between physical and functional domains each time he or she moves down the functional or goal tree. Suh (1990) argues that "a good designer can identify the most important FRs at each level of the functional tree by eliminating secondary factors from consideration. Less-able designers often try to consider all the FRs of every level simultaneously, rather than making use of the hierarchical nature of FRs and DPs. So, the design process becomes too complex to manage." The use of functional requirements and structural descriptions in models of conceptual design for concurrent engineering is discussed extensively in Chapter 3.

Quality Function Deployment: A Descriptive Model for Planning and Design

Quality Function Deployment (QFD) is a descriptive model that uses a structured approach to create quality design by invoking the "voice of the customer" at each phase of product planning, design, manufacturing, and marketing.

Quality Function Deployment starts with customer requirements which are usually fuzzy and loosely stated, such as: looks good, easy to use, works well, feels good, safe, comfortable, luxurious, or lasts long. These are important to the customer but often defy quantification and are difficult for the company to act on (American Supplier Inst., 1987). The QFD allows the designer to convert the customer specifications into internal company requirements, which are called design or functional requirements. These are generally global product characteristics. It also enables a designer to exploit the global product characteristics rather than design at the system, subsystem, or part level. The global design requirements must then be translated into specific parts and the critical characteristics of these parts that cause the essential function to be performed. The use of parts is quite appropriate for products that are assemblies of mechanical components. The concept applies equally well to other types of products that are combinations of ingredients or materials, as well as to nonphysical products that are combinations of services (American Supplier Inst., 1987).

Quality Function Deployment is accomplished through a series of charts (Fig. 1.6). It starts with a list of objectives, or the WHAT's that are needed in the context of developing a new product. A list of customer requirements is often called the "voice of the customer." The items contained in this list are usually general, fuzzy, and difficult to implement directly, requiring further detailed definition. For example, a comfortable chair has a wide variety of meanings to different people. This is a highly desirable product feature, but it is not directly actionable.

The first chart (product planning) is often called "the house of quality" because of the rooflike structure of its top (Fig. 1.7). The house of quality represents the relationships between the WHAT's, the rows (customer requirements) and the HOW's, the columns (technical requirements or functional requirements). The WHAT's evolve into HOW's and their relationships are entered into the matrix. The HOW's are related to each other and the correlations are established (the roof of the house). The trade-off decisions are made using judgment and analysis, assisted by the competitive assessment and importance ratings.

Each of the initial WHAT's requires further definition. The list is refined to the next level of detail by listing one or more HOW's for each WHAT. This process is similar to the process of refining the marketing specifications. Quality Function deployment allows the customer requirements to be mapped onto global product characteristics or functional requirements. These functional requirements have measurable characteristics that can be evaluated on the completed product. The comfortable chair requirement might be translated into the angle between backrest and seat, the ability to adjust the backrest, or the ability to move the chair easily.

The items on the HOW list represent greater detail than those on the original WHAT list, although they are themselves often not directly actionable, requiring yet further definition. This further definition is accomplished by treating each HOW as a WHAT and defining a new, more detailed list of HOW's required to support the WHAT's. This is done by creating a new chart in which the HOW's

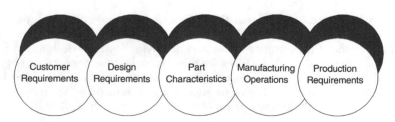

FIG. 1.6. QFD consists of the series of charts.

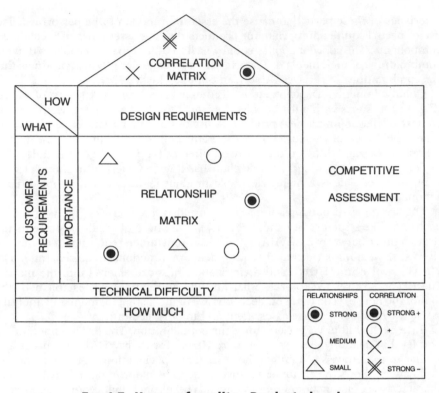

FIG. 1.7. House of quality—Product planning.

of the previous chart become the WHAT's of the new chart (Fig. 1.8). The HOW MUCH values are usually carried along to the next chart to facilitate communication and ensure that the objective values are not lost.

Quality Function Deployment allows the coupling of functional requirements (WHAT's) and design structures (HOW's). Therefore, at each level of refinement some of the HOW's may affect more than one WHAT, sometimes adversely. The designer must minimize the adverse affects of HOW's by selecting those that are not in conflict and which also fulfill the customer requirements most effectively.

Recent literature suggests that the Japanese companies that have used QFD achieved impressive results. One of the key benefits of QFD is a better understanding of what the customer wants and deploying it in the design and manufacturing of the product. The QFD model is well suited for concurrent engineering in which the marketing staffs, designers, and product and process engineers participate in a team effort. It may be regarded as a "blue print" for the operation of such a product development team (American Supplier Inst., 1987).

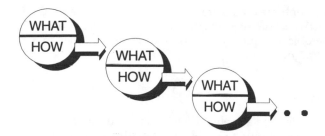

FIG. 1.8. The HOW's of the previous chart become the WHAT's of the new chart.

Computational Models of Design

The general problem solver model (GPS) epitomizes how various control choices can be assembled into an overall problem solver model (Winston, 1984). For many problems, it is natural to think in terms of the current situation and the desired situation. The collection of facts that specify the problem and its status represent the current state. The objective is to get from the current state to the goal state (Winston, 1984). Winston (1984) argued that procedures are selected according to their ability to reduce the observed differences between the current state and the goal state.

Simon (1969) described design as a problem-solving process of searching through a state space where the states represent the design solution. The main task of a designer is to make decisions based on the functional requirements (goals) and design constraints (Simon, 1969). This decision-making process in the general problem solving model of design provides the heart of the matter. Many techniques such as simulation, optimization, artificial intelligence, fuzzy logic, and neural networks can be borrowed from various fields of science (e.g., operations research, computer science, mathematics, artificial intelligence, etc.), in order to assist the decision-making process of design activity.

Optimization

Mathematical programming techniques can be used to identify the potential design configuration by optimizing it based on functional requirements and goals. In general, the solution of the problem is developed by solving the mathematical model consisting of an objective function that is to be optimized and a set of constraints representing limitations on resources. Any model can be represented in a standard form as follows:

$$\begin{aligned} &\textit{Maximized} \quad Z = f(X) \\ &\textit{Subject to} \quad g(X) = 0 \\ &\textit{Where} \quad\quad X \geq 0, \ \text{for } X = [x_1, x_2, \dots x_n] \end{aligned}$$

Optimization can provide a vital solution in cases where a design problem can be formulated based on the objective and functional requirements. The main problem with optimization techniques is that they do not address the question of how to arrive at the objective functions. Designers generally do not think in terms of the objective functions or optimization, and they may not easily relate to these techniques.

Simulation

Simulation is based on a problem-solving method that has been in use for many years, sometimes referred to as the model-building method or, more commonly, the scientific method (Graybeal, 1980). Design can utilize simulation as it exploits optimization techniques to compute decision variables. These variables are then evaluated against the functional requirements to determine whether the design satisfies the input requirements. If the design is not found to be acceptable, then the decision variables may be modified and the process is repeated. However, the main shortcoming of the simulation technique is that there is no way to tell how good the final design is in comparison with other possible designs (Coyne et al., 1990).

Prototype Model of Design

A prototype typifies, or exemplifies, a class of designs, and thus serves as a generic design. A description of a class of designs may also be prototyped; knowledge or rules can even constitute a prototype (Coyne et al., 1990). The prototype model of design is very similar in nature to the object oriented paradigm. The fundamental contribution of the prototype model is the abstract data type approach: Rather than describing the individual designs, one must concentrate on the patterns that are common to a whole class of design. A particular design can then be instantiated or exemplified from the class (prototype) of designs.

Lansdown (1987) argues that innovation arises from incremental modification of existing tried and true ideas rather than from entirely new approaches. Lansdown believes that the transformation from initial to final description is continuous and that design is more like fine-tuning a set of already working ideas rather than inventing something new, although the results might not resemble anything previously imagined. A prototype model of design expiates the common form of design and it can be argued that it is more useful than searching for a highly innovative design (Lansdown, 1987).

Gardiner (1986) describes the prototype model of design as "one that brings together several new divergent lines of development to form a new 'composite' design, which is internally adjusted to form a new consolidated design which is then further developed as a variety of 'stretched' design."

It has been shown that the key to creativity is knowledge. For instance, creative people know a great deal about the subject in which they are being innovative. Lansdown believes that one can conclude from this and from observation of the work and working methods of creative people, that their memory or their notebook is a fruitful source and even the most creative designers do not arrive at new ideas out of a vacuum (Lansdown, 1987). Lansdown defines "prototype" as an especial representation or abstract example of a set of particular objects; for instance, a prototype chair would be one that has four legs, a seat which is roughly 430 mm above the ground, and a backrest of certain height (Lansdown, 1987). The prototype model of design can explain the idea generation of an ordinary office chair, but it would be difficult to typify a beanbag chair or typists' kneeling chair (Lansdown, 1987).

A prototype model consists of three activities: modification, adaption, and creation. Prototype *creation*, which is known as conceptual or original design, is where the new prototypes materialize, as in design of the first airplane (Coyne *et al.*, 1990). Prototype *modification* involves working within the constraints of a particular class of design. Prototype *adaptation* pertains to extending the boundaries of a particular class of design.

1.5 DESIGN THEORIES AND AXIOMS

It is important to keep in mind that there is a significant difference between the theoretical statements and the real world system that theory tries to explain. The theoretical systems never match the real systems perfectly, but they can come close in describing real world phenomena (Dixon, 1987).

Dixon believes that the major components of theories are

(1) Data or observations from the real system
(2) Generalization of data or observations
(3) Explanations of why the generalizations are what they are

Keep in mind that generalizations are not theories; theories emerge from describing and figuring out why a generalization of phenomena is the way it is (Dixon, 1987).

Toward Design Axiom and Scientific Theory

Hongo (1985) provides definitions for a design science or scientific study of design activities. Scientific study of design activity is a collection of logically connected knowledge such as design methodology and design technique. Design technique consists of three sections: the applied knowledge from natural and human science, the theory of machine systems, and, finally, the theory of design processes. A narrower definition of design theory is a

> system of methodical rules that determine the classes of possible procedures and actions that are likely to lead on a planned path to the accomplishment of desired aim. Types classified according to method of thinking (intuitive or discursive), according to aim and application (methods for solution search, evaluation, calculation). (Hongo, 1985)

Hongo argues that design cannot be explained by one theory and that this may discourage people who are seeking one generally acceptable theory of design. Hongo (1985) believes that the inherent multiplicity of design comes from differences in an observer's point of view: "From a viewpoint of a high level of abstraction one can see a good perspective, however details can be observed only through a microscope on a concrete standpoint." He debates that even if one observes the design activity from the same point of view, some points may be ignored (unconsciously or intentionally) for the simplicity of description or for making a point (Hongo, 1985).

The theory of design can be inferred from the following observations (Hongo, 1985):

(1) The theories of design must be derived from facts.
(2) During design process only the law of nature is absolute and unchangeable.
(3) Design methodology or method used by designer to attain desired goal must be the main guide of the designer.
(4) The design methodologies are useful only in the conscious mode of design activities.
(5) Intuitive design activity should supersede all other activities, including the design methodology.

Design Axioms

Suh (1990) defines design as the culmination of synthesized solutions in the form of product, software, processes, or system by the appropriate selection of design parameters (DPs) that satisfy perceived needs through the mapping from functional requirements (FRs) in the functional domain to DPs in the structural domain. This mapping process is not unique and more than one design may result from the generation of DPs that satisfy the FRs. Therefore, there can be an infinite number of feasible design solutions and mapping techniques (Fig. 1.9). Suh's design axioms provide the principles that the mapping technique must satisfy the input requirements of which in order to produce a good design and provide a framework for comparing and selecting designs (Suh, 1990). Suh's design axioms are the *independence axiom* and the *information axiom* (Suh, 1984; Suh *et al.*, 1978). These axioms are defined as follows:

(1) *Independence axiom.* In an acceptable design, the DPs and the FRs are related in such a way that specified DP can be adjusted to satisfy its corresponding FR without affecting other functional requirements.
(2) *Information axiom.* The best design is a functionally uncoupled design that has minimum information content.

Design Mapping Paradigm

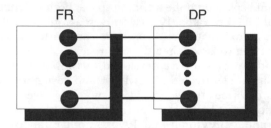

FIG. 1.9. Design mapping paradigm.

Suh's information axiom coincides with an important principle in design known as "simplicity." Simplicity is a word that has been used by designers and aestheticians for many centuries and remains a principle of primary concern. What does the designer mean when he or she applies the word *simple* to a work of art? The designer is not speaking of a mental deficiency. Simple in the design means being able to reduce it to the fewest possible lines, shapes, and subparts, without reducing its functional requirements or violating its specifications. Simple designs will reduce the assembly time and product cost, and increase reliability by many orders of magnitude. A good design is one to which no more can be added, and at the same time, one from which nothing can be subtracted without causing an incomplete design (Tyng, 1984). In other words, good design must not be restrained with nonessential details.

The information axiom does not imply that a part has to be broken into two or more separate physical parts, or that a new element has to be added to the existing design. Functional coupling may be achieved without physical separation, although in some cases such physical decomposition may be the best way of solving the problem. The information axiom does imply that the concept that "my design is better than yours because it does more than what was intended" is misguided (Suh, 1990). A design should only fulfill the precise needs defined by the FRs and nothing more and nothing less.

General Theory of Design

Yoshikawa (1985) and Tomiyama (1990) have developed a general design theory and its major achievements are the mathematical formulation of the design process and the justification of the knowledge representation techniques in a certain situation. General design theory, according to Tomiyama, is a descriptive model that tries to explain how design is conceptually performed in terms of knowledge manipulation. In general design theory, a design process is regarded as a mapping from the functional space onto the attribute space, both of which are defined on an entity concept set (Tomiyama, 1990). Tomiyama argues that from this formalization based on an axiomatic set theory, one can mathematically derive interesting theory that can well explain a design process.

Yoshikawa and Tomiyama have developed the design theory under two circumstances. Design under the ideal knowledge and design under the real knowledge. Tomiyama describes that in the ideal knowledge we know all of the elements of the entity set and each element can be described crisply by the abstract concept without ambiguity (Tomiyama, 1990). Another important property of the ideal knowledge is that design can be viewed as a mapping process from the functional space onto the attribute space, which immediately terminates when the specifications are described. Because everything is known in the ideal knowledge, one can completely describe the specifications in terms of function and the solution is obtained in terms of attributes. Figure 1.10 depicts the Yoshikawa and Tomiyama view of design as a mapping process. The following are the design axioms in the ideal knowledge.

(1) *Axiom 1 (axiom of recognition).* Any entity can be recognized or described by attributes and/or other abstract concepts.
(2) *Axiom 2 (axiom of correspondence).* The entity set S' and the set of entity concept (ideal) S have one-to-one correspondence.
(3) *Axiom 3 (axiom of operation).* The set of abstract concept is topology of the set of entity concept.

The real knowledge unlike the ideal knowledge is fuzzy and one must take into consideration the following characteristics:

(1) Design is not a simple mapping process, but rather a stepwise refinement where the designer seeks the solution that can satisfy constraints.
(2) Use of the behavior instead of function.
(3) The ideal knowledge does not take physical constraints into consideration.

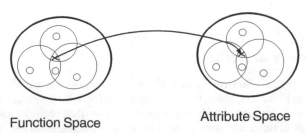

Function Space   Attribute Space

FIG. 1.10. Design as mapping in the ideal knowledge.

In the ideal knowledge, design is a direct mapping process from the functional space to the attribute space, whereas in the real knowledge, design is a stepwise, evolutionary transformation process (Fig. 1.11).

Tomiyama admits that the general design theory does not completely support the cognitive model of design, and the cognitive model of design process can be derived from the results of design experiments. He argues that the design process can be decomposed into small design cycles. Each cycle has the following subprocess (Tomiyama, 1990):

(1) *Awareness*. Identifying problem comparing the object under consideration and the specification.
(2) *Suggestion*. Suggesting the key concept needed to solve the problem.
(3) *Development*. Developing candidate from the key concepts by using design knowledge.
(4) *Evaluation*. Evaluating the alternatives in various ways such as structural computation, simulation of behavior, and so on. If a problem is found as the result of evaluation, it also becomes a new problem to be solved in another design cycle.
(5) *Conclusion*. Selecting a candidate for adaptation and modification.

Tomiyama has distinguished between action level and object level activities in a cognitive model of design process (Fig. 1.12). Object level activities are concerned with the operations about the design object, whereas action level activities are more or less related to the design process.

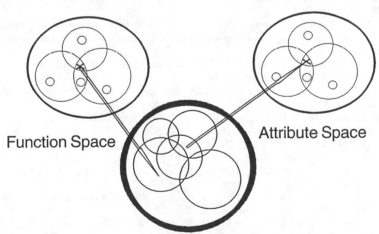

Function Space

Attribute Space

Metamodel Space (Physical Phenomenon Space)

FIG. 1.11. Design as a stepwise refinement process in the real knowledge.

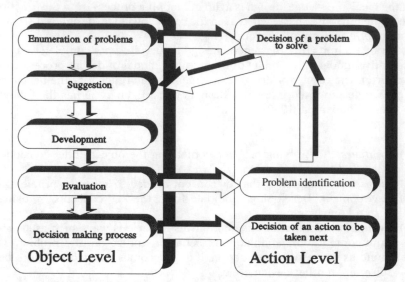

FIG. 1.12. The cognitive model of design process.

REFERENCES

Alexander, C. 1964. *Notes on the Synthesis for Form*. Cambridge, Massachusetts: Harvard University Press.

American Supplier Institute. 1987. *Quality Function Deployment Manual*. Dearborn, Michigan.

Anderson, J. R. 1977. Induction of augmented transition network. *Cognitive Science* 1 (2):125–157.

Asimow, W. 1962. An overview of the structure of the design process. In *Emerging Methods in Environment Design and Planning*, ed. G. T. Moore, 285–307. Cambridge, Massachusetts: MIT Press.

Coyne, R. D., Rosenman, M. A., Radford, A. D., Balachandran, M., and Gero, J. S. 1990. *Knowledge-Based Design Systems*. Reading, Massachusetts: Addison-Wesley.

Dixon, J. R. 1987. On research methodology towards a scientific theory of engineering design. AI EDAM 1 (3):145–157.

Duvvuru, S., Stephanopouls, G., Logcher, R., *et al.* 1989. Knowledge-based system applications in engineering design: Research at MIT. *AI Magazine* 10 (3):79–96.

Encyclopedia Britannica. 1986. s.v. "The Art of Architecture."

Gardiner, J. P. 1986. Robust and lean designs with state of the art automotive and aircraft examples. In *Design, Innovation and Long Cycles in Economic Development*, ed. C. Freeman. London: Frances Pinter.

Graybeal, W. J., and Pooch, U. W. 1980. *Simulation: Principles and Methods*. Cambridge, Massachusetts: Winthrop Publishers.

Hongo, K. 1985. On the significance of the theory of design. In *Design and Synthesis*, ed. H. Yoshikawa. Amsterdam: Elsevier Science Publishers.

Jones, J. C. 1970. *Design Methods*. New York: Wiley.

Kuhn, T. S. 1970. *The Structure of Scientific Revolutions*. Chicago: University of Chicago Press.

Lansdown, J. 1987. The creative aspects of CAD: A possible approach. *Design Studies* 8 (2):76–81.

Luckman, J. 1967. An approach to the management of design. *Operational Research Quarterly* 18 (4):345–358.

Markus, T. A., Whyman, P., Morgan, J., Whitton, D., *et al.* 1972. Building performance. *Applied Science*, London.

Serbanati, L. D. 1987. Iterform: A CAD system for program development. *IEEE 9th International Conference of Software Engineering*, pp. 190–197.

Simon, H. A. 1969. *The Science of the Artificial.* Cambridge, Massachusetts: MIT Press.

Suh, N. P., Bell, A. C., and Gossard, D. C. 1978. On an axiomatic approach to manufacturing systems. *Journal of Engineering for Industry, Transactions of ASME* 100 (2):127–130.

Suh, N. P. 1984. Development of the science base for the manufacturing field through the axiomatic approach. *Robotics and Computer Integrated Manufacturing* 1 (3/4):399–455.

Suh, N. P. 1990. *The Principles of Design.* New York: Oxford University Press.

Tomiyama, T. 1990. Intelligent CAD systems. *Eurographics.* Switzerland.

Tyng, A. 1984. *Beginnings.* New York: Wiley.

Winston, P. H. 1984. *Artificial Intelligence.* Reading, Massachusetts: Addison-Wesley.

Yoshikawa, H., and Warman, E. A. eds. 1987. *Proceedings of the IFIP W.G. 5.2 Working Conference 1985* (Tokyo). Amsterdam: North Holland.

Chapter 2

Computational Models for Conceptual Design

Sridhar Kota
Design Laboratory
Department of Mechanical Engineering and Applied Mechanics
University of Michigan
Ann Arbor, Michigan

2.1 INTRODUCTION

Design can be viewed as the process of transforming an idea or concept into a description of a physical system. This definition presupposes the existence of the idea or concept. In other words, before the design process can begin, a design *concept* must be generated. This stage is generally referred to as *conceptual design* and it is usually the most difficult stage of the entire design process. Later stages become more routine as the design space gets progressively narrower downstream. The difficulty of the conceptual stage arises from the fact that a choice must be made from a number of alternatives, but there are no established systematic methods for enumerating and evaluating the alternatives. Therein lies the main problem facing automation of this activity. Designers find this initial activity to be intuitive rather than scientific. Communication between designers about this level of thought is therefore limited, and it is difficult to extract organized information from the designers for the construction of a computational model. Therefore the main problem to be overcome before an attempt can be made at automation is the development of a means for effectively communicating information at a conceptual level—a *design language*.

In order to describe and solve design problems at a conceptual level, the *language of functions* serves as a meaningful abstract representation of knowledge about existing devices. The term *function* describes the design intent—the relationship between inputs and outputs. In conceptual design, a function diagram describing essential functions and subfunctions is established. Function diagrams represent *what* needs to be accomplished without any reference to *how* a particular function is implemented (Pahl and Beitz, 1984). This chapter highlights two important design concepts, discretization of the design space and development of function diagrams (also called *functional configuration*), and discusses in detail how these concepts have been applied to the automation of the conceptual design process, illustrating some of the techniques currently being applied toward achieving this difficult goal.

2.2 CLASSES OF DESIGN TASKS

Design problems can be categorized. For instance, Brown and Chandrasekharan (1984), among others, describe three classes: class 1, class 2, and class 3. Pahl and Beitz (1984) categorize design tasks into original design, adaptive design, and variant design. An *original design* requires configuring subfunctions (and corresponding physical devices) and their relations (how they are connected). Typically, this creative task demands not only task decomposition, but also evaluation of different working principles (such as mechanical, hydraulic, electromechanical, or magnetic principles) based on systems-level constraints (such as overall weight, cost, and load cycles) to determine an optimum distribution of subfunctions among compatible working principles while fulfilling global constraints. *Adaptive design* involves adaptation of a known solution principle to fulfill new design requirements. Synthesis of a hydraulic system, for instance, is an example of adaptive design, because the nature of the components (such as valves, cylinders, and hydraulic pumps) that make up the final design are typically known *a priori*. The task, however, requires establishing individual subfunctions by task decomposition and determining appropriate components and their arrangement to fulfill the systems-level constraints (such as maximum pressure, flow rate, and cost). A *variant design* or parameter design task is one in which the configuration and the components are already established and what is required is essentially the *sizing* of the components.

An important distinction between the three design classes is the level of conceptualization required to perform a given task. Conceptualization involves decomposition of the task into subtasks and identification of appropriate working principles so that systems-level constraints are satisfied. Task decomposition is associated with original design (class 1) and adaptive design (class 2), but not variant design (class 3). Conceptual design involves reasoning with *functions*. Furthermore, a routine parameter design task of selecting and sizing the individual components for a preestablished configuration involves *constraint-based reasoning*, where the constraints are nonfunctional requirements such as cost or reliability. To carry out configuration design, we perform functional reasoning to establish a functional configuration and then select components (and component parameters, hence parametric design is involved) for each subfunction.

2.3 CONCEPTUAL DESIGN

Conceptual design is that part of the design process in which the basic solution path is created through the elaboration of a solution concept (Pahl and Beitz, 1984). The process of conceptualization involves

(1) Understanding the essential nature of design requirements
(2) Identifying of the essential problems through abstraction
(3) Establishing functional diagrams to aid in the search for appropriate solution principles

The first step is to clarify the design specification in terms of overall function and global constraints. Once the overall function is understood, the next step is to break down complex functions into simpler subfunctions, a process called *function decomposition*. The combination of individual subfunctions results in a functional configuration representing the overall function. The optimum method of breaking down an overall function—that is, the optimum number of sub-function levels and also the number of subfunctions per level—is determined by the relative novelty of the problem and also by the method used to search for a solution.

In the case of original designs, neither the individual subfunctions nor their relationships to each other are generally known. Therefore, the search for, and establishment of, an optimum functional configuration constitute some of the most important steps of the conceptual design phase. The basis of a functional configuration is the *specification* and the *abstract formulation* of the problem. In the case of adaptive designs, on the other hand, the general structure with its assemblies and components is much better known, so that a functional configuration can be obtained through an analysis of the product to be developed. Depending on the special demands of the specification, that functional configuration can be modified by the variation, addition, or omission of individual subfunctions or by changes in their combination. Functional configurations are intended to facilitate the discovery of solutions: they are not ends in themselves. Because varying the functional configuration introduces distinct solutions, establishing functional configurations constitutes a first step in the search for solutions. Functional analysis of existing designs helps to develop *variants* to open the path for other solutions, for subsequent optimization, and for development of modular products.

Working principles have to be identified for each subfunction, and these principles must eventually be combined. A working principle must reflect the physical effect needed for the fulfillment of a given function and also its form–design features. A systematic classification of various solution principles, through abstractions, is necessary in order to help conceptualize alternate working solutions to a given design task. In the search for a solution, it is often difficult to make a clear distinction between the physical effect and the form–design features. A solution field can be constructed by variation of the physical effects and the form–design features.

The established functional configuration reflects logical and physically possible useful associations of the subfunctions. In combining subfunctions, it is important to ensure the physical and geometrical compatibility of the solution principles. It is also important to select technically and economically favorable combinations of principles from a large field of theoretically possible combinations. At this relatively abstract conceptual phase, it may not be advantageous or even possible to employ computers in the decision-making process—the feasibility of any kind of reasonable computer assistance varies widely from one domain to other. For instance, in the case of purely logical function or in domains of known elements and assemblies, such as electronic or hydraulic circuits, a systematic computer-based combination of subfunctions to yield overall desired function is in fact possible. However, in the mechanical domains, it could be excruciatingly difficult to decompose and recombine subfunctions systematically in a meaningful way. The reasons for this formidable difficulty is partly due to the three-dimensional nature of mechanical designs and the nonmodular nature of the constituent elements. Mechanical components (e.g., bushings) are not as well behaved as components of modular digital systems (e.g., resistors) in terms of input–output relationships.

Establishing a functional configuration via abstraction, systematic enumeration of different working principles, and searching for appropriate physical implementation of subfunctions all help reduce the risk of "getting it wrong," or, in other words, they reduce conceptual vulnerability. These systematic methods help to diversify the approaches to the problem, prompt inventive steps, and reduce the chance of overlooking them. The purpose of developing computer-based models is to create a framework within which knowledge about existing designs and components is abstracted, classified, and compiled in such a way that the resulting computer program suggests alternate solution concepts and checks for any inconsistencies during early stages of product design.

2.4 AN EXAMPLE OF FUNCTIONAL CONFIGURATIONS— TIME MEASURING DEVICES

Although defining time presents difficulties, measuring it does not; it is the most accurately measured physical quantity. A time measurement assigns a unique number to either an epoch, which specifies the moment when an instantaneous event occurs, in the sense of time of day; and/or a time interval, which is the duration of a continued event. *The progress of any phenomenon that undergoes regular changes may be used to measure time.* Such phenomena make up much of the subject matter of astronomy, physics, chemistry, geology, and biology, and, hence, time measurements based on manifestations of gravity, electromagnetism, rotational inertia, and radioactivity have been developed (EB Vol. 28). The *Encyclopedia Britannica* defines a clock as a "machine in which a device that performs *regular movements* in equal intervals of time is linked to a counting mechanism that records the number of movements. All clocks, of whatever form, are made of this principle." The basic needs for time measurement are, therefore, a source of regular movements and a means of counting them.

A brief review of the history of watches, including the invention of modern day watches, is given here to illustrate the notion of abstraction and the significance of functional configurations. We will see that various physical configurations of timepieces, such as a grandfather clock or a quartz watch, can all be traced back to a single functional configuration. The differences in their physical structures are a result of differences in the working principles or physical means that have been adopted to fulfill various functions necessary to time measurement.

The water clock was invented by Ctesibius in about 250 BC. This was a device in which water dropped at a *constant rate* into a container, the level of water indicating the time. Ctesibius improved it by having a float raise a rack that turned a pinion connected to a pointer on a drum. Variations on this theme led to the development of mechanical clocks. The oldest surviving mechanical clocks date from the late 1300s. Gears transmitted the constant movement of a regulator to the hands or to a bell. A good regulator appeared only with the discovery of the pendulum in 1581 by Galileo, who timed a swinging chandelier with his pulse and realized that the time taken for each swing was always constant. But it took nearly a century after Galileo's discovery of a pendulum before the first pendulum clocks appeared. The first domestic clocks were smaller versions of large public clocks, and they appeared late in the fourteenth century. There can be little doubt that the first watches appeared shortly after 1500, when Peter Henlein introduced the mainspring as a replacement for weights in driving clocks. These were the first portable timepieces, representing one of the great strides in horology. The early balance wheel was subjected to no systematic constraint, and it was not possible to define its period of oscillation. Controlling the oscillations of a balance with a spring (hair spring or balance spring) was another important step. Minute hands did not appear until 1670, and there were no glass covers until the seventeenth century.

Electricity then replaced weights or springs as an energy source. Electric-powered watches use one of three drive systems:

(1) The galvanometer drive, consisting of the conventional balance–hairspring oscillator and kept in motion by the magnetic interaction of a coil and a permanent magnet;
(2) The induction drive, in which an electromagnet attracts a balance containing soft magnetic material; or
(3) The resonance drive, in which a tiny tuning fork driven electrically provides the motive power.

Types (1) and (2) use mechanical contact actuated by the balance motion to provide properly timed electric-drive pulses. Type (3) is inherently more accurate because it operates at a frequency higher than that customarily used with balance-type watches, and the tuning fork is a fairly stable source of frequency. The higher frequency requires the replacement of a mechanical contact by a transistor. In 1929, the quartz crystal was first applied to time-keeping; this invention was probably the single greatest contribution to *precision* time measurement. Because the frequency of vibration, 100,000 Hz, is too high for convenient time measurement, it is reduced by a process known as demultiplication (it is subjected to a combined electrical and mechanical gearing reduction of 6,000,000) and applied to a synchronous motor connected to a clock dial through mechanical gearing. The vibrations are so regular that the maximum error of an observatory quartz clock is only 1 second in 10 years (EB Vol. 3).

The progressive miniaturization of electronic components in the late twentieth century made possible the development of multifunctional, all-electronic watches, in which the necessary transistors, resistors, capacitors, and other elements were on one or several miniature integrated circuits or chips (EB Vol. 12).

Functional Analysis of Clocks and Watches

What are the functions and features that are common among different clocks and watches from the ancient water clock to the present-day quartz clock? A

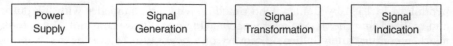

FIG. 2.1(a). Essential functions of a time-indicating device.

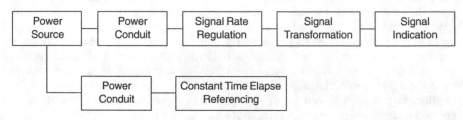

FIG. 2.1(b). A functional network of a time-indicating device showing the basic subfunctions.

common ground can be established by describing the essential functions of a watch. This common semantic model for different designs can be represented by a functional configuration or network that charts the different subfunctions and their connectivity.

Figure 2.1(a) shows the basic functional configuration of a timepiece. This is an abstract description of the overall function of a timepiece in terms of its subfunctions. The word "signal" does not necessarily imply an electrical signal, but any source of regular movements or changes. A more detailed network that results from further decomposition is shown in Fig. 2.1(b). Figure 2.2 shows a structural configuration using mechanical working principles. Figures 2.3, 2.4, 2.5, and 2.6 illustrate physical configurations of a pendulum clock, quartz clock, quartz LCD, and a mechanical watch, respectively. These result from specific implementations of the subfunctions in Fig. 2.2. All these physical configurations can be traced back to the original functional configuration, which can, in turn, be derived from any one of the physical configurations. The development of a timepiece can be explained in terms of different means of implementing the individual subfunctions. For instance, the water head (in a water clock) is replaced by weights (in a pendulum clock), by a mainspring (in a portable watch), and finally by an electric battery for the energy reservoir subfunction. Similarly, there is the constant time elapse referencing function as implemented by a pendulum in a pendulum clock, by a balance–wheel–hairspring in a mechanical watch, and by a quartz crystal in a quartz watch. The point is that by *abstracting* the functions of various components or subassemblies of existing designs one can generate a functional configuration that could help generate alternate means of accomplishing individual functions. Abstractions help "chunk out" knowledge so that the search for solutions can be performed more efficiently. It is, therefore, important that a methodology to represent design knowledge at different levels of abstraction be developed.

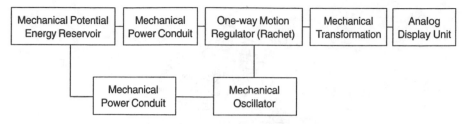

FIG. 2.2. A network of basic physical
building blocks in a mechanical clock.

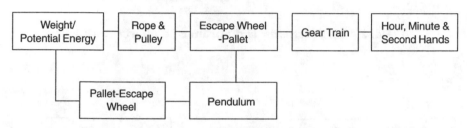

FIG. 2.3(a). Structural configuration of a pendulum clock.

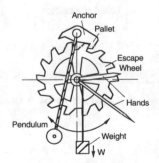

FIG. 2.3(b). A schematic diagram of a pendulum clock.

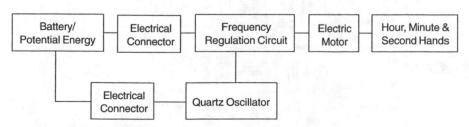

FIG. 2.4(a). Structural configuration of a quartz clock.

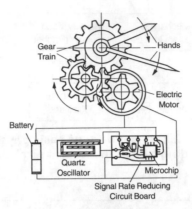

FIG. 2.4(b). A schematic diagram of a quartz clock.

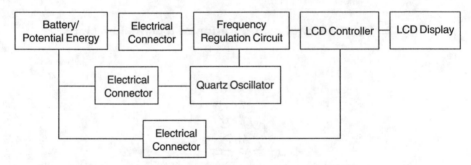

FIG. 2.5(a). Structural configuration of a quartz clock with LCD.

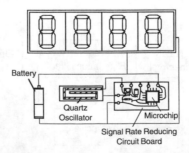

FIG. 2.5(b). A schematic diagram of a quartz clock with LCD.

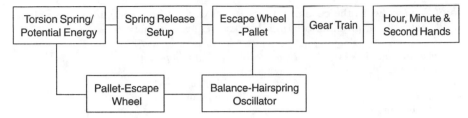

FIG. 2.6(a). A structural configuration of a mechanical watch.

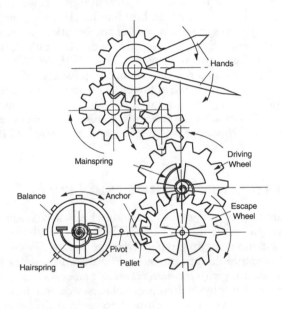

FIG. 2.6(b). A schematic diagram of a mechanical watch.

In the timepiece analysis, one can identify basic functions that need to be fulfilled in order to achieve the overall function. These basic functions are defined as the *functional building blocks*. In this example, the functional building blocks, as shown in the functional configuration, are power supply, pulse or signal generation (or a means to dissipate energy at a constant rate), signal regulation, signal transformation that is suitable for display, and signal indication or display. These functional building blocks can then be mapped to the physical domain in a number of different ways. For instance, by considering different physical working principles for the pulse generation function, we can map to a pendulum or a crystal oscillator (quartz watch) or metered fluid flow (water clock). Similarly, physical components and subassemblies can be abstracted as *physical building blocks*. In the case of a mechanical watch, the physical building blocks and instances of physical building blocks are given below.

Physical Building Blocks	*Instances or Physical Components*
Energy storage devices	Weights, springs
Power conduit	Shaft (rigid or flexible)
Oscillator	Tuning fork, pendulum
Intermittent motion device	Ratchet
Transmission	Gears (external, internal, epicyclic), chains-and-sprockets, belts-and-pulleys
Analog display	Hour, minute, and second hands

Each physical building block is an abstraction of a class of similar physical devices. Design abstractions, such as building blocks and functional configurations, promote the process of seeking useful combinations of existing implementations of subfunctions and can thus lead to a novel overall solution. They enable the designer to think in completely abstract terms in the beginning and gradually move into the physical domain. This can open up aspects of the problem previously unnoticed and remove some of the blocks to creativity. Care must be taken, however. Functional configurations are a tool and not an end in themselves. *The key is to intelligently map abstract functions to physical components without generating meaningless abstractions and without violating compatibility constraints.*

2.5 DISCRETIZATION OF THE DESIGN SPACE

So far, the significance of design abstraction has been discussed in terms of establishing a functional configuration. The first step in developing computational models for systematic design is to *discretize* the design domain. For functional reasoning in conceptual design, the term *discretization* implies identifying, representing, and reasoning with the *design building blocks* which are the functional building blocks *and* the physical building blocks. For constraint satisfaction in parameter design, the term discretization implies identifying, representing, and exploring design *subspaces*.

Each building block represents, in an abstract way, a subspace of the entire design space. There might exist a number of feasible physical designs within a subspace; as in numerous variations of "gear train." General modification rules can be developed to help generate variations of a given building block that correspond to various points within the design subspace (Kota, 1990; Kota and Lee, 1990). Once the design space is "properly" discretized, these building blocks should combine to generate new configurations. The notion of a finite set of building blocks describing the domain and modification rules generating mutations of the building blocks is like piecing together the design subspaces that were originally discretized. *Such discretization and recombination is fundamental to the development of computational models for conceptual design.*

Computerization requires discretization of a continuous design space into "chunks" of subspaces and a means of representing and reasoning with the subspaces (building blocks) at different levels of abstraction. Discretization of the design space is one of the fundamental requirements for automating the design process. The concept of design–space–discretization works well if the design elements are *modular*. Digital circuit design has been discretized (and automated as in VLSI circuits) because the electrical components are modular and well behaved. The mechanical design world, on the other hand, is *continuous*. As the design parameters are varied, the behavior of a mechanical system does not always vary in a systematic way throughout the design space. Knowledge representation at different levels of abstraction becomes difficult. Discrete design spaces are natural to the electrical domain and hence VLSI was possible. It will be a challenging task to discretize the continuous design space of the mechanical world. One of the major reasons for difficulty in discretizing mechanical designs into functional and physical building blocks is the overlapping of functions and features in existing designs. For instance, in the mechanical watch example discussed earlier, a component, such as the escapement wheel, participates in performing the function of signal regulation as well as signal transmission. In other words, the escapement wheel is a multifunctional component; it shares both functions. This aspect of *function sharing* makes the process of associating unique functions with each component difficult. In such cases, it may be helpful to consider only the primary function of each component; in the escapement wheel case, the primary function being signal regulation.

The distinction between functions and physical features blurs due to the presence of multifunctional features. This is especially true in the case of so-called "efficient" or multifunctional mechanical designs. Nonetheless, one should be able to distinguish between primary and secondary or incidental functions of each component and index each feature by it's primary function. It is important to note that "efficient" designs probably started out as modular designs and were later refined to embed multiple functions in individual components. Although it has been prescribed here that design knowledge should be compiled as a hierarchical set of functional and physical building blocks, designs that result from combinations of these blocks would probably be modular and even "inefficient." The aspects of modularity versus function sharing could potentially explain why design automation can be successfully carried out in modular domains whereas it is excruciatingly difficult in a nonmodular mechanical domain. However, if there is success in developing a computational model for conceptual design that synthesizes building blocks and generates alternate modular designs as first-cut solutions, improvisation with the resulting "inefficient" designs can be performed by a human designer.

Cam Synthesis as an Example of Discretization

The geometry of a cam profile dictates, to a great extent, the function of a cam. The function of a cam is described in terms of the mating follower. The follower displacement is a continuous function. However, the desired functional relationship (including first-, second-, and higher-order derivatives) is usually approximated by a combination (piecewise) of standard library functions (cycloidal, harmonic, trapezoidal, polynomial functions, etc.). This library can be viewed as building blocks for cam profile synthesis, because one can systematically synthesize an entire cam profile by piecing together the individual profile segments (subfunctions). Therefore, conceptually, numerous output motions could be created by novel combinations of finite building blocks.

2.6 A FUNCTIONAL FRAMEWORK FOR CONCEPTUAL DESIGN

The process of conceptualization needs to be formalized so that it can be traced using computers. To formalize the design process, one must discretize the design space into design building blocks, both functional and physical. A systematic conceptual design process begins with function decomposition and proceeds to determine working principles based on given systems-level constraints. The subfunction/working principle pairs are then mapped to physical building blocks by taking the prescribed constraints into consideration.The granularity (size, complexity, or level of detail) of the building blocks is one of the fundamental issues in any systematic design process. If the granularity of the building blocks is too fine, combinatorial explosion occurs. If it is too coarse, then novel synthesis with building blocks will be hindered. Obviously, there should be an appropriate granularity that precludes combinatorial explosion and permits novel synthesis. In order to at least partially address the problem of defining "appropriate" granularity in an automated design scheme, one must abstract the functionality of individual components into the functionality of subassemblies in organizing the domain knowledge.

Organization of Knowledge

In a functional framework developed by Kota and Lee (1990), the given design specifications are first dissected into functional requirements, performance goals, and constraints as shown in Fig. 2.7. A function describes the intended behaviors of the artifact to be designed. Constraints describe the circumstances under which the artifact is expected to operate, i.e., the limits of design variables, cost limits, space restrictions, and so forth. A design based purely on function might produce the desired behavior, but it might be too expensive to manufacture and maintain, or too bulky to install, or it might fall apart after a few hours of operation. Therefore, a functionally synthesized design is *not* a complete design solution in itself. Conversely, if the designed artifact cannot be operative (cannot function), it is immaterial whether it is cost effective, easy to assemble, or compact.

The fundamental assumption is that the conceptual design phase begins with reasoning about functions before fulfilling constraints. This ordering of functions and constraints is essential to developing a systematic procedure for the conceptual design process. Whenever an order or discipline is imposed on an open-ended process, such as conceptualization, the need inevitably arises to focus on

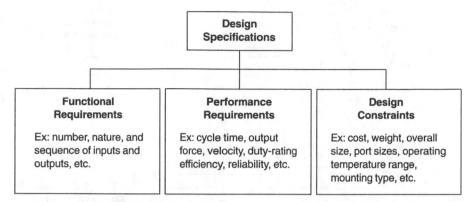

FIG. 2.7. Separation of functions, performance goals, and constraints in design specifications.

certain aspects of a problem first and set aside the others until later stages. This does not mean that constraints are not important or even less important than functions. It only means that a functional design should first be created before constraints come into play.

In view of this assumption, the design knowledge can be organized into three tiers: the top tier contains hierarchically organized, domain-independent functions; the middle tier contains generic physical devices, each representing a chunk of design subspace; and the bottom tier contains descriptions of catalog components (points within a given design subspace). A gross outline of the knowledge organization is shown in Fig. 2.8. Starting with design specifications, basic functions are first identified, and each function is then mapped to one or more feasible generic devices that meet performance criteria and constraints. Specific catalog components are then identified for each generic device by taking into account constraints, tolerances, and weighting factors.

Functions

One of the key aspects of this framework is the hierarchical organization of *domain-independent* functions (Fig. 2.8). Numerous functional modules are arranged in hierarchies (similar to a road map) and connected by "AND" or "exclusive OR" junctions. An AND junction is a decomposition point that breaks down a function into its subfunctions. An exclusive-OR junction connects (two or more) functions that are *different* at their level of abstraction into a *single* higher-level function. Whereas a choice between the alternatives is only *relative* at an OR junction, the choice is *absolute* at an exclusive-OR junction. The choice between power switching and power multiplexing is absolute because the former implies exercise of control on how the power is to be distributed to various branches, and the latter implies no control whatsoever. In Fig. 2.8, the *number* of suffixes denotes the level of decomposition, and the suffixes themselves indicate the path

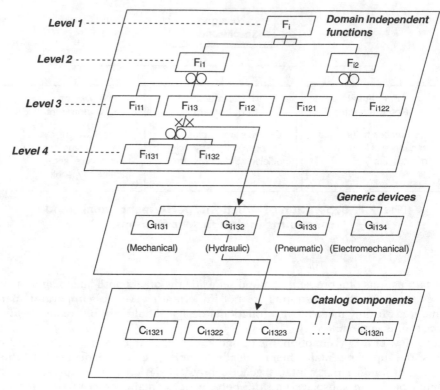

FIG. 2.8. Organization of design knowledge.

taken along the hierarchy. For example, function F_i is decomposed into F_{i1}, and F_{i2}. F_{i12} is the second node in the decomposition of F_{i1}.

Mapping of functions to generic devices exists, at least in theory, at the different levels. Functions at different levels map to different generic devices. Even a higher-level function can theoretically be mapped to a generic device. Such mapping could, however, be futile if the performance goals and constraints specified in a given task are not satisfied. The higher-level function should then be decomposed into lower-level subfunctions until a feasible map is established. The process of decomposition is interleaved with mapping and systems-level constraint evaluation.

Each function may be decomposed into several subfunctions; this decomposition continues until each subfunction is mapped to a catalog component. Depending on the mode of decomposition or function-level choices, different design configurations can be generated. If a particular function at a higher level of abstraction can readily and successfully be mapped to a catalog component, thus fulfilling all the given constraints, it is implied that the resulting design is less likely to be original. In other words, the depth of function decomposition required before a successful mapping to a physical building block can be achieved directly corresponds to the originality of the resulting design. Alternatively, a more stringent set of design constraints demands that one traverse deeper down the function decomposition tree. Therefore, the extent of originality that is required for a given design task or a subtask dictates how far down the function decomposition tree should be traversed before one can successfully identify a physical component that can meet all the design requirements.

Functions are abstracted in such a way that some of the higher-level functions map to subsystems, whereas the lower-level functions map to individual components. Additionally, higher-level functions that map to subsystems or a self-contained multifunctional component under certain performance requirements and constraints might fail to do so under a different set of prescribed constraints. Mapping is therefore *context dependent*. As shown in Fig. 2.8, links exist from functions at various levels to different generic devices and between functions and subfunctions. In actual implementation, the former links take priority over the latter links.

The choice of the particular level at which mapping occurs depends on the prescribed constraints and performance criteria. It will be shown later in this chapter that there is a direct correlation between the stringency of the design constraints and the level at which the mapping could take place. The more stringent the set of design constraints, the deeper the function decomposition tree must be traversed before feasible generic devices are identified for implementation.

Generic Devices

The working principles of existing devices serve as bridges that connect functional descriptions to the physical domain. A working principle is a vehicle that delivers an intended function through a particular set of structural characteristics. Generic devices are classified according to their working principles (Fig. 2.9). These are arranged hierarchically and are connected together by OR junctions only. An OR junction is a selection point that connects alternate physical implementations to their generic physical devices.

Each generic device represents a *class* of catalog components. For instance, a linear actuation function can be accomplished by a solenoid or a hydraulic cylinder. A solenoid would be considered a generic physical device that embodies electromagnetic principles. Similarly, a hydraulic cylinder would be a considered a generic physical device that embodies hydrostatic principles. Each generic device represents a *range* of performance characteristics, costs, and environmental characteristics that it can deliver. Thus, each generic device represents a subspace within a multidimensional design space. For instance, in terms of performance, a hydraulic cylinder could easily deliver up to several hundred pounds of output force, whereas a solenoid is limited to a few pounds of output force. Specific values of performance, cost, size, and so forth depend on the specific device under consideration (a point within the subspace) within a given class.

The notion of a generic device representing a subspace is carried into the computational model for identifying a *feasible range* for each design parameter (para-

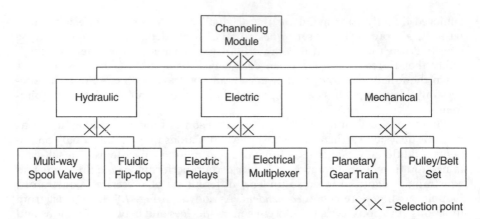

FIG. 2.9. **Organization of generic physical devices.**

metric design). The parametric design scheme takes as fundamental the notion of a discretized design space. In the hydraulics domain, certain characteristics are identified that allow all specifications and generic devices to be described in terms of their values. Now, each characteristic has a *domain* to which its values are restricted. Two types of domain are defined: interval-equipped domains and point domains. In the case of interval-equipped domains, a value in that domain is normally accompanied by an interval of values within which the value falls. Characteristics like "system pressure" have interval domains because the pressure must be within a certain interval. Usually, such characteristics are defined by a specific desired value within the interval. In the case of point domains, a value is not accompanied by an interval. Characteristics like "type of fluid" have point domains. These characteristics are thus dimensions of a design space, which is discretized into a finite number of partitions, each represented by a generic device thought of as occupying its center. The n_c characteristics define an n_c-dimensional *design space*, which may be thought of as the Cartesian product of the domain of the characteristics. The dimensionality of the design space is first reduced by matching certain critical characteristics and thus eliminating them. A search is then conducted in this reduced domain to find a generic device(s) that matches the given specifications most closely. The design paradigm assumes that a designer is presented with a specification that allows flexibility in the sense that various values may be renegotiated within fixed limits. The parametric design scheme here screens various generic devices and performs initial selection. Given a specification (set of performance requirements and constraints), it finds one or more generic devices that are promising initial designs for meeting the specification.

To clarify the preceding description, a simplistic example is presented. The design object is a hydraulic valve. There are several *characteristics* to be considered that have different types and ranges of values.

Generic Physical Device: Hydraulic multiway valves
Instance: Multiway spool valves

Characteristics ($n_c = 9$)	Domain type	Values
Number of shifting positions	point	integer (2, 3, 4 or 5)
Number of input ports	point	integer (2 or 3)
Number of output ports	point	integer (2, 3, 4, 6, or 8)
Type of operation	point	symbol (solenoid, manual, pilot, etc.)
Flow type	point	symbol (closed-centered, open-centered, etc.)
Pressure drop	interval	range of real numbers
Flow capacity	interval	range of real numbers
Port size	point	real number
Mounting type	point	symbol (side, front, etc.)

A computation network implemented within the knowledge-based design tool measures how well a generic device matches the given design specifications and returns the goodness-of-match value. The network propagates and consolidates individual goodness-of-match values that are computed for each of the characteristics in order to establish feasibility of a generic device to provide a desired function while meeting the performance requirements and constraints.

The Design Process

The design process of this configuration design method can be summarized in the following three steps:

Step 1. Separate the functional requirements from the design constraints. Establish a basic network of domain-independent functional modules Fi based on functional requirements [Fig. 2.10(a)]. Figure 2.10(a) shows three functions in a function diagram or function network. For instance, in an energy domain, functions F_1, F_2, and F_3 might represent power supply, power distribution, and motion actuation functions, respectively.

Step 2. For each functional module F_i:

(a) Identify a feasible generic physical device Gij that meets performance goals and satisfies constraints, or

(b) Decompose into simpler subfunctions F_{ik} using domain-independent function decomposition hierarchies and repeat step 2(a).

FIG. 2.10(a). A preliminary functional network.

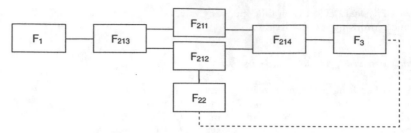

FIG. 2.10(b). A network of basic functions as an initial skeletal design.

A complete network of necessary and implementable functions, the functional configuration [shown in Fig. 2.10(b)], is thus developed by replacing some or all (depending on the constraints) of the original functions by simpler subfunctions.

Step 3. For the feasible generic device G_{ij} identified in step 2, a specific catalog component is identified that can fulfill all the constraints and designer preferences. For each feasible generic device, the most suitable catalog component that satisfies absolute constraints is then determined using a computation network. The computation network computes, propagates, and consolidates goodness-of-match indices for each of the functional and structural characteristics and selects the "best" component. The feasible device might fail to identify a suitable catalog component, in which case backtracking to step 2 may be necessary. Feasibility of a generic device is established by matching individual constraints against the domain of generic devices. New constraints are introduced as each generic device is added to the design network.

Alternate Configurations

For a given task, functional requirements are first met by identifying the basic functions that are needed. These functions and their interconnections are represented as a functional network. For a given task, basic functions that were identified in step 1 remain unchanged. In principle, alternate physical designs can be generated in three distinct ways:

(1) By enumerating alternate topologies of the same set of functions,
(2) By choosing alternate working principles (generic devices), or
(3) By selecting alternate components within a particular class of generic devices.

However, generally the performance criteria and the design constraints impose severe restrictions on the number of feasible designs that fulfill the specifications. In this method, alternates at each stage are evaluated against performance criteria and constraints. Typically, when more than one alternate design paths exists at any given stage, the path that seems "most promising" is pursued. The design process backtracks to an alternate path when it either fails to identify a feasible component or simply reaches a dead end.

2.7 COMPUTATIONAL SCHEMES FOR CONFIGURATION DESIGN METHODICAL GENERATION OF FUNCTION STRUCTURES

Methodical Generation of Function Structures

Hundal (1990) describes the computer implementation of a systematic design method for use in the early stages of the design process. The method is the classical one that breaks the process into Task Clarification, Conceptual Design, Embodiment Design, and Detail Design. Hundal and Byrne (1990) have developed a computer program that is used to develop the specifications list and functional block diagram, to search for solutions, and to develop concept variants and the final solution concept. It is basically a configuration design aid. The final product of the program is a solution concept in the form of a pictorial functional schematic of the product and process. The program has subprograms that serve the following purposes:

(1) Check input data
(2) Determine the logical event
(3) Determine the physical effects
(4) Determine the solution principles
(5) Determine the overall concept and produce the documentation

The program first aids the user in constructing the specifications list. Then, the user builds a functional block diagram of the system. The program checks for compatibility between blocks and helps the user by suggesting possible functions from a function database to satisfy any necessary transformations. The six basic categories of functions are convert, change magnitude, channel, connect, branch, and store/supply. The next step is to develop functional variants. The methods used are

(1) Subdividing complex functions
(2) Combining two or more sequential functions
(3) Relocating functions in an existing block diagram
(4) Moving the system boundary

The next step is to find solutions for each of the subfunctions. The program uses a database of solutions for each of the functions given in the function database. These are stored in a morphological matrix. At this stage, the solutions are given only in a rudimentary form. Concept variants are then formed by various combinations of the subsolutions and these are then evaluated by using value analysis.

The program is general in nature and has several distinct advantages. It helps the designer proceed in a methodical manner. It suggests alternatives at different steps of the process and ensures that none are overlooked. It also evaluates alternative design ideas and helps dispel prejudice toward a specific solution.

Configuration Task Modeling

Mittal and Frayman (1989) have addressed the need for precisely defining the task of configuration design. This aids in the development of a general theory of configuration design and more efficient problem solving methods. Their definition of a configuration task is as follows:

GIVEN:
  (1) A fixed, predefined set of components, where a component is described by a set of properties, ports for connecting it to other components, constraints at each port that describe the components that can be connected at that port, and other structural constraints,
  (2) Some description of the desired configuration, and
  (3) Possibly some criteria for making optimal selections

BUILD:
  (1) One or more configurations that satisfy all the requirements, where a configuration is a set of components and a description of the connections between the components in the set, or
  (2) Detect inconsistencies in the requirements

According to this definition, one cannot design new components, and the components cannot be modified to get arbitrary connectivity. Also, a solution must not only specify the actual components but also how to connect them. Mittal and Frayman then define a restricted version of the task, identifying two important assumptions: (1) the kinds of functional roles that need to be fulfilled within a configured artifact are known, and (2) for each functional role, one or more components can be identified as "key components." A problem solver for the task thus defined needs three kinds of knowledge: (1) available components, (2) functional decomposition specified by the given architecture, and (3) knowledge for mapping from functions to key components. To enable the mapping, the component-level knowledge is augmented to include knowledge about the functions provided and other functions needed in support of the former function.

Computational Conceptual Design—Novel Combination

Ulrich and Seering (1987) describe a computational technique for performing the task of specifying a schematic description of a system of components that will meet a behavioral specification. Their "design and debug" strategy is to generate an initial solution that meets the nominal input–output behavioral specifications of the problem and then to debug this prototype design until it meets the full behavioral specifications. They use bond graphs for representing designs. Bond graphs are a formal language for describing the exchange of energy in systems composed of lumped-parameter elements like masses, springs, resistors, and capacitors.

The space of possible bond graphs that may represent designs that implement any desired behavior is infinite. There are four key ideas that enable the pruning of this space to controllable dimensions:

(1) Limit the size of the design prototype and its bond graph.
(2) Precisely specify the input and output of the design by specifying chunks of bond graph to represent each.
(3) Use design precedents to limit the search.
(4) Enforce type consistency. The "type" of a bond graph chunk is the medium (electrical, fluid, etc.) associated with the chunk.

The next step is to use an algorithm to generate bond graphs corresponding to prototype designs that meet the nominal specifications of the design problem. Transfer function analysis is then used to evaluate the designs and debug them. A more detailed bond graph "grammar" is described by Finger and Rinderle (1989). They describe a transformational approach defining two main types of transformations: behavior-preserving transformations and component-directed transformations.

An important aspect of any configuration design task is the simultaneous implementation of several functions with a single structural element called *function sharing*. Ulrich and Seering (1987a, 1987b, 1988, 1989) view function sharing as a computational design procedure that produces efficient designs from modular designs. They define it as a correspondence between several elements in a device schematic description and a single element in a device physical description. The key idea that allows function sharing to be performed computationally is that most of the properties of a structural element in a design description are secondary and incidental to the properties that allow it to implement its intended function. The procedure they outline consists of three steps:

(1) A structural element is eliminated from the design
(2) Physical features that can provide alternative implementations of the functions of the deleted element are found
(3) Modifications are made to the design to accentuate the desired properties of the features found in step 2

One of the key concepts behind their research (Ulrich and Seering, 1987) is that most new designs come from knowledge of old designs: "*Novel Combination* is the process of extracting individual structural attributes from each of several known devices and combining these attributes in novel ways to create structural descriptions of new devices" (1987a). All designers do this, whether it is done consciously or not. This is, in fact, the basis for the effectiveness of functional analysis. Alternative means for accomplishing subfunctions come from previous experience with what are often completely unrelated designs. Identifying this activity and understanding it can be of great help in automating this aspect of conceptual design. Ulrich and Seering (1987a) describe a computer program that demonstrates these concepts in the domain of mechanical fasteners. They attempt to define a "design language" to control and manipulate information at a conceptual level. An important result of this research is the realization that using knowledge of existing successful designs to guide synthesis of novel designs greatly reduces the complexity of the design task.

2.8 A COMPUTATIONAL MODEL FOR THE CONFIGURATION DESIGN OF HYDRAULIC SYSTEMS

Hydraulics is one of the oldest branches of mechanical engineering. Hydraulic power systems are extensively used in modern aircraft, automobiles, heavy industrial machinery, and many kinds of machine tools (Henke, 1983). Hydraulic systems were selected as an application domain because they occupy a middle ground between digital and mechanical systems. Although the components of hydraulic systems are generally more modular than pure mechanical artifacts, they are less modular than elements of electronic digital circuits. The component choices in the hydraulics domain are, in general, wider than in digital systems.

Typically, a hydraulic system has an electric motor-driven or an engine-driven hydraulic pump as input that draws the fluid from a reservoir and delivers it to output devices such as linear (hydraulic cylinder) or rotary (hydraulic motor) actuators. The system may have multiple inputs and multiple outputs. The fluid is transported via pipes from one component to another. The distribution of power to various output devices is controlled by various valves such as directional control valves, pressure control valves, and flow control valves. Valves may either be controlled electrically by a signal that triggers a solenoid located inside the valve, or mechanically, for example, by a cam. Pump size determines the flow rate (gallons per minute), and the external load (e.g., the output cylinder working against an inertial load) influences system pressure. Protective devices, such as filters, relief valves (which bypass the fluid if a sudden overload causes the system pressure to reach the maximum), and emergency push buttons ensure safe and reliable operation. Figure 2.11 shows a simple hydraulic circuit consisting of a motor (M), a pump (P), a three-position, four-way directional control valve (V), and an output, double-acting cylinder (O). As the fluid flows to one end of the cylinder via port $p1$, the piston rod extends. As the piston rod reaches the end of the stroke, a limit switch (L) transmits a signal by a feedback loop to actuate the solenoid (S) of the valve (V) causing the valve to shift. The fluid is then directed into the cylinder via port $p2$ and out of the cylinder from port $p1$, back to the reservoir or tank (T).

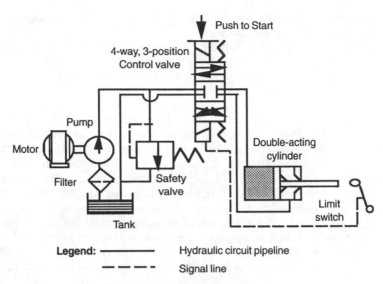

Push to Start

4-way, 3-position
Control valve

Pump

Motor

Filter

Safety
valve

Double-acting
cylinder

Limit
switch

Tank

Legend: —————— Hydraulic circuit pipeline

— — — - Signal line

FIG. 2.11. A simple hydraulic circuit.

Hierarchal Building Blocks and Knowledge Compilation

As described earlier, a functional building block is a black box that fulfills an abstract function while the means of accomplishing the function is of no concern. For example, a higher-level functional building block called the *power distribution model* is a black box that carries a generic function of distributing the input power to the output destinations. The knowledge base consists of numerous functional building blocks arranged in hierarchies containing AND, OR, and D junctions. An "AND" junction is a decomposition point that breaks down a function into its subfunctions. An "OR" junction is a selection point that connects alternative functions to their generic function. A *discrimination* (or D) junction combines (two or more) functions that are *different* at their level of abstraction into a *single* higher-level function. For instance, "power switching" and "power multiplexing" (Fig. 2.3) are two different functions in this context. These two functions are abstracted to a single, higher-level function called "power distribution" and are connected at a D junction. Whereas a choice between the alternatives is only *relative* at an OR junction, the choice is *absolute* at a D junction. The choice between power switching and power multiplexing is absolute because the former implies exercise of control on how the power is to be distributed to various branches, and the latter implies no control whatsoever.

There are five super classes of functional building blocks:

(1) A *power supply module* supplies power to operate the system
(2) A *motion actuation module* transforms the input power into the desired motions

(3) A *power distribution module* distributes the power from the input(s) to the motion actuation modules

(4) A *power regulation module* regulates the power level (pressure, torque, and force) and power rate (flow rate and speed)

(5) A *protection module* protects the system and its operators

Consider, for example, the power-switching function branch in Fig. 2.12. To implement this function, one must configure two subproblems: (1) the number of power flow routes (branches), and (2) a means to perform the switching itself. Note that these functional abstractions of hydraulic subsystems help formalize the design reasoning process. Traversing down the power-switching branch shows that a routing module and an activation control module are the two generic functions that are needed to perform the power-switching function. Routing requires configuration of a network of channeling modules. The elements of an activation control module sense triggering activities and then schedule and shift the accompanying routing module. The routing module is the *subject* on which the activation control module *acts* to accomplish its parent function of power switching.

Corresponding to each of these functional modules, one can identify implementable physical building blocks. For instance, a channeling module is a black box that channels (partitions or merges) power flows. A generic device, such as a two-way valve cavity, which has three power flow ports to provide two-way power flow channels, is an instance of the abstract channeling module. When combined with associated physical building blocks (which are actuators that implement the associated motion actuation modules), the multiway valve cavity forms a complete multiway valve. Depending on the working (operating) principles of the associated actuators, a two-way valve can evolve, for example, either into a solenoid-operated, two-way directional control valve, when the actuators are electromechanically operated, or into a sequence valve, when the actuators are hydraulic pressure operated.

The choice of physical building blocks is only an intermediate step between subfunctions and cataloged components. As noted later, the selection of a specific component from a catalog, given its generic function, is essentially a routine parametric design problem. The global parameters (systems-level constraints) are established while mapping subfunctions to physical building blocks. The nonfunctional constraints, such as cost and reliability, are considered in selecting catalog components after the functional requirements and the systems-level constraints (such as system pressure) are established. For instance, there are numerous physical components that fulfill the function of a three-way direction control valve with a maximum operating pressure of, say, 3000 psi. To select from a host of possible valves, all other characteristics are *matched* (compared) against local constraints, compatibility constraints (generated during the functional reasoning process), and the designer's preferences. These characteristics represent a minimum set of structural parameters required to specify catalog components. For instance, in the case of a three-way directional control valve, the parameters are (to name but a few) the pressure range, the duty rating, the flow capacity range, the pressure drop, and the operator type (solenoid or mechanically operated).

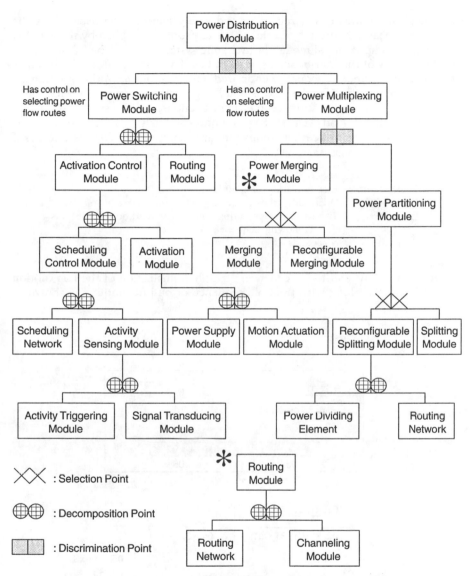

FIG. 2.12. The power distribution function decomposition hierarchy.

Design Example

A design example is presented in this section to illustrate a systematic method of configuration. The design specifications consist of descriptions of inputs and outputs, including the sequence of output motions, the operator interface, the operating environment, and reliability and safety factors. The user enters the design specifications through a series of menu prompts supplied by the HYSYN program, a computational model for hydraulic system design. The following is a brief summary of the user-defined specifications. For instance, the user specifies the number, nature, and sequence of desired outputs motions. Although numerical values are not given for the sake of simplicity, they must be specified for loads, speeds, cycle time, duty rating, geometric restrictions, desired system efficiency, and so on. Based on load cycle, HYSYN not only establishes the number and type of hydraulics power sources or pumps that are required, but also determines if an accumulator is necessary.

Power source: Electrical 120 volts, 60 Hz
Input: Operator pushes a button to start the cycle
Output: Two linear reciprocating and coordinated output motions
     per following sequence
Cycle time: N seconds

Output motions and their sequence: a graphic illustration of the two motion sites, S1 and S2, along with the time sequence of output motions is shown in Fig. 2.13.

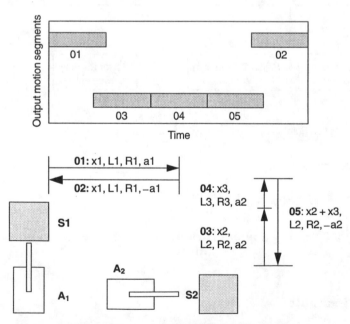

FIG. 2.13. Design specifications for a hydraulic systems design task.

(1) Inertia load L_1 lb should be moved through a distance x_1 at speed (power rate) R_1 in the direction a_1 at the site S_1 (motion segment O_1 in Fig. 2.13).

(2) The load L_1 must be held stationary while

    (a) Another inertial load L_2 is advanced through distance x_2 at speed (power rate) R_2 in the direction a_2 at site S_2 (motion segment O_3 in Fig. 2.13).

    (b) The inertial load L_3 is advanced at speed (power rate) R_3 through a distance x_3 in the direction a_2 at the site S_2 (motion segment O_4 in Fig. 2.13).

    (c) The load L_2 is advanced rapidly through a distance $x_2 + x_3$ in the negative direction a_2 at the site S_2 (motion segment O_5 in Fig. 2.13)

(3) Retract the inertial load L_1 through a distance x_1 in the negative a_1 direction at the site S_1 (motion segment O_2 in Fig. 2.13).

Selection and Decomposition of Functional Building Blocks

The first step in this configuration design process is to analyze the functional requirements and identify a set of basic functional building blocks. The basic functional building blocks are the root nodes of the function decomposition hierarchies that are stored in the knowledge base. In the design example, the basic functional modules are the power supply module, the power distribution module, and the motion actuation modules, as shown in Fig. 2.14. Because the desired output motions are specified at two different sites, it is inferred that two separate motion actuation modules are needed. Among these three basic functional modules, only the motion actuation modules are readily implementable and hence require no further function decomposition. The other two basic modules are broken down into their subfunctions to seek physical implementations. The function decomposition process is guided by the precompiled generic function decomposition trees (similar to road maps). The power distribution hierarchy shown in Fig. 2.12 is one such tree and is used to expand the power distribution node of Fig. 2.14.

Because the desired output motions are required to be sequenced, a control is needed for the power distribution function. Therefore, the power-switching branch (of the power distribution tree) is explored. The power-switching node is not readily implementable and is decomposed into its subfunctions: a routing module and an activation module. The routing module is decomposed into a network of channeling modules according to a generalized routing rule, discussed in the following paragraph. These channeling modules are implemented

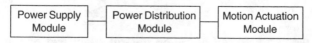

FIG. 2.14. A preliminary functional network of basic functions.

by channeling devices (or multiway valve cavities) as physical building blocks. The activation control module is broken down into a scheduling control module and a set of activation modules. In this design example, a network of activity sensing modules is algorithmically constructed to fulfill (partially) the function of the activation control module. Individual activity sensing modules are implemented as limit switches or other alternatives, such as hydraulic pressure sensors.

Generalized operators at the function level help construct functional networks. Each operator provides an operational guideline on ways to connect different functional modules according to a given overall function. The operators are problem independent and they are derived at the time the generalized knowledge is compiled as function decomposition trees. One of the generalized operators in this system is a generalized routing network algorithm that determines the flow paths based on the number and the nature of the input–output motion segments. In the example, there are five output motion segments organized into four motion sections (two for each actuator—forward and reverse). By applying the routing algorithm to the four motion sections, the routing network shown in Fig. 2.15 is generated. The channeling modules shown in Fig. 2.15 are default (four-way) channeling devices. As the design progresses, the default devices could be replaced by catalog components that meet all the constraints.

Based on the prescribed load cycle, back-of-the-envelope type calculations (or

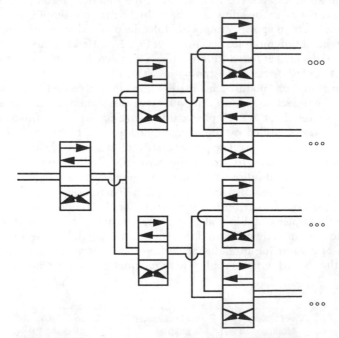

FIG. 2.15. Based on given design specifications, a routing network with default channeling modules is generated by the routing algorithm of HYSYN.

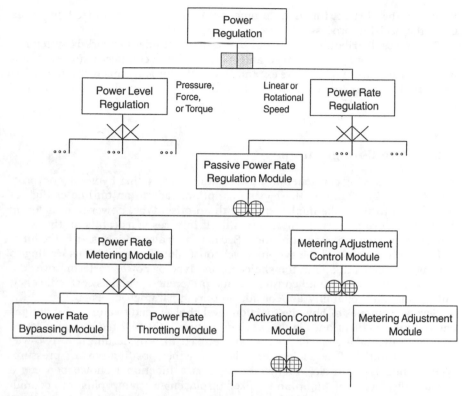

FIG. 2.16. Power regulation functional tree.

quantitative inferences) are performed to size the pump and any required auxiliary power supply units, such as an accumulator. The system pressure is also calculated. Such systems-level parameters help constrain the number of choices in the downstream design process. For instance, if the system pressure is established at an early stage, the number of feasible alternatives during the component selection process is reduced.

Once the primary functions are decomposed down to the implementation level (where they are implementable with physical building blocks), secondary functions are considered. In this design example, the primary function is to provide a sequence of linear-reciprocating motions. The secondary function is to fine-tune to the specified speed and the loading level by regulating the power from the power source. The power regulation function tree (precompiled and stored in the knowledge base) indicates that the power can be regulated by controlling either the power *rate* (speed) or the power *level* (force or torque) or both (Fig. 2.16). The speed regulation function provides a choice of either increasing or decreasing the nominal speed. The functional choices are (1) an autonomous power supply (that stores and restores power), (2) a passive power-rate regulation, or (3) an active power supply. Subject to various constraints and preferences in the design specifications, the abstract function decomposition trees and generalized operators guide the decision process.

The power distribution module of the basic functional network is systematically expanded using precompiled abstract function decomposition trees. Similarly, other nodes of Fig. 2.14 are expanded to seek physical implementations. The complete functional network, in which all the nodes are readily implementable, is shown in Fig. 2.17.

Alternative Configurations

Power-rate metering can generally be accomplished by either bypassing or throttling (Fig. 2.17). Choosing the bypassing option leads to an off-line configuration that in turn can be implemented with an offset-type, power-rate metering method. Choosing a bypassing function itself imposes constraints on the selection of a metering-adjustment method. Because both alternatives satisfy the functional requirements and the systems-level constraints, configurations leading to both will be generated, and the choice of one type of power metering over the other will not be made until constraints and preferences, such as cost, efficiency, duty rating, and reliability, are considered during parametric design.

Several examples of how the function-level choices lead to alternative designs can be given. As mentioned in the previous section, either a three-way, electromechanical valve or a sequence valve can be used to provide alternate two-way power distribution. The choice depends on whether position-type or pressure-type sensing is desirable. Another example is a functional choice between a variable-displacement pump and a fixed-displacement pump plus an accumulator. Either choice accommodates large variations in the load cycle. In these

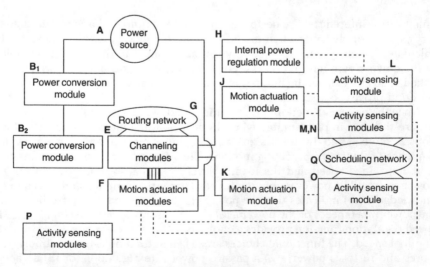

FIG. 2.17. A complete network of essential functions.

two examples, functional alternatives are enumerated and later evaluated against nonfunctional requirements, such as cost and reliability.

Parameter Design

A detailed account of the discretization of a parameter design space into "nominal design models" is discussed earlier to help select catalog components. Once all the functional building blocks in the established functional network are found implementable, the physical building block hierarchies (one such building block for each subfunction) are traversed. The chosen physical building blocks are guaranteed to fulfill the functional attributes of the functional building blocks. Nonfunctional constraints and preferences should be satisfied during the final component selection process. For instance, a four-way directional control valve is a composite physical building block (consisting of a four-way valve cavity and its associated operators). This description, however, is still too vague for ordering catalog components, even though the pressure range and the flow rate are already established.

The component characteristics are grouped into two factors: *systems-level performance requirements*, consisting of medium (fluid-type), power-flow rate, power level, or operating pressure, and *component-specific requirements*, consisting of cost, reliability index, duty rating, response frequency, pressure drop, port size, mounting type, size, weight, and so on. Systems-level performance requirements are derived from quantitative inferences made during the configuration design stage, and these requirements must be satisfied by all the components in the designed circuit. The component-specific requirements are different for different components. For instance, the component-specific requirements for linear actuators cover such parameters as single/double acting, stroke length, mounting type, port size, and rod end type. The design specifications are matched against the characteristics of the stored design models, which are classes of catalog components. Each design characteristic is associated, on the one hand, with a value and a tolerance band for specifications and, on the other hand, with a value and an "achievable region" for stored design models. The matching process involves computing a value between 0 and 1 that indicates the goodness-of-match, 1 being a perfect match. Individual goodness-of-match values are propagated to the solution nodes, and an overall best component is selected. (Weights are used to indicate the designer's preferences.)

Based on the functional network shown in Fig. 2.17 and the parametric design procedure just described, a complete hydraulic circuit, shown in Fig. 2.18(a), is synthesized for the given design specifications (described in Fig. 2.13). Alternative circuit configurations can be generated by traversing either alternative functional decomposition branches or alternative paths in the physical abstraction hierarchies. One possible alternative configuration in this design example consists of a sequence of valves instead of a four-way directional control valve and its accompanying limit switch (see Fig. 18(b)). Such an alternative configuration is systematically determined by choosing an alternative working principle, namely, a hydraulic *pressure* sensor instead of a *position* sensor.

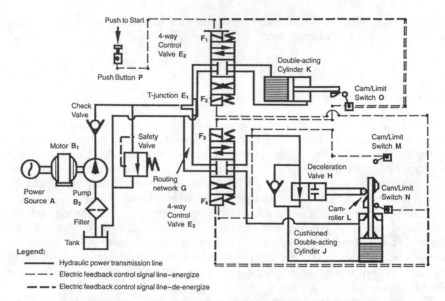

FIG. 2.18(a). Hydraulic system configuration derived from the functional diagram shown in Fig. 17. Component labels shown here match corresponding function labels shown in Fig. 17.

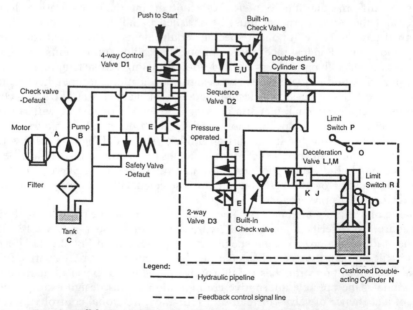

FIG. 2.18(b). An alternate hydraulic circuit generated by HYSYN by choosing a pressure sensor instead of a position sensor to implement the activity-sensing subfunction shown in Fig. 17.

2.6 CONCLUSION

Although the hydraulics domain may be more modular than other mechanical domains, the multitude of components and their variations pose a nontrivial configuration task. The methodology and the KBS are applicable to multiple-input, multiple-output systems. The functional methodology described here has been tested on practical complex hydraulic applications, such as deep-hole drilling, hydraulic presses, and hydraulic steering and drive systems. Knowledge compilation (giving functional and physical building block hierarchies) covers most of the industrial hydraulic systems domain. Interested readers are encouraged to contact the author for details.

The methodology underlying this approach to configuration design can be extended to other domains as well, such as automotive power trains. Discretization of the design space into design building blocks is the driving force behind the methodology presented here. In conceptual design, the domain is discretized into a set of interrelated functional and physical building blocks at different levels of abstraction. Once the system configuration is established, the parameter design process is applied. This process is governed by the discretization of the parameter space into nominal design models. (See Chapter 4 on parametric design for details.) The concept of design-space discretization works well if the elements of design are modular, as in digital circuits. Here, the design building blocks for hydraulic systems have been identified and abstracted. Kota (1990) shows similar building blocks for mechanisms design, which is another mechanical design application domain.

The key to generalizing this functional design methodology to other domains is the ability to describe the design building blocks at different levels of abstraction. General mechanical design spaces are continuous. By identifying design building blocks, one is "chunking out" the subspaces inside a continuous design space. Each building block represents, in an abstract way, a subspace of the entire design space. Variations of each building block represent physical variations of the concepts that building blocks represent.

The methodology presented here also suggests that the granularity of building blocks should be such that there exists a one-to-one mapping from function/working-principle pairs to physical building blocks. This controls the combinatorial explosion and permits synthesis of new (or novel) design configurations. The notion of one-to-one mapping need not preclude generation of alternative designs or new designs because functions are represented at different levels of abstraction. Depending on the nature of the desired functions and constraints in a given design task, one may find it necessary to decompose each function to different levels until a suitable physical implementation is reached.

REFERENCES

Brown, D. C., and Chandrasekharan, B. 1984. Expert systems for a class of mechanical design activity. *IFIP WG5.2, Working Conference on AI in CAD*, p. 259.

Finger, S., and Rinderle, J. R. 1989. A transformational approach to mechanical design using a bond graph grammar. *Proc. 1989 ASME Design Technical Conference (Design Theory and Methodology)*, 1989.

Henke, R. W. 1983. *Fluid Power Systems and Circuits*. Cleveland, Ohio: Penton Publication.

Hundal, M. S. 1990. A systematic method for developing function structures, solutions and concept variants. *Mech. Mach. Theory. Vol. 25, No .3.*

Hundal, M. S. and Byrne, J. F. Computer-aided generation of function block diagrams in a methodical design procedure. *ASME Design Theory and Methodology Conference.*

Kota, S. 1990. A qualitative matrix representation scheme for the conceptual design of mechanisms. *1990 ASME Design Technical Conferences, 21st Biennial Mechanisms Conference* New York: ASME.

Kota, S., and Lee, C. 1990. A functional framework for hydraulic systems design using abstraction/decomposition hierarchies. *Proc. 1990 ASME International Computers in Engineering Conf.* New York: ASME.

Mittal, S., and Frayman, F. 1989. Towards a generic model of configuration tasks. *Proc., 11th Joint Conf. on Artificial Intelligence, Vol. 2, 1989.*

Pahl, G., and Beitz, W. 1984. *Engineering Design*. London: Springer-Verlag.

Ulrich, K. T., and Seering, W. P. 1987a. Conceptual design as a novel combination of existing device features. *Advances in Design Automation, Vol. 1.*

Ulrich , K. T., and Seering, W. P. 1987b. Conceptual design: synthesis of novel systems of components. *1987 ASME Winter Annual Meeting, Symposium on Intelligent and Integrated Manufacturing Analysis and Synthesis*. New York: ASME.

Ulrich, K. T., and Seering, W. P. 1988. Function sharing in mechanical design. *AAAI 88, 7th National Conference on Artificial Intelligence.*

Ulrich, K. T., and Seering, W. P. 1988. Synthesis of schematic descriptions in mechanical design. *Research in Engineering Design, Vol.1, No.1, 1989.*

Chapter 3

Models of Conceptual Design for Concurrent Engineering

Mazin M. S. Al Hamando, and Soundar R. T. Kumara
Intelligent Design and Diagnostics Research Laboratory
Department of Industrial and Management Systems Engineering
Pennsylvania State University
University Park, Pennsylvania

3.1 INTRODUCTION

The traditional design and production process has been often understood as a sequential process begun by satisfying some functional requirements, then planning and producing a product. This process is usually divided into phases, with an individual or a team performing each task and making decisions in isolation from the others based on the knowledge required for each particular stage. Such a procedure commits the engineer to design decisions that impact all aspects of the product such as manufacture, process planning, maintainability, and other product life cycle issues. This procedure has influenced and dominated engineering design both in practice and in research and education.

Concurrent engineering is a perspective that attempts to represent and integrate all issues of designing, producing, and utilizing a product, from conception to disposal, under consideration at the early stages of the design process. For example, it enables the designer to determine the time required for producing various design features, evaluate the ease of product manufacture, or estimate the production cost while simultaneously trying to meet the functional needs. Computer technology such as artificial intelligence (AI) can be useful not only in making needed knowledge available to the designer at the beginning of the process, but also in providing techniques to handle the complexity of the design process. Research in concurrent engineering would contribute to an improved understanding of the design process, enhance design methods, help develop new design theories, and improve design education within engineering schools. However, this chapter also has to address problems such as methodology for abstraction, decomposition, acquisition, and organization of knowledge relevant to the product's design and life cycle in a cross-disciplinary and communicable format (Finger and Dixon, 1989b). The current practice in design, both in the profession and in engineering schools, does not support such methods as these and, in many cases, the approach is limited to normative design methods, largely ignoring the cognitive aspects of the design process.

In addition to design methods, the field of engineering design has also suffered from a lack of serious design theories. This is mostly due to a lack of a cross-disciplinary formalism that could capture the essence of the design process. One of the most important aspects of understanding the process of design and hence in formulating a theory is to understand the function–behavior–structure concept of design and to model it through a rigorous AI-based paradigm. Some design theories have attempted to introduce the notions of function and structure into the description of the design process. Significant contributions in this area have been made by Freeman and Newell (1971), Yoshikawa (1981), Chandrasekaran and Mittal (1983), Gero et al. (1988), and Suh (1990). However, these notions are in the development stage and further work is needed.

The main objective is to develop a domain-independent formalism for the basic concepts of design that is capable of providing communication links for concurrent engineering models. This chapter investigates the concept that the delineation of function–behavior–structure is an essential ingredient for models of conceptual design.

3.2   BASIC IDEA OF DESIGN

Definition

Design is an extremely complex process and is incompletely understood because it relies on creativity, intuition, and imagination, as well as on experience, learning, and the successful application of scientific principles (Kalay, 1987). Our understanding of engineering design is still elementary, and probably the most ill-understood aspects of it lie in its earliest stages, or what is known as the *conceptual design stage*. This is exacerbated by the lack of a universally accepted definition of the process or its elements. A review of the literature uncovers many definitions, as various authors and references define it differently with emphasis on certain elements of design. Most definitions present design as a process of putting together or relating ideas and objects in order to create a whole—products, processes, and systems—which is expected to attain a certain purpose or perform desired functions. These definitions focus on the purpose of the designed object, which is the *intended function* of the artifact. The concept of the intended function will be discussed in more detail later.

Elements of Design

The diversity in understanding and performing design stems from its complexity, although it can be reduced to some basic elements. In a broad sense, there are three basic elements involved in design activity. The first element is the *prod-*

uct, i.e., the final output of the design activity, which is the design as an artifact. The second is the *designer* who performs the activity, whether it is a human, a machine, or an interaction of the two. The third element is design itself as a *process*. Given these elements, the schools of thought in design theory can be presented. The cognitive school and the engineering school are the most common of these (Kumara *et al.*, 1989).

The central issue in the cognitive school is the involvement of the human designer and how a human performs a certain mental task. The main focus is on the second element of design—the designer—with secondary focus on the third element—the process. The cognitive mode of thinking can be described as the imagination and externalization of thought through action and its external representation, usually through drawings (Bridges, 1985; Dixon, 1987; Kumara *et al.*, 1989). Of primary concern to this school is the knowledge possessed by the designer, which usually reflects the designer's own personality and bias.

The engineering school of thought is concerned with the *practice* of engineering design, is based mainly on normative design methods. Ultimately, it is concerned with having prescriptions that specify how design should be done in particular circumstances and for particular products. These prescriptions are guided by specialized empiricism, experience, and intuition (Dixon, 1987), usually in specified domains. In other words, it describes how the design process should proceed in a sequence of phases, mainly analysis, synthesis, and evaluation. The main element of concern in this school is the first element, the product, that it determines the third element, the process, with little or no consideration for the second element, the designer.

The intention behind reducing design to some basic elements and comparing the cognitive and engineering schools of thought is to show that a more comprehensive school could be established by the positive merging of the two. It is hoped that the approach presented in this chapter will be one step in this direction.

Design Theories

Design theory is new as a field of research. Although there have been some design theories, most of them were derived from designers' long experience with the design activity. The existing design theories have followed different approaches. These approaches can be classified into three major categories according to their level and basis of abstraction: conceptual, relational, and axiomatic.

The *conceptual* approach deals with design at the lowest level of abstraction of functionalities, where design is based on a set of known *a priori* descriptions. The design process is accomplished by either conjuncting or disjuncting these descriptions to generate a new design (Yoshikawa, 1981). The *relational* approach deals with design at the component level, where each component is specified by a set of attributes of known and well-defined variables. New designs for a specific functionality can be derived by combining the attributes and deriving the values for the attribute. The *axiomatic* approach focuses on axioms as the basis for design (Suh, 1990).

3.3 THE DESIGN PROCESS

Phases of the Design Process

The engineering design process often occurs over a long period of time and involves more than one person, depending on the complexity of the problem at hand and the innovation involved. Because of this, design is often regarded as a process that occurs in phases. The major phases are the conceptual, configuration, and parametric design phases. *Conceptual design*, the first phase, is the transformation of the functional requirements into physical embodiments, structural descriptions, or configurations (Finger and Dixon, 1989a; Ulrich and Seering, 1987b). *Configuration design* is the transformation of the physical concept into a configuration with a defined set of attributes, but with no particular values assigned (Finger and Dixon, 1989a). In other words, the emphasis of this phase is on the realization and representation of the geometry and spatial relationships among parts, addressing the issues of connectivity and organization of assemblies. *Parametric design* is concerned with the assignment of definite values to the attributes.

Although these phases are regarded as separate entities by many researchers in the design community, it has to be noted that there are no clear lines that separate them. Rather, the design process is regarded as a continuous process despite the adoption of these terms. This view is strengthened by the fact that many researchers who adopt these terms disagree about the boundaries of these phases, and about the input and output of each phase.

Although there has been much research devoted to the configuration and parametric design phases, such as in CAD/CAM/CAE, there has been little work done in the conceptual design phase. Few design textbooks deal explicitly with this phase. This is mostly due to the fact that conceptual design is a very challenging realm in design research. The difficulty stems, in part, from the significance of the designer's creativity and the intimate involvement of the physical principles in the development of physical form embodiments from functions (Finger and Dixon, 1989a).

Concepts, concept formation, and concept representation are ways in which humans efficiently store and organize information and images of the world, such as objects and events. In psychology, concepts refer to mental representations of classes of equivalent entities that can be described by a small set of attributes and statements. For the purposes of design, a concept represents the basic functional and structural attributes of a class of entities. Generic functions are represented in an English-like formalism as concepts. The function concept of *joining* is associated with parts, static equilibrium, transforming forces, connection, and adhesion. Concepts are formed by abstraction, which is an important idea in design at the beginning of the process; i.e., the conceptual phase. In design, abstraction occurs at various levels. A model for abstraction is proposed in this chapter. It is based on the FSP design paradigm. Because the function initiates and drives the design process, abstraction is based on functional reasoning which identifies subfunctions, borrowing from heuristic classification and subgoal generation.

Classes of Design Problems

Design is an activity that is generally attributed to a wide range of solutions to design problems. In terms of the creative effort involved, these solutions belong to a wide spectrum, beginning from the simple modification of a few parameters of an existing product, to creating a whole new line of products, and ending with the invention of a completely new product with no precedent.

The segregation of these activities is obviously based on the innovation involved in the realization of the product. Because it is very hard to measure or quantify the innovativeness of a certain design, these categories are considered only as a guideline. In many cases, the decision of how to categorize a certain design on a certain scale is rather relative—with regard to some reference point—and subjective. Pahl and Beitz (1984) divide design into variant, adaptive, and original design. Similarly, Brown and Chandrasekaran (1988) classify design effort into three types or classes: creative, innovative, and routine design.

In creative design new primitives, which have no obvious relation to previous configurations, are created, usually by means of revolutionary methods or grouping of methods. The result is a major invention or an entirely new product (Brown and Chandrasekaran, 1988). Innovative design is the process of applying known principles to a problem that is largely different from those to which the principles are usually applied. The sources for the knowledge that has to be used are usually identified before attempting to solve the problem. However, the strategies for solving the problem are not known in advance (Brown and Chandrasekaran, 1988). The major element for this type of design is understanding the principles involved in the concepts and configurations of existing designs. In order to achieve such a capability, it seems that it is necessary to capture the causal knowledge of a certain domain. Routine design problems are concerned with slightly modifying certain features to improve the performance of or change a functional attribute. The structure of the object is assumed to be fixed, and the methods of designing the object or its components are known and well documented. The task of the designer in these problems is to select from previously known sets of well-understood design alternatives.

Often, in engineering design, the initial attempt to get a final product does not satisfy some or all of the intended functional requirements or might fail to meet the design restrictions. Then, the designer has to go back to an earlier stage of the design process and change some or all of the elements involved in the current solution. This process is called *redesign*. Sometimes a designer performs this feedback process, despite the fact that the product is meeting all its requirements, in order to achieve a better or an optimum solution.

Design Paradigms

From the earliest civilizations, humans have always attempted to achieve capabilities that were not naturally available to them by inventing new tools and designing new products. These tools and products became more and more sophisticated as new discoveries, new sources of energy, and new technologies were made available. Driven by ever-continuing societal needs and human aspirations for achievement, new discoveries were made at an increasing pace. Each scientific breakthrough triggered new products to be designed that made use of and were made possible by the new discoveries.

Whether the relationship between society and science and technology is teleological or ontological is not within the scope of this chapter. However, it is this interaction that drives designers to invent a new product based on a social need and a new technology. Yoshikawa (1985) distinguishes two types of technological innovation based on two different driving forces:

(1) Innovation that is guided by new scientific knowledge or a new scientific paradigm, such as nuclear power and electrical machines which were guided by new paradigms in physics and new electrical theory, respectively.

(2) Innovation that is created by a new design principle or a technological paradigm. The novelty of this type of technology stems from the novelty of its function; i.e., the technology is based on a new design principle to create a new function. Examples are the steam locomotive, computer aided design, and robots.

The design or invention of a new design paradigm usually takes decades or even centuries to be realized and completed.

If a new paradigm happens to be successful, economically and socially, it begins to grow based on the diversity of users' needs and market demands and starts to develop distinct types or prototypes that differ significantly from each other, although still relying on the same principles and sharing some basic properties. The definition of *prototype* here is borrowed from Gero *et al.* (1988). They define a prototype as "a generalization of groupings of elements in a design domain which provides the basis for the commencement of a design. A prototype comprises function, structure, and knowledge" (Maher *et al.*, 1989). These terms, according to Gero *et al.* (1988) and Maher *et al.* (1989) mean a set of interpretations (either of required interpretations or required performance), a set of vocabulary of elements, and the knowledge about them and their relationship. Some examples of prototypes of the same paradigm are cars, trucks, and buses. The design of a new product usually takes a few years or maybe a few decades.

Each prototype can grow further into more distinct types that are called *classes*. These classes of objects share some common characteristics, but differ in some design features. Each model of a car manufacturer can be considered a class of objects. Each different product of each class is an *instance* of that class. For example, a Honda Accord 1990 is an instance that is different from the others, but still shares most of the basic properties with instances of the same class.

The evolutionary and hierarchical structure of the design paradigm into pro-

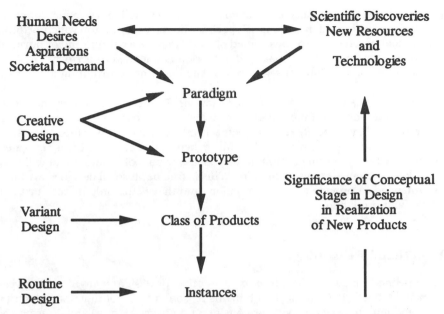

FIG. 3.1. Hierarchical organization of conceptual knowledge.

totypes, classes, and instances is shown in Fig. 3.1. The vertical arrow at the right represents the significance of the conceptual design stage in designing new products. The higher the product on the tree, the more significant is the role of the conceptual design stage. This is because in an entirely new design paradigm, the designer is involved in a creative activity of defining new primitives through the use of certain physical principles to achieve the functional requirements that have to be translated to structural descriptions. This significance is illustrated by the approximate description of the class of design involved in these products, shown at the left side of the diagram.

The present discussion is aimed at identifying the classes of artifacts that designers deal with and the degree of creativity and effort involved in each one. By relating this scheme to the previous classifications of the design process, one can realize the significance of the conceptual design phase at each level. This scheme is helpful in formalizing a framework for a design methodology and will be referred to later.

3.4 FUNCTIONAL AND CAUSAL REASONING IN DESIGN

Functionality in Engineering Design

Engineering design is basically concerned with providing an artificial device that can be used to achieve a desired function, or as Simon (1969) described it, "the process of devising artifacts to attain goals." *Webster's* dictionary defines *function* as "the action for which a thing is specially fitted, used, or for which a thing exists," and in reference to constructed objects "implies a definite end or purpose that object serves or a particular kind of work it is intended to perform." Also, it refers to function as "one of a group of related actions contributing to a larger action."

People think and reason in terms of functions. They often refer to the designed objects based on the function they provide, like a can opener or a sewing machine, or they associate these objects with their functions like the association between a house and a place to live in, or between a cup and drinking water. Humans, when observing an unfamiliar device or part of a device, immediately speculate or inquire about its function. This is true because all designed artifacts are intended to provide a certain function, and that is the only reason for their design and production.

Functional Reasoning

The intended function of an object is the motive for design in engineering. Freeman and Newell (1971) argue that humans reason in terms of functional description, and tend to select objects for consideration in problem solving in terms of their functional description. Based on the tendency of humans to design in terms of functions, they presented an approach based on functional reasoning where the basic model of the design task environment consists of a set of structures and a set of functions. In essence, the approach is based on the assumption that existing structures could be combined into new ones to achieve the desired function. The basic environment is in the format: *given* a set of structures and their functional specifications, *construct* a structure with desired functional specifications. The relationship between the function and structure is the essence of the design problem.

Function–Structure Relationship in the Design Process

In a given design problem, the transformation from functional requirements to structures could be achieved basically in two ways: a top–down approach and a bottom–up approach. Other approaches can be derived from the basic two schemes, such as a meet-in-the-middle approach (Thorp and Peeling, 1987) and a most-critical-component-first approach (Freeman and Newell, 1971). All methods have a combinatorial, heuristic search character where at each point, a set of possible actions is available to advance the process.

Top–Down Approach

Top–down schemes start with the desired function and progressively transform it into structural descriptions, working backwards toward the available structures. The logic that drives the process is to find the structure that provides a certain function. So a typical step in a top–down approach would be

$$f - requires \rightarrow S$$

The stipulation can be structural or functional. In the former case, the step is linking the function directly to the structural attributes, whereas in the latter, the function is being further refined and broken down into subfunctions.

This process allows an incremental binding of the design leading into further detailing without overcommitting the designer. The final result is achieved when all the functional requirements are satisfied. This process is analogous to a backward heuristic search procedure (Freeman and Newell, 1971). The outcome of a successful design is an object composed of either the available structures or some combination of their structural descriptions. The result might not match a real physical object, thus further detailed functionalities or constraints have to be added until a physical description is implicit in the functional specifications.

Bottoms–Up Approach

The bottom–up scheme starts with the available structures, and by constructing successively larger structures, a design is found that satisfies the functional requirements. The structural elements of known functionality form the design space. A new structure can be constructed from a set of structural elements that form functional connections. A step in a bottom–up approach usually would be

$$s - provides \rightarrow F'$$

where s is an existing or constructed structure and F' is a function or a set of functions that are provided by that specific structure. A structure satisfies the desired functional specifications if, and only if, it provides functions which include those desired, i.e., if F is a subset of F', and if for each desired function the required function matches exactly those desired (Freeman and Newell, 1971).

The bottom–up scheme is an exact heuristic search in terms of the operations. The disadvantage of such schemes is that they require an extensive library of components for realistic chances of achieving successful designs. Thus, the search process would be extremely large and difficult to accommodate. This scheme seems to be more appropriate for modular design domains where the modules are already known designs, and some components seem to be dominant elements in the new designs.

Meet-in-the-Middle Approach

This scheme is a combination of the previous two approaches and is probably the way designers actually work (Thorp and Peeling, 1987). The advantage of this approach is the reduction of the search space and difficulty, because design can be initiated from either side depending on a given situation. Thus, this scheme requires two libraries, or the ability to extract one from the other (Kumara et al., 1989).

Most-Critical-Component-First Approach

This approach is most suitable for design problems where the design depends mainly on one component or part, or when the significance of its components can be ranked according to some criteria. So the initial step here is to assume functional specifications of the structure that are most critical in the design and solve them first.

Function–Structure Design Model

The essence of this work is that it defines the design process as the process of transformation of functional requirements into structure. The Freeman and Newell (1971) model of design can be simply represented, where the direction of the arrowhead would depend on the approach followed by the designer:

Function ← *transforms* → **Structure**

The significance of the Freeman and Newell model is that it was one of the first to introduce the notion of functional reasoning as a basis for design, with a clear delineation of function and structure. However, the confusion of the multiple functionalities of an object is primarily caused by the failure of the model to distinguish between the notion of a function and the behavior of a structure, which was introduced later by other models along with other lines of reasoning. The work that followed this pioneering functional reasoning based model attempted to avoid some of its shortcomings. One of these shortcomings was the lack of a clear abstraction of function and structure.

Function–Structure Abstraction

The first function–structure design model did not elaborate on the nature of the function, discuss its composition, or propose a scheme for its decomposition. The same was true for the structure, because a device or an object was basically treated as a simple collection of components. In other words, there was no clear structural organization for the designed object at the conceptual stage. Moreover, the model did not develop or suggest any theme or theoretical framework for abstracting the function or the structure of a device, nor did it provide any guidelines for establishing the function–structure relationships. Later models further developed these concepts. The formal definition of the abstraction of both the function and the structure to sets of lower levels of functional requirements and physical components is an important concept that supports the function–structure design model.

The structure of a device in most design problems could be organized as a collection of assemblies, or subassemblies, and their components. This decomposition is a common method for abstracting devices structurally. The function of a device can also be decomposed into sets of lower-level functions. The concept of functional decomposition itself is not new. Although this theme has been commonly used, there has been no well-defined method for abstracting a device functionally. For example, Rinderle (1988) proposed the establishment of a functional hierarchy for devices. However, in the scheme that he presented, the functional abstraction was established in order to evaluate the designer's proposed preliminary configurations. In other words, there was no specific reference to the role of functional abstraction in the conceptual design phase. Instead, it was being proposed—along with the structural abstraction—as a procedure to help the designer to evaluate several alternative configurations and to choose among them.

From the preceding discussion, the functional and structural abstractions of a device are assumed to be related, as they represent the same object. Earlier, the function–structure relationship was discussed in terms of the search strategy. These strategies do not indicate how these relationships are established nor how they are mapped. The ability of a designer to determine the function of a certain physical configuration is usually attributed to experience. However, the fundamental basis for this relationship is basically embodied in the physical laws that determine the behavior of a given structure or assembly of structures. The concept of behavior and its relation to the function–structure design model is presented in the following section.

Function–Behavior–Structure Relationship

Behavior is broadly defined as the manner in which an object responds to stimulation from its environment. The introduction of the notion of behavior to design requires the modification of the definition of function. Bobrow (1985) defined function as "the relation between a goal of a human user and the behavior of a system."

The concepts of function and behavior are often misunderstood and interchangeably used because of their close interaction depending on the domain in which they are being used. Bobrow distinguishes between function and behavior by indicating that functionality is a different level of description than behavior. For example, the behavior of the hour hand of a clock can be described in terms of rotation around a point, where its function is to indicate the hour to an observer. The function of a component of a system relates the behavior of that component to the function of the system as a whole. In the same example, the function of the system or the device—the clock—is indicating the time in hours, minutes, and seconds. Thus, behavior, according to Bobrow refers to "the time course of observable changes of state of the components and the systems as a whole. Each component has some associated behavior, and the behavior of the system as a whole results from the interactions of the behaviors of the components through specific connections." These connections are believed to be causal.

Similarly, Davis (1985) defined structure as "information about the interconnection of modules," organized either functionally—how the modules interact—or physically—how they are packaged. According to this definition, the term *structure* was replaced by *functional organization* and *physical organization*. Based on the fact that every component has both a functional and physical description, two interconnected description hierarchies are developed for each, linked at their terminal nodes. This link will represent the relationship between the structure and function of a component at the lowest level.

The significance of these concepts is in the representation of functional organization of function, and the segregation of the behavior from the function. The limitation of this concept is that it is more oriented toward diagnosis and application of the same principles to design. The major difference between the two is that in diagnosis, the configuration of the entity is already known, and the connection to the function is much easier to establish. Also, these principles were applied to electrical design only, a domain that is modular with one-to-one mapping between function and structure. This limited application would make it difficult to generalize these principles to all domains of design.

Causal Reasoning

The definitions of both function and structure are modified on the introduction of the concept of behavior. Similarly, the definition of design also has to be modified to accommodate these changes. Hence, design can be defined as "any arrangement of the world that achieves a desired result for a known reason" (Genesereth, 1985).

The basic difference between the definitions is that while both explained design as a process of transformation between function and structure, the latter presented a base for this transformation on which the designer deliberately—not accidentally—proceeds through the process. Although this concept seems to be simple and obvious to most designers, it remains an essential and rather unconscious procedure during the progress of design. Our understanding, and hence the definition, would be incomplete without its full incorporation into the transformation process. The previous design model should be modified accordingly. A simplified representation of the model is

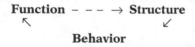

The remainder of this chapter attempts to organize design knowledge and develop this design model by incorporating the basic concepts presented so far. The function–behavior–structure abstraction presents a cross-disciplinary knowledge representation that facilitates the concurrent consideration of life cycle issues using this abstraction for knowledge representation. Thus, the designer can simultaneously attempt to satisfy the requirements for producibility, reliability, safety, and maintainability, as well as functionality, performance, and quality. Moreover, this abstraction should allow the concurrent development of production planning along with the design, because this scheme facilitates the exchange of information between disciplines. This model will be presented theoretically and through the use of an example from engineering applications.

Formalization of the Abstraction Process

Design has been defined as a process that basically deals with function, structure, and behavior. In order to define the formal relationships among these three components at the conceptual level, an abstraction scheme is proposed for use in developing the functional and causal design model.

Functional Abstraction

The process of design, as discussed earlier, is motivated by and associated in most cases with a single need, which is the main function for its intended use. This function is denoted as f^*. In engineering design, a need can be satisfied by constructing a device. In engineering problems, this need is only a broad concept that motivates the designer to create an entity to satisfy the need. In other words, the need itself in most cases is not explicitly defined as constituting the functional specifications for engineering design problems. Hence, the designer has to convert this concept, based on the specific design situation and constraints, into specific functional requirements F that consider all life cycle issues. The desired function is usually associated with other functions abstracted from other domains: $f_1, f_2, \ldots, f_n$. In real-life situations, the designer commences the design process by performing this step.

$$\text{Need} - \textit{translate} \rightarrow F = \{f_1, f_2, \cdots, f_n\}$$

Establishing the functional specification is an important step in defining the problem, triggering the early stages of the conceptual design phase, guiding the design process, and thus determining the outcome or final solution. The process of arriving at functional specifications will be discussed in detail with an example.

Structural Abstraction

Any designed artifact is composed of one or more structures. These structures are not necessarily physical objects, as in the case of software design where the artifact is a computer program composed of lines of code or subroutines. The structures could be described in different ways, in terms of their structural attributes or structural descriptions sd. Any structural entity Sd_i has an infinite number of attributes or descriptions:

$$Sd_i = \{sd_{i1}, sd_{i2}, sd_{i3}, \ldots\}$$

These attributes fully describe that entity and distinguish it from all others. A designed device is an assembly of structural descriptions, connected in a certain manner in order to achieve the desired function. Hence, the physical device Pd_1 could be described as

$$sd_1 \wedge sd_2 \wedge \ldots sd_k \rightarrow Pd_1$$

If at least one of these structural attributes is changed, the resulting device would be different. The significance of the difference would depend on the significance of that particular attribute to the design:

$$sd_1 \wedge sd_3 \wedge \ldots sd_m \rightarrow Pd_2$$

Behavioral Abstraction

Each attribute of any device Pd_i that interacts with its environment, behaves in a certain fashion b_i if certain conditions or input exist. If the device exhibits more than one behavior, then the behavioral description of the device consists of a set of behaviors $\{b_{i1}, b_{i2}, \ldots, b_{in}\}$. Thus an axiom could be introduced:

$$F(Pd_i) \rightarrow B_i = \{b_{i1}, b_{i2}, b_{i3}, \ldots, b_{in}\}$$

where $F(Pd_i)$ is the set of functions derived by a physical device Pd_i. Because

$$F(Pd_i) = \{f_{i1}, f_{i2}, f_{i3}, \ldots, f_{ik}, f^*, \ldots, f_{in}\}$$

the mapping process can be represented as

$$\{f_{i1}, f_{i2}, \ldots, f_{ik}, f^*, \ldots, f_{in}\} M \{B_i = \{b_{i1}, b_{i2}, \ldots, b_{in}\}\}$$

where M is a mapping function. Any single behavior or more than one of a given attribute can contribute to achieving the desired functionality. Some of the behaviors of structural entities are not known or well understood, so this set cannot be assumed to be exhaustive.

If a certain structural entity has potential behaviors that can partially satisfy the functional requirements, then by changing one or more of its attributes the designer can achieve the functionality or get closer to achieving it. It is also possible that the desired functionality might not be achieved. This might lead to a different physical device. A theorem could be derived postulating that changing a structural attribute will change at least one behavior of a given structure. This theorem is derived from the previous axiom. Currently, the proof is by verification only.

The exhibited behavior of the device is caused by its interaction with the environment. The environment at a given time t can be described as a set of conditions $C = \{c_1, c_2, \ldots, c_n\}$. The abstraction scheme presented can be a tool to formally represent the design process. Given the preceding definitions, it can be summarized as

$$F = \{f_1, f_2, \ldots, f^*, f_n\}$$
$$S = \{sd_1, sd_2, \ldots, sd_n\}$$
$$B_i = \{b_{i1}, b_{i2}, \ldots, b_{in}\}$$
$$C = \{c_1, c_2, \ldots, c_n\}$$

where $f_1, f_2, \ldots, f_n$ are functions and f^* is the intended function; $sd_1, sd_2, \ldots, sd_n$ are structures; $b_1, b_2, \ldots, b_n$ are behaviors; and $c_1, c_2, \ldots, c_n$ are constraints. At the conceptual level and before any abstraction, F is at least a singleton set. These sets represent the abstractions for device i. Achieving these sets would result in the design of the needed device.

The design problem in essence is the process of abstracting the functional specifications and mapping them onto structural descriptions, based on known causalities. The mapping functions are denoted as M_1, M_2, ..., and so on where M_i could correspond to processes, machines, and so on, thus incorporating the concept of concurrent engineering.

Among the characteristics of this mapping process is the possibility of obtaining one function by using more than one structure. This characteristic, adding to the difficulty of the design problem, implies the following:

$$f^* \rightarrow \{sd_i\}$$
$$f^* \rightarrow \{sd_j\}$$
$$f^* \rightarrow \{sd_k\}$$

The implication of this multiple mapping is that the same device could be obtained by a variety of combinations of different structural descriptions. At the same time, the use of one or more of the structures that provides the desired function does not guarantee a device that provides the desired function, depending on the interaction with the other structures that collectively form the device. In other words, the use of some structures that provide a function with different components might lead to different devices, such as

$$sd_1 \wedge sd_2 \wedge sd_3 \wedge \ldots sd_k \rightarrow Pd_1$$
$$sd_1 \wedge sd_3 \wedge sd_5 \wedge \ldots sd_n \rightarrow Pd_2$$
$$sd_1 \wedge sd_3 \wedge sd_4 \wedge \ldots sd_j \rightarrow Pd_3$$
$$\vdots$$

The interaction of the set of environmental conditions with the device, described by its structural descriptions, causes the device to exhibit a certain set of behaviors. This could be represented as follows:

$$\{c_1, c_2, \ldots, c_n\} m_1 \{sd_1 \wedge sd_2 \wedge sd_3 \wedge \ldots sd_n\} \rightarrow B_i$$
$$\{c_1, c_2, \ldots, c_n\} M_2 \{sd_1 \wedge sd_3 \wedge sd_5 \wedge \ldots sd_k\} \rightarrow B_j$$
$$\vdots$$
$$\{c_1, c_2, \ldots, c_m\} M_1 \{sd_1 \wedge sd_2 \wedge sd_3 \wedge \ldots sd_k\} \rightarrow B_k$$

where M_i is a mapping function. The transformation process from the initial set of the required functions to the conceptual device is illustrated in Fig. 3.2.

The set of behaviors B_i is assumed, in a successful design, to include at least one element b_{ij} that is equivalent to the desired function f^* (j refers to the device). If B_i does not include such an element, then the device does not satisfy the functional requirements of the design problem. Thus, the process has to go to the redesign phase at the conceptual level.

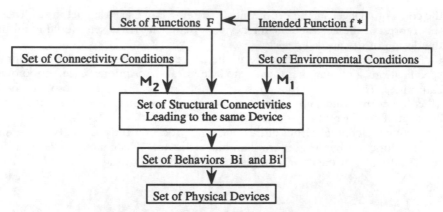

FIG. 3.2. Schematic for the abstraction process.

3.5 EVOLUTION OF THE CONCEPTUAL DESIGN

The approach presented in this chapter assumes that this process of functional abstraction and evolution is done at several levels, where the complexity of these levels depends on the problem at hand and the class of the design activity. It requires an accurate understanding of the need, which is done by identifying and refining the functional attributes for the desired entity based on the higher-level context of the design and its environment. The outcome of this process is the initial identification of the paradigm that the problem belongs to, which is the first step in shaping the conceptual design.

Once the designer matches the need with an existing paradigm, the concept inherits the general functional and structural attributes of that paradigm. Given these attributes, along with the functional requirements at hand, the designer moves to match the current state of the entity with an existing prototype by breaking down the functional requirements into lower levels. This, in turn, will generate more functional requirements to be satisfied, and hence will further guide the process.

In order to elaborate on this process, we need to understand how designers perform this process. Gero *et al.* (1988) suggest that when faced with the task of designing an object, a novice designer needs to refer to references in order to commence, needing both general and more problem-specific information. Experienced designers rarely do so because they have acquired the needed knowledge for that design situation. They have also chunked this knowledge into a generalized model, as a prototype, that makes it available across the entire range of design (Gero *et al.*, 1988). These prototypes have, semantically and syntactically, certain general properties. Hence, when a designer proposes a solution derived from a prototype, the design will inherit these general properties.

Yoshikawa (1981) and Tomiyama *et al.* (1989) assume that design is a process of evolution and transformation of the state of the design objects. However, they did not elaborate on the evolution of the functional requirements. As presented in this chapter, this process is in fact an evolution and refinement of the need from its initial general form into abstract functions in relation to the design and manufacturing constraints and other life-cycle issues. This process is called the *function transformation* (Al Hamando, 1990). Generally, it is possible to map functions to structural descriptions at almost any level of abstraction. However, the deeper the level of the functional abstraction is, the more detailed the structural description will be. For example, if the required function is to "provide a place to live in," then this function could be mapped to a house, an apartment, or a hut. Matching the general function to this structural description, which represents a prototype, does not provide enough information to derive a design solution, yet it is the step where most designers begin.

space to live – *mapped to* → House

So the designer would usually transform the general function into another level of functional abstraction, according to the given design situation. In the case of the preceding example, this would correspond to a space to sleep, a space to eat, a space to cook, a space to wash, and so on for the functions that are associated with living. The second level functions would be mapped to a lower level of the structural description that might start defining the spatial composition of the entity. The space to sleep would be mapped to a bedroom, the space to eat might be mapped to a dining room, and so on. Again, this structural description is far from being sufficient to identify a solution, but is obviously the early stages of forming the conceptual design.

This process of function transformation continues until the level of the functional abstraction is either at its lowest level or is sufficient to identify a detailed design instance. Each iteration of the function transformation adds more functions to the set of the functional requirements. This set is then mapped to the structural attributes that can causally provide the desired function. These structural descriptions are then synthesized into structural components that in turn determine the form of the device. The output of these iterations is an evolution from the conceptual design to the early stages of the configuration design. This process is illustrated in Fig. 3.3. The model is illustrated through an example in the following section.

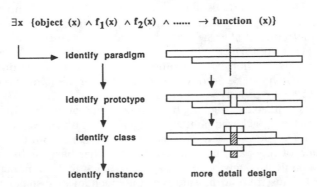

$$\exists x \; \{object \; (x) \wedge f_1(x) \wedge f_2(x) \wedge \ldots \ldots \rightarrow function \; (x)\}$$

Identify paradigm

Identify prototype

Identify class

Identify instance   more detail design

FIG. 3.3. Evolution of the conceptual design.

3.6 MECHANICAL FASTENERS

Joining in Engineering Design

The problem of joining is often encountered in engineering design. Most design elements are usually composed of several components or parts that have to be joined together in a certain fashion. Even objects that are composed of one component might need to be made of several subcomponents or pieces, because of possible limitations on the size or shape of the components. Moreover, the designed or manufactured artifacts often have to be joined to other existing parts (Ray, 1985). Joining, according to *Webster's* dictionary, is the act of "putting, connecting, or bringing together so to form a unit." Therefore, the desired function is to "join" two or more parts together.

Paradigms for Joining in Engineering

Most of the known methods for joining can be classified into three basic design paradigms: metallurgical processes, mechanical fasteners, and adhesive bonding (Ray, 1985).

Metallurgical processes are used mainly for joining metals together. The processes are based in most cases on applying temperature to the metals to produce a *permanent* joint. Within this paradigm, it is possible to identify three main prototypes: soldering, brazing, and welding (Ray, 1985). Soldering is the adhesion between the parent metal and a fusible, filler-metal alloy, which is the solder. Brazing is based on capillary attraction. Welding is a high temperature process that is above the melting point of the parent metal, producing a joint that is pressure tight and as strong as the parent metal but with the possibility of many defects. These prototypes can be classified further into classes and subclasses. For example, welding processes can be divided into fusion (nonpressure), resistance processes (pressure), and heating (Ray, 1985).

Adhesive bonding is a relatively new process using polymer resins in industrial applications. It is usually considered as a less reliable and less durable joining method than the others. It provides a lighter and more economical joint than the traditional joining methods in mechanical engineering and, more recently, in structural engineering. The bond is formed due to the attractive force between atoms and molecules that is generated by the movements of electrons (Lees, 1984). Joints that are formed by this method are usually considered *permanent* joints, and are used when light loading is expected. The exception is anaerobic adhesives which can be used when dismantling of the joint is required. Lees (1984) lists 12 major prototypes of adhesives.

Fastening is defined as attaching by pinning, tying, or nailing. In other words, mechanical fastening is based on the use of a physical object to join two or more parts together. Fastening in general was used by humans from the beginning, in the fabrication of tools and in connection with other basic skills necessary for survival. Mechanical fasteners specifically date back to Herculaneum in 79 AD (Blake, 1986). Thus it could be said that the mechanical fastener as a distinct paradigm for joining evolved at that period. Today, there are thousands of fastener types available for different purposes. Among the most common prototypes of fasteners are rivets, threaded fasteners, and pins.

The realm of mechanical fasteners is an important field in most engineering design disciplines because they are used in most constructed systems. Despite their small size in relation to the whole system, they are remarkably complex elements and are an important factor in the success of any engineering design. Mechanical fasteners are used in huge numbers in complex systems, and are capable of developing and transferring tremendous forces. To illustrate their complexity, in a screw thread there are over 125 separate geometrical features and dimensional characteristics in their design and construction, each with its own term and definition (Blake, 1986). Thus the problem of mechanical fastener design is an appropriate illustration of the basic concepts being presented in this chapter.

Formal Definition of Fastener Design Problem

To formally define the problem, a comprehensive description of the design situation has to be presented in order to encompass all the basic ideas of concurrent engineering. The need within a particular design situation will initiate the process of identifying the functional specifications, manufacturing and production constraints, and the product's life cycle concerns of utilization and disposal which should guide the design process. These functionalities and constraints will help identify the design paradigm. The logical process in identifying the conceptual design follows the scheme that was presented in section 3.3.

If in a design problem, two elements, y and z, are to be joined together to form a physical device, Pd_i (or to become a component of it), then the general utilization of the component A_i and/or the device will influence the transformation of the function which, in this case, is to "join."

$$object(x) \land element(y) \land element(z) \land join(x,y,z) \rightarrow component(A_1) \in Pd_1 \land Pd_2$$

The functional representation of the object x would be

$$F(x) = \{f^*\}$$

where

F = set of conceptual functional specifications of x
$f*$ = join

Hence, the design problem at this stage can be stated as "Is there an object x that can join element y to element z?" This problem can be represented formally as

$$\exists_x \forall y \forall z \{object(x) \land join(x,y,z) \rightarrow join(x,y,z)\}?$$

This function, at this stage of the process, can be mapped onto several design paradigms where the solution could be a process (paradigm 1), a catalytic component (paradigm 2), or a physical object (paradigm 3). The designer has to abstract the functionality conceptually, guided by two factors. The first factor is the constraints of the end use and the design situation, such as the environmental conditions and the cost of producing the joint. The second is the functions and life cycle issues associated with joining. The functions associated with joining are strength and reusability. Some of the life cycle issues are the maintainability and producibility of the joint. Obviously, the more specific the use or location of the joint itself within the device, the more precise and explicit the functional abstraction will be because the functional specifications and constraints vary depending on the end use.

For example, assume that the fastener is used in a vehicle. The general utilization of the vehicle will set functional constraints on f^*, such as the expected life of the device, strength of the joints, and a range of environmental conditions over which the entire vehicle is expected to operate (Ritchie, 1967). The vehicle could be an aerospace, ground, or underwater vehicle. Each one of these broad categories will imply several functional constraints and inferences. Furthermore, an aerospace vehicle could be a commercial aircraft, a manned military vehicle, an unmanned military vehicle, or a space vehicle. If, for example, the two parts to be joined will be a component of a physical device within a commercial aircraft, then it can be expected that the device would have long operational but short storage life. This implies that the device and its components would require frequent maintenance, which, in turn, means that the joint should be strong and dismantleable for maintenance or replacement. Thus, x should be strong and removable. The designer would include the first attribute in the functional specifications. The representation of the problem is now:

$$\exists x \, \forall y \, \forall z \, \{object(x) \, \wedge \, join(x,y,z) \, \wedge \, strong \_ join(x) \, \rightarrow \, join(x,y,z)\}$$

Again, this functional description could be mapped to more than one paradigm. Therefore other attributes are necessary for further abstraction. The design abstraction in this stage could be represented as

$$\exists x \, \forall y \, \forall z \, \{object(x) \, \wedge \, join(x,y,z) \, \wedge \, strong \_ join(x) \, \wedge \, removable(x) \, \rightarrow \, join(x,y,z)\}$$

This functional decomposition process continues until it is possible for the designer to map the functional attributes to a paradigm. In the preceding example, the functional attributes could be mapped only to mechanical fasteners.

$$\forall x \, \forall y \, \forall z \, \{object(x) \, \wedge \, join(x,y,z) \, \wedge \, strong \_ join(x) \, \wedge \, removable(x) \, \rightarrow \, fastener(x)\}$$

Thus the early conceptualization phase of the design has been accomplished by the identification of a design paradigm. If it is not possible to map the function onto any known paradigm, then the designer is faced with a creative design problem where the paradigm definition is the major part of the design task.

Once mechanical fastening is identified and chosen as the paradigm for this joining situation, then the design will inherit the functional, behavioral, and structural attributes of this paradigm. Some of the functions and life cycle issues that are associated with joining, based on the fastener paradigm, are reusability of the fastener, strength of the joint and fastener, and producibility of the fastener, hole, and joint. These attributes are added to the functional set $F(x)$. The functional specifications could be added to the set either randomly or in a predetermined order according to the importance of the functionality. This can be represented as

$$F(x) = \{f^*, f_1, f_2, f_3\}$$

where

  F = set of conceptual functional specifications
  $f*$ = join
  f_1 = reusability
  f_2 = strength
  f_3 = producibility

The common structural attributes for fasteners are drive (sd_d), head (sd_h), shank (sd_s), tip (sd_t), and locking device (sd_{ld}). These attributes are added to the structural set Sd:

$$Sd = \{sd_d, sd_h, sd_s, sd_l, sd_{ld}\}$$

    The constraints that are imposed on joining in vehicles usually are the cost of producing the joint (c_1) and the environmental conditions, which are the thermal capability (c_2), fluids compatibility (c_3), corrosion resistance (c_4), vibration resistance (c_5), negative pressure (c_6), and material compatibility (c_7).

$$C = \{c_1, c_2, c_3, c_4, c_5, c_6, c_7\}$$

The designer then proceeds to the next step, which is prototype identification. Thus, the designer has to further decompose the functionality. The first function in the example is reusability of the fastener. That functionality is added to an *open* set. The value of that functionality will be passed to a second level transformation function specific to that functionality which will further decompose the function into another level of functional abstraction in order to establish the causal links to the structural descriptions.

    The notation used is intended to support the hierarchical division of function and structure. Thus, a function f_n, when abstracted, will result in more functions. In order to indicate the derivation of those functions, the notation of the lower level functions is f_{ni}. The functions further derived from this function would similarly be notated as f_{nij}.

    The reusability of a fastener is associated with its accessibility, removability, and actuation force. Thus the decomposition of f_1 is

$$f_1 = \{f_{11}, f_{12}, f_{13}\}$$

where

f_1 = set of functions associated with the reusability of a fastener
f_{11} = accessibility
f_{12} = removability
f_{13} = actuation force

In other words, in order for a fastener to be reusable, first, it has to be accessible, second, it has to be removable in a manner that will not affect its basic joining configuration or strength, and third, it should be installed with adequate force that would make it properly removable. This can be represented as

$$\forall x \; \{fastener(x) \land f_1(x, high) \rightarrow f_{11}(x, high) \land f_{12}(x, high) \land f_{13}(x, min)\}$$

The new level functionalities will be added to the *open* set. The values of those functionalities will be passed, if necessary, to specific mapping functions to be further decomposed or mapped to structural attributes. The accessibility of the fastener is determined by the accessibility of its head, its tip, and its locking device.

$$f_{11} = \{f_{111}, f_{112}, f_{113}\}$$

where

f_{11} = set of functions associated with accessibility of a fastener
f_{111} = head accessibility
f_{112} = tip accessibility
f_{113} = locking device accessibility

High accessibility of the fastener means that the head, tip, and the locking device should be accessible. These attributes will be added to the open set and passed to other mapping functions to infer the structural attributes. For example, the accessibility of the fastener's head f_{111} will influence the structural description of the head and will determine-along with other behaviors-the type of head for the fastener:

$$\forall x \; \{fastener(x) \land f_{111}(x, high) \rightarrow sd_{h1}(x, out)\}$$

where sd_{h1} is the head type of the fastener. Similarly, the required accessibility of the tip and the locking device (if any) of the fastener will influence the structural description of the tip sd_{t1} and the locking device sd_{ld1}. Once this mapping is accomplished, the designer proceeds to the second functionality in the open set, which is f_{12}, and so on. The process of functional abstraction of f_1 and the mapping process to abstract structural descriptions are partially shown in Fig. 3.4.

In some cases, the specifications and constraints of the design problem would not uniquely determine the design values. In this case, a default value would

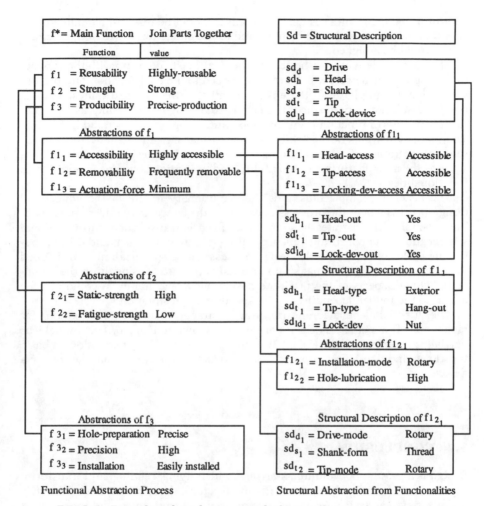

FIG. 3.4. Functional and structural abstraction and mapping process.

be assigned, usually according to previous design experience. In all the preceding steps, temporary values are assigned to all the functionalities and structural attributes. Then, before assigning a final value, it is checked whether specific functionality or structure was previously examined and assigned by other branches. If it is already included in the open set, then the values would be compared. If the values coincide, then they would be reinforced. If there is a conflict, then an attempt would be made to resolve it locally according to the significance of the determining factor. If that could not be resolved, then the values would be kept until the final synthesis, and the conflict would be resolved globally. In the case that neither value would be preferred to the others for any reason, a default value would be assigned.

The output values are synthesized in the final step to come up with the conceptual design of the device, which are then passed to the configuration and parameterization design phases. If there is any conflict in the assigned values, a global conflict resolution is performed. The conceptual design of a fastener as an evolutionary process of function transformation and mapping is illustrated in Fig. 3.5. The model illustrates how this abstraction formalism can facilitate the concurrent consideration of some of the fastener's life cycle issues because it includes some of the manufacturing, producibility, and utilization concerns in addition to functionalities.

The fastener example illustrates the evolutionary nature of the conceptual design process where the progress is based on the concepts that were presented. The example demonstrates how an initial need is transformed into functional specifications and constraints, incorporating manufacture, cost, and other product life cycle concerns into the design process. These specifications are mapped to structural descriptions that simultaneously take into consideration these concerns. Other aspects of the product's development and life cycle could also be added to the model depending on the specific design situation.

The functional–behavioral–structural abstraction and transformation for mechanical fasteners as a design paradigm is shown in Fig. 3.6. This model was partially implemented on the IBM 3090 using lisp/vm. The system follows a basic top–down and depth-first approach in constructing the conceptual design for a device.

3.7 CONCLUSION

Design is a process of evolution, starting by identifying, refining, and transforming the basic functional requirements to structural descriptions that ultimately define a physical device. All knowledge of processes, machines, and tools can be used at this stage, and through a series of abstractions the conceptual design can be accomplished. Hence, design is perceived as being guided by the functional specifications and constraints that lead to the synthesis of the structure.

The overall goal is to develop a knowledge-based methodology for conceptual design on the basis of reasoning about function and structure. The proposed method is aimed at capturing the design knowledge that is based on the basic physical laws that govern the behavior of a structural entity of a certain configuration, to achieve the desired functionality at the conceptual level. The foundation of this method is the function-to-structure transformation.

The future objective of research in this area is to formally define and include manufacturing processes and other life cycle issues, along with a library of generic functions and structures, in the existing model. This would entail adding knowledge of various engineering disciplines based on further and more detailed implementation of these concepts in various domains of engineering design.

$\exists x$ {object (x) ∧ join (x, y, z) → join (x, y, z)}

$\exists x$ {object (x) ∧ strong(x) → join (x, y, z)}

$\exists x$ {object (x) ∧ strong(x) ∧ remove-join (x, y, z) → join (x, y, z)}

$\forall x$ {object (x) ∧ strong(x) ∧ remove-join (x, y, z) ⊃ fastener (x)}

$\exists x$ {fastener (x) ∧ reusable (x) → join (x, y, z)}

$\forall x$ {fastener (x) ∧ reusable (x) ⊃ removable(x) ∧ accessable (x)}

$\forall x$ {fastener (x) ∧ reusable (x) ∧ removable (x) ⊃ accessable (d) ∧ accessable (t) ∧ rotary (dm) ∧ accessable (x)}

$\forall x$ {fastener (x) ∧ reusable (x) ∧ removable (x) ∧ accessable(d) ⊃ external (d) ∧ external (h) ∧ accessable (d) ∧ accessable (t) ∧ rotary (dm) ∧ accessable (x)}

$\forall x$ {fastener (x) ∧ reusable (x) ∧ removable (x) ∧ accessable(d) ∧ accessable(x) ⊃ ....}

$\exists x$ {fastener (x) ∧ external (d) ∧ external (h) ∧ .... ⊃ join (x, y, z)}

$\forall x$ {fastener (x) ∧ .... ⊃ ext-int (d) ∧ rotary (dm) ∧ .... }

Fig. 3.5 Conceptual design of a fastener.

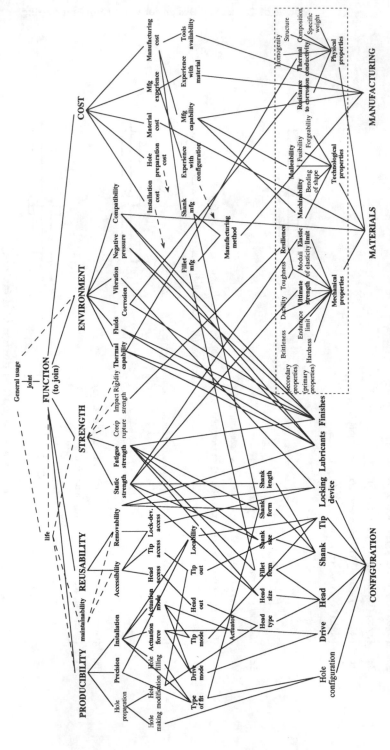

Fig. 3.6 Function-behavior-structure abstraction for the conceptual design of mechanical fasteners.

REFERENCES

Al Hamando, M. 1990. A design methodology for mechanical fasteners based on functional and causal reasoning, M.S. thesis in Industrial and Management Systems Engineering, Pennsylvania State University, University Park, Pennsylvania.

Blake, Alexander. 1986. *Threaded Fasteners: Materials and Design*. New York: Marcel Dekker.

Bobrow, D. G. 1985. *Qualitative Reasoning About Physical Systems: An Introduction*. Cambridge, Massachusetts: MIT Press, pp. 1–5.

Bridges, A. H. 1985. Any progress in systematic design? *ICCAAD*, Delft, The Netherlands, pp. 5–15.

Brown, D. C., and Chandrasekaran, B. 1988. Expert systems for a class of mechanical design activity. In *Expert Systems in Engineering*, ed. D. T. Pham, Berlin: Springer-Verlag.

Chandrasekaran, B., and Mittal, S. 1983. Deep versus compiled knowledge approaches to diagnostic problem-solving," *International Journal of Man-Machine Studies* 19 (5):425–436.

Davis, R. 1985. Diagnostic reasoning based on structure and behavior. In *Qualitative Reasoning About Physical Systems: An Introduction*. ed. D. G. Bobrow, pp. 347–410.

Dixon, John R. 1987. On research methodology towards a scientific theory of engineering design, *AI EDAM* 1 (3):145–157.

Finger, Susan, and Dixon, John R. 1989a. A review of research in mechanical engineering design. Part I: Descriptive, prescriptive, and computer-based models of design processes. *Research in Engineering Design* 1, (1):51–67.

Finger, Susan, and Dixon, John R. 1989b. A review of research in mechanical engineering design. Part II: Representations, analysis, and design for the life cycle. *Research in Engineering Design* 1, (2):121–137.

Freeman, P., and Newell, A. 1971. A model for functional reasoning in design. *Proc, 2nd IJCAI*, London, pp. 621–640.

Genesereth, M. R. 1985. The use of design descriptions in automated diagnosis. In *Qualitative Reasoning about Physical Systems: An Introduction*, ed. D. G. Bobrow, Cambridge, Massachusetts: MIT Press, pp. 411–430.

Gero, J. S., Maher, M. L., and Zhang, W. 1988. Chunking structural knowledge as design prototypes. *Artificial Intelligence in Engineering: Design*, ed. J. S. Gero. Amsterdam: Elsevier.

Kalay, Y. E. 1987. *Computability of Design*. New York: Wiley.

Kumara, S., Ham, I., Al Hamando, M., and K. Goodnow, 1989, "Causal Reasoning and Data Abstraction in Component Design. *CIRP Annals* 38 (1):145–148.

Lees, W. A. 1984. *Adhesives in Engineering Design*. London: Springer-Verlag.

Maher, M. L., Zhao, F., and Gero, J. S. 1989. An approach to knowledge-based creative design. In *Proc. of the NSF Engineering Design Research Conference*, Amherst, Massachusetts, pp. 333–346.

Pahl, G., and Beitz, W. 1984, *Engineering Design*. London: Springer-Verlag.

Ray, Martyn S. 1985. *Elements of Engineering Design: An Integrated Approach*. Englewood Cliffs, New Jersey: Prentice-Hall.

Ritchie, Oscar. 1967. Design trade-offs that determine fastener selection. *SAE*, New York, pp. 1–7.

Rinderle, James R. 1988. Function and form relationships: A basis for preliminary design. *Proc. from the NSF Workshop on the Design Process*. ed. M. B. Waldron, Oakland, California.

Simon, Herbert. 1969. *The Sciences of the Artificial*. Cambridge, Massachusetts: MIT Press.

Suh, N. P. 1990. *The Principles of Design*. Oxford: Oxford University Press.

Thorp, T. L., and Peeling, N. E. 1987. The role of HDLS in the digital design process. In

VLSI 87:VLSI Design of Digital Systems, ed. C. H. Séquin, pp. 29–44. Amsterdam: North-Holland.

Tomiyama, T., Kiriyama, T., Takeda, H., Xue, D., and Yoshikawa, H. 1989. Metamodel: A key to intelligent CAD systems. *Research in Engineering Design* 1 (1):19–34.

Ulrich, Karl, and Seering, Warren. 1987a. A computational approach to conceptual design. In *Proc. ICED 87*, Boston, pp. 689–696.

Ulrich, K. T., and Seering, W. 1987b. Conceptual design as novel combination of existing device features. *Advances in Design Automation*. Boston: ASME.

Yoshikawa, H. 1981. General design theory and a CAD system. In *Man-Machine Communication in CAD/CAM*. Amsterdam: North-Holland.

Yoshikawa, H. 1985. Paradigm change in technology. In *Proc. of 3rd Seminar of Joint Japanese-Hungarian Project for Expert Systems on the History of Science and Technology*, Veszprém, Hungary, August 21–23.

Chapter 4

Computational Models for Routine Design

Sridhar Kota
Design Laboratory
Department of Mechanical Engineering and Applied Mechanics
University of Michigan, Ann Arbor

4.1 INTRODUCTION

Routine design or parameter design is typically considered to be that stage of design where the solution configuration has already been established and the remaining task is to assign appropriate values to the defining parameters of various components. *Routine* design tasks lend themselves well to the methods of artificial intelligence. This chapter discusses various approaches to classifying design tasks and describes a few computational models that have been implemented to automate the routine design process. The last section focuses on one model in particular, the Intelligent Design System (IDS), which is based on the work described in Esterline and Kota (1992).

4.2 ARTIFICIAL INTELLIGENCE IN MECHANICAL DESIGN

The design task can be considered as an interactive process between the designer and the realm of possible solutions to the problem at hand. The purpose of design, as defined by Mostow (1985), is to develop a structure description that satisfies the given specifications, conforms to certain limitations, meets requirements on performance and resource usage (e.g., time, space, power, and cost) and satisfies design criteria on the form of the artifact (e.g., style, reliability, and manufacturability).

Early computer-aided design (CAD) applications primarily addressed computer-aided drafting—the downstream design process. As programming techniques grew more sophisticated and this early CAD became widely accepted, attention began shifting further upstream. More sophisticated design tools such as finite element method (FEM) software and kinematic/dynamic modeling packages were developed. But these are, in a pure sense, tools for analysis, not design, which enter the design process only after a trial design has been developed. Analyses are usually used to simulate or predict the performance of a design, and therefore, a design must exist before any such analysis can be performed. Good analysis is important for good design, but design cannot be done by analysis alone (Dixon, 1986). This understanding gave rise to a differentiation between pure design activity and the analysis that precedes iteration, which is an essential part of the overall design process. This differentiation, in turn, has formed the foundation for focused studies in design theory and methodology, a fast-growing interdisciplinary area of research. A large amount of work is being done in fairly downstream areas such as parametric design, as well as in upstream stages like conceptual design. Parallel to these advances have been advances in the field of artificial intelligence, more specifically in knowledge-based systems. This parallel development has led to a natural confluence of the two streams. The reasons for this are explained in the following paragraphs.

Simon (1981) brings attention to the fact that a human being can store away in memory a great deal of information that can be evoked by appropriate stimuli. He further states that this memory may be viewed less as part of the organism itself than as part of the environment to which it adapts. There are only a few "intrinsic" characteristics of the inner environment of humans that limit or influence the adaptation of thought to the shape of the problem environment. Everything else in behavior is artificial or learned and is subject to improvement through the invention of improved design and memory storage. If this line of reasoning is accepted, it follows that design is essentially a knowledge-intensive task. Artificial intelligence (AI) addresses the mechanization of such tasks and is thus a natural discipline for the study of design. Shank (1987) states that the primary goal of AI is to build an intelligent machine. The second goal is to find out about "the nature of intelligence." To even attempt the first goal, some progress has to have been made toward the second. The search for the nature of intelligence is a more global view of the attempt to define the design process. If the nature of intelligence can be defined to suit certain purposes, i.e., automating the design process, then building an intelligent machine becomes the next logical step towards this goal.

Because we accept that human behavior is subject to improvement, AI may be defined as the science of endowing programs with the ability to change themselves for the better as a result of their own experiences (Shanck, 1987). Consider for a moment the widely accepted point of view that the essential nature of mechanical design is iterative. Therefore, to construct an AI program that can design, the iterative processes need to be intelligently guided so that acceptable designs can be produced efficiently. A model of the design process is needed in order to formulate design problems, acquire and represent design knowledge, and develop design inference engines.

One factor to be considered is the importance of *geometry* in the mechanical design process. Geometry is the natural language of mechanical design. Mechanical designers think in terms of three dimensional geometric forms. There is no mathematical connection between the mental image or concept of a design and its visual representation in a drawing. A mechanical design solution is a description of a 3-D object. Learning how to represent the geometry of designs is, therefore, a key issue for applying AI to mechanical design. Dixon (1986) argues that the best way to represent geometry is probably in terms of features, where he defines a feature as "any geometric form or entity whose presence or dimensions in a domain are germane to manufacturing evaluation or planning, or to automation of functional analyses." Another important issue in mechanical design is material selection. Knowledge of material properties is quantitative, but a material choice is not found by a mathematical procedure. Manufacturing concerns also play a critical role in mechanical designs. Knowledge of manufacturing processes is mostly qualitative and symbolic, not numerical. Thus there are two more important issues to be dealt with in constructing an AI design program. Materials must be represented so that programs can reason about them. Manufacturing processes and machine tools must be represented so that programs can be written that consider the manufacturability of designs and possibly plan the production process. Finally, mechanical designs are predominantly nonmodular in nature. Cost considerations often lead to attempts to reduce the number of parts by combining as many functions as possible into a single component, whenever possible. This creates difficulties in developing an effective representation scheme for mechanical parts or components.

The definition of AI just presented above and the discussion of factors influencing mechanical design may seem to be in opposition to the presumption that AI is a viable tool for automating the design task. But this is not so. Routine mechanical design remains a knowledge-intensive task and is well suited to AI methods. Dixon (1986) highlights the difficulties that could be encountered in this task, and his discussion serves as a foundation for the desired definition of "the nature of intelligence." *Identifying the nature of the mechanical design process is the key to building an intelligent design machine.*

4.3 CLASSES OF DESIGN TASKS

Brown and Chandrasekharan (1984) have analyzed design problem solving as an information-processing task. Chandrasekharan (1988, 1989) presents a classification of design based on the difficulty of the subtasks. He gives three classes as follows:

(1) *Class 1 Design*. This is an open-ended, "creative" design. It is the type of design that leads to major inventions or completely new products. Far from routine design, it may be considered as extremely innovative behavior and is not easily characterized.

(2) *Class 2 Design*. This is the type of design where the structure of the system (e.g., automobiles, bicycles) is well understood and remains more or less unchanged. Although it does not involve revolutionary changes on a large scale, several of the components in the product may undergo major technological changes.

(3) *Class 3 Design*. This is relatively routine design, though it is not necessarily trivial. Effective problem decompositions are known, compiled design plans are known, and actions to take on failure of design solutions are also known. These routine design problems that still require knowledge-based problem solving lend themselves well to AI methods.

A simpler definition is given by Pahl and Beitz (1984), who use a different terminology to identify essentially the same classes of design. They qualify their classification by emphasizing that the boundaries of these types of design are not precisely fixed.

(1) *Original design*. This involves elaborating an original solution principle for a system with the same, a similar, or a new task.

(2) *Adaptive design*. This involves adapting a known system to a changed task, the solution principle remaining the same. Here original designs of parts or assemblies are often called for.

(3) *Variant design*. This involves varying the size and/or arrangement of certain aspects of the chosen system, the function and solution principle remaining the same. This also covers work in which only the dimensions of individual parts are changed, sometimes called *fixed principle design*.

On the other hand, Snavely *et al.* (1990) define four mutually exclusive types of design. First, however, they define certain terms: a *catalog* is a database to which the design system has access. The catalog contains individual pieces of data called *catalog entries*. A *topology* is a structure representing the relationship between slots, where a *slot* is a location into which a catalog entry may be placed. Using this vocabulary, the four types of design are defined as follows:

(1) *Type 1 Design—Invention*. The process of creating a new entry to a catalog that cannot be created by combining existing catalog entries.

(2) *Type 2 Design—Innovation*. The process of filling the slots of a variable topology with catalog entries.

(3) *Type 3 Design—Routine design*. The process of filling the slots of a fixed topology (or a predetermined set of fixed topologies) with catalog entries.

(4) *Type 4 Design—Procedural design*. An algorithmic process for filling the slots of a topology with a single combination of catalog entries.

This classification is not really that different from the two previously described. The difference lies in the precision with which the tasks have been treated, leading to defined rather than fuzzy borders between the four types.

A useful subclassification of routine design tasks has been discussed by Morjaria (1989). He classifies routine design into four subtasks.

(1) *Component selection task*. Given a set of components, the selection of one which meets some specified requirements.

(2) *Component parameter design task*. The design of a component by choosing certain values for it's parameters, given some performance requirements. Component selection is a more specific case of this task.

(3) *Configuration selection task*. The selection of a configuration using a specified architecture and a known set of components to meet given requirements. An important characteristic of this task is the connectivity between components.

(4) *Configuration design task.* The development of a configuration consisting of a set of components to meet given requirements. This is a more general task than configuration selection because the development of a specific architecture is also involved.

A different approach to classifying mechanical design problems has been presented by Dixon *et al.* (1988). Their taxonomy defines a problem in terms of initial state (six types) and final state (six types) states of knowledge. A basic problem type is then identified by specifying the initial and final knowledge states. The initial state of knowledge is classified into *perceived need, function, physical phenomena, embodiment, artifact type,* and *artifact instance.* The final desired state of knowledge is classified into *function, physical phenomena, embodiment, artifact type, artifact instance,* and *feasibility.* There are then seven major problem types. These are *functional* (perceived need—function), *phenomenological* (function—phenomena), *embodiment* (phenomena—embodiment), *attribute* (embodiment—artifact type), *parametric* (artifact type—artifact instance), *preliminary* (function—artifact type), and *conceptual* (function—embodiment). Feasibility studies form another class of problem types: *X-feasibility* (X-initial state—feasibility). There are, of course, many more possible combinations of knowledge states, but these are the ones most frequently encountered. It must be noted that this taxonomy identifies problem types and not design processes.

Dixon's method classifies design as ranging from conceptual to parametric design. Although in the past this has been seen as levels of routineness, Brown (1991) states that it is not so. He proposes that levels of routineness and the differentiation between conceptual and parametric levels of design form two orthogonal axes of a general design space (Fig. 4.1). The first axis is the *routine–nonroutine* axis, reflecting the level of experience with a certain type of

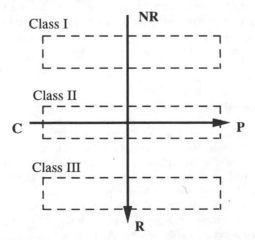

FIG. 4.1. Classes of design in relationship to the design axes.

design. The second axis is the *conceptual–parametric* axis. This axis shows the abstractness of the decisions being made; the solutions becoming more constrained as the design activity progresses. The three classes of design described earlier lie along the routine–nonroutine axis. The design space is thus divided into four categories of design activity, represented by the four extreme points at the limits of the axes:

(1) *RC: Routine, conceptual design.* At this point, the designer is making very abstract decisions (conceptual) and has well-formed methods for deciding them (routine).

(2) *RP: Routine, parametric design.* Here, the designer is deciding values for parameters (parametric) and has well-formed approaches to deciding them (routine).

(3) *NRC: Nonroutine, conceptual design.* Here again, the designer is making abstract decisions (conceptual), but now he or she does not have any well-formed methods for making them (nonroutine). This is the area about which the least is known.

(4) *NRP: Nonroutine, parametric design.* The designer is deciding values for parameters (parametric), and does not have any well-formed approach to make them (nonroutine).

4.4 SOME COMPUTATIONAL MODELS OF ROUTINE DESIGN

Since the initial emergence of artificial intelligence as a design tool, a vast amount of research has been devoted to building computational schemes to simulate the design process. One reason for the popularity of this field is the very real possibility of industrial advancement by the use of AI. Another is the fact that researchers from what were mutually exclusive fields are working toward common goals. In any case, most computational models of design are application specific. There have not been too many generalized schemes whose principles may be successfully applied to a variety of problems.

The Importance of Design Theory for CAD

The need for a general, scientific design theory for the construction of practical CAD systems has been well described by Yoshikawa (1983). Good CAD systems require good cooperation between the human designer and the other available resources. It is therefore necessary to acquire a better understanding of the designer's thought processes, both for proper organization of CAD systems and for replacement of the designer's elementary processes with automatic ones toward the full automation of design. A formal theory of design as an intelligent process is therefore a prerequisite to design automation.

Most models of the design process are derived from phenomenological observations. Though important, this does not always result in scientific objectivity. The theory should describe design as a process in which a concept, describable in languages, symbols, and figures is transformed into an entity with attributes recognizable by scientific means. This entity must satisfy the requirements described in the concept. The knowledge looked for is about the structure of data in a designer's memory and the procedures by which a designer describes specifications. The results are summarized as follows:

(1) The designer's knowledge is represented by entity concepts and abstract concepts.
(2) Abstract concepts include several categories, which are functional, attributive, morphological, and so on.
(3) Design process is a mapping from the space of function onto that of attribute.
(4) Mathematical formulation of the mapping is not available because of the insufficient structure of a designer's concept set.

Design Refinement

Brown and Chandrasekharan (1984, 1985) have been developing an approach to problem solving in class 3 design that views a complex body of knowledge as being decomposed into a hierarchy of conceptual specialists containing different domain expertise, engaging in collective, cooperative action, and solving the problem in a distributed manner, top down. The upper levels of the hierarchy deal with the more general aspects of component design and the lower levels deal with subsystems or subcomponents.

The design agents involved are defined as follows. A *specialist* can make design decisions in it's own area of expertise and can utilize the services of other specialists below it. A specialist follows a plan to achieve its part of the design. A *plan* consists of a sequence of calls to specialists or tasks. A *step* is a design agent that can make one design decision. A *task* is expressed as a sequence of steps, possibly with interspersed constraints. A *constraint* is an agent that tests for a particular relationship between two or more attributes at some particular stage of the design. Specialists refine the design independently, tasks produce further values, constraints check on the integrity of the decisions being made, and the plan gives the specific sequence in which the agents may be invoked. Each plan is the product of past planning, refined by experience.

The design activity is divided into four phases. First, the requirements of the user are collected and verified for consistency. The next stage is called "rough design." The effect of this is to prune the design search space and to provide a starting point for the design process. Then, the design phase begins as previously described. Here, parts of a plan may indicate that some constraints cannot be satisfied. This is regarded as failure. If any such failures occur, then a redesign phase is entered. If this is successful, a return is made to the design phase.

Constraint Programming

Bowen and O'Grady (1990) have developed a constraint programming language called Galileo that is geared toward the writing of design advice programs for life cycle engineering. They use a generic programming technology, based on constraint networks, that can be used to produce on-line design advisors. A constraint network is "a collection of objects that are interlinked by constraints that specify relationships that must be satisfied by the values that are assumed by the objects." The network can explicitly represent the mutually constraining influences that exist between the various aspects of a product's life cycle. An important feature of these networks is that the constraints can support nondirectional inference. When any one of the objects acquires a value, values can be inferred for other objects attached to the constraint. The designer may, therefore, approach the task from any perspective, deciding on values for objects in any order. When a user sets an object value, the consequences are propagated through the network, and any violation of constraints is immediately recognized. The system then either automatically resolves the violation or provides suggestions on how to resolve it.

Case-based Reasoning in Design

Case-Based Reasoning (CBR) is an AI approach that has been applied with success to computational design models. It is used in two ways: interpretive/classification CBR, used for strategic planning and legal reasoning, argues that a new specification should or should not be treated like a past case whose interpretation or classification has been settled; problem-solving CBR, used in expert systems for design, formulates a solution, retrieving similar cases from the case base, which may then be modified.

Case-based reasoning retrieval uses features of the new case that have been found to be relevant in past cases as indices into the databases of cases or the case base. The retrieved cases should support predictions about the new case, and so support the reasoning involved in subsequent steps. Previous cases are used as starting points for new solutions and to alert the reasoner of potential failure. Once a set of similar cases is retrieved, it is winnowed down to one or a few most-on-point candidates as the foundation of a new solution. Sycara and Navinchandra (1989) note that human designers use previous designs extensively to avoid earlier mistakes and to re-use previous approaches. The major challenge they cite for automating CBR in design is finding a representation and indexing mechanism for case retrieval. Their solution is to use a multilayered representation of cases. Surface features are described linguistically with basic functional keywords and context description. The current and previous problems are represented using black boxes with functional relations between outputs and inputs.

More deeply, the structure of a previous solution is represented by a causal network, and relations in this network are described in the language of qualitative physics. Thus, a behavioral description of the previous solution is also available. An attempt to find a previous case similar to the current case begins by attempting a direct match on surface features. If no relevant cases are found, the black box description of the function is used for indices, and matching may be relaxed by generalizing along object and concept hierarchies. If required, new relations may be generated by propagating relations with simple combination and propagation rules. If relevant cases are still not found, indices may be reformulated or generated to access previously inaccessible cases.

4.5 INTELLIGENT DESIGN SELECTION: A GENERAL PARADIGM FOR ROUTINE DESIGN

Overview

Esterline and Kota (1992) have developed an expert system shell that implements a domain-independent paradigm of the Intelligent Design Selection (IDS) of a model to satisfy a specification in routine engineering design. For a given design domain, certain characteristics are identified that allow all specifications and models in that design domain to be described in terms of their values. These characteristics are thus dimensions of a design space, which is discretized into a finite number of partitions, each represented by a model thought of as occupying its center. These models are shallow in the sense that they represent neither the interdependencies of the values of the characteristics nor the reasons for these values. Each such model, however, is associated with a deep model, which contains sufficient information for the modeled device, process, or system to be realized. Despite the fact that the models inhabiting the space are shallow, the paradigm comprises a relatively rich mathematical structure. The IDS paradigm also presents a convenient and structured framework for acquiring and representing domain knowledge. Work has also been done on an enhanced version of IDS, which attempts iterative redesign directed by the particular mismatch between a specification and an otherwise promising model. To date, IDS has been applied in a variety of design domains, including mechanisms design, hydraulic components, assembly methods, and nondestructive testing methods.

Intelligent design selection demonstrates the usefulness of the design paradigm that takes as fundamental the notion of a discretized design space. This concept is relatively simple to execute if the design elements are modular. The "building blocks" arising from discretization can, generally speaking, be functional building blocks, physical building blocks, generic components, or specific instances of generic components. Further downstream in the design process, the design space under consideration changes from a continuous space with fuzzy divisions to a modular space with distinct elements. This is especially so with mechanical design, where well-defined components enter the picture only at a fairly late stage. In the case of IDS, the partitions in the design space are well defined. Subsequently, in areas where IDS has already been applied or will be applied, the building blocks are generic components, as in material selection or pulley assembly methods (Kota and Boerger, 1990). It has also been used for component selection in the design of hydraulic systems (Kota and Lee, 1990). Here, the building blocks are specific instances of generic components. Thus, IDS serves as a tool for *routine* or *procedural design, variant design,* or *class 3* design depending on the terminology used. More specifically, it is applicable to the tasks of *component selection* and *component parameter design,* as defined by Morjaria (1989). Using Dixon's taxonomy (Dixon *et al.,* 1988), these can be called *attribute design* (transforming an embodiment into an artifact type) and *parametric design* (transforming an artifact type into an artifact instance), respectively. Brown's classification (1991) using orthogonal axes would place these tasks in the *routine parametric* quadrant of the general design space.

This interpretation of IDS centers on the initial selection of components and their possible redesign. Complex mechanical design problems, however, are decomposed recursively into smaller subproblems until each subproblem can be solved by a single component (Kota and Lee, 1990). This gives a hierarchy of interdependent subproblems. Verrilli, Meunier, and Dixon (1987, 1988) describe a hierarchy of "managers each with exclusive control over it's subordinates, configured so that all communication among subdesigners is via the hierarchy." Managers pass specifications to their subdesigners, who return the best possible designs, along with useful suggestions and requests for specification changes. Managers then integrate the subdesigns they receive, evaluate the resulting system, and form respecifications until an acceptable solution is achieved. Brown and Chandrasekharan (1984, 1985) present a similar hierarchical decomposition ("specialists" instead of "managers") and node communication architecture in their "design refinement." A collection of IDS-based systems may be organized in a similar hierarchy. One reason for this is that what counts as a component is relative. More fundamentally, a specification need not be supplied by a human. It could just as well be supplied by a manager/specialist forming part of an automated design system. In this context, the specification–model duality reflects the top–down versus bottom–up and goal-driven versus data-driven dualities familiar from general problem-solving methodologies. Although IDS is currently being used as a tool for routine design, it could itself act as a building block in the construction of an automated hierarchical design management system. The difference at each level of the hierarchy would be in *what* constitutes a "component" and, correspondingly, *how* a "specification" is defined.

As mentioned before, the IDS paradigm has much in common with CBR. This is especially so when one considers that IDS checks whether the current specifications are similar to specifications that have been solved in the past. The retrieval scheme used by Sycara and Navinchandra (1989) requires a representation of cases that is considerably deeper than the representation of shallow models used by IDS. Also, their matching scheme is much more elaborate and nonuniform than that of IDS. Still, their schemes do not give sufficient insight into the structure of the design space, as this space is occupied by shallow models. Indeed, CBR has tended to rely on deeper, causal models and to bypass formalization of the sort of heuristic knowledge that abounds in industry, which must be captured by disciplined knowledge acquisition. Part of the appeal of CBR is that it involves a form of learning and thus promises to ameliorate the knowledge acquisition bottleneck. The IDS paradigm, in contrast, ameliorates this bottleneck by supplying a clear framework for acquiring and representing domain knowledge. A major motivation for this is that the design space for a design domain is of interest beyond its use in a particular software system.

The IDS System: A General Description

The IDS system is a shell that implements a certain design paradigm in the design domain to which it is applied. A *design domain* is characterized by a type of function and an abstract working principle. Examples of domains in which IDS has been used are mechanisms design, hydraulic component selection, and automotive pulley assembly methods. The design paradigm assumes that a designer is presented with a specification that allows flexibility in the sense that various values may be renegotiated within fixed limits. There exists both a basic IDS system and an extended version. An application of the basic system performs initial selections; given a specification, it finds one or more models that are promising initial designs for meeting the specification. An application of the extended system performs redesign as well; given a promising model, it modifies this model in ways to better meet the specification. The models in question are shallow in the design domain in question and are represented as sets of characteristic-value pairs. For a fixed design domain, initial formulations of models may differ in the number of characteristics they involve. It is required, however, that the design domain be sufficiently well analyzed so that a fixed set of characteristics may be used in each model. These models are shallow because they do not capture the structures of the devices, systems, or processes, nor do they record the dependencies among the values of the characteristics; in particular, there is no indication of compatibility. But each shallow model must be associated with a unique, deep model, which does describe the structure and compatibility of the artifact, and so may be considered to contain the essential information needed to realize the artifact or to redesign the initial selection.

Some of the basic terminology of IDS will now be explained. By way of explanation, the problem of selecting engineering materials in design is used as an example in Fig. 4.2. The ellipses signify characteristics, e.g., surface finish, color, formability, weldability, cost/lb, corrosion resistance, impact strength, and so on. For instance, for impact strength, the user would have to input the desired value and some acceptable tolerance limits. Each characteristic has a *domain* to which its values are restricted. For purposes of describing characteristics, domains are of two types. For a domain of one of these types, a value in that domain is normally accompanied by an interval of values (in the same domain) within which the value falls. An obvious example is the set of real numbers, or any dense subset thereof, equipped with the usual total order relation $\leq$. For a domain of the other type, a value in that domain is not accompanied by an interval. An obvious domain of this type is an enumerated set of values. Because for such a domain there is no need for the notion of a value between other values, there is no need

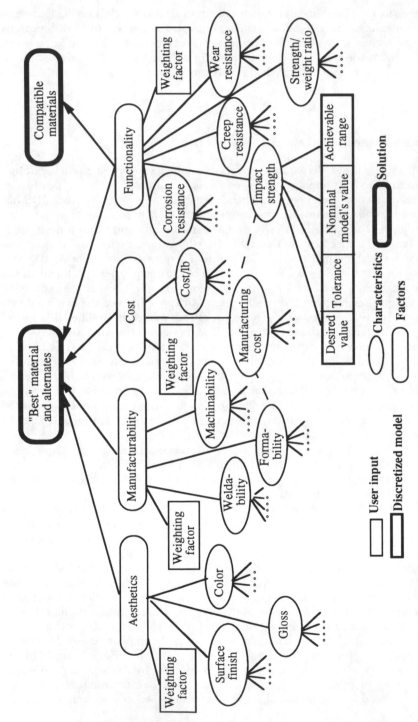

FIG. 4.2 Selection of engineering materials in design using IDS expert system shell.

for such a domain to be equipped with an order relation. Domains of the first type will be called *interval-equipped* domains; those of the second type, *point* domains. Note that an interval-equipped domain might be discrete. For example, a sufficiently large subset of integers may be an interval-equipped domain. On the other hand, when a sufficiently small subset of the integers is considered a point domain, the usual order relation ≤ is ignored, and the domain is essentially just an enumeration. The surface finish of the material may have an interval-equipped domain, signifying an acceptable range of finish. The same could be the case for machinability or manufacturing cost. Characteristics like color, on the other hand, probably have point domains. There may only be a few acceptable colors for the material required. If there are three such colors, the domain would be a three-point domain. Although IDS supplies a few predefined domains, most domains are defined by the knowledge engineer in implementing an IDS-based system. Therefore a fixed design domain is assumed and, hence, a fixed specification of IDS.

The n_c characteristics define an n_c-dimensional *design space*, which may be thought of as the Cartesian product of the domain of the characteristics. Each point in the design space is then represented by an n_c-tuple. Now, imagine that the design space is partitioned into regions (to picture this, imagine a metric defined on this n_c-dimensional space and that it is divided into convex regions). Imagine also that for each region there is a representative prototype near its "center" (again, this is pictured by invoking the fictional metric function). See Fig. 4.3. Each prototype, then, is a *shallow model*. Such a model thus describes a point in the design space because associated with it is a value for each characteristic. A model is also representative of a region because associated with it is an interval for each characteristic with an interval-equipped domain. An interval associated with a model is called an *achievable interval*. To be concrete, an achievable interval can generally be thought of as indicating the values of the characteristic in question that are easily achieved by minor *redesign* the corresponding deep model. For instance, a high-carbon steel model may have "hardness" as one of its interval-equipped characteristics. Depending on the nature of the heat-treatment process (redesign) applied to the material, various degrees of hardness can be achieved.

In many applications, n_c is sufficiently large to obscure the structure of the design space and its partition into regions. The dimensionality of the design space is thus reduced in two ways. First, certain characteristics are classified as *critical*. If a specification and a model do not match on a critical characteristic, then there is no hope for that model as an initial selection in the process of satisfying the specification. For a material, a critical characteristic could be some desired value of corrosion resistance, wear resistance, or thermal-expansion coefficient. The IDS system, given a specification, first eliminates those models that fail to match the specification on some critical characteristic. Because the remaining models all match perfectly on these characteristics, there is no further need to consider these characteristics. Thus, if there are n_{cc} critical characteristics, the initial step reduces the dimensionality of the design space from n_c to $(n_c - n_{cc})$. The dimensionality of the design space is further reduced by partitioning the remaining $(n_c - n_{cc})$ characteristics into subsets, called *factors*. These factors are motivated both by the inherent nature of the problem and by

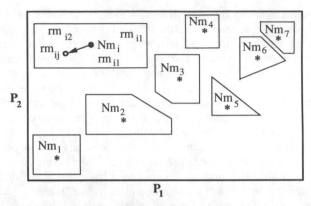

FIG. 4.3. A two-dimensional design space discretized into seven models (or subspaces). Initial design involves selecting nominal models. Redesign heuristics help adjust nominal model's parameters (generate rm_{ij} to meet specifications more closely).

the fact that they facilitate analysis of the problem by modularizing it. The example problem design domain (Fig. 4.2) has been partitioned into aesthetics, manufacturability, cost, and functionality. Thus, if there are n_f factors, $n_f < (n_c - n_{cc})$, a model is located not only in an n_c-dimensional design space, but also in a simpler $(n_c - n_{cc})$-dimensional space, and, further, in a still simpler (because coarser) n_f-dimensional space. Furthermore, a model is representative not only a region in the n_c-dimensional space, but also of a region induced by reduction of dimensions in the $(n_c - n_{cc})$-dimensional space, and, indeed, it is representative of a region, induced by the partition of noncritical characteristics into factors, in the n_f-dimensional space. Thus, the conceptual basis of IDS involves the notion of a design space that may be reduced in dimensionality both by eliminating certain dimensions straightaway when initial selection for a specification is considered, and by "factoring" dimensions together. Figure 4.2 shows the network of characteristics and factors leading to solutions for the material selection problem.

This design paradigm leads naturally to a knowledge acquisition methodology that is particularly apt for use by experts who have evolved a coherent heuristic model of their domain through years of experience, but who may lack a deep, theoretical understanding of the domain. Such experts are common in industry, and so a significant function of IDS is to record in a useable form expertise that otherwise would be restricted to one or few designers. The discretized design space concept also naturally leads to a conceptualization of redesign as moving from the center of one of the subspaces, occupied by one of the models that better matches the specification, to a point nearer its boundary. The direction of movement is dictated by the characteristics on which the model and the specification poorly agree. Because redesign involves deep as well as shallow models, the enhanced IDS system presents difficulties that are lacking in the basic system.

Chair Design Example

To clarify the preceding description, a simplistic example is presented. The design object is a chair. There are several characteristics to be considered that have different types and ranges of values (Fig. 4.4). For instance, choosing whether to incorporate an armrest or casters are characteristics whose values may be either YES or NO, i.e., two-point domains. Comfort, aesthetic, and durability indices are characteristics of *discrete* interval-equipped domains, i.e., their values lie in the interval (1,10), but they may only assume certain fixed values, integers in this case. Height and weight are examples of characteristics with *continuous* interval-equipped domains, i.e., their values may lie anywhere within the specified domains. Thus, there is initially an 11-dimensional design space. The options of having armrests, casters, and a rocking-type chair have been selected as critical. The dimensionality of the design space is therefore reduced to eight. Now, these are grouped into three factors on the basis of the "kind" of characteristic, i.e., performance, structural, or economic. Some of the possible models that can result are listed here.

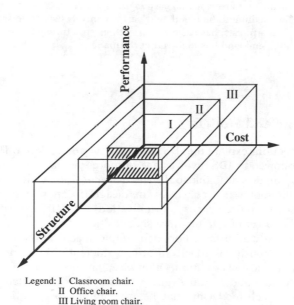

Legend: I Classroom chair.
       II Office chair.
      III Living room chair.

FIG. 4.4. A three-dimensional parameter design search space for selection of chair designs.

Characteristics ($n_c = 11$)	Values
Armrests	Yes/No
Casters	Yes/No
Rocking type	Yes/No
Comfort index	An integer value between 1 and 10
Asthetic index	An integer value between 1 and 10
Durability index	An integer value between 1 and 10
Height	Interval (e.g., 18 in. to 24 in.)
Weight (portability)	Interval (e.g., 10 lb to 35 lb)
Occupied floor space	Interval (e.g., 2 sq ft to 4 sq ft)
Cost	Interval (e.g., $40 to $70)
Warranty period	Interval (for instance 0.5 yr to 1 year)

Critical Characteristics ($n_{cc} = 3$)
Armrests, casters, and rocking type.

Factors ($n_f = 3$)
Performance (comfort, durability, and aesthetics)
Structural (height, weight, and occupied floor space)
Economic (cost and warranty period)

Models
Classroom chair (has no armrest, no casters, does not rock, is structurally small, economically low end, and performance is also toward low end)
Living room chair (has armrests, no casters, does not rock, is structurally large, economically medium to high end, and performance is usually toward high end)
Office chair (has armrests, has casters, can rock, is structurally midrange, economically high end, and has high-end performance)

Specifications and Models

The following sections explain the IDS paradigm in greater detail. The fundamental paradigm followed by IDS involves one or more specifications supplied by the user and several models available to the shell. *Specification* is defined in the sense of a set of requirements that constrain the design (in another sense of "specification," each such requirement is a specification). The IDS system breaks each specification into a set of one or more specifications that are simple in a sense that will be presently discussed. For each simple specification, if the IDS-based system finds a previously solved specification sufficiently similar to it, the system simply returns the previous solution. Otherwise, it returns a list of pairs (m_i, gm_i), where m_i is a model and gm_i, $0 \leq gm_i \leq 1$, is a measure, called the *goodness-of-match*, of how well model m_i matches the simple specification in question. Generally, there is some threshold *th* such that, if $gm_i < th$, then the pair (m_i, gm_i) is not included in the output list. If the output list is empty, then the simple specification has no solution (given the current model base). Note that the gm_i rank the different models m_i as the best, second best, and so on, solutions for the simple specification. Also note that when the IDS-based system finds a previously solved specification S_2 sufficiently similar to the current simple specification S_1, the previous solution it returns is a list of pairs (m_i, gm_i) for S_2. If S_2 really is sufficiently similar to S_1, then a nearly identical list would be computed for S_1, so computational resources are spared by simply returning the already computed list.

In this paradigm, it is generally easiest to think of a specification and a model as belonging to the same category. For example, a model may be a model of an intermittent-motion mechanism, and a specification may be a partial description of an intermittent-motion mechanism to be designed. This partial description may be thought of as constraints that must be satisfied by any design that solves the design problem stated by those constraints. The IDS-based system for this problem would then return (ignoring any previous solutions) a list of pairs (m_i, gm_i), where a model m_i is a promising type of intermittent-motion mechanism for the problem. The greater gm_i, the easier it should be to complete the design using this type. The specifications and models, however, may sometimes be more naturally thought of as belonging to different categories. For example, a model may be a type of nondestructive test and a specification may be a component-flaw pair. The (m_i, gm_i) pairs that the IDS-based system would return for this problem would give tests m_i for detecting the stated flaw in the stated component, where gm_i indicates how easy it is to adapt the test to the current problem. But note that the component-flaw pair itself can be thought of as the specification, hence partial description, of a test; it is a partial description insofar as it describes what the test detects.

A simple specification is characterized as a set of ordered pairs (CD_i, W_i), where W_i, $0 \leq W_i \leq 10$, is a real number called the *weight* and CD_i, called the *characteristic description*, is itself an ordered pair or ordered triple. If the domain of a characteristic is a point domain, then the corresponding CD_i is an ordered pair (Ch_i, Val_i), where Ch_i is the characteristic in question and Val_i is the value of this characteristic that any solution of the problem posed by the specification is expected to have. If, on the other hand, the domain of the characteristic in question is an interval-equipped domain, then the characteristic description CD_i is an ordered triple (Ch_i, Val_i, Int_i). Here Ch_i, as before, is the characteristic in question. But now there is an interval of values, Int_i, such that a solution to the problem will be acceptable, as far as characteristic Ch_i is concerned, as long as its value for Ch_i is within that interval. This interval is called the *acceptable interval*. The value Val_i is the preferred value for Ch_i: other things being equal, a solution with the value Val_i for characteristic Ch_i will be preferred to one with any other value for Ch_i. The weight W_i indicates the importance of the characteristic Ch_i for the problem at hand. If $W_i = 0$, then, in effect, nothing is required concerning Ch_i. W_i is allowed to range between 0 and 10 because it is anticipated that almost always the 11 integers in this range will allow the level of importance to be expressed; W_i is allowed to take on nonintegral values in this range just in case a user finds need to express importance more finely.

Similarly, a model may be characterized as a set of elements, one for each characteristic. Here, however, there is no notion of weights, so the elements are simply the characteristic descriptions. Furthermore, the components of these descriptions are interpreted somewhat differently. If the domain of the characteristic Ch_i is a point domain, then the characteristic description CD_i is, as before, an ordered pair (Ch_i, Val_i). Here, as before, Ch_i is the characteristic, but now Val_i is interpreted as the only value an instance of this model can assume for characteristic Ch_i. If, on the other hand, Ch_i is an interval-equipped domain, then (again as before) CD_i is an ordered triple (Ch_i, Val_i, Int_i). Int_i is now interpreted as the interval of values, called the *achievable interval*, that can be produced by instances that, even though they are not identical with the model regarding Ch_i, may still reasonably be said to conform to the model on this characteristic. V_i, accordingly, is now interpreted as the value of characteristic Ch_i of an instance that follows the model with no deviation on Ch_i.

A model may thus be thought of as a prototype described in terms of characteristics. For any kind of design problem, the specifications and models will all have the same number, say n, of characteristics. The characteristics thus define an n-dimensional space called the *design space*. Now consider a fixed model, and, for any characteristic of that model whose domain is a point domain, trivially define an achievable interval for that characteristic as the singleton set whose only element is the value associated with that characteristic—this guarantees that there is an achievable interval for each of the n characteristics. The Cartesian product of these n achievable intervals forms a convex set in the design space with the same dimensionality as the design space; this set is called the *achievable region* for the model. The n-tuple of values for the characteristics (given by the model) is a point, called the *default point*, within the achievable region. The distance from the default point to any point p in the achievable region indicates the effort required to redesign the model, thought of as the set of characteristic-default value pairs, to give exactly the values of the characteristics represented by p. This conception of a model is consonant with a certain straightforward paradigm of design that has been found to be appropriate for several areas. In such cases, the design space has some continuous dimensions, yet is conceptualized discretely in terms of a reasonable number of models (usually less than 100). A model is characterized by a flexible kernel prototype and some notion of the difficulty of modifying the prototype to achieve closely related designs.

A simple specification, ignoring the weights, can be interpreted analogously in the design space. The Cartesian product of the acceptable intervals is called the *acceptable region* and the point described by the values, which must lie in the acceptable region, is called the *optimal point*. Determining how well a simple specification and a model match is not as simple as this geometrical interpretation would suggest, for there can be some sort of match even when the achievable and acceptable regions do not intersect. Still, for a nonzero goodness-of-match, there are some characteristics on which they must overlap. These characteristics are called *critical*. If the projections of the acceptable and achievable regions overlap on some characteristics and on all critical characteristics (if any) then disjointness on some noncritical characteristics, although significantly penalizing the goodness-of-match, is nonetheless consistent with the hope of redesigning the prototype to meet the constraints of the problem or of compromising on the specification to fit the models.

Several terms contribute to the goodness-of-match. One is the nearness of the optimal point to the default. This is found by taking the distance d between the two in each dimension, normalized to the interval $(0,1)$, taking the complement

$(1 - d)$ of each, and using the weights supplied by the simple specification to form the weighted sum of the results. Similar component-wise computations are performed to judge how near the default point is to the "center" of the acceptable region, how near the optimal point is to the "center" of the achievable region, and how much the acceptable and achievable regions overlap. In general, one works with the projections of points and regions onto single dimensions. Goodness-of-match indicates the ease of redesigning the prototype (represented by the default point) to satisfy the specification, a bonus being given for coming near the optimal point.

A complex specification describes several optimal points. Such a specification will have one or more characteristics whose descriptions contain sets as values. When a characteristic with an interval-equipped domain is involved, the set of optimal points could be dense. For simplicity, this possibility is ignored; it is, in any case, handled by an easy extension that works with the overlap of intervals rather than with the identity of points. Intelligent design selection splits a complex specification into a set of simple specifications by selecting one element from each value set. The size of the set of simple specifications is thus the product of the sizes of the value sets. Because this set could become unmanageably large, it would be desirable to have constraints to eliminate unlikely combinations; however, this subject is not pursued here.

Basic Structure of IDS System

Figure 4.5 presents a data-flow diagram of the basic IDS system. Arrows show the progress from data in the form of specifications (input) to data in the form of solutions (output). The circles represent processing components. Because IDS is a shell, the basic IDS system must be supplemented with a knowledge base to produce a usable IDS-based system. The components of the knowledge base are represented in Fig. 4.5 as double-lined rectangles. An IDS-based system maintains a database of previous solutions to compare against new problems; this database is represented by a single-lined rectangle.

The first processing component in Fig. 4.5 breaks specifications into simple specifications as previously discussed. The last processing component is the

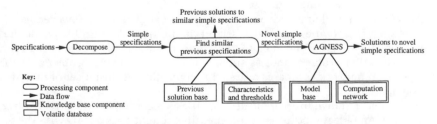

FIG. 4.5. The data-flow diagram of the basic IDS system.

major part of the system and is discussed in the next section. This component consists of the AGNESS expert system shell and matches simple specifications, which are input, with models available from the knowledge base. For each simple specification S that is input, this component returns a list of (m_i, gm_i) pairs, where m_i is the name of a model and gm_i is the goodness-of-match between S and m_i; such a pair is included in the output only if gm_i meets or exceeds a certain threshold, as explained before. A different model base must be supplied for each IDS-based system. Also, each IDS-based system has its own computation network, which is the computational structure that is interpreted by AGNESS to compute the output. The threshold values and characteristics must be supplied to this processing component as part of the knowledge base forming a particular IDS-based system. Note that to get accurate goodness-of-match values, while still enjoying some increase in efficiency, the system could carry on to the next processing component even when a sufficiently similar previous solution is found; the savings would be achieved by restricting the models to those that are listed in the previous solution.

AGNESS

This is the last processing component in Fig. 4.5. An IDS computation network, along with representations of models and specifications, is implemented using the AGNESS expert system shell (Slagle, 1986). AGNESS uses a computation network (a generalization of the scheme introduced by PROSPECTOR), as opposed to production rules, to represent domain knowledge. There are several advantages that a network-based shell has over a rule-based shell. For example, in a network-based system, there is no need to search for rules to fire, as all applicable rules are directly connected to the currently active network node. The price for such direct connection is that rule combinations are predetermined. AGNESS partially alleviates this rigidity by the generality of the inference methods it permits in the nodes.

An AGNESS network has the form of a directed acyclic graph (DAG). Each node represents a general proposition. A *context* is an *n*-tuple of objects or types of objects used to instantiate the general proposition represented by a node. A value is associated with each node in a given context. Because domain-specific knowledge is relatively fixed, it is represented in the computation network. User supplied and problem-specific knowledge, on the other hand, is more volatile and so is stored in a separate database.

AGNESS is aimed at a wide variety of domain applications; however, as with all shells, some activities are better served than others. AGNESS is particularly useful for matching entities. The matching problem is really a generalization of the classification problem and, as such, is a widely occurring problem. An IDS computation network compares a design specification against a set of models in the same area.

Every object known to an application of IDS is recorded in an AGNESS *object-type lattice*. An object-type lattice is most easily thought of as a DAG with the *universe* as its unique top node, with *objects* as leaves, and with *types* as the interior node. An arc between types (thought of as going toward the top of the lattice) indicates that objects in its source type are also in its destination type, i.e., that its source type is a subtype of its destination type. Note that the subtype relation is transitive: if T_1 is a subtype of T_2, and T_2 is a subtype of T_3, then T_1 is a subtyle of T_3. An arc from an object to a type indicates that the object is of the given type. An object, then, not only is of the type or types immediately indicated by arcs, but also of all types of which these types are subtypes. Note that the same object or type may be the source for several arcs, giving a sort of multiple inheritance; clearly, the same type can be the destination of several arcs. A general IDS computation network is a specialization of a general AGNESS network.

Outline of IDS Network

In gross outline, an IDS network has the form of a tree, as shown in Fig. 4.6. Here antecedents are shown below their consequences. To picture how this works, suppose that there are N specifications and M models, and the network finds goodness-of-match values for all $N \times M$ specification–model pairs in parallel. (The parallelism, of course, is simulated.) Consider one such pair s-m, which will serve as a context for all nodes in the network. Initially, there are copies of s-m at each leaf node. Each leaf node corresponds to a characteristic Ch and computes a goodness-of-match for s-m on this characteristic, giving a datum for this node and context s-m. All characteristic nodes are thought of as executing in parallel. The copies of s-m then advance in parallel to be combined at the intermediate nodes. These nodes are called factors; each computes a goodness-of-match for s-m by combining the goodness-of-match values of s-m at its antecedent characteristics. The copies of s-m at the factors then proceed in parallel to be combined at the root solution, which computes the overall goodness-of-match for s-m by combining the goodness-of-match values of s-m at the factors. At this point, there is a datum for s-m each node in the network. Although the solution to the overall problem is given at the root, the user interface encourages inspection of values at any node.

The role of factors in this scheme is important, and, in fact, the general structure of Fig. 4.6 can be modified to allow factors as antecedents of factors. Factors allow characteristics to be grouped, giving intermediate concepts that mediate their impact on the solution. This is consonant with the way designers conceptualize problems in many areas. Factors allow IDS to supply sufficient structure to mirror top–down or bottom–up approaches to problems, and are almost a necessity when there is a large number of characteristics. Multiple levels of factors indicate a more structured problem domain. Factors also facilitate the search for the strengths and weaknesses of a modal vis-à-vis a given specification: the user can isolate strengths and weaknesses at certain factors and then concentrate on the characteristics that are antecedents of those factors.

Two features spoil the tree form of an IDS network. First, critical characteristics are actually antecedents not only of factors but also of other characteristics. If a specification–model pair fails on a critical characteristic, then the node for that characteristic sends a signal to nodes higher up telling them to ignore that

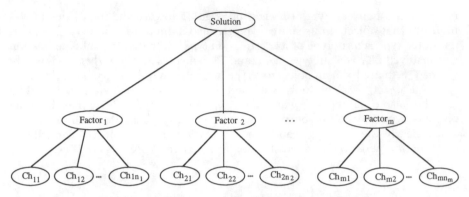

FIG. 4.6. The gross outline of an IDS network.

pair. If the pair does not fail, then the node sends the goodness-of-match value to its consequent factors. The second feature spoiling the tree form of IDS networks is the position of nodes (not shown in Fig. 4.6) representing the weights of characteristics. The node representing the weight of characteristic Ch is an antecedent not only of the factor belonging to Ch, but also of the solution node.

Iterative Design Refinement

The next task is to enhance IDS so that it can generate new models located in the design space near those models that are promising. This results in a hill-climbing behavior. For simplicity, suppose only one simple specification is being handled. The original set of models is scattered rather evenly through the design space. Suppose further that several of these models give high goodness-of-match values that still are not over the threshold. The system then makes what easy modifications it can to the promising models using heuristics that are sensitive to the discrepancies between the specification and an individual model. The new set of models (there may be several per modified model) is then used as the model base in another application of the basic IDS system, and the new goodness-of-match values are computed for these models. This generate-and-test procedure repeats until either (1) the goodness-of-match value for some specification–model pair reaches the acceptance threshold, or (2) all new models on some iteration give at best negligible improvement (relative to the models from which they were derived), or (3) a predetermined maximum number of iterations is reached. Such a scheme is plausible as long as the original set of models gives a fine enough sampling of the design space so that local maxima may be discriminated on the first iteration. Subsequent iterations then move toward the local maxima that have been singled out and eventually allow them to be (perhaps roughly) identified and compared. Note that the representation of models already supplies some foundation for this hill-climbing approach in that achievable ranges, which may be thought of as sensitivity estimates, contribute to the goodness-of-match values and thus can direct the system in directions that are, when modifications are allowed, promising. The advantage of this iterative scheme is that it relieves the knowledge engineer of the burden of meeting an implicit completeness requirement for the set of models he or she formulates. The requirement is that there must be many sufficiently different models so that a reasonable initial selection may be made for any given part of the design space.

This iterative approach, however, is appropriate for only some problem domains. For the necessary conclusions about characteristics to be drawn from suggested modifications, there must be available, not just shallow models, but also models that are deep in the sense that they involve the first principles of the problem domain. Furthermore, for the system to be practical, the redesign (or modification) heuristics must give simple changes to a deep model, and there must be a tractable way to deduce default values and achievable ranges from the modified deep model for every characteristic of interest. Finally, the design space must be sufficiently unpredictable to warrant this iterative approach, yet not so unpredictable as to vitiate hill climbing. The basic system, after all, already presents a usable paradigm and relies only on shallow knowledge available by quite straightforward knowledge acquisition. The suggested enhancement, even with the most tractable problem domain, requires a considerably deeper and more varied knowledge base and shifts the balance between the general shell and the problem-domain-specific knowledge base in the direction of the latter. Concerning the burden on the knowledge engineer, one must weigh the burden of the model set completeness requirement for the original system against the deeper and more diverse knowledge base required by the enhancement.

Figure 4.7 is a data-flow diagram of the enhanced system in which all aspects of redesign and deep reasoning are summarized into the last (right most) processing component. The first two components summarize the basic system (see Fig. 4.5). The first component summarizes the first two components in Fig. 4.5. The remaining components in Fig. 4.7 are enhancements to the basic system. If the basic system finds a specification–model pair with goodness-of-match over the acceptability threshold, then the run is complete. Otherwise, the n best specification–model pairs are passed to the enhancement, where n is a parameter for the problem domain and "best" is in terms of goodness-of-match. For simplicity, it is assumed that there is only one simple specification s. If there are $m > 1$ specifications, then there are m problems that are independent except for the number of candidate models for each, and the effect of n is, first, to restrict the number of models generated in an attempt to satisfy any one specification, and, second, to force out unpromising specifications. Figure 4.8 expands the last component in Fig. 4.7, which creates new models, into a sequence of constituent components, knowledge bases, and temporary stores; it represents that part of the enhancement that involves redesign and deep reasoning. This discussion will assume that each shallow model is correlated with a "deep model" that is a device, system, or process that *explains* its constituent characteristics, i.e., is cognizant of the relationships between them. Our assumption of a one-one correspondence between shallow and deep models may be too restrictive because in many problem domains there are often several deep models that achieve the same shallow model. One way to avoid this difficulty is to introduce enough discriminating characteristics into the shallow models to ensure the assumed correspondence.

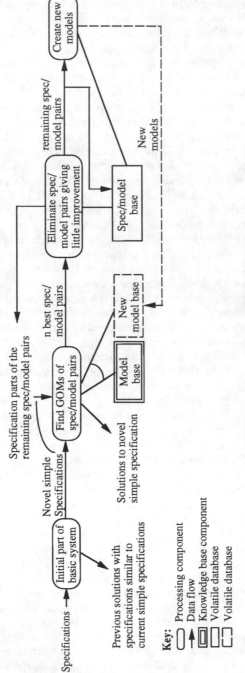

Fig. 4.7 The data-flow diagram of the enhanced IDS system. All aspects of redesign and deep reasoning are summarized into the processing component labeled "Create new models" (on the right).

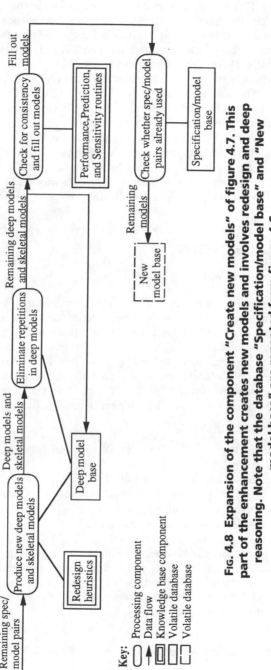

FIG. 4.8 Expansion of the component "Create new models" of figure 4.7. This part of the enhancement creates new models and involves redesign and deep reasoning. Note that the database "Specification/model base" and "New model base" are repeated from figure 4.6.

Like CBR, the IDS redesign component needs models that are deeper than the shallow models that inhabit an IDS design space. Guidelines for such models remain to be formulated in a principled way; a functional representation scheme and a causal network both have attractive features. The IDS redesign component differs from most CBR design schemes in that evaluation is conducted at the shallow level, where a uniform, straightforward representation exists for each problem domain. The contact between the shallow and deep levels, which is less than explicit in many CBR schemes, occurs in IDS when the skeletal shallow models are filled out with values for performance characteristics. The results of deep analysis are also carried through to the shallow realm in the form of achievable intervals for characteristics with interval-equipped domains. These intervals represent possibilities for future modifications in a way that is more direct than what is available to a case-based reasoner, and in a way that can be related to the intuitions of experienced designers with diverse backgrounds.

Other Applications of IDS

Pulley Assembly Methods

The pulleys employed in automotive industry drive systems often consist of a two-piece assembly. A multitude of fastening techniques are used in completing the assembly. There are numerous assembly methods and a variety of distinct pulley configurations dictated by the various automobile manufacturers in accordance with individual accessory drive requirements. Kota and Boerger, (1990) have applied the IDS methodology to evaluate the merit of multiple assembly alternatives for a specific pulley application. The IDS system provides a consistent evaluation tool for assembly alternatives, balancing the influence of the following factors:

(1) Product cost (cost of filler/fastener, of two components being assembled, and assembly cost)
(2) Process capability (tolerance required and process variability)
(3) Relative strength (assembly strength in terms of ultimate tensile strength, applied load, and reliability merit)
(4) Quality considerations (serviceability, etc.)

The expert system judges the acceptability of various pulley assembly techniques (spot weld, resistance braze, projection weld, annular projection weld, press fit, semipierce, extrude, cap screw, solid rivet, etc.), assigning "merit values" between 0 and 1 to the designs based on how well they fit the specific application. Better designs get higher values.

Selection of Hydraulic Components

Kota and Lee (1990) have used a functional framework for developing a systematic design methodology for hydraulic systems (circuits) design using abstraction/decomposition hierarchies. They use IDS in the final stage of component selection. The first step is function decomposition and establishment of the functional network. The second step is mapping candidate functional building blocks to structural building blocks (generic component descriptions). In the third stage, mapping is done from generic to specific components by taking into consideration system level requirements (system pressure, flow rate), cost, and component specific constraints. Figure 4.9 shows the IDS network for selecting directional control valves. The "component functionality" node and its children nodes vary for different components, whereas the "system requirements" node and its children nodes remain the same because all the components in a hydraulic system are expected to comply with given or derived system requirements. For example, in the case of rotary actuators, the subnodes of the component functionality node may be "rotation degrees," "torque," and so on.

Determination of Nondestructive Testing Methods for Composite Components

Gomes and Kota (1990) have applied the IDS technique to formalize the knowledge domain of nondestructive quality control of automotive composite components with organic (resin) matrices and to develop a prototype knowledge-based system called NICC, for Nondestructive Inspection of Composite Components, to determine the nondestructive test methods that should be applied to a given composite component in order to ensure its quality. The knowledge base from which to identify, select, and develop appropriate methods (for nondestructive inspection) for application to specific quality problems is growing rapidly. An expert system is a promising solution to the problem of controlling and using this expanding information base. Gomes and Kota (1990) have demonstrated that it is feasible to both compile and represent this domain knowledge and translate it into an efficient, automated tool capable of giving reliable expertlike advice at low cost by doing just this, for a specific problem.

The structural fitness of composite components may be compromised by a great variety of flaws; some flaws are due to material imperfections and others are due to existing manufacturing process limitations. Given a component and information about the particular situation and environment, the system makes an intelligent guess at the nature of the flaws that the component may have and determines the type of nondestructive tests that are needed to detect these flaws. Geometric and bonding characteristics of parts and assemblies are taken into account. A basic assumption is that it is possible to determine what flaws might be present in a given component, based on a limited amount of easily accessible information about this component.

Knowledge Acquisition

Knowledge acquisition has been recognized as the major bottleneck in constructing expert systems. The most obvious way to try to acquire knowledge from an expert is by direct questioning. But there are problems with this, most fundamentally the fact that skilled knowledge is typically tacit and intuitive and not

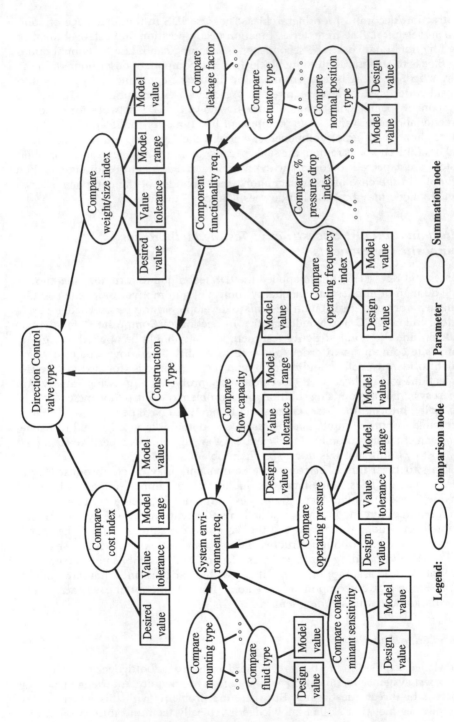

Legend: ⬭ Comparison node   ◯ Parameter   ▢ Summation node

FIG. 4.9 Selection of hydraulic directional control valves using IDS.

directly accessible to consciousness. *Knowing how*, which allows skilled performance because the knowledge is second nature and manifested tacitly, is generally distinguished from *knowing that*, which involves knowledge that is consciously accessible so that it can be applied to totally novel cases and can be easily communicated. In computational terms, knowing-how relates to *procedural* knowledge, as might be incorporated into a program, whereas knowing-that relates to *declarative* knowledge, which is represented propositionally and must be interpreted. With experience, declarative knowledge becomes compiled into procedural knowledge. This leads to what has been called "the paradox of expertise": the most valuable problem-solving knowledge is that which experts are least able to articulate. When an expert is asked to verbalize his or her problem-solving strategies, the expert is apt to articulate what he or she was taught as a novice, not the tacit methods that are actually used. Such articulated, *reconstructed* reasoning methods are endorsed by entire communities in textbooks. The need, in contrast, is to elicit the *authentic* reasoning methods that determine the expert's actual behavior.

REFERENCES

Bowen, J., and O'Grady, P. 1990. A technology for building life cycle design advisors. *ASME Computers in Engineering Conf. 1990.*

Brown, D. C. 1993. Routineness revisited. *Mechanical Design: Theory and Methodology*, eds. M. Waldron and K. Waldron. To be published by Springer-Verlag in 1994.

Brown, D. C., and Chandrasekharan, B. 1984. Expert systems for a class of mechanical design activity. *IFIP WG5.2, Working Conference on AI in CAD*, p. 259.

Brown, D. C, and Chandrasekharan, B. 1985, Knowledge and control for design problem solving. Technical Report, Ohio State University. Laboratory for Artificial Intelligence Research.

Chandrasekharan, B. 1988. Design: An Information Processing Level Analysis. Technical Report, Ohio State University, Laboratory for Artificial Intelligence Research.

Chandrasekharan, B. 1989. A framework for design problem-solving. *WAID 89, Workshop on Research Directions for AI in Design.*

Dixon, J. R. 1986. Artificial intelligence applied to design—A mechanical engineering view. *Proc., AAAI 86, 5th National Conference on Artificial Intelligence.*

Dixon, J. R., Duffy, M. R., Irani, R. K., Meunier, K. L., and Orelup, M. F. 1988. A proposed taxonomy of mechanical design problems. *Proc. International Computers in Engineering Conf.*

Esterline, A., and Kota, S. A general paradigm for routine design—Theory and implementation. *Artificial Intelligence for Engineering Design, Analysis and Manufacturing*, 6 (2): 73–93.

Gomes, E., and Kota, S. A knowledge representation scheme for nondestructive testing of composite components. *SAE International Congress and Exposition.*

Kota, S., and Boerger, J. G. 1990 A network-based expert system for comparative analysis of pulley assembly methods. *SAE International Congress and Exposition.*

Kota, S., and Lee, G. 1990. A functional framework for hydraulic systems design using abstraction/decomposition hierarchies. *Proc. 1990 ASME Int'l. Computers in Engineering Conf.*

Morjaria, M. 1989. Knowledge-based systems for engineering design. *Conf. AUTOFACT '89.*

Mostow. Towards better models of the design process. *AI Magazine*, 6 (1): spring 1985.

Pahl, G., and Beitz, W. 1984. *Engineering Design*. Design Council London: Springer-Verlag.

Simon, H. A. 1981. *The Science of the Artificial*. 2nd ed. Cambridge: The MIT Press.

Shank, R. C. 1987. What is AI, anyway? *AI Magazine* Vol. 8, No. 4, Winter.

Slagle, J., Wick, M., and Poliack, M. 1986. AGNESS: A generalized network-based expert system shell. *Proc. of the 5th National Conference on Artificial Intelligence*, Philadelphia.

Snavely, G. L., Pomrehn, L. P., and Papalambros, P. Y. 1990. Toward a vocabulary for classifying research in mechanical design automation. *1st Int'l. Workshop on Formal Methods in Engineering Design, Manufacturing and Assembly*.

Sycara, K. P., and Navinchandra, D. 1989. Integrating case-based reasoning and qualitative reasoning in engineering design. *Proc. 2nd Int'l. Conf. on Industrial & Engineering Applications of AI and Expert Systems*.

Verrilli, R. J., Meunier, K. L., and Dixon, J. R. 1987. Iterative respecification management: A model for problem-solving networks in mechanical design. *Proc. 1987 ASME Int'l. Computers in Engineering Conf. & Exhibition*.

Yoshikawa, H. 1983. CAD framework guided by general design theory. *IFIP*, p. 241.

Chapter 5

Desirable Functionalities of Intelligent CAD Systems

Varol Akman
Department of Computer Engineering and Information Science
Bilkent University
Ankara, Turkey

Paul J. W. ten Hagen
Department of Interactive Systems
Center for Mathematics and Computer Science
Amsterdam, The Netherlands

Tetsuo Tomiyama
Department of Precision Machinery Engineering
University of Tokyo
Tokyo, Japan

5.1 INTRODUCTION

Computer-aided design programs assist a designer in specifying an artifact. The assistance can range from merely registering the design results to analyzing the proper functioning of the designed object, perhaps through simulation or, more properly, through envisioning (de Kleer, 1975). More advanced forms of assistance include problem-solving activities such as optimization and routing, to even suggesting a solution based on the given specifications. The latter activities become more dominant when the assistance can be extended to the earlier and more difficult phases of design.

The design process can be defined as transforming a set of specifications into a set of attributed objects, which together perform as required by the specifications. The process can be structured in terms of stages (analysis, synthesis, and evaluation). Moreover, there may be forms of backtracking, iteration, detailing, and so on. In fact, the design process can be characterized by the way it interacts with the design object. An important goal is to find appropriate means for describing the design process and to define the semantics in terms of design transactions (Mostow, 1985).

Much of a designer's activities consist of manipulations of the design object, modifications, and inspections. The context in which these take place may vary.

Even the purpose of such activities may initially be left unspecified. This could, in some cases, influence the way in which the corresponding transactions are visualized. A design object must be properly represented to identify the status of the object information: proposed, decided, and so on. Interaction between process representations and object representations depends on the status information. In particular, the status information must be allowed to be incomplete, inaccurate, and even inconsistent in a given intermediate situation (Purcell, 1988).

Mechanical part design is the domain under discussion here because it probably has the strongest industrial appeal. As a well-established, integral part of Computer-Integrated Manufacturing (CIM), mechanical CAD is the backbone of today's highly industrialized world. It helps engineers develop products ranging from the simple and ordinary to the complex and sophisticated. It multiplies the productivity many times and renders, using CIM techniques (Yeomans *et al.*, 1985), robust products.

However, it is commonly accepted that current CAD systems are difficult to master and inflexible to growing needs. They can only deal with limited domains and occlude attempts at integration. They do not properly support a crucial ingredient of design, i.e., interaction. What is worse is that they lack the distinguishing characteristic of human designers: they have little or no intelligence (Simon, 1979). As technologies advance, it is conjectured that only systems that embed advanced reasoning capabilities will be able to deal with the complexity arising from the management of large quantities of design data.

Efforts to provide a wider perspective of CAD are now underway at several companies, universities, and research institutes. Because design is a highly mental activity, researchers have long felt the need for making CAD systems more intelligent (Akman *et al.*, 1989). It should, on the other hand, be remarked that design is not basically a mental activity. Design is basically a physically creative activity. It is only since the industrial revolution that certain kinds, such as mechanical design, have become so abstracted from the associated physically creative (manufacturing) aspects that design can now appear to be a purely mental activity.

The work this chapter is based on advances the theory and practice of intelligent CAD systems. It is based on IIICAD (Intelligent, Integrated, and Interactive CAD) which employs artificial intelligence (AI) techniques and knowledge engineering tools to obtain a system that is potentially more substantial than expert systems (Lansdown, 1988). This chapter gives an overview of the IIICAD philosophy.

5.2 PROBLEMS WITH EXISTING CAD SYSTEMS

Sutherland's revolutionary SKETCHPAD (Sutherland, 1963) generated much enthusiasm for using interactive graphics in engineering. SKETCHPAD allowed geometric shapes to be represented and various conditions to be specified over these shapes in terms of constraints. This, in turn, provoked a stormy decade when turnkey, two-dimensional drafting systems gradually replaced drawing boards in the professional environment. Finally, the dust settled with their general acceptance by industry. Three-dimensional modeling systems became available and they were also widely accepted as indispensable tools in product development.

Nevertheless, borrowing an analogy from Bobrow *et al.* (1986), it can be claimed that all these systems follow the "low road" approach. They are programmed in an ad hoc manner and regard design from a singular viewpoint, i.e., as a mainly geometric activity. Thus, despite their popularity, there are problems with the existing CAD systems. Even the recent research cannot escape various inherited pitfalls. In this section, these problems are highlighted.

Methodology

As with any other discipline, a critique of CAD systems presupposes a starting point, i.e., a vision of design. Briefly, design can be seen as an intellectual activity performed by human designers where the essential thing about a designer is that she builds her vision of the world. Thus, design systems should provide a framework in which designers can exercise their faculties at large. With this view, the idea of apprentice (as opposed to autonomous) CAD systems can be more or less supported. This chapter challenges some of the commonly held views about the nature of design such as:

(1) Design is a routine process
(2) Design is an innovative process
(3) Design is a problem-solving process
(4) Design is a decision-making process
(5) Design is an optimization process

The first view treats design as a rather straightforward activity where the designer selects from a known set of well-understood alternatives. A recent example is the AIR-CYL system (Brown and Chandrasekaran, 1986). Clearly, this view is ingenuous and does not reflect the intricate nature of design. The second view goes to the other extreme and embraces the exciting ideas of AI to create novel devices via brainstorming and discovery heuristics. It is quite early to predict whether this can be achieved in domains more involved than the usual micro worlds of AI; thus, EDISON is only a toy system (Dyer *et al.*, 1986). Although the remaining views in the preceding list regard design as an activity requiring intelligence and creativity, they underplay its holistic nature. They are mostly implemented as expert systems which solve the specific problems of a specific design process. An example of this "middle road" approach is the PRIDE system (Mittal *et al.*, 1986). An annoying and often cited problem with expert systems is that they cannot deliver genuinely expert performance because they have no underlying mechanism with which to understand what is going on (Doyle, 1985). This problem manifests itself when a particular expert system is unable to solve a simple problem in spite of its proven expertise with difficult problems. This discrepancy has contributed to the emergence of terms like *deep* and *shallow*.

"High road" systems are deep systems and IIICAD is aimed at them. The knowledge of such systems is to represent the principles and theories underlying the discipline of design. This requires demystifying several aspects of design by way of formal, mathematical methods. Clearly, such a formalization may not say much about what goes on during the design process, serving as a post hoc rationalization of it. In the case of IIICAD, the fundamentals of a general design theory that is based on axiomatic set theory can be found in Tomiyama and Yoshikawa (1987). A comprehensive and detailed model of design is not easily available. There are many domain-specific sides to design. For instance, VLSI design is mostly two-dimensional, whereas mechanical design is inherently three-dimensional. IIICAD hopes to incorporate the similarities in design processes, leaving the application-dependent issues for further consideration. Only through a clean design theory and formalization can one arrive at testable conjectures of design; logic is the principal instrument in this endeavor (Hayes, 1977; Moore, 1985; Akman and Tomiyama, 1989).

Key Problems

CAD Systems Support Few Design Processes/Models and Lack Integration

Producing final drawings is where current CAD systems excel. This clearly depends on what is meant by final drawings, but in the usual sense of them being what is handed to a production engineer, CAD systems are not that good even at producing final drawings; they cannot yet handle many of the details involved, such as tolerances, finishes, and materials. Also, they are virtually powerless with respect to initial sketching. There are systems that can accept rough drawings, but there is no system that can handle such information during the design process.

Another weakness in terms of design processes can be seen by comparing software development and machine design cycles. There is no corresponding tool in mechanical CAD for what is known as *formal specifications* in software. The same goes for *documentation*, which is de rigueur in software engineering. Last but not least, there are few established methods other than testing to guarantee the correctness of manufactured design objects.

Integration of models is essential because mechanical design deals with complicated gadgets. A design object must be viewed from various angles using different models, e.g., the kinematic, dynamic, finite element, and control theoretic models of a robot manipulator (Forbus, 1988). In general, the present trend is to integrate CAD systems around models concerning products. In fact, models should be process-oriented and the so-called conceptual design stage should be supported by tools. Thus integration will be a synthesis of (1) design subsystems, (2) design models and views based on an integrated data description scheme, and (3) design processes (especially those of the early design stages).

CAD Systems Do Not Support Error Checking

Current CAD systems are not fully able to recognize inconsistencies in their input data. To worsen the situation, final outputs of conventional systems are so impressive that many errors go unnoticed for they exceed the capacity of the designers. A remedy is to provide continuous error checks and to make sure that only the correct commands are accepted. Unfortunately, semantic error checks are difficult. A few systems provide good user interfaces to make suggestions against simple mistakes, but this is only a small part of what is eventually needed.

Data Entry Is Problematic

This has to do with the lack of task-domain terminology in the system. Because a conventional CAD system has no commonsense knowledge of machine design and cannot follow the designer's intentions (McCarthy, 1968), one is likely to enter a good deal of information to state simple requests like "Here I need a hole to insert the shaft I just created." When one inputs raw data manually, errors and misunderstandings during man–machine communication are inevitable (Akman, 1988). The ultimate solution is that CAD systems must accept substantially reduced yet comprehensive data instead of raw data. For instance, they should accept commands like "Generate an object with such and such properties" or "You have been supplied the minimum requirements, so proceed as you think fit."

Temporality, Ambiguity, and Inconsistency Are Not Allowed

In design, instead of sticking to one particular idea, one may want to experiment with several ideas; e.g., when using top–down stepwise refinement (Wegner, 1984). This brings a time dimension to design. A designer may purge things previously built, introduce things that have not been considered before, or require that the system temporarily forget a particular facet of a design object that for the moment is not being worked on.

Designers also frequently want to separate the structure of a design object from the values of its attributes so that they can first decide about its shape during the conceptual design stage. For example, it is more important to recognize first the topology of a mechanical part if it is going to be inserted in another part. Similarly, a designer may sometimes wish to acknowledge the existence of a point rather than specify its exact location. A similar problem has been studied in database theory where it is known as *null values* (Levesque, 1984).

Unstructured Code Is Commonplace

Software engineering requires that maintainable software be modular both "in the small" (to allow modification of minor components in specific applications) and "in the large" (to allow changes in major components based on, e.g., advances in technology) (Brooks, 1975). It is difficult to observe these characteristics in today's CAD systems, which are not open-ended, because they are not developed on a strong theoretical basis and consist of large amounts of code with unclear specifications, functions, and interactions. More often than not, efficiency is made a central concern and this gives rise to cryptic programs.

Data Exchange May Cause Deterioration of Meaning

When there is a three-dimensional solid modeling system based on, say, Boundary Representation (B-rep), data cannot easily be exchanged, data with another solid modeling system based on, say, Constructive Solid Geometry (CSG). This problem has connections with a fundamental philosophical problem known as *intensional* versus *extensional* descriptions and will be touched on later in this chapter (Tomiyama and ten Hagen, 1987).

Symbolic and Numerical Computing Are Not Coupled

Mechanical engineering systems normally use complex numerical and optimization procedures during design. However, in many cases, insight into the problem is not present. Insight is also needed to interpret the outcome of some computations. As Richard Hamming once said (Kitzmiller and Kowalik, 1986), "The purpose of computing is insight, not numbers." Traditionally, mechanical design systems contain numerical knowledge in the form of bulky libraries of numerical code but nothing else. Users are left alone in analyzing the results of long, confusing computations. Recent research in coupled systems is directed toward integrating the explanatory and problem-solving abilities of expert systems with the precision of numerical computing.

5.3 IIICAD PRINCIPLES

The architecture of IIICAD is directly inspired by, if not derived from, the theory. A central model of the design object, a metamodel, is maintained. From this metamodel more specific models will automatically be derived. Changes to the latter can be promoted to permanent changes in the metamodel and propagate from the metamodel to the other models.

Architecture

The Supervisor (SPV) is at the core of IIICAD and controls all information flow. It adds intelligence to the system by comparing user actions with scenarios (which describe standard design procedures) and by performing error handling. Although the SPV corrects user errors, it does not have the initiative for the design process because IIICAD is envisaged to be a designer's apprentice, not an automatic design environment. *Scenarios* are design process descriptions. External information is further exchanged with the user interface module and with the application modules.

Thus, IIICAD should (1) have a control mechanism to guide the designer,

(2) compare user actions with scenarios, and (3) be a designer's apprentice. Point (1) suggests that the system have control knowledge that is applied to the human designer, point (2) suggests that the system check the actions of the human designer against some control knowledge, and point (3) suggests that the system be trained by the human designer (like a human apprentice who is trained by a master craftsman).

The Knowledge Base (KB) is divided into two parts: an object store where all objects and their internal structures can be found, and a rule store where the relations between several objects are defined in terms of definite program clauses, as in Prolog. The parts of the design artifact and their internal structures are kept in the object store, whereas facts and interrelationships among the parts are furnished by the rule store. Functions "connect" the object store and the rule store.

All information about the design objects, including their attributes and functions (or using the object-oriented terminology, instance variables and methods [Goldberg and Robson, 1983]), as well as the relationships among the objects, will be stored in the KB. It can contain both procedural and declarative descriptions of the artifact that is being designed. Some form is given to this by the object-oriented programming paradigm to describe the objects and by the logic programming paradigm to describe the interrelations among the objects (Bobrow, 1985; Stefik and Bobrow, 1986).

It should be noted that the rule store is most dynamically used during the design process. To provide flexibility to this dynamical behavior, the SPV should provide a mechanism to partition the rule base and group the clauses for specific purposes. The advantage of this is twofold: (1) logical computation becomes efficient because only a relatively small amount of knowledge is passed to the inference mechanism, and (2) consistency is easier to maintain because less information will be considered.

IIICAD has a kernel language called the Integrated Data Description Language (IDDL) used by all system elements. The IDDL is the means used to code the design knowledge and the design objects, and guarantees integrated descriptions systemwide.

In addition to the preceding above principal elements, IIICAD has a high-level interface called the Intelligent User Interface (IUI), which is also driven by scenarios written in IDDL. The IUI accepts messages from other subsystems and sends them to lower level interface systems. Syntactical user errors are processed by the IUI, whereas semantic errors can be processed, as much as this is possible, by the SPV. The goal is to manipulate more user-oriented concepts; this is the basis for more direct communication (i.e., without intermediate command repertoire). To support it, the IUI must be provided with sufficient information about the semantics to recognize the symbols being used, both for input and output. Such a system can be built as a two-layer interface system. The lower layer is a user interface. The upper layer interprets the syntactically accepted constructs of the lower layer on the basis of declarative knowledge that has been made available by the SPV. Semantic recognition can drive typical user interface processes such as anticipation, error correction, default handling, and focusing.

The Application Interface (API) secures the mapping between the central model descriptions about a design object and the individual models used by the application programs. The following list is a first-order approximation to the desirable application programs: conceptual design systems to handle vague information, consultation and problem-solving systems for engineering applications, basic/detailed design systems coupled with geometric modelers, engineering analysis systems such as finite element packages, and product modelers.

User Interface

There are several useful ways of looking at intelligent CAD user interface architecture. The following dichotomies are quite common (David, 1987): CAD versus automated design (AD), designer's apprentice versus autonomous design system, and glass box versus black box.

The boundary between CAD and AD is indeed hard to delineate. One view is that the ultimate aim of design computerizationt design is to arrive at automatic design systems which can compete with and even surpass the best human designers. However, the interactive nature of design will probably dictate that for a long time to come, CAD as man–machine cooperation must dominate. The same holds true for apprentice versus autonomous systems. An apprentice system has less hard-wired knowledge than an autonomous system, but it knows better how to interact and has a generic model of design. An autonomous system is powerful for narrow domains. It is relatively easy to extend an apprentice system by teaching it new "skills." It is unwieldy to extend an autonomous system because its very constitution warrants myopia.

A more natural look at these dichotomies is via the metaphor glass box versus black box. If a CAD system has a glass box structure, then the user can, at any time, look through it to see partial results and processes. On the other hand, a black box system resembles a batch processing environment—one submits tasks to be executed and the system reports back with results.

The seasoned researchers of CAD may remember those times when ideas such as "general CAD" became fashionable (Jacquart *et al.*, 1974). Today, demands for integration suggest reconsideration of that sweeping panorama of design. The view which regards design as a large collection of intelligent tools is different from the view which regards a design system as a framework. The intelligent tool approach assumes that if one has a cooperating set of experts who can communicate with each other, then one can solve many problems. The framework approach regards the "shell" of the design systems as their biggest advantage; the domain-specific issues can be dealt with separately, using the facilities provided by the shell.

5.4 STRATEGIES

There are two caveats in the development of IIICAD. The first is that everything should be based on a formal theory to avoid the infamous hacker trap, i.e., assorted features that overwhelm the user. The second caveat is to be careful about software development: while knowledge engineering is different from software engineering, the KB will still have to be maintained (Ramamoorthy *et al.*, 1987).

A well-founded design theory may serve as a basis for specification and implementation of intelligent CAD systems. To be useful for this purpose, a theory must be realistic in the sense that it has a close relation to design practice; it must describe design processes as they are in practice or as users would like or are accustomed to. A design theory must also have a logical basis so that there are guarantees that a system, developed according to the theory, will take sound steps. Thus, logical representations of incomplete descriptions of objects, patterns of reasoning involved in design (Simon, 1977), and multiple worlds (which are described later) are to be allowed.

There are three ontological aspects of design: processes, models, and activities. A theory of CAD is then an aggregate of the following:

(1) A theory that describes the design processes and activities (Tomiyama and Yoshikawa, 1987).
(2) A theory that deals with the models of design objects (Akman and ten Hagen, 1989). For this discussion, this must be a theory of machines (Minsky, 1967); in VLSI design, it would be a theory of VLSI, and so on.
(3) A metalevel theory that describes existing knowledge about design.

The Role of Logic

In General Design Theory (Tomiyama and Yoshikawa, 1987), a design process is regarded as a mapping from the function space onto the attribute space. Both spaces are defined on an entity set. A design process evolves about a metamodel. During design, new attribute descriptions will be added (or existing ones will be modified) and the metamodel will converge to the design solution. In other words, design specifications will initially be presented in functional terms and the design will be completed when all relevant attributes of the artifact are determined so as to be able to manufacture it. To further illustrate the design process, three major components need to be recognized: (1) entities, (2) attributes of entities, and (3) relationships among entities. A design process is thus a sequence of small steps (forward and backward) to obtain complete information about these components.

It was mentioned before that to control the stepwise refinement of the design process, a designer needs to express unknown, uncertain, and temporal information about the design object. This can be accomplished using an amalgam of intuitionistic logic, modal logic, and temporal logic (Veth, 1987). It is taken for granted that descriptions of a design object are given by a set of propositions (such as well-formed formulas in first-order logic). A simplified view of design is then as follows. A sequence of metamodels is generated from an initial specification. If they cannot pass a feasibility check, then a compromise is made or backtracking is applied. The models derived from the metamodels are, in the meantime, evaluated for consistency. Thus,

> Specification: $s = T[0] --> \ldots --> T[n] --> \ldots --> T[N] = g$
>
> Metamodel: $M[0] --> \ldots --> M[n] --> \ldots --> M[N]$
>
> Propositions: $q[0] --> \ldots --> q[n] --> \ldots --> q[N]$

Here, s is the original design specification and g is the design goal. Each design step has an associated set of propositions that are denoted by $q[n]$. Two central concerns are (1) how to choose $q[n]$ (i.e., how to proceed with design) and (2) what if it is discovered that $\sim q[n]$ (i.e., how to deal with contradictions). The following definitions are therefore given:

$$q[n] = p[0] \& \ldots \& p[i] \& \ldots \& p[k]$$

where each $p[i]$ is a fact concerning the metamodel,

$$q[n], C[n] |- m[n]$$

where $|-$ is the syntactic turnstile, $m[n]$ is a model, and $C[n]$ is control knowledge, and

$$q[n], m[n], D[n] |- r$$

where $D[n]$ is detailing knowledge and r is a proposition that should be added to $q[n]$ to arrive at the next description, $q[n + 1]$. Knowledge appearing right before the syntactic turnstile is used in the derivations as metaknowledge. With this notation, the following classification of design suggests itself:

Invention: Given s, determine $q[n]$, $C[n]$, $D[n]$, and g.

New product development: Given s and $C[n]$, determine $q[n]$, $D[n]$, and g.

Routine design: Given s, $C[n]$, and $D[n]$, determine $q[n]$ and g.

Parametric design: Given s, $q[n]$, $C[n]$, and $D[n]$, determine g.

Logic with modes of truth, i.e., modal logic with necessity and possibility, can be used as a notational tool. Here, there are not only affirmations that some proposition is true, but also stronger ones, such as that p is necessary (denoted Lp) and weaker ones, such as that p is possible (denoted Mp). If p is asserted to be necessary, then it can also be asserted that p is true. If p is asserted as true, then we can also assert p as possible. The following equalities can be used:

$$Lp = \sim M \sim p$$
$$Mp = \sim L \sim p$$

Three well-known modal logic systems are T, S4, and S5. T is characterized by the axiom schemata of the predicate calculus plus the following:

$$Lp => Lp$$
$$L(p => q) => (Lp => Lq)$$

There is a rule of inference (referred to as necessitation) in T which allows derivation of Lp from p. S4 is obtained by the addition of

$$Lp => LLp$$

to T, and S5 by by the addition of

$$Mp => LMp$$

For temporal logic, let $t >> p$ ($t << p$) denote that p holds after (before) time t. Let $t[1] \ldots t[2]$ denote the time interval whose end points are $t[1]$ and $t[2]$. Then,

$$t >> \sim p = \sim (t >> p)$$

$$t >> (p|q) = (t >> p|(t >> q)$$

$$t >> (p \& q) = (t >> p) \& (t >> q)$$

$$t[1] \ldots t[2] >> p = (t[1] >> p) \& (t[2] << p) \& (t[1] < t[2])$$

Using temporal logic, inference control (usually called metalevel control) can be described. For instance, in Prolog, the order of rules matter (Bobrow, 1985). In general, this knowledge is embedded in the interpreter of the language. By disclosing this control, more supple control may be introduced. For example, D[n] may be a set of rules of the following sort:

$$(t[1] >> q[1]) \& (t[2] >> q[2]) \& (t[1] < t[2]) => (t[2] >> q[3])$$

$$(t[1] >> q[1]) \& (t[2] >> q[2]) \& (t[1] > t[2]) => (t[2] >> q[4])$$

That is, if q[1] holds after t[1], q[2] holds after t[2], and t[1] is earlier than t[2], then a new property, q[3], holds after t[2]. Otherwise, another property, q[4], holds.

Intuitionistic logic can be blended with temporal logic. Let t[p] >> p be defined as tt (true). Now, introducing a logical symbol uu (unknown), intuitionism can be formalized in terms of temporality:

$$t[p] << (p| \sim p) = uu$$

$$t[p] >> (p| \sim p) = tt$$

Naive Physics

In machine design, it is not yet precisely known by which symbolism one should describe the functions of machines. There is, however, a view that functions can be represented in terms of the physical phenomena that the machine exhibits (de Kleer and Brown, 1984). Therefore, the representation of functions can be reduced to the representation of physical phenomena and the qualitative reasoning about them.

> When a particular machine is described to us, we do not first ask questions about its material construction. Given an engineering drawing, a circuit diagram, a patent description, something must first convince us that we understand how it works *in principle*. That is, we must see how it is "supposed" to work. We inquire only later whether this member will stand the stress, or whether that oscillator is stable under load, etc. But the *idea* of a machine centers around some *abstract* model or process.... The abstract idea of a machine, e.g., an adding machine, is a *specification* for how a physical object *ought* to work. If the machine that I build wears out, I censure *it* and perhaps fix it. Just as in physics, the parts and states of the physical object are supposed to correspond to those of the abstract concept. But in contrast to the situation in physics, we criticize the *material* part of the system when the correspondence breaks down. [Emphasis removed in various places.] (Minsky, 1967, pp. 5–6)

In order to give the reader a better appreciation of the kind of physical reasoning being sought, a quick look at geometric reasoning is provided. This is also an example of general knowledge, which needs to be applied in specific situations. For geometry, the emphasis is on generating the appropriate representation in order to answer queries as directly as possible. One obvious solution is to encode the essential knowledge procedurally. This kernel is surrounded by declaratively described methods about how it is to be used. A given specific problem, described declaratively, is matched with the "geometry base" and the nearest answer is used as a starter. This is in the spirit of de Kleer's (1975) Random Access Local Consequent Methods (RALCMs).

In qualitative physics, the reduction of information is arrived at by creating an abstract layer (the naive or qualitative layer) which may, strictly speaking, be incorrect but sufficiently correct for the problem at hand. Naive physics observes that people have a different kind of knowledge about the physical world. This knowledge can best be described as common sense, and is attained after years of interaction with the world (McCarthy, 1968; Akman *et al.*, 1989). Naive physics ideas are useful in machine design and should be codified in the IIICAD system. To this end, the proposal in Hayes (1985) is followed with the hope of capturing naive physics in logic. Additionally, qualitative physics is used as a mathematical tool based on symbolic manipulations.

Consider the following concepts underlying "change" in physical systems: state, cause, equilibrium, oscillation, force, and feedback. Qualitative physics regards these concepts in a simple qualitative way. It maps continuous variables to discrete variables, taking only a small number of values (+, −, 0). Accordingly, differential equations are mapped to qualitative differential equations (also known as confluences) (Kuipers, 1986).

Qualitative techniques may cause ambiguities. Assume that a certain quantity M varies with N/L, i.e., M is proportional to N/L. If N increases (decreases) while L remains constant, then M also increases (decreases). However, a finer knowledge of the individual changes is required if we are told that both N and L increase (or decrease). The techniques of order of magnitude reasoning are designed to handle precisely this kind of problem without requiring knowledge of the numerical values involved (Raiman, 1986).

In qualitative reasoning, a "mechanistic" world view is adopted. This asserts that every physical situation is regarded as a device made up of individual components, each contributing to the overall behavior. Nevertheless, the laws of the substructures may not presume the functioning of the whole: the principle of no-function-in-structure (de Kleer and Brown, 1984). Additionally, assumptions that are specific to a particular device should be distinguished from the class-wide assumptions that are common to the entire class of devices. A simplistic view of modeling devices comprises three kinds of constituents: materials, components, and channels. Channels transfer material from one component to another.

After modeling a device, designers can reason about it. Envisioning starts start with a structural description to determine all possible behavioral sequences, momentarily forgetting about the real values of the problem variables while trying to see all possible outcomes (Kuipers, 1986). Naive physics concepts are required for design because a design object will have a physical existence and, accordingly, obey natural laws. If designers want to create designs that correspond to physically realizable design objects, then they will have to refer to naive physics notions (Akman et al., 1990). Furthermore, if they want to reason about a design object in its destined environment, envisioning, simulation, and diagnostics tools need to be available (Forbus, 1984).

Intension Versus Extension

In order to discuss design, the entities, their properties, and the relationships among them need to be described. In an extensional description method, the fact that an entity e has property p is described by p(e) and the fact that entities e and f stand in relationship r is described by r(e,f). In an intensional description method, these two facts can be represented by e(p) and rel(e,r,f), respectively. Extensional descriptions do not imply any preconceptions, whereas intensional descriptions make assumptions. When an intensional description has to be changed, it results in a modification of those predefined conditions. For instance, a shaft might be represented intensionally by shaft(diameter,length,bearing_1,bearing_2). If we now want to add a new attribute, such as power, the addition results in a redefinition of the predicate shaft. On the other hand, an extensional description might consist of the following facts: shaft(s), equal(diameter(s),D), equal(length(s),L), supported_by(s,b_1), supported_by(s,b_2), bearing(b_1), and bearing(b_2).

Thus, in an extensional description we need to write numerous obvious descriptions. However, modifying such a representation is easy: just add or delete facts. On the other hand, an intensional description is difficult to modify but shows better performance. CAD applications demand a flexible data description scheme that is easy to modify (Tomiyama and ten Hagen, 1987). Independent multiple views of a design object demand independent small partitionings of the database. This is easily achieved by an extensional description method because only the relevant facts have to be picked up.

5.5 RAPID PROTOTYPING

IIICAD will evolve over time, with the definition of its purpose being refined as it becomes a fuller system. This suggests that recent techniques of software engineering such as exploratory programming (Ramamoorthy *et al.*, 1987) and rapid prototyping are not to be overlooked. These techniques are more permissive than the rigid method of formal specifications in that they advocate iterative enhancement. This leads to an evolutionary software life cycle. One starts with a skeletal implementation and adds new modules until the system is reasonably complete for demonstration. In rapid prototyping, the interest is in perceiving a glimpse of a future system in order to assess its strengths and weaknesses (Brooks, 1975).

Smalltalk and Loops

With regard to exploratory programming and rapid prototyping, Smalltalk is a fine implementation tool which is appreciated for two reasons. First, is the emphasis of Smalltalk on interactive graphics and its sophisticated user interface (Goldberg and Robson, 1983). Second, Smalltalk is not just an isolated programming language; it is a programming environment. For instance, the ability in Smalltalk to inspect any data structure recursively gives the programmer a great ability for exploratory programming. Smalltalk's insistence to express everything as objects and messages using a simple syntax is conceptually powerful and consistent.

Experience with Smalltalk also suggests that it is not yet perfect (Nielsen and Richards, 1986). First and foremost, using it effectively is not an easy task. Long chains of message passing make it difficult for the novice to understand how some action takes place. The scale of the system and its generalist design may frustrate even the professionals with a wide background in other programming languages. The class hierarchy is rigid. The inheritance mechanism, even when it is enriched with multiple inheritance, is seen as a drawback for CAD systems (Veth, 1987). A scheme called *delegation* is currently being popularized for pliable sharing of knowledge in object-oriented systems. In its most common form, inheritance is a way to arrange classes in a tree so that they inherit methods from other classes. Delegation is more general: an object can delegate a message to an arbitrary object rather than being limited to the paths of a class hierarchy (or lattice, in case of multiple inheritance).

Loops is also becoming increasingly popular due to its multiparadigm nature (Stefik *et al.*, 1986). It supports a mechanism for annotated values. This helps programmers monitor arbitrary values without previously planning such access. There are two kinds of annotated values: property annotation and active value. The latter associates with any value a demon. The former associates with any value an optional property list.

From a CAD viewpoint, another useful construct of Loops is as a composite object. Composite objects contain other objects as parts. A car may be described structurally as consisting of a body, a mechanical system, and an electrical system. The body has four doors, six windows, and so on. Parts can contain other parts, e.g., a door has an ashtray and a handle. Objects may belong to more than one structure, e.g., the power window controller can be viewed as a component of the mechanical system or the electrical system.

Loops introduces *perspectives*, which are a form of composite object and which provide a way to implement the multiple views of the same design object. Thus a pressure regulator may be represented using perspectives like mech_assembly, disp_object, and func_box. The first two perspectives both treat coordinates, but with different interpretations. In the first perspective, the coordinates refer to physical dimensions of the regulator to be manufactured whereas in the second perspective, they are just measures on a display screen. The third perspective concerns the functioning of the regulator as a control theoretic device with feedback. Loops offers a remedy to the complicated method hierarchy of Smalltalk. In Loops, a method is defined over a set of classes. This means that methods do not belong to a particular class.

5.6 IDDL: A DESIGN BASE LANGUAGE

Every human-controlled production process for some artifact contains numerous tasks. Only a few of these are supported by computerized design tools. IDDL contains new constructs which support writing code for a wide range of design tasks.

Design is a complex activity. Consequently, the motives for improving design support can be quite different, e.g., making designing more economical, improving the quality of designs, and making designing more independent of expertise. Such general objectives have to be analyzed in order to distill a number of problem areas for which adequate scientific and technical treatment would provide better support. The problems are classified in such a way that language constructs needed for formulation of design support methods can be gradually introduced. With each new facility added, both the language and the application domain will grow.

Representational Issues

A typical CAD system must have three major components: (1) a design object component, (2) a design process component, and (3) a user interface component. Improvements in the representation of design objects is a necessity for integration of design tasks. On the other hand, a satisfactory design process representation is necessary for enlarging the scope of design tasks. A good user interface is crucial to be able to directly specify domain-specific terminology. This requires semantic processing of user transactions. The user interface must be directly coupled to the object and process representations.

A design process representation is a list of actions, which, when executed in a meaningful order, may specify a design object. Each action is preceded by a condition that expresses when the action is possible: in this case, execution will contribute something to the design object. Actions can be structured in design scenarios. A scenario exists for each design task. The status of the design process can be explicitly maintained in a rule base. The status of the artifact is maintained in the same rule base. Status information and user input together form the operands of the conditions that precede the action rules. The conditions, therefore, represent the control structure of a scenario. The control structure of the entire design process is obtained by adding to this scenario structures which consist of a subscenario hierarchy and the option to activate several scenarios concurrently.

The design object is represented by atomic objects and object relations, which can be used to create composite objects. Hence, all object structuring is obtained explicitly by asserting relations. These relations together make up the object status previously mentioned. Equally, the design process status can be represented as object relations. This makes it possible to take a close look experimentally at how a design object and its generating process are interrelated.

The part of an artifact and the design process status that is relevant for a given scenario is called a *world*. Much of the potential of IIICAD will depend on the flexibility of the world mechanism being built. A world can create a particular, restricted view on the artifact. In a world, one can execute the actions of the corresponding scenario more efficiently.

All automated parts of the design process now follow the same scheme: If a condition is defined over a process status, and an object status holds, then action is taken as specified in the consequence of the condition. This action may lead to a new status for both the object and the process, for which another rule may apply, and so on. This process comes to a halt when new input from the user is needed to continue.

The KB consists of the collection of all objects that are created and the collection of all relationships that hold among these objects. In addition, every object has its current status, e.g., the values of its attributes. Most objects have attributes that are represented by functions which map objects onto attribute values. A set of such functions forms the "inside" structure of an object.

One can identify a particular configuration of objects and their relationships, e.g., a world. Worlds as a configuration of objects and their relationships partition the KB in a straightforward manner. At any point in time, a functional separation of the KB is achieved by calling the set of available objects an "object base" and the relationships among them a "rule base."

Requirements for IDDL

The IDDL will be the base language on which the subsystems of IIICAD will be built. This section summarizes the requirements for IDDL (Veth, 1987).

The IDDL, as a language used to construct the knowledge base, should support incremental programming and easy maintenance. It should be able to describe not only design objects but also design processes. It must embed the stepwise nature of the design process and should be able to describe the knowledge to detail a metamodel, to check metamodel feasibility, and to control the detailing process. It also should allow a myriad of views of a design object; these views are possibly independent but still correlated.

The IDDL should incorporate positive and negative information, known and unknown, and modalities such as "necessary" and "possible." This requires that

IDDL consolidate logics such as modal, intuitive, and temporal. Inconsistencies need to be resolved with some sort of truth maintenance when transferring to the next metamodel. In other words, design problem solving can also be seen as selecting among plausible alternatives. One naive method for exploring the search space is to enumerate its points and test. It is more advantageous to find solutions that meet some criteria of acceptability. This implies the ability to compare partial solutions. A world is demarcated by a set of assumptions and defines a possible solution. Different assumptions on the same range are clearly contradictory. That is, the KB that records the different worlds will be inconsistent. A Truth Maintenance System (TMS) is needed to work safely with an inconsistent database. It records the inferences made by the problem-solver and then avoids repeating the same inferences. Once a contradiction is found, the world it belongs to is no longer considered. Via dependency-directed backtracking, a TMS is able to remove contradictions from the database and rebuild a consistent world (de Kleer, 1986).

To control the behavior of the system, the IDDL must have metaknowledge that selects which rule to apply at a certain moment. It should also have a "focusing control" mechanism which can create a small world where it is clearly defined what kind of information is accessible. From the viewpoint of interactive design, it is desirable for the human designer to be able to mark intermediate design stages, and to later go back to examine or resume from there. Consequently, the stages of design evolution must be representable on the level of IDDL.

Design produces intermediate results that are incomplete and even inconsistent during a time spanning a series of transactions. The design object's representation must allow assumptions to be used for the evolution of the design object. The IDDL, using nonmonotonicity, should be able to retract assumed (but eventually unconsidered or disproved) propositions.

In spite of the slight weaknesses cited earlier, object-oriented programming languages deliver extensibility, flexible modifications of code, and reusability. Important issues in object-oriented programming are data encapsulation and information hiding. Thus an object can be regarded as an independent program that knows everything about itself. It is an additional benefit of object-oriented programming systems that they offer incremental compilation, dynamic binding, system building tools, and good user interfaces. Therefore, object-oriented programming is a good choice for creating IIICAD. On the other hand, logic programming is powerful because it can reflect the reasoning process most naturally. IDDL uses the logic programming paradigm to express the design process, whereas the object-oriented programming paradigm is utilized to express design objects.

A Multiworld Mechanism

During the course of design, it is vital that an intelligent CAD system allows the designer to represent the design object in various ways. These various descriptions are called *models of the design object*. Four examples of such models are

(1) A functional specification of the design object in terms of the constraints that should be met

    (2) A geometrical model which creates a visual representation of the design object

    (3) An FEM (finite element method) model enabling strength predictions to be made on complex mechanical constructions

    (4) A cost analysis model to calculate the manufacturing costs

Models are able to communicate with each other by means of the metamodel. This is a central description of the design object to which all models refer to and depend on. All changes that occur in a certain model are propagated through the metamodel to all other models, which are then updated appropriately. Although the different models may use different languages internally (e.g., C for the cost analyzer, a CSG language for the solid modeler), the interface between a metamodel and the other models is realized in IDDL. This is achieved by the multiworld mechanism (Akman *et al.*, 1988). A model is created by a call to a scenario which in turn opens a world. A world is a part of the design object description together with some information that belongs to the particular model that is created. The multiworld mechanism lets the designer open several worlds simultaneously; in other words, several models may be active at the same time. For instance, the designer may input new constraints and examine the results of these in a CSG model and an FEM model concurrently.

Moreover, the multiworld mechanism allows the designer to create multiple descriptions of the design object in parallel. Here, a distinction is made between dependent versus independent worlds. *Dependent* worlds result in a unique design object description; they reflect the same metamodel. *Independent* worlds, however, can result in different design object descriptions; they do not reflect the same metamodel. In a nutshell, dependent worlds are used to create multiple views of the design object, whereas independent worlds give rise to alternative design solutions.

The multiworld mechanism is embedded in the scenario part of IDDL. Scenarios specify how many worlds exist simultaneously and how they relate to each other. Special care is taken for constructs that close or update a world, thereby transferring some of its properties to the metamodel. This control mechanism also checks the validity of the worlds with respect to the metamodel and propagates changes in the metamodel to all applicable worlds.

5.7 CONCLUSION

IIICAD is a unifying framework for describing and using design knowledge. Theoretical ideas of AI such as naive physics, formal tools such as logic, and practical software techniques such as prototyping are essential to IIICAD. IIICAD clarifies, on an abstract level, what the design process is in relation to the design object. No distinction is drawn between the parts of the process carried out by the designer and by the assisting program.

Smalltalk is used as an implementation language on top of which IDDL and a Prolog-like inference engine can be built. Except for the hierarchical constructs, IDDL can take advantage of the already existing object-oriented constructs of

Smalltalk in order to represent the objects in the object base. The hierarchical structure of the objects can then be fully implemented as clauses in the rule base.

REFERENCES

Akman, V. 1988. Geometry and graphics applied to robotics. In *Theoretical Foundations of Computer Graphics and CAD*, ed. R. A. Earnshaw, pp. 619–638. Berlin: Springer-Verlag.

Akman, V., and ten Hagen, P. J. W. 1989. The power of physical representations. In *Intelligent CAD Systems 2: Implementational Issues*, eds. V. Akman, P. J. W. ten Hagen, and P. Veerkamp, pp. 170–194. Berlin: Springer-Verlag.

Akman, V., and Tomiyama, T. 1989. The role of logic and commonsense reasoning in intelligent CAD. In *Proc. of 3rd IFIP WG 5.2 Workshop on Intelligent CAD*, Osaka, Japan, pp. 15–20.

Akman, V., ten Hagen, P. J. W., Rogier, J. L. H., and Veerkamp, P. 1988. Knowledge engineering in design. *Knowledge-Based Systems* 1:67–77.

Akman, V., Franklin, W. R., and Veth, B. l989. Design systems with common sense. In *Proc. of 3rd Eurographics Workshop on Intelligent CAD Systems: Practical Experience and Evaluation*, Texel, The Netherlands, pp. 317–322.

Akman, V., Ede, D., Franklin, W. R., and ten Hagen, P. J. W. 1990. Mental models of force and motion. In *Proc. of IEEE International Workshop on Intelligent Motion Control*, ed. O. Kaynak, pp. 153–158. IEEE Press.

Bobrow, D. 1986. If Prolog is the answer, what is the question? or What it takes to support AI programming paradigms. *IEEE Transactions on Software Engineering* 11:1401–1408.

Bobrow, D., Mittal, S., and Stefik, M. 1986. Expert systems: Perils and promise. *Communications of the ACM* 29:880–894.

Brooks, F. P.1975. *The Mythical Man-Month*. Reading, Massachusetts: Addison-Wesley.

Brown, D.C., and Chandrasekaran, B. 1986. Knowledge and control for a mechanical design expert system. *IEEE Computer* 19:92 100.

David, B. T. 1987, Multi-expert systems for CAD. In *Intelligent CAD Systems 1: Theoretical and Methodological Aspects*, eds. P. J. W. ten Hagen and T. Tomiyama, pp. 57–67. Berlin: Springer-Verlag.

Doyle, J. 1985. Expert systems and the myth of symbolic reasoning. *IEEE Transactions on Software Engineering* 11:1386–1390.

Dyer, M.G., Flowers, M., and Hodges, J. 1986. EDISON: An engineering design invention system operating naively. *Artificial Intelligence in Engineering* 1:36–44.

Forbus, K. 1984. Qualitative process theory. *Artificial Intelligence* 24:85–168.

Forbus, K. 1988. Intelligent computer-aided engineering. *AI Magazine* 9:23–36.

Goldberg, A., and Robson, D. 1983. *Smalltalk-80: The Language and Its Implementation*. Reading, Massachusetts: Addison-Wesley.

Hayes, P. J. 1977. In defense of logic. In *Proc.of 5th International Joint Conference on Artificial Intelligence* (IJCAI-77), Cambridge, Massachusetts, pp. 559–565.

Hayes, P. J. 1985. The second naive physics manifesto. In *Formal Theories of the Commonsense World*, eds. J. R. Hobbs and R. C. Moore, pp. 1–36. Norwood, New Jersey: Ablex.

Jacquart, R., Regnier, P., and Valette, F. R. 1974. GERMINAL: Towards a general and integrated system for computer aided design. In *Proc. of 11th Design Automation Workshop*, Denver, Colorado, pp. 352–358.

Kitzmiller, C. T., and Kowalik, J. S. 1986. Symbolic and numerical computing in knowledge based systems. In *Coupling Symbolic and Numerical Computing in Expert Systems*, ed. J. S. Kowalik. Amsterdam: Elsevier.

de Kleer, J. 1975. Qualitative and quantitative knowledge in classical mechanics. Technical

Report AI-TR-352, Artificial Intelligence Laboratory, Massachusetts Institute of Technology, Cambridge, Massachusetts.

de Kleer, J. 1986. An assumption-based TMS. *Artificial Intelligence* 28:127–162.

de Kleer, J., and Brown, J. S. 1984. A qualitative physics based on confluences. *Artificial Intelligence* 24:7–83.

Kuipers, B. 1986. Qualitative simulation. *Artificial Intelligence* 29:289–338.

Lansdown, J. 1988. Graphics, design, and artificial intelligence. In *Theoretical Foundations of Computer Graphics and CAD*, ed. R. A. Earnshaw, pp. 1153–1174. Berlin: Springer-Verlag.

Levesque, H. J. 1984. The logic of incomplete knowledge bases. In *Conceptual Modeling*, eds. M. L. Brodie, J. Mylopoulos, and J. W. Schmidt, pp. 165–186. New York: Springer-Verlag.

McCarthy, J. 1968. Programs with common sense. In *Semantic Information Processing*, ed. M. Minsky, pp. 403–418. Cambridge, Massachusetts: MIT Press.

Minsky, M. L. 1967. *Computation: Finite and Infinite Machines*. Englewood Cliffs, New Jersey: Prentice-Hall.

Mittal, S., Dym, C. L., and Morjaria, M. 1986. PRIDE: An expert system for the design of paper handling systems. *IEEE Computer* 19:102–114.

Moore, R. C. 1985. The role of logic in knowledge representation and commonsense reasoning. In *Readings in Knowledge Representation*, eds. R. J. Brachman and H. J. Levesque, pp. 336–341. Los Altos, California: Morgan Kaufman.

Mostow, J. 1985. Toward better models of the design process. *AI Magazine* 6:44–57.

Nielsen, J., and Richards, J. T. 1986. Comments on the learnability and usability of Smalltalk for casual users. Technical Report RC-12080, IBM T. J. Watson Research Center, Yorktown Heights, New York.

Purcell, P. A. 1988. Computer environments for design and designers. *Design Studies* 9:144–149.

Raiman, O. 1986. Order of magnitude reasoning. In *Proc. of American Association for Artificial Intelligence (AAAI-86)*, Philadelphia, 100–104.

Ramamoorthy, C., Shekhar, S., and Garg, V. 1987. Software development support for AI programs. *IEEE Computer* 20:30–40.

Simon, H. A. 1977. The structure of ill-structured problems. In H. A. Simon, *Models of Discovery (and Other Topics in the Methods of Science)*, pp. 304–325. The Netherlands: D. Reidel, Dordrecht.

Simon, H. A. 1979. The science of design: Creating the artificial. In H. A. Simon, *The Sciences of the Artificial*, pp. 55–83. Cambridge, Massachusetts: MIT Press.

Stefik, M., and Bobrow, D. 1986. Object-oriented programming: Themes and variations. *AI Magazine* 6:40–62.

Stefik, M., Bobrow, D., and Kahn, K. 1986. Integrating access-oriented programming with a multiparadigm environment. *IEEE Software* 3:10–18.

Sutherland, I.E. 1963. SKETCHPAD: A man-machine graphical communication system. In *Proc. of AFIPS Spring Joint Computer Conference*, pp. 329–346. Baltimore: Spartan Books.

Tomiyama, T., and ten Hagen, P. J. W. 1987. Representing knowledge in two distinct descriptions: Extensional vs. intensional. Technical Report CS-R8728, Center for Mathematics and Computer Science, Amsterdam.

Tomiyama, T., and Yoshikawa, H. 1987. Extended general design theory. In *Design Theory for CAD*, eds. H. Yoshikawa and E. A. Warman, pp. 95–130. Amsterdam: North-Holland.

Veth, B. 1987. An integrated data description language for coding design knowledge. In *Intelligent CAD Systems 1: Theoretical and Methodological Aspects*. eds. P. J. W. ten Hagen and T. Tomiyama, pp. 295–313. Berlin: Springer-Verlag.

Wegner, P. 1984. Capital-intensive software technology. *IEEE Software* 1:7–45.

Yeomans, R. W., Choudry, A., and ten Hagen, P. J. W. 1985. *Design Rules for a CIM System*. Amsterdam: North-Holland.

Chapter 6

Reasoning About Symbolic Descriptions of Mechanical Parts

Gerald M. Radack and Leon S. Sterling
Department of Computer Engineering and Science
and
Center for Automation and Intelligent Systems Research
Case Western Reserve University
Cleveland, Ohio

6.1 INTRODUCTION

Human designers and engineers often must deal with complicated objects during design. They cope with the complexity during the earlier stages of design by leaving many of the details unspecified, and by reasoning about them implicitly. In contrast, current computer-aided design (CAD) systems insist on specifying all the details from the beginning of the design stage, and are really little more than electronic drafting tools. Consequently, it is difficult to use current CAD systems to design complex parts, particularly in the early stages of design.

It is essential for CAD systems to support implicit reasoning about partially specified objects if CAD systems are to become real design aids. This chapter studies how implicit reasoning may be achieved by describing parts with symbolic representations and reasoning with constraints in the description to fill in specific details of a part as necessary. This will show that symbolic reasoning can be used to represent significant portions of the designer's intent and raise the level of CAD tools.

What is a symbolic description? A symbolic geometric representation of a mechanical part is a description of the object in terms of shape primitives whose parameters may be symbolic variables instead of numbers. The symbolic variables may be related using constraints. Manipulating the part occurs through reasoning about the symbolic values and the constraints. The details of this symbolic representation scheme, and examples, are covered in Section 6.2.

There are several reasons why one might be interested in symbolic reasoning. Two are stressed here. The first reason is to avoid overspecification of parts during design which may cause premature and inappropriate design decisions. As a corollary, the designer must be allowed to reason more generically about underspecified objects. The second reason is to avoid problems with inexact arithmetic. Most CAD models suffer from inconsistencies due to rounding of numeric values which can be avoided if expressions are manipulated symbolically.

This chapter describes several examples of reasoning with symbolic representations, including:

- Reasoning about manufacturing features to give the designer feedback early in the design cycle as to possible interactions between features
- Reasoning about dimensioning and tolerancing information
- Performing Boolean operations on underspecified parts
- Drawing underspecified part descriptions on a terminal screen or hard copy device

The first example concerns designing a part using higher-level features. When specifying a part, a designer must give its shape and often specifies other properties such as surface finish, color, and manufacturing method. It is clear that the designer has semantic features in mind which a helpful system could manipulate. The experimental system presented here manipulates simple features such as slots and through holes where these features are expressed symbolically. The system deduces consequences of feature interaction, e.g., whether all given features can fit together on a part. These interactions should be transparent to the designer. The second example demonstrates how tolerances can be incorporated into a feature-based design system. This is important for inspection. The prototype system checks if a symbolically described part lies in some tolerance zone. This checking involves solving constraints; the part is described in terms of features and may have additional constraints.

The final examples concern underconstrained objects. To manipulate parts described symbolically, modified algorithms have been developed for the set operations, union, intersection, and difference. The algorithms handle symbolic values, reason about constraints, and generate new constraints where appropriate. The overlapping polygons are described by lists of edges and crossing points. There are many ways polygons can overlap, and a program in Prolog to generate all the possibilities on backtracking has been written. The goal was to draw a representative from each possibility. By adding suitable heuristics capturing aesthetic criteria about convex figures, and using the constraint logic programming language CLP($\neg$), representative examples of these symbolically specified objects could be drawn.

Although this chapter emphasizes the importance of symbolic reasoning, in fact, the work is more general. The same code can often be used both for symbolic and numeric values—a unique feature of this approach. This flexibility is true for both the first and second examples. The flexibility stems from using a logic programming language that evaluates constraints if there are actual values, but treats them symbolically if there are symbolic values. A mixture of symbolic and numeric values are also handled by the same code.

This work is related to a larger project to develop a "rapid design system" (RDS). RDS is intended to support the fast and economical design of mechanical parts. It is being developed with the cooperation of a machine shop which specializes in custom modification of aircraft (e.g., to add new instrumentation) and production of replacement parts that are not available from the manufacturer. In some cases, prints are no longer available for such parts, so they must be redesigned. Both types of jobs are characterized by low production runs—sometimes quantities of one. In such situations, reducing the design time can significantly lower costs. The objective of the RDS project is to speed the design process. It aims to provide both an intelligent CAD interface which enables the designer to get his or her design into the computer faster than current systems allow, and integrated tools for checking a design for manufacturability and inspectability.

6.2 SYMBOLIC DESCRIPTIONS WITH CONSTRAINTS

This chapter advocates using constraint logic programming for representing parts and reasoning about them and attempts to be self-contained. To this end, Section 6.8 gives a summary of the basic terminology of logic programming used here. Some additional terminology is introduced as needed. The syntax used derives from the syntax of logical terms and, specifically, is the syntax of Edinburgh Prolog. (For further information on logic programming or Prolog, see, e.g., Sterling and Shapiro, 1986).

Symbolic Representations

A part is, in essence, a connected piece of material that performs some function, often as a component of a larger assembly. The designer of a part must specify its shape, and possibly other properties such as surface finish, color, and manufacturing method. The problem of specifying the shape of a part is focused on here.

It is assumed that complicated shapes are built from simpler geometric primitives. A number of ways of representing geometric shapes have been developed (Requicha, 1980). Any representation scheme will fall into one of two classes: volumetric or boundary representation (B-rep). In a volumetric representation, primitive volumes (or areas in 2-D) are combined to describe the object's shape. In a B-rep, the object's boundary is described by primitives (faces in 3-D or edges in 2-D). Each face in 3-D is in turn described by its enclosing edges.

This work deals primarily with boundary representations because of the requirements of the RDS system. Furthermore, for pedagogic purposes, mainly 2-D parts are considered. It is straightforward to extend much of the work to 3-D, however the practicality of reasoning symbolically in 3-D remains an open question.

The following is a brief outline of the B-rep used in the examples. The primitives are assumed to be *vertices*, which are denoted by V_i, and *edges*, which are either straight lines or circular arcs. For simplicity, circles rather than circular arcs are used in the examples. Straight lines are specified by two vertices, a beginning point V_1 and an end point V_2, and are denoted edge(V_1,V_2). A term circle(C,R) denotes a circle whose center is the vertex C and whose radius is the scalar value R. Edges are connected together by making the end point of one edge the beginning point of the next. A closed sequence of connected edges form a *boundary*. A *face* is an area enclosed by a boundary. A 2-D part is a face, possibly with holes. Holes can themselves be specified by boundaries.

The representations are symbolic and are orientation invariant because the coordinates are removed from vertices, and parts are conceived of as logical entities. Orientation invariance makes sense when describing parts for design because the position is not an intrinsic property of a part. Consequences of this view will be illustrated. Thus a vertex V denotes a particular, though unspecified, point.

Note that the information included in the representation described so far is more topological than geometric in nature, and many details of the geometry—such as lengths of edges or angles between adjacent edges—cannot be specified. This geometric information will be specified using *constraints*.

Reasoning about terms is done with logical inference (refer to Appendix I at the end of the chapter for formal definition of terms). Rather than building an inference engine, however, existing logic programming technology is used. By writing descriptions of parts in a logic programming language, and also rules expressing relationships between parts, it is assumed that the computational mechanisms of the language will perform the inference.

A triangle, then, is specified by its boundary of three straight lines and can be denoted

$$[edge(V_1, V_2), edge(V_1, V_3), edge(V_3, V_1)]$$

Lists are used to represent sequences of elements. The syntax for lists is as follows. The empty list is denoted [ ], whereas [a,b,c] denotes the sequence of three elements a, b, and c. Note that the edges are connected, which is indicated by the endpoint of one edge of the triangle being the same variable as the starting point of the next edge. This is known as *variable sharing*. Further, the endpoint of the final edge is the same as the first vertex of the first edge, so the triangle is enclosed.

The representation of a part is a term, part_desc(OuterBoundary,InnerBoundaries), where OuterBoundary is a list of edges constituting the boundary of the part, and InnerBoundaries is a list of boundaries of holes in the part. To represent the triangle as a part, then, we need to consider whether it has any inner boundaries. For a solid triangle with no holes, the part description is

$$part\_desc([edge(V_1, V_2), edge(V_2, V_3), edge(V_3, V_1)], [\ ])$$

The generic part description of the preceding triangle can be used to check whether a particular object X is a triangle by matching the part description of the triangle with that of X. For example, the part description part_desc([edge(x,y),edge(y,z),edge(z,x)],[ ]) would match the generic triangle description. Both part_desc([edge(x,y),edge(a,b),edge(m,n)],[ ]) and part_desc([edge(x,y),edge(y,z),edge(z,x)],[circle(c,r)]) would fail to match, the former because the edges are not connected, and in the latter case because there is a circular hole inside the part. Matching, or more technically, unification is the process of making two logical terms identical. For details, refer to Sterling and Shapiro (1986). For the purposes of this chapter, an intuitive sense of matching is sufficient.

There are a range of possible triangles—equilateral triangles, right triangles, and so on. These classes of triangles are distinguished by the relationships that exist between the subentities of the parts in the classes. To continue with this theme, triangles are distinguished by the relationships between the sides. An equilateral triangle has all sides the same length, whereas a right triangle has one pair of edges that are mutually perpendicular. In a symbolic description, relationships between entities are expressed using constraints. Specifically, a *constraint* is an implicit relation between several (logical) variables. It can be expressed by a predicate that holds between the variables or, more directly, by the sharing of variables.

Table 6.1 contains some constraint relationships that have been used in the authors' work on symbolic reasoning. Variables of the form V_i refer to vertices, whereas variables of the form E_i refer to edges. The meanings of the predicates are self-evident.

To continue with triangles, an equilateral triangle is a triangle with the additional constraint that distance(V_1,V_2,L), distance(V_2,V_3,L), and distance(V_3, V_1, L) hold. The comma denotes logical conjunction, again adopting the convention of Edinburgh Prolog. All three of the distance relationships must be satisfied for the triangle to be equilateral. A right triangle can be specified by insisting that two of its edges, e.g., E_1 and E_2, say, satisfy the relationship perpendicular(E_1,E_2).

In practice, some of the constraint relationships will be primitive. Other constraints will be defined in terms of the primitives. For example, three edges meeting at a corner in 3-D might be defined as follows:

$$\text{blockcorner}(E_1, E_2, E_3) \text{ "} \text{perpendicular}(E_1, E_2),$$
$$\text{perpendicular}(E_1, E_3), \text{perpendicular}(E_2.E_3).$$

The choice of primitives will be application dependent in general. For some examples, determining that two edges are parallel will be a constraint that will not be evaluated. In other examples, slopes of lines may be reasoned about more generally, in which case the parallel constraint can be expressed in terms of a slope predicate as follows:

$$\text{parallel}(E_1, E_2) \text{ "} \text{slope}(E_1, S), \text{slope}(E_2 S).$$

Table 6.1. Common Relationships Among Primitives

distance (V_1, V_2, L)
angle (V_1, V_2, V_3, T)
crosses (E_1, E_2)
parallel (E_1, E_2)
perpendicular (E_1, E_2)
X_1 rel op X_2, where rel op is one of $<, >, =, \leq, \geq$

Computing slopes presumes a coordinate system where slopes can be evaluated. Many of the examples have used symbolic coordinates for vertices, as will be seen. Nevertheless, the examples remain as abstract as possible by using coordinates in rules only when necessary.

Symbolic Reasoning

A logic program is a collection of facts and rules that express relationships between objects. A logic program is queried by asking if a certain relationship logically follows from the collection of facts and rules constituting the program. Parts are reasoned about by querying a program containing the facts and rules that describe the parts of interest. The basic relationship used for describing parts is part(Name,PartDescription), which associates a part description with the name of an object. The generic triangle is defined by the fact

$$part(triangle, part\_desc([edge(V_1, V_2), edge(V_2, V_3), edge(V_3, V_1)], [\ ])).$$

The following rule tests whether an object is a triangle. The rule states that an object is recognized as a triangle if its part description matches the part description of a generic triangle.

$$is\_triangle(Object) \ \cdots \ part(Object, PartDescription),$$
$$part(triangle, PartDescription).$$

Constraints are used to refine descriptions of parts. They can be represented in one of two ways. The first way represents them explicitly by adding an argument, which is a list of constraints that hold between the subentities of the part, to the part description. Using this representation, a possible description of an equilateral triangle is

$$part(equilateral\_triangle, part\_desc([edge(V_1, V_2), edge(V_2, V_3), edge(V_3, V_1)], [\ ])$$
$$[distance(V_1, V_2, L), distance(V_2, V_3, L), distance(V_3, V_1, L)]).$$

When the constraints are explicitly stated in the part description, a procedure is needed to check that the constraints hold. For symbolic descriptions, that means being able to handle symbolic values. There are essentially two ways to reason symbolically in a logic programming language. One is to use symbolic variables for arguments, as previously discussed, when matching objects against the generic triangle description. An example of a sophisticated program written using symbolic values is the PRESS system for solving symbolic equations (Bundy and Welham, 1981; Sterling *et al.*, 1988).

Here, logical variables are used to represent symbolic values. The primary reason is to take advantage of the built-in constraint solver provided in the logic programming language CLP($\neg$) (Jaffar and Lassez, 1987). CLP($\neg$) is similar to Prolog but has replaced unification with a more general mechanism to solve constraints between variables, taking values over real numbers.

The second way of representing constraints in part descriptions is to add them as goals to the body of a rule. This has the effect of changing part facts into part rules. For example, an equilateral triangle can be defined as

part(equilateral_triangle, part_desc([edge(V_1, V_2), edge(V_2, V_3), edge(V_3, V_1)], [ ])
  " distance(V_1, V_2, L), distance(V_2, V_3, L), distance(V_3, V_1, L).

Querying the part results in the constraints being explicitly solved. Matching a symbolic description against a part description can have one of three outcomes. The first is *success*, where the symbolic description is an example of the part. The second is *failure*, where the symbolic description is not an example of the part. The third and most interesting, outcome is *specifying conditions* (constraints), whereby the part will match the part description. Providing such an answer is beyond the scope of the usual inferences of Prolog, but can be done with CLP(¬).

Here is a small example to illustrate the desirability of providing constraints as answers. Consider a relationship in_range(X,Lower,Upper) which will be true if X lies between Lower and Upper. This can be defined logically by the following rule:

in_range(X, Lower, Upper) " Lower £ X, X £ Upper.

The query in_range(X,10,20)? can be used to check if some (possibly known) value of X lies between 10 and 20. If X is in fact unknown, Prolog would fail due to the attempt to solve the goal "10 £ X"? However, a better answer, and what would be expected from a more helpful system, is that 10 £ X, X £ 20. Note that if in fact the value of X was known, the query could be evaluated; therefore, when programming/designing with the relation in range, the programmer/designer does not care if the value is known or not known.

Returning to the example of a triangle, there is a better, more concise way to describe an equilateral triangle. The idea is to define an equilateral triangle in terms of a generic triangle and abstract the property of the sides having equal length. Note that this representation generalizes more readily to other regular shapes such as squares. Using a predicate equilateral(Edges,L), which is true if all edges in the list Edges have length L, an equilateral triangle can be defined as

part(equilateral triangle, part_desc(Edges, [ ]))
  " part(triangle, part_desc(Edges, [ ])), equilateral(Edges, L).

Straightforward code for the predicate equilateral is

equilateral([], L).
  equilateral([edge(X, Y)|Edges], L) " distance(X, Y, L), equilateral(Edges, L).

To summarize, part descriptions have the form "part(Name,PartDesc) " Constraints."—where one of the constraints in the (possibly conjunctive) goal "Constraints" may be a description of a more general part. In general, part descriptions represent classes of shapes rather than a particular object. An alternative view, which can be taken when designing with a part description, is that an underconstrained object is being manipulated. Sections 6.4 and 6.5 are concerned with manipulating and visualizing underconstrained objects.

Examples of Parts

A simple part, perhaps describing a bearing, is a pair of concentric circles. This part is called an *annulus*. Its part description is

$$\text{part(annulus, [circle(C, R_1)], [circle(C, R_2)])} \; \cdots \; R_1 < R_2.$$

The shared variable "C" indicates that the two circles are concentric. The concentricity could also be expressed by an explicit equality constraint, but the former is the preferred representation. The annulus is clearly underconstrained and can be readily constrained further. For example, adding the condition that $R_2 - R_1 < R_1/4$ may give a thin annulus, whereas $R_2 - R_1 > 2 * R_1$ would give a fat annulus. The next example is a four-hole plate, shown in Fig. 6.1. It will be used to illustrate reasoning about tolerances.

The four-hole plate has a square as the outer boundary, and four holes forming the inner boundaries. The vertices of the square are labeled V_1 through V_4 as shown, and the centers of the holes are labeled C_1 through C_4. The part description is then:

$$\text{part\_desc([edge}(V_1, V_2), \text{edge}(V_2, V_3), \text{edge}(V_3, V_4), \text{edge}(V_4, V_1)],$$
$$\text{[circle}(C_1, R), \text{circle}(C_2, R), \text{circle}(C_3, R), \text{circle}(C_4, R)]).$$

It remains to specify the relative alignment of the centers of the circular holes. Two approaches are suggested here. The approaches have consequences for reasoning about tolerances to be described in the next section. The first approach is to give symbolic coordinates to each of the four centers and specify that the *x*-coordinate of C_1 is the same as that of C_2, the *y*-coordinate of C_1 is the same as that of C_4, and so on. The second approach is to define a new circle whose center C is at the center of the plate. The centers of the four holes are then equidistant

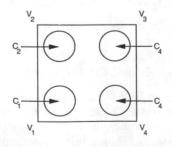

FIG. 6.1. A four-hole plate.

from C and the lines from the separate centers to C are mutually perpendicular.

The final example uses a volumetric representation rather than a B-rep. It will be used in the next section to demonstrate the rationale for using constraints. The part uses two 2-D volumetric primitives, box(X,Y,W,H), which denotes a rectangular box of height H and width W whose bottom left-hand corner is at the coordinate (X,Y), and disk(X,Y,R), which denotes a circular disc of radius R whose center is at the coordinate (X,Y). This example does not worry about the orientation.

Figure 6.2 is a drawing of the part, a flange with two bolt holes. The volumetric representation is also given. The symbol "+" denotes set union, whereas "−" denotes set difference. This part is the union of a box and a disk with three disks cut out from it. To be consistent with the symbolic representation, shared variables in Fig. 6.2 indicate common values. For example, both bolt holes have the same radius.

Volumetric representations need different syntax for part descriptions. An appropriate syntax models the symbolic build-up of primitives directly using ">>"

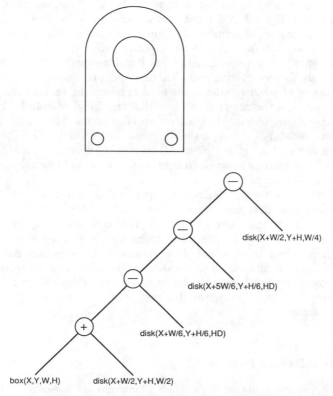

FIG. 6.2. A two-holed flange and its volumetric representation.

and "\" for union and difference, respectively. In Prolog, where addition and subtraction are uninterpreted function symbols, "+" and "−" can be used for union and difference. In CLP(¬), different functors would be needed. The following logic programming rule defines the two-hole flange. The syntax of constraints is from CLP(¬). More will be said about the part in the next section.

> part(twoholeflange, part _ desc(box(X, Y, W, H)
> >> disk(XD, YD, RD)\disk(XD1, YD1, RD1)\
> disk(XD2, YD2, RD2)\disk(XD3, YD3, RD3)) ¨
> $RD = W/2, XD − X = W/2, YD − Y = H, RD1 = W/4, XD1 = XD,$
> $YD1 = YD, RD2 = RD3, YD2 = YD3, XD2 − X = X + W − XD3.$

6.3 CONSTRAINT-BASED DESIGN

Constraints have become widely advocated in recent years. Nevertheless, the potential of constraints and constraint programming languages has not been sufficiently stated. Here is a brief discussion of why constraints are essential.

Consider the expressive power of constraints in the context of the two-hole flange pictured in Fig. 6.2. A designer could build such an object with standard CAD tools. The geometric primitives of lines and circles would be specified and the sketch quickly accomplished by an experienced user.

The inadequacy of standard CAD tools becomes readily apparent when the designer wants to modify the part. There is no provision for expressing the designer's intent or what relationships hold between the various dimensions in the flange. Suppose the designer decides that the flange should be bigger. In a current CAD system, she would click on an edge of the flange and drag it to a new position. What should happen to the remaining features? Several of the possibilities are pictured in Fig. 6.3. The CAD system has no way of deciding between them. With the constraint style given here, new values could be calculated immediately in terms of the old.

Further, there is no provision for representing commonsense knowledge that engineers and designers share. For example, suppose the aspect ratio (height/width) must lie between 1 and 1.5. This fact can be expressed easily as a constraint, but has no obvious place to be attached in a standard CAD system. Bolt holes come in standard sizes. Again, the information can be readily expressed as a constraint. Another constraint that might emerge from manufacturability considerations is that the bolt holes must be more than twice the bolt hole diameter from the edge. Again, it is easily expressed within a constraint programming language.

Parametric Design Systems

The type of reasoning just outlined exists in current cutting-edge systems under the guise of "parametric design." In a parametric design system (Lukas, 1988;

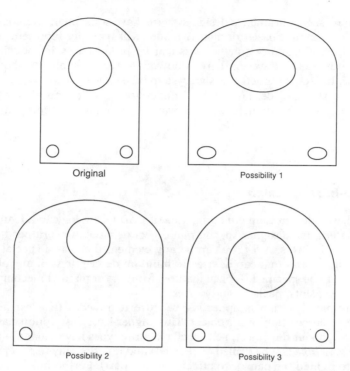

Original

Possibility 1

Possibility 2

Possibility 3

FIG. 6.3. Scaling two-hole flange.

Gregory, 1989), a model is represented using a tree that represents a part–subpart hierarchy. At each node in the tree, the user can define parameters (variables) and give either constants or expressions for the parameter values. Expressions can refer to variables at other positions in the tree (typically in an ancestor of the node containing the parameter being defined). In addition to ordinary expressions, conditional code can be used. This allows a change in a few key parameters to control the entire model in subtle ways. Each expression can be thought of as a constraint in the explicit form

$$y = f(x_1, x_2, \ldots, x_n)$$

However, unlike in a true constraint-based system, changes in parameters can only filter through the model in one direction; that is, in the preceding example, changes in values of the X_i parameters would cause Y to be recalculated, but the reverse is not true. Thus, the person creating the model must decide, in effect, what are the independent variables and what are the dependent variables for a given problem. This can only be done effectively if the design problem is well understood *a priori*.

As can be seen, parametric design systems have some characteristics in common with constraint-based design. A model will typically represent a class of objects. Specific instances of the class can be produced by introducing values for the parameters. However, there is no way to reason explicitly about a class of designs. In fact, parametric design systems are typically used to generate variations on a standard design in a well understood application area, e.g., boiler design. They can be thought of as a way of automating a company's design standards.

Feature-based Design

Feature-based design is an emerging area of CAD technology. In a feature-based design system, the designer specifies an object using features rather than using geometric primitives. A *feature* can be any element that has a special meaning to the designer, and that can be used to build up descriptions of any object that might need to be specified. Typical features from the domain of mechanical parts include holes, slots, pockets, and bosses.

Feature-based design is appealing because it provides the designer with a higher-level description of an object. This higher-level description has implicit information about the object; i.e., specific feature types have modes of manufacturing (e.g., a hole can be drilled or reamed) and functionality (e.g., a pocket can be used to lighten the part or to attach another part). Furthermore, the description is more compact because each feature will typically replace several surfaces of a conventional description.

Features can be easily accommodated within constraint-based design. Each feature is represented as one or more surfaces, with a given set of relationships (i.e., constraints) to each other and to the surrounding surfaces on the part boundary. The relation feature(Name,FeatureDescription) can be used to represent the features. The rule for features will have the form

feature(Name, FeatureDescription) $\because$ Constraints

and will be in the same style as the representation of parts by part descriptions.

Design is accomplished by adding features to parts. Different types of features need to be considered separately. For example, *positive features* (features that protrude from the surrounding surfaces) such as ribs are intrinsically different from *negative features* (features that are depressed into the surrounding surfaces) such as holes and pockets.

Code is needed to build parts from simpler parts and features. At an abstract level, the constraint-based design system might have the following rule construct. There would be an analogous rule for negative features using a procedure remove feature. The constraint solver would ensure that all the constraints attached to the part and to the feature would be solved.

construct(Part, Feature, NewPart) ∵

   part(Part, PartDescription),

   feature(Feature, FeatureDescription),

   positive(Feature),

   add_feature(PartDescription, FeatureDescription, NewPart).

The procedure needs to handle symbolic descriptions. This is inevitably a difficult problem. Adding a slot, say, to an annulus will change the annulus into a "C" shape. Adding a blind hole to an annulus puts a constraint on the length, lest the blind hole become a through hole or slot. There is a need for general procedures for symbolic intersection, union, and difference. Progress on this is discussed in section 6.4. The manipulation of features is well developed for parametric design systems. It can be anticipated that symbolic algorithms will abstract current well-understood algorithms just as the symbolic intersection algorithm given in the next section abstracts polygon intersection algorithms.

Building a robust system will require careful knowledge engineering to be useful for designers. Designers often view features as manufacturing operations rather than geometric primitives; e.g., thinking of holes in terms of the drilling operations that are available rather than in terms of hole size. The CAD system builder needs to accommodate different views.

Checking Design Rules

There is a need for commonsense mechanical knowledge to simplify parts. Human language usage is inherently ambiguous and people use context to disambiguate all the time. A drafter of a description knows and can make assumptions about how the part will be built. One way to capture this is to use design rules. It is straightforward enough to represent semantic constraints and just add them to the constraint solver. The problem is knowing what sets of constraints will be useful and which will not. For that, a real engineer will have to tinker and play with the design.

The primary advantage of symbolic reasoning is the ability to reason about classes of parts rather than individual parts. In this subsection, a simple design rule checker is sketched which exhibits such reasoning. The idea is to design rules as logical rules. By querying whether a given part description satisfies the design rules, it can be determined whether the design rules hold.

The syntax of design rules is as follows: Each rule has a name, a part description, and a procedure definition which specifies the logical conditions that the design rule is checking. As an example of a design rule, one might want to test whether there is room inside a part for all of the holes given in the part description. If two holes must overlap due to lack of space, for example, the designer's intent is probably not being met. Assume that this design rule is named "room inside," and that there is a predicate room_inside(OB,IBs) which is true if there is room inside for all the objects in the list of inner boundaries IBs to fit inside the part enclosed by the outer boundary OB without any of the inner boundaries overlapping. A design rule fact presenting that information is

design_rule(roominside, part_desc(OB, IB), roominside(OB, IB)).

To check that this design rule succeeds on a particular part description means calling the procedure "room inside" on the appropriate outer boundary and inner boundaries. It is a straightforward exercise to program a general design checker.

Writing the code for room inside for general symbolic descriptions is nontrivial to say the least. However, there are some simple cases that might be usefully checked, e.g., testing whether two circular holes can fit inside a circular boundary. The design rule checker comes up with constraints that must be true about the radii of the circles. Invoking the design rule checker is easiest done as the designer requests. It is also possible to have design rules more proactive, suggesting constraints as changes are being made. This has been done for a tolerance checker. Only by experimenting in real design situations can it be determined how important such features are. Another issue is interactive modification of design rules. This is possible and is a matter of software engineering. In general, such user interface issues are ignored in this chapter.

Reasoning about Dimensions and Tolerances

Computer-aided design systems represent parts by using geometric primitives, all of which describe ideal shapes. On the other hand, actual manufactured parts are necessarily imperfect approximations to an ideal. It is necessary to specify dimensioning and tolerancing information during design so that it can be decided whether a manufactured part is acceptably close to the designed ideal during inspection.

Current commercial CAD systems either ignore tolerancing completely or provide a simple mechanism for adding tolerances to a model by hand. These tolerances are often little more than notations in the drawing—the system is incapable of reasoning about them. Systems such as ValiSys can do tolerance evaluation, but are designed to be used after the model is created. They do not allow the designer to reason about dimensions and tolerances as an integral part of the design process. The designer is left with the responsibility of ensuring that the tolerances are complete and consistent. The systems do not ensure that tolerances are reasonable or meaningful. Checking if a part lies in some tolerance zone is precisely solving constraints. Some of the constraints can, in fact, be solved during the design phase.

The framework presented here for constraint-based design ought to be applicable for expressing tolerance information. This subsection sketches some research in that direction. The authors have developed a prototype system for checking whether a specific part meets a tolerance specification. The part is described with a symbolic representation, possibly with features. The system is intended to reason about both underconstrained parts and specific parts.

The first issue to discuss is representing dimensions and tolerances, using the four-hole plate given in Fig. 6.1 as an example. In Fig. 6.4, the part is reproduced together with tolerance information expressed in plus/minus notation.

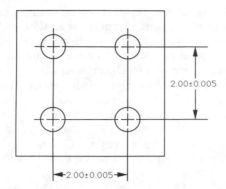

FIG. 6.4. A toleranced four-hole plate, 2.000 ± 0.005.

It is straightforward to reproduce the style of parts with constraints to represent the dimensions and tolerances. The dimensions are symbolic values that are constrained to be in the desired range. Matching is used to check whether a specific part matches the extra constraints proposed by the tolerances. Some of the constraints for this example are distance(C_1,C_2,X), in_range(X,1.995,2.005) where C_1 and C_2 are the centers of two of the holes. It is easy to write code to go from plus/minus notation to in-range information.

Geometrically specified constraints can be handled similarly. Geometric conditions about points being equally spaced around a circle, for example, are translated into constraints on the relative positions of the points. The representation of particular geometric conditions is left as an exercise in logic programming.

Is Constraint-based Design Practical?

This section concludes with a discussion of the practicality of constraint-based design. This is a real concern. Many computationally intractable problems can be thought of as "simply" solving constraints. Research in analysis of algorithms in computer science has revealed that some easily described problems have no effective solution method. Further, there is a class of problems, called *NP-complete* problems, that have solution methods that are feasible only for the smallest examples. It is easy to translate an NP-complete problem into a constraint-solving problem. Thus it is impossible to create a completely general constraint solver. There are many problems for which no practical solution method can exist. Analysis is needed to work out what sets of constraints can be efficiently solved and which cannot. Computer-aided design tools can only hope to deal with easily solvable sets of constraints.

CLP(¬) currently works well only for sets of linear constraints over the field of real numbers. Constraining sides to be parallel and/or perpendicular leads to nonlinear sets of constraints over the coordinates of the vertices. So, for example, specifying that a part is a parallelogram, giving the lengths of a pair of adjacent sides and the coordinates of one vertex, fully determines the part. CLP(¬) cannot fill in the coordinates for points except for special cases. This can be partially overcome by adding redundant constraints. However, CLP(¬) does behave correctly in the sense that a set of constraints are returned in answer to any query. It is just that the set of constraints has been insufficiently simplified to be useful.

Research needs to be done on developing efficient constraint solvers for interesting and useful special cases. One direction that merits investigation is taking techniques from algebraic geometry. The constraint logic programming language CAL (Aiba *et al.*, 1988) bases its constraint solver on an algorithm for computing the Grobner basis of a set of polynomials. CAL has proved some interesting geometric theorems, which suggests it may be useful for CAD applications.

6.4 INTERSECTION OF SYMBOLICALLY DESCRIBED OBJECTS

The Boolean operations of intersection, union, and set difference are some of the most important operations that are used in CAD systems to build complex shapes from simpler shapes. This section explores the problem of computing the intersection of symbolically described objects. The case of planar polygons will be presented.

The intersection of two polygons is normally accomplished in two stages. In stage 1, it is determined which edges of the two polygons cross, and in stage 2, the portions of the edges of the original polygons are selected which make up the boundary of the new intersection polygon. When a conventional representation is used, stage 1 is straightforward, because essentially one just compares each edge of the first polygon against each edge of the second and compute whether they intersect.

If the polygons are represented symbolically, stage 1 is more complex, because there may be many ways that the edges may cross and still satisfy the constraints. An algorithm is presented for performing stage 1 for symbolically represented polygons. The polygons are assumed to be convex. The input consists of two polygons, described using a boundary representation, and some additional constraints which may be added to "tie together" the two polygons.

The principle behind the algorithm is to "walk around" (traverse) the boundary of the second polygon, checking each vertex and edge for intersection with the first polygon. The algorithm makes use of convexity in several ways to rule out impossible situations. From convexity, we can deduce the following rules:

(1) An edge can intersect with the other polygon in at most two discrete points or one interval. In other words, the situation in Fig. 6.5 is impossible, but that shown in Fig. 6.6 is allowed.
(2) If P_1 and P_2 are two consecutive points of intersection of the boundary of the second polygon with that of the first, then they are also consecutive points of intersection of the boundary of the first polygon with that of the second. In other words, the situation in Fig. 6.7 is impossible.

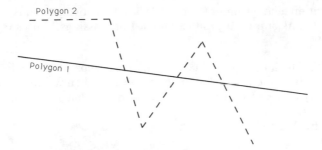

FIG. 6.5. Impossible situation for convex polygons.

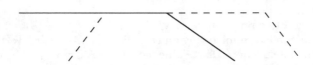

FIG. 6.6. Possible situation for convex polygons.

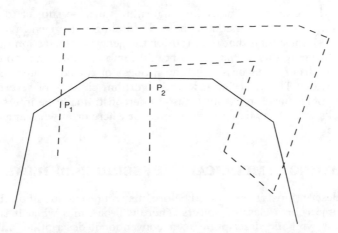

FIG. 6.7. Impossible situation for convex polygons.

The algorithm takes as input the boundaries of the two polygons, described as lists C_1 and C_2. As output, it produces a list I of crossings. It uses the following variables:

- A flag W which has value "in" or "out." This keeps track of whether one is currently inside or outside the first polygon when walking around the boundary of the second polygon. "Flipping" W changes it from "out" to "in" or "in" to "out."
- Edges E, F, and G.

Because the polygons are convex and have straight sides, there must exist a vertex of one polygon that is outside the other polygon. Therefore the "walk around" the boundary of the second polygon can be started at a point outside the first polygon. If the second polygon happened to be entirely inside the first polygon, this would fail, and the roles of the two polygons would have to be reversed.

The algorithm, called the *symbolic crossing algorithm* is as follows:

(1) Decide nondeterministically whether the two contours intersect at all. If not, determine nondeterministically whether to return C_1, C_2, or the null intersection.
(2) Initialize I to empty. Initialize W to "out."
(3) Choose nondeterministically an edge E of C_1 whose first vertex is outside the intersection. Delete all edges up to E from C_1.
(4) Nondeterministically do one of steps 5, 6, or 7.
(5) Determine that E does not intersect at all with C_2.
(6) Determine that E has one intersection with C_2 at edge F. Add i(E,F) to I. Flip W.
(7) Determine that E has two intersections with C_2 at edge F and G. Add i(E,F) and i(E,G) to I.
(8) If W is "out," then one may (nondeterministically) decide to return. Otherwise go to step 4.

Each of the tests in the preceding algorithm must be subject to the input constraints. A simplified version of the code for stage I is given in section 6.9. This code is simpler than that required for the general intersection of symbolically described polygons in that it does not take into account constraints on such things as lengths of edges or angles, and it does not consider intersections that occur at vertices. Thus, the input to the algorithm consists of severely underconstrained polygons. The output is also underconstrained; the intersection list returned tells whether two edges cross, but not where or at what angle.

6.5 DRAWING SYMBOLICALLY DESCRIBED OBJECTS

Symbolic descriptions, as mentioned before, may represent an impossible object, a unique object, or a class of objects. There will be times when it is required to convert a symbolic description to a conventional description. In the case where the symbolic description represents a class of objects, a single conventional description cannot be produced. Instead, a conventional description of a "representative" member of the class is produced. The definition of "representative" will depend on the intended use for the conventional description. Among the reasons for producing a conventional description are

- For export to a conventional CAD system
- For export to analysis packages (e.g., finite element analysis)
- For graphical display of the object

The problem of finding a representative conventional description corresponding to a symbolic description is explored by considering the problem of drawing the configurations of intersecting polygons which are produced by stage 1 of the intersection algorithm described in the previous section. Once the conventional description is produced, one can apply well-known computer graphics algorithms in order to draw the objects on the screen. Therefore, the term "draw the objects" is used to mean solving the problem.

To the greatest extent possible, the pictures produced should be aesthetically pleasing and should not contain polygons that appear distorted or odd-shaped. Therefore, we would like the following conditions to hold:

- Both polygons are convex.
- Both polygons are regular.
- All intersections between edges occur at the midpoints (if an interior point intersection is specified), or at the appropriate vertex, as specified in the list of crossings.
- Intersections split edges into equal-sized segments.
- Edges intersect at 90-deg. angles.

Unfortunately, such an ideal picture either may not exist for a given problem instance, or it may be too computationally expensive to find it. Therefore, the following are more realistic goals:

- Both polygons are convex.
- The first polygon is regular.
- The second polygon is piecewise regular. This means that the boundary can be broken up into sections, each of which exhibits regularity, i.e., equal angle and edge lengths. (This notion will be precisely defined later).
- Intersections between edges occur at interior points or at vertices as specified in the input.
- When an intersection occurs at an interior point of an edge, it occurs at least D units from each vertex where D is a tolerance value. Otherwise, it might appear in the drawing to be at the vertex.
- Intersections split edges into segments that are as equally sized as possible. Angles of intersecting edges are as close to 90 deg. as possible.

Problem Formulation

The input to the algorithm consists of polygons as described in section 6.2, and the intersection list I produced by the algorithm described in the previous section. Entries in I distinguish between intersections that occur at interior points of edges and intersections that occur at vertices, but do not give either the absolute or relative position of an intersection, or the angle between two edges. For example,

$$[i(edge(u_1, u_2), v_4), i(edge(u_4, u_5), edge(v_1, v_2))]$$

says that the edge u_1u_2 of the first polygon intersects vertex v_4 of the second polygon, and edge u_4u_5 of the first polygon intersects edge v_1v_2 of the second polygon. The intersection list I is assumed to be a complete list of intersections; that is, edges or vertices should intersect in the drawing as specified in I, and no intersections should occur that are not specified in I. This problem is treated as a constraint satisfaction problem. This algorithm is implemented in CLP(¬) and makes use of its built-in constraint solution facilities where possible. Because CLP(¬) can automatically solve constraints over the real numbers, the input is converted into a set of constraints over a set of real variables. Variables are introduced to represent the coordinates of the vertices, as well as angles between adjacent edges and lengths of certain edges. A search method is then used to find a solution to these constraints.

Because CLP(¬) contains an equation solver, equations can be asserted in implicit form without having to decide which variables will be ground at the time of solution. CLP(¬) only handles linear constraints but contains a delay mechanism which delays nonlinear equations until enough variables are ground to make the constraint linear. This powerful delay mechanism is used to create a test-and-generate scheme. That is, first all constraints (tests) are set up, then, values for all the variables are generated. This greatly speeds up the solution time compared to the traditional test-and-generate scheme. More information about the test-and-generate paradigm can be found in Sterling and Shapiro (1986).

The problem can be formulated as a nonlinear optimization problem on the coordinates of the vertices. The objective function would be a penalty function designed to give no penalty for an ideal picture and increasing penalties the further away from the ideal picture. This penalty function would then be minimized over constraints specifying that the polygons are convex, that all intersections occur as specified, and that there are no extra intersections. However, basic properties in two-dimensional geometry, e.g., that a vertex is on the outside of a polygon or at a minimum distance from an edge, makes the optimization problem concave. A concave nonlinear optimization problem is particularly hard to solve. In fact, no reasonable and efficient solution method may exist.

Notation and Terminology

The vertices of a polygon, labeled V_i, $0 £ i £ N$, for some N, are ordered in clockwise direction around the polygon. The vertex V_i has coordinates (X_j, Y_j). A vertex

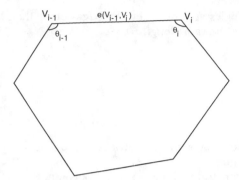

FIG. 6.8. Notation for a polygon.

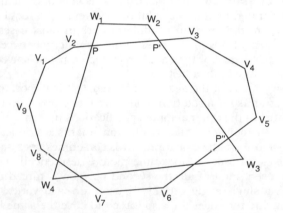

FIG. 6.9. Two intersecting polygons.

angle q_i is the inside angle between the edge $e(V_{i-1}, V_i)$ and the edge $e(V_i, V_{i+1})$ (Fig. 6.8.).

A *vertex intersection* is an intersection between two polygons that occurs at the vertex. An *edge intersection* is an intersection that occurs somewhere other than at a vertex of the edge. An *edge out-to-in intersection* between two polygons is an intersection between an edge $e(V_i, V_{i+1})$ and an edge or vertex where V_i is on the outside and V_{i+1} is on the inside of the other polygon. A *vertex out-to-in intersection* is an intersection where the vertex V_i, is on the border, V_{i-1} on the outside, and V_{i+1} on the inside of the other polygon. The edge and vertex in-to-out intersections are defined as the reversed case.

A *boundary chain* is a sequence of edges of one polygon spanning two intersections with the other polygon. In Fig. 6.9, PW_1W_2P' is a boundary chain, as is $P'V_3V_4V_5P''$. A polygon is said to be "piecewise regular" if for each boundary chain, the vertex angles are equal and the edges other than the initial and final edge segments have the same length.

Algorithm

The algorithm consists of three steps:

(1) Generate coordinates for the vertices of the first polygon so that it is a regular polygon.
(2) Set up the constraints for the second polygon.
(3) Generate values for the parameters obtained from step 2 until a solution to the constraints is found.

A test-and-generate algorithm is used to generate the geometric objects, meaning that all the constraints on the objects are specified first, then, values for the variables are generated to obtain a solution. However, the requirements for the objects presented in the problem formulation are in most cases impossible to fulfill. Although step 1 leads to an undesirable asymmetry between the two polygons, it reduces the degree of the equations which must be solved, and allows a solution to be generated much faster.

The complicated part of the algorithm is step 2. It is important to obtain the right set of constraints for a solution. There are really two objectives: creating a drawing that satisfies the original input specifications in terms of edge crossings and convexity of the polygons, and creating one that is aesthetically pleasing. In order for CLP($\neg$) to solve the constraints, it is sometimes necessary to introduce auxiliary variables. In order to make the picture aesthetically pleasing, several approaches are used. First of all, the second polygon is forced to be piecewise regular; that is, a single angle variable is used for each vertex angle within a boundary chain, and the edges are also forced to have the same length. Second, when performing step 3 of the algorithm, the values of these variables that are most likely to meet the aesthetic criteria should always be tried first.

The Constraints for the Second Polygon

The constraints that will result in a reasonable picture are divided into the following five groups:

(1) *Global inside constraints* specify that vertices of one polygon which are inside the other polygon according to the input, are in fact inside in the drawing.
(2) *Global angle constraints* state that the sum of all vertex angles for each polygon is the appropriate value, namely $p(N - 2)$.
(3) *Intersection constraints* state that edges intersect as specified in the input.

(4) *Positional constraints* for the vertices of the second polygon which are inside the first polygon ensure that the piecewise regularity condition is met.
(5) *Positional constraints* for the vertices of the second polygon which are outside the first polygon ensure that the piecewise regularity condition is met.

These constraints result in a set of parameters which will be passed to the generate part of the algorithm (step 3).

Space limitations prevent a complete discussion of all of the preceding types of constraints. Only one group of constraints, the intersection constraints, will be discussed in detail. Further details on the algorithm and the other constraints can be found in Andersson and Radack (1989).

Intersection Constraints

Intersection constraints ensure that the boundaries of the polygons intersect as specified in the input. There are actually three different kinds of intersections between boundaries if the ordering is disregarded: edge–edge, edge–vertex, and vertex–vertex.

Let P be the position of an edge–edge intersection, as shown in Fig. 6.10. Then, use the parametric equation of a line to get:

$$P = (1 - t)V_i + t V_{i+1}$$
$$P = (1 - u)W_i + t W_{i+1}$$

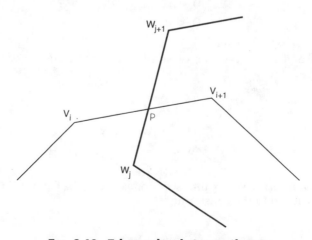

FIG. 6.10. Edge–edge intersection.

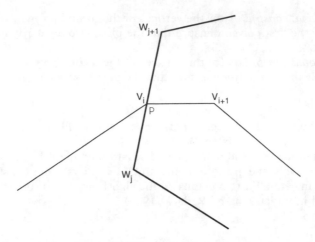

FIG. 6.11. Vertex–edge intersection.

In order for P to fall between the vertices,

$$0 < t < 1$$
$$0 < u < 1$$

However, in order to prevent P from appearing to lie on a vertex, it must be at least a tolerance D away. Thus,

$$D < t < 1 - D$$
$$D < u < 1 - D$$

In the case of an edge–vertex or vertex–edge intersection, as shown in Fig. 6.11,

$$P = V_i$$
$$P = (1 - u)W_i + t\,W_{i+1}$$
$$D < u < 1 - D$$

In the case of a vertex–vertex intersection, as shown in Fig. 6.12, the following constraint is added to the constraint set:

$$W_j = V_i$$

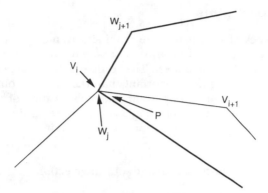

FIG. 6.12. Vertex–vertex intersection.

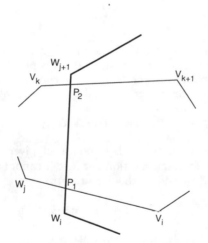

FIG. 6.13. Double intersection.

In the case of a double intersection, i.e., an edge intersecting two other edges or vertices, as shown in Fig. 6.13, the following constraints are added:

$$W_j = (1 - u)W_{j+1} + uP_1$$
$$Wj + 1 = (1 - V)W_j + vP_2$$

The parameters u and v are passed on to the third step of the algorithm and determine the positions of the intersection points P_1 and P_2.

Solving the Constraints

Four different types of parameters are obtained from step 2 in the algorithm; they are the angle parameter, the position parameter, the outside offset parameter, and the outside length parameter. The vertices on the inside of the first polygon are considered to be more important than those on the outside. The angle is also considered to be more important than the position of the intersection, that is more important than the outside length and the outside offset. Thus, the following order of search in the solution space is obtained:

- Inside angle
- Positions for the out-to-in and in-to-out intersections
- Outside angle
- Positions for out-to-out intersections
- Outside offset
- Outside length

Implementation

As explained earlier, CLP($\neg$) delays all nonlinear constraints until enough variables become ground to solve the constraints. This problem is solved by adding extra constraints which permit the CLP($\neg$) interpreter to solve apparently nonlinear constraints. For example, consider the following intersection constraint:

$$P = (1 - t)V_i + tV_{i+1}$$

If P and V_{i+1} are known and V_i needs to be found, given some other constraint on V_i, CLP($\neg$) will fail to find a solution because it cannot solve the nonlinearity. This problem is solved by adding the constraint:

$$Vi = (1 - u)P + u\,V_{i+1}$$

which allows CLP($\neg$) to solve the constraints.

To compensate for numerical errors in the overdetermined equation system, the machine zero is set to be 10^{-4} instead of the default value of 10^{-9}. This may seem to be too inaccurate, but considering the application to produce pictures at a resolution of around 1000 by 1000 pixels, this is accurate enough.

Because in general there will not be a unique solution to the constraints generated, a specific solution—preferably, the one which produces the best picture—must be found. Each rule in step 2 of the algorithm does two things. First, it asserts one or more constraints. These constraints are then stored in a canonical form by CLP($\neg$). Second, it appends the names of all variables introduced by those constraints to a list. A typical entry in the list would be ip(T), indicating that T is an intersection parameter. In step 3, specific values for all variables in this list are found. If a variable is nonground, different values are tried, starting with the preferred values for the given type. In this case, the preferred value for an intersection parameter is 0.5, which means that the intersection will occur in the middle of the edge. The implementation in CLP(R) is a program containing 227 rules in 1535 lines.

6.6 RELATED WORK

There has been a significant amount of work done with constraints, especially for specifying pictures more compactly. Pioneering work was achieved by Sutherland when he developed his Sketchpad system (Sutherland, 1963). Constraints in this system are taken from a limited set, e.g., point equality, horizontal and vertical relationships, and line length equality, and are solved numerically using relaxation. Ideal (Van Wyk, 1981) is a picture generation language that serves as a preprocessor to the troff typesetting language. It solves constraints using a linear equation solver and substitution of known values. A CAD system incorporating variational geometry was developed by Lin, Gossard, and Light (1981). Constraints between points were used to establish an object's geometry. Constraints were solved numerically. The innovation in the work of the present authors is solving constraints symbolically, as well as numerically, using a higher-level language.

Bruderlin describes research aimed at automating geometric proofs and constructions (Bruderlin, 1988). He also uses logic programming methodology to describe and reason about geometric objects at a more abstract level than the present work and because of the different application area, proving geometric theorems, the details of his research are substantially different.

The recent literature suggests a consensus for higher-level abstractions, and more sophisticated mathematics, to improve computer-based tools for designers of mechanical parts. There is too much relevant recent work to be reviewed here—the references provide pointers to some of the more interesting studies. The work in this chapter is sympathetic to the attempts to incorporate artificial intelligence techniques. Many, if not all, are readily expressed within the paradigm of constraint-based design presented here. For example, the constructions described by Smithers (1989) about shaft diameters, when arguing for the need for higher-level knowledge, would fit well into this work's framework of constraints.

6.7 CONCLUSION

An approach to the representation of geometric objects characterized by the use of symbolic rather than numeric values, and by the use of constraints was presented. It was demonstrated how algorithms can be developed to manipulate objects described symbolically. This approach shows promise for solving some of the problems inherent in current CAD systems. Much research remains to be done, however, before practical tools will emerge. In particular, there is a need for incorporating powerful symbolic equation solvers, especially for nonlinear equations.

LOGIC PROGRAMMING TERMINOLOGY

In contrast to traditional *procedural* programming languages such as BASIC or Pascal, logic programming is a *declarative* approach to problem definition and solution. Ideally, the user specifies *what* is known about a problem rather than specifying *how* to solve it. Logic programming languages have an inferencing mechanism that is capable of deducing consequences of facts and rules.

In more formal terms, logic programming involves the use of a restricted set of first-order predicate logic. Specifically, a *logic program* is a finite set of clauses. A *clause* or *rule* is a logical sentence containing a single conclusion that is implied by the conjunction of zero or more goals. It is written in the form

$$A \text{ '' } B_1, \ldots, B_n \quad n \geq 0.$$

A is called the *head* of the rule, whereas the B_i's are its *body*. Rules can be read declaratively: "A is implied by the conjunction of the B_i's." Rules serve as procedure definitions and have an associated procedural reading. In this case, "to execute a procedure call A, execute the procedure calls $B_1, \ldots, B_n$." If n = 0, the rule is known as a *fact* and is written as

$$A.$$

meaning that A is true under a declarative reading, and procedure call A is executed immediately under the procedural reading.

Each goal is of the form $p(t_1, t_2, \ldots, t_n)$, where p is a predicate symbol and the arguments, the t_i's, are terms. A goal posits that the relationship p holds among its arguments.

The data structure in logic programs is a *term*. A term is a constant, a variable, or a compound term. Constants denote particular individuals, such as integers and names, whereas variables denote a single but unspecified individual. The symbol for a name can be any sequence of alphanumeric characters, including underscores, which begin with a lowercase letter. The symbol for a variable can be any sequence of alphanumeric characters, including underscores, which begin with an uppercase letter. A *compound term* comprises a *functor* and a sequence of one or more terms called *arguments*. A functor is characterized by its name and *arity* or number of arguments. Syntactically, compound terms have the form $f(t_1, t_2, \ldots, t_n)$, where the functor has name f and it is of arity n, and the t_i's are the arguments.

A *query* is a goal, possibly conjunctive. A computation of a logic program checks whether a query logically follows from the rules and facts in the program. When the query contains variables, the computation finds values for the variables in a query so that the query is logically implied by the program. A restricted form of resolution is used to make logical inferences. Backtracking is used to find multiple solutions if they exist. Particular logic programming languages are only approximations to the declarative ideal of logic programming. For example, Prolog interpreters use the order of goals in the body of the clause as sequencing information to know which goal to solve next, and try clauses in the order they are written in the program. This use of order deals with issues of nondeterminism present in the computational model for logic programming related to scheduling procedure calls and cases where several rules match a procedure call. Clause terms can act as either input or output procedure parameters—which alternative depends on the calling context.

A LOGIC PROGRAM FOR SYMBOLIC INTERSECTIONS

This section gives the central logic program for generating symbolic intersections of two convex polygons. The program has been run under both Prolog and CLP(¬). It follows the description of the algorithm given in section 6.4, although not exactly. In particular, the choice of which vertex to start with in the part is made outside the scope of this code. Conversely, the choice of whether two polygons intersect at all is contained within the crossings code, which is the central procedure whose description follows:

$$/^*crossings(Part1, Part2, W, Names, Vertices, Crossings)^{..}$$

Crossings is a list of intersections representing the intersection of two convex polygons Part1 and Part2. The polygons are represented symbolically by a sequence of straight lines edges. *W* is a flag keeping track of being inside or outside the polygon, as described in section 6.4. *Names* is a list of new names with which to label vertices produced as intersection points. *Vertices* is a list of vertices in the parts which have been labeled to show if the vertex is inside or outside the intersection. Difference lists (Sterling and Shapiro, 1986) are used to handle the labeled vertices.

The nondeterministic choice of whether the chosen edge of the first part crosses two, one, or zero edges of the second part is reflected in the first three rules for crossings. The final crossings rule is bookkeeping, which labels remaining vertices in the second part.

```
*/
crossings([E|Es], Fs, out[N1, N2|Ns], [V|Vs]\Vs0,
        %edgeEcrossesedgesF1andF2
    [i(E, F1), i(E, F2)|Crossings])
    label_leading_vertex(out, E, V),
    remove_upto(Fs, F1, Fs1, in, Vs\Vs1),
    remove_upto1(Fs1, Fs, Fs2, out, Vs1\Vs2)
    crossings(Es, Fs2, out, Ns, Vs2\Vs0, Crossings).
crossings([E|Es], Fs, OutIn, [N|Ns], [V|Vs]\Vs0, [i(E, F)|Crossings])
        %edgeEcrossesedgeF
    label_leading_vertex(OutIn, E, V),
    remove_upto(Fs, F1, Fs1, InOut, Vs\Vs1),
```

```
                    opposite(OutIn, InOut),
                    crossings(Es, Fs1, InOut, Ns, Vs1\Vs0, Crossings).
          crossings([E|Es], Fs, OutIn, Ns, [V|Vs]\Vs0, Crossings)
                        %edgeEcrossesnoedges
                    label_leading_vertex(OutIn, E, V),
                    crossings(Es, Fs, OutIn, Ns, V\Vs0, Crossings).
          crossings([ ], Fs, out, Ns, [V|Vs]\Vs0, [ ])
                    remove_upto(Fs, F, [ ], in, Vs\Vs0).
          /*remove_upto(Part, Edge, RestEdges, OutIn, Vertices)
```

(Nondeterministically) choose an Edge from the Part and remove all edges up to it leaving RestEdges.

The list of vertices in Vertices are labeled as being out or in using the OutIn information.

```
                    */
                    remove_upto([E|Es], E, Es, OutIn, Vs\Vs).
                    remove_upto([E|Es], F, Fs, OutIn, [V|Vs]\Vs0)
                        label_leading_vertex(OutIn, E, V),
                        remove_upto(Es, F, Fs, OutIn, Vs\Vs0).
```

/* remove_upto1 is a variant of remove_upto with a different boundary condition.

```
                    */
                    remove_upto1([E|Es], E, [E|Es], OutIn, [V|Vs]\Vs)
                        label_leading_vertex(OutIn, E, V).
                    remove_upto1([E|Es], F, Fs, OutIn, [V|Vs]\Vs0)
                        label_leading_vertex(OutIn, E, V),
                        remove_upto1(Es, F, Fs, OutIn, Vs\Vs0).
                    /*opposite(OutIn, InOut)
```

Flip the flag OutIn, determining whether the algorithm is inside or outside the polygon.

```
                    */
                    opposite(out, in).
                    opposite(in, out).
                    /*label_leading_vertex(OutIn, Edge, Vertex)
```

Label the leading vertex of Edge as either out or in depending on the flag OutIn and return the result as Vertex.

$$*/$$

label_leading_vertex(out, edge(V1, V2), out(V1)).
label_leading_vertex(in, edge(V1, V2), in(V1)).

REFERENCES

Aiba, A., Sakai, K., Sato, Y., Hawley, D. J., and Hasegawa, R. 1988. Constraint logic programming language CAL. *Proc. 2nd Intl. Conference on Fifth Generation Computer Systems*, Tokyo, Japan, pp. 263–276.

Andersson, M., and Radack, G. 1989. Generating polygon intersection configurations from a symbolic description using CLP(R). Technical Report, CES-26-89, Computer Engineering and Science, Case Western Reserve University, December, 1989.

Bruderlin, B. 1988. Automatizing geometric proofs and constructions. In *Computational Geometry and its Applications*, ed. H. Noltemeier, 232–252. Lecture Notes in Computer Science 333. Berlin: Springer-Verlag.

Bundy, A., and Welham, R. 1981. Using meta-level inference for selective application of multiple sets of rewrite rules in algebraic manipulation. *Artificial Intelligence* 16:189–212.

Gregory, J. G. 1989. Rule-based definition of geometric models. *SIAM Conference on Geometric Design*, Tempe Arizona, November.

Jaffar, J., and Lassez, J. L. 1987. Constraint logic programming. *Principles of Programming Languages Conference*, Munich, January.

Lin, V. C., Gossard, D. C., and Light, R. A. 1981. Variational geometry in computer-aided design. *Proc. SIGGRAPH Conference ACM*, pp. 171 177.

Lukas, M. P., and Pollock, R. B. 1988a. Automated design through artificial intelligence techniques. *Artificial Intelligence and Advanced Computer Technology Conference*, Long Beach, California, May.

Lukas, M. P., and Meerbaum, M. L. 1988b. Improving productivity by capturing and automating design/manufacturing knowledge. Technical report TP-88-20, Bailey Controls, Wickliffe, Ohio.

Requicha, Aristides A. G. 1980. Representations for rigid solids: Theory, methods and systems. *ACM Computing Surveys* 12(4):437–464.

Requicha, Aristides A. G. 1983. Toward a theory of geometric tolerancing. *International Journal of Robotics Research* 2(4):45–59.

Smithers, T. 1989. AI-based design versus geometry-based design. *Computer-Aided Design* 21(3):141–149.

Sterling, Leon S., and Shapiro, E. Y. 1986. *The Art of Prolog*. Cambridge, Massachusetts: MIT Press.

Sterling, Leon S., Bundy, Alan, Byrd, Lawrence, O'Keefe, Richard, and Silver, Bernard. 1988. Solving symbolic equations with PRESS. *J. Symbolic Computation*.

Sutherland, I. E. 1963. Sketchpad—A man-machine graphical communication system, Ph.D. thesis, MIT.

Van Wyk, C. J. 1981. A graphics typesetting language. *Proc. ACM SIGPLAN Symposium on Text Manipulation*, Portland, Oregon, June 1981, pp. 99–107.

Chapter 7

IDEF3 Process Descriptions and Their Semantics

**Christopher Menzel, Richard J. Mayer,
and Douglas D. Edwards**
Knowledge Based Systems Laboratory
Texas A&M University
College Station, Texas

7.1 INTRODUCTION

The central way of describing what happens in the world around us, and in particular for describing how a given or prospective system works, is to relate a story in the form of an ordered sequence of events or activities. The term used here is *process description*. This chapter concerns defining a rigorous method for capturing process descriptions that (1) can be used by engineering and manufacturing domain experts to express the normal content of a commonsense process description, and (2) is structured enough to allow for computerized representation, automated interpretation, and intelligent support for uses of the language in capturing process descriptions. The underlying motivation for such a method is that before one can provide any sort of information-based application for a user within a particular domain—manufacturing and engineering in particular—one must have an accurate description of the user's understanding of the structure of the domain. This chapter investigates one approach to the representation of process descriptions as a basis for supporting knowledge-based applications known as IDEF3.

IDEF is the name of a family of methods developed under Air Force funding for use in integrated systems development. The original IDEFs were developed for the purpose of enhancing communication among people who needed to decide how their existing systems were to be integrated. IDEF0 was designed to allow a graceful expansion of the description of a systems' functions through the process of function decomposition and categorization of the relations between functions (i.e., in terms of the Input, Output, Control, and Mechanism classification). IDEF1 was designed to allow the description of certain information that an organization deems important to manage in order to accomplish its objectives. The third IDEF, IDEF2, was originally intended as a user interface modeling method. Though still in use in some quarters, it has not garnered the support or attention the other IDEFs enjoy. IDEF3 will be described here. IDEF4 was developed to support the design of object-oriented software systems programmed in such languages as C++, Flavors, CLOS, or SmallTalk. IDEF5 is a method for capturing domain ontologies.

7.2 BACKGROUND AND MOTIVATION

Descriptions Versus Models

It is important first of all to distinguish between models and descriptions (Mayer, 1988). We emphasize that although models may well be constructed from descriptions, the task here is not the construction of models but the formal representation of descriptions and the information they convey.

To get at the distinction, a *model* can be characterized as an idealized system of objects, properties, and relations that is designed to imitate in certain relevant respects the character of a given real world system. The power of a model comes from its ability to simplify the real world system it represents, and to predict certain facts about that system in virtue of corresponding facts within the model.[1] A model is thus itself, in a certain sense, a complete system. For in order to *be* an acceptable model of a given or imagined real world situation, it must satisfy certain "axioms" or conditions derived from the real world system.

A *description*, on the other hand, is a recording of facts or beliefs about the world around us. Because such descriptions are generally partial, a person giving a description may omit facts that do not seem to be relevant, or which have been forgotten in the course of describing the system. There are no preconditions on an acceptable description, no "axioms" to be satisfied short of simple accuracy as far as it goes; descriptions, it might be said, are assumed to be true, but incomplete.[2] The accumulation of descriptions is thus prior to and distinct from the construction of models. Indeed, generally, the conditions one puts on acceptable models are derived from descriptions one receives from domain experts, they are, so to say, the data from which models are built.

Descriptions are essential to the model building process. An accurate treatment of such descriptions requires two components, one having to do with the descriptions themselves as linguistic entities—the *syntactic* component—and the other having to do with their content and with the information they convey—the *semantic* component. That is, on the one hand, it is important that there be an effective means of representing the descriptions themselves, a means of capturing their "logical form." On the other hand, there must also be a rigorous account of their information content.

On the syntactic side, as will be shown, IDEF3 makes use of the standard language of first-order logic as its formal base. This permits a rich and flexible means of expressing the logical form of most any typical descriptive statement. Semantically, a variant of first-order semantics is used here, enriched to represent the temporal information so crucial to process descriptions. This approach,

---

[1] See Corynen (1975) for a detailed analysis of this phenomena.
[2] In fact, one very powerful use of models is to fill in the gaps in descriptions.

unlike that of typical simulation languages, enables interpretation of the intended meaning of a given description in terms of a semantic structure that corresponds in a natural way to the real world situation being described.

Phenomenological and Linguistic Motivations

What is a Process?

In order to understand the idea of capturing process descriptions, it is first necessary to know what is meant by a process. The term is not in fact being used in a technical sense, but rather in an ordinary language sense, in keeping with IDEF3's role as a methodology for acquiring the intuitive knowledge of domain experts. Unfortunately, the term *process* is quite ambiguous in English, for several reasons. We will need to refine our understanding of process terminology in ordinary language before we can characterize the intended sense of process more clearly.

Because there is a need to capture a human's understanding of the world and how it works, it is necessary to characterize the concept of a process in view of that understanding. Such a characterization is bound to be difficult because the notion of *change*—a notoriously slippery notion—is basic to the concept of process. Intuitively, process is used to describe an isolable event or occurrence. As such, it can be assigned a more or less definite starting point, typically associated with the satisfaction of certain antecedent conditions, and continue indefinitely. A process will generally involve objects with certain (perhaps changing) properties standing in specified (perhaps changing) relations. A process can also stand in relations with other processes: e.g., a process can start, suspend, and terminate other processes; objects or information about objects can be shared between processes; one process can change the properties of such a shared object and "cause" the exclusion of another process execution, and so on.

It is crucially important to distinguish between *process types* and *process instances* or *individual processes*. (Indeed, it is important to distinguish generally between types and instances with regard to many other kinds of entities as well.) An *individual* process can be thought of as a concrete occurrence located at a specific time and place. Process *types* may be thought of as *classes* of individual processes or *properties* that individual processes may have. It is an unfortunate feature of the English language that it does not distinguish between process types and individual processes; the word "process" can refer to either. In this chapter, however, the distinction will be rigorously maintained whenever it matters. (It does not always matter; for instance, it does not matter in very general contexts (as the preceding) or where process occurs as an integral part of phrases like "process flow description capture" or "process model.") Process types may vary from general to specific. An individual process p which is among those picked out by a process type P will be called an *instance* of P. If process types P and Q are such that any instance of P is also an instance of Q, then P is said to be a *subtype* of Q. Similar terminology is used for types and individuals of varieties other than processes.

One important note about the more general use of the term *individual*: not all individuals are concrete entities. Some types, like *number*, may have instances that are abstract entities; these instances are nonetheless individuals. In fact, "individual" is really more or less synonymous with "instance"; a thing is called an individual only with a tacit reference to some type, of which it is an instance.

Narrow and Broad Senses of "Process"

Another problem in describing processes in English arises from the language's intense focus on the details of temporal succession, characteristic of the Indo-European languages.

There is one sense of "process" in which the word is distinguished from "event," "state of affairs," "eventuality," "occurrence," and any number of other words of this general class. In fact, there are several such senses of "process," each stressing a different kind of distinction between processes and other things of this general kind. For instance, in one sense, processes are supposed to have internal structure, as opposed to events, which are pointlike. In another sense, each instance of a given process type is supposed to be divisible into temporal subparts which are process instances of the same process type. This would not be true for events. The linguist and philosopher Zeno Vendler (Vendler, 1967, 1968), among others, has gone into great detail in classifying things of this kind, coining individual terms for concepts represented by variations in meaning in English.

On the other hand, there is another sense of "process" in which it is synonymous with "event." In this sense, the extensions of any of the other terms listed in the preceding paragraph would be subsets of the class of processes; a process is *anything* of the general kind described in the preceding paragraph. It is this broadest sense of "process" with which we are concerned in IDEF3; the Vendlerian classification is irrelevant to our purposes. (IDEF3 has its own ways of distinguishing one kind of process from another based on the internal structure of the instances.) The precise technical term invented here for processes (in this broad sense) is *unit of behavior* (UOB), which simply means *a process or event, in the most general senses of those terms.* "Process" will continue to be used where it is clear that any UOB is meant, not just a process in some narrower sense.

IDEF3 Versus Other Process Formalisms

Various disciplines have their own special perspectives on the task of describing processes. In the world of simulation, for instance, "modeling" a process means constructing a model which can be used to simulate the process. In the literature on robot planning in artificial intelligence a plan is a kind of process description.

Process modeling and planning, however, are only two ways in which processes might be described. IDEF3 aims at producing high-level, general-purpose descriptions of processes. These are *IDEF3 models*, not to be confused with "process models" in the simulation sense. There are many purposes for which the IDEF3 approach is useful, including:

- Determining the impact of an organization's information resources on the major operation scenarios of the business
- Documenting the decision procedures affecting the states and life cycles of critical shared data
- Organizing the user supplied descriptions of user operations to assist in requirements decision making and system design

Additionally, an IDEF3 model can be used in the early stages of defining a knowledge-based system, a simulation study, a robot plan, or some other kind of special-purpose model of a process. This use of IDEF3 as an *early, fact-gathering and organization aid* can save time and reduce complexity in early design. As in every design activity, it is easier to discover *how* to do something once you know *what* you want to do. Furthermore, because IDEF3 carries less of the technical baggage of various entrenched disciplines than do most other process formalisms, it will be relatively easy for a domain expert, without extensive training in any process formalism, to use IDEF3 to *communicate* with designers of many different kinds of systems (software, simulation, shop floor machining systems, etc.). IDEF3 will thus be a powerful tool for knowledge acquisition.

With this background, then, a more precise account of IDEF3 can be given, beginning with some formal prerequisites.

7.3 THE SYNTAX AND SEMANTICS OF FIRST-ORDER LOGIC

IDEF3 diagrams have a definite syntax. Furthermore, diagrams constructed in accordance with that syntax are intended to represent certain chunks of the world accurately and informatively; that is to say, the diagrams have semantic content. All too often the syntax of information representations of various kinds is ill defined, and the intended semantic content of such representations—how they are supposed to hook up with the world—is vague and imprecise. IDEF3 attempts to avoid these problems by providing an explicitly defined syntax—so that it is clear exactly what does and what does not count as an IDEF3 diagram—and a corresponding mathematically precise semantics—so that it is clear exactly what sorts of structures are representable by IDEF3 diagrams.

To help achieve this goal, the syntax and semantics of first-order logic are heavily relied on. There are several reasons for this decision. First of all, first-order logic is as clearly understood as any extant scientific or mathematical theory. This enables us to proceed in confidence that the most basic theoretical foundations of our work are sound. Second, although the language of first-order logic was originally designed to express propositions of mathematics with clarity and precision, it soon became clear that much of natural language could also be clearly represented in this formal language. This is especially true for constrained fragments of natural language such as one might find in a manufacturing, engineering, or database setting[3] which makes first-order logic a natural and effective choice for capturing the propositional content of process descriptions in a rigorous and precise way. Finally, for all its rigor, the theory of first-order logic is intuitive and relatively simple to understand. The language is a straightforward idealization of ordinary discourse, and its semantics, or *model theory*, provides especially natural mathematical representations of the phenomena to be modeled.

Because familiarity with first-order logic is not assumed, this section covers enough of the basic theory to enable one to follow the exposition of the foundations of IDEF3. Some knowledge of basic set theory will be presupposed.

First-Order Languages

First-order logic is expressed in a *first-order language*. Such a language *L* is a *formal* language. That is, it is a formal object consisting of a fixed set of basic symbols, often called the *vocabulary* of *L*, and a precise set of syntactic rules, its *grammar*, for building up the sentences or *formulas* of the language—those syntactic objects that are capable of bearing information.

Vocabulary

The basic vocabulary of a first-order language consists of several kinds of symbols:[4]

- Constants
- Variables
- Predicates
- Logical symbols

Constants are symbols that correspond to names in ordinary language. For many purposes, it is useful to use abbreviations of names for constants straight out of ordinary language, e.g., *j* for "John," *wp* for "Wright-Patterson," *v* for "Venus," *e* for "Elevator 1," and so on.[5] When languages are being described in general and there is no specific application in mind, the letters *a*, *b*, *c*, and *d*, will be used, perhaps with subscripts; it is assumed that no more than a finite

---

[3]There is in particular a large literature on the uses of logic in database design. See, for example, Frost (1986), Ch. 5, for a good introduction to logical database theory, and Gallaire and Minker (1978) or Jacobs (1982) for more detailed treatments.

[4]Function symbols are omitted for purposes here, though they would be present in a complete account of the theory.

[5]Most uses of quotation marks are terribly inconsistent, as the previous sentence indicates. The general policy here will be to use quotation marks when necessary for clarity, and to avoid them otherwise, e.g., avoid quoting elements of a language *L*.

number of subscripted constants will be added to the language.[6] Constants are usually lowercase letters, with or without subscripts, but this is not necessary. Indeed, it is often useful to use uppercase.

Often an "arbitrary" constant is used as a way of talking about all constants, much as one might talk about an arbitrary triangle *ABC* in geometry as a way of proving something about all triangles in general. For this purpose it will not do to talk specifically about a given constant, because what is described needs to apply to all constants. This requires that when talking *about* the formal language presented here special *metavariables* need to be used whose roles are to serve as placeholders for the arbitrary constants of this language, much as *ABC* serves as a placeholder for arbitrary triangles. Thus, metavariables are not themselves part of the first-order language *L*, but rather part of the extended English being used to talk about the constants that *are* in the language. Lowercase sans serif characters a, b, c will be used for this purpose. Next on the list are the variables, whose purpose will be clarified in detail. The lowercase letters, x, y, and z, possibly with subscripts, will play this role, assuming there to be an unlimited store of them. The characters, x, y and z will be used as metavariables over the store of variables in this language. The third group of symbols consists of n-place predicates, $n > 1$. One-place predicates correspond roughly to verb phrases like "has insomnia," "is an employee," "is activated," and so forth, all of which express properties. Two-place predicates correspond roughly to transitive verbs like "begat," "is an element of," "weighs less than," "enters," and "lifts," and these express two-place *relations* between things. There are also three-place relations, such as those expressed by "gives" and "between," and with a little work one could come up with relations of more than three places, but in practice there is little cause to go much beyond this. When speaking generally, uppercase letters such as *P*, *Q*, and *R* will be used for predicates. Occasionally, these may appear with numerical superscripts to indicate the number of places of the relation they represent, and if necessary, with subscripts to distinguish between those with the same superscripts. Once again, in practice it is often useful to abbreviate relevant natural language expressions. Most languages contain a distinguished predicate for the two-place relation "is identical to." The symbol ≈ will be used for this purpose; and once again, the corresponding sans serif characters P, Q, R, and so on will serve as metavariables. The last group of symbols consists of the basic logical symbols: ¬, ∧, ∨, ⊃, and ≡, about which more will be said shortly. (For ease of exposition, here, quantifiers are omitted, although these would be present in a thorough treatment.) Parentheses will also be needed and perhaps other grouping indicators to prevent ambiguity.

Grammar

Now that the basic symbols are decided, one needs to know how to combine them into grammatical expressions, or *well-formed formulas*, which are the for-

---

[6]The restriction to a finite number of constants here is not at all essential, but constraint languages in general will use only finitely many; the same holds for predicates and function names.

mal correlates of sentences. These will be the expressions that will encode the propositional content of process descriptions (and more besides). This is done recursively as follows.

First, all namelike objects are grouped into a single category known as *terms*. This group includes the constants and, for reasons discussed later, it includes the variables as well. Next, the basic formulas of the language are defined. Just as verb phrases and transitive verbs in ordinary language combine with names to form sentences, so too in this formal language predicates combine with terms to form formulas. Specifically, if P is any n-place predicate, and $t_1, \ldots, t_n$ are any n terms, then $Pt_1 \ldots t_n$ is a formula, and in particular an *atomic* formula. To illustrate this, if H abbreviates the verb phrase "is happy," and a the name "Annie," then the formula Ha expresses the proposition that Annie is happy. Again, if L abbreviates the verb "loves," b the name "Barbara," c the name "Charlie," then the formula Lbc expresses the proposition that Barbara loves Charlie. The lowercase Greek letters φ, ψ, and θ will be used as metavariables over formulas.

Often when one is using more elaborate predicates drawn from natural language, e.g., if *LIFTS* were used instead of L in the previous example, it is more readable to use parentheses around the terms in atomic formulas that use the predicate and separate them by commas, e.g., *LIFTS(b,x)* instead of *LIFTS b,x*. Thus, more generally, any atomic formula $Pt_1 \ldots t_n$ can be written also as $P(t_1, \ldots, t_n)$. Furthermore, atomic formulas involving some familiar two-place predicates like $\approx$, and a few others will be introduced, are more often written using *infix* rather than *prefix* notation, i.e., with the predicate between the two terms rather than to the left of them. For example, one usually expresses that a is identical to b by writing $a \approx b$, rather than $\approx ab$. Thus it is stipulated that formulas of the form Ptt' can also be written as tPt'.

Now to begin introducing the logical symbols that allow more complex formulas to be built. Intuitively, the symbol $\neg$ expresses negation; i.e., it stands for the phrase "It is not the case that." Because any declarative sentence can be negated by attaching this phrase onto the front of it, there is a corresponding rule in the formal grammar that if φ is any formula, then so is $\neg\varphi$. The symbols $\wedge, \vee, \supset$, and $\equiv$ stand roughly for "and," "or," "if ... then," and "if and only if," which are also (among other things) operators that form new sentences out of old in the obvious ways. Unlike negation, however, each takes *two* sentences and forms a new sentence from them. Thus, the corresponding rule that if φ and ψ are any two formulas of the language, then so are $(\varphi \wedge \psi), (\varphi \vee \psi), (\varphi \supset \psi)$, and $(\varphi \equiv \psi)$. So to illustrate once again, using the preceding abbreviations, $(Lcb \supset (Hb \wedge \neg Ha))$ expresses that if Charlie loves Barbara, then Barbara is happy and Annie is not.

Finally, we turn to the quantifiers $\exists$ and $\forall$. Recall that variables were introduced without explanation. Intuitively, $\exists$ and $\forall$ stand for "some" and "every," respectively; one of the central tasks of the variables is to enable them to play this role in the formal language. (They will have another crucial role to play in IDEF3, as will be seen). Consider the difference between "Annie is happy," "Some individual is happy," and "Every individual is happy." In the first case, a specific individual is picked out by the name "Annie" and the property of being happy is predicated of her. In the second, all that is stated is that some unspecified individual or other has this property. And in the third, it is stated that every individual whether specifiable or not, has this property. This lack of specificity in the latter two cases can be made explicit by rephrasing them like this: for some (resp., every) individual x, x is happy. Because the rule for building atomic formulas counts variables among the terms, the means for representing these paraphrases is provided. Let H abbreviate "is happy" once again; then the paraphrases can be represented as $\exists xHx$ and $\forall xHx$, respectively.

Accordingly, the final rule to this grammar is added: if φ is any formula of this language and x is any variable, then $\exists x\varphi$ and $\forall x\varphi$ are formulas as well. In such a case, the variable x is *bound* by the quantifier $\exists$ (resp. $\forall$), and the formula φ is the *scope* of the quantifier $\forall$ in $\forall x\varphi$ and the quantifier $\exists$ in $\exists x\varphi$.

First-Order Semantics: Structures

The construction of the grammar has been motivated by referring to the intended meanings of the logical symbols and by letting constants and variables abbreviate meaningful expressions out of ordinary language. But from a purely formal point of view, all there is in a language is a bunch of uninterpreted syntax—it remains to be shown how to assign meaning to the elements of a first-order language. A *structure* for a first-order language L consists simply of two elements: a set D called the *domain* of the structure, and a function V known as an *interpretation function* for L. Intuitively, D is the set of things one is describing with the resources of L, e.g., the natural number, major league baseball teams, objects flowing through a manufacturing system, the people and objects that make up an air force base, or the records inside a database. The purpose of V is to fix the meanings of the basic elements of L—in the present case, constants and predicates—in terms of objects in or constructed from D.

Interpretations for Constants

Variables will not receive a specific interpretation, because their meanings can vary within a structure (they are *variables* after all). They will be treated with their own special, but related, semantic apparatus. Constants on the other hand, being the formal analogues of names with fixed meanings, are assigned members of D once and for all as their interpretation; in symbols, for all constants c of L, $V(\text{c}) \in D$.

Interpretations for Predicates

For any one-place predicate P, let $V(\text{P})$ be a subset of D—intuitively, the set of things that have the property expressed by P. And for any n-place predicate R, $n > 1$, let $V(\text{R})$ be a set of n-tuples of elements of D—intuitively, the set of n-tuples of objects in D that stand in the relation expressed by R. Thus, for example, if L is to abbreviate the verb "loves," and domain D consists of the population of Texas, then $V(L)$ will be the set of all pairs $\langle \mathbf{a}, \mathbf{b} \rangle$ such that $\mathbf{a}$ loves $\mathbf{b}$. Formally, then, for all n-place predicates P, $V(\text{P}) \subseteq D^n$, where D^n is the set of all n-tuples of elements of D. If one wishes to include the identity predicate $\approx$ in one's language, and have it carry its intended meaning, then one needs an additional, more specific semantical constraint on the interpretation function V. Identity, of course, is a relation that holds between any object and itself, but not between itself and any other object. This additional constraint is easy to express formally: if language L contains $\approx$, then the interpretation of $\approx$ is the set of all pairs $\langle o, o \rangle$ such that o is an element of the domain D, i.e., more formally, $V(\approx) = \{\langle o, o \rangle | o \in D\}$.

Truth Under an Assignment

The goal now is to define what is required for a formula to be *true* in a given structure $M = \langle D, V \rangle$. First, the notion of a *variable assignment* is needed, or *assignment* for short. An assignment might be thought of as a *temporary* interpretation function for variables: like an interpretation function on constants, it assigns members of the domain to variables; but within the same structure many different assignment functions are used. This reflects the semantic variability of variables as opposed to constants and predicates. Now, given the structure M and an assignment α one can define interpretations for *terms*, i.e., constants *and* variables generally, relative to α: the interpretation $V_\alpha(t)$ of a term t under an assignment α is just $V(t)$, if t is a term, and $\alpha(t)$—the object in D assigned to t by α—if t is a variable.

Atomic Formulas

Given a general notion of an interpretation for terms under an assignment α, one can now define the notion of *truth under an assignment* in a structure M. Truth *simpliciter* in M will then be defined in terms of this notion. For convenience, a formula's being "true$_\alpha$ in M" is used instead of being "true in M under α."

To start, define truth under an assignment for atomic formulas. Let φ be an atomic formula $Pt_1 \ldots t_n$. Then φ is true$_\alpha$ in M just in case $\langle V_\alpha(t_1), \ldots, F_\alpha(t_n) \rangle \in V_\alpha(P)$. Intuitively, then, where $n = 1$, Pt is true $_\alpha$ in M just in case the object in D that t denotes is in the set of things that have the property expressed by P. And for $n > 1$, $Pt_1 \ldots t_n$ is true$_\alpha$ just in case the n-tuple of objects $\langle o_1, \ldots, o_n \rangle$ denoted by $t_1, \ldots, t_n$, respectively, is in the set of n-tuples whose members stand in the relation expressed by P, i.e., just in case those objects stand in that relation. To help fix these ideas, construct a small language L^* and build a small structure M^*. Suppose there are four names a, b, c, and d, a one-place predicate H (intuitively, to abbreviate "is happy"), and a three-place predicate T (intuitively, to abbreviate "is talking to ... about"). The distinguished predicate $\approx$ is also included, although no real use of it will be made until later. Use x, y, and z for the variables. For the structure M^*, take the domain D to be a set of three individuals, {Beth, Charlie, Di}, the interpretation function G will be defined as follows. For constants, $G(a)$ = $G(b)$ = Beth, $G(c)$ = Charlie, and $G(d)$ = Di. (Beth thus has two names in this language; this is to illustrate a point to be made several sections later.) For predicates H and T, let $G(H)$ = {Beth, Di} (so, intuitively, Beth and Di are happy), and $G(T)$ = {$\langle$Beth, Di, Charlie$\rangle$,$\langle$Charlie, Charlie, Di$\rangle$} (so, intuitively, Beth is talking to Di about Charlie, and Charlie is talking to himself about Di). Following the rule for $\approx$, let $G(\approx)$ = {$\langle$Beth, Beth$\rangle$,$\langle$Charlie, Charlie$\rangle$,$\langle$Di, Di$\rangle$}. Finally, for the assignment function α, let $\alpha(x)$ = $\alpha(y)$ = Charlie, and $\alpha(z)$ = Di. Now check that Hd and $Tbdx$ are true in M^* under α. In the first case, by the preceding, Hd is true$_\alpha$ in **M*** just in case $G_\alpha(d) \in G_\alpha(H)$, i.e., just in case Di is an element of the set {Beth, Di}, which she is. So *Hd* is true$_\alpha$ in **M***. Similarly, *Tbdx* is true$_\alpha$ in **M*** just in case $\langle G_\alpha(b), G_\alpha(d), G_\alpha(x) \rangle \in G_\alpha(T)$, i.e., just in case $\langle G(b), G(d), \alpha(x) \rangle \epsilon$, and i.e., just in case $\langle$ Beth, Di, Charlie$\rangle \in \{\langle$ Beth, Di, Charlie$\rangle, \langle$ Charlie, Charlie, Di$\rangle\}$. Because this obviously holds, the formula *Tbdx* is true$_\alpha$ in **M***. A formula is *false*$_\alpha$ in a structure **M**, of course, just in case it is not true$_\alpha$ in **M**. It is easy to verify that, for example, *Hc*, *Hx*, and *Tdbc* are all false$_\alpha$ in **M*** under α.

Digression on Variables, Types, and Instances

The distinction between types and instances has been emphasized. It is important to see how this distinction is captured to a certain extent by the apparatus of variables and assignments. Although there is no specific semantic object corresponding to types, *intuitively*, formulas with unassigned variables can be thought of as expressing types of situations.[7] For example, the formula *Hx*, *independent of any assignment*, can be thought of as expressing the type of situation in which someone or other is happy; when that variable is assigned, or *anchored* to a given individual, e.g., Charlie, then one gets a determinate instance of that situation type. Again, *Tzcw*, can be thought to express the type of situation in which someone is talking to Charlie about someone, an assignment of some object, e.g., Beth, to *z* yields the somewhat more determinate situation type in which Beth is talking to Charlie about someone or other, and a further assignment of an object to *w* then yields a determinate instance of the latter two types.

This reflection of the type/instance distinction in the assigned/unassigned variable distinction plays a crucial role in representing the process type/process instance distinction in IDEF3. More will be said about this presently.

Conjunctions and Negations

Now for the more complex cases. Suppose first that φ is a formula of the form $\neg\psi$. Then φ is a true$_\alpha$ in a structure **M** just in case ψ is *not* true$_\alpha$ in **M**. In so defining truth for negated formulas, it is ensured that the symbol $\neg$ means what is intended. Things are much the same for the other symbols. Thus, suppose φ is a formula of the form $\psi \wedge \theta$. Then φ is true$_\alpha$ in **M** just in case both ψ *and* θ are true. If φ is a formula of the form $\psi \vee \theta$, then φ is true$_\alpha$ in **M** just in case either ψ *or* θ is true. If φ is a formula of the form $\psi \supset \theta$, then φ is true$_\alpha$ in **M** just in case either ψ is false in **M** or θ is true$_\alpha$ in **M**. And if φ is a formula of the form $\psi \equiv \theta$, then φ is true$_\alpha$ in **M** just in case ψ and θ have the same truth value in **M**. To test for comprehension of these rules, verify that $\neg H(\psi)$ and $(Tbcz \wedge Txxc) \supset Hc$ are both true in **M*** under α.

Quantified Formulas

Last are the quantified formulas. (This section can be omitted without impairing the reader's understanding, since the examples in this chapter do not involve quantified statements.) The intuitive idea is this. When the quantifiers were intro-

---

[7]The notion of a *situation* is at the heart of much recent work in natural language semantics, philosophy, logic, and artifical intelligence, especially around Stanford University. See especially Barwise and Perry (1983) and Barwise (1989).

duced it was noted that "Some individual is happy," i.e., $\exists xHx$, can be paraphrased as "for some individual x, x is happy." This in turn might be paraphrased more linguistically as "for some value of the variable x, the expression "x is happy is true." This is essentially what the formal semantics for existentially quantified formulas will come to. That is, $\exists xHx$ will be true in a structure **M** under α just in case the *un*quantified formula Hx is true in **M** under some (in general, new) assignment α' such that $\alpha'(x)$ is in the interpretation of H. It is easy to verify that this formula is true in the little structure **M*** under α, when looking at a new assignment function α' that assigns either Beth or Di to the variable x. Thus, $\exists xHx$ should come out true in **M*** under α. But care is needed in defining truth in a structure formally, because some formulas—*Tbxz*, for example—contain more than one unquantified, or *free*, variable. Thus, when evaluating a quantification of such a formula—$\exists zTbxz$, say—one has to be sure that the new assignment function α' does not change the value of any of the free variables—in this case, the variable x. Otherwise, one could change the sense of the unquantified formula in midevaluation. So, intuitively, under the preceding assignment α, $\exists zTbxz$ intuitively says that Beth is talking to Charlie about someone (recall that $\alpha(x)$ = Charlie), and this should turn out to be false$_\alpha$ in **M*** because Beth is not talking to Charlie about anyone, i.e., there is no triple in $F(T)$ such that Beth is the first element and Charlie the second. But suppose all that is required to make an existentially quantified formula true under α is that there be some new assignment function α' such that $Tbxz$ is true under α'. Then, it could also turn out that $\alpha'(x)$ is Di and $\alpha'(z)$ is Charlie. But then the formula $Tbxz$ would be true in **M*** under α', because Beth is talking to Di about Charlie, i.e., $\langle$Beth, Di, Charlie$\rangle \in G_\alpha(T)$. And that is clearly not wanted.

All that is needed to avoid this problem is a simple and obvious restriction: When evaluating the formula $\exists zTbxz$, the new assignment α' that is used to evaluate $Tbxz$ must not be allowed to differ from α on any variable except z (and even then it *need not* differ from α. More generally, if φ is an existentially quantified formula $\exists x\psi$, then φ is true in a structure **M** under α just in case there is an assignment function α' just like α except perhaps in what it assigns to x such that the formula ψ is true in **M** under α'. And if φ is a universally quantified formula $\forall x\psi$, then φ is true in **M** under α just in case for *every* assignment function α' just like α except perhaps in what it assigns to x, the formula ψ is true in **M** under α'. That is, in essence, φ is true in **M** under α just in case ψ is true in **M** no matter what value in the domain is assigned to x (while keeping all other variable assignments fixed).

Truth and Realization

Now, finally, a formula can be defined to be *true* in a structure **M** *simpliciter* just in case it is true$_\alpha$ in **M** for all assignments α, and *false* in **M** just in case it is false$_\alpha$ in **M** for all α. Note that for most any interpretation, there will be formulas that are neither true nor false in the interpretation. The previous example $\exists zTbxz$, for instance, is neither true nor false in **M***. Such formulas will of course always have free variables because it is the semantic indeterminacy of such variables that is responsible. However, note that some formulas with free variables—e.g.,

$Hx \wedge \neg Hx$—will nonetheless be true or false in certain models, though these will typically be logical truths or falsehoods, i.e., formulas which are not capable of true (resp. false) interpretation.

A structure **M** is said to be a *realization* of a given set Σ of formulas just in case every formula in Σ is true in **M**.[8] For example, the structure **M*** is a realization of the set $\{Hd, Hx \supset Hx, Tbdc \wedge \neg Hc, \forall x(Hx \vee \exists y(Tydx))\}$. The notions of truth and realization will be central to the semantics for IDEF3.

Temporality and Index Semantics

First-Order Logic and the Problem of Temporality

Despite its success in numerous domains, there are areas of potential application where plain vanilla first-order logic and its semantics come up short. Most notable among these are domains involving time. A standard first-order structure "freezes" the world, as it were, at a certain moment, and this seriously hinders the representation of dynamic processes. For present purposes, then, first-order logic needs some supplementation. The answer, or at least one good answer, is index semantics.

Roughly speaking, *index* semantics is just plain vanilla first-order semantics writ large. That is, instead of a single interpretation, in an index semantical structure one finds many plain vanilla interpretations, each distinguished from the other (in addition to internal differences) by a unique index. The idea then, in the temporal case, is that each index can represent a certain moment, or interval of time, and the structure it indexes represents the world at that moment or during that interval.[9] In effect, one overcomes the static representation of a single first-order interpretation by stringing together a series of related snapshots. The result, though somewhat artificial, nonetheless adds great expressive power and flexibility to unadorned first-order languages and their semantics.

Elaborations

This section introduces extensions to the first-order language L and the semantics appropriate to the task at hand. To the language is added a new class of temporal constants $k_1, k_2, \ldots$ and temporal variables $i_1, i_2 \ldots$, and a distinguished class of n-place temporal predicates. Intuitively, the temporal constants will serve as

---

[8]It is more common in logic to say that such a structure is a *model* of Σ. But this term is already so overextended in the area of information modeling (case in point) that it was thought best to avoid the standard terminology here.

[9]Though there were several precursors to full-blown index semantics, most notably the work of Prior (1957), it reached its maturity in the "possible world" semantics that Saul Kripke provided for modal languages, i.e., languages with such operators as "necessarily," "possibly," "it has always been the case that," "it will be the case that," etc. See Kripke (1963) for a readable overview, Chellas (1980) and Hughes and Cresswell (1968) for more formal developments.

names of intervals, e.g., 12 noon (on a particular day), 9 a.m. to 12 a.m., and so on. Temporal variables will take temporal intervals as values, and the predicates intuitively express properties of, and relations among, intervals, e.g., duration properties like *5 minutes in length*, and significant temporal relations—precedence and inclusion in particular.

Temporal terms and predicates will not be allowed in formulas of the original language. Rather, they are the elements of a separate, and for purposes here, simpler temporal language whose only logical symbols are the Boolean connectives (and hence there are no temporal quantifiers). The resulting formulas will be called *temporal* formulas, and formulas from the original language *standard* formulas. Formulas of both sorts will be used in the construction of a new kind of expression that is called an *elaboration*, consisting of a temporal interval variable, temporal formulas involving that variable, and a collection of nontemporal formulas. More specifically, let i be a temporal interval variable, $\psi_1, \ldots, \psi_n (n \geq 0)^{10}$ temporal formulas, and $\varphi_1, \ldots, \varphi_m (m > 0)$ are standard formulas, $[i, \{\psi_1, \ldots, \psi_n\}, \{\varphi_1, \ldots, \varphi_m\}]$ is an elaboration.[11] i will be called the *dominant* temporal variable of the elaboration.

Intuitively, to anticipate things a bit, temporal formulas in an elaboration put conditions on the value of the temporal variable i, e.g., that it be before noon, or have a duration of 20 minutes; subject to these conditions, the elaboration is to be thought of as "asserting" that each of its standard formulas is true throughout the value of i. An elaboration thus represents (at a certain level of detail) what is occurring within a particular temporally extended situation—type or instance, depending on whether or not there are free variables occurring in the elaboration. An instance of a process, then, thought of roughly as a sequence of actual events, can be represented by a corresponding sequence of *determinate* elaborations—elaborations containing no free variables. A general process *description* will be represented by a structured cluster of *indeterminate* elaborations—elaborations with free variables among the formulas—that can be instantiated in many different ways, corresponding to the different possible runs of the general process captured in the description. The graphical syntax of these clusters will be described.

Temporal Structures

To be able to represent these ideas semantically, temporal indices are added to the plain vanilla structures. Specifically, a *temporal* structure $\langle D, TI, dom, V \rangle$ consists now not only of a domain D and an interpretation function V, but two other elements as well. First, there is a set of temporal intervals, or more exactly, a triple $TI = \langle T, \leq, \sqsubseteq \rangle$, where T is a set, and $\leq$ and $\sqsubseteq$ are two binary relations on T—intuitively, $\leq$ represents the relation of temporal precedence (last Tuesday pre-

---

[10]In the case where n = 0, the sequence $\psi_1, \ldots, \psi_n$ is the empty sequence.

[11]The restriction to temporal *variables* i is not a genuine restriction, because for any temporal constant k can be included the condition i = k among the formulas ψ_j, thus in effect eliminating the restriction. Using only variables in the definition, however, makes for a smoother statement of the semantics for the instantiation graphs.

cedes last Thursday), and $\sqsubseteq$ the relation of temporal inclusion (today's lunch hour is included in the period from 8:00 this morning to 5:00 this evening). Familiar temporal properties and relations can be defined in terms of these notions. For example, an *atomic* interval can be defined as an interval that includes no intervals but itself.

Further conditions will be imposed on the temporal structure of the intervals. In particular, it will be assumed that every interval has a beginning (and ending) point. This can be stated in the preceding terms as the condition that every interval τ includes an interval that precedes (is preceded by) every other interval included in τ. Under this condition, one interval τ *meets* another τ' just in case the ending point of τ is the beginning point of τ'.

In most real-world settings, not every object exists across every temporal interval. In life, people die, others are born; in a manufacturing system, new objects are constructed, others leave the system; in a database, new records are added, old ones deleted; and so on. Thus, there must be the flexibility to have different domains of objects associated with different intervals of time; more exactly, the plain vanilla structures have to be indexed by different intervals to be able to have different domains. That is the job of the second new element *dom* in temporal structures. Specifically, in a temporal structure $\langle D, TI, dom, V \rangle$, D is to be thought of as the set of all the objects that exist in *any* of the temporal intervals represented by TI (i.e., all the objects that exist in any temporal interval in the real-world setting that the structure is designed to represent). *dom* then assigns to each interval in TI the set of objects that exist in that interval—i.e., intuitively, the objects that exist (at least) from the beginning of the interval to the end and at every point in between. The same object, of course, might, and generally will, exist in many different temporal intervals. Thus, if one were modeling the run of a manufacturing system over a 24-hour period, D would consist of all the objects that occur in the system during any interval within that period—parts, employees on their various shifts, finished jobs from the time of their completion to the time they leave the system, and so on.

Just as conditions are placed on $\leq$ and $\sqsubseteq$ to ensure that they capture the desired properties of temporal intervals, a similar condition must also be placed on *dom*. Specifically, as just noted, if an object exists throughout a certain interval of time, then it exists throughout every subinterval. However, nothing that has been said so far about the formal structures proper guarantees that *dom* will represent this fact, i.e., that it will assign all the objects in a given interval τ also to every subinterval of τ. It can be guaranteed with the following condition, stated explicitly in terms of the semantical apparatus: for any interval $\tau \in T$, and for any object $o \in D$, if $o \in dom(\tau)$, then for any $\tau' \in T$, if $\tau' \sqsubseteq \tau$, then $o \in dom(\tau')$. The converse is not required, of course, because an object could come to exist during a subinterval τ' of τ that does not exist throughout all of the larger interval τ.

The interpretation function V in a temporal structure also needs to be slightly revised. One of the most salient features of temporal processes is that things *change* over time. This has generated a venerable philosophical problem: how can an object be different at one time than at another and still be the very same object? Greek, medieval, and some contemporary philosophers put things in terms of substance and accident: the same substance can nonetheless alter those *accidental* properties that are not essential to its being that very substance.

Thus, a woman's height, for example, is not essential to her, and hence it can change over time without her ceasing to be who she is. The same cannot be said however of the woman's being a human being. That property is essential to her; she could not, say, come to be a stone, an alligator, a daisy, or otherwise come to lack it and still be herself.[12]

However the metaphysics of change are viewed, it is undeniable that the ordinary conceptual scheme—as reflected in the sort of ordinary language reports whose content IDEF3 is intended to capture—permits one and the same object to have different properties over time. This is implemented in the formal semantics by relativizing the interpretation of predicates to intervals. Specifically, for a given n-place predicate P, and any interval $\tau \in T$, let $V(P, \tau)$ be a subset of D. In this way, an object $o \in D$ might be in the interpretation of P during one interval τ, i.e., one might have $o \in dom(\tau)$ and $o \in V(P, \tau)$, and not be in the interpretation of P during another interval τ', i.e., one might also have $o \in dom(\tau')$ and $o \notin V(P, \tau')$.

It is not required, analogous to the preceding condition on dom, that if an object has a property over a given interval, then it has that property over every subinterval. For although this is true of many properties, e.g., running, it is not true of all. Obvious cases are ones that involve some sort of average measurement, e.g., a manufacturing system over a given 24-hour period might have the (average) property of putting out 52 jobs per hour, although it might be that in no single hour subinterval of that period were there actually exactly 52 jobs put out. It thus has to be added specifically for each predicate in an IDEF3 representation whether or not its interpretation at a given interval τ is to be nested within each subinterval of τ.

It is also not required that the interpretation of a predicate at an interval contain only objects that "exist" at that interval. Intuitively, this is because there are many meaningful predicates that seem to contain objects that no longer exist. For example, Lincoln intuitively is in the extension of the predicate FORMER PRESIDENT. Or for a more manufacturing-oriented example, suppose that in the course of constructing a given widget W, one first needs to use a certain gadget G that is destroyed in the process before W is complete. After its construction, however, at a certain time τ, one might want to be able to list which parts played a role in the construction of W, and hence one might want some sort of predicate PART USED IN CONSTRUCTION OF W that is true at τ of G, even though G no longer exists at τ, i.e., $G \notin dom(\tau')$. Of course, for certain purposes, one might for one reason or another wish to enforce the condition that the interpretation of a predicate at an interval only take objects that exist during that interval, and such a condition could of course be added unproblematically, but for greater generality it is omitted.

Interpretations for constants are given just as before: for any constant c, $V(c) \in D$. Assignment functions also work as before, assigning arbitrary objects in D to free objects variables, and arbitrary intervals in TI to free temporal variables.

---

[12]The concepts of substance, essence, and accident have in recent years generated a voluminous literature, much of it spawned by Kripke's formal work in the semantics of modal logic. For a good introduction to the issues, see Schwartz (1977).

Truth and Realization in Temporal Structures

Atomic Formulas and Connectives

Truth in temporal structures is now just a simple extension of truth in ordinary first-order structures. Specifically, let I be a temporal structure $\langle D, TI, dom, V \rangle$, and a an assignment for I. Then truth$_\alpha$ is defined just as before, only relative to the interval indices: in the simplest case, an atomic formula Pc is true$_\alpha$ in I relative to τ just in case the object that c denotes, i.e., $V(c)$, is in the set $V(P, \tau)$ of things that have the property expressed by P at the interval t; if instead there is a variable x instead of c, then $\alpha(x)$ is looked at instead. Similarly for atomic formulas constructed from n-place predicates. Connectives work just as before, modulo the relativization to intervals.

Quantified Formulas

Quantifiers present two options. (Again, not included in the examples given here.) On the one hand, given a quantified sentence $\exists x \varphi$, one can interpret the quantifier as ranging over all objects in the domain D independent of the interval τ at which the formula is being evaluated, or one can relativize them to those objects in the domain of τ. For a variety of reasons, one should opt for the latter. Thus, $\exists x \psi$ is true$_\alpha$ at t just in case there is some object that exists at τ, i.e., some $o \in dom(\tau)$, and assignment function α' that differs from α at most in that it assigns o to x, such that ψ is true$_{\alpha'}$. That is, in essence, $\exists x \psi$ is true$_\alpha$ in $\mathbf{M}$ at τ just in case ψ is true$_\alpha$ in $\mathbf{M}$ for some value *in the domain $dom(\tau)$ of* τ that α' assigns to x (while keeping all other variable assignments fixed). Similarly, $\forall x$ is true$_\alpha$ in $\mathbf{M}$ at τ just in case ψ is true in $\mathbf{M}$ for all values in $dom(\tau)$ that are assigned to x (while keeping all other variable assignments fixed).

Truth and Realization for Elaborations

As before, *truth* for a formula φ at an interval τ in an interpretation I is just for φ to be true$_\alpha$ at τ for all assignments α. Otherwise put, for a formula to be true at an interval in an interpretation is for it to hold during that interval no matter what values of the domain are assigned to the free variables of the formula.

Given all this, a notion analogous to truth at an interval can be defined for elaborations. Specifically, an assignment α *realizes* an elaboration $E = [i, \{\psi_1, \ldots, \psi_m\}, \{\varphi_1, \ldots, \varphi_n\}]$ in I just in case each ψ_1 and each φ_j is true$_\alpha$ at $\alpha(i)$.[13]

As it happens, in IDEF3, the notion of an assignment realizing an elaboration will play a much more prominent role than the notion of an elaboration simply being realized, and hence the notion of truth under an assignment will play a more prominent role than straight truth. The reason for this is that, first, different variable assignments for the same elaboration provide a natural representation of the idea of different objects instantiating the same process across

---

[13]In a somewhat fuller development, a second type of elaboration would be added that requires only that the formulas φ_1 be true at some *sub*interval of τ. This enables one to capture descriptions that are less than precise about what *exactly* goes on during some period of time.

time, and second, assignment of the same object to the same variable across different elaborations provides a natural representation of the flow of a given object through a process. These are the chief ideas for which IDEF3 is intended to be a flexible and powerful representation tool.

7.4 IDEF3 GRAPHICAL SYNTAX

Turning now to the more explicit development of IDEF3 proper, in addition to the (supplemented) first-order component already noted, the syntax of IDEF3 also has a graphical component, used for constructing figures that are vivid and especially useful for real world applications. There are several types of basic elements of the graphical syntax for IDEF3: boxes, labels, arrows, and junction symbols. With the exception of junction symbols, of which there are two, & and X, there is an inexhaustible (i.e., countably infinite) supply of elements of each type. Boxes and labels join to form *labeled boxes*, or *l-boxes*, and boxes and junction symbols join to form *junctions*: &-junctions and X-junctions, respectively. (In practice, labels serve as concise abbreviations or descriptions of the state of affairs described by an elaboration associated with the box in a graphical diagram. For formal purposes, lowercase letters with subscripts are used.) The preferred two-dimensional (2-D) representations of these constructs are depicted in Fig. 7.1.

Both labeled boxes and junctions are called *nodes*. Nodes are joined with other nodes to form what are called *prediagrams*. The joining of one node a to another a' by an arrow r can be represented as a triple $\langle a, r, a' \rangle$. r is called an *outgoing* arrow of a, and an *incoming arrow* of a'. The natural way to represent $\langle a, r, a' \rangle$ two dimensionally is of course simply to draw the 2-D representation of r from the 2-D representation of a to the 2-D representation a'. Henceforth, the examples will often not distinguish between graphical elements of IDEF3 syntax and

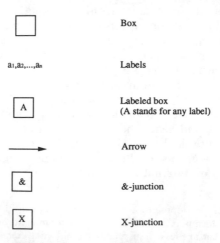

□	Box
$a_1, a_2, \ldots, a_n$	Labels
A	Labeled box (A stands for any label)
→	Arrow
&	&-junction
X	X-junction

FIG. 7.1. 2-D graphical lexicon.

their 2-D representations, often speaking informally, e.g., of "drawing" an arrow from one node to another, of two nodes being "connected" by an arrow, of "connecting" an arrow to a node, and so on. In particular, the rules for constructing diagrams—mathematically, these are *graphs* of a certain sort—will be stated in these more informal (but no less rigorous) terms.

Not just any way of drawing arrows between nodes is a legitimate prediagram. Indeed, most ways of doing so are not. Most yield diagrams that are semantically unwieldy at best, and incoherent at worst. Here, order is imposed on the construction box and arrow figures out of the graphical syntactic elements by means of the following *recursive* definition of notion of a prediagram, i.e., a definition that begins with basic instances of the notion, and then proceeds to define more complex instances in terms of the less complex. The syntatic rules will be stated first; detailed explanation of each rule follows.

(1) For $n > 2$, the result of drawing n arrows from an &-junction (resp., X-junction) to n distinct l-boxes is called *basic open &-split* (resp., *basic open X-split*).

(2) The result of drawing an arrow from each l-box in a basic open &-split (resp. basic open X-split) is a *closed &-split* (resp., *closed X-split*).

(3) l-boxes, open and closed splits (basic or not) are *prediagrams*. Two-dimensional representations of open and closed splits are provided in Fig. 7.2.

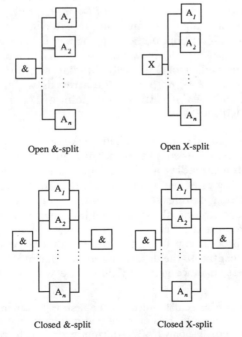

Open &-split   Open X-split

Closed &-split   Closed X-split

FIG. 7.2 Open and closed splits.

(4) The l-boxes and junctions of a prediagram are called its *nodes*. A node in a prediagram with no outgoing arrows is called *extensible*.

(5) A *path* in a prediagram is a sequence $\langle a1, \ldots, a_n \rangle$ of nodes such that for $i < n$, there is an arrow from a_i to a_{i+1}. In this case, $\langle a_1, \ldots, a_n \rangle$ is a path *from a_1 to a_n*. Sequences with a single element are to be considered limiting cases of paths. A node a' in a prediagram π is *accessible from* a node a of π iff (i.e., if and only if) there is a path from a to a'. A path p is said to *traverse* a node a iff a is an element of p. a and a' are *basically incomparable* iff either (a) there is no path from a to a' or from a' to a, or (b) there is a junction j such that both a and a' are accessible from j but every path from one to the other traverses j.[14] a is *essentially accessible from a'* iff a *is accessible* from a', and a and a' are not basically incomparable.

(6) A node p in a prediagram D is a *leftmost point*, or *L-point*, of D iff every node of D is accessible from p. p is a *rightmost point*, or *R-point*, of D iff p is accessible from every node of D. D is *L-pointed* if it has a unique L-point, *R-pointed* if it has a unique R-point, and *closed* if it is both L-pointed and R-pointed.

(7) The result of replacing any l-box b in a closed split (of either sort) with a closed prediagram D by attaching the arrows coming into b to the L-point of D and the arrow coming out of b to the R-point of D is a closed split. It follows from this rule that every split is closed in this sense. The area between the L-point and R-point of a closed split S is called the *scope* of S. If a is the L-point of S and b the R-point, then b is said to be *a's R-counterpart*, and *b's L-counterpart*.

(8) The result of drawing an arrow from an extensible node of a prediagram F to the L-point of another prediagram is itself a prediagram.

(9) The result of drawing an arrow from an extensible node a of a prediagram D to any node a' of D is itself a prediagram iff (a) a is essentially accessible from a', (b) no part of the arrow is within the scope of a closed split, and (c) a' is neither the L-point of D nor the R-point of a closed split within D.

Further discussion of these rules will help make their function clear. As noted, the preceding definition is recursive in that it begins by introducing the basic cases of certain notions (prediagram, closed split) and then uses further rules to extend the notions after establishing the basic cases. Rules (1) and (2) give further initial elements to help get things started. Intuitively, open &-splits represent processes (both types and instances) that diverge into several distinct subprocesses, and open X-splits represent process types that have a "conditional branch," i.e., a point where the process can flow in one and only one of several ways. Such splits are obviously central to the description of indeterminate cycles within process types. A process instance generally flows one way rather than another at

---

[14]The second condition here actually includes the first as a vacuous case, but this way of putting it makes the idea a bit clearer. Note that paths between basically incomparable nodes will be made possible only by (9), which provides for the construction of cycles within diagrams.

a branching point depending on whether or not some condition is met. If it is not, then the process instance loops back to an earlier point in the process type, eventually returning to the branching point. When the satisfaction of the relevant condition cannot be determined in advance, the cycle in the process is indeterminate.

The difference between open &-splits and closed &-splits is that the branches of a process represented by the former are not conceived ever to converge at some later point back into a single stream. In closed &-splits they are. In and of themselves there is no essential difference between open X-splits and closed ones, because in both cases there can only be a single process that emanates from the branching point. However, in the context of a larger diagram there is a crucial difference. For only closed X-splits can be used to place conditional branches in the midst of a larger process that is to be construed as a single stream. An open X-split represents two possible wholly divergent paths a process can take; a closed X-split represents a mere option to jog one way or another on the path to a single end.

Rule (3) together with (1) and (2) actually give the base case for the recursion. (Compare the basic splits with atomic formulas in the grammar for first-order languages.) Note, however, that the definition is not restricted only to *basic* splits. This allows counting of other, more complex sorts of splits to be defined in (7) as well. Rules (4) through (6) define some important auxiliary notions. Rule (4) defines the notion of an extensible node, and (5) some useful graph theoretic concepts, and the notion of essential accessibilty needed in (9).

Regarding (6), L-points and R-points in a prediagram intuitively represent definite beginning and ending points of a described process or subprocess. If some event is, in fact a beginning point of a process, then everything that follows in that process can be traced back to that beginning point; this idea is captured in the requirement that all points in the prediagram—representing the events that make up the process—be accessible from the L-point. Analogously, if an event marks a definite end point to a process, then one should be able to trace back from that point to all preceding events in the process; thus the requirement that an R-point be accessible from all other nodes in the prediagram.

Rules (7), (8), and (9) are the constructive parts of the definition; they define complex prediagrams in terms of less complex parts. Specifically, given the notion of a closed prediagram, (7) gives a recursive rule for generating more complex closed splits from properly closed prediagrams and less complex closed splits. The rough idea is that if a description represents a process that splits, then any of the descriptions of the subprocesses that branch off can be replaced by still more complex descriptions. Rule (7) also defines the important notion of the *scope* of a split, which will be returned to shortly.

Rules (8) and (9) tell how to build more complex prediagrams by drawing new arrows. Rule (8) allows one to draw an arrow from an extensible node in one diagram to the L-point of another, a natural way in which one might put together prediagrams constructed from descriptions of different parts of a single system. The explicit purpose of (9) is to provide for the construction of diagrams that represent processes with (determinate or indeterminate) cycling. As previously noted, this can only be done by drawing an arrow from some extensible node in a prediagram to some "preceding" box. This is captured by the requirement that the l-box a out of which the arrow is drawn must be accessible from the l-box a' to which the arrow is drawn. Consider for example a process that might be described as follows:

> After its construction, a car body enters the painting area where it activates the paint-jets. It moves through the area and receives a coat of paint. Then it enters the drying area where it activates the dryers, and stays there for 20 minutes until it is dry. At that point, sensors check to see if the car body has received enough paint. If it has, it is shunted off down the line; if not, it is put through the paint-dry cycle again, and continues in the cycle until it receives enough paint.

Consider then how one might capture this description using the preceding syntax. First, a box is drawn to represent the construction of a car body. Because (suppose) one is not at present interested in the details of the construction, a single l-box labeled "Construct Car Body" (CCB) is used to represent that process. A second box labeled "Enter Paint Area" (EPA) is then introduced with an arrow [using Rule (8)] drawn from the first box to the second. Three more boxes are labeled "Paint Car Body" (PCB), "Enter Drying Area" (EDA), and "Dry Car Body" (DCB) in the same fashion, each connected to the previous box by an arrow [by (8) once again]. The two possible outcomes of checking the paint are represented by an open split involving an XOR junction, with one box of the split labeled "Enough Paint" (EP) and another labeled "Not Enough Paint" (not-EP). This open split can now be joined to the DCB box by (8) once again. A further box is introduced along the top branch of the split to represent (or summarize) the process that a car body enters on completing the paint/dry cycle. All that remains is to represent the loop back into the cycle from the not-EP l-box. This is allowed by (9) because the not-EP box is essentially accessible from the PCB box, and the desired arrow is not within the scope of a closed split, nor connected to "illegal" l-boxes.

The condition that arrows cannot be drawn into or out of the scope of a closed split stems from the idea that processes emanating from the L-point of a closed split should be *isolable*, i.e., that the only way in or out of a process represented by a closed split is from its beginning. If a subdiagram within a closed split accurately pictures a certain distinct process outside the scope of the split, then in constructing a prediagram one should simply copy the relevant section where it is needed, rather than to cross a split's logical boundaries.

The prediagram resulting from the preceding construction is shown in Fig. 7.3. (The box labeled "Decomposition of CCB" dangling off the CCB box serves as a pointer to its more detailed meaning, or *decomposition*; this will be discussed later.)

The requirement (9) that a be *essentially* accessible from a' is added in order to rule out the use of (9) to generate certain pathological cycles that would arise by allowing arrows between l-boxes a, a' that are accessible only because of a loop—generated by a previous application of (9)—from a, e.g., back to another a'' from which both a and a' are accessible. That a' cannot be the R-point of a closed split, as required by (c), stems from the fact that such nodes mark the end of a split process, and hence should only have arrows coming into it from within the split. That it can't be the L-point of the diagram represents the idea

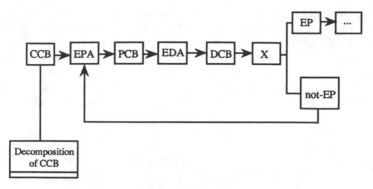

FIG. 7.3. Prediagram for paint/dry cycle.

that processes typically have a unique starting point, though this condition is dispensable.

Several further remarks are in order. First, note that except for the "target" node in a cycle, no node in a prediagram has more than one incoming arrow. At first blush, this might lead one to believe that IDEF3 is incapable of representing convergent processes, where several processes in parallel converge to a single event. In IDEF3, however, convergence is to be represented by the convergence of several arrows to a single &-junction at the end of a closed split. In representing convergence by a closed split, the presupposition here is that all parallel convergent processes have a common initial path, that tracing back down each parallel process will reveal a common origin from which they all split—perhaps only the signing of a purchase order, or the system timer striking 8:00 a.m.—but a common origin nonetheless. For otherwise there seems no initial ground that "parallelizes" the processes that converge in the first place.

Second, a number of constructs that will appear in IDEF3's more practical guise have been omitted here. For example, a common junction is *inclusive* OR, whereas only *exclusive* OR have been included. The reason for this omission is that inclusive disjunction can be defined in terms of the other two.[15] Thus, for theoretical purposes it is redundant. In practice, of course, inclusive OR is quite convenient, indeed, perhaps essential, because, e.g., it cuts down greatly on the size of certain prediagrams. It is also the most natural meaning of many ordinary uses of the word *or* in common process descriptions, and hence is needed in order to capture such descriptions in the most natural way.

A second construct that for convenience is also being omitted is *relational links*. These are links that can encode a wide variety of temporal and other information about events within a given process. These, like inclusive disjunction, are easily added to the theory.

---

[15]Specifically, an OR-split can be defined in terms of an X-split, with each branch leading to a possible conjunction of all the branches of the OR-split that could occur.

Third, along the same lines, further refinements on junctions can be defined that are useful in practice. For instance, it is possible to distinguish between *synchronous* &-junctions, where all the events represented by a given split must occur simultaneously, and *asynchronous* &-junctions, where this is not required. Because these are all definable in terms of the current apparatus, it will be omitted to avoid needless complexity. (These junctions and links, and more besides, can be found in the "user-oriented" version of IDEF3 sketched in the last section of this chapter.)

Finally, it is noted that certain decisions have been made that take form in corresponding restrictions on the syntax. There is a great deal of flexibility here, and that, within limits, alternative choices and views could be embodied in alternative definitions of the syntax.

Elaboration Tables and Decompositions

This section brings together first-order syntax with graphical syntax. As noted previously, the label on a box is just an abbreviation for or terse description of (the content of) an associated elaboration. Theoretically, labels are superfluous; one could just as easily attach elaborations to boxes directly. But in practice, where one actually *uses* the 2-D graphical syntax, because there are no limits placed on the complexity of elaborations, there needs to be a more concise way of identifying the state of affairs a box represents. This is the role of the labels. The boxes in a prediagram are associated directly with elaborations via what is called here, an *elaboration table*—essentially, just a one-to-one mapping from boxes to elaborations. In practice, of course, an elaboration table might take any one of a number of forms depending on the relevant implementation of IDEF3: a pencil-and-paper implementation might use an actual written table on a separate sheet, whereas in a graphic-based computational implementation, boxes might take the form of a data structure, one of whose elements is a pointer to an associated elaboration. However it is done, the point is that both labels and elaborations will appear in any implementation of IDEF3. Therefore, because the theoretical cost of retaining labels in the theory is negligible, it is best at this point to keep the formal theory more in step with practice.

Formally then, where π is a prediagram, an *elaboration table* τ for π is a function that maps each l-box of π to an associated elaboration. This is illustrated by taking the paint/dry cycle prediagram to the next stage in the construction of a complete IDEF3 diagram. Because the details of the actual construction of a car body are being suppressed while focus is on the paint/dry cycle per se, the elaboration of the CCB box might be no more than $[i_1, \{\}, \text{Constructed}(x)]$. (The empty braces indicate that (as yet) no conditions have been placed on the temporal intervals during which the car body construction process occurs.) The EPA box's elaboration would be something like $[i_2, \{\}\{\text{On}(x \text{ CB-carrier}), \text{Enters}(x, \text{paint-area}), \text{Activates}(x, \text{paint-jets})\}]$, and that of the PCB box something like $[i_3, \{\}, \{\text{On}(x, \text{CB-carrier}), \text{Moving}(x), \text{Activated}(\text{paint-jets}), \text{Being-painted}(x)\}]$. The EDA box's elaboration, analogous to the EPA's, might be $[i_4, \{\}, \{\text{On}(x, \text{CB-carrier}), \text{Enters}(x, \text{drying-area}), \text{Activates}(x, \text{dryers})\}]$, and that of the DCB box might be $[i_5, \{20\text{-minutes}(i_5)\}, \{\text{On}(x, \text{CB-carrier}), \text{Moving}(x), \text{Activated}(\text{dryers}),$

CCB: $[t_1, \{\}, \{\text{Constructed}(x)\}]$

EPA: $[t_2, \{\}, \{\text{On}\{x, \text{CB-carrier}), \text{Enters}(x, \text{paint-area}),$
Activates(x, paint-jets)$\}]$

PCB: $[t_3, \{\}, \{\text{On}(x, \text{CB-carrier}), \text{Moving}(x),$
Activated(paint-jets), BeingPainted(x)$\}]$

EDA: $[t_4, \{\}, \{\text{On}(x, \text{CB-carrier}), \text{Enters}(x, \text{drying-area}),$
Activates(x, dryers)$\}]$

DCB: $[t_5, \{\text{20-minutes}\}, \{\text{On}(x, \text{CB-carrier}), \sim\text{Moving}(x),$
Activated(dryers), Drying(x)$\}]$

EP: $[t_6, \{\}, \{\text{On}(x, \text{CB-carrier}), \sim\text{Moving}(x),$
Activated(paint-sensors), Value-of(paint-sensors, 1)$\}]$

not-EP: $[t_6, \{\}, \{\text{On}(x, \text{CB-carrier}), \sim\text{Moving}(x),$
Activated(paint-sensors), Value-of(paint-sensors, 0)$\}]$

FIG. 7.4. Elaboration table for paint/dry cycle.

Drying$(x)\}]$; that of the EP box might be $[i_6, \{\}\{\text{ON}(x, \text{CB-carrier}), \text{Moving}(x),$
Activated(paint-sensors), Value-of(paint-sensors, 1)$\}]$, and that of the not-EP box
$[i_6, \{\}, \{\text{On}(x, \text{CB-carrier}), \text{Moving}(x), \text{Activated(paint-sensors)}, \text{Value-of(paint-}$
sensors,0)$\}]$; and as with the process prior to the paint/dry cycle, the process
that continues after the paint/dry cycle is suppressed and summarized by a single box. This possible elaboration is depicted in tabular form in Fig. 7.4.

The notion of suppressing detail in a diagram can be understood in a rigorous way in IDEF3. The box noted attached to the CCB box serves as a pointer
to another prediagram/elaboration table combination $\langle \pi', \tau' \rangle$, one which, so to
speak, turns up the power of the descriptive microscope on the CCB box and
represents its contents in greater detail. This is (roughly) what is referred to as
a *decomposition* of the CCB box. A possible decomposition prediagram for the
CCB box is pictured in Fig. 7.5.

Decompositions, along with prediagrams and elaboration tables, are the final
ingredient of full-blown IDEF3 diagrams. Informally, an IDEF3 diagram will consist of three elements: a prediagram π, an elaboration table ϵ, and a *decomposi-
tion function* δ; the diagram itself can thus be thought of as a triple $\langle \pi, \epsilon, \delta \rangle$ consisting of these elements. A decomposition function for an IDEF3 diagram is a
partial function—i.e., a function that is not necessarily defined everywhere in its
domain—on the l-boxes of π that takes each box on which it is defined to another
IDEF3 diagram.

The decomposition of any given box in a prediagram δ should not contain
that very box, or for that matter any other box in δ, or any of the boxes in *its*
decomposition (if it has one). A decomposition, after all, is a closer look at some
event within a larger process; hence it seems quite reasonable that no smaller part
of that event could contain within itself the original event, or any other part of the

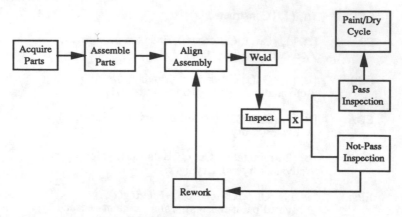

FIG. 7.5. CCB box decomposition prediagram.

larger system. This conception of processes, in fact, comports well with the way one would draw decompositions if one were using a large sheet of paper: each decomposition would consist in entirely new boxes drawn below the decomposed box of the original diagram.

At the same time, "nested" decompositions are allowed. That is, it should be possible to raise the power of the descriptive microscope even farther than at a given point in the course of description capture. Thus, boxes within decompositions themselves are allowed to admit further decomposition, and boxes within those decompositions to admit of yet further decomposition, and so on without bound.

To achieve all this in a rigorous fashion, proceed as follows. First, because the set B of boxes is infinite, we can divide it up into infinitely many mutually disjoint infinite sets B_0, B_1, and so on. (Labels, as noted, are theoretically superfluous and can be ignored in the present context.) Use the first of these sets, B_1, to define an initial, base set $diag_0$ of $basic$ IDEF3 diagrams, all of the decomposition functions of which are everywhere undefined; no box in a diagram at this stage, has a decomposition. (Recall that decomposition functions are partial, and therefore need not be everywhere, or even anywhere, defined.) At the next stage, build a new set $diag_1$ of IDEF3 diagrams out of the boxes in B_2, only now they are allowed to contain decomposition functions that take 1-boxes to diagrams in the base set $diag_0$. This will satisfy the condition that the decomposition of a given box b cannot contain b itself, or any other box b' at the same "level" as b in the diagram.

This is not quite enough, however. For, as they are defined here, boxes in IDEF3 diagrams all represent temporally nonoverlapping events, i.e., events that intuitively could have no common parts. Hence, it is also required that the decompositions of any two distinct boxes b, b' of π must not contain any common box. (In fact, IDEF3 can be generalized to allow temporal overlap, but even in this case it turns out to be most convenient still to enforce this conditions and represent even the common parts of overlapping events by distinct boxes in each decomposition.[16]

One further condition must be imposed given the distinction between closed and nonclosed prediagrams. Let π be a prediagram constructed out of boxes in B_1. Any given box b of π cannot be allowed to be mapped to just any diagram in $diag_0$. For if b is nonextensible, i.e., if b has an outgoing arrow, then it can only be mapped to a *closed* diagram.[17] The events represented by such boxes intuitively do not branch at their end but continue in a single stream. Speaking more syntactically, because a decomposition only represents a closer look at a given event, one should always be able to replace any box in a diagram with its decomposition. The only way to do so in the case of a nonextensible box is to attach its incoming arrows to the L-point of its decomposition, and its outgoing arrow to the R-point of its decomposition. This can only be done if the preceding condition is imposed.

Diagrams at successive levels $diag_n, n > 1$ are defined in just the same way. In general, that is, for $n > 0$, an nth-*level diagram*, i.e., an element of $diag_n$, is a triple $\langle \pi, \epsilon, \delta \rangle$ such that π is a prediagram whose boxes are in B_n, ϵ is an elaboration table for π, and δ is a partial function from the boxes of π to the diagrams in $diag_{n-1}$ satisfying the preceding conditions. The set of all diagrams is then defined to be the union of the $diag_m$, for $m \geq 0$. This definition thus allows for the nesting of diagrams within diagrams to any finite degree.

A couple of brief remarks are in order. First, note that the condition that the decomposition function for an nth-level diagram only take values in $diag_{n-1}$, and not $diag_m$ for all $m < n$ is not at all restrictive because each level contains a "copy" of all previous levels.[18] Thus, there is no diagramatic structure available for decomposition functions at one level that is unavailable at successive levels.

Second, the more computationally minded reader will likely have noted similarities between the structure of IDEF3 diagrams and dynamic record types in high level languages like Pascal. In addition to a variety of standard fields, such record types can contain one or more fields whose value for a given record consists of a pointer to a record of the same type. In the same way, a decomposition function for a given IDEF3 diagram (applied to a box in the diagram) points to yet other diagrams. Unlike true dynamic record types, however, the hierarchical construction rules out the possibility of diagrams that point back to themselves.

Now to make the definition entirely formal for good measure. For a given graph π constructed out of the elements of IDEF3 graphical syntax, let $boxes(\pi)$ be the set of boxes that occur in π, let $PD(\pi)$ mean that π is a prediagram, and let

---

[16]This condition streamlines the semantics considerably, because, as will be seen, the definition of realization for prediagrams in $diag_0$ serves for all prediagrams generally.

[17]Where a diagram $\langle \pi, \epsilon, \delta \rangle$ is *closed* just in case π is closed.

[18]For example, because decomposition functions are partial and each B_i is infinite, $diag_1$ contains in particular all the diagrams that can be formed from the boxes of B_1 that, like the basic diagrams, have decompositions that are undefined everywhere. There will thus be an isomorphic copy in $diag_1$ of each basic diagram in $diag_0$, and similarly for all succeeding levels.

$ET(\epsilon, \pi)$ mean that ϵ is an elaboration table for π. Where $a = \langle \pi, \epsilon, \delta \rangle$, let $(a)_1 = \pi$. Then:

$diag_0 = \{\langle \pi, \epsilon, \delta \rangle | PD(\pi) \text{ and } boxes(\pi) \subseteq B_0 \text{ and } ET(\epsilon, \pi) \text{ and } \delta = \emptyset\};$

$diag_n = \{\langle \pi, \epsilon, \delta \rangle | PD(\pi) \text{ and } boxes(\pi) \subseteq B_n \text{ and } ET(\epsilon, \pi) \text{ and } domain(\delta) \subseteq boxes(\pi)$

and $range(\delta)$

$\subseteq diag_{n-1}$ and $\forall x \in domain(\delta),$ if $not-EXTENSIBLE(x),$ then $CLOSED(\delta(x)),$

and $\forall x, y$

$\in domain(\delta), boxes((\delta(x))_1) \cap boxes((\delta(y))_1) = \emptyset\},$ for $n > 0;$

$diag = \bigcup_{m \geq 0} diag_m.$

7.5 IDEF3 SEMANTICS

Now a semantics for IDEF3 graphs needs to be given that will hook them up with all the more standard first-order apparatus that have been developed here. Intuitively, an l-box in a diagram represents a (or a part of a) process that is described by the associated elaboration $E = [i, \{\psi_1, \ldots, \psi_m\}, \{\varphi_1, \ldots, \varphi_n\}]$. An *instance* of that process will exist if during the temporal interval represented by i (i.e., if at the value of i under some assignment) all the sentences ψ_i, φ_j are true. As noted already, the use of variables is crucial to this idea, because object variables can have different objects assigned to them as values, and temporal interval variables different temporal intervals. This allows instantiation of the same elaboration in many different ways, thus capturing the different ways in which a general process might be realized.

Realizations

Instantiation Graphs

Interpretations provide mathematical models of the general structure of a described process. Interpretations together with variable assignments enable one to model, or *realize*, specific instances of the general process.

To fix a given IDEF3 diagram $\langle \pi, \epsilon, \delta \rangle$ written in some language L: For any l-box $b \in boxes(\pi)$, let $\epsilon(b)$ be the elaboration associated with b by the elaboration table ϵ. Given an interpretation I for L, an L-I-assignment α can be said to *realize* the l-box b just in case it realizes $\epsilon(b)$.

Now, with every prediagram π can be associated a set (generally infinite) of associated graphs which characterize the possible ways in which the system the prediagram describes can be instantiated. Thus, these associated graphs are called *instantiation graphs* for π. If π has no cycles (i.e., no paths that begin and end at the same node), then its instantiation graph (there is only one in this case, up to isomorphism) is especially easy to characterize, because it will look just like π itself except with its junctions removed. That is, roughly, form the instantiation graph for π by beginning, first, with the L-point of π, and then, tracing down from the L-point, add as nodes all the l-box "children" of any &-junction one comes to, and only one of the l-box children of any X-junction one comes to until one cannot continue. The procedure for generating instantiation graphs from prediagrams π with cycles is similar, only one must in addition allow an instantiation graph to "unfold" the cycles some finite number of times (if possible–some legitimate prediagrams with unconditional cycles have only infinite instantiation graphs).

It might be wondered why junctions are removed from instantiation graphs. The reason is that junctions are needed primarily because of the two ways in which a process might split that are recognized in IDEF3—conjunctive splits and exclusive disjunction splits. If there were only one sort, then multiple arrows could come straight out of an l-box. In an actual process *instance* there is, in fact, only the first sort of splitting; where a diagram has an X-split, representing possible continuations of the process represented by the diagram, any corresponding instance of the process goes either one way or the other; there is no actual disjunctive splitting at the instance level. The splitting is only at the type level. Thus, in an instantiation graph, because there is only one kind of splitting—where the process flow diverges into several streams—junctions are superfluous.[19]

Despite the simplicity of these ideas, it takes a little work to give them formal expression. To begin, let $\Delta = \langle \pi, \epsilon, \delta \rangle$ be an IDEF3 diagram, and let $\Gamma = \langle V, A \rangle$ be a graph such that all the vertices $x \in V$ are of the form $\langle a, n \rangle$, where a is a node of π, and n is a natural number greater than 0. As usual, A—the set of edges, or arcs, of the graph—is a set of pairs of members of V (hence a set of pairs of the form $\langle \langle a, n \rangle, \langle b, m \rangle \rangle$; intuitively, each pair represents an arc from the first member to the second). If a and b are nodes of π, then b is a *successor* of a (in π), and a is a *predecessor* of b, if there is an arc from a to b in π.

Now, say that Γ is π-*generated* iff, first, $\langle a, 1 \rangle \in V$ iff a is the L-point of π, and for

---

[19]There is a further reason for retaining &-junctions. The syntactic rules allow *nested* &-junctions (and X-junctions), i.e., junctions that are successors of other junctions. In these cases &-junctions can serve as grouping delimiters that might well put constraints on the relations between events that instantiate a diagram. For example, one might want to distinguish two cases where three events branch off from a given event: on the one hand, one might want to allow the three to begin at any three times after the given event; on the other hand, one might want to group two of the events and constrain matters such that the two must begin either before or after the third, and therefore they cannot "sandwich" the third temporally. The most natural way to group the two with this syntax would be to represent them as a small closed split whose L-point is, along with a box representing the third event, an immediate successor of another &-junction. But then, if junctions are eliminated in instantiation graphs, it seems that this grouping information would be lost.

However, as already noted, the syntax of IDEF3 allows one to put additional constraints on temporal intervals other than the intervals represented by the dominant temporal interval of an elaboration. The chief reason for allowing this is to put constraints on the temporal intervals associated with the distinct branches of branching processes. Thus, one can simply transfer the grouping information carried by the nested &-junctions explicitly into the elaborations in terms of the appropriate conditions. (Note how this capability is captured in the semantics in Clause 4 of the definition of realization for instantiation graphs given in the next section.)

all nodes a of π and all natural numbers n, if $\langle a, n \rangle \in V$ and a has any successors, then

(1) If a has a unique successor b, then
    (a) If b is a box, or the L-point of a split, or the R-point of a closed X-split, then $b \in A_{n+1}$ and $\langle\langle a, n \rangle, \langle b, n+1 \rangle\rangle \in A$;
    (b) If b is the R-point of a closed &-split, then $(i)\langle b, n+j \rangle \in V$, where j is the least number such that for each of b's predecessors $c, \langle c, i \rangle \in V$, where $m < i < n + j$, where m is the largest number $< n$ such that $\langle b', m \rangle \in V$, where b' is b's L-counterpart, and $(ii)\langle\langle a, n \rangle, \langle b, n+j \rangle\rangle \in A$.
(2) If a does not have a unique successor, then
    (a) If a is the L-point of an &-split, then all of a's successors are in A_{n+1}, and for each such successor $b, \langle a, n \rangle, \langle b, n+1 \rangle\rangle \in A$;
    (b) If a is the L-point of an X-split, then exactly one of a's successors b is in A_{n+1}, and $\langle\langle a, n \rangle, \langle b, n+1 \rangle\rangle \in A$.

Intuitively, if a is not a junction, a vertex $\langle a, n \rangle$ in a π-generated graph represents an occurrence of an instance of the event represented by a in the prediagram π at a certain stage in a run of the system represented by the entire prediagram. The need for indexing a with a number n arises from the possibility of cycles in the system—different indices paired with the same box a represent different instances of the same event. The rather complex 1(b) in particular ensures that the R-point of a closed split is assigned the right index relative to its predecessors for a given possible run of the system.

These ideas are illustrated in Fig. 7.6, which shows a prediagram π and an associated π-generated graph. For formal purposes, labels are ignored by simply tagging the boxes of the prediagram directly (in a full-fledged prediagram, of course, a_2, a_4, and a_8 would all have to be junctions). Note that π contains a cyclic X-split down one path of an &-split. This allows for indeterminate cycling from instances of box a_3 to instances of box a_6 and back again. The π-generated graph represents a process instance in which there is just one such cycle before the process flows from (an instance of) a_3 to a_7, and finally to a_{11}. Note that the two traversals of a_3 are distinguished by two different indices, 3 and 6 respectively.

Now, the prediagram intuitively requires that instances down each path be complete before there can be an instance of a_{11}. This means that one needs to have arcs running from the "last" event down each branch to the same instance of a_{11}, in this case represented by $\langle a_{11}, 11 \rangle$. So $\langle a_{10}, 4 \rangle$ has to "wait" until the upper branch is completed before being connected to the close of the split a_8; one cannot index a_8 with the number 5 and define an arc from $\langle a_{10}, 4 \rangle$ to $\langle a_8, 5 \rangle$, because $\langle a_8, 5 \rangle$ would indicate a different point in time than does $\langle a_8, 11 \rangle$. This is ensured by 1(b). To see this, let $\langle a, n \rangle$ in the definition be $\langle a_{10}, 4 \rangle$, and let b be a_8 (the R-point of the preceding closed &-split; then the definition requires that for each of a_8's predecessors c—in this case only a_7 is relevant—if $\langle c, i \rangle$ is a node—in this case $\langle a_7, 9 \rangle$—then where j is the least number such that when added to n the sum is greater than any such i (so j is 6 in our example) $\langle a_8, 4 + 6 \rangle$, i.e., $\langle a_8, 10 \rangle$ must be a vertex of the π-generated graph, and there must be an arc from $\langle a_{10}, 4 \rangle$ to

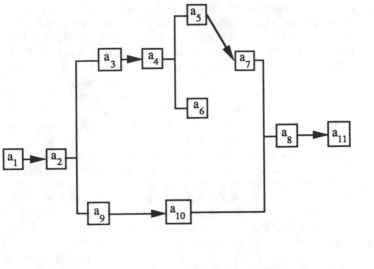

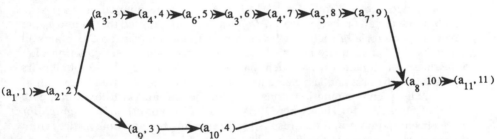

FIG. 7.6. Prediagram μ with π-generated graph.

$\langle a_8, 10 \rangle$. The number m in the definition (which is the number 2 here and plays no significant role) ensures in general that one is dealing with instances within the same subprocess represented by the entire closed split, because they too can be traversed more than once in a given large process. Such multiple traversals would be indicated by different indexed occurrences of a_2. The role of m is to ensure that one is always dealing with instances of events within an instance of the split that have occurred since the most recent traversal of a_2.

A π-generated graph $\Gamma = \langle V, A \rangle$ is said to be π-*admissible* iff it has no proper π-generated subgraph.[20] The reason for this definition stems from the fact that nothing in the idea of a π-generated graph rules out the possibility of all sorts of extra "junk" getting thrown into the nodes or arcs of such a graph over and above what is sanctioned by the definition alone. For instance, the sorts of graphs discussed here are *simple*, i.e., they have at most one arc between any two given

[20]Where a graph $\Gamma' = \langle V', A' \rangle$ is a *subgraph* of a graph $\Gamma = \langle V, A \rangle$ iff V' V and A' A. Γ' is a *proper* subgraph of Γ if it is a subgraph and either $N' \neq V$ or $A' \neq A$.

nodes; but, e.g., an extraneous arc can be added between any two nodes of a π-generated graph and the result will still be a π-generated graph. For the definition only tells what must be present in such a graph, not what must *not* be present. Thus, such graphs at a given stage n do not necessarily represent the state of a given run of the system being represented by π at that point. Such unintended graphs are thus filtered out of consideration by focusing on only the "smallest" graphs that satisfy the definition, hence those with no extraneous nodes or arcs. The π-generated graph of Fig. 7.6 is also π-admissible; it could be transformed simply into an inadmissible graph by, say, adding a new unconnected node $\langle a_3, 17 \rangle$ to the set of vertices.

Given a π-admissible graph $\langle V, A \rangle$, the final task is to eliminate all the junctions from V and revise A in the obvious way to obtain the graph $\langle V^*, A^* \rangle$. That is, in the simplest case, where a and c are boxes of π and b is a junction, if $\langle\langle a,n \rangle,\langle b,m \rangle\rangle,\langle\langle b,m \rangle,\langle c,m+1 \rangle\rangle \in A$ (that is, if there is an arc from $\langle a,n \rangle$ to $\langle b,m \rangle$ and from $\langle b,m \rangle$ to $\langle c,m+1 \rangle$), then b and the preceding arcs are removed from V and A, respectively, and a new arc is defined from $\langle a,n \rangle$ to $\langle c,m+1 \rangle$, i.e., we add the arc $\langle\langle a,n \rangle,\langle c,m+1 \rangle\rangle$ to A^*.

More formally, then let $\Gamma = \langle V, A \rangle$ be a π-admissible graph. Let V^* be $V - \{\langle a,n \rangle \in V \mid a$ is a junction of $\pi\}$, and let A' be $A - \{r \in A \mid r$ contains a junction of $\pi\}$. Now, let S be the set of all paths $\langle\langle a_1, n_1 \rangle, \ldots, \langle a_m, n_m \rangle\rangle$ of $\Gamma, m > 2$, such that a_1 and a_m are boxes of π, and for all i such that $1 < i < m, a_i$ is a junction of π. So S contains all the paths of Γ between two boxes whose intervening nodes are all junctions. Let S' be the set of all pairs $\langle a_1, a_m \rangle$ such that $\langle a_1, \ldots, a_m \rangle \in S$, i.e., the set of all pairs consisting of the first and last elements of some path in S; S' is thus the result of deleting all the intervening junctions between the first and last boxes in a path in S. Let A^* be $A' \cup S'$. Then where Γ^* is $\langle V^*, A^* \rangle$, Γ^* is an *instantiation graph* for π. The instantiation graph that results from removing the junction vertices from the π-generated graph of Fig. 7.6 is illustrated in Fig. 7.7.

Realization for Instantiation Graphs

This section describes the realization of an instantiation graph by a class of associated assignment functions (in a given interpretation). A correlation is set up

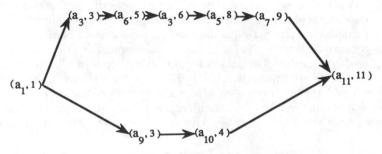

FIG. 7.7. Instantiation graph resulting from π-generated graph of Fig. 7.6.

between each node of an instantiation graph and an associated assignment function for the elaboration associated with that node. In order for the assignment functions as a whole to realize the graph, they have to interpret it jointly in such a way as to represent a given run of the system; e.g., they have to map adjacent vertices to adjacent temporal intervals and interpret identical variables in the corresponding elaboration tables of adjacent vertices by means of the same objects to capture object flow through the system, and so on.

The apparatus is straightforward, but a bit involved. First, the relevant syntactic apparatus is set up. Let L be a first-order language of the sort previously defined, $\Delta = \langle \pi, \epsilon, \delta \rangle$ be an IDEF3 diagram whose language for its elaborations is L, and let $\Gamma = \langle V, A \rangle$ be an instantiation graph for Δ. For a given box a, of π, let i_a be the dominant temporal variable of the elaboration $\epsilon(a)$ associated with a. It will be assumed for ease of exposition that $\epsilon(a)$ contains no quantified formulas for every box a of π.

Thus, for the corresponding semantic apparatus, let I be an interpretation for L, and let F be a mapping of the vertices in V to assignment functions such that for all $\langle a, n \rangle \in V, F(\langle a, n \rangle)$ is defined on *only* the variables in $\epsilon(a)$.[21] α_n^a represents the assignment $F(\langle a, n \rangle)$. For any such assignments α, α', "$\alpha \sim \alpha'$" is defined to mean that α and α' agree on all the variables on which they are both defined.

Given all this, it can be said that F *realizes* Γ just in case, for all $\langle\langle a, n \rangle, \langle b, m \rangle\rangle \in A$,

(1) α_n^a realizes $\epsilon(a)$ and α_m^b realizes $\epsilon(b)$;
(2) $\alpha_n^a \sim \alpha_m^b$;
(3) If $\langle b, m \rangle$ is $\langle a, n \rangle$'s only successor and $\langle a, n \rangle$ is $\langle b, m \rangle$'s only predecessor, then $\alpha_n^a(i_a)$ meets $\alpha_m^b(i_b)$;[22]
(4) If $\langle a, n \rangle$ has more than one successor, then (a) for all its successors $\langle c, l \rangle, \langle c', l' \rangle, \alpha_l^c \sim \alpha_{l'}^{c'}$, (b) there is one successor $\langle c, l \rangle$ such that α_n^a (ia) meets $\alpha_l^c(i_c)$, and (c) for all remaining successor's $\langle c', l' \rangle, \alpha_n^a(i_a)$ meets or precedes $\alpha_{l'}^{c'}(i_{c'})$;
(5) If $\langle a, n \rangle$ has more than one predecessor, then (a) for all its predecessors $\langle c, l \rangle, \langle c', l' \rangle, \alpha_l^c \sim \alpha_{l'}^{c'}$, (b) there is one predecessor $\langle c, l \rangle$ such that $\alpha^c l(i_c)$ meets $\alpha_n^a(i_a)$, and (c) for all remaining predecessor's $\langle c', l' \rangle, \alpha_{l'}^{c'}(i_{c'})$ meets or precedes $\alpha_n^a(i_a)$.

Condition (1) is an obvious enough requirement; for F to realize Γ, the assignment it associates with each vertex must realize the corresponding elaboration. The reason behind (2) relates back to object flow. As noted, the same free variable occurring in the elaborations of connected boxes represents the flow of a single object from one event to another. Thus, it is required that for F to realize an instantiation graph, assignments for adjacent vertices must agree on

---

[21] It is not only more convenient to use such "partial" assignments, but it also corresponds more closely to the way in which assignments would be implemented in a computational tool. In a more detailed treatment, the notion of a partial assignment would be defined more explicitly.

[22] Where, recall, an interval T meets another τ' iff the end point of T is the beginning point of τ'.

the free variables common to the boxes in those vertices. This is just what (2) requires.

Condition (3) captures the idea that boxes connected by an arrow represent temporally contiguous events within a larger process. This is a rather stringent requirement adopted primarily for ease of exposition. In fact, the apparatus can be generalized to allow virtually any temporal relation to obtain between any two given boxes. Temporal contiguity serves here only as a convenient default.

Similar remarks apply to (4). Splitting in an instantiation graph represents the branching of a process into several parallel subprocesses. Chosen as a default semantics is that the event represented by the vertex that splits meet at least one of the branches, and that it meet or precede all the others. This is captured by 4(b) and 4(c). 4(a) places the additional requirement that any two of the assignments associated by F with the successors of the branching vertex agree on free variables on which they are both defined. This permits placement of additional temporal constraints on the intervals occupied by the branches of branching processes, e.g., that one of the branches precede another, that two begin together and precede a third, and so on.

Condition (5) is essentially the "dual" of (4) for the "back end" of a splitting process that eventually converges.

It can be said that I realizes a basic IDEF3 diagram[23] $\langle \pi, \epsilon, \delta \rangle$ iff, for any assignment function α on the variables of the elaboration $\epsilon(p)$ of the L-point p of π that realizes $\epsilon(p)$, there is an instantiation graph Γ and a mapping F from the vertices of Γ onto assignment functions such that (a) $F(p,1) = \alpha$, and (b) F realizes Γ. (Intuitively, this captures the idea that anytime the initial process of a system occurs, the entire system will be instantiated in some way.) Although details are avoided here, it should be quite clear that any nonbasic IDEF3 diagram Δ can in principle be "expanded" to a basic diagram Δ'—called its *basic expansion*—that explicitly includes all of Δ's nested decompositions.[24] I *realizes* an IDEF3 diagram Δ generally just in case it realizes its basic expansion.

7.6 OVERVIEW OF USER ORIENTED IDEF3

The bulk of this chapter is devoted to establishing the theoretical foundations of IDEF3. Those foundations, however, are rather austere and unfriendly from a practical point of view. The intention, however, is that IDEF3 be a usable and useful method, and it should not be the case that one has to *master* its theoretical foundations in order to *use* it in designing and modeling activities, any more than an engineer should have to master the theoretical foundations of analysis in order to use the calculus to build a bridge. Therefore this section suggests a way in which the formal methodology can be enhanced and enlarged by certain constructs which, although not explicit in the formal foundations proper, nonetheless are *definable* in terms of the basic apparatus (or in terms of straight-

---

[23]That is, recall, a diagram with no decompositions.

[24]That is, all the decompositions of the boxes in Δ's prediagram, all the decompositions of the boxes in those decompositions, and so on.

forward extensions of the apparatus), and hence possess (or can easily possess) a well-defined semantics. This follows common mathematical practice. Often, it is easiest to work out the foundations of a given mathematical theory, to strip it down to its barest and most abstract form in order to have the fewest number of concepts to deal with. After those foundations are well established and one wishes to *use* the theory, one is able in full confidence freely to introduce new concepts in terms of the old.

Thus, this section provides a sketch of a user-oriented version of IDEF3, which is called IDEF3*. The idea is to provide a flexible mechanism for capturing descriptions precedence and causality relations between situations and events in a form that is natural to the domain experts in an environment. The trick is to provide an organizing language framework that does not impose a particular set of process modeling idealizations. IDEF3* differs from formal IDEF3 as described in the previous sections in that it contains a number of shortcuts for describing commonly occurring description structures that would be awkward to describe in the formal language proper (e.g., inclusive OR junctions and relational links). It also contains forms for the capture and organization of the process elaboration descriptions to avoid the first-order predicate syntax which many domain users find intimidating. It is important to note, however, that all the constructs of this section are capable of being defined in terms of either the basic apparatus, or straightforward extensions thereof, so that no syntactic construct is introduced here that does not have a well-defined semantics.[25]

The following subsections describe the basic language elements of IDEF3*. Combinations of these language elements are used to form descriptions of the domain. The IDEF3* language is a graphical language, using the familiar box-link network as its basic stucture. A process description captures a network of relations between UOBs (units of behavior) in a specified scenario. The basic symbol set of the IDEF3* process model is displayed in Fig. 7.8.

Scenarios

The basic organizing structure provided to the domain user in the IDEF3* method process flow descriptions is the concept of a scenario, which provides both focus and boundaries for a process description. Conceptually, a *scenario* is

---

[25] IDEF3* is currently in use by engineering and manufacturing domain experts to express the normal content of a common sense process descriptions primarily in support of integrated information system developments. It is also being employed as the method for describing system development frameworks (Zachman, 1986) in a form that can serve as a process schema in an ISO Conceptual Schema information integration architecture. Finally, it has proven useful for design of man–machine interaction scenarios (Blinn et al., 1989). An automated tool has been constructed that supports the creation, storage, and manipulation of IDEF3* process descriptions (Mayer et al., 1990). Research is ongoing in the use of process descriptions as the basis for automated simulation model design (Mayer, 1988; Lin, 1990).

UOB Box

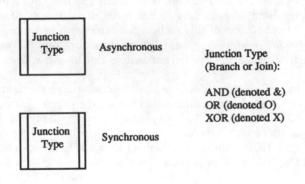

Function	Process
Activity	Operation
Action	Event

Junction Boxes

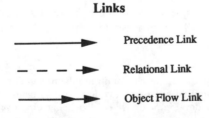

Asynchronous

Synchronous

Junction Type
(Branch or Join):

AND (denoted &)
OR (denoted O)
XOR (denoted X)

Links

→ Precedence Link

- - - → Relational Link

⟹ Object Flow Link

FIG. 7.8. IDEF3* symbol set.

simply a typical problem-solving activity or recurring situation.[26] The following are examples of typical process flow scenarios:

(1) Develop Die Design for Side Aparture Panel
(2) Process Customer Complaint
(3) Process Engineering Change Request

The method recommends that a scenario name be an action verb or phrase. It should be specific enough to allow the readers to make judgments about the appropriateness of the contents of the process description. The role of a scenario is to establish an initial context for the process description.[27] It also forms a top level abstraction for the process description. That is, any UOB can be considered to be the "scenario" for UOB networks that reference it as their context.

Units of Behavior

In capturing a description of "what's going on" within an organization or any complex system, there are a number of "language primitives" that must be accounted for, including function, activity, action, act, process, operation, event, scenario, decision, and procedure. Each of these terms is used in common language to describe "states of affairs" and changes in the world around us. In IDEF3*, a choice had to be made about which of these objects would be explicitly represented. During the design of IDEF3, it was noted that each of these terms refers to some "circumscribed" behavior. That is, when someone refers to the "Planning activity" or "Make/Buy decision" or the "Contract award event," that person is carving up the world around us into chunks of time (and generally space as well) to allow the description of "whats going on" in that chunk separate from the rest of the world. Therefore, in IDEF3* a decision was made to provide a generic unit of behavior concept which can be used to represent any of the previously listed states of affairs or states of change. Whether a unit of behavior is classified as an "event," a "process," a "function," and so on, is left to the analysis of the description of that UOB and the structure surrounding it.

Each UOB in an IDEF3* process flow description is denoted by a box. The label inside the box is the *display name* of the UOB. Associated with the UOB is a unique "name," which is formed out of a verb or verb phrase.[28] Each UOB can have associated with it both a description in terms of other UOBs and a description in terms of a set of participating objects and their relations. The former is referred to as a *Decomposition* of a UOB and the latter as an *elaboration* of a UOB. These, of course, are the IDEF3* correlates of the formal notions just defined.

An IDEF3* description of a scenario consists of a set of UOBs and constraints (special relations) among the UOBs. Because IDEF3* provides a "description" of

---

[26]Scenarios may often be taken directly from activities in a corresponding IDEF0 model (if one exists).

[27]In this respect it is similar to the "Context" statement of an IDEF0 model except that multiple scenarios can be part of a process description.

[28]Just as in IDEF0.

an organization or system it must be "partial." That is to say, no claim is made by the modeler about the "completeness" of the description. What claim is made is that the description that is provided is "factual" (i.e., the objects and relations described in the individual UOBs do in fact exist in the real world and stand in the prescribed relations.) This is in contrast to other types of methods (e.g., IDEF2, Petrie nets, and IDEF0) where the models represent an "idealization" of the real world and are assumed to be complete. Furthermore, in IDEF3*, a UOB can have many decompositions.[29] This allows for the capture of different "perspectives" of "whats going on" in the UOB itself. These perspectives are referred to as *views*. Multiple views of a given scenario are illustrated in Fig. 7.9.

Elaboration Language

A UOB elaboration is expressed in the IDEF3* elaboration language. One of the features of this language is that it supports the naming or description of specific objects, places, times, and relations as well as the naming or description of indeterminate objects, places, times, and relations.[30] This is a consequence of the fact that descriptions of how things work include both specific information about particular objects, and also general descriptions about what happens to arbitrary objects at arbitrary times within a system. Each object can be tagged as an *agent* if that object is considered to be an active causal agent in the UOB. Similarly, an object can be tagged as *affected* if the relations to that object are created or changed by/during the UBO. Again, an object can be tagged as a *participant* if no causality or transformation is associated with that object as a part of the UOB description. Finally, an object may be tagged as *created* or *destroyed* by a particular UOB. These classifications are optional. However, if supplied, they allow automated analysis as described in a later section of this document.

The first level IDEF3* elaboration language is intended to be captured on an elaboration form. An *elaboration form* captures the information of the sort just described from the area expert in structured natural language textual descriptions and presents this information in a structured manner. This elaboration form includes (1) an object list, (2) a fact list, and (3) a constraint list. Through the use of reference pointers, additional forms of elaboration information may be attached to a UOB.

Link Types

In IDEF3*, links are used to denote distinguished relations between UOBs. The elaboration language within IDEF3* provides a mechanism for describing virtu-

[29]This is a point at which IDEF3* goes beyond what is explicitly definable in IDEF3, which as it stands allows for only a single decomposition for each box, i.e., each "UOB". The theory is easily extended to accommodate multiple decompositions.

[30]This allows the IDEF3* modeler to easily describe both specific UOBs and also UOB types. A UOB type is defined as any UOB whose elaboration contains an indeterminate. It should be noted that in practice most of the UOBs contained within a model will be UOB types rather than specific UOBs.

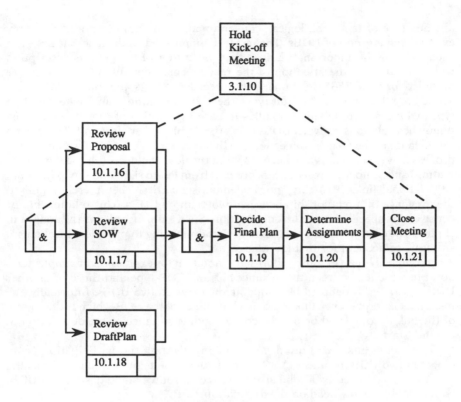

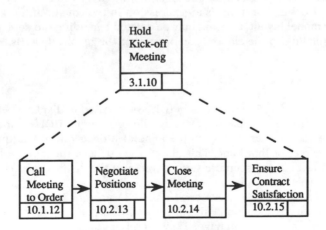

Fig. 7.9. Multiple decompositions.

ally any type of temporal, logical, conventional, or natural constraint that may exist among a group of UOBs. The term "distinguished" indicates that links are used to highlight important relations that the author of the process description wishes to draw to the attention of the reader. Three default types of links are provided for in IDEF3*, relational links, precedence links, and object flow links. These are referred to as "default types" because the author can create new link types with his own default semantics to ease the display of the particular distinguished relations between UOBs that arise in his or her situation. There is no significance to the area of connection of a link to a box or junction. By convention, process flow descriptions are laid out so that the flow of objects (physical or information) and temporal precedence is ordered from left to right and top to bottom.

Relational links (RL) carry no predefined semantics. They merely highlight the existence of a relationship between two or more UOBs. This relationship or constraint is specified in the link description. Such a link use allows the analyst to capture knowledge about a relationship without having to provide a mechanism structure to account for that knowledge.

Precedence links (PL) are a short-hand notation for expression of simple, temporal precedence between the instances of one UOB type and those of another UOB type. A PL is denoted by a solid arrow between two UOBs. Informally, the meaning of a precedence link is that each instance of the UOB which is the source of the link is completed before the corresponding instance of the destination of the link starts.

Object flow links (OL) are a means of highlighting the participation of an object in two UOB instances. An OL carries the same temporal semantics as the PL. An OL is denoted by a solid arrow between a source and a destination UOB, with a double arrow head on the destination UOB.

Each link type has a unique label in a model, as well as an elaboration which (like a UOB elaboration) is an expression in the constraint language. For clarity in the model layout, any link may be deleted by adding the description associated with the link to the elaboration of each of the involved UOBs.

Junctions

As in formal IDEF3, junctions in IDEF3* are used to display special types of constraints on the possible sequencing relations among UOBs. Junctions in IDEF3* can be used to describe both the logic of a decision making procedure as well as the effect of that logic. This allows the effect of the logic to be displayed at a higher level in the scenario description and the detailed description of the logic to be relegated to a lower level decomposition.

Also as in IDEF3, junctions in IDEF3* are not UOBs; they do not have an elaboration or a decomposition. In fact, it is perhaps best to consider them as macros of the link language. They merely allow commonly used constraints to be expressed quickly and concisely.[31]

---

[31] This remark corresponds to the fact in IDEF3 that the temporal information carried by the arrows in an IDEF3 diagram could in principle be imported into the temporal conditions within elaborations.

There are three major types of junctions in IDEF3*: AND, OR and XOR. These junction types come in both a synchronous and asynchronous interpretation. There is also a different interpretation for the use of junctions to initiate a branching, and junctions used to terminate a number of links (fan-out interpretation versus fan-in interpretation). Finally, there are special interpretations for the use of combinations of junctions (e.g., a branching that begins with an AND junction and ends with an OR junction.) A complete description of the types of structures that can be formed with these junctions is beyond the scope of this chapter. Interested readers are referred to Mayer *et al.* (1989) for a complete description of the IDEF3* methodology.

7.7 CONCLUSION

In this chapter an overview of some of the issues of process description has been given along with a proposal for a formal methodology—IDEF3—for capturing such descriptions. A less formal version of the methodology, IDEF3*, which is aimed at the real-world user has also been presented. Many research issues still remain in regard to the syntactic and semantic representation of process descriptions. Of particular importance are those surrounding the continuity of time and change. The preceding discussion should serve as a promising foundation for this research.

ACKNOWLEDGMENT

Funding for this project was provided by the Air Force Human Resources Laboratory, Logistics and Human Factors division (AFHRL/LR), Wright-Patterson AFB, Ohio. We are in particular deeply indebted to Captain Mike Painter for his dedication, enthusiasm, and support. Our thanks also go to Tim Ramey for his support and his insight into the process of process modeling. The authors wish to note that IDEF3 has undergone significant development in the time since this paper was submitted. Although the general shape of the method remains the same, many elements of the formalization have changed. Most notably, the formal foundations are now based more overtly on situation theory.

REFERENCES

Barwise, J. 1989. *The Situation in Logic*. Stanford: Center for the Study of Language and Information.

Barwise, J., and Perry, J. 1983. *Situations and Attitudes*. Cambridge, Massachusetts: MIT Press/Bradford Books.

Blinn, T., Mayer, R., Bodemiller, C., and Cook, S. 1989. Automated IDEF3 and IDEF4 system design specification. Interim Technical Report, Contract No. 055, NASA Cooperative Agreement No. NCC9-16, Project No. IM.15, NASA RICIS Program, University of Houston, Clear Lake, Texas.

Chellas, B. 1980. *Modal Logic: An Introduction*. Cambridge: Cambridge University Press.

Corynen, G. C. 1975. A mathematical theory of modeling and simulation. Ph.D. dissertation, Department of Engineering and System Science, University of Michigan.

Curry, G., Deuermayer, B., and Feldman, R. 1989. *Discrete Simulation: Fundamentals and Microcomputer Support*. Oakland: Holden-Day.

Frost, R. 1986. *Introduction to Knowledge Base Systems*. New York: McGraw-Hill.

Gallaire, H., and Minker, J. 1978. *Logic and Databases*. New York: Plenum Press.

Hughes, G. E., and Cresswell, M. J. 1968. *An Introduction to Modal Logic*. London: Methuen and Co.

Jacobs, B. E. 1982. On database logic. *Journal of the Association for Computing Machinery* 29: 310–332.

Kripke, S. 1963. Semantical considerations on modal logic. *Acta Philosophica Fennica* 16: 83–94.

Lin, M. 1990. Automated simulation model design from a situation theory based manufacturing system description. Ph.D. dissertation, Department of Industrial Engineering, Texas A&M University.

Mayer R. 1988. Cognitive skills in modeling and simulation. Ph.D. dissertation, Department of Industrial Engineering, Texas A&M University.

Mayer, R., Menzel, C., and Mayer, P. 1989. IDEF3 technical reference report. IISEE Program Interim Technical Report, AFHRL/LRL, Wright-Patterson Air Force Base, Ohio.

Mayer, R., Blinn, T., Cook, S., and Bodemiller, C. 1990. Automated support tool for IDEF3 and IDEF4. Final Technical Report, Contract No. 055, NASA Cooperative Agreement No. NCC9-16, Project No. IM.15, NASA RICIS Program, University of Houston, Clear Lake, Texas.

Prior, A. 1957. *Time and Modality*. Oxford: Oxford University Press.

Schwartz, S. 1977. *Naming, Necessity, and Natural Kinds*. Ithaca, New York: Cornell University Press.

Vendler, Z. 1967. *Linguistics in Philosophy*. Ithaca, New York: Cornell University Press.

Vendler, Z. 1968. *Adjectives and Nominalizations*. The Hague: Mouton.

Zachman, J. 1986. A framework for information systems architecture. Report No. G30-2785, IBM Los Angeles Scientific Center, California.

Chapter 8

Manufacturing Feature Identification for Intelligent Design

Alice E. Smith
Department of Industrial Engineering
University of Pittsburgh
Pittsburgh, Pennsylvania

Cihan H. Dagli
Department of Engineering Management
University of Missouri-Rolla
Rolla, Missouri

8.1 OVERVIEW

Design is the first and most influential manufacturing activity. It is also the most creative and least structured. Design relies greatly on the designer's expertise, judgment, and use of heuristics. Recent developments in computer-aided design (CAD) have improved the speed and quality of design; however, intelligent techniques can further assist the process. Knowledge-based systems are built to contain human reasoning ability so that investigations and decisions are made in an efficient, comprehensive, and standardized way. Knowledge-based systems can be used in manufacturing design to replicate human abilities to assemble, manipulate, and specify features in an acceptable, and even creative, design. Artificial neural networks are excellent pattern classification techniques when dealing with noisy and complex data. They adapt well to new and changed data. Neural networks offer assistance with feature identification tasks by classifying low-level features, or their components, for use by higher-level methods (e.g., knowledge-based systems or human designers) to manipulate and combine. The objective in using intelligent computing for design is to consistently and efficiently develop product designs that are robust during manufacture. The design should also result in functionally adequate, quality products that are economical to manufacture.

This chapter starts with an overview of design in a manufacturing context and with an explanation of why features are the fundamental building blocks of design. There are serious limitations to expert systems for feature identification, and these introduce the need for neural network pattern recognition. Various artificial neural network paradigms are described here, with emphasis on the multilayered perceptrons trained with backpropagation. Previous work describing and building neural network based feature design systems will be discussed. Finally, the current problems with neural networks are presented along with the outlook for composite intelligent systems.

This chapter uses the terms *expert system* and *knowledge-based system* interchangeably although, strictly speaking, the latter is more descriptive. Design systems are based on knowledge from different sources, and do not generally replicate one expert. The terminology used for neural networks is common although other names do exist (e.g., *neurons* can be called *processing units*).

8.2 INTRODUCTION TO THE DESIGN PROCESS

The design process begins the manufacturing life cycle by specifying shapes, dimensions, materials, tolerances, performance and assemblies of products, and parts and mechanisms. After design, process planning, production, quality control, distribution, and service take place. Design is important for these downstream activities. It affects process planning, i.e., the choice of manufacturing methods, tools, routing, and sequencing. Design impacts the inventory and supplier process by specifying parts and materials. It affects the manufacturability of the product, which has a direct bearing on the unit cost and quality of the end product. It also determines, in part, the product functionality and durability, which can have ultimate effects on marketing, sales, and profitability. The final impact of design ranges from 65% to 75% of total manufactured cost (Khoshnevis and Park, 1988; Suri and Shimizu, 1989; Swift, 1987). Design seeks to balance cost efficiency and manufacturability with quality and functionality, and therefore must satisfy many, sometimes conflicting, constraints.

When viewing the design function, three classes emerge (Brown and Chandrasekaran, 1988; see Ch. 4, secton 4.3 for more detail about classification). Class 1 design is innovative, breaking barriers to develop a new product or process. Class 2 involves new techniques or requirements for known products or problems. Class 3 selects previously known alternatives—it is still complex because there are many components and numerous combinations. Present intelligent systems are best capable of addressing class 3 design efforts because they are not sophisticated enough to create new and innovative design solutions.

Design tasks are normally done in a linear sequence beginning with fundamental shapes and components, and refining these until the desired part is reached. Generic steps are (1) identify needs, (2) set strategies, (3) establish design concept, (4) select feasible alternatives, (5) select and specify parameters, and (6) evaluate and implement (Suri and Shimizu, 1989). Design must specify these aspects of each part:

- Shapes
- Dimensions
- Materials

- Tolerances
- Static and kinetic interactions
- Assemblies

CAD systems support engineering functions such as mass properties calculations, interference checking, and geometry definitions for finite elements, drafting, and numerical control, but considerable human interaction is still needed for successful design (Shah and Rogers, 1988). This is because CAD systems fall short in two important areas of design: feature identification and synthesis, and creativity and heuristic use. Intelligent systems can replicate some of the human abilities of recognition and reasoning needed in these two areas, especially for class 3 designs which do not require creativity or innovation.

8.3 IMPORTANCE OF FEATURES

Mechanized systems addressing design, such as CAD solid modelers, are based on features. *Features* are primitive or low-level designs, with their attributes, qualifiers, and restrictions, that affect functionality and manufacturability. Features can describe form (size and shape), precision (tolerances and finishing), or materials (type, grade, properties, and treatment) (Shah and Rogers, 1988), and vary with product and manufacturing process. Table 8.1 partially lists typical features for the major manufacturing processes.

Table 8.1 Typical Features for Manufacturing Processes (adapted from Cunningham and Dixon, 1988)

Forging	Extrusion	Stamping
Planes	Webs	Slots
Ribs	Ribs	Fingers
Bosses	Tongues	Corners
Fillets	Walls	Holes
Webs	2-D intersections	Cut-outs
3-D corners	Hollowness	Notches
Bends/twists	Corner breaks	Windows
Casting	**Tool and die**	**Structural**
Planes	Circles	Plates
Cylindricality	Webs	Shells
Projections	Walls	Beams
Depressions	Corner breaks	Frames
Hulls	Slots	Trusses
Solids	Hollows	Columns
Holes	Tongues	Arches

To accomplish design, features must be created, deleted, modified, copied, moved, detailed, interrogated, and have attached properties, attributes, and restrictions (Pratt, 1988). Existing CAD systems have been successful at improving design through manipulating geometric data rapidly and precisely, in both a two-dimensional (surface) and three-dimensional (solid or volume) format. Volume representation is natural and useful in defining machining operations, whereas surface representation is needed to access the faces of the volumes for positioning, attaching attributes, and tolerancing (Kusiak, 1990). Drawing storage, modification, and costing have also been greatly eased through mechanization. Because design implies subsequent redesign, the ability to quickly generate alternate versions of a design is vital, and CAD fulfills this need.

Central to a feature-based CAD system is the library of features. This library contains the features needed for product design with their associated properties. The library eliminates the need to define and create features during the design process. The designer selects from the library, then modifies the feature to suit the product. Dimensions, tolerances, orientation, placement, materials, and so on are individualized, then, the product is constructed by combining the individualized features. Although the library is efficient for features stored within, new and fundamentally changed features or properties cannot be accommodated without expanding or modifying the library.

8.4 OVERVIEW OF KNOWLEDGE-BASED SYSTEMS

CAD systems cannot replicate heuristics and reasoning when combining and specifying features to form a product. To standardize and improve the quality and quantity of design, expert systems can be used to supplement human abilities, which vary significantly with the person, the design task, and the environmental conditions and constraints. Knowledge-based systems, also known as expert systems, are formulated to replicate and improve on human reasoning, handling symbolic processing and logical structures well (Harmon and King, 1985). Knowledge is commonly stored either in production rules or in frames, creating the knowledge base. The former are structures normally of If/Then type (*modus ponens* reasoning) with antecedent conditions, attribute matching, and consequent actions or conclusions. Frames store information according to components with attributes, a type of object-oriented programming. Components are arranged hierarchically so that they may inherit, pass on, and relate to attributes of other components.

The reasoning of a knowledge-based system is accomplished by the inference engine, which directs the query of the knowledge base. Inference engines are forward chaining (data driven or antecedent reasoning) and/or backward chaining (goal driven or consequent matching) (Swift, 1987). Forward chaining systems begin with the known facts and search solution avenues until each is exhausted, or until a conclusion is reached. This type of reasoning is inefficient when large numbers of facts and possible solutions exist. Backward chaining begins with desired goals and works through antecedent conditions until all are matched with known facts, or avenues are exhausted. Some hybrid manufacturing systems have effectively combined both types of reasoning (Kusiak, 1990).

8.5 APPLYING KNOWLEDGE-BASED SYSTEMS TO FEATURES

The design area is broader than many others which apply expert systems—there are enormous ranges of artifacts, tasks, and domains (Kusiak, 1990). Many prototypic and operational systems have been developed for different processes of manufacturing design. Some are rule based and some are frame oriented, some are integrated with CAD modelers and others are not. For feature extracting expert systems, a hierarchical set of features is normally developed to reduce combinatorial explosion, then forward chaining logic is applied because the starting point (the input geometric model) is completely known (Hirschtick and Gossard, 1986). This hierarchy of features is essentially analogous to the feature library discussed earlier.

CASPER is a frame-based LISP system operating with a color CAD system to assist aluminum casting design (Luby et al., 1986). First-Cut is also object oriented and is integrated with a solid modeler (Cutkosky et al., 1988). It assists machining design, and also formulates high-level process plans. Impard similarly uses a solid modeler to advise on injection molding part manufacturability with a limited number of features (Vaghul et al., 1985). Rules are also used in Extrusion Advisor (Hirschtick and Gossard, 1986). It takes a different approach by identifying features which will cause difficulties in manufacturing, using characteristic patterns for walls, hollows, and edges. Standard roller chain-drive design and process selection was addressed by CDDES, a system combining frames and rules that converses in English and Chinese (Wang and Yu, 1988). Swift developed a rule-based system integrated with a two-dimensional modeler consisting of 246 rules aimed at assembly (Swift, 1987). It advises the designer of difficulties the proposed design presents for automatic handling, suggests remedies, and estimates the equipment cost for the designed components. Another approach partitioned a knowledge base for design based on dynamically acquired user preferences and on operational information (Sykes and White, 1991). This approach improved the search for good design solutions, and was more readily accepted by users because of the preference capability.

There are two large classes of problems when using knowledge-based systems for feature recognition and design. First, the recognition itself is still best done by humans with their faculty for categorizing visual images into groups, although knowledge-based systems can effectively work with the features once they are identified. To design a set of rules or frames so that a given feature can be properly identified is difficult and lengthy. For example, an expert system may be fed the geometry of a heat sink with two fins and identify it as three walls or eight milled surfaces (Hirschtick and Gossard, 1986).

A second inherent problem with expert systems is their somewhat brittle approach to problems. Systems cannot interpolate or extrapolate knowledge and must work with a well defined, clearly bounded domain. Decisions are dependent on the situational factors fitting the knowledge base. Closely related to the brittleness problem, is that knowledge-based systems rely on how the problem domain was originally defined and how the knowledge was extracted and recorded. Problem selection and knowledge engineering are crucial to any intelligent system's performance, and the latter is the primary development bottleneck.

8.6 APPLICABILITY OF NEURAL NETWORKS

Feature recognition is best accomplished by humans whose eye–brain system is capable of immediate and robust performance. Artificial neural networks were originally designed to replicate some of this human ability, and although the technology is still far from reaching human standards, it does offer significant advantages over other computing options for feature recognition. Based on the biological brain's process of thought transmission, stimuli recognition, and physical response, neural networks are massively parallel computing mechanisms. They are valued because they deal successfully with noisy, uncertain, and partial inputs, and they are fault tolerant and degrade gracefully. They are useful for feature recognition because they can generalize their knowledge to corrupted, partial, modified, or new inputs. Instead of a static library of features, a neural network is capable of interpolating between features and of learning new features.

There are many neural network paradigms and variations, and the reader is directed to comprehensive works such as Lippmann (1987), Simpson (1990), and Wasserman (1989). All networks do share common aspects and mechanics, which are described briefly here. A network works by directing vectorized input through parallel and serial elements where it is evaluated and combined, and finally directed to a meaningful vectorized output state, as shown in Fig. 8.1. Most neural networks capture input/output relationships by storing a distributed model as fixed weights along each connection between neurons.

In most neural network paradigms, weights are initially random and allowed to change during training as the network seeks the best combination of weights to represent the input/output model. Training can be done by guiding the network toward the optimum model using desired output, or teacher vectors. This guiding is called *supervised training* and has the advantage of explicitly declaring the outputs the final neural network should model. A second form of training is *self-organization* or *competitive learning*, where the network changes its connection weights so that similar input vectors are grouped together. This, too, forms an input/output model, but the exact form of the model cannot be specified precisely prior to training.

The number of neurons may vary from layer to layer, as may the evaluation and combination algorithms. Combination is typically done by summing the input times the weight of each connection across all neurons, sometimes with an added bias term. The summation is compared to a threshold value and then subjected to a transfer function (often the sigmoid, step, or linear threshold) which calculates an output. Feedforward networks have connections only to

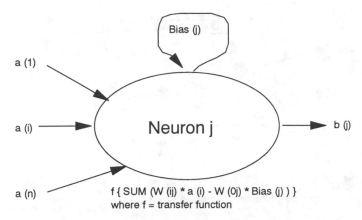

FIG. 8.1. Generic components of a neural network.

the next layer, whereas feedback or recurrent networks have connections to the next layer, to a previous layer, or within a layer. Recurrent networks are usually used to model relationships that have a temporal aspect, whereas feedforward networks generally handle static relationships.

Generic pattern classification or recognition is accomplished by preprocessing an input into binary and/or continuous vector components. A supervised network will have been trained to signal an output class based on the input vector. Again, the output may be binary or continuous, but most pattern classification networks use binary outputs where a "1" signals a match with that class of patterns. Pattern classification can be heteroassociative, i.e., association of an input vector with a class grouping. Another aspect of pattern recognition is not the classification of patterns, but the output of an exemplar pattern when the input pattern is partial or noisy. This is termed *content addressable* or *auto-associative memory* (input of degraded pattern A outputs complete pattern A).

8.7 MULTILAYERED PERCEPTRONS TRAINED BY BACKPROPAGATION

The most well known and commonly used neural network paradigm is the multilayered perceptron trained by backpropagation (Rumelhart *et al.*, 1986). This is popularly called a backpropagation network and is shown in Fig. 8.2. This network is discussed in length here because it is versatile, simple, and handles well pattern classification tasks, of which feature identification is one. Backpropagation can accommodate both binary and continuous input or output. From a statistical viewpoint, backpropagation is the optimal supervised training method, as it converges to a nonlinear estimator with the maximum likelihood of being true (Movellan, 1990; Werbos, 1988). Backpropagation is readily available in software form and, increasingly, in hardware form. For these reasons, backpropagation,

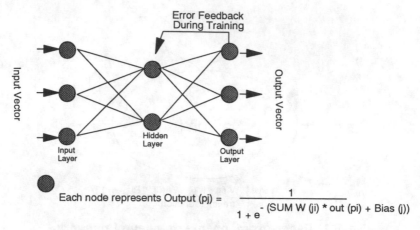

FIG. 8.2. Typical backpropagation network during training with sigmoidal transfer function.

or a variation of backpropagation, is often the network of choice for pattern classification when teacher data is available.

A backpropagation network is a feedforward network, typically consisting of an input layer, one or more hidden layers, and an output layer all containing varied numbers of neurons. It has been arithmetically proven that this network, with at least three layers (input, output, and one hidden layer), and a nonlinear transfer function can implement any function (Hornik *et al.*, 1990; Hornik, 1991). However, for continuous input vectors, the superiority of using two hidden layers has been theoretically and empirically noted (Lapedes and Farber, 1988; Smith and Dagli, 1991).

Backpropagation works by using the theory of least squares—calculating the derivatives of error with respect to the connection weights, and adjusting the weights based on steepest error surface descent. Weights are modified during training until they reach a stable state (convergence); this translates to the network achieving a state of error minimization. Because weights are usually adjusted after each vector input instead of after the whole training set, the resultant descent is not necessarily the steepest, but closely approximates it (Khanna, 1990). Although classical backpropagation cannot escape from local minima during its descent along the error surface, in practice a local minimum significantly far from the global minimum is rarely encountered (Smith *et al.*, 1991).

There are several critical factors when formulating and training a backpropagation network:

(1) Number of input neurons
(2) Number of output neurons
(3) Number of hidden layers
(4) Number of neurons in each hidden layer
(5) Size and composition of training set

(6) Size and composition of test set for trained network validation

(7) Training rate and modifications

The number of input and output neurons are usually dictated by the problem (e.g., a network categorizing features, each described by an input vector of length 40, into four categories might have 40 input neurons and 4 output neurons).

Practically speaking, the choice of the number of hidden neurons is tied to the choice of the number of hidden layers. Hidden layers can provide translation and scaling invariance (Roth, 1990), i.e., the positioning and size of the feature would not be critical to its identification. In applications, the choice of the number of hidden layers is generally confined to one or two. Once the number of hidden layers is selected, the size of each layer can be estimated. The objective is to find the least number of hidden neurons that can achieve adequate performance. Decreasing the number of hidden neurons increases generalization and is more computationally efficient, but impairs the network's ability to learn. Overfitting with too many hidden neurons tends to decrease generalization because of training set "memorization," and is computationally inefficient. Estimating optimum hidden neurons is usually done by trial and error. Some heuristics involving the similarity and regularity of the training set have been proposed (Ahmad and Tesauro, 1989; Baum and Haussler, 1989; Gutierrez et al., 1989; Kung and Hwang, 1988; Perugini and Engeler, 1989).

The size and composition of the training set are critical. It should be a sample with fixed probability distribution chosen randomly from the expected values, which also have a fixed probability distribution (Hecht-Nielsen, 1989). The training set is presented to the network many times during training. It should be in random order and contain all the training features. Upper and lower bounds for the number of training pairs have been directly related to the numbers of neurons and weights, and the rate of classification error (Baum and Haussler, 1989). It has also been shown that as training set size increases, so does probability of correct network pattern classification (Ahmad and Tesauro, 1989).

A disadvantage of backpropagation is the long training time it often takes a network to work its way down to the bottom of the error surface. This is in part determined by the step size or training rate. A large training rate implies a large step size which will decrease convergence time; however, moving too quickly down the error surface increases the chance of nonconvergence (Kung and Hwang, 1988) and paralysis (Wasserman, 1989). A small learning rate avoids these problems but increases training time. The learning rate is often constant through training, but can be decreased during training to avoid network instability. It may also be somewhat randomized so that the network can arbitrarily "jump" out of local minima. The training rate can be sized based on the number of hidden neurons (Kung and Hwang, 1988).

The training disadvantage of backpropagation is not significant when building feature identification systems. Training can be assumed to be an off-line, infrequent task and therefore speed is not essential. The requirement of teacher vectors is also not a problem for feature identification as they are readily available. A problem that is significant with backpropagation for feature identification is that once a network is trained, new patterns cannot easily be added to its internal model. It is usually best to build and train a new network to incorporate the new features.

8.8 OTHER NEURAL NETWORK PARADIGMS USEFUL FOR FEATURE IDENTIFICATION

Although backpropagation is the network of choice for many pattern classification tasks, there are other neural network paradigms which offer some advantages in specific areas. The other networks discussed here are counterpropagation networks, adaptive resonance theory, probabilistic networks, and fuzzy networks. These networks have certain capabilities for feature identification.

Counterpropagation Networks

Counterpropagation networks were introduced by Hecht-Nielsen as a combination of two established neural network paradigms, backpropagation and the Kohonen self-organizing network (Hecht-Nielsen, 1987). Because of the long training times for backpropagation networks, counterpropagation aims at the same mapping functionality but with less generality, and significantly less required training cycles. A counterpropagation network can work equally well for binary and continuous vectors. It is essentially a "look up" table for stored patterns.

The counterpropagation network is defined to be five layers, fanning in and then fanning out. Layers 1 and 5 are normalized input layers, layer 3 is a Kohonen layer (Kohonen, 1984), and layers 4 and 5 are Grossberg outstar layers (Grossberg, 1982). Normalized vector input is directed to the Kohonen layer, which self-organizes, then is passed to the Grossberg layers, which are trained, through supervision, for output.

The Kohonen layer works by classifying similar vectors together without the benefit of a teacher vector. It is trained through competitive learning, where only one Kohonen neuron outputs a 1 (turns on or fires) for a given input. All other Kohonen neurons are inactive (output = 0). The winning Kohonen neuron is that which has the largest summation of the dot products between each input vector from layers 1 and 5, and their weights to layer 3. During training, weights are adjusted only for the winning Kohonen neuron so that eventually training causes each of the weights from the input layers to each Kohonen neuron to become like the average of those vectors being classified (turned on) by that neuron. By itself, the Kohonen layer approximates the probability density function of the input vectors (Jakubowicz and Ramanujam, 1990; Lippmann, 1987). In addition the final weights are organized so that topologically close neurons are sensitive to physically similar inputs (Lippmann, 1987).

This network is advantageous in that it is a good classifier of input vectors without extensive training times and can be used for rapid prototyping (Wasserman, 1989). The number of classifications must be known *a priori*, and a large amount of training data must be available. In one hard pattern classification task, a counterpropagation network was found to converge more quickly than backpropagation but provide poorer recognition (Shea and Lin, 1989).

Adaptive Resonance Theory (ART)

Adaptive resonance theory, better known as ART, is a good candidate for feature identification because of its unusual ability to acquire new knowledge to an existing network (Carpenter and Grossberg, 1987a; Grossberg 1976). ART is a combination of self-organizing and supervised learning, where like patterns are grouped together, but the fineness of the groups is controlled *a priori* by the user through use of a vigilance factor. When new inputs are entered, the network checks its stored patterns to see if the new pattern is close to any stored pattern. If it is acceptably close, the closest stored pattern is signaled as the correct classification. If the new pattern is not close to any stored pattern, the new pattern is stored as an additional pattern in the network memory. In this way, new features or significantly altered features can be added to the network memory dynamically without retraining or rebuilding.

ART 1, the original ART network, only handles binary inputs and outputs, but ART 2 handles continuous inputs as well (Carpenter and Grossberg, 1987b). ART 3 is a parallel search version of ART designed for network hierarchies (Carpenter and Grossberg, 1990). ARTMAP is a recent version that rapidly self-organizes to stable class mappings of optimal size (Carpenter et al., 1991). ARTMAP handles only binary inputs and outputs. A new version of ARTMAP is fuzzy ART, which will be discussed shortly.

ART does have disadvantages, particularly in tuning the fineness of the classes using the vigilance factor. The network must be tuned so that it only adds new stored patterns when the pattern is novel enough, as defined by the user. This is often not easy to determine, and successful use of ART may require some trial and error. Besides ART 2 and Fuzzy ART, the paradigm handles only binary inputs and outputs, and ART 2 handles only binary outputs. These may be limiting depending on how feature identification is handled.

Probabilistic Networks

Probabilistic networks are supervised, feedforward classifying networks which use an exponential transfer function, and approximate Bayes classifiers (Specht 1990a, 1990b). The principle advantage of a probabilistic network over a backpropagation network is the much shortened training time because only one pass through the training set is required. Two other advantages over backpropagation are that the network trains successfully with sparse data, and new patterns can overwrite old when retraining.

The probabilistic network stores each and every training pattern, which makes it infeasible for very large domains. It is not clear from the research whether performance of probabilistic networks is equal to backpropagation, but they are an alternative when training time is critical or only a small training set is available. They can also be used for quick prototyping and exploration.

Fuzzy Networks

There are several versions of fuzzy networks. All share a common base in the seminal work of Zadeh in fuzzy set theory (Zadeh, 1965). Although the reader is directed elsewhere for an adequate discussion on fuzzy set theory (e.g., Klir and Folger, 1988), briefly, fuzzy set theory attempts to capture *imprecision*. An object belongs to a set with a membership degree, usually between 0 and 1, where 0 indicates the object is definitely not a member of the set and 1 indicates the object is definitely a member of the set. Values in between indicate degrees of membership of the object in the set. Fuzzy set theory provides an ordered method to combine and infer fuzzy relationships.

This folds in nicely with feature identification because of the potential imprecision of some features classes, especially when dealing with identification of new, corrupted, or altered features. Several neural network paradigms incorporating fuzzy concepts have been described recently. Probably the most well known is the fuzzy associative memory (FAM) which combines evidence of membership degree with conflict resolution (Bahrami *et al.*, 1991; Kong and Kosko, 1992; Kosko, 1992). FAMs can be trained by supervision, such as backpropagation, or by self-organization, called adaptive FAM. Each FAM rule, or instance, provides a sample point in the model. Unfamiliar input to FAM is estimated by combining known FAM rules through fuzzy set theory. FAMs are especially noted for their robustness.

Other network paradigms incorporating fuzzy concepts include a fuzzy version of backpropagation (Hunt *et al.*, 1991). This can improve standard backpropagation classification accuracy by including membership degrees in the error calculation during training. Another major paradigm adapted for fuzzy use is ART. Fuzzy ART is a continuous extension of ART 1 by using a minimum operator instead of an intersection operator (Carpenter *et al.*, 1991).

8.9 FEATURE RECOGNITION WITH NEURAL NETWORKS

A trained network can be assigned identification tasks based on features, and then automatically integrate diverse features into a set. For networks to process features, physical attributes must be translated into meaningful input. Preprocessing of data takes the form of devising a compact scheme which uniquely represents the important differences among features. Fig. 8.3 shows two variations of input vector coding.

For more complex feature detection, more complex preprocessing is needed. First, the number of features must be limited and the ones selected must sufficiently discriminate among classes (Roth, 1990). Aspects such as orientation, size, placement and edge detection must be considered. One schema involves breaking at inflection and orientation discontinuities, and keying on the ratio of

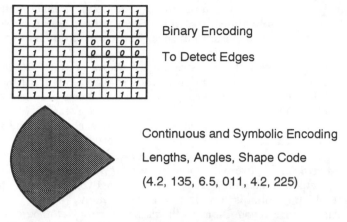

Binary Encoding

To Detect Edges

Continuous and Symbolic Encoding

Lengths, Angles, Shape Code

(4.2, 135, 6.5, 011, 4.2, 225)

FIG. 8.3. Two schemes for preprocessing input vectors.

chord to arc length, the relative lengths scaled to the longest contour, the number and degree of corners, and the degree of inflections and discontinuities (Krishnan and Walters, 1988). By concentrating on the piece parts of features, rather than whole objects, some robustness with regard to differences in size and position is gained.

Besides the features themselves, networks can be trained for typical attributes, or for a range of attributes. One approach trained a neural network on randomly chosen attribute values from a typical range so that the network could recognize infeasible attribute values (Knapp and Wang, 1992). For example the feature "hole" was input with typical values of its attributes; depth, diameter, size tolerance, positional tolerance, circularity, straightness, and surface finish.

A problem is that the combination of features and attributes is explosive, and the proposed neural network could quickly grow unwieldy in size and training set. One approach to alleviate this is to combine hierarchies of networks, some of which may even be of different paradigms. The first level of network might separate features into broad categories based on outstanding differences, perhaps through self-organization. The second level could discriminate among the broad class by finer aspects of the feature. A third level could group the identified features by attribute value. Because neural networks work well in hierarchy, the potential for this approach is good. This approach is also modular, which reduces the need for retraining when new features or attributes must be added.

8.10 LIMITATIONS OF NEURAL NETWORKS

As an immature technology, neural computing has many drawbacks for operational applications. Foremost, there are few commercially available neural network chips, either electronic or optical. Therefore, implementation of this technology usually now depends on simulation by traditional serial computers with special software, and sometimes hardware. There is little doubt, however, that widespread use of neural networks in the near future will rely on hardware implementations.

A second problem is that the construction of neural network architectures is nondeterminative. First, a paradigm or cascade of paradigms must be selected. This task alone is significant as new paradigms are being prodigiously developed, and each paradigm has its own advantages and drawbacks. Most developers select several paradigms and evaluate the results of each before going forward with one (Orlando *et al.*, 1990; Shea and Lin, 1989). Next, the number of neurons, connections, and layers must be chosen. As discussed earlier in this chapter, this is a trial and error procedure with some known properties and some heuristics. The training method and training set also affect the network, as does determining the point at which training is complete and operation may begin.

Structuring feature recognition problems so that they can be conveniently input and output as vectors, either binary or continuous, to neural networks or hierarchies of neural networks is quite a difficult problem by itself. Features must be selected and coded in such a way as to distinguish between classes, but not overly encumber data pre- and postprocessing. The selection of the training set will ultimately determine the neural network model, therefore the training set must properly reflect the population of features and attributes to be classified. Bias or incompleteness of the training set can cause an incorrectly operating network even though networks are fairly robust to less than optimal training sets (Twomey and Smith, 1992).

8.11 COMPOSITE INTELLIGENT SYSTEM ARCHITECTURES

Given a knowledge-based system to assist design, integrating it with both a CAD system to model geometrically and kinematically, and neural networks to recognize and classify features will have synergistic results. The knowledge base serves as user interface, integrator, and reasoner. John Hopfield, a pioneer in neural networks, believes that composite systems will be the venue for using neural networks (Myers, 1990). Expert systems are good at logic, whereas neural networks excel at fuzzy analysis and pattern recognition. Hopfield believes the two will not compete, but rather neural networks will act as front ends to logical back ends. These so-called expert networks are becoming popular (Caudill, 1991). A prototype expert network for feature identification uses neural networks to extract features from a machine vision system for use by an expert system that previously relied on manual selection of features (McAndless *et al.*, 1991). Figure 8.4 shows a generic intelligent system for feature identification.

The knowledge base contains heuristics and analytic rules on the combination and manipulation of features for product design. Features are recognized via pattern recognition neural networks by transforming low-level features and attributes into vector representations. A neural network can dynamically feed a CAD feature library. CAD acts as the workhorse, receiving direction from the

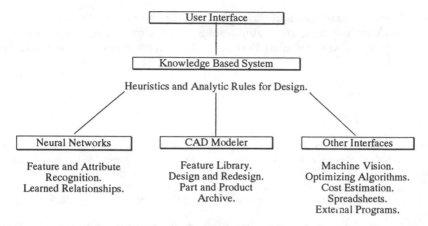

FIG. 8.4. Generic composite system architecture.

neural nets on feature identification and from the knowledge base on how to assemble them. CAD saves and stores designed parts for later redesign. It acts as a geometric modeler, feature library, and drawing and specification archive.

8.12 CONCLUSION

Because manufacturing design is becoming largely automated through use of CAD modelers, adding intelligence in the form of knowledge-based systems and neural networks is synergistic. The designer need not search a catalog of applicable features and attributes, and apply them consistently. The system can perform these tasks. Designers can also be more productive in both quantity and quality by being assisted in applying the proper design rules to ensure functionality and manufacturability.

Expert system technology is becoming mature and has many operational systems. Modeling by integrating an expert system with CAD has been studied in research and application with good results. A shortcoming of this approach—the inability to robustly recognize and classify features—can be addressed by neural networks. Although this technology is far from mature, it has been applied on a limited scale to feature extraction and classification.

Several substantial drawbacks to the intelligent system approach remain. Intelligent systems are all customized, thereby demanding substantial development and testing. Knowledge acquisition varies depending on the problem definition and the available expert sources. Temporal reasoning and kinetic knowledge expansion are areas that need improvement. Preprocessing features and their attributes to vectors to be recognized and classified by neural networks or hierarchies of neural networks requires considerable effort and much trial and error. Selecting neural network paradigms and training the networks are very much based on heuristics and expertise. Training can be lengthy and dependent on network architecture, and training set and technique. Most neural networks are currently software simulated on serial computers at quite a computational cost.

REFERENCES

Ahmad, Subutai and Tesauro, Gerald. 1989. Scaling and generalization in neural networks: A case study. In *Advances in Neural Information Processing Systems I*, ed. David S. Touretzky, pp. 160–168. San Mateo, California: Morgan Kaufmann Publishers.

Bahrami, Ali, Dagli, Cihan, and Modarress, Batoul. 1991. Fuzzy associative memory in conceptual design. *Proc. of the International Joint Conference on Neural Networks*, I, pp. 183–188.

Baum, Eric B., and Haussler, David. 1989. What size net gives valid generalization? *Neural Computation*, 1:151–160.

Brown, D. C., and Chandrasekaran, B. 1988. Expert systems for a class of mechanical design activity. In *Expert Systems in Engineering*, ed. T. Pham. Exeter, U.K.: Springer-Verlag.

Carpenter, Gail A., and Grossberg, Stephen. 1987a. A massively parallel architecture for a self-organizing neural pattern recognition machine. *Computer Vision, Graphics, and Image Processing* 37:54–115.

Carpenter, Gail A., and Grossberg, Stephen. 1987b. ART 2: Stable self-organization of pattern recognition codes for analog input patterns. *Applied Optics* 26:4919–4930.

Carpenter, Gail A., and Grossberg, Stephen. 1990. ART 3: Hierarchical search using chemical transmitters in self-organizing pattern recognition architectures. *Neural Networks* 3:129–152.

Carpenter, Gail A., Grossberg, Stephen, and Rosen, David B. 1991. Fuzzy ART: Fast stable learning and categorization of analog patterns by an adaptive resonance system. *Neural Networks* 4:759–771.

Caudill, Maureen. 1991. Expert networks. *Byte* 16:108–116.

Cunningham, J. J., and Dixon, J. R. 1988. Designing with features: The origins of features. *Proc. of the ASME Conference on Computers in Engineering*, p. 237.

Cutkosky, M. R., Tenenbaum, J. M., and Muller, D. 1988. Features in process-based design. *Proc. of the ASME Conference on Computers in Engineering*, p. 557.

Grossberg, Stephen. 1976. Adaptive pattern classification and universal recoding, II: Feedback, expectation, olfaction, and illusions. *Biological Cybernetics* 23:187–202.

Grossberg, Stephen. 1982. *Studies of Mind and Brain*. Dordrecht, Holland: D. Reidel Publishing Co.

Gutierrez, Mario, Wang, Jennifer, and Grondin, Robert. 1989. Estimating hidden unit number for two-layer perceptrons. *Proc. of the International Joint Conference on Neural Networks*, I, pp. 677–681.

Harmon, Paul, and King, David. 1985. *Expert Systems*. New York: John Wiley & Sons, Inc.

Hecht-Nielsen, Robert. 1987. Counterpropagation networks. *Proc. of the International Joint Conference on Neural Networks*, II, pp. 19–32.

Hecht-Nielsen, Robert. 1989. Theory of the backpropagation neural network. *Proc. of the International Joint Conference on Neural Networks*, I, p. 593.

Hirschtick, J. K., and Gossard, D. C. 1986. Geometric reasoning for design advisory system. *Proc. of the ASME Conference on Computers in Engineering*, Vol. 1, p. 263.

Hornik, Kurt. 1991. Approximation capabilities of multilayer feedforward networks. *Neural Networks* 4:251–257.

Hornik, Kurt, Stinchcombe, Maxwell, and White, Halbert. 1990. Universal approximation of an unknown mapping and its derivatives using multilayer feedforward networks. *Neural Networks* 3:551–560.

Hunt, B. R., Qi, Y. Y. and DeKruger, D. 1991. Fuzzy classification using set membership functions in the back propagation algorithm. In *Intelligent Engineering Systems Through Artificial Neural Networks*, eds. C. H. Dagli, S. R. T. Kumara, and Y. C. Chin, pp. 267–276. New York: ASME Press.

Jakubowicz, Oleg, and Ramanujam, Sridhar. 1990. A neural network model for fault-diagnosis of digital circuits. *Proc. of the International Joint Conference on Neural Networks*, II, pp. 611-614.

Khanna, Tarun. 1990. *Foundations of Neural Networks*. Reading, Massachusetts Addison-Wesley.

Khoshnevis, Behrokh, and Park, Joo. 1988. Real time manufacturing process planning. *University of Southern California Working Paper*.

Klir, George J., and Folger, Tina A. 1988. *Fuzzy Sets, Uncertainty, and Information*. Englewood Cliffs, New Jersey: Prentice-Hall.

Knapp, Gerald M., and Wang, Hsu-Pin. 1992. Neural networks in acquisition of manufacturing knowledge. In *Intelligent Design and Manufacturing*, ed. A. Kosiak, pp. 723–744. New York: Wiley.

Kohonen, T. 1984. *Self-Organization and Associative Memory*. Berlin: Springer-Verlag.

Kong, Seong-Gon, and Kosko, Bart. 1992. Adaptive fuzzy systems for backing up a truck-and-trailer. *IEEE Transactions on Neural Networks* 3:211–223.

Kosko, Bart. 1992. *Neural Networks and Fuzzy Systems: A Dynamical Systems Approach to Machine Intelligence*. Englewood Cliffs, New Jersey: Prentice-Hall.

Krishnan, Ganapathy, and Walters, Deborah. 1988. Psychologically plausible features for shape recognition in a neural network. *Proc. of the International Joint Conference on Neural Networks*, II, p. 127.

Kung, S. Y., and Hwang, J. N. 1988. An algebraic projection analysis for optimal hidden units size and learning rates in backpropagation learning. *Proc. of the International Joint Conference on Neural Networks*, I, pp. 363–370.

Kusiak, Andrew. 1990. *Intelligent Manufacturing Systems*. Englewood Cliffs, New Jersey: Prentice Hall.

Lapedes, Alan, and Farber, Robert. 1988. How neural nets work. In *Neural Information Processing Systems*, ed. D. Z. Anderson, pp. 442–456. New York: American Institute of Physics.

Lippmann, Richard P. 1987. An introduction to computing with neural nets. *IEEE ASSP Magazine* 4:4–22.

Luby, S. C., Dixon, J. R,. and Simmons, M. K. 1986. Creating and using a features data base. *Computers in Mechanical Engineering* 5:25.

McAndless, Elizabeth, Stacey, Deborah, Rueb, Kurt, and Wong, Andrew K. C. 1991. A hybrid artificial neural network/rule based approach to a real-time machine vision system. In *Intelligent Engineering Systems Through Artificial Neural Networks*, eds. C. H. Dagli, S. R. T. Kumura, and Y. C. Chin, pp. 909–914. New York: ASME Press.

Movellan, Javier R. 1990. Error functions to improve noise resistance and generalization in backpropagation networks. *Proc. of the International Joint Conference on Neural Networks*, I, pp. 557–560.

Myers, Ware. 1990. Artificial neural networks are coming. *IEEE Expert* 5:3–6.

Orlando, Jim, Mann, Richard, and Haykin, Simon. 1990. Radar classification of sea-ice using traditional and neural classifiers. *Proc. of the International Joint Conference on Neural Networks*, II, p. 263.

Perugini, N. K,. and Engeler, W. E. 1989. Neural network learning time: Effects of network and training set size. *Proc. of the International Joint Conference on Neural Networks*, II, 395–401.

Pratt, M. J. 1988. Synthesis of an optimal approach to form feature modeling. *Proc. of the ASME Conference on Computers in Engineering*, p. 263.

Roth, Michael W. 1990. Survey of neural network technology for automatic target recognition. *IEEE Transactions on Neural Networks* 1:28.

Rumelhart, David E., McClelland, James L., and the PDP Research Group. 1986. *Parallel Distributed Processing*, Vol. 1 Cambridge, Massachusetts: MIT Press.

Shah, J. J., and Rogers, M. T. 1988. Feature-based modeling shell: Design and implementation. *Proc. of the ASME Conference on Computers in Engineering*, p. 255.

Shea, Patrick M., and Lin, Vincent. 1989. Detection of explosives in checked airline baggage using an artificial neural system. *Proc. of the International Joint Conference on Neural Networks*, II, 31–34.

Simpson, Patrick K. 1990. *Artificial Neural Systems: Foundations, Paradigms, Applications, and Implementations*. New York: Pergamon Press.

Smith, Alice E., and Dagli, Cihan H. 1991. Relating binary and continuous problem entropy to backpropagation network architecture. In *Applications of Artificial Neural Networks II*, Vol. 2, pp. 551–562. Bellingham, Washington: SPIE.

Smith, Alice E., Dagli, Cihan H., and Raterman, Elaine R. 1991. An empirical analysis of backpropagation error surface initiation for injection molding process control. *Proc. of the 1991 IEEE International Conference on Systems, Man, and Cybernetics*, pp. 1529–1534.

Specht, Donald F. 1990a. Probabilistic neural networks and the polynomial adaline as complementary techniques for classification. *IEEE Transactions on Neural Networks*, 1, 111–121.

Specht, Donald F. 1990b. Probabilistic neural networks. *Neural Networks*, 3, 109–118.

Suri, Rajan, and Shimizu, Masami. 1989. Design for analysis: A new strategy to improve the design process. *University of Wisconsin—Madison Technical Report*, No. 89-3.

Swift, K. G. 1987. *Knowledge Based Design for Manufacture*. Englewood Cliffs, New Jersey: Prentice-Hall.

Sykes, Edward A., and White, Chelsea C. III. 1991. Multiobjective intelligent computer-aided design. *IEEE Transactions on Systems, Man, and Cybernetics* 21:1498–1511.

Twomey, Janet M., and Smith, Alice E. 1992. An examination of performance measures for pattern classification backpropagation neural networks. In *Intelligent Engineering Systems Through Artificial Neural Networks*, Vol. 2, eds. C. H. Dagli, L. I. Burke, and Y. C. Shin. New York: ASME Press, pp. 343–348.

Vaghul, M., Dixon, J. R., and Sinsmeister, G. E. 1985. Expert systems in a CAD environment: Injection molding part design as an example. *Proc. of the ASME Conference on Computers in Engineering*, p. 77.

Wang, Q., Zhou, J., and Yu, J. 1988. A chain-drive design expert system and CAD system. In *Expert Systems in Engineering*, ed. D. T. Pham. Exeter, U.K.: Springer-Verlag.

Wasserman, Philip D. 1989. *Neural Computing: Theory and Practice*. New York: Van Nostrand Reinhold.

Werbos, Paul J. 1988. Backpropagation: Past and future. *Proc. of the International Joint Conference on Neural Networks*, I, 343.

Zadeh, Lotfi. 1965. Fuzzy sets. *Information and Control* 8:338–353.

PART II

Concurrent Engineering:
Use of Intelligent Systems

Products introduced to the marketplace are getting more complicated, which means that design and manufacturing of these products becomes involved. The increase in demand for high quality places an extra burden on the manufacturing processes, demanding tight control with minimum variance between products being produced. The minimization of variance from the increasingly complicated manufacturing processes must be done through improved manufacturing procedures and automation of the manufacturing processes themselves.

One of the most successful methods employed to shorten the development cycle, from design concept to market, is concurrent engineering. Concurrent engineering abandons the traditional "serial" approach to product design. After the product specifications are completed, the design team is charged with designing a product that conforms to the specifications. When the design team has completed the design, it is turned over to the manufacturing department so the processes for producing the parts for the designed product can be defined. Next, the design and process plans are turned over to the production department where assembly plans are created. Also, at this time the service department is given the designs so that plans are initiated on how to service the product once it has reached the customer. It is not until the product reaches the customer that the true test of customer satisfaction is done. In the traditional product design process, first the "functionally" is designed in, then the "manufacturability" is determined, then the "assembleability" is analyzed, along with the "serviceability." Finally, and only when the product is shipped to the customer, the most importance aspect of the design, the "satisfiability," is determined.

Concurrent engineering is a methodology for shortening the development cycle. A useful approach of implementing concurrent engineering is through automation of the product design and manufacturing processes. This automation can range from the automated generation of process flow charts to systems that automatically design, manufacture, and package products.

Chapters 9 through 13 cover various aspects of concurrent engineering.

In Chapter 9, the application of neural networks in design and manufacturing is examined. The system incorporates three neural network paradigms such as fuzzy associative memory, backpropagation, and adaptive resonance theory to achieve its task. The fuzzy associative memory approach is utilized for automation of mapping the marketing characteristics into predesigned structures. Adaptive resonance theory is utilized for object identification. A backpropagation neural network is used for camera calibration and another backpropagation neural network is used to control the speed of the robot arm based on the size of a workpiece. This unique application of neural networks in design and manufacturing can be extended to more sophisticated tools for concurrent engineering.

The example selected in Chapter 9 demonstrates the integration issues and the use of intelligent systems to automate the process using neural networks. The concepts introduced in this chapter reinforce the need for the application of concurrent engineering methodologies and specific technologies based on artificial intelligence.

Chapter 10 examines the impact of design on manufacturability and manufacturing cost. Manufacturing engineers are able to impact a significant portion of the costs. Therefore, the check for manufacturing friendliness of a design solution should be done as early as possible. To obtain a manufacturing friendly product, one should design it for manufacturing, i.e., consider the factory dependent restrictions into account in an early design phase. Another approach is not to restrict a designer but to analyze the design solution afterwards. The first case study uses a hybrid of these two approaches, while the last two cases analyze manufacturability after the design has been completed.

The knowledge associated with process plans should be implemented in such a form that it could be reused for manufacturability evaluation. An extra effort is required and it may be frustrating to implement a module that performs just manufacturability analysis. Furthermore, when the manufacturing methods are continuously developed on the shop floor, it is difficult to maintain the knowledge. Hence it is firmly believed that it is most reasonable to use the knowledge stored in the process planning system.

In Chapter 11, a method is presented for automated generation of assembly plans. The plan is generated from the geometry of parts and topology model, and thus explicit specification of mating relations between parts is not required. The approach not only eliminates the time-consuming specifications of mating relations by the user, but also prevents wrong mating relations from being presented, and does not require checking of validity. Algorithms are presented for finding a collision-free path to yield disassembly motions. To disassemble an MSW the parts or subassemblies are determined that can separate themselves from the MSA after a series of translational and rotational motions. The problem of deducing such motions is posed as one of determining changes in the number of degrees of freedom of subassemblies due to either translational or rotational motion. After the motions are deduced, a series of transformations is performed on the model of the MSA to accomplish disassembly.

In Chapter 12, an intelligent system is discussed that generates assembly sequences and formulates a task-level assembly plan utilizing the geometry of the assembly. A rule-based approach has been demonstrated to be effective for solving this type of planning problem. The purpose of the intelligent assembly system is to assist an engineer and to enhance the design process by analyzing, optimizing, evaluating, and formulating the design. To provide intelligent systems with compatible interfaces, some research issues need to be addressed. In addition to considering the number of tool changes and directions, one needs to consider fixture complexity, manipulability of parts, and locality. A future assembly planning system can be improved by allowing the user to select appropriate criteria and assigning weights to indicate their relative importance.

It is generally recognized that the practice of designing products for manufacturing can shorten the product design and manufacturing time, minimize development cost, improve product quality, and ensure a smooth transition into production. To fully exploit the cost and quality advantages of automation, a suitable design approach is needed. Chapter 13 provides a brief review of the design models and tools available, and proposes a design methodology for automated manufacture. To automate the design process, a considerable effort is required to develop the necessary support tools. For example, tools should be developed for automated examining of technology alternatives, automated tolerance specification, and analysis of complex assemblies. With the availability of these design automation tools, designers can direct more effort into creative thinking to generate innovative designs.

Chapter 9

Integrating Product and Process Design Through Intelligent Systems

Ali Bahrami
Computer Information Systems
Rhode Island College
Providence, Rhode Island

Mark Lynch
Department of Mechanical and Industrial Engineering
Louisiana Tech University
Ruston, Louisiana

Cihan H. Dagli
Department of Engineering Management
University of Missouri-Rolla
Rolla, Missouri

9.1 INTRODUCTION

The face of manufacturing has changed forever. A new manufacturing environment exists which includes global competition and an explosion of new technologies. Because of this new manufacturing environment, manufacturers are seeing shorter product life cycles, smaller margins, and greater demand for high quality products with low product costs. In order for manufacturing firms to stay competitive, they must shorten the product development cycle, and automate the product design and manufacturing processes.

Products being developed and introduced to the marketplace are getting more complicated. This means that both the design and manufacturing of these products are also becoming more complex. To take the burden off the design teams, the design processes can be automated using new technologies to assist the designers in performing their tasks better and faster, as well as relieving them from some of the mundane aspects of the design process. The increase in demand for high quality also puts an extra burden on the manufacturing processes, demanding tight controls with minimum variance between products being produced. The minimization of variance from an increasingly complicated manufacturing processes must be done through improved manufacturing procedures and automation of the manufacturing processes themselves.

One of the most successful methods employed to shorten the development cycle, from design concept to market, is through concurrent engineering. Concurrent engineering abandons the traditional "serial" approach to product design. In the traditional approach, the specification for the new product is compiled first, usually from the marketing department. After the specification is completed, the design team is charged with designing a product to conform to the specification. When the design team has completed the design, it is turned over to the manufacturing department so that the processes needed to produce the parts for the designed product can be defined. Next, the design and process plans are turned over to the production department so that assembly plans can be created for the manufactured parts. Also at this time, the service department is given the design so that plans can start on how to service the product once it has reached the customer. It is not until the product reaches the customer that customer satisfaction can truly be tested. So in the traditional product design process, first the functionality is designed in, then the manufacturability is determined, then the assemblability is analyzed along with the serviceability. Finally, and only when the product is shipped to the customer, is the most important aspect of the design, the "satisfiability," determined.

The problem with the traditional approach lies in the serial nature of the process. Once the design is completed and turned over to manufacturing, it becomes very expensive to make design changes to improve the manufacturability of the part. Another problem is that each step in the process is done only by designers with expertise in their area (i.e., design, manufacturing, or assembly). These domain experts are only consulted when it comes to be their time in the product design cycle.

With concurrent engineering, the different domain experts are brought into the design process from the start. Every expert (manufacturing, assembly, servicing, etc.) has access to the design and can influence the final product. Even customers can get involved in the design process in order to obtain a product that they will be satisfied with. The coextensive nature of concurrent engineering will produce better all-around products at lower costs, and that are easier to produce.

Concurrent engineering is one methodology for shortening the development cycle. A useful technique in implementing concurrent engineering is the automation of the product design and manufacturing processes. This automation can range from the automatic generation of process flow sheets and routers using computer-aided design drawings, to systems that automatically design, manufacture, and package products. An example of such an automated system is presented in this chapter. The desire for creating totally automated design and manufacturing systems has motivated continuous research activities. The current trend is to build autonomous, automated systems that can adapt to changes in the environment, including manufacturing systems.

Decision complexity is and will continue to be an issue in manufacturing systems because excessive design and operation alternatives exist in the products to be produced and the choice among appropriate combinations is not an easy task. The global market necessitates flexibility in manufacturing systems in order to compete effectively with companies emerging around the world. There is a definite trend toward customized products with short life cycles, responding to market changes almost instantaneously. The flexibility needed can only be obtained through integration among the basic functions of manufacturing, namely, product and part design, process planning, programming for machines, robots, automated guided vehicles, production planning, manufacturing, receiving, storage, and shipping. Manufacturing flexibility demands customized high-quality, and low-cost products with inexpensive components. This translates into autonomous machine setup procedures, automation of design and process planning, and well-integrated manufacturing information systems. Hence, flexibility requires intelligence, and this needs to be integrated with real-time control to be able to adapt to changes both in the market and in the manufacturing environment at the shop floor.

The emergence of intelligent systems has been a welcome development for manufacturing. The "intelligence" embedded in the intelligent systems can take many forms. In the traditional intelligent systems, emerging out of the artificial intelligence community, the knowledge in the form of rules regarding domain decisions constitutes "intelligence." These rules are provided by domain experts and the systems are thus called *expert systems*. An advantage of the expert systems is that once the knowledge is embedded into the system, there is no longer a need to rely upon the expert being present at crucial times. Another advantage of these expert systems is that experts from different domains can be used to create a system with expertise in several domains.

Another emerging form of intelligent system is created from artificial neural networks. The intelligence is distributed throughout the system in the form of weights along the paths interconnecting the processing elements or neurons of the artificial neural network. The knowledge is embedded into the network typically through a training process. The network is exposed to many examples of correct domain decisions and it learns the relationships that determine good and bad decisions. It is also possible to combine the different types of intelligence, along with conventional programming techniques, to form hybrid intelligent systems. With the development of hybrid systems, the advantages of the various intelligent systems can be exploited to produce an optimal system.

This chapter presents an application of artificial neural networks used in design and manufacturing. In order to best illustrate the ability of artificial neural networks, a nontrivial example is presented. The design and automation problem selected is that of selecting a chair design from a set of standard chair designs that best meets the criteria established by a given customer. A design solution for this problem is presented along with a description of the prototype system. In the system, the chair design function has been automated by retrieving a design from a database of design solutions that satisfies the market demands. Once the appropriate design is retrieved from the database, the system locates the required parts for the selected design within an inventory area and moves the parts to a packaging area. The parts are arranged to provide shipment in the smallest container feasible. Figure 9.1 shows a list of the system network components.

The system is best described as having two major subsystems, which are further broken down into modules. The two major subsystems are the automatic design retrieval system (ADRS) and the intelligent packaging system (IPS).

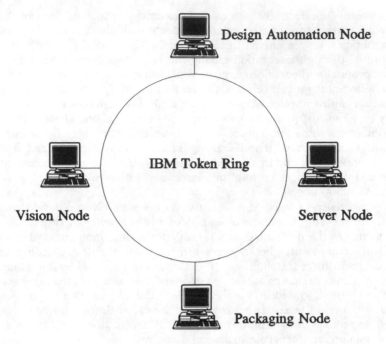

FIG. 9.1 System network.

Automatic Design Retrieval System (ADRS). The ADRS evaluates and maps the functional specification, as provided from marketing data, onto a set of physical structures based on the *predesigned* substructures and the knowledge of existing designs (chair designs) for automating the design process.

Intelligent Packaging System (IPS). The IPS consists of two modules, the vision and robot controller modules. These modules represent two major areas in manufacturing automation: machine vision and automated manufacturing operations through use of robotics. *Machine vision* concerns understanding the surrounding environment through the acquisition and processing of video images. This processing provides the sensory inputs needed for the manufacturing automation process. It allows for the creation of intelligent automated systems that can sense their environment and adapt their actions accordingly. The use of robotics has enabled a lot of the physical activities required in manufacturing to be automated. Robotics has been successfully applied to a variety of tasks involved with the manufacturing, assembly, or moving of parts.

The machine vision subsystem processes images in order to identify and locate chair parts in both the inventory and packaging areas of the system. The processing consists of data transformations, which start with raw video images and end up with a set of parts, their location, and their orientation within the area being analyzed.

The *robot controller* moves the required chair parts from the inventory area to the packaging area. In moving the pieces, the robot controller considers the size, position, and orientation of each object. The pieces are moved one at a time at a speed which minimizes the packaging time while also minimizing the chance of the robotics arm losing the piece during movement.

9.2 ARTIFICIAL NEURAL NETWORKS

Artificial Neural Networks (ANNs) are a new information processing technique that simulates biological neurons using computer programs. Although biological details are disregarded by this hardware/software model, artificial neural networks retain enough structure to work like a biological neural processing unit. They are mathematical models of theorized mind and brain activity. ANN provides a greater degree of robustness or fault tolerance because of the massive parallelism in their design. Neural networks are used in situations where only a few decisions are required from a massive amount of data, or when a complex nonlinear mapping needs to be learned.

In this section three ANN paradigms that have been incorporated in the proposed system are examined. These are Fuzzy Associative Memory (FAM), Backpropagation neural networks (BP), and Adaptive Resonance Theory (ART1).

Fuzzy Associative Memory (FAM)

Fuzzy associative memories (Kosko, 1987) are knowledge-based information processing systems. However, unlike the bivalent rules as symbols in expert systems, the FAM rules consist of numerical entities. These rules are not single-value propositions, but are an embodiment of multivalued sets. These numerical entities of associations (rules) relax or deemphasize the articulated, expertly precise nature of the stored knowledge. In the real-world application of knowledge bases (expert systems), a knowledge engineer can hardly capture the articulated rules; incorporating them inexactly and imprecisely.

FAM is a two-layer *feedforward* network—where signals allow information to flow among nodes or Processing Elements (PEs) in one direction only (Fig. 9.2). FAM is *heteroassociative* because it stores the pattern pairs $(C_1, S_1) \cdots (C_m, S_n)$. Therefore, it operates as a fuzzy classifier that stores an arbitrary fuzzy spatial pattern pair (C_k, S_k) using fuzzy Hebbian learning, where the kth pattern pair is represented by the fuzzy sets $C_k = \{c_1^K, \cdots, c_n^K\}$ and $S_k = \{s_1^K, \cdots, s_p^K\}$. Fuzzy composition is defined as:

$$M = C^T \circ S$$

or, in pointwise notation (Simpson, 1990) as:

$$m_{ij} = \min\left(\mu_C(c_i^K), \mu_S(s_j^k)\right)$$

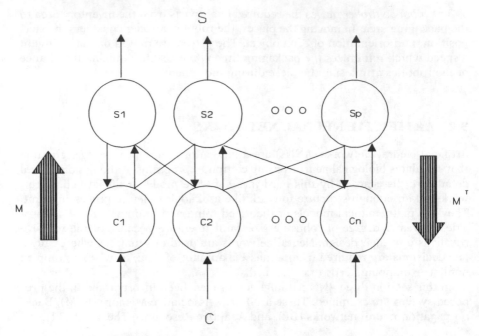

FIG. 9.2 FAM is two-layer feedforward fuzzy classifier.

Where $\mu_C(c_i^k)$ is the degree of membership of the ith member of the fuzzy set C (with the range of 0 to 1), m_{ij} is a fuzzy connection strength from the ith to the jth neuron or the max–min composition between the two layers of the network.

Backpropagation Neural Networks

The backpropagation neural network (BP) paradigm has been the most widely used paradigm. The elementary backpropagation is a three-layer feedforward network with feedforward connections (no feedback connections) from the input layer to the hidden layer, and feedforward connections from the hidden layer to the output layer of the network. Figure 9.3 shows an example of a backpropagation neural network. In general, it is possible to have several hidden layers, connections that skip over layers, and lateral connections. Backpropagation uses supervised learning and a multilayer gradient descent error correction encoding algorithm. It is heteroassociative and capable of storing arbitrary analog spatial pattern pairs. It learns off-line and operates in discrete time. Outputs of backpropagation networks are not restricted to just binary patterns and can take on analog values (Simpson, 1990).

Classification is performed by training the network to respond correctly to the set of training data, made up of the input vectors and the output classification

OUTPUT VECTORS

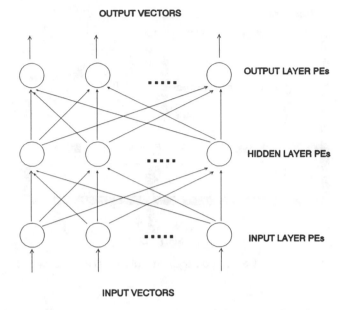

OUTPUT LAYER PEs

HIDDEN LAYER PEs

INPUT LAYER PEs

INPUT VECTORS

FIG. 9.3 An elementary backpropagation topology.

codes. The backpropagation algorithm performs the input to output mapping by minimizing a cost function to make connection weight adjustments according to the error between the computed and desired output. The cost function is minimized using the squared error, which is the squared difference between the computed output value and the desired output value for each PE.

Adaptive Resonance Theory

Binary adaptive resonance theory (ART1) neural networks are two-layer, nearest neighbor classifiers that store an arbitrary number of binary spatial patterns (Simpson, 1990). The topology of an ART1 neural network is shown in Fig. 9.4. The network does not require training. When a binary pattern is presented to the network, the network compares the input to the patterns stored in its memory. If the input is significantly close to a stored pattern, a match is made. If no pattern is found that closely matches the input pattern, the input pattern is stored in a new location within the network.

Input feature vectors are presented to the inputs of the ART1 network. The inputs are propagated through the first layer to the second layer. At the second layer, all the neurons compete with each other to produce a single neuron with an output of one commonly called the *winner-takes-all*. The winning neuron sends a signal back through the network's top-down weights creating a new vector called X. The X vector is compared to the input vector and the difference of the two

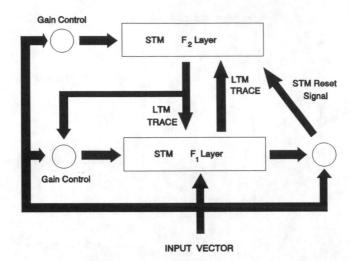

FIG. 9.4 The basic features of ART1 neural network.

vectors is divided by the sum of components in the input vector. This result is compared to a parameter called the vigilance factor. If the result exceeds the vigilance factor, the input vector is recognized as a match to a pattern in memory. If the result does not exceed the vigilance parameter, then no match is made and the winning neuron is removed from the set of possible matches for the input vector. Then, the process is repeated with the reduced set of possible matches for the input vector. This process is repeated until the pattern is matched to an existing pattern or stored in memory as a new pattern.

The setting of the vigilance factor determines how similar the input pattern must be to a stored pattern in order to match. A high vigilance factor will mean the input vector and stored pattern have to be very close to one another before a match is recognized. Using a high vigilance factor prevents false matches to previously stored objects. The similarity of the objects the system is expected to distinguish between will have to be considered when setting the vigilance factor.

9.3 AUTOMATIC DESIGN RETRIEVAL SYSTEM (ADRS)

The main objective of ADRS is to automate design receival by retrieving a design based on how well a design solution satisfies the marketing demands and user specifications (Bahrami and Dagli, 1992). Design involves continuous interplay between what we want to achieve and how we want to achieve it (Suh, 1990). A designer usually associates sets of fuzzy functional requirements with sets of physical structures. Then, during the design process, design solutions are retrieved from memory to solve the design problem.

Customers and the design–build team usually communicate through a natural and somehow ambiguous language that cannot be modeled by conventional two-valued logic. Fuzzy sets can exploit the complexity and ambiguity that may result from communication gaps between users and designers and turn them into manageable problem domains without ignoring the important factors involved. Fuzzy sets give the building blocks for dealing with imprecise and overwhelming complex representation problems of input requirements. For instance, the class of comfortable chairs can be viewed as a fuzzy set. An executive chair is definitely a member of this fuzzy set with a high degree of membership (close to 1), and a classroom chair is more out of the set than it is in it. Because of the fuzzy characteristics of the functional requirements and design parameters, and the capability of mapping a fuzzy spatial pattern pair of FAM, this paradigm has been selected for the ADRS.

The Design Problem

Given sets of fuzzy functional requirements (FRs) and design constraints (Cs), generate the design solution(s) that can satisfy the input requirements. For instance, the input requirement for designing a chair may be stated as:

> *Design a very comfortable chair that can be used more or less in public.*
>
> FR_1 = The chair must be *very comfortable.*
>
> C_1 = *Use more or less in public.*

Having defined FRs and Cs, how are the design solutions generated, namely a *very comfortable chair* that can be *used more or less in public.* Design constraints have been differentiated from functional requirements because they basically concern the boundary of the design, such as size, weight, and cost (the input constraints), or capacity, geometric shape, and usage (the system constraints) (Suh 1990). The use of fuzzy associative memory in automatic design retrieval will now be illustrated.

Fuzzy Knowledge Representations

To experiment with the concept, six generic functional requirements and eleven design constraints have been generated for designing various classes of chairs. Functional requirements are defined as:

(1) Ability to adjust the chair (FR_1)
(2) Ability to move the chair (FR_2)
(3) Ability to fold the chair (FR_3)
(4) Stability (FR_4)
(5) Ability to stack the chair (FR_5) and
(6) Comfortability (FR_6)

Design constraints are defined as cost (C_1), size (C_2), weight (C_3), use for dining

(C_4), use for office (C_5), use for relaxation (C_6), use for home (C_7), use for classroom (C_8), use for public (C_9), use for typing (C_{10}), and aesthetic look (C_{11}). The crisp universal sets, FRs of the functional requirements and Cs of design constraints, are defined as follows:

$$\text{FRs} = \{FR_1, FR_2, FR_3, FR_4, FR_5, FR_6\}$$
$$\text{Cs} = \{C_1, C_2, C_3, C_4, C_5, C_6, C_7, C_8, C_9, C_{10}, C_{11}\}$$

A database of 11 different design solutions has been created, as shown in Fig. 9.5. Associated with each design solution is a list of required parts along with their positions in the final packaging configurations. Each design solution (chair) satisfies a certain set of functional requirements and design constraints. For instance, an executive chair may be defined as:

$$\text{frs (chair2)} = \{1.0/FR_1, 1.0/FR_2, 1.0/FR_6\}$$
$$\text{cs (chair2)} = \{1.0/C_5, 0.7/C_6, 0.3/C_7, 1.0/C_{11}\}$$

The above fuzzy sets may be interpreted in English as follows: *An executive chair is a chair that is very comfortable with a high degree of adjustability and movability, furthermore it is used more in the office than in the home, it also can be used for relaxation; finally the appearance is very important.*

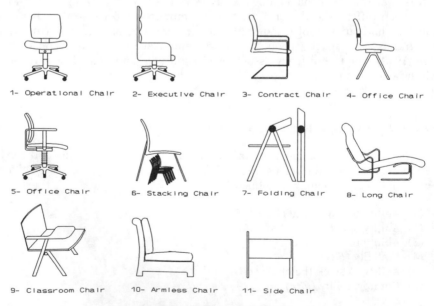

1- Operational Chair 2- Executive Chair 3- Contract Chair 4- Office Chair

5- Office Chair 6- Stacking Chair 7- Folding Chair 8- Long Chair

9- Classroom Chair 10- Armless Chair 11- Side Chair

FIG. 9.5. Design solutions.

Triggering and Conflict-Resolution Strategy

Fuzzy associative memory is used to retrieve a design solution based on how well a design satisfies the user's specifications. The primary disadvantage of FAM is in one-pair-storage capacity. Therefore, for each pattern pair (a design), a separate network must be created. The main problem in implementing the multi-FAM model is the selection of a network based on an incoming pattern.

An algorithm has been formulated to associate an incoming vector to the most applicable network (a design solution). The proposed algorithm consists of two components: triggering and conflict-resolution procedures. During triggering, the incoming vector is fed forward and backward through all the networks and triggers each network to generate a vector. A conflict-resolution procedure resolves the conflict by selecting the network that has stored the closest vector to the incoming vector.

Trigger Procedure

Assume that there are n networks, one for each design solution or associations as follows:

$$M_i = C_i^T \circ S_i, \quad i \in N_n$$

Where C_i and S_i are the antecedent and consequent, respectively, of the FAM rule i. Now suppose that an *l-dimensional* input fuzzy vector R is the fuzzy input requirement to the system.

The vector R is fed through the first layer of each network and fires every FAM rule in parallel, but to a different degree. Each FAM rule generates an *m-dimensional* fuzzy output vector P_i, where $i \in N_n$.

$$P_i = R_i \circ M_i^T, \quad i \in N_n$$

Next, pattern P_i is fed back through the second layer (output layer) of each network. Each FAM generates pattern Q_i.

$$Q_i = P_i \circ M_i^T, \quad i \in N_n$$

Conflict-Resolution Procedure

The conflict-resolution module compares pattern Q_i with the incoming pattern R. The following equation is used for measuring the similarity of patterns R and Q_i (Bahrami *et al.*, 1991):

$$S(R, Q_i) = \sum_{j=1}^{n} Q_{ij} R_j - \left| \sqrt{\sum_{j=1}^{n} (R_j - Q_{ij})^2} \right|$$

The network with the maximum value of S is the winner and it will be selected to do the mapping.

Network Topology and Data Set

The input as discussed earlier, consists of two fuzzy sets, FRs and Cs. For the purpose of simplicity, these two sets have been represented as a list. Further, the symbolic representation has been replaced by the positional importance of the degrees of memberships in the list. The input layer is designed to have 17 neurons: one neuron for every functional requirement and design constraint. For example, the functional requirements and design constraints for executive chair (chair 2) are represented as follows:

$$C_2 = (1.0 \quad 1.0 \quad 0 \quad 0 \quad 0 \quad 1.0 \quad 0 \quad 0 \quad 0 \quad 1.0 \quad 0.7 \quad 0.3 \quad 0 \quad 0 \quad 0 \quad 0 \quad 1.0)$$

The first value corresponds to FR1 (*ability to adjust the chair*), the second to FR2 (*ability to move the chair*) and so on. Each degree of membership is assigned to a separate neuron.

The output (second) layer of FAM is designed to have 11 neurons, one for every class of chair. For instance, Chair 2 is represented as

$$S_2 = (0 \quad 1.0 \quad 0 \quad 0 \quad 0 \quad 0 \quad 0 \quad 0 \quad 0 \quad 0 \quad 0)$$

9.4 INTELLIGENT PACKAGING SYSTEM (IPS)

The machine vision subsystem provides two functions. The first function is the identification, location, and orientation of the standard chair parts located in the inventory area. The second function is packaging of the required parts and monitoring the packing area to ensure that the parts have been moved and packaged correctly.

In determining the location and orientation of the standard part, the vision system acquires an image of the inventory area. Figure 9.6 shows a raw video image acquired of the inventory area. The image consists of 480 lines of pixels with each line having 512 pixels. The intensity of each pixel is represented by a number between 0 (darkest intensity) to 255 (brightest intensity). This video image is processed to extract the identification, position, and orientation of each part found in the inventory area. The location and orientation of the desired parts in inventory will be passed, along with the packaging locations, to the robotics subsystem for packaging of the parts for final shipment.

The monitoring of the packaging area ensures that the correct parts are included in the final package. A camera located above the packaging area acquires a video image of the area. This image is processed to locate the container that the chair parts will be packaged in, and once the parts are packaged, locate the standard parts within the package.

FIG. 9.6. Raw video image of the inventory area.

Machine Vision and Object Identification Module

Most of the neural network applications in vision have been for object recognition systems (Barnard, 1989). In these applications, the images are processed to classify the objects found in the images for proper identification. In practical applications, the objects in the images have undergone some type of transformation, such as magnification, translation, rotation, or a combination of these three. Classification techniques must be capable of handling all the transformations.

Conventional classifiers divide the feature space into hyperplanes or hyperquadrics. Neural network classifiers are capable of piecewise linear or piecewise quadric decision boundaries (Barnard, 1989). Although the most popular neural network classifier is backpropagation, many other paradigms are available to choose from with varying capabilities and memory capacities. However, because ART1 provides on-line learning capability and is able to distinguish small differences in the input patterns, it has been selected for the vision module object classification. Object identification is divided into two sections, image preprocessing and object classification. Figure 9.7 shows the knowledge transformations that occur during the processing of the images.

Image Preprocessing

In order to process the scenes as seen from the cameras, digital representations must be obtained. Images are acquired from the cameras, digitized, and stored as two-dimensional arrays—of size 480 rows by 512 columns—for processing. Each

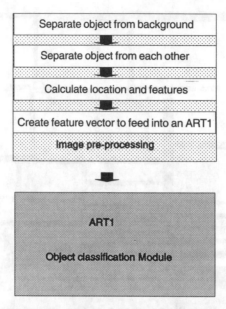

FIG. 9.7. Knowledge transformations in image processing module.

location of the array holds one byte (8 bits) of information indicating the intensity level of the corresponding pixel. A value of 0 represents the darkest intensity, while a value of 255 represents the brightest pixel value. The following is the algorithm used for the preprocessing:

begin
        Threshold the image to form a binary image of parts.
        The thresholding operation will separate the objects from the
            background.
        Process the binary image to separate and label the different objects.
  while (there is an object) **do**
  begin
        Identify each object and calculate its position and orientation.
  end
end

The outcome of the preprocessing operation is a feature vector that will be fed to a ART1 network for classifications. The feature vector should contain enough information so that the classifying network will be able to distinguish between different objects, while still being able to recognize the same objects located at different locations and orientations within the field of view of the camera. After all of the parts have been identified and located, a database of parts and their location and orientation is created.

Noise Suppression and Thresholding

The purpose of thresholding is to separate the objects from the background. The result of thresholding is to create a two-level image called a *binary image*, in which the background is at one level (0) and the objects are at the other binary level (1). The following formula illustrates the operation:

$$f(x,y) = \begin{cases} 1 & if \, \xi_{xy} \geq T \\ 0 & otherwise \end{cases}$$

where $f(x,y)$ is the resulting binary image, ξ_{xy} is the original gray-level image, and T is the thresholding level.

Object Separation

With the objects separated from the background, the next step is to differentiate the objects in the image. Two approaches are commonly used to separate and label different objects: the *recursive* and the *sequential* labeling algorithms (Horn, 1986).

The sequential algorithm was selected for labeling because it avoids recursive calls and thus requires less system memory, providing a straightforward procedure for object labeling. The sequential algorithm scans the image sequentially and labels the components in one pass. In this algorithm a pixel is analyzed along with three of the pixel's immediate neighbors, located directly to the left, top, and upper left (diagonal).

begin
    V_A :=   The value of the pixel under consideration for labeling
    V_B :=   The value of the pixel on top of A pixel
    V_C :=   The value of the pixel to the left of A pixel
    V_D :=   The value of the pixel to upper left corner of A pixel
    while (there is a pixel) **do**
    begin
            if VA = 0 **then** *continue*
            if V_A = 1 **and** V_D is *labeled* **then** V_A := V_D
            if V_B is *labeled* **then** V_A := V_B
            if V_C is *labeled* **then** V_A := V_C
            if V_B = V_C **and** both are *labeled* **then** V_A := V_B (or V_C)
            if VB $\leftrightarrow$ VC and both are labeled then VA := VB or VA := VC
            (Note the two labels are equivalent and correspond to same object.)
    end
end

The algorithm successfully labeled the objects, regardless of their position and orientation.

Position and Orientation Calculations

With all the separate components labeled in the image, calculations are performed to compute the area, the center of mass, the angle of the principal axis, the length along the principal axis, and the length of a line perpendicular to the principal axis. The following formula illustrates the moment calculations being performed on each object:

$$M_{ij} = \int_{-\infty}^{+\infty} \int_{-\infty}^{+\infty} x^j y^k f(x,y)\,dxdy$$

where j and k take on all nonzero values, and $f(x,y)$ is the binary image. There are two first-order moments M_{10} and M_{01}. The moments along with the area are used to calculate the center of gravity (centroid) for each object. The center of gravity (X_{cog}, Y_{cog}) is calculated with the following formulas:

$$X_{cog} = \frac{M_{10}}{M_{00}} \qquad Y_{cog} = \frac{M_{01}}{M_{00}}$$

The center of gravity is used for the location of each object in camera coordinates.

Central moments are used to compute the orientation of each object. The following formula is used to perform this computation:

$$\mu_{ij} = \int_{-\infty}^{+\infty} \int_{-\infty}^{+\infty} (x - x_{cog})^j (y - y_{cog})^k f(x,y)\,dxdy$$

In designating orientation, the angle of the principal axis is calculated with the following formula:

$$\tan 2\theta = \frac{2\mu_{11}}{\mu_{20} - \mu_{02}}$$

Once the angle of orientation is computed, the length of the object along the principal axis can be calculated. The length along the principal axis is created by starting at the centroid of the object and moving along the principal axis looking for the object's border. Once the border is found, that point is saved. The next step is to go back to the centroid and move along the principal axis in the other direction, again looking for the object's border. When the border is found in that direction the point is saved. The length along the principal axis is the distance between the two edge points found along the principal axis. A similar procedure is used to find the length along a line perpendicular to the principal axis. The only difference is instead of moving along the principal axis from the centroid, one moves along a line projected perpendicular to the principal axis.

In creating the feature vectors, the lengths are broken up into several ranges. Each range is represented by a couple of bits in the feature vector. When the two lengths (along the principal axis and perpendicular to the principal axis) are calculated, the bits corresponding to the range the lengths fall into are set to one, with the rest of the bits set to zero. With the length and width of the objects making up the feature vector, each object is classified with the neural network classifier.

Object Classification Through ART1

The parts are classified through a neural network classifier. A feature vector is calculated for each object and fed into an ART1 neural network. The network performs a nearest neighbor classification of the feature vector. If the feature vector does not match sufficiently close to any patterns already stored in the network, a new class is created, signifying that a new part has been presented to the neural network classifier.

The feature vector consists of two part attributes which are the object's area and the length of the object about the principal axis. Because all of the standard parts are rectangular in shape, these two features will allow the recognition of all parts. These two features can be quickly created for each object because most of the calculations have been performed during the preprocessing stage. When a feature vector is presented to the network, the network compares the input patterns to the patterns stored in its memory. If the input is significantly close to a stored pattern, a match is made. If no pattern is found that closely matches the input pattern, the input pattern is stored in a new location within the network. If an object is presented to the network for the first time, the system will consult the database to retrieve the name of the part and then create a new class for the object, but if the object has been already classified, the system will add the part to the already created class and display it in that class color with its name. Figure 9.8 shows an example where the parts are identified within the inventory area.

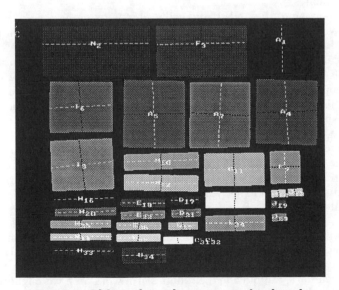

FIG. 9.8. Objects have been recognized and labeled by utilizing ART1 neural network.

System Calibration with Backpropagation Neural Network

System calibration is an important step in any machine vision application. Before obtaining accurate location or measurement information, the cameras of the vision system must be calibrated to a global coordinate system. Because the objects are going to be moved by a robotics arm, it is convenient to use the robot arm's coordinate system as the global coordinate system. The calibration procedure establishes the transformation of points from image coordinates to global coordinates (robotics arm coordinates). The complexity and accuracy of the calibration is determined by the requirements of the application.

The purpose of developing the ANN-based calibration system is to investigate whether the system can be inexpensively trained, with sufficient accuracy, to transform points from image to robotics coordinates. The setup must be straightforward and easily automated, should the network perform adequately, and any fixturing or test objects needed in the calibration must to be easily produced.

The first question to consider when attempting to perform the calibration with a back-propagation network is what advantages the approach offers over more conventional techniques that are available. The main advantage of the proposed system over other techniques is that it does not require an elaborated model of the imaging system that is needed by conventional approaches. Another advantage that the proposed method offers is that no *a priori* knowledge of camera placement, the effective focal length of the camera lens, or the pixel spacing of the pixel array is required. Other techniques estimate these parameters in order to establish the relationship between the camera and robot coordinates. Although the neural network does not estimate these parameters explicitly, the parameters are learned as the network trains on how to transform image coordinates into robot coordinates.

A disadvantage of the ANN-based calibration is its moderate accuracy of calibration. Whereas the network was accurate enough for the application it was developed for, it does not obtain the accuracy of less than a millimeter claimed by the other calibration techniques. A second disadvantage with the neural network approach is that it cannot provide the real-time calibration that can be performed by other approaches. The training of the neural network needs to be performed off-line. This disadvantage is not a vital limitation because the camera remains fixed in a single position, requiring calibration only if the camera is moved relative to the robotics arm.

The cameras to be calibrated are located approximately 70 in. above the work table of the robotics arm. The ANN-based calibration procedure is designed to learn the relationship between the camera coordinate system and the robotics arm coordinate system. The field of view of the cameras for the system are approximately 2 ft by $1\frac{1}{2}$ ft.

The first step in the calibration procedure is to place objects in known locations within the field of view of the camera. In this setup, 20 white Plexiglas blocks, a half-inch square, were picked up by the robotics arm and placed evenly throughout the field of view of the camera. Points that were within the field of view of the camera, but outside the robotics arm work area were ignored. Figure 9.9 illustrates the setup from a top view looking down on the robotics arm work space.

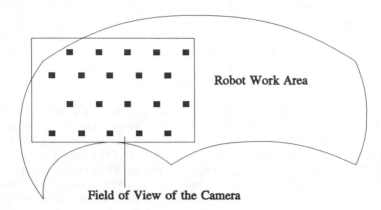

FIG. 9.9. Robot arm area and camera field of view.

The next step in the calibration procedure is to train the neural network to learn the transformation between image coordinates and robot coordinates. The network is a four-layer network consisting of one input layer, two hidden layers, and one output layer. The input layer has two input neurons corresponding to the normalized x and y of the object's centroid from the camera. There is also two neurons in the output layer corresponding to the object's centroid in robot coordinates. Each of the hidden layers contains 20 neurons. Each vector pair was presented to the network and the network weights were modified appropriately. Training continued until an acceptable accuracy was obtained. During each pass, a network error was calculated for the entire training set. The network error was the accumulated sum of the difference between the desired and actual output. The following formula illustrates the error calculation:

$$\text{Net Error} = \sum_{i=1}^{i=20} |\text{output}_{\text{desired}} - \text{output}_{\text{Network}}|$$

The network was trained until the accumulated error for the entire 20-vector training set was 0.0049. The initial training of the network took place over several days in order to obtain this level of accuracy. After the initial training session, if the camera was moved slightly (< 1 in.) the system could be recalibrated to this accuracy with only an additional hour of training. So once the initial calibration network has been trained, any recalibration can be done relatively quickly. The results were encouraging and the average error was less than 0.04" and the maximum error was 0.056". The accuracy of the calibration network can be improved by adding more test objects throughout the camera's field of view and spacing them closer together. However, this claim requires further research.

Robot Controller Module

The robot controller module constitutes the last part of the IPS. It is composed of two components, an IBM 7335 robot used for packaging and a host computer to control it. The input to the module are the pick-and-place coordinates of each of a chair's parts that are needed for packaging. The pick coordinates are obtained from the vision system after a series of image processing, as described in the previous sections. The place coordinates are determined by the design module.

The sequence generator portion of the module reads the information supplied by the vision system and the design, i.e., the pick-and-place coordinates, and determines a valid sequence of pick and place. The second step involves the dynamic programming of the robotics arm in AML (A Manufacturing Language). AML is a high-level robotics programming language. The dynamic program generator, which is an object-oriented software program written in C++, generates the AML code with correct syntax in ASCII format. Thus the output of the second step is an AML code consisting of a sequence of pick-and-place function calls with unique pick-and-place coordinates in each call. The third step involves compiling the AML code into a machine language of the robot. This is performed by another C++ member function that invokes the AML compiler and provides as input the AML program. The result is another file with the machine instructions ready to be transmitted to the robot.

The fourth step is executed by a robot interface program. This program is responsible for sending the file, consisting of a series of machine instructions, to the robot controller by using an RS-232 communication protocol. This is essentially a serial communication channel and involves a good amount of handshaking for ensuring error free transmission.

At the beginning of the fifth step, the robot controller has in its memory a sequence of machine instructions for controlling the robot. The controller reads these instructions sequentially and decodes them into the necessary electrical signals to make the robot move and perform an operation. After the assembly is complete, the robot moves back to its home position and is ready for the next operation. The result of this step is a packaged product that is ready to ship.

ANN-Based Robot Velocity Control

A backpropagation neural network has been used to control the velocity constraints for each part based on the part's length and width. The network architecture consists of three layers: one input, one hidden, and one output layer. The input layer consists of 8 neurons, the hidden layer consists of 15 neurons, and 2 neurons are used in the output layer.

The training set is composed of dimensions of sample parts and the recommended speeds for each. Table 9.1 shows a list of dimensions (in inches) and the recommended speeds. The length and width parameters together form the 8-bit input vector to the network and the 2-bit speed parameter represents the desired output of the network. The speed is divided into four classes, namely: *very slow* (0), *slow* (1), *moderate* (2), and *fast* (3).

Table 9.1. Representative of Component Dimensions and Their Recommended Speeds

Length	Width	Feature Vector (Input Vector)	Speed	Desired Output Vector
6 = (0 1 1 0)	2 = (0 0 1 0)	0 1 1 0 0 0 1 0	Very Slow	0 0
8 = (1 0 0 0)	6 = (0 1 1 0)	1 0 0 0 0 1 1 0	Slow	0 1
4 = (0 1 0 0)	2 = (0 0 1 0)	0 1 0 0 0 0 1 0	Moderate	1 0
4 = (0 1 0 0)	4 = (0 1 0 0)	0 1 0 0 0 1 0 0	Fast	1 1

Similar to the calibration procedure, training continued until an acceptable accuracy was obtained.

9.5 IMPLEMENTATION

The system has been implemented based on the ideas discussed in this chapter. The intelligent design retrieval and packaging system is composed of four IBM PCs, networked through an IBM token ring (Fig. 9.1). Table 9.2 shows the list of the computers used in the system.

The ADRS is divided into two separate sections, front end and back end. The front end section provides the user interface, and the back end consists of fuzzy associative memory. The front end, itself, is divided into two sections, preprocessor and postprocessor. The preprocessor communicates with the designers and assists them in setting up the functional requirements and design constraints. The postprocessor on the other hand converts the recall vector of the FAM to a design solution. The back end does the actual mapping of input requirements to the design solutions.

The network server provides the shared resources for the system. The server is set up to share a hard disk as well as a virtual disk. The system monitor runs on this system. The monitor program checks the status of the system and facilitates communications between the different processes running concurrently. This

Table 9.2.

Function	Computer Type
Automatic Design Retrieval System (ADRS)	PS/2 Model 80
Machine Vision	PS/ Model 30
Network Server	IBM 7552
Robot Controller	IBM AT

Table 9.3. System Modules and Implementation Languages

Module	Computer Language
ADRS Pre-processor	LISP
ADRS Post-processor	LISP
Fuzzy Associative Memory	C++
Vision Pre-processing	C++
Backpropagation Neural Network	C++
Image Classification ART1	C++
Robot Controller	C++
Monitor	C++

communication is accomplished through shared data files residing on the network. Each subsystem has a data file in which status information can be written. The monitor program writes a certain code to the appropriate data file when a subsystem should start operation. The subsystem, in turn, writes a different code in the file when it has completed its operations. The entire system's status can be seen by looking at the codes stored in the system data files. The use of shared data files on the network allows for an easy interface between system modules and provides a language-independent way to communicate throughout the system. Table 9.3 shows the various modules of the system and the programming language used for their implementation.

9.6. CONCLUSION

In this chapter the application of neural networks in design and manufacturing has been examined. The system has incorporated three neural network paradigms, fuzzy associative memory, backpropagation, and adaptive resonance theory (ART1) to achieve its task. FAM is utilized for automating the design retrieval or mapping the marketing characteristics to predesigned structures. ART1 has been utilized for object identification of the vision module. A backpropagation neural network has been used for camera calibration; another backpropagation neural network was used to control the speed of the robot arm based on the size of a given part. This unique application of neural networks in design and manufacturing can be extended to more sophisticated tools for concurrent engineering and future automated factory.

The example used here demonstrated the integration issues and the use of intelligent systems to automate design through manufacturing using newly emerging technologies such as artificial neural networks. The concepts introduced in this chapter are reinforced in more detailed descriptions of the problems of concurrent engineering and the specific technologies proposed for their solution through the use of artificial intelligence.

ACKNOWLEDGMENTS

We wish to acknowledge the programming efforts of Mr. Vellanki M. Kumar. This work was supported in part by AT&T, and in part by IBM, and in part by Intelligent Systems Center, University of Missouri-Rolla.

REFERENCES

Bahrami, A., and Dagli, C. H. 1992. From fuzzy input requirements to crisp design. *International Journal of Advanced Manufacturing Technology*, 8:52–60.

Bahrami, A., Dagli, C., and Modarress, B. 1991. Fuzzy associative memory in conceptual design. *Proc. of IEEE International Joint Conference on Neural Networks (IJCNN)*, **I**, 183-188, Seattle, Washington.

Barnard, E., and Casasent, D. 1989. Image processing for image understanding with neural nets. *Proc. of IEEE International Joint Conference on Neural Networks (IJCNN)* **I**, 111-115, Piscataway, New Jersey.

Horn, B. 1986. *Robot Vision*. Cambridge: MIT Press.

Kosko, B. 1987. Fuzzy associative memories. In *Fuzzy Expert Systems*, ed. A. Kandel. Reading: Addison-Wesley.

Simpson, P. 1990. *Artificial Neural Systems*. New York: Pergamon Press.

Suh, N. P. 1990. *The Principles of Design*. Cambridge: Oxford University Press.

Chapter 10

Manufacturability Analysis as a Part of CAD/CAM Integration

Jussi Opas and Helge Bochnick
Bremer Institut für Betriestechnik und
angewandte Arbeitswissenschaft and
der Universität Bremen (BIBA)
Bremen, Germany

Jukka Tuomi
Helsinki University of Technology
Laboratory of Information Processing Science
Espoo, Finland

10.1 INTRODUCTION

An automated production needs a complete product model. Therefore, a design system that provides the necessary product model is a basic requirement for an integrated CAD/CAM system. A CAD system should not be only an electronic drafting board—a product model should be in use in all phases of the manufacturing process, including assembly and testing activities. This information should be accommodated into a factory database.

Traditionally, the designer's task has been to introduce functional requirements of products. Manufacturability and functions like tool design, assembly, testing, and service, which also have an effect on total costs, have been left to a secondary stage. The current CAD systems have been developed to make design processes easier, but they do not support consideration of the other mentioned functions.

A CAD/CAM system database must be uniform and it should be used in all phases of the design process. Figure 10.1 presents a simplified model of design and manufacturing processes in which a product model is first developed in the design phase and afterwards it is used in the manufacturing phase (Ohsuga, 1988).

This chapter describes the work being done on manufacturability analysis and process planning on the basis of the feature modeling taking place at the Helsinki University of Technology and at BIBA, the Bremer Institut für Betriebstechnik und angewandte Arbeitswissenschaft.

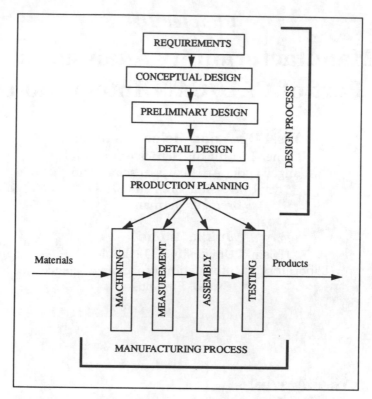

FIG. 10.1. Basic procedure of design and manufacturing (Ohsuga, 1988).

10.2   DESIGN AND MANUFACTURABILITY

The Effect of Design on Manufacturing Costs

In the beginning of the design phase, the most important parameters of the product are determined. If design is divided into sketching, designing, and drafting, then the most important phase of design is sketching. In that phase, the most important physical properties, functional principles, and the size of construction are selected. The designer's ability to estimate manufacturing costs rises during the design process and is at its best in the drafting phase when the possibility of affecting manufacturing costs is at its lowest (Fig. 10.2).

Especially in one-of-a-kind production, the typical policy is to make a cost analysis just before or just after manufacturing. The designer also gets feedback in this way, but the benefits of cost consciousness cannot be put into use in the design tasks. A more powerful practice is to obtain information about manufac-

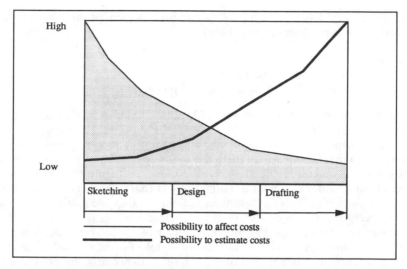

FIG. 10.2. The possibilities of designer to estimate affect on costs.

turing costs during the sketching phase when the possibility of affecting manufacturing costs are best. When this is done, the cost analysis will take place in the design process along with the other technical analyses. For example, strength calculations comprising iterations and reviews are an obvious part of the design process.

Definition of Manufacturability

Courtright has done a case study on manufacturability analysis (Courtright, 1988). He defines manufacturability in a specific instance of a flexible manufacturing cell with so-called manufacturability parameters. In the implemented manufacturability analyzer, Courtright checks manufacturability with respect to the capabilities of a manufacturing cell. The implemented system reveals features, that cannot be manufactured, but it does not make proposals for improvement. While manufacturability analysis is done, whether there are sufficient raw materials and cutting tools is also being checked. Thus the analyzer is also performing process planning. Therefore the problems of manufacturability are closely related to those of process planning.

Now to look at the aspects that are implemented into the technological manufacturability analyzer and the generative process planning system (Mäntylä *et al.*, 1987, and Opas and Mäntylä 1988). HutCAPP, a machining operation planner, considers machining operations performed in a three-axis machining center. The operations addressed include milling, boring, reaming, sinking, and so on.

Manufacturability depends on the following three aspects of the manufacturing complexity of the product (Tuomi, 1989):

(1) Fixturing of workpiece
(2) Precision or accuracy requirements
(3) The form and dimensioning of a workpiece

First, the design of workpieces should be such that they can be machined in one setup. When this is not possible, the designer should take into account that in different setups it is difficult to reach concentricity, which requires a very precise setup. In a machining center, there are several possibilities to make fixturing: directly into the machine, directly into the pallet, in a turning table, and so on. In a machining center the most essential thing is that workpieces can be manufactured in one setup. This leads to the requirement that the workpiece must be accessed freely from each needed machining direction.

Precision requirements determine the number of needed operations and thus also the machining costs. The surface finish should not be set to higher values than the functionality of the workpiece requires. Especially the points, where more expensive manufacturing operations become necessary, should be considered carefully. In tolerancing, factory-dependent standarization should be taken into account. An *increment* is the smallest movement that a machine tool can do. Deflection and backlash can cause the repetition accuracy of a machine tool to rise, usually up to 0.01 mm or 0.005 mm.

When the design of the workpiece is detailed, the designer should take into account possible manufacturing methods and the tools to be used. Workpieces should be machined with standard tools. Consequently, roundings, filletings, hole bottoms, and other such details should match the tool geometry. Although manufacturing features, such as holes or faces to be machined, are located in the workpiece, it should be noted that the tool and spindle need extensive space in machining.

10.3 MANUFACTURABILITY ANALYSIS AND CAD/CAM INTEGRATION

Problems in CAD/CAM Integration

There are several problems to be solved before design, planning, and manufacturing can be integrated into a computerized environment. The most important problems are:

(1) Insufficiency of conventional product models
(2) Poor portability of CAPP systems
(3) Lack of common process planning logic
(4) Uncompleteness of CAPP systems
(5) Contradicting goals of process planning.

These problems are further explained in the following paragraphs.

Conventional computer internal product descriptions are not sufficient to support all the design tasks, let alone process planning and manufacturing execution tasks. An obvious defect of purely geometric product representation is that there is no parametric knowledge about tolerances, surface finishes, or material conditions. Product models have been mainly developed to visualize products, therefore things like paralellism requirement of two surfaces or number of holes in one direction cannot be asked. Another shortcoming is that geometric models represent mechanical parts in terms of low-level geometric entities. When intelligent functions like manufacturability analysis are integrated with CAD/CAM systems, means must be introduced to represent parts in terms of their functionally significant aspects, such as holes, grooves, and surfaces. Feature modeling offers these missing means (see Shah *et al.*, 1988). By means of a feature library, design and manufactring knowledge can be stored and utilized. When a feature-based CAD/CAM system is used, a conventional geometric modeler is still useful to visualize parts.

Manufacturing environments are continuously evolving, old machine tools are retracted and new ones are introduced. The same cycle is happening to other manufacturing equipment (Eversheim, 1989). A process planning system needs to be implemented so that it can be ported into new manufacturing environments with a minimum of effort. Ideally, a process planning system or a manufacturability analyzer can be launched in a new factory just by writing the description of the facility, the factory model, once. One problem is that the technology used in manufacturing may vary considerably from factory to factory. Some facilities are using advanced technologies, while the same manufacturing processes may be carried out manually in another facility.

One important difficulty in implementing a process planning system is that planning logic for different kinds of parts varies considerably. The planning logic for hole processes has its own characteristics when compared to milling processes like pocketing and groove milling. When other technologies like sheet metal works, which include flame cutting, nibbling and bunching, and turning operations, are taken into account it is impossible to define a common planning procedure.

In the current state of the art in CAPP systems, it is impossible to include all the manufacturing processes existing in a real factory. It may be a little bit provocative for the people who are working with CAPP systems, but it makes sense to try to implement computerized methods to the 20% of the manufacturing processes that can solve the 80% of the manufacturing problems. Full automation will not be reached in manufacturability analysis and process planning, but there can still be a level of satisfaction with computer-aided methods.

One of the difficulties of computer-aided process planning is that the goal of its various subtasks are contradictory; hence, the overall planning problem cannot be decomposed into independent subproblems (Mäntylä *et al.*, 1989). One instance of this difficulty is given by setup and tool selection planning. The global goal of setup planning is to keep the number of needed work directions at a minimum; even if the machining center to be used is capable of machining a workpiece from several directions without a new setup, fixturing design will be simplified if fewer directions are used. On the other hand, the local goal of tool selection is to select the most appropriate method and hence the best tool to manufacture a feature.

Manufacturability Analysis and a CAD/CAM Integration Model

Eversheim proposes that in new developments of CAPP systems, specific attention should be given to the flexible structuring of automation stages, extendable interfaces and data models, and new flexible system architechtures (Eversheim, 1989). Here, a model for CAD/CAM integration is presented that puts special emphasis on manufacturability analysis for part design solutions and aims to produce feedback information from downstream planning phases to upstream design phases (Fig. 10.3).

Here, CAD/CAM integration is divided into four phases:

(1) Design
(2) Technological analysis
(3) Proposing
(4) Binding

In the *design* phase, the product designer makes his or her creative and intellectual work, and produces a functional product description. It is possible to use existing CAD systems and to some extent recognize meaningful manufacturable entities, but ideally, design work is done in terms of design features. The concepts and methods used in early phases of design and the kind of conversion or mapping processes that must be applied are not discussed here, but the assumption is that the result of a designer's work will be a *feature model of the product* available for analysis and planning tasks. Moreover, the feature model should also have significance for the manufacturing point of view, not only the function.

The designer should be able to check the quality of the design as early as possible. Therefore, *technological analysis* should take place during design or immediately after completion of detailed design. The design of a product may still be incomplete when the designer wants to make the first check of manufacturability. This phase uses *common analysis knowledge*, which can be tailored by using *factory parameters*, describing the capabilities of each manufacturing facility. They consist, for instance, of predefined hole sizes or tested tolerancing practices. One source for common analysis knowledge is for example industrial standards. The output from the technological analysis is *enumerated and evaluated properties* of the product. When *impossible properties* are flagged, the product designer must change the design.

Process planning itself is divided into two phases, *proposing*, which could also be called the front end of process planning, and *binding*, which could also be called the back end of process planning. Dividing process planning into two phases is important, because it allows a shift from product-focused and factory-independent planning to manufacturing method-focused and factory-specific planning. The planning done in the proposing phase can be done more roughly than the detailed planning done in the binding phase. The proposing phase is

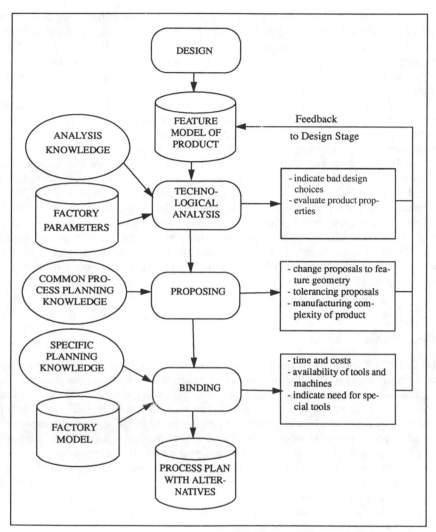

FIG. 10.3. A CAD/CAM integration model with manufacturability analysis.

generative in its nature, whereas the binding phase has characteristics in common with variant process planning.

In the proposing phase, *common manufacturing knowledge* is used. The phase aims to do preliminary setup planning by first enumerating the whole solution space and, afterwards, by minimizing the needed cutting directions. The solution space is restricted so that feasible or good alternative process plans can be proposed that reveal the *manufacturing complexity* of the product. *Geometric change proposals* can also be done. Both product designers and manufacturing engineers should perform the proposing phase of process planning, which enables a fluent shift of the responsibility of product and production toward the shop floor. When the proposed process plan is flexible and has alternatives, it can be used repeatedly and interpreted in different ways in binding, depending on the dynamic situation.

In the *binding phase*, a proposed process plan is bound to the actual restrictions of the manufacturing facility. Hence *factory model* and other *factory-dependent manufacturing knowledge* are used. The factory model should describe the static data of the factory, e.g., machine tools, fixturing equipment, and cutting tools, and dynamic data, e.g., load of machine tools, tool wearings, and accuracies of fixturing equipment. Factory-dependent manufacturing knowledge includes scheduling strategies and NC-programming practices. From the binding phase comes such manufacturability information as unavailable cutting tools and machining time, which can reveal the *exact manufacturing costs*. The output from binding phase is a *process plan*, which includes routing, setups, cutting tools, fixturing equipment, and NC-programs for each manufacturing step. The factory model and the generated process model are later used to control the manufacturing process.

10.4 CASE STUDIES

The CAD/CAM integration model, especially the idea of how to distribute manufacturability analysis into the model, is demonstrated with three case studies. The first case demonstrates technological manufacturability analysis, the second one demonstrates the proposing phase of process planning, and the last case demonstrates the ideas of the binding phase of process planning. The first two examples consider manufacturing operations that are performed in a machining center, such as milling, drilling, or turning (although the sample parts presented do not require any operations to be performed on a lathe). The technology of the third case concerns another kind of part family, sheet metal parts, which are manufactured by such methods as nibbling or punching. The implemented software for the first two cases have been integrated with each other, whereas the last case is demonstrated with stand-alone software.

Technological Manufacturability Analysis

Properties

A *property* is a feature in a part that affects the manufacturability of the part. A property may be a surface finish in a certain area, the shape of a hole pattern, or the perpendicularity of a hole. One feature may include one or more properties. Some of the properties may be refined by several features or parts of features. The sample part in Fig. 10.4 is first divided into features, after that the properties of the part are enumerated. In the sample part, there are only a few

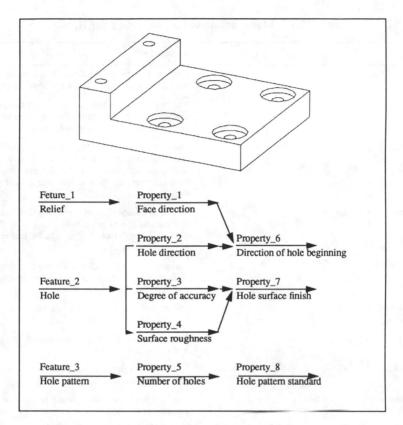

FIG. 10.4. A sample part and some of its properties.

different features, but they have several different properties. In Table 10.1 there are descriptions of properties for holes.

Property Grades and Scoring

The properties of a part are classified into quality classes, i.e, grades. The *grade* of a property may vary from 0 to 4. If the grade number of a property is 1, then that property of the part is optimal in a manufacturing point of view. If the grade of a property is, for example 3, then the design of the part can be changed to a better one so that the grade of the property is raised to 2 or even 1. In practice, that means, for example, the reduction of different hole sizes from 3 to 1.

All the grades of properties are scored such that the worst grade is zero or one point. The score of the grade is zero if it cannot be manufactured at all or if the manufacturing costs make no sense. Properties with a grade of zero must always

Table 10.1.   Manufacturability Properties for Holes

Property	Explanation
Hole-direction	Only a few hole directions should be used, because they affect into number of needed setups.
Hole-beginning	The beginning of a hole should be flat and perpendicular to its surface. In the case of a tilted beginning surface, a cutting tool may break.
Hole-ending	The end surface of a trough hole should be flat and perpendicular to the beginning surface. When ending surface is oblique, the tool may break. Under through hole there should be free space for drill.
Number-of-diameters	As few as possible hole diameters should be used, because this affects number of needed tools. The diameter of drills should be same as the diameters of free holes in part.
Hole-depth	The depth of hole should not be more than five to eight times the diameter, because otherwise a special tool is needed.
Hole-bottom-type	The bottom of a hole should be conical because the drill ends are conical.
Hole-bottom-angle	The bottom angle of blind holes should be same as standard angle of drill end.
2D-hole	Diameters of concentric holes should be same as standard angle of drill end.
Hole-sink-angle	The sink angle of a hole should be same as in standard profile drill.
Hole-accuracy	The accuracy of holes has remarkable effect on number of needed cutting tools.
Hole-surface-finish	Hole surface finish has remarkable effect on number of needed cutting tools.
Hole-diameter	The diameter of holes should be standardized according to standard tools.
Hole-pattern	The radius of circular hole patern should be standardized and number of holes in circular hole pattern should be standardized, too.

be changed. In Figure 10.5 there is a sample property that cannot be manufactured. In the bottom of a deep hole lies a ream, which has a considerably larger diameter.

All the grades of the properties are scored from best to worst. The first grade has the highest scores, the second grade has a little lower score, and so on. The absolute score number does not tell everything about the property, but the change in score when a property moves from one grade to a higher one, describes a change in manufacturability. In some properties, movement to the next upper

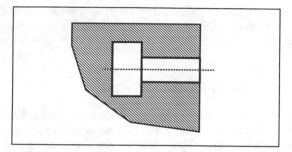

FIG. 10.5. A manufacturing-hostile property.

grade makes manufacturability better than another property changing over two grades. In Fig. 10.6 there is a sample case that demonstrates the scoring of grades. The design of the lower part is better from a manufacturing point of view, although the grade of the property "number of hole diameters" is 3. Drilling

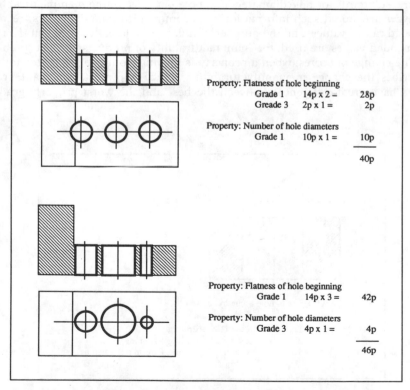

FIG. 10.6. Two sample workpieces with two properties.

a hole with a "twist drill" in the upper design is almost impossible. Thus the scores reached in the upper design (40 points) are a lot lower than the scores of the lower design (46 points).

Parametrization of Manufacturability Rules

Manufacturability rules include parametric values like hole diameters and surface finishes. Also the score numbers that belong to the property grades are used in the manufacturability rules. The grade scores are enumerated in a parametric list. This parameter list can be used to enhance the manufacturability analyzer for a specific factory. For example, recommended diameter values can be updated. When machine tools are changing in a factory, the reachable hole accuracies can be updated from the parameter list. In Fig. 10.7 there is a manufacturability rule (property) that determines manufacturability (grade) according to the costs of needed operations. If the manufacturing facility has machine tools that are able to produce the hole accuracy IT 10, then it can be updated on the manufacturability parameter list.

From the point of view of product and factory standardization, the parameter list is a useful database. Within the factory standardization belongs, among others, standards for hole diamaters and hole patterns. In the manufacturability analyzer are stored such information as recommended hole diamaters, recommended radius values, and the number of holes for hole patterns. When the recommended values are used, the manufacturability of products stay acceptable.

The change of scores, when a property is moving from one grade to another, describes the change in manufacturability. Hence, the most significant properties have great differences between the best and the worst property grades.

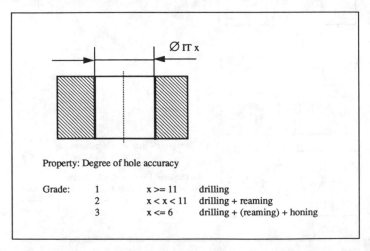

Property: Degree of hole accuracy

Grade:	1	$x >= 11$	drilling
	2	$x < x < 11$	drilling + reaming
	3	$x <= 6$	drilling + (reaming) + honing

Fig. 10.7. Manufacturability rules that concern hole accuracy.

Accordingly, the less important propereties have smaller differences between grade scores.

Figure 10.8 is an example of how to prioritize properties in relation to each other. The manufacturability of workpieces in Fig. 10.8 is estimated by using two different scores. The example concerns the property "perpendicularity of holes." If the difference from grade one to grade three is 5 points (12p - 7p), then the upper design alternative is more manufacturing friendly than the lower one. If

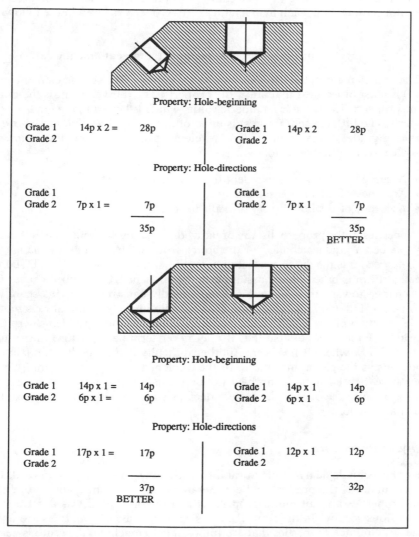

FIG. 10.8. Priorization of properties by adjusting scores of grades.

the difference is 10 points (17p - 7p), then the lower design alternative should be chosen with a total score of 37.

Property List

When the system analyzes the manufacturability of the part, it simultaneously generates a property list for the part. A property list consists of properties which the system has scored when it analyzed the manufacturability of the part. The property list is modified so that in reading it the user gets information on basis of which he or she is able to make changes to the construction of the product. The information about each manufacturability property is given in the following format:

(property (features) grade score (scores) (comment and advice))

The first element in the list is the analyzed property. The second element (features) is a list of features that affect the property. The third element is the grade of the property. The score is a numeric value, which is bound to the grade of the property. The fifth element (scores) is a list of numeric values that are bound to the better grades of the property. The last element in the list includes comments or advice, which may be as follows:

- Accuracy of the hole is excellent to manufacture
- Accuracy of the hole is satisfactory
- Accuracy of the hole is very difficult to reach

Properties in the property list are organized so that by changing the first property to a better grade, a change for the better score will be greatest. A change for the better score is the difference between the first atom of "(scores)" and "score." The algorithm is based on the assumption that the change described causes the best change toward more manufacturing friendly construction. This search is known as a "hill-climbing" algorithm. The hill-climbing algorithm always moves in the direction of the locally steepest ascent. These are some problems with this algorithm. First, it is possible that it may never terminate because the system does not know where it has been. Another difficulty is that the local maximum is not always the global maximum. In the implemented manufacturability analyzer, these theoretical problems have not prevented the use of hill-climbing algorithms, because the user of the system decides which geometric changes to the design are made.

Analysis Procedure

When the technological manufacturability analysis system is run, it first reads the feature model of the product and enumerates the manufacturability properties of it. Properties are put into a property list in the order that was described in the previous section. In the enumeration step, forward chaining rules are used. If the system finds properties that are impossible to machine (the score is zero), then it gives to the user a property list consisting of the manufacturing-hostile properties. The part geometry must be changed to eliminate the properties that are impossible to manufacture. The system stays in this loop until there are no properties that are impossible to manufacture.

Next, the system defines the manufacturability of the part as a whole. Manufacturability is the sum of all the scores that are bound to the properties. When changes to the design are done and manufacturability becomes worse than in the previous version, then the system returns back to the previous version. If manufacturability has became better or the part is again in the original state, the system accepts the changes and once again makes the property list. The analysis procedure can be run as many times as the user wants.

The output of this system is a manufacturing-oriented product model. Changes to geometry have been done by the user, with advice from the manufacturability analysis expert system. See Fig. 10.9.

Summary of Technological Analysis

The output of manufacturability analysis is characteristically similar to the proposing phase of HutCAPP (see the next section), in which geometric change proposals concerning the design of the product are suggested. The analysis tells the user what to change in the product design, but it does not tell how to make the changes.

The manufacturability analyzer considers the product as a whole so that it does not propose changes that make single features more manufacturing efficient but which make the product worse to manufacture as a whole. This is ensured so that different versions of the product are evaluated and the changes to the product model are accepted only if manufacturability as a whole becomes better.

If a product has properties that are classified as impossible to manufacture, the system generates for the user a list of the impossible properties. The manufacturing-unfriendly properties must be changed before the manufacturability of the product can be defined any further.

Proposing Phase of Process Planning

The purpose of this section is to demonstrate the front end of process planning, i.e., proposing. In the proposing phase, HutCAPP is capable of manufacturability analysis by using the so-called *relaxed features*. The phase is called *proposing* because feasible alternative process plans are proposed and changes which make a product's construction more manufacturing friendly are also proposed. One reason to divide process planning into two distinct phases is that *proposing* uses common manufacturing knowledge and the *binding* phase uses factory model and factory-dependent manufacturing knowledge.

Relaxed Feature Models

The proposing phase of HutCAPP works in terms of manufacturing features. There are several problems to be solved before a product model is described in terms of any *manufacturing features*. Discussion of design by features and feature

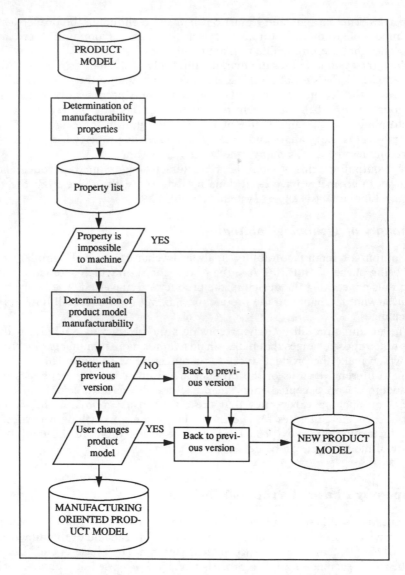

FIG. 10.9. Manufacturability analysis procedure.

recognition is out of the scope of this chapter. For an extensive review of feature research see Shah *et al.* (1988). Mäntylä *et al.* (1989) give the following caveats of product models described by manufacturing features:

(1) Overspecification of geometric models persists in any process planning system based on feature recognition from geometric models. This leads to premature commitment to certain manufacturing solutions.

(2) Parts can often be represented by means of several feature models, each representing a commitment to a certain way of manufacturing the part. A process planning system working on the basis of a single interpretation only cannot take into account the manufacturing opportunities offered by other interpretations.

The problem of premature commitment to a certain view of a part and to a certain way to manufacture it can be overcome if the process planner is able to make feature conversion. This means that a planner is able to modify and augment a feature model to take into account such manufacturing alternatives that are not explicitly covered by the original feature model.

Conversion capabilities are based on the idea that features themselves are able to take into account alternative interpretations. This kind of model is called a *relaxed feature model*.

Sample relaxation groups are:

(1) External-slot (through)	Three-way-slot
(2) External-slot (not through)	Break-slot
(3) Internal-filleted-relief	Internal-edged-relief
(4) External-filleted-relief	External-edged-relief

The relaxation cases are illustrated in Fig. 10.10. For example, the external slot that goes through the part should basically be machined with an endmill from the top or bottom, if the side direction is used, two tools should be used, an endmill and a ball-ended mill. Therefore, if the rounding is removed, i.e., the type of the feature is changed to a three-way-slot, a groove that is open to three directions, then it can be machined with an endmill from the side or with a sidemill from the front or back. The other relaxation groups, (2), (3), and (4) are described according to the same principles.

Feature relaxation introduces a certain vagueness into the product description. The original feature specification is not treated as being completely fixed, but as a loosely defined part model that denotes a whole family of vaguely similar parts, whose geometric details can be changed. By systematically searching this space of similar parts, a planner can reveal manufacturing alternatives that were not present in the original feature model.

Cutting Strategies

HutCAPP aims at near-optimal overall machining efficiency by considering all potentially useful machining processes for each feature. To be able to understand how the planning procedure of HutCAPP runs and how the system makes a manufacturability analysis in the proposing phase, cutting strategies must first be introduced. A *cutting strategy* is a combination of a tool and its working direction, i.e, the direction of the rotating spindle of a machining center or a milling machine.

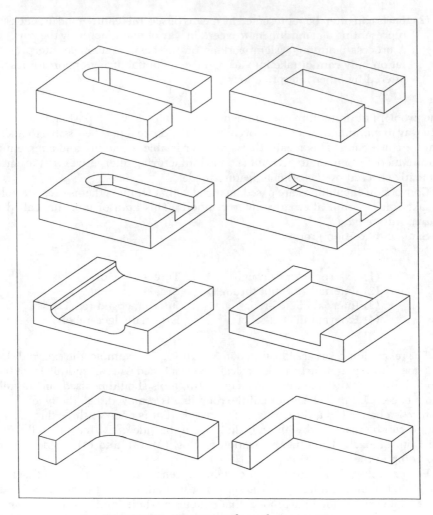

FIG. 10.10. Feature relaxation groups.

Cutting strategies are divided into two sets according to feature relaxation groups (or, vice versa, the feature relaxation groups are defined according to cutting strategies). Figure 10.11 presents cutting strategies for a relief feature. A relief is an area in a product that must be machined away from a blank part.

The part in Fig. 10.11 has three relief features. The second relief feature is highlighted. For instance, relief2 can be machined from the direction of the negative x-axis with an endmill, which is indicated with the combination ⟨xn, endmill⟩. It has three other cutting strategies.

The *alternative cutting strategy* becomes applicable if the geometry of the feature is changed, for instance, by adding or removing a rounding or a fillet. If

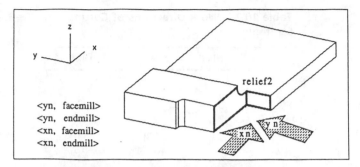

FIG. 10.11. Cutting strategies.

a rounding is inserted into relief2, then new process types and work directions become applicable. Figure 10.12 shows the alternative cutting strategies for the feature.

Manufacturability Analysis Procedure

After all the applicable cutting strategies have been enumerated, it becomes possible to consider the part as a whole and form the cutting plans. The reliefs of the sample part offer the work directions described in Table 10.2, where 1 indicates that the feature can be machined from the direction indicated in the row.

Thee information in the table is used to compute all such combinations of working directions that form minimal covers in the sense that all the features can be machined and no unnecessary directions are used. This computation can

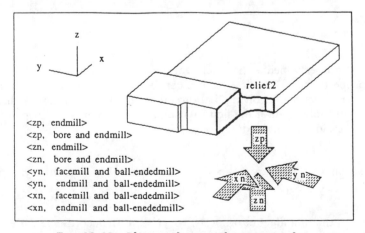

FIG. 10.12. Alternative cutting strategies.

Table 10.2. Work Directions of Cutting Strategies

	relief1	relief2	relief3
xp	1	-	-
xn	-	1	1
yp	1	-	-
yn	1	1	1
zp	1	-	1
zn	-	-	1

be expressed by means of a simple lattice algebra. In order to ensure that relief1 can be machined, it can be seen from the first column that at least one of the directions xp, yp, yn, or zp must be used. This requirement can be symbolized by the expression:

$$xp + yp + yn + zp$$

where "+" can be read as "or." The whole table can be expressed as

$$(xp + yp + yn + zp)^\circ(xn + yn)^\circ(xn + yn + zp + zn)$$

where the multiplication symbol reads as "and." When the resulting expression is evaluated by using a special algebra, the desired list of covering work directions can be obtained. The two properties of the algebra are

(1) $x^\circ x = x$
(2) $x + x^\circ y = x$

The first property means that each feature must be machined only once. The second property states that if a feature can be machined from some direction, all the other directions involving that direction and one other can be discarded. When the multiplication of the first two sums in brackets is performed, the following expression is obtained:

$$\langle=\rangle(xp^\circ xn + xp^\circ yn + xn^\circ yp + xn^\circ yp + xn^\circ yn + yn^\circ yn + xn^\circ zp + yn^\circ zp)^\circ$$
$$(xn + yn + zp + zn)$$

According to the first algebra property, $yn^\circ yn = yn$. In accordance with property (2), all the pairs where yn appears can be canceled. Consequently, the product of the sums can be shortened as follows:

$\langle=\rangle$ $(xp°xn + yn + xn°yp + xn°zp)°(xn + yn + zp + zn)$

$\langle=\rangle$ $xp°xn°xn + xp°xn°yn + xp°xn°zp + xp°xn°zn + xn°yn + yn°yn + yn°zp$
  $+ yn°zn + xn°xn°yp + xn°yp°zp + xn°yp°zp + xn°yp°zn + xn°xn°zp$
  $+ xn°yn°zp + xn°zp°zp + xn°zp°zn$

Now the first property can be applied:

$$xp°xn°xn = xp°xn$$
$$yn°yn = yn$$
$$xn°xn°zp = xn°zp$$
$$xn°zp°zp = xn°zp$$

Thus, the equation can be reduced as follows:

$\langle=\rangle$ $xp°xn + xp°xn°yn + xp°xn°zp + xp°xn°zn + xn°yn + yn + yn°zp + yn°zn$
  $+ xn°yp + xn°yp°yn + xn°yp°zp + xn°yp°zn + xn°zp$
  $+ xn°yn°zp + xn°zp + xn°zp°zn$

According to algebra property (2), yn absorbs each pair where it appears and xp°xn absorbs each triplet where it appears; besides xn°zp and xn°yp°zp appear twice, so the duplicates can be canceled. Thus the sum of products can be reduced to the following sum:

$$\langle=\rangle xp°xn + yn + xn°yp + xn°yp°zp + xn°yp°zn + xn°zp$$

Finally, xn°yp and xn°zp absorb the corresponding triplets and the sum can be written:

$$\langle=\rangle yn + xp°xn + xn°yp$$

These are the minimal covering machining directions for the sample part. The same calculation can be made when the geometric changes are taken into account. The calculation is done in Table 10.3, where the directions of applicable alternative strategies zp and zn are inserted into relief2.
From the product of the sums

$$(xp + yp + yn + zp) ° (xn + yn + zp + zn) ° (xn + yn + zp + zn)$$

the following sum of products can be calculated:

$$yn + zp + xp°xn + xp°zn + xn°yp + yp°zn$$

which indicate the minimal covering work directions for compound cutting and alternative cutting strategies.

Table 10.3. Work Directions of Cutting and Alternative Cutting Strategies

	relief1	relief2	relief3
xp	1	-	-
xn	-	1	1
yp	1	-	-
yn	1	1	1
zp	1	1	1
zn	-	1	1

Now a sequence of preliminary cut plans can be formed. First, the plans including only one direction are inserted by putting the directions calculated from the cutting strategies first, and after that, those calculated from compound cutting and alternative cutting strategies. Thus the sequence begins:

$$\langle\ yn,\ zp,\dots\rangle$$

Next to the sequence are the potential cut plans, which include two directions. First, the direction from the minimal covering cutting strategies. Hence the sequence continues:

$$\langle\ yn,\ zp,\ xp°xn,\ xn°yp,\dots\rangle$$

Next the cut plan candidates, which are formed from a combination of cutting and alternative cutting strategies, are put into the sequence:

$$\langle\ yn,\ zp,\ xp°xn,\ xn°yp,\ xp°zn,\ yp°zn,\dots\rangle$$

The sequence can now be further extended by combining the directions yn and zp by any other direction. After this, all the candidate cut plans including one or two machining directions are sequenced. By combining these directions or pairs of directions further with any other direction, all the possible triplets can be enumerated. By using the same logistics, all possible combinations are enumerated until the most complex cut plan, where all the machining directions are present, is put last into the sequence. The first directions in the sequence, here yn and zp, are called *optimal* directions.

After sequencing the candidate cut plans, a feasibility study is done for all of them by scoring and analysis. The feasibility study checkes whether the dimensions of each feature satisfy the requirements of the potential tool type. For a more precise explanation of the feasibility study, see Opas and Mäntylä (1988).

When fewer work directions need to be used by applying feature relaxation, then geometric changes are proposed for some features. For instance, an insertion of rounding may be proposed with the requirement that it must be at least 3.5 mm. When there are several potential geometric improvements in the part, the proposal done by the current implementation may be partly contradictory. The system is also capable of enhancing geometric changes automatically into the feature model of the part, when the user indicates which features are to be relaxed.

Another output from the proposing phase is a *process plan framework* that has alternative cut plans for the part. From this process plan framework, the user can see the manufacturing complexity of the product, i.e, the number of needed machining directions, tool types, and number of tools. Figure 10.13 shows a process plan framework that is proposed by the system for one relaxed feature model for the part that is presented in Fig. 10.11 and Fig. 10.12. In Fig. 10.13, heavy arcs represent "and" relationships; thin arcs are "or" relationships, i.e., alternative processing paths.

When the user accepts a process plan proposal for a part, the proposed process plan can be further restricted by generating restrictive values for the main dimensions of the selected tool type. These restrictions look like the ones shown in Table 10.4. It should be noted that the model does not yet have any statement about the sequence of machining operations. The sequencing is consciously left out of the proposing phase because fixturing decisions and selection of physical tools from the tool library affects sequencing considerably.

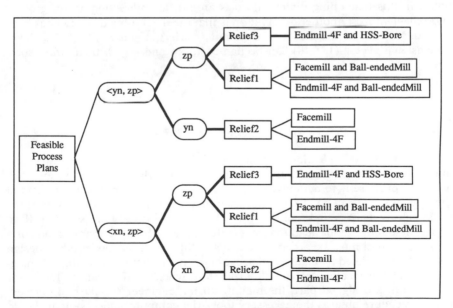

Fig. 10.13. A proposed alternative process plan. Heavy arcs represent "and" relationships; thin arcs are "or" relationships.

Table 10.4. Restrictions on Toolitems

Toolitem	Endmill
Number of flutes	4
Cutting length	Longer than 12.5 mm
Diameter	From 2.5 mm to 12 mm
No. of needed cuts	Between 2 and 5

Criticism of the Planning Procedure

The advantage of enumerating the whole solution space is that a feasible solution is always found, if the product design allows it. A shortcoming of the procedure is that the solution space is large—when six machining directions are concerned, 6! possible work direction combinations can be enumerated, which makes a total of 720 candidate cut plans. Further, when the number of work directions grows, it expands the number of candidate cut plans exponentially. This exponential expansion has not caused problems for the part families, which the project has been working with, because the parts until now have been orthogonal prismatic parts having at a maximum six possible machining directions.

As can be guessed, holes force their machining directions to be used because they have only one possible machining direction, or two in the case of through holes. In this machining direction, holes are not as interesting as are grooves and relief features. Another observation is that the machining direction has been named. Naming of the direction does not restrict its generality, e.g., a three-dimensional vector (1, 0, 0) can be named to xp and (-1, 0, 0) to xn, respectively.

Tool Selection Program for Sheet Metal Parts

In this section a tool selection program called TSP is introduced. TSP is an experimental stand-alone program that is implemented with the expert system shell ART. The purpose is to demonstrate the binding phase of process planning and the feedback that can be given to upstream planning and design stages from the latest phase where actual tools from the factory tool library are selected. If an appropriate tool cannot be found for a feature, the tool must either be made or a new special tool must be ordered. To keep tooling expenses low, product design should be completed by taking into account the restrictions of existing tool magazines that the machine tools hold. Therefore when no tool can be found for a feature in a designed part, the manufacturing engineer should be informed. If the procedure obtains the necessary tools, the computer-aided system should command the attributes to be fulfilled and the tool to be used.

Sheet Metal Parts

Because the part families addressed by TSP are sheet metal parts, which are manufactured by operations such as nibbling and punching, the features involved in these part families will be discussed first. The outer contour shape of a sheet metal part must be either a rectangle or a circle. This is not a completely necessary restriction, but at the moment these two shape rules have been implemented for manufacturing. It is possible to extend the system by adding other shapes and rules for manufacturing. The features that appear in sheet metal parts are holes. The holes currently implemented in the tool selection program are circles, rectangles, and keyslots. These features are illustrated in Fig. 10.14.

An interesting property of the features in sheet metal parts are the so-called segments, "internal geometries" inside features. Figure 10.15 shows the segments of a keyslot feature. For the one-punch manufacturing method (a hole can be manufactured with one punch), only one segment exists that has the shape of the keyslot itself. Another method, continous punching, has three segments: two circles and one rectangle.

Holes in a sheet metal part can be arranged into patterns. Currently, there are two kinds of patterns, one and two directions (Fig. 10.16 and Fig. 10.17). The shapes of the holes in a workpiece are not necessarily restricted to those presented here because TSP uses the structural file of the BRITE-2406 project. New shapes can relatively easily be added into the system. An example of how a sheet metal with six workpieces can look is shown in Fig. 10.18.

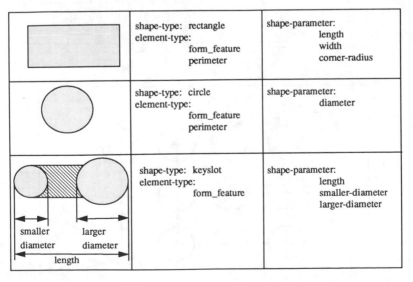

FIG. 10.14. Feature types covered by TSP.

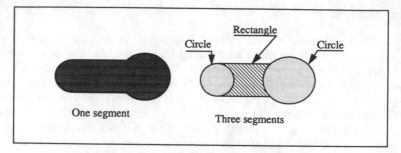

FIG. 10.15. Segments of a keyslot.

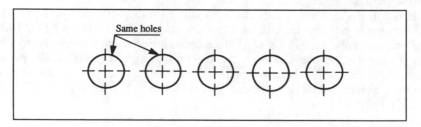

FIG. 10.16. Pattern in one direction.

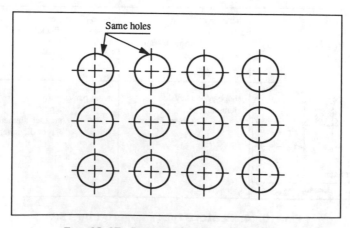

FIG. 10.17. Pattern in two directions.

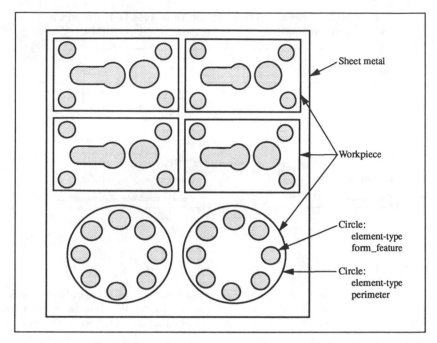

Fig. 10.18. An example of a sheet metal part.

One of the main difficulties in solving the problem of tool selection for a sheet metal part is to find a suitable knowledge representation schema. For this exercise of using an expert system to select tools, the knowledge representation from the BRITE-2406 project was used. The exact description can be found in the "Structural File" Tilley and Selleslagh (1989). Only a short explanation is given here.

A sheet metal part is represented by using a structured group of objects. These objects are the holes of the sheet metal part that has to be manufactured. There exist two different so-called element types for holes, perimeter and form-feature (Fig. 10.18). A *form-feature* is the description of a hole, i.e., internal or external. The corresponding shape must have only one contour. Thus the hole can be punched out with a single stroke. A *perimeter* defines the contour of the workpiece. In this application, the perimeter shapes are restricted to rectangles and circles.

In the tool selection program feature attributes are represented by slots and their values. For instance, one slot is the element type. Other slots are the shape type (rectangle, circle, etc.), the position on the sheet metal (or the workpiece), the size of the hole, and some other attributes. An example of the data for a hole is shown in Table 10.5. The tools to manufacture the holes are represented in a similar format.

Table 10.5. Frame Representation of a Hole Feature and a Tool (Units in [mm])

Hole Frame Slot	Value	Tool Frame Slot	Value
Shape type	rectangle	Tool class	rec20x05
Element type	perimeter	Tool type	rectangle_cp rectangle_pn
Length	150.0	Length	20.0
Width	60.0	Width	5.0
X-coordinate	200.0	Corner radius	0.1
Y-coordinate	120.0	Possible machines	behrens625

Tool Selection Method

First, the data of a sheet metal part and the data of the available tools are loaded. The information for each hole and each tool can be studied before or after tool selection program execution. The knowledge of features and tools is stored in the expert system schemata. (A schema is the name of a data structure that is more widely known as a frame.) In browsing a schemata, it is possible to give every hole a name so that the schemata get the same name. Tools always have the same name as their schemata. From a data format, the data of holes and tools are transformed into schemata. Some more information is derived before the rules for tool selection can be applied.

The manufacturing knowledge of features is implemented by using the ART rule system. Rules to produce a hole are fixed by the element type and shape of a hole. So for each allowed combination of these two slot values, a rule exists on how to produce that kind of hole. A check is done to see whether a tool exists that satisfies conditions on the left-hand side of a rule (the conditional side). Often, several methods can be used to manufacture a hole. For this reason, a hierachy of methods is represented. If a hole can be punched out with one stroke, this method has a higher priority than punching it out with multiple strokes. The program always tries to find a tool for the current "highest" method. So after successfully finding out all tools for a special method, no other methods will be checked because the next method will have a lower priority.

In a bad case, no tool can be found to produce the hole. Each possible method will then be checked, and for each method, an ideal tool can be ascertained later. All the tools having the right manufacturing method but not the right size can also be browsed to find out which size parameter failed. On the basis of this information, it is possible to add the right tool to the tool library. At the end of using the rule system, information about the tools will exist which can be used to manufacture the sheet metal part. The next step is to select the minimal set of tools that are needed for the whole sheet metal part.

Table 10.6. Sample Data for a Sheet Metal Part

Shape Type	Element Type	Coordinates	Parameters	Pattern
Rectangle	Perimeter	(100 100 0)	(150 60 0)	-
Keyslot	Form feature	(-30 0 0)	(35 15 10)	-
Circle	Form feature	(-65 -20 0)	(11)	(1 40 90 1 130 0)
Circle	Form feature	(30 0 0)	(20)	-

Examples

Take a sheet metal part consisting of one workpiece with its features. Sample data is shown in Table 10.6.

The first row in the table describes the workpiece (characterized by the value perimeter). The other entries are the hole features in the workpiece. The sample workpiece can be seen in Fig. 10.19, where there is an illustration of the user interface of a tool selection program for sheet metal parts.

When a hole is picked with the left mouse button, a window showing the selected tool is displayed. In the example (Fig. 10.20), two holes were picked. The window of the keyslot hole shows that the hole can be manufactured with the method "cont_punch," i.e, by continuous punching. After each segment, the name of an appropriate tool that can be used for each segment is displayed.

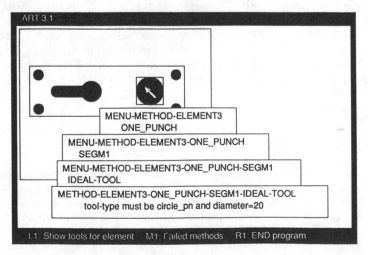

FIG. 10.19. The user interface of a tool selection program.

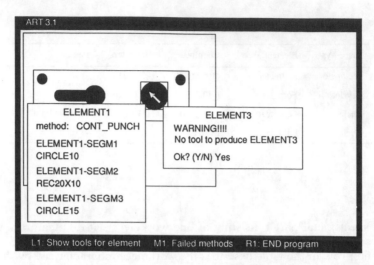

FIG. 10.20. Feedback information from tool selection program.

The other window belongs to the large circle hole on the right of the keyslot hole. For that circle hole no tool could be found in the tool library. Therefore a warning message is shown. No appropriate tool could be found for the feature "Element 3." Before continuing, the user must first confirm the warning message. If a negative confirmation is given, then the tool selection program stops.

By pointing to a feature with a mouse, the user is able to get a menu of the manufacturing methods for which no tool was found (see Fig. 10.19). A method can be selected and a menu of segments will appear. Now, a segment can be selected and a menu of tools appears. It consists of the possible tools for the selected method; they have the same shape as the selected segment. There is also a menu item named "ideal-tool," if selected, it shows the main dimensions of the ideal tool to manufacture the selected segment. Further, if the tool is selected, the application will show why it cannot be used to make the feature.

10.5 CONCLUSION

Design has the greatest effect on manufacturability and manufacturing costs. Manufacturing engineers are able to affect a portion of the costs. Therefore, checking for the manufacturing friendliness of a design solution should be done as early as possible, preferably during the design phase or immediately after the design has been completed. To obtain a manufacturing friendly product, one may perform design for manufacturing, i.e., take the factory-dependent restrictions into account. Another approach is not to restrict the designers capabilities, but to analyze the design solution afterwards. The first case study uses a hybrid of these two approaches, whereas the last two cases analyze the manufacturability afterwards, when the design solutions have already been done.

Manufacturability analysis is a nontrivial task, which, in fact, is closely related to the same problems in process planning. Therefore, manufacturability analysis cannot be wholly implemented into a design system, but should be distributed into different modules of an integrated CAD/CAM system model. The first analysis step, technological analysis, should be relatively "light" and it should be done closely with design. This step should enhance the standardization that is used in specific manufacturing facilities and be incorporated into design.

Process planning is run in two phases, proposing and binding. The first phase is generative, whereas the binding phase has properties in common with variant process planning. In the proposing phase, product design is considered as a whole and more generally, alternative process plans, which reveal manufacturing complexity, are proposed. Using relaxed feature models changes and improvements to the design can also be proposed. The binding phase concentrates on more detailed issues like optimal manufacturing parameters, the actual tool which is used to machine a feature, the tool path, and so on. Factory-dependent static and dynamic constraints are applied to proposed alternative process plans and the final manufacturing decisions are made.

It is extremely useful to implement modules that are capable of incorporating manufacturability analysis into CAD/CAM systems. A process planning system must have a vast amount of knowledge of the capabilities of a factory and it should be implemented in such a form so that the same knowledge can also be used in manufacturability evaluation. This requires extra effort, but otherwise it may be frustrating to implement a module that only makes manufacturability analyses. Further, when the manufacturing methods are continuously developed on the shop floor, it becomes even more difficult to take care of the life cycle of the enhanced knowledge. Therefore it is more reasonable to use the knowledge stored in process planning systems.

When automation in factories increases, the planning and programming effort needed grows too. Because of the vast amount of required preparation work, there is a danger of losing the flexibility that should have been reached with higher automation level. Hence it will be of strategic importance to be able to introduce more and more advanced computer-aided methods to integrate the vital design, planning, and manufacturing cycles. Since writing this chapter, the european research project on sheet metal manufacturing has successfully been finished (Knackfuss, *et al.* 1991). We also have been able to make further progress with other related tasks like feature modeling, variant process planning, fixturing planning, and also with part program generation in another european project (Hämmerle, *et al.* 1991).

ACKNOWLEDGMENTS

This chapter is based on work done at the Laboratory of Information Processing Science, Helsinki University of Technology and at BIBA, Bremer Institut für Betriebstechnik und angewandt Arbeitswissenschaft. Professor Hirsch provided good working conditions in the institute. The chapter was written while J. Opas was visiting BIBA in Bremen. He gratefully thanks Walter Ahlström Foundation and the Academy of Finland for the financial support making the visit possible. The chapter has certainly benefited from the instruction of professor Martti Mäntylä from the Helsinki University of Technology.

REFERENCES

Courtright, M. J. 1988. Manufacturability analysis for a flexible manufacturing cell. Master's thesis, Department of Mechanical Engineering, University of Maryland, College Park, Maryland.

Eversheim, W. 1989. Process planning in computer integrated manufacturing—developments and experiences (in German), *Industrie Anzeiger 85/89*.

Mäntylä, M., Opas, J., and Puhakka, J. 1989. Generative process planning of prismatic parts by feature relaxation. Presented in ASME Conference in Montreal, September 1989, 18 pp.

Mäntylä, M., Opas, J., and Puhakka, J. 1987. A prototype system for generative process planning of prismatic parts. *Proc. AMPS 87*, North-Holland, Amsterdam, 599–611.

Ohsuga, S. 1988. Towards intelligent CAD systems. *Valokyna 4/86*.

Opas, J., and Mäntylä, M. 1988. HutCAPP—A machining operations planner. *Robotics and Manufacturing*, Volume 2. New York: ASME Press, pp. 901–910.

Shah, J. J., Sreevaslan, P., Rogers, M. T., Billo, R., and Mathew, A. 1988. *Current Status of Feature Technology*, Report R-88-GM-04, CAM-i, Inc., Arlington, Texas

Tilley, S., and Selleslagh, G. 1989. Structural File General Description. *Int. Report of the BRITE Project*, No. 1406.

Tuomi, J. 1989. Manufacturability analysis in a feature-based CAD/CAM system (in Finnish). Master's thesis, Espoo, Finland. Laboratory of Mechanical Engineering, Helsinki University of Technology.

Chapter 11

Generating Assembly Plans From 3-D Solid Modeler

Raju S. Mattikalli
Department of Mechanical Engineering
Carnegie Mellon University
Pittsburgh, Pennsylvania

Pradeep K. Khosla
Department of Electrical and Computer Engineering
Carnegie Mellon University
Pittsburgh, Pennsylvania

Yangsheng Xu
The Robotics Institute and
Engineering Design Research Center
Carnegie Mellon University
Pittsburgh, Pennsylvania

11.1 INTRODUCTION

Current production practice is iterative: product designs evolve as they move back and forth from the designer to the manufacturing engineer. This is due to the fact that the designer cannot always foresee problems that might occur during the manufacturing process. This iterative cycle results in a significant loss of time and is, consequently, expensive and counterproductive. One approach to alleviate this problem is to speed up the design and modification process, using better tools for design representation and communication. Another approach is to look at the design–manufacture cycle as a whole, and provide solutions that reduce the number of iterations involved.

Designers are increasingly using computers to represent, display, analyze, and modify their designs. Designs are typically represented using CAD software and solid modeling systems. This new approach makes the design process more convenient in terms of design representation and communication, but it does not address the problem of reducing the design–manufacture cycle time in an integrated manner. Also, schemes for *modeling* mechanical assemblies within current CAD and solid modeling systems are not powerful enough to support the detailed inquiry that knowledge representations require in order to make inferences about the manufacturability of designs. Typically, most CAD and solid modeling systems are used as high-tech drafting tools. The present authors believe that geometric modelers that embody powerful representations, coupled with software tools that evaluate designs for ease of manufacture, will make a notable contribution to streamlining the process of engineering design.

Software tools that evaluate the manufacturability of a design would allow the designer to anticipate potential problems that may arise during the manufacture of a product; i.e., they would help the designer to *design for manufacturability*. By providing useful feedback to the designer during the design of a product, these tools will help reduce the design–manufacture cycle time. The manufacture of any product could include a number of processes such as casting, forging, stamping, drawing, molding, machining, assembly, and so on. Each of these processes are distinct and hence require different methods of analysis and different bodies of knowledge for the evaluation of a design. This chapter addresses the process of assembly. Feedback about assembly concerns could be as simple as a YES/NO answer regarding the assemblability of the design on a given facility, or it could be something more complex that would identify certain assembly tasks that cannot be carried out and include suggestions for redesign of the component. In either case, in order to be useful and practical, such tools should have complete models of the assembly and the manufacturing facility. A system that could critique a design and provide useful feedback for redesign is still far from the horizon, but a substantial amount of present-day research is being targeted toward the development of important parts of such a system.

The long-term goal of the work presented in this chapter is to develop a methodology for automated assembly analysis. Such tools could provide valuable help to the designer in addressing downstream assemblability concerns. The authors are developing a system that will accept a 3-D geometric description of an assembly and a model of assembly facilities, and that will reason about the assembly to answer the question: Can the given assembly be automatically assembled on the available facility? In order to answer this question, the process must

- Create a suitable representation of the assembly
- Generate the sequence of assembly operations
- Create a representation of the facility
- Allow reasoning about the assemblability, using the assembly operations and the facility model

If the mechanical system can be assembled on the given facilities, each assembly task is automatically planned and programmed as a sequence of standardized actions corresponding to the specific assembly task. These programs could be downloaded onto the real assembly facilities to perform the assembly. The block diagram in Fig. 11.1 gives an overview.

The authors' research group in the Engineering Design Research Center at Carnegie Mellon has developed a geometric modeler *Noodles* (Gursoz *et al.*, 1980). The work described in this chapter utilizes *Noodles* to create 3-D representations of assemblies. Starting from this representation, a strategy has been developed, based on kinematic constraints, that automatically determines the assembly sequence of the given Mechanical System/Assembly (MSA).

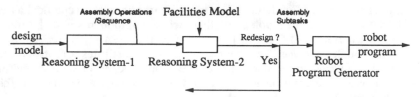

FIG. 11.1. Overview of assembly operations and facilities model.

This chapter presents work on automatically determining the assembly sequence from a 3-D geometric modeler description of an assembly. Meaningful subassemblies that can be assembled using combinations of translational and rotational motions are identified. By posing it as a problem of reasoning about changes in degrees of freedom of geometric subassemblies due to their movement within the assembly, sequences of rotational and translational motions can be determined. Algorithms have been developed that compute collision-free translational and rotational motions. This work is an important step toward developing software tools to evaluate the assemblability of mechanical assemblies.

One of the early works in evaluating and reducing assembly costs is by Boothroyd and Dewhurst (1972). They rated the efficiency of a design based on a classification of the various geometric features of the components comprising the assembly. These features are used to estimate the full cost of automation using heuristic knowledge. Here, it is proposed to make assembly evaluations using detailed process knowledge. Using a *geometric model* of an MSA, the assembly tasks that assemble the MSA are systematically determined. Two principal steps are involved: (1) identifying subassemblies, and (2) finding detailed assembly motions of the subassemblies. Knowledge about the capabilities of the available assembly facilities and the relative difficulty of each assembly task is used to make a more comprehensive evaluation of assemblability.

Based on the sequence of motions generated using the method presented in this chapter, it is possible to categorize groups of assembly motions as a predefined library of *tasks*. (Future work will define such a library of tasks, and find a mapping from the assembly motions and the geometric features on the subassemblies (given by the current system) to one of the task libraries.) For each task, the assemblability can be finally evaluated based on the facility model being developed. In the case where the design is not assemblable, design modifications are suggested using the available facility model, or additional facilities are selected without modifying the design. When the design can be assembled, the assembly task is automatically planned and programmed as a sequence of standardized detail actions corresponding to the specific assembly task.

11.2 REPRESENTATION OF THE MSA

In modeling MSAs for assembly analysis, the following attributes are important: form, material, dimensions, surface quality, tolerances, geometric features, and mating conditions. Fundamental to most abstractions of mechanical assemblies is the geometry and topology of the various components and the mating between them. Here, a 3-D geometric model of the MSA is created using the geometric modeler *Noodles*. This geometric model constitutes a representation in terms of low-level geometric primitives (i.e., nodes, edges, faces, and regions). The geometric representation is augmented by a topological framework (constructed within *Noodles*). Most of the higher-level abstractions can be derived from this topology- and geometry-rich model; others, such as abstractions representing function and behavior, may require human input to augment the model.

In general, the success of an automatic reasoning system depends significantly on the abstraction used in representing the entity that is being reasoned about. In particular, the ability to reason about mechanical assemblies using computer models is limited by the abstraction of the assembly that is created in the computer. If the model is a good one, it responds to inquiries about it in the same way as the original object would. Of primary importance in the effort to determine assembly operations are the geometric descriptions and higher-level abstractions relating to part mating and spatial occupation. Such higher-level attributes are represented implicitly within the geometric modeler, although the derivations from the geometric model involve varying degrees of complexity. Sedas and Talukdar (1987) used a stick model to represent spatial occupation and to reason about the disassembly. This abstraction limits the utility of their approach to symmetric MSAs. In this work, inquiries about spatial occupation are made directly to the *Noodles* model. Mating relationships are represented in the form of a graph that is sufficiently general to represent any MSA. As will be evident later, the reasoning mechanism makes extensive use of part mating information. It is for this reason that a separate representation of part mating has been created.

The internal representation of *Noodles* facilitates the generation of other abstractions of a MSA that are required for the reasoning system. *Noodles* provides a powerful representation scheme for describing the geometry and topology of mechanical systems (Gursoz *et al.*, 1988). Geometric models of individual components are created by the designer using functions provided by *Noodles*. The models of these individual components are then combined to create a model of the MSA.

The Geometric Modeler *Noodles*

As described earlier, a model of the MSA is created using the geometric modeling system *Noodles*. This modeler uses a surface boundary representation scheme, i.e., it models objects by their enclosing shells. In particular, it employs a nonmanifold scheme for surface boundary representation. One significant advantage of the nonmanifold scheme for describing geometry is that geometric elements of all kinds, 0-D, 1-D, 2-D, and 3-D can be represented and manipulated uniformly. The fundamental geometric elements (namely, nodes, edges, faces, and regions) are interpreted as point sets in R^3. The entire space is categorized into disjoint point sets, consisting of these four fundamental elements.

Although these elements are disjoint, there is a relationship of immediate neighborhood among them. The geometric data is augmented with topological information using support elements (also referred to as topological elements) which have explicit notions of the surrounding space around nodes, directionality of edges, use of faces, and neighborhood and containment of regions. As a result of attempting to categorize space and explicitly represent the topology, *Noodles* demonstrates a significant improvement over contemporary geometric modelers in its receptiveness to interrogations from Reasoning Systems I and II (Fig. 11.1) about the geometry and topology of assemblies.

With reference to a model of a mechanical assembly, connectivity and neighborhood of components can be easily inferred as they correspond to the neighborhood of the fundamental geometric elements. Moreover, a group of components (a subassembly) can be handled just as if it were a single component. Because *Noodles* possesses the notion of universal space, topological elements that neighbor free space can also be determined. This is useful for querying about the accessibility of components and subassemblies for the purpose of clasping, probing, moving, or other such assembly operations. The following describes some of the relevant elements of the data structure of *Noodles*. The abstract entity that each of these represents is indicated. A detailed description of *Noodles* can be found in Gursoz *et al.* (1988).

- Group. This represents a point set. The elements of the point set could consist of one or more of the geometric elements (nodes, edges, faces, and regions).
- Region [geometric]. This represents a volumetric entity of R^3. The boundary of a region is represented by one or more *seals*.
- Seal [topological]. This represents the bounding surface of a region. A *seal* is composed of a topologically connected set of *walls*.
- Wall [topological]. This is an element of a *seal*, and is an area entity. A *wall* represents one side of a *face*.
- Face [geometric]. This represents what is traditionally also referred to as a face in geometric modeling. In *Noodles*, each *face* has two *walls* associated with it. A *wall* could also be thought of as being one of the two "uses" of a *face*.

Referring to the elements of the data structure, each component is represented as a *region*. Subassemblies are represented as a *group* whose point set consists of the regions corresponding to the components in that subassembly. The mating between components can be extracted from the fact that a *face* exists that has each of its *walls* belonging to the *seals* of two different *regions*. To understand what a model of an MSA looks like within the *Noodles* representation, refer to Fig. 11.2. It shows a model of a simple assembly (in cross section) consisting of three components (and one void space). Each bold line is a single *face*; each fuzzy line is a *wall*. A *seal*, which is a list of connected *walls*, defines the boundary of a region in space, either a component or free space. By creating new lists of *walls* which surround a different portion of R^3, the subassemblies can be defined. This is how single components and subassemblies are handled in a unified manner for reasoning about assembly operations.

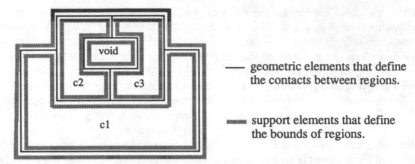

— geometric elements that define the contacts between regions.

▬ support elements that define the bounds of regions.

FIG. 11.2. An MSA as represented within the *Noodles* data structure.

To create the model of the MSA from component models, each component model must be placed at a given position in space, relative to other components in the assembly. In the assembly data structures introduced by Wesley *et al.* (1980), the location and orientation of each component is specified by a 4×4 transformation matrix. Such a method is quite cumbersome and error prone. Rocheleau and Lee (1987) have developed a technique that allows the designer to interactively create an assembly of components by specifying mating conditions between components. These conditions consist of *virtual links* which represent mating conditions such as *against* and *fits*.

Locations and orientations of components are specified interactively by the designer. This is accomplished by using a set of movement and orientation operators. With the help of a graphic display of the components, the designer can interactively locate components in their assembled positions. A merge operation (defined in *Noodles*) is performed on this set of components to obtain the model of the MSA.

Abstraction From the Geometric Model

Apart from the geometric model, a MSA is also represented at another level of abstraction. This abstraction emphasizes the matings between components and subassemblies and will be referred to as the *component graph*. The purpose of this abstraction is to have a knowledge representation that is more appropriate for the high-level reasoning for assembly plan generation and task generation. Also, as described later, the assembly procedure is represented in the form of an AND/OR graph, which could be thought of as another abstraction of the MSA. The geometric representation, however, forms the basis of these abstractions.

The Component Graph

The component graph is an undirected graph that represents the mating between the components in a subassembly (a topologically connected group of components). The graph data structure is a powerful abstraction for representing and manipulating relational data, and is ideal for the purpose of representing mating relations between components and subassemblies. *Nodes* in the graph represent either individual components, subassemblies, or void regions; *links* represent the mating conditions between the nodes. *Mating* consists of the faces that are shared by the two concerned nodes. One very useful addition has been made to the component graph: a node that represents the region of space that surrounds the assembly. In the context of the graph, this special node has links to all components that are accessible from the outside. This information is valuable to the Reasoning System-I, as will be seen in section 11.3. This graph is constructed automatically by making inquiries into the geometric model. The following paragraph briefly describes the procedure for constructing the component graph.

Consider two components, c1 and c2, that have physical contact (Fig. 11.3). A set of *faces* exists that corresponds to the surface of contact. Every *face* has two *walls*: the two sides to any *face*. A *face* that is part of a contact surface has one *wall* that defines part of the boundary of component c1 and the other *wall* which defines part of the boundary of component c2. A collection of all such *faces* between any pair of components forms part of the link between the pair of nodes that represent the two components.

Each node in the component graph contains the following information:

- An identifier that indicates whether the node is currently active or not. To reason about a subassembly rather than an individual component, a new node is created in the component graph which represents the subassembly. The need for creating a representation of this subassembly is temporary, and many different subassemblies are created in succession. Thus, whenever a subassembly representing a set of components

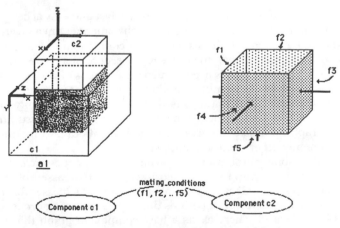

**FIG. 11.3. (a) Peg-in-hole assembly.
(b) Mating *faces*. (c) *Link* between c1 and c2.**

$C_1, C_2, \ldots, C_n\}$ is created, it is attached to the original component graph by pushing the nodes that represent components $C1>, C2, \ldots, Cn\}$ to the background, and superposing the new node with its new links onto the graph. A node can be made to fall to the background by *deactivating* the node and the links that lead to the node. After the need for the subassembly is over, the superimposed node and its links are removed and the original nodes are reactivated.

- An identifier that indicates the *type of entity* that is represented by the node, i.e., whether the node represents a component, a subassembly, a void region, or the outer region.
- A list of *walls* that bound the entity that the node represents.

If the node represents a component, then the following properties are also included.

- A transformation matrix, which defines the position and orientation of the local frame of reference of the component with respect to a global reference frame.
- The degrees of freedom of the component with respect to its local frame of reference.

If the node represents a subassembly, then it also contains a list of pointers to nodes, each of which represents a component in the subassembly.

A link l between a node pair $N1, N2$ consists of the following information:

- An identifier that indicates whether link l is active or not (active and inactive having the same meaning as that described for a node).
- A list of *faces*: These are the *faces* that are common to node $N1$ and $N2$, i.e., their "mating" *faces*.

The purpose of the component graph is to give fast and easy access to information about the immediate neighborhood of each component in a given subassembly. Based on the mating conditions between a component and its neighbors, an evaluation of the constraints on the degrees of freedom of a component (or group of components) is made. This is used to recognize groups of components as being part of a meaningful subassembly. Another merit in constructing this intermediate representation of part matings is that it makes the assembly task generation routines independent of the geometric modeling system, assuming that the component graph can make the necessary inquiries about part matings and part geometry from any other representation scheme.

During the reasoning process, when various subassemblies are being reasoned about, the component graph is modified to represent subassemblies of varying constituent components. Because a number of different subassembly representations are required, each for brief periods during the reasoning process, a *two-tier* graph has been devised. There exists a base component graph that was created with each component as a node. When a subassembly with components $\{C_1, C_2, \ldots, C_n\}$ needs to be created, the nodes in the base graph that represent the components $\{C_1, C_2, \ldots, C_n\}$ are deactivated and a new node is created at the upper tier.

Given the model of any MSA, the first objective is to determine a sequence of assembly tasks that would assemble the MSA. With a similar objective, Lee and Ko (1987) developed a method for automated generation of an assembly procedure for an assembly. Their procedure requires the designer to input the mating conditions and give qualitative descriptions of the kind of mating (namely: against, fits, tight-fits, and contact) between components. From the constructed graph, they create a *hierarchy of components* based on the number and type of links that connect to each node. They mainly focus on the relationships between components as represented within their **graph**. Subassemblies are determined based on the number and type of links that are incident on a given set of components. Their work demonstrates the power of using a graph that has been augmented with various assembly relevant characteristics. Their approach, however, does not involve any geometric considerations, such as accessibility for grasping, ease of grasping, and so on, to determine meaningful subassemblies. Knowledge about the detailed geometry of assemblies allows automation of the evaluation of assembly characteristics and behavior, without requiring detailed human input. The work presented here involves a more geometric approach. In most computer-aided design efforts, the designer creates a geometric model of the design. By fully utilizing this geometric knowledge, the present approach does not additionally burden the designer.

The central idea behind the method to generate assembly tasks is to *disassemble* the MSA. The disassembly procedure is part of the reasoning system and is described in section 11.3. The result of the disassembly procedure (and possible alternatives) is recorded in the form of an AND/OR graph, which will be referred to as the *disassembly graph*. This graph represents the assembly tasks that would assemble the MSA.

The Disassembly Graph

When the Reasoning System-I "disassembles" the MSA, it generates a set of disassembly tasks. The affect of applying a disassembly task/operation on a subassembly results in it being split into two smaller subassemblies. If this *splitting operation* is applied recursively to each emerging subassembly that consists of more than one component, the MSA would be disassembled. The disassembly procedure is represented using an AND/OR treelike data structure, with the original MSA as the root, subassemblies as branch points, and components as leaves; disassembly operations are represented on the interconnecting links. If similar subassemblies are generated, they are represented as the same node, which makes the AND/OR tree an AND/OR graph. If a given subassembly can be disassembled in more than one way, then an OR node is formed; each of the immediate successors of the OR node represent AND nodes. Each AND node represents one way in which the subassembly can be disassembled.

The disassembly graph that is created is similar to the one described to represent assembly sequences in Homen de Mello and Sanderson (1986). The link between an AND node and its children nodes represents a disassembly task. At the end of the disassembly, a hierarchical structure of disassembly tasks is generated. Note that within this task hierarchy, there is an implicit hierarchy of subassemblies and components. Previous work, such as that by Lee and Ko (1987), attempted to generate a hierarchy of components and then determine assembly operations based on this part hierarchy. However, arranging components in an hierarchical order and determining assembly tasks from them is rather artificial. A hierarchy should be constructed only as a tool for analysis or representation. Imposing a hierarchy on sets of components is rather like working in reverse, as the hierarchical decomposition should emerge from the assembly process, and not the other way around. Thus the real hierarchy *emerges* at the task level, and not at the component level.

An example of an MSA and its corresponding disassembly graph is shown in Fig. 11.4. As can be seen, the root node represents the complete assembly of four components. The first disassembly operation corresponds to the unscrewing of component c4 from component c3. Because there is no alternative disassembly operation, the root node would be an AND node. In case some alternatives were found, the root node would be an OR node, with each of its children nodes representing each alternative. Thus, in this case, the root node gives rise to two children nodes, corresponding to the component c4 and the rest of the assembly components c1, c2, and c3. Because node n1 represents a single component, it is a terminal node. Node n2 can now be treated as a new subassembly, and the splitting procedure is applied to node n2. This process is continued to generate the complete component hierarchy. In this case, because there is only one disassembly sequence, there are no OR branches in the tree, generally they would be present.

A number of issues have to be addressed before one can successfully carry out an assembly task on an assembly facility. These include issues such as part acquisition, gross motion planning for approach to and departure from the vicinity of the assembly, fine motion planning to carry out the assembly, determination of forces, positional accuracy, and so on. The focus here is on how the geometry of the MSA influences this process of assembly, so that the designer can make

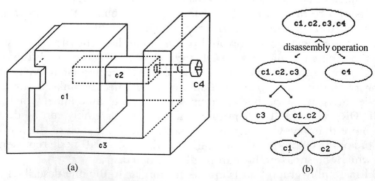

(a)   (b)

FIG. 11.4. (a) An example of an assembly. (b) The Disassembly Graph.

appropriate design modifications, if necessary. Part geometry plays an important role in determining grasps and in fine motion planning, though it is also of some importance in other aspects of the assembly process as well. Note that the use of the term *fine motion* refers to the motion of the components (and hence the facility) when in close vicinity of other components just before they reach their final assembled positions. This work attempts to determine these fine motions and check whether they can be carried out on the facilities. When using the word *assembly* (or *disassembly*) task in this chapter, it refers to this kind of part motion only, although in the future, other issues such as gross motion planning and part handling will be addressed. The definition of an assembly task depends on part motions as well as the geometry of the components that are involved. Depending on the type of assembly task, the motions would be different. Each assembly task can be defined in terms of a set of *primitive assembly operations*. If these primitive operations are defined at a sufficiently low level, a set of primitive assembly operations could emerge that are *independent* and *complete*.

The requirement of independence and completeness would be of importance when attempting to generate sets of primitive operations from the description of the part motions and part geometry. An assembly task is defined by a list of attribute-value pairs, with each type of task having its own list of attributes. The Reasoning System-I determines feasible subassemblies and their motions out of the MSA. Based on the geometry and the motions of the moving subassemblies, a set of assembly tasks are identified. There has been some past effort to define assembly tasks. Kondelon (Owen, 1982) studied a number of products and their assembly methods and came up with a set of 12 primitive tasks associated with the assembly process. Kondelon's 12 tasks are:

(1) Peg insertion
(2) Push and twist (e.g., bayonet lock)
(3) Multiple insertions (e.g., electronic components)
(4) Insert peg and retainer (one component keyed to the other, usually in the cross direction)
(5) Screw
(6) Force fit
(7) Remove location peg
(8) Flip parts over
(9) Provide temporary support
(10) Crimp
(11) Remove temporary support
(12) Weld or solder

The preceding set of tasks includes four tasks, (7)–(9) and (11), that merely assist the assembly process. The family of assembly tasks of interest here does not involve deformations of components; these are assembly tasks (1) through (6). The preceding tasks give some understanding as to what assembly tasks look like. It is desirable to define tasks at a lower level of breakdown; at a level that more appropriately reflects the exact manner in which these assembly tasks would be carried out. For example, when a sliding motion occurs, it is classified based on the number of degrees of freedom that the moving part possesses. Thus the case of sliding contact with respect to only one plane would be classified as a different task compared to sliding contact with respect to two planes. The difference is that the moving body is constrained differently in the two cases, therefore requiring different considerations during the actual assembly. When attempting to reason about the assembly tasks vis-à-vis the assembly facilities, there must be available a detailed description of the exact nature of the assembly tasks. A high-level description (like that described in Owen, 1982) would make the reasoning process cumbersome. It is for this reason that assembly tasks are defined at the *action* level of breakdown rather than at a higher-level description.

The next section describes Reasoning System-I: how the abstractions are used, how subassemblies are generated, how the disassembly algorithm works, and how collision-free part motions are determined. A more detailed description of Reasoning System-I is presented in Mattikalli and Khosla (1989).

11.3 REASONING SYSTEM-I

Reasoning System-I generates a sequence of assembly tasks using as input a model of an MSA and its component graph. Whitney and De Fazio (1987) have described a method for generating all assembly sequences, based on the responses of the user to a set of questions. The assembly is characterized by a network of nodes and liaisons. The questions concern the *order* in which these liaisons are performed during the assembly process. In their network, nodes represent components and liaisons represent user-defined matings between these components. Any assembly step is characterized by the establishment of one or more liaisons.

In comparison, although the goal here is not to determine *all* assembly sequences, a more direct procedure is adopted—determine assembly operations and their sequence, without attempting to specify any precedence explicitly. Precedence relations fall out implicitly as a consequence of performing a *disassembly*. Sedas and Talukdar (1987) have described a *disassembly expert* that imitates the human method of trial and error to simulate a disassembly process. In most cases, the sequence of assembly operations can be created by reversing the sequence of disassembly operations. Similarly, the assembly operations required to assemble an MSA can be determined effectively by studying the way in which the MSA is disassembled. Each assembly task can be thought of as being some process by which the degrees of freedom of the components involved in that operation get constrained. An unassembled component has 6 degrees-of-freedom, 3 translational and 3 rotational. An assembly process has the effect of constraining some or all of these degrees of freedom. Using this philosophy, each of the assembly actions that assembled the MSA can be deduced. The next section provides a description of Reasoning System-I. The output of this system is a disassembly graph accompanied by a graphic display of the disassembly process.

Reasoning System-I is best explained in terms of modules. At the heart of Reasoning System-I is the module *Split*. It consists of three main parts: *Find_Subassembly*, *Determine_Motions*, and *Identify_Tasks*. Module *Split* identifies a "split" in the model of the MSA into two subassemblies, formed as a result of a disassembly operation. Module *Find_Subassembly* accepts a subassembly consisting of n components, and finds a suitable division of these n components into two groups (or two subassemblies) such that one of them possess some degrees of freedom (dof). The word *subassembly*, as used in this chapter, refers to a grouping of components based on their topological connectedness, i.e., they must be topologically connected. Once a suitable subassembly has been chosen, module *Determine_Motions* starts moving the subassembly out of the parent assembly. Thus *motions* that separate the subassembly from the rest of the MSA are determined. Based on the two subassemblies that are generated and the motions that bring about a separation, module *Identify_Tasks* identifies the set of primitive assembly operations that generate the motions. It also defines the parameters that define this primitive operation uniquely. Module *Find_Subassembly* works as follows.

Consider an input subassembly consisting of a set $\mathbf{R}$ of n components. The aim is to find a subset of $\mathbf{R}$ that possesses at least one dof. This set $\mathbf{R}$ must also satisfy some other conditions, such as accessibility from the outside, availability of grasp surfaces, and so on. If such a subset can be identified, the degree of freedom would suggest a direction of disassembly of that subset from the rest of the components. The space of all possible subassemblies is represented as a tree structure, with subassemblies at higher levels having a progressively larger number of components. To determine such a group, a breadth-first search with a look ahead of one level is carried out in the space of all possible subassemblies. When a set $\mathbf{G}$ of components is to be treated as a subassembly, the component graph is modified to represent the set $\mathbf{G}$ as one entity. This modification has been previously described.

If more than one disassemblable group is found at any level (including higher levels), then they are represented as branches of an OR node in the disassembly graph. No attempt is made here to determine all such possibilities, but rather the first group that satisfies the set of conditions is accepted. In case there is a need to represent alternatives, this data structure would still be adequate. In that case, to choose the actual assembly sequence, decisions at OR nodes would be made using a set of heuristics.

A lot of past work, including that by Boothroyd and Dewhurst (1972), has studied the rules of thumb that lead to better designs from the point of view of ease of assembly. Such rules of thumb could be expressed in terms of heuristic functions that would make decisions at OR nodes to determine a "good" assembly sequence among possible alternatives. These decisions would be based partly on the geometry of parts from which criteria such as the stability of the subassembly, its size, the availability of part features for grasping, and so on, can be determined. Also, the motions that each subassembly may require for its disassembly can be used in heuristic functions. For example, a commonly recommended heuristic is that top–down assemblies are easier to perform than sideways assemblies and should be preferred. As can be expected, there could be conflicting criteria in which case some weighting can be assigned to each of these heuristics. A change in these heuristics would result in potentially choosing a different subassembly and consequently a different assembly plan. In the current implementation, simple grouping criteria have been used though we plan to incorporate better heuristics in the future.

An important part of this splitting procedure is the determination of collision-free motion of the subassembly out of the parent assembly. Module *Determine_Motions* performs this function. In case no collision-free motion can be determined, a backtracking mechanism is initiated such that other subassemblies can be generated by *Find_Subassembly*. The method presented here for determining collision-free motions takes advantage of the nature of the problem at hand. Any motion is composed of primitive translational and rotational motions. Emerging from this module is an ordered set of primitive motions which when applied to the MSA would disassemble it. The next section describes this module in detail.

The module *Identify_Tasks* takes as input the set of primitive motions and the description of the subassembly that is being disassembled. From these, it identifies "assembly tasks" that bring about these motions. As described earlier, a library of assembly tasks is defined. A task represents an action on a subassembly. The definition of each task contains a list of primitive motions which when made to act on a subassembly results in the subassembly being assembled. It also contains information on what kinds of geometric features need to be present on the subassembly if this task could act on it. The need to include the description of geometry within the task definitions can be seen from the following example. Consider the multiple-peg insertion task. This has to be distinct from the (single) peg insertion task because different considerations of force compliance, and so on are involved when the task is actually performed using the available facilities. Thus, the geometric specification in this task definition would require that there be at least two pegs and two corresponding holes on the subassemblies involved. Module *Identify_Tasks* chooses the correct set of primitive tasks and assigns the motions and geometric feature parameters to them.

Table 11.1 presents pseudo code that describes the main parts of the implementation of the *Split* module. The procedure calls have names that indicate their function. The algorithms have been implemented on the SUN workstation in C programming language. The following paragraph illustrates the working of the *Split* module and the *Determine_Motions* module using the MSA in Fig. 11.5 as an example. The main purpose of this example is to demonstrate the authors' method of identifying subassemblies; subassemblies that are created using information about part constraints that are derived directly from part geometry. This technique of creating subassemblies is most natural from the assembly point of view. It also outlines the manner in which the rest of the Reasoning System-I works.

Figure 11.5(a) shows an MSA that consists of seven components. Component c1 is a *base component* (one over which most of the components are placed). Heuristics are defined such that a base component is not disassembled in the initial disassembly operations. The first disassembly operation requires the construction of a subassembly consisting of components c3, c4, c5, c6, and c7. After the *Split* module reaches level 5, it determines that this subassembly possesses a degree of freedom, and thus deduces the first disassembly operation. After the parameters of the disassembly task are deduced, the component graphs representing the two newly formed subassemblies are generated. The disassembly graph is modified to record this disassembly operation. If either of the subassem-

Table 11.1.   Pseudo Code Describing the "Split" Module

(CG) = component graph of a subassembly having (say) n components.
In the following piece of code, lines with comments begin with **.

function Split-A (CG)
(1) out_node = Get_OutNode ();
    ** *'out node' represents the outside of the subassembly.*
(2) for (all nodes that have links to out_node) do
    ** *let 'b_node' represent the border node.*
    (a) dof = Degrees_Of_freedom (b_node);
    (b) if (dof) then
        (i) Get_Global_Directions_Of_DOF (b_node);
        (ii) group = Get_Group (b_node);
        (iii) Append_To_List (p_list, group);
        end.
    ** *'p_list' is a list of potential groups for disassembly.*
    end.
(3) if (Size_Of (p_list) > 0) then
    Apply_Hueristics (p_list);
        ** *puts components in order of preference.*
        ** *may delete some unsuitable components from p_list.*
    if (Size_Of (p_list) > 0) then
        group = Item_At_Head (p_list);
        return group, Global_Dir_Of_DOF(group).
    end.
    end.
(4) for (all nodes that have links to out_node) do
        ** *let 'c_node' be such a node.*
    for (all nodes that have links to c_node) do
        group = Take_NodeA_With_NodeB (c_node, out_node);
        if (group) then
            Append_To_List (p_list, group);
        end.
    end.
    end.
(5) if (Size_Of (p_list) > 0) then
    Apply_Hueristics (p_list);
(6) if (Size_Of (p_list) > 0) then
    group = Item_At_Head (p_list);
    return group, Global_Dir_Of_DOF(group).
    else
    return Split-B (CG).
    end.
End Split-A.

function Take_NodeA_With_NodeB (nodeA, nodeB)
    (a) dof1 = Degree_Of_Freedom (nodeB
            assuming nodeA is absent);
    (b) if (dof1) then
        (i) Get_Global_Directions_Of_DOF (nodeB);
        (ii) for (each direction of freedom) do

Table 11.1. (*Continued*)

```
        **let dir be the direction.
            if (Dir_Is_Free (nodeA, dir)) then
                group = Form_Group (nodeA, nodeB);
                return group;
            end.
        end.
    end.
End Take_NodeA_With_NodeB.

function Split-B (CG)
(1) nodes = Component_Nodes (CG);
(2) while (nodes) do
    Explore_Next_Level (CG, nodes, group, new_nodes);
    if (group) then
        return group, Global_Dir_Of_DOF (group);
    else
        nodes = new_nodes;
    end.
(3) return nil.
    **in this case no disassembly could be found.
End (Split-B).

function Explore_Next_Level (CG, nodes, group, new_nodes)
    **'group' is the subassembly that has been identified to be
    **disassemblable. If no such group can be identified,
    **new_nodes contains the set of nodes that represent
    **all subassemblies at that level. This set of nodes is used
    **in the next cycle to test subassemblies in the next level.
(1) for (each element of nodes) do
    **let 'a_node' be such a node.
    for (all nodes that have a link to a_node) do
        **let 'b_node' be such a node.
        new_node = Merge_Nodes (a_node, b_node);
        if (new_node) then
            Modify_Component_Graph (CG, new_node);
            Append_To_List (new_nodes, new_node);
            for (all nodes that have links to new_node) do
                **let 'c_node' be such a node.
                group = Take_NodeA_With_NodeB(c_node, new_node);
                if (group) then
                    Append_To_List (p_list, group);
                end.
            end.
            if (group) then
                goto (2).
            end.
        end.
    end.
end.
```

```
(2)  if (Size_Of (p_list) > 0) then
        Apply_Hueristics (p_list);
        group = Item_At_Head (p_list);
        if (group) then
          Empty_List (new_nodes);
        end.
(3) return.
End Explore_Next_Level.
```

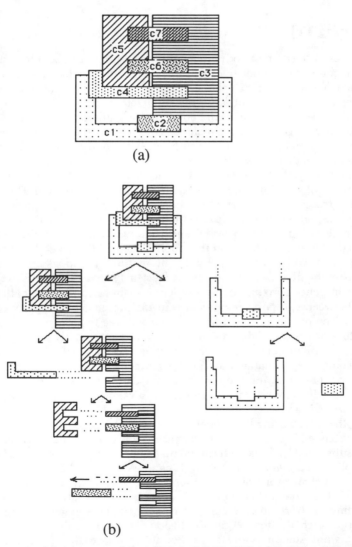

(a)

(b)

FIG. 11.5. **(a) An assembly model. (b) The disassembly process.**

blies consists of a single component, then that node of the disassembly graph is the leaf node. The *Split* module is applied to every subassembly, until all leaf nodes in the disassembly graph are generated. The hierarchy that is generated for the MSA in Fig. 11.5(a) is shown graphically in Fig. 11.5(b). If this graph is traversed from bottom to top, and each of the disassembly operations are made to act in reverse, then the assembly sequence can be deduced. Alternate assembly sequences could be generated from the partial orderings of assembly operations obtained from this graph.

Generating Valid Disassembly Motions

The degrees of freedom of nodes in a component graph can be inferred from the links that connect that node to other nodes. This information is used in identifying a suitable subassembly S_1 that can potentially be disassembled, as well as in proposing a direction of motion of the subassembly out of the parent assembly A_1. But this does not ensure a valid collision-free path for the moving subassembly S_1. In order to generate *valid* disassembly motions, the reasoning mechanism must be able to find a collision-free path for S_1 out of A_1. In its most general formulation, this is thus a *find-path* problem.

Lozano-Perez (1981, 1983) and Lozano-Perez and Wesley (1979) have described the configuration space approach to solving this problem. Brooks (1983) represents free space as generalized cones and presents an algorithm to find collision-free paths. However, these methods are fairly difficult to implement for 3-D objects that are translating and rotating. One critical difference exists between the kinds of problems in this application and the general *find-path* problems, i.e., this work is concerned with the motion of a subassembly within its parent assembly that has or had *constrained* this subassembly in a well-defined manner; the general @i (find-path) problem is to find a continuous path of a polyhedron between two positions in space in the presence of arbitrary polyhedral obstacles. The problem here of finding collision-free motions has obstacles that are in close proximity of the moving objects (in fact, they are usually in contact with the moving objects). This is the key information.

By making a systematic study of the geometric constraints imposed by the stationary subassembly on the moving subassembly, the problem can be formulated differently. If looked on as a search for a valid path, in this new premise, a *generate-and-test* approach does not involve extensive search. Moreover, by augmenting the search using knowledge of the geometric features that constrain the moving subassembly, as well as those features present on (and surrounding) the moving subassembly, the search can be made fairly efficient. So instead of posing this problem as a *find-path* problem, it can be considered as a problem in reasoning about changes in dof of subassemblies due to translational and rotational motions. When done using geometric models, this is a rather interesting problem; adding to efforts toward computer-based spatial and geometric reasoning. The heart of such a system requires collision detection capabilities between moving objects and stationary obstacles. For this purpose, the authors have developed efficient translational and rotational collision detection algorithms, which are described in the following paragraphs. These would apply to any surface boundary-based geometric representation which approximates the object shape using planar facets.

Determining Translational Motion

Given a subassembly and the direction in which it can potentially be disassembled, this module detects whether motion of the subassembly in that direction will cause a collision with the rest of the assembly, and if so, the module determines the amount of allowable motion. The module uses a simple swept volume method; i.e., it generates a volume that is formed when the subassembly moves in the given direction and checks whether this volume intersects with any of the stationary components. Information about containment shells of subassemblies, directions of the normals of facets, bounding boxes, and so on, is used to reduce the number of intersection calculations (face-face, face-edge, and edge-edge). Because a complete geometric model of the MSA exists, such information can be extracted at will. The problem of trying to reduce the number of intersection calculations also occurs in the field of computer graphics. In ray tracing procedures, data structures which support efficient geometric search makes it possible to look at only a small percentage of the facets that model the surface of the components in the assembly to determine the closest intersection (Kay and Kajiya, 1986; Fussell and Subramanian, 1988). These techniques should make the intersection module computationally more efficient. Once a collision is detected, the process of finding new motions continues after moving the subassembly to the point where the collision occurred. The motion is recorded and the disassembly is continued.

Determining Rotational Motion

This section describes an approach to efficiently compute rotational dof within assemblies. Using this information, disassembly operations that involve rotational motions can be deduced. One class of subassemblies that potentially possess rotational dof are those that have a peglike cylindrical shape feature, which mates with a cylindrical holelike feature (referred to as a cylindrical *peg-in-hole* type of mating). Thus, in order to check for rotational dof, a peg-in-hole type of mating feature would have to be identified. It must be pointed out that such shape features could be found within individual components or within subassemblies (the latter case would involve more than a single component contributing to the feature). Within the context of a geometric modeler that employs a boundary representation scheme with linear facets, this task of *recognizing* cylindrical shape features is a fairly substantial one, and is a major part of on-going research. In this work, it will be assumed that such features can be identified using either help from the user or some other automatic feature-recognition techniques. The axis of the cylindrical set of features is the *axis of rotation* of the subassembly.

Given an axis $\mathbf{A}$ in space and a subassembly $\mathbf{S}_1$ that has a rotational dof about $\mathbf{A}$, we need to determine the amount of rotation of $\mathbf{S}_1$ about $\mathbf{A}$. The *amount* of rotation is determined by the state of the final position of S_1: either it cannot rotate any more (in which case a collision has occurred), or its dof have changed to some desirable value. The actual rotation of S_1 would result in its being completely disassembled, or, would lead to a *state* where some subassembly (not necessarily S_1) has its dof modified. Most often, it is @b[S@down{1}] that has one of its translational dof modified, which means that after the rotation is performed on S_1, it can be translated to continue the disassembly process. This is what is meant by a desirable value of dof of S_1. A simple example is the twist-and-pull-out action (e.g., bayonet lock) which requires a rotation of the peg by a certain amount resulting in a state in which the peg is free to translate along its axis. Figure 11.6 is an example of rotational intersection. The following paragraphs describe an efficient method of determining the amount of rotation that a subassembly can make about an axis before it collides with a part of the remaining assembly. This forms an important module of the proposed reasoning mechanism.

An Algorithm to Efficiently Determine Rotational Intersections

Consider an assembly of n components. Let C_s be a set of stationary components, and C_r be a set of components that is being rotated about axis A. Note that C_r is the complement of C_s about the set of all components within the given assembly. The problem is to determine whether C_r collides with C_s during the course of its rotation about A, and if so, through what angle does it rotate before collision occurs. The broad outline of the algorithm is as follows. The description of the model is transformed from the Cartesian coordinate system to the cylindrical coordinate system (actually, the transformation is performed only for faces and edges that form part of the outer shell of C_r and relevant elements of the shell

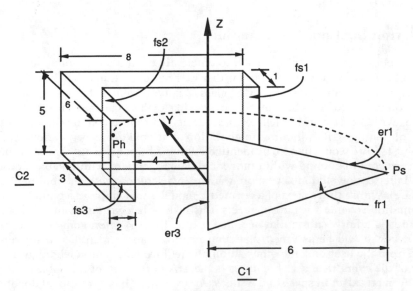

FIG. 11.6. Example illustrating rotational intersections.

of C_s. *Cylindrical bounding boxes* are created around such edges and faces. The volume traversed by C_r during rotation is swept out by a subset of the edges and faces of C_r. The set E_r of all such edges and faces F_r are identified. Faces and edges that belong to C_s and that form the neighborhood of the rotating subassembly are grouped into face set F_s and edge set E_s. Each member of E_r is checked for collision in a rotating frame with the members of F_s. In a similar fashion, each member of E_s is tested with members of F_r, but with the rotation in the reverse direction. This final check is equivalent to keeping C_r fixed and rotating C_s in the opposite direction. Emerging from this algorithm is information about the amount of rotation that C_r can make about the given axis before collision. The algorithm is described using a simple case of one rotating component and one stationary component. Figure 11.6 shows the stationary component C_2 and one of the faces of C_1. C_1 is rotating about the Z axis and the goal is to determine the amount of rotation that the face fr_1 can make before colliding with C_2. It would be worthwhile to spend a few moments visualizing as to how fr_1 would rotate and collide with C_2. What happens in this case is that edge er_1 hits face fs_2. But suppose that fr1 was located a little closer to C_2 (say one unit along the Y axis), then edge er_3 would collide with face fs_2.

(1) Transformation of Coordinates. Within the geometric modeling environment, the spatial locations of nodes are described in terms of Cartesian coordinates (x,y,z). Reasoning about *rotations* becomes cumbersome in this domain, whereas, as the task suggests, a cylindrical coordinate system (r,θ,z) would be far more effective both in determining rotational motions as well as in representing them. Thus a transformation from Cartesian to cylindrical coordinates is made for all elements of F_s, E_s, F_r, and E_r (this collection of elements will be referred to as set S). A coordinate frame is defined on axis A and the transformations are made with respect to this local frame.

Referring to Fig. 11.6, the following sets are defined.

$F_s = \{fs_1, fs_2, fs_3,\}$

$E_s = \{es_1, es_2, \ldots, es_9, es_{10}\}$

$F_r = \{fr_1,\}$

$E_r = \{er_1, er_2, er_3\}$

(2) Cylindrical Bounding Boxes. When the components in C_r are rotated, members of C_s constitute *obstacles* in the path of motion. In order to check for collisions efficiently, the approximate locations of the members would be required so as to discard nonobstructing faces. To do so, *cylindrical bounding boxes* are computed for each of the elements of set S. These boxes store range data for the (r,θ,z) values of elements, and are used extensively during collision detection. They are useful in reducing the number of intersection computations between rotating edges and stationary faces (or vice versa), and are not used to actually compute intersection values.

(3) Rotating Edges and Stationary Faces. When a face rotates around an axis, it is the *edges* of the face that define the boundary of the swept volume. Referring to Fig. 11.6, the volume generated by face fr_1 is defined by edges er_1, er_2, and er_3. Thus, at the lowest level of geometry, modeling edges rotating among arbitrary obstacles would give a measure of the rotational degrees of freedom of subassemblies. To do so, one needs to calculate the intersection between a rotating edge and a stationary face. When such collision tests are made for all edges in $\mathbf{E_r}$ in relation to the faces in $\mathbf{F_s}$ (e.g., edge er_1 and face fs_2), and edges in $\mathbf{E_r}$ in relation to the faces in $\mathbf{F_s}$ (the rotation in this case being done in the reverse direction), then one can obtain the rotation $\mathbf{C_r}$ makes before colliding. To understand as to why one needs to consider the second class of edges, consider the following. An edge $\mathbf{E}$ from set $\mathbf{E_r}$ could collide with a face $\mathbf{F}$ from set $\mathbf{F_s}$ in either of two ways: first $\mathbf{E}$ could *pierce* the flesh of $\mathbf{F}$, and, second, $\mathbf{E}$ could *hit* an edge of $\mathbf{F}$. But it could also happen that before $\mathbf{E}$ collides with $\mathbf{F}$, an edge from $\mathbf{E_s}$ could collide with a face from $\mathbf{F_r}$. It is for this reason that the second class of edges' intersections have to be carried out. The following paragraphs describe in brief how the pierce and hit conditions are detected and the appropriate angles computed.

The *pierce* condition results when a node $\mathbf{N}$ of an edge $\mathbf{E}$ collides with a face $\mathbf{F}$ (just like an arrow hitting and lodging in a tree). In the example, er_1 and fs_2 would be one possible $\mathbf{E}$ and $\mathbf{F}$ respectively. The set of points that lie on the edges that bound $\mathbf{F}$ and which have the same z value as $\mathbf{N}$ are calculated (only two points in this example). The extreme pair of points $(\mathbf{P_1}, \mathbf{P_2})$) are selected. The line joining $(\mathbf{P_1}, \mathbf{P_2})$) has on it a point $\mathbf{Ph}$ (refer to Fig. 11.6) that lies at the same distance from the axis of rotation as node $\mathbf{N}$. If $\mathbf{Ph}$ lies inside face $\mathbf{F}$ (which in this example it does), then there is potentially a pierce condition, except for one last test, which will be referred to as the *Normal* test. The normal of face @b{F} is rotated in the direction opposite to the actual rotation of the edge by an amount that would bring the $\mathbf{N}$ to lie on the wall, had it been rotated (i.e., in this example, $fs2$ is rotated to make points $\mathbf{P_h}$ and $\mathbf{P_s}$ coincide). The angle between the rotated normal of $\mathbf{F}$ and the tangent of edge $\mathbf{E}$ that points in the direction of @b {N} is calculated. If this angle happens to be obtuse, then it can be concluded that there is a pierce condition. In any other case, there is no pierce condition between $\mathbf{N}$ (belonging to edge $\mathbf{E}$) and $\mathbf{F}$. The preceding test is also carried out for the other node of $\mathbf{E}$ with $\mathbf{F}$. In case an edge does pierce a face, the difference between the θ values of point $\mathbf{P_h}$ and node $\mathbf{N}$ gives the required angle through which the edge can rotate before colliding.

The *hit* condition results when a rotating edge $\mathbf{E_r}$ collides with one of the edges (say $\mathbf{E_s}$) of a stationary face $\mathbf{F}$. If point $\mathbf{Ph}$ (previously defined) lies outside the face, or an edge fails the *Normal* test, then it is potentially a hit condition.

In both these tests, in order to check for rotational intersections between edges, the two edges are projected onto the $(\mathbf{R}, \mathbf{Z})$ plane. Note here the projection is not a projection by translation but by a rotation. In the projected space, the intersections are computed, and then projected back to the real space. To summarize, a method has been developed to compute rotational collisions between arbitrary polyhedral objects by using cylindrical coordinate transformations and intersection algorithms between rotating edges and stationary faces developed specifically for the cylindrical domain. This makes a notable contribution to the effort in reasoning about rotational disassembly tasks using geometric information about assembly parts. The preceding algorithm has been implemented and the computed values of angles of rotation are being used to determine disassembly tasks.

11.4 EXAMPLE

The capabilities of the proposed disassembly method are demonstrated in this section using an example which has been taken from Hoffman (1989). Figure 11.7 shows a series of snapshots during the disassembly of the MSA, as generated automatically by the authors' program. The MSA consists of four parts: (1) a box which has a slotted block inside it, (2) a door, which fits onto (3) a cylindrical bar

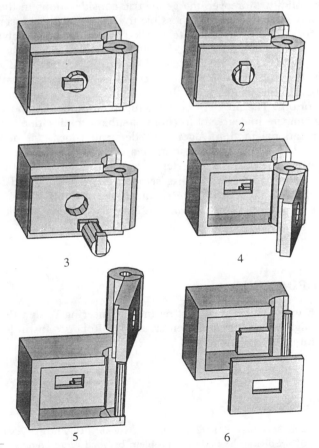

FIG. 11.7. Example showing disassembly process.

which is on the box and acts like a hinge, and (4) a key which passes through the slot in the block and gets locked in the slot. The program is supplied a model of the complete MSA [as in Fig. 11.7(1)]. The purpose in selecting this example is to highlight the generation of *translational* and *rotational motions* to disassemble an MSA.

11.5 CONCLUSION

This chapter has presented a method for the automated generation of an assembly procedure for a given assembly. The procedure is generated from the parts geometry and topology model, and thus explicit specification of mating relations between parts is not required. The approach not only dispenses with the time-consuming specification of mating relations by the user, but also prevents wrong mating relations from being presented and makes unnecessary the need to check for validity. Moreover, the geometric considerations in the generation of the assembly sequence makes it possible to directly evaluate assembly performance and, further, to easily generate detailed assembly plans, such as grasping, transferring, and manipulation, based on the given geometry of the assembly.

Algorithms are created to find a collision-free path to yield disassembly motions. To disassemble an MSA, one determines the parts or subassemblies that can separate themselves from the MSA after a series of translational and rotational motions. The problem of deducing such motions is posed as one of determining changes in degree of freedom of subassemblies, due to either translational or rotational motion. Algorithms determine locations at which collisions occur between moving subassemblies and the rest of the parent MSA. After the motions are deduced, a series of transformations is performed on the model of the MSA to accomplish disassembly. The efficiency and feasibility of the algorithms were demonstrated. Recent progress of this work can be found in the papers by authors [Khosla *et al.* (1992), Mattikalli and Khosla (1992), and Xu *et al.* (1991a), and Xu *et al.* (1991b)].

ACKNOWLEDGMENT

This research was supported in part by the Engineering Design Research Center, an NSF Engineering Research Center, and the Robotics Institute at Carnegie Mellon Institute.

REFERENCES

Boothroyd, G., and Dewhurst, P. 1972. *Design for Assembly*. Boothroyd Dewhurst Inc.
Brooks, R. A. 1983. Solving the find-path problem by good representation of free space. *IEEE Trans. on Systems, Man, and Cybernetics* SMC-13, No. 3.

Fussell, D. and Subramanian, K. R. 1988. Fast ray tracing using K-D trees. *Technical Report, Dept. of Computer Sciences*. The University of Texas at Austin TR-88-07.

Gursoz, L., Choi, Y., and Prinz, F. 1988. Vertex-based representation for nonmanifold boundaries. In *Geometric Modeling for Product Engineering*. New York: North-Holland, 107–130.

Hoffman, R. 1989. Automated assembly in a CSG domain. *Proc. IEEE Conference on Robotics and Automation*, 210–215.

Homem de Mello, L., and Sanderson, A. 1986. AND/OR graph representation of assembly plans. *Technical Report, The Robotics Institute*. CMU-RI-TR-86-8.

Kay, T. L., and Kajiya, J. T. 1986. *Ray Tracing Complex Scenes*. Vol. 20, No. 4.

Khosla, P. K., *et al.* 1992. CMU rapid assembly system. In *Video Proc. of the IEEE Conference on Robotics and Automation*. Nice, France, May 12–14, 1992.

Lee, K,, and Ko, H. 1987. Automatic assembly procedure generation from mating conditions. *CAD* 19(1):3–10.

Lozano-Perez, T. 1981. Automatic planning of manipulator transfer movements. *IEEE Trans. on Systems, Man, and Cybernetics* SMC-11:681–698.

Lozano-Perez, T. 1983. Spatial planning: A configuration space approach. *IEEE Trans. on Computers* C-32, No.2:108–120.

Lozano-Perez, T., and Wesley, M. A. 1979. An algorithm for planning collision-free paths among polyhedral obstacles. *Comm. of the ACM* 22, No.10:560–570.

Mattikalli, R. S., and Khosla, P. K. 1989. A system to determine assembly sequences. Technical Report, EDRC-24-16-89, Engineering Design Research Center, Carnegie Mellon University.

Mattikali, R. S., and Khosla, P. K. 1992. Motion constraints from contact geometry: Representation and analysis. In *Proc. of the IEEE Conference on Robotics and Automation*, pp. 2178–2185. Nice, France, May 12–14, 1992.

Owen, T. 1982. *Assembly with Robots*. Prentice Hall.

Rocheleau, D., and Lee, K. 1987. System for interactive assembly modeling. *CAD* 19(2):65–72.

Sedas, S., and Talukdar, S. 1987. Disassembly expert. Technical Report, EDRC-01-03-87, Engineering Design Research Center, Carnegie Mellon University.

Wesley, M., *et al.* 1980. A geometric modeling system for automated mechanical assembly. *IBM Journal of Research and Development* 24(1):64–74.

Whitney, D., and DeFazio, T. 1987. Simplified generation of all mechanical sequences. *IEEE Journal of Robotics and Automation* RA-3(6), December, 1987.

Xu, Y., Mattikalli, R. S., and Khosla, P. K. 1991a. Two-disk motion planning strategy. In *Proc. of the IEEE Conference on System, Man, and Cybernetics*, pp. 991–996. Charlottesville, Virginia, October 13–16, 1991.

Xu, Y., Mattikalli, R. S., and Khosla, P. K. 1991b. Generation of partial medial axis for dissambly motion plan. In *Proc. of the IEEE Conference on System, Man, and Cybernetics*, pp. 997–1003. Charlottesville, Virginia, October 13–16, 1991.

Chapter 12

Intelligent Assembly System for Sequence Generation and Task Planning

C. L. Philip Chen
Department of Computer Science and Engineering
Wright State University
Dayton, Ohio

12.1 INTRODUCTION

As the complexity of systems and products increases, there is an increasing need for computer design tools to aid the designers during the design process. Computer-aided design and manufacturing (CAD/CAM) systems were developed to assist engineers in creating, modifying, and evaluating their product designs. An intelligent system is able to support design information that influences the designer's ability to create designs, make decisions, perform problem solving, and correct design errors. There has been considerable recent progress in computer-aided design. These efforts try to close the gap between design and manufacturing, most importantly, using the CAD system to transfer the abstract design concept to the desired type of problem. There has been much research that has tried to map this abstraction level to the real world design in the areas of mechanical assembly design and planning.

Mechanical assembly plays a fundamental role in the manufacture of most products. Parts that have been individually formed and machined are assembled into a configuration that achieves the functions of the final product. The manufacturing industry is placing extensive effort to implement flexible assembly systems (FAS) to improve the efficiency and cost effectiveness of assembly operations (Homen de Mello and Sanderson, 1990). Assembly using intelligent machines represents the leading edge of scientific and technological development in today's manufacturing industry. A truly intelligent assembly automation will not be achieved until the interaction between humans and computerized machines has been remarkably simplified. The problems of building an intelligent mechanical assembly system and reducing man–machine interaction are important economic factors in the manufacturing industry. Two fundamental factors need to be addressed to design such an intelligent assembly system. The first factor is the assembly executor, which consists of operations of flexibility of the assembly machines. The assembly executor specifies control of the assembly machines used for each assembly step and the operation of the machines.

The second factor is the assembly planner, which generates assembly plans that enable machines to perform certain tasks and that control the sequences of the machines' movements to accomplish the tasks.

The assembly plan is generally expressed in terms of a series of operation descriptions in transforming the assembly operation from one state to another (Fu *et al.*, 1987). Many robot languages have recently been developed to express these assembly operations (Mujtaba *et al.*, 1982; Popplestone *et al.*, 1978). These languages specifically describe physical constraints of the world model to enable a robot to perform precise assembly operations. Several researchers (Wolter, 1988; Homem de Mello, 1989; Huang, 1991) have presented a detailed review of such robot assembly planning systems. Recently, building an intelligent assembly system by integrating the CAD model to cope with the geometric constraints of generating assembly plans has been developed (Nnaji *et al.*, 1988; Delchambre, 1991; Huang, 1991; Chen and Wichman, 1992). These assembly systems combine both assembly planner and assembly executor to achieve intelligent assembly operation. Previous works indicate that one of the main problems of assembly planning is to generate the sequences for the assembly executor that transforms the assembly operation from the initial state to a goal state.

Thus to achieve cost-effective assembly operations, the assembly planner must generate all possible assembly sequences and determine the most promising one to be used for assembling the mechanical object. This chapter discusses assembly sequence generation and an assembly planning system that generates task-level assembly plans. Generally, the assembly process is either to attach two parts together or to cohere part(s) with a formed sub-object. This process can be executed repeatedly until the desired object has been obtained. To achieve such a process usually involves the precedence relation among the parts; that is, the order of assembly operations crucially determines whether the desired object is able to be constructed from the parts. This precedence relation results from the geometric and physical constraints of the assembly. Thus to generate all the feasible assembly sequences, one must consider these important factors.

The precedence relations among parts are usually obtained from the answers to questions about the relation between a pair of parts posed by a design engineer. De Fazio and Whitney (1987) refined the approach that Bourjault (1984) developed to generate assembly sequences based on a set of answers expressed by the precedence relationship. Usually, the precedence knowledge is expressed as the symbolic precedence logic form, and the constraints are either expressed as precedence direct graph or as predicate logic form, which are used to deduce all the feasible assembly sequences (Jentsch and Kaden, 1984; Chen and Wichman, 1992). Here, the concept of State-Constrained Traveling Salesperson Problem (SCTSP) will be introduced to generate all possible feasible assembly sequences. Different with standard TSP [E. L. Lawler ed. 1985. The traveling salesman problem: A guide tour of combinatorial optimization. Wiley, N.Y.], SCTSP restricts the movements of the next states.

12.2 ASSEMBLY SEQUENCE GENERATION

The first part of this chapter focuses on automatically generating all the assembly sequence of the assembly planner and presents a novel approach for obtaining all the assembly sequences. Here, a precedence knowledge acquisition, derived from the concept of SCTSP, is presented that reduces the time to obtain such knowledge. The AND/OR predicate logic precedence representation and the proposed precedence knowledge representation are shown to be equivalent. For the precedence knowledge acquisition, the proposed approach is much more general than the one discussed in De Fazio and Whitney (1987) and Chang and Lee (1988).

Based on the precedence knowledge obtained in the planning state and the cost or resources arrangement between tasks and robots, the assembly sequence scheduler must find the best sequence of the assembly task. The sequencing problem can be solved either by *Cost-Constrained* TSP (CCTSP) or *State-Constrained* TSP (SCTSP). The solution of the CCTSP usually is solved by setting the cost of all the prohibited moves between two cities (or tasks) to very large values to satisfy the desired constraints. This approach only restricts the movement from one city, x, to the next city, y (e.g., visit city x *immediately* before visiting city y), by checking the cost between two cities, which is usually called the *immediate predecessor–successor* relationship. But during the acquisition of the precedence knowledge, the *immediate* predecessor–successor relationship is insufficient. Instead, the characteristics of the precedence relationship between two tasks is only expressed as a predecessor–successor relationship; i.e., only the knowledge of the precedence order of the tasks is given, not the detailed relationship between pairs of liaisons. During the process of precedence knowledge acquisition, the immediate predecessor–successor relationship acquisition needs considerable effort. For example, a precedence constraint "visit city x before visiting city y," is easily satisfied rather than having to specify the exact order between city x and y. This general expression implies that any city can be visited after visiting city x as long as city y is visited after city x. The pseudo-cost arrangement, like the CCTSP method, is insufficient to exactly express this relation. The SCTSP proposed here can easily solve this problem from the proposed knowledge representation by restricting the movement of the generation of next valid cities.

Another advantage of the SCTSP over CCTSP is the computation time of finding the best assembly schedule. To obtain the best assembly schedule, the CCTSP method needs to solve the standard TSP

$$\prod_{q=1}^{K} M_q N_q$$

(Chang and Lee, 1988), where M_q and N_q are the number of the OR precedence operators in one precedence form and K is the total number of the precedence forms. The best solution results in the best assembly schedule. The SCTSP method presented here needs to solve the standard TSP only *one* time. This improvement comes from the arrangement of the precedence knowledge acquisition and representation. Detailed algorithms, analyses, and examples are presented to show the feasibility of the proposed method in both precedence knowledge acquisition and assembly sequence and schedule generation.

Recursive Decomposition of Assembly Problem

This section discusses the concept of partitioning and decomposing all the feasible assembly sequences. System models, formulations, and algorithms are based on this concept.

Representation of System Model

In general, the parts that construct a mechanical object, O, can be represented by an undirected network $N = (P, L)$ consisting of a finite nonempty set of vertices P, $P = \{\sum P_i | P_i \in N, i = 1, 2, \ldots\}$ and a set of finite edges L, $L = \{L_i | L_i \in N\}$, $|L| = l$, connecting them. Each vertex, p_i, represents a part and each edge, L_i, represents the liaison that connects the two parts. An example of a ballpoint pen adopted from (De Fazio, 1987) is shown in Fig. 12.1. For a given partition S_j, let ϕ_k, $l \leq k \leq q$ (where max $q = n$) be a block of a certain partition of the given N such that

$$\bigcup_{K=1}^{q} \phi_k = P$$

and $\phi_h \cap \phi_k = \varnothing$, $h \neq k$. The assembly problem is to find permutations of parts or

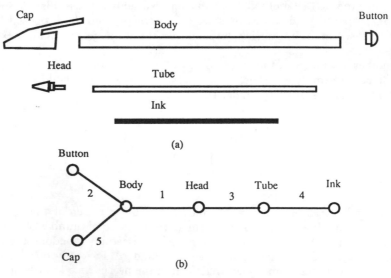

(a)

(b)

FIG. 12.1. Assembled parts of ballpoint pen (Adapted from De Fazio 1987).

liaisons within each block and permutations among blocks such that the object can be constructed.

Liaison Flow Assembly Sequence Tree

Given a network representing the topology of a mechanical object, the assembly operation can be represented by a tree structure called the *liaison flow assembly sequence tree*. There are two kinds of nodes in the tree, the part nodes and the liaison nodes. The part nodes are the nodes with no predecessors, and the liaison nodes specify the connectivity between part nodes and/or liaison nodes. The arcs in the tree correspond to the order of execution sequence and connectivity between two part nodes or two liaison nodes. The execution order of an assembly is to assemble the parts connected by a liaison nodes from left to right across the top of the liaison flow assembly tree. Thus, the liaison flow assembly tree specifies the order of operations. The concept of the liaison flow assembly tree representation is analogous with the data flow graph representing the computation program. The advantages of the liaison flow representation are the part nodes that specify the order of parts entering an assembly and the liaison nodes that specify the liaison information indicating the necessary mechanical operations (such as mate, insert, screw, etc.). Although only the sequence problem is focused on here, the mechanical operations will be an important aspect of the assembly planning problem after the sequences are generated. An example expressing two assembly sequences of the ballpoint pen as the liaison flow assembly tree is shown in Fig. 12.2.

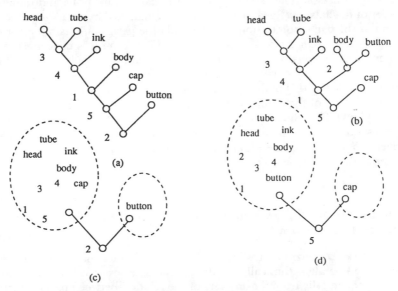

FIG. 12.2. Two liaison flow assembly trees.

Recursively Removing Nodes

The feasible assembly sequences can be obtained using the concept of the liaison flow assembly tree. Each liaison flow assembly tree is an assembly sequence. The execution order of the assembly sequence can be interpreted by tracing liaison nodes from left to right and from top to bottom. In a liaison flow assembly tree, the terminal node is the last operation to assemble the object. This last operation is performed either to combine a part with the formed sub-object Fig. 12.2(a) or to cohere two formed sub-objects together Fig. 12.2(b). Given an object, several last assembly operations that completely assemble the object can be found. Two groups of liaisons and parts in the liaison flow assembly tree can be formed. Each group is attached to the arc connected to the last operation. Currently last assembly operations can be found recursively within each group. Examples of this process are shown in Fig. 12.2. Here, two last operations (liaisons 2 and 5) can be identified. Two groups of liaisons and parts are connected to each of the last operations. For liaison 2, the group on the right side is the part *button*, whereas the group on the left side consists of the rest of the liaisons and parts with unknown connectivity. Similarly for the liaison 5 group. Thus, all the feasible assembly sequences can be found by performing the following steps repeatedly:

(1) Identify all currently last operations to assemble the object.
(2) Update liaisons set by removing the currently last operation from current liaisons set.

Transforming Liaisons Flow Assembly Tree to Expansion Tree

The preceding liaison flow assembly tree gives part connections and the execution order of the liaisons. Because two parts are connected by a liaison, if the data structure of the parts' connection is given, only the permutations of liaisons are needed to generate all the assembly sequences. Based on this concept, the execution order of liaisons of an assembly sequence can be simply expressed by a path of an expansion tree with the execution order tracing the path from bottom to top. The nodes in this path represent the liaisons. The last liaison operation, thus, is on the top of the path, and the first liaison operation is on the bottom of the path. Figure 12.3 shows all 12 feasible sequences of assembling a ballpoint pen represented as an expansion tree. Thus, to find all the feasible sequences is equivalent to generating the expansion tree such that all the paths on the tree satisfy precedence constraints.

Precedence Knowledge Acquisition and Assembly Sequence Generation

Previous work (De Fazio and Whitney, 1987) has shown that all the assembly sequences can be algorithmically obtained from a series of rules. The rules are generated sequentially from the answers of the relation between parts, which are called *liaisons*. Here, liaisons L_i and tasks T_i are used alternatively.

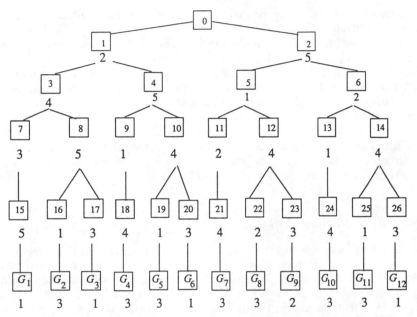

FIG. 12.3. State-space representation of the assembly sequences for the ballpoint pen example. Squared numbers indicate node expansion order, and a path from a G_i node to the initial node indicates the assembly sequence number *i*.

De Fazio and Whitney (1987) have proposed the modification method differentiating from Bourjault's work, which requires 2*l* questions to be answered in a precedence logical form (where *l* is the number of liaisons). This simplification method is used to include a small set of questions regarding the conditions of liaisons establishment and is represented in a more compact form. The series of questions

For *i* = 1 *to l* do

(Q1) What liaisons must be done prior to doing liaison *i*?

(Q2) What liaisons must be left to be done after doing liaison *i*?

Both questions are to be answered for each liaison. By expressing the answers in the precedence or the logical relations, all the assembly sequences can be generated by logic induction. The answers to all the liaisons are expressed in the form:

$$(L_j \lor (L_k \land L_m)) \rightarrow L_i \tag{1}$$

$$L_i \rightarrow (L_s \lor (L_t \land L_u)) \tag{2}$$

The symbol → is read "must precede" and ∨ and ∧ are logic OR and AND operators, respectively.

Based on the location of a single task with respect to →, two precedence relationship forms are identified: *post*-precedence ((Q1) or Eq. (1)) and *pre*-precedence ((Q2) or Eq. (2)). This approach is to obtain all possible *pre*- and *post*-AND/OR combinations by asking each liaison. Thus, the number of questions asked is $2l$ for a given object with l liaisons (or a given assembly operation with l tasks) to be completed. Given these precedence constraints, all the feasible sequences are shown to be generated by logic induction.

A novel approach based on the concept of constrained TSP to acquire all the precedence knowledge and further to generate all the feasible assembly sequences will be introduced in the following section.

Assembly Sequences Problem and TSP

The Traveling Salesperson Problem, a well-known combinational problem, is to find the shortest tour taken by a salesman based on the costs of the visited distances. The constrained TSP is restricted to the next city visited by the salesman. For the assembly schedule problem, the cost from the final city to the initial city is ignored. This terminology is similar to the generation of the feasible assembly sequences, which is constrained by the AND/OR precedence conditions during the state expansion.

As previously noted, there are two kinds of constrained TSP, the cost-constrained TSP (CCTSP), and the state-constrained TSP (SCTSP). The CCTSP method artificially sets the cost of prohibited moves at a very large value ensuring that the constraints are satisfied. Given this terminology, the CCTSP method can only solve immediate predecessor–successor constraint problems. This can be shown in Fig. 12.4, where L_1 *immediate* → L_3 gives the precedence constraint specifying that task L_3 must be done immediately after performing task L_1. The elements (1,2) and (1,4) of this matrix are artificially set at very large values to allow movement from L_1 *to* L_3 only. Similarly, elements (2,3), (3,1), and (4,3) of this matrix are artificially set at very large values to prohibit movement from L_2 to L_3, L_3 to L_1, and L_4 to L_3, thus the sequences are L_1, L_3**, $*L_1L_3*$, and $**L_1L_3$, where the * is a wild card sign specifying any tasks that can be allocated in these positions as long as a tour is valid.

Instead of setting large values in the cost matrix, the SCTSP method restricts the movements of the next states. The SCTSP is quite feasible in terms of prece-

$$\begin{bmatrix} \square\dagger & \infty\ddagger & 2 & \infty \\ 5 & \square & \infty & 1 \\ \infty & 4 & \square & 5 \\ 1 & 6 & \infty & \square \end{bmatrix}$$

FIG. 12.4. An example of the cost matrix with the precedence L_1 *immediate* → L_3.

dence knowledge acquisition. For example, given an $L_1 \rightarrow L_3$ relationship, during the assembly sequence generation, whenever the city (i.e., state) L_3 is going to be generated one can answer the question, "*Is there any city left to be visited named L_1?*" If the city L_1 is not in the set of cities left to be visited, then the city L_1 must have been visited before L_3, thus this precedence constraint is satisfied. Otherwise, the precedence constraint is violated. All the feasible assembly sequences satisfying this precedence constraint are L_1L_3**, L_1*L_3*, L_1**L_3, $*L_1L_3*$, $*L_1*L_3$, and $**L_1L_3$ orderings. Obviously, the immediate predecessor–successor relationship is a subset of the predecessor–successor relationship. If only immediate predecessor–successor sequences are pursued, they can also be obtained by applying the SCTSP method (Chen, 1991). Given a series of AND/OR precedence rules, the solution of an assembly schedule can be solved by using CCTSP (Chang and Lee, 1988). Based on the concept of SCTSP, precedence knowledge acquisition can easily be done and its advantages will also be discussed.

Precedence Knowledge Acquisition

The concept of precedence knowledge acquisition is derived from the process of finding the solution of a SCTSP. Given a set of cities to be visited, the solution of the TSP can be formulated as a state–space expansion tree. Here, a state of the tree represents a city. The root node of the tree is the last city to be visited, a terminal node of the tree is the first city to be visited. A *tour* is a path from a terminal node to the root node. Based on this paradigm, the solution of the TSP is the path from a terminal node to the root node with minimum cost.

Similarly, for the precedence-constrained assembly problem, if the root node of the tree is the desired object, a state of the tree is an assembly operation, and a path from a terminal node to the root node is an assembly sequence. For the assembly problem, there exist precedence relationships among tasks, thus during the next state generation process, the next states must be carefully selected such that the precedence constraints among tasks are satisfied.

Based on the definition of the state–space expansion tree, a path of the tree can be easily divided into three groups: the state x, and the groups above and below the state x. States above the state x of a path are the assembly operations performed after performing the operation x, whereas states below the state x are the assembly operations performed before the operation of state x. This is explained in Fig. 12.5. For the precedence-constrained problem, the elements of these two groups must be constrained during the expansion; i.e., to constrain the task execution above and below the task x. The task group located below the task x comprises the tasks that can be performed before the execution of task x, whereas the task group located above the task x are the tasks that can be performed after the execution of task x. This leads to precedence knowledge acquisition by asking: If the task x is not done, what tasks combined *cannot* be done and what tasks combined *can* be done?

Because there are l tasks in an assembled object and $1 \leq x \leq l$, every task needs to be performed. Thus the total number of states of a given path in the state–space expansion tree is l. Based on this analysis, the minimum number of

{ .. }

..

..   States (or assembly operations) above the state x are

..   the operations after performing the x operations.

..

x State x

..

..   States (or assembly operations) below the state x are

..   the operations before performing the x operations.

..

{ .. }

FIG. 12.5. Divide a path of an expansion tree into three groups.

questions asked to obtain all precedence knowledge is l. This yields the following proposition.

Proposition: The minimum number of questions asked to obtain precedence knowledge for an l liaison object is l.

Obviously, one can move task x along a path and ask what tasks combined cannot be done and what tasks combined can be done if task x is in the mth position of the path. Because there are l tasks, $1 \leq x \leq l$, and l states in a path, $1 \leq m \leq l$, this feature requires at least l_2 questions to be answered. Thus, in order to achieve the minimum number of questions asked, the designed question must treat task x in any position along a path (i.e., reduce m from l to 1) when this question is asked.

When applying the designed question, even though some combined tasks cannot be done, it is still possible that these tasks can combine with other tasks to make the rest of the assembly operations possible. Because there are several combinations among the tasks that can be done, the answers must be well designed so that they can be obtained easily and concisely. Using the definition of *dominant tasks* avoids the pursuit of combinations of tasks with tasks that cannot be done to obtain answers of l questions. Tasks are said to be *dominant tasks* if these tasks, when combined with tasks that cannot be done, make the rest of the assembly operations possible.

With this definition, now the question is If task x is not done, what combined tasks cannot be done and what are the dominant tasks? To answer this question, the assembly engineer must know the relations among the parts and liaisons to construct the object. The number of assembly sequences generated depends on the format of the answers given. Some of the unfeasible assembly sequences might appear if answers are incorrect, or some of the feasible sequences might disappear if some of the eligible combined tasks are ignored. Thus to generate all the assembly sequences, it is necessary that all the questions be answered correctly without errors or omissions.

Proposed Precedence Knowledge Acquisition and AND/OR Precedence Knowledge

Equations (1) and (2) show *post-* and *pre*-precedence conditions of each liaison. The proposed precedence knowledge acquisition method not only can solve both precedence conditions (*post-* and *pre-*), but also solve a general precedence nominal form that combines both Eqs. (1) and (2) expressing more complicated precedence relationships of assembly operations.

A nominal set of AND/OR precedence knowledge can describe the precedence relationship among tasks. A nominal set of AND/OR precedence relationships can be expressed as:

$$
\bigvee_{i=1}^{M} \left(\bigwedge_{j=1}^{m} T_j \right)_i \rightarrow \bigvee_{k=1}^{N} \left(\bigwedge_{l=1}^{n} T_l \right)_k , \tag{3}
$$

where $(\wedge_{j=1}^{m} T_j)$ is a series of tasks called "And-Tasks-Group" (ATG) relating by $\wedge$ operator, and i varies from 1 to M specifying M sets of ATG related by $\vee$ operator.

Another standard form of nominal AND/OR precedence knowledge is

$$
\bigwedge_{i=1}^{M} \left(\bigvee_{j=1}^{m} T_j \right)_i \rightarrow \bigwedge_{k=1}^{N} \left(\bigvee_{l=1}^{n} T_l \right)_k , \tag{4}
$$

where $(\vee_{j=1}^{m} T_j)$ is a series of tasks called "Or-Tasks-Group" (OTG) relating by $\vee$ operator, and i varies from 1 to M specifying M sets of OTG related by $\wedge$ operator.

The nominal set of AND/OR precedence forms describes all the possible precedence constraints of the assembly problem. Any $\wedge$ or $\vee$ combinations of tasks can be derived by the logical distributive or associative properties and can be expressed as Eqs. (3) or (4). Previous work has only discussed post- and pre-precedence constraints acquisition; general nominal precedence constraints are not indicated explicitly. Because the precedence relationship is embedded in each answer, the proposed precedence knowledge acquisition can solve an assembly operation with a general nominal precedence constraint. Here, the proposed precedence knowledge that can express the general precedence nominal form of Eq. (3) is addressed. Another general precedence nominal form of Eq. (4) can be applied similarly.

Given an assembly operation, shown in Fig. 12.6, components a and b are tightened on the supporting desk using screws d, e, and f. Component c is attached to either component a or b by screw g as long as either a or b is tightened. The precedence knowledge can be obtained as follows:

$i = 1$: If task 1 is not done, task 4 and task 5 cannot be done, but task 3 can combine with tasks 4 and 5 to make the rest of the assembly operations possible. Thus, task 3 is the dominant task.

$i = 2$: If task 2 is not done, task 4 and task 5 cannot be done, but task 3 can

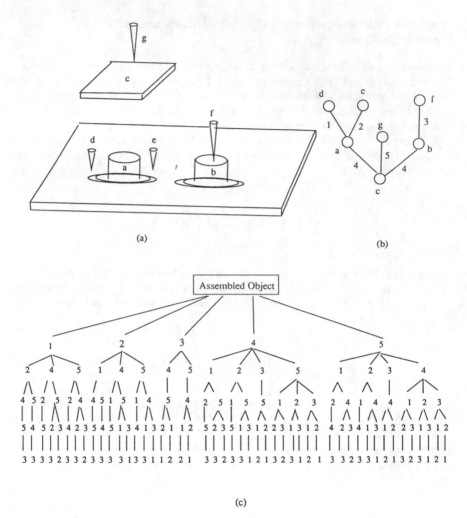

(a)

(b)

(c)

FIG. 12.6. An assembled object for Example, which shows general nominal precedence knowledge.

combine with tasks 4 and 5 to make the rest of the assembly operations possible. Thus, task 3 is the dominant task.

$i = 3$: If task 3 is not done, task 4 and task 5 cannot be done, but tasks 1 and 2 can combine with tasks 4 and 5 to make the rest of assembly operations possible. Thus, tasks 1 and 2 combined are the dominant tasks.

$i = 4$: If liaison 4 is not done, everything can be done.

$i = 5$: If liaison 4 is not done, everything can be done.

The precedence relationship of this assembly operation is listed in Table 12.1.

Table 12.1. Precedence Knowledge for Fig. 12.6, Which Is Equivalent to General Nominal Precedence Relationship Expressed as $(1 \wedge 2) \vee 3 \rightarrow 4 \wedge 5$

Question Number (i)	$\omega_1(i)$	$\omega_2(i)$	$\omega_3(i)$
1	{1}	{{4}, {5}}	{{3}}
2	{2}	{{4}, {5}}	{{3}}
3	{3}	{{4}, {5}}	{{1, 2}}
4	{4}	—	—
5	{5}	—	—

The precedence knowledge of this example is equivalent to the general nominal AND/OR precedence relationship expressed as

$$(1 \wedge 2) \wedge 3 \rightarrow 4 \wedge 5$$

The proposed precedence knowledge acquisition method can obtain combinations of %andsign% and %orsign% operators on both sides of → operator by simply embedding precedence relationships into "cannot be done" and "dominant" combinations. Based on the precedence knowledge, the assembly sequence generation algorithm will be discussed next.

Assembly Sequence Generation and the Pattern-Matching Algorithm

Based on the proposed precedence knowledge acquisition method, all the feasible assembly sequences can be generated. As previously discussed, the assembly sequences can be represented as a state–space expansion tree. The state–space expansion tree paradigm is defined by a triple (U, R, G) where U is a set of initial states, R is a set of operators on states, and G is a set of goal states. The state–space is represented by an expanded tree in which each node is a state and the application of an operator to a node results in transforming a state to a successor state, a process commonly called *node expansion*. A solution to the generating assembly sequence problem is a path in the state–space defined by a sequence of operators. From the foregoing concept of obtaining the last liaison operation of the assembly sequence, the root node of this tree is the desired object. A path from a goal state to the start state is an assembly sequence. The state–space tree representation of generating all the assembly sequences is formulated as follows:

(1) *State Representation.* Let a set $U(m) = A(m)$ denote a liaison operation at a node m of the expansion tree. The set $F(m)$ is the set of liaisons left to be performed. For any states of a path $F(m) = L - \cup_m A(m)$, where L

is the set of all liaisons. The set $A(m) = \{L_i\}$ in the node m means that the liaison L_i is to be performed.

(2) *Initial State.* The initial state of the expansion tree is the desired object, $U(m) = \varnothing$; i.e., $A(m) = \varnothing$ and $F(m) = L$.

(3) *Operators.* Operators are the means for transforming the sequence problem from one state to another. The application of an operator to a node is to let $A(m)$ be a new liaison L_i which is removed from $F(m)$. Let the set $R_c(m) = \{L_j | L_j \in L\}$ be a set of candidate liaisons. Each liaison removed from $F(m)$ must satisfy the pattern-matching algorithm imposed on the set $\omega_1(i)$, $\omega_2(i)$, and $\omega_3(i)$, which will be explained next. Then, the operator updates the set $A(m)$ by assigning one liaison from the set $R_c(m)$ to it, and updates the set $F(m)$ as the difference of the old set $F(m)$ and $R_c(m)$.

(4) *Goal State.* Any state $U(m)$, $F(m) = \varnothing$ is a goal state.

Consider the problem of assembling l liaisons to form an object. The assembly sequence generation problem is represented by an expansion tree. The currently last liaison operation represents a branching (or expansion) at a node corresponding to the given liaison to be removed from the set $F(m)$. Starting with the object that consists of l assembly liaisons, each liaison removed is subject to the constraints obtained from the pattern-matching algorithm. A path from a goal node to the start node (or root node) corresponds to an assembly sequence. A pattern-matching algorithm is used to correctly expand all the qualified nodes to satisfy precedence constraints from the root node to the goal node. This algorithm is introduced next.

From the state–space tree representation, the pattern-matching algorithm is used to find the set $R_c(m)$ in each node m of the expansion tree. Recall that in the state space representation of the expansion tree, liaisons L_i are continuously removed from the set $F(m)$ as the nodes are expanding. Based on the characteristics of the designed question and the definition of ω's sets, if the $\omega_2(i)$ set is an empty set, then the task in the set $\omega_1(i)$ is a candidate task to be expanded. If $\omega_2(i)$ is not an empty set, then one needs to check whether all the tasks in the $\omega_2(i)$ set match the tasks in the set $(F(m) - L_i)$. If matching fails, then the remaining tasks do not contain tasks that cannot be done, thus the task in the set $\omega_1(i)$ is a candidate task to be expanded. If matching occurs (even if only one element in the set $\omega_2(i)$ matches the set $(F(m) - L_i)$), then one needs to check whether there are any dominant tasks left, which will make assembly operations possible, and expand the task in the set $\omega_1(i)$. If indeed there are dominant tasks, one should check whether these dominant tasks are in the set $(F(m) - L_i)$ (recall that $F(m)$ is the set of tasks left to be done). If not, no expansion can be done; otherwise, the task in the set $\omega_1(i)$ is still a candidate task. The flowchart of the pattern-matching algorithm is shown in Fig. 12.7. The pattern-matching algorithm is summarized in the following.

Algorithm PM (*Pattern-Matching Algorithm*). Given a series of sets $\omega_1(i)$, $\omega_2(i)$, and $\omega_3(i)$, the sets $A(m)$, and $F(m)$ at node m of the state–space expansion tree, this algorithm obtains a set of candidate tasks, $R_c(m)$, for expansion.

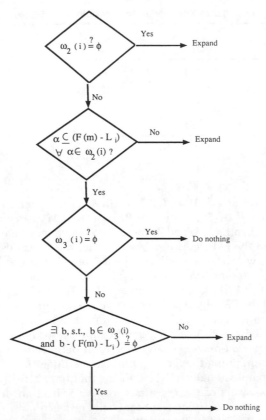

FIG. 12.7. Flow chart for Pattern-Matching Algorithm.

P1. [Initialization] Set $R_c(m) = \emptyset$, $F(m) = L - \bigcup_m A(m)$.
P2. [Matching test] For every $L_i \in F(m)$ do
P2.a If $\omega_2(i) = \emptyset$, go to step P3.
   Else
P2.b   If $\alpha \not\subseteq (F(m) - L_i)$ for all $\alpha \in \omega_2(i)$, go to P3.
    Else
     If $\omega_3(i) \neq \emptyset$
P2.c   If *exist* b such that $b \in \omega_3(i)$ and $b - (F(m) - L_i) = \emptyset$, go to P3.
P2.d   Else exit
P2.e   Else exit;
P3. [Constructing $R_c(m)$ set] $R_c(m) = R_c(m) \cup \omega_1(i)$.
END PM

Using the ballpoint pen example shown in Fig. 12.1, by applying this proposed precedence knowledge acquisition method, a series of ω's(i) are given in Table 12.2. With reference to Table 12.2, the PM algorithm, and Fig. 12.3, one has the

Table 12.2. Precedence Knowledge for Ballpoint Pen Shown in Fig. 12.1

Question Number (i)	$\omega_1(i)$	$\omega_2(i)$	$\omega_3(i)$
1	{1}	{{5}}	—
2	{2}	—	—
3	{3}	{{4}, {1,2}}	—
4	{4}	{{1,2}}	—
5	{5}	—	—

start state $A(0) = \emptyset$ and $F(0) = \{1,2,3,4,5\}$. When $i = 2$ and $i = 5$, the liaisons in the sets $\omega_1(2)$ and $\omega_1(5)$ satisfy step P2.a of the PM algorithm. Thus, $R_c(0) = \{2,5\}$. Whereas when $i = 1, 3$, and 4, these liaisons cannot be expanded because of the step P2.e of the PM algorithm. The next candidate expansion nodes are the liaisons 2 and 5, which means either liaison 2 or 5 is the last liaison operation to assemble the ballpoint pen. Similarly, for $A(1) = \{2\}$, and $F(1) = \{1,3,4,5\}$, one can obtain $R_c(1) = \{4,5\}$ from $\omega_2(4)$ and $\omega_2(5)$ in Table 12.2, which satisfy steps P2.b and P2.a of the PM algorithm, respectively. Thus, one can generate the next two branches shown in Fig. 12.3. For each of these branches, the liaisons that can be done are liaisons 1, 3, and 5 (connect *cap-head-body-tube*), and liaisons 1, 3, and 4 (connect *head-tube-ink-body*). For each path, the ballpoint pen can be constructed by combining the liaisons that can be done (i.e., the liaisons below the currently expanded one) with the liaisons that have already been expanded.

Because the answers of the questions may vary, it might happen that some tasks in the set $\omega_2(i)$ or $\omega_3(i)$ are a subset of the tasks contained in the same set. According to step P2.a of the PM algorithm, if $\beta, \eta \in_2 (i)$ and $\beta \subseteq \eta$, then η can be deleted from the set $\omega_2(i)$. Similarly, according to step P2.c of the PM algorithm, if $\lambda, \gamma \in \omega_3(i)$ and $\lambda \subseteq \gamma$, then λ can be deleted from the set $\omega_3(i)$. This *merging* operation can reduce expansion time during sequence generation.

The algorithm FASG (Feasible Assembly Sequence Generation) that generates all the feasible assembly sequences by using the pattern-matching algorithm is detailed in the following description.

Algorithm FASG (*Feasible Assembly Sequence Generation Algorithm*). Given n parts and l liaisons that construct a mechanical object, this algorithm generates all the feasible assembly sequences from the sets of liaisons obtained from the proposed precedence knowledge acquisition and the pattern-matching algorithm.

F1. [*Initialization*] Put the start node I on a list of unexpanded nodes, called *FORMOBJ*. Note that in the initial state I, $F(I)$ is the liaison set L and $A(I)$ is an empty set.

F2. [*Find a node from the FORMOBJ list*] Select from the *FORMOBJ* list a node m. If several nodes qualify, choose a node arbitrarily.

F3. [*Move the node from the unexpanded list to the expanded list*] Remove node *m* from the *FORMOBJ* list and place it on a list of expanded nodes, called *SEQUENCE.*

F4. [*Check the goal node*] If *m* is a goal node (i.e., $F(m) = \emptyset$), an assembly sequence has been determined; if $F(m) = \emptyset$ and *FORMOBJ* is an empty list, all the assembly sequences have been generated; exit with success; otherwise, continue.

F5. [*Expand node m*] Using operators generated from the *PM* algorithm applicable to node *m*, expand node *m* and create all its successor nodes. For every successor node m_s of node *m*:

(5a) Obtain $A(m_s)$ and $F(m_s)$ according to the algorithm *PM*.

(5b) Add m_s to the *FORMOBJ* list with $A(m_s)$ and $F(m_s)$. Attach a pointer from node m_s back to its predecessor node *m* (in order to trace back an assembly path from a goal node to the start node once the goal node is found).

F6. [*Loop*] Go to Step F2.
END FASG.

In the same ballpoint pen example, according to the algorithm FASG and Table 12.2, a total of 12 assembly sequences are generated and shown in Fig. 12.3. All the sequences are obtained that satisfy all the precedence constraints by tracing the liaison from a terminal node to the root node. Here, squared numbers indicate the node expansion order. The assembly sequence number *i* is a path from a goal node (G_i) to the initial node of the expansion tree as shown in Fig. 12.3. Detailed node expansion and element of the states are listed in Table 12.3. All the feasible assembly sequences of the first example are shown in Fig. 12.6(c) by applying PM and FASG algorithms. By using the proposed precedence knowledge acquisition, the nature of the FASG and PM algorithms are similar to that of SCTSP. Furthermore, the solution of the optimal assembly schedule can be easily obtained if cost or resource arrangements between assembly liaisons are properly defined, compared to the CCTSP method proposed by Wilson and Rit (1990) in which obtaining the optimal assembly schedule requires solving standard TSP

$$\prod_{q=1}^{K} M_q N_q$$

where $M_q N_q$ is the number of the "OR" precedence operators in one precedence form and *K* is the total number of precedence forms. The optimal assembly schedule obtained, based on the concept of SCTSP, saves tremendous computation time.

De Fazio and Whitney (1987) have shown that it requires $2l$ of questions to be answered to obtain such precedence knowledge, where *l* is the total number of the tasks to be performed. Based on the approach just described, the proposed scheme only requires *l* questions to be answered. This scheme reduces the time of the acquisition process by 50%.

Table 12.3. Elements of Expansion Tree

Node Number (m)	$A(m)$	$F(m)$	$R_c(m)$
1	{2}	{1,3,4,5}	{4,5}
2	{5}	{1,2,3,4}	{1,2}
3	{4}	{1,3,5}	{3,5}
4	{5}	{1,4,3}	{1,4}
5	{1}	{2,3,4}	{2,4}
6	{2}	{1,3,4}	{1,4}
7	{3}	{1,5}	{5}
8	{5}	{1,3}	{1,3}
9	{1}	{3,4}	{4}
10	{4}	{1,3}	{1,3}
11	{2}	{3,4}	{4}
12	{4}	{2,3}	{2,3}
13	{1}	{3,4}	{4}
14	{4}	{1,3}	{1,3}
15	{5}	{1}	{1}
16	{1}	{3}	{3}
17	{3}	{1}	{1}
18	{4}	{3}	{3}
19	{1}	{3}	{3}
20	{3}	{1}	{1}
21	{4}	{3}	{3}
22	{2}	{3}	{3}
23	{3}	{2}	{2}
24	{4}	{3}	{3}
25	{1}	{3}	{3}
26	{3}	{1}	{1}
G_1	{1}	Ø	—
G_2	{3}	Ø	—
G_3	{1}	Ø	—
G_4	{3}	Ø	—
G_5	{3}	Ø	—
G_6	{1}	Ø	—
G_7	{3}	Ø	—
G_8	{3}	Ø	—
G_9	{2}	Ø	—
G_{10}	{3}	Ø	—
G_{11}	{3}	Ø	—
G_{12}	{1}	Ø	—

Equivalency of AND/OR Precedence Knowledge and Proposed Precedence Knowledge Acquisition

In the previous section, it was shown that combinations of ∧ and ∨ operators can be derived by logical distributive or associative properties and expressed as

Table 12.4. Equivalent Precedence Knowledge for
$(1 \vee 2) \wedge (3 \vee 4) \rightarrow (5 \vee 6)$

Question Number (i)	$\omega_1(i)$	$\omega_2(i)$	$\omega_3(i)$
1	$\{1\}$	$\{\{5,6\}\}$	$\{\{2,3\},\{2,4\}\}$
2	$\{2\}$	$\{\{5,6\}\}$	$\{\{1,3\},\{1,4\}\}$
3	$\{3\}$	$\{\{5,6\}\}$	$\{\{1,4\},\{2,4\}\}$
4	$\{4\}$	$\{\{5,6\}\}$	$\{\{1,3\},\{2,3\}\}$
5	$\{5\}$	—	—
6	$\{6\}$	—	—

Eqs. (3) and (4). In fact, Eq. (4) can also be transformed into Eq. (3) by distributive or associative properties and vice versa. The equivalency between the general AND/OR precedence nominal forms and the proposed precedence knowledge acquisition and representation is addressed in this section.

Given a general AND/OR precedence nominal form similar to Eq. (4) with

$$(1 \vee 2) \wedge (3 \vee 4) \rightarrow 5 \vee 6 \tag{5}$$

This form can be transformed into a nominal form similar to Eq. (3) using the distributive and associative properties

$$(1 \wedge 3) \vee (2 \wedge 3)(1 \wedge 4) \vee (2 \wedge 4) \rightarrow 5 \vee 6 \tag{6}$$

Based on Eq. (5) and the concept of the PM algorithm, the proposed knowledge obtained in Table 12.4 is equivalent to the precedence knowledge shown in Eq. (5). In Table 12.4, question number 1 states that if task 1 is not done, tasks 5-6 combined cannot be done, and tasks 2-3 combined or 2-4 combined are the dominant tasks. Because in a path of the expansion tree, if task 1 is not done, tasks 5-6 combined cannot appear below the task 1 node, but as long as $F(m)$ contains tasks 2-3 or 2-4 pairs, task 1 can be expanded. The rest of the entries can be applied similarly.

The proposed precedence knowledge can also be obtained based on Eq. (6) and the concept of the PM algorithm. According to this precedence relationship, at least one set of ATG must be completed before tasks 5-6 combined, thus in a path of the state expansion tree, if task 1 is not done, tasks 5-6 combined cannot appear below the task 1 node, but as long as $F(m)$ contains tasks 2-3, or 1-4, or 2-4 pairs, task 1 can be expanded. Similar reason can be applied to rest of tasks. The equivalent proposed precedence knowledge is shown in Table 12.5. In fact, Table 12.5 can be reduced using the merging operation mentioned earlier. Notice that in question number 1 of Table 12.5, the element $\{1,4\} \in \omega_3(1)$ is known. Recall in step P2.c of the PM algorithm, if $L_i = 1$, $\{1,4\}$ can never be a subset of $F(m) - L_i$, thus the element $\{1,4\}$ can be deleted from $\omega_3(1)$. The rest of the entries can be explained based on this reasoning. Thus, in fact, Table 12.5 is equal to Table 12.4. This example demonstrates that not only can the gen-

Table 12.5. Equivalent Precedence Knowledge for
$(1 \wedge 3) \vee (2 \wedge 3) \vee (1 \wedge 4) \vee (2 \wedge 4) \rightarrow (5 \vee 6)$

Question Number (i)	$\omega_1(i)$	$\omega_2(i)$	$\omega_3(i)$
1	{1}	{{5,6}}	{{2,3},{1,4},{2,4},}
2	{2}	{{5,6}}	{{1,3},{1,4},{2,4},}
3	{3}	{{5,6}}	{{2,3},{1,4},{2,4}}
4	{4}	{{5,6}}	{{1,3},{2,3},{1,4},}
5	{5}	—	—
6	{6}	—	—

eral AND/OR nominal precedence knowledge forms be transformed, but also the proposed precedence knowledge forms. The preceding example also shows the equivalency of the proposed precedence knowledge forms and the general nominal AND/OR precedence forms. It also shows that both pre- and postprecedence knowledge forms shown in previous subsections, and the complicated nominal AND/OR forms expressed in Eqs. (3) and (4), can be represented by the proposed scheme.

12.3 ASSEMBLY PLANNING SYSTEM

Although the preceding method can generate all possible assembly sequences in an efficient way, this method is only suitable for the design engineer who manually answers all the constraint questions. An intelligent assembly system would be able to identify these precedence constraints based on geometric information. Together with currently developed geometric representation, a knowledge-based system can be designed to deduce the geometric relationship of the assembled parts. Furthermore, an intelligent assembly planning system can be developed to generate task-level assembly plans automatically. The design of planning systems has been part of artificial intelligence (AI) since its earliest days. Two approaches have been taken to solve planning problems: (1) understand and solve the general problem such that the planning system can be expected to work for a reasonably large variety of application domains, and (2) use domain-specific heuristics to control the planner's operation. The bulk of AI research can be found in the former area of domain-independent research, mainly due to the fact that it is a more difficult problem and its solution is still elusive. In the latter area, practical systems are successfully being developed and making their way from the research labs to everyday use. The majority of these successful domain-dependent systems are implemented using a rule-based approach (i.e., expert system) which demonstrates the utility of this new-found tool.

In general, assembly plans specify a valid series of assembly tasks that will result in a completed assembly. Cost-effective planning systems unite with existing CAD systems to utilize geometry of the individual components and the configuration of the components with respect to the complete assembly. The development of robot programming languages (RPL) over the past several years has been with a trend toward higher levels of abstraction and greater use of world knowledge (Fu *et al.*, 1987). There are basically three levels of RPL. The lowest level is joint-level (or actuator-level) languages which describe the robot operations via control commands that drive individual motors or actuators of the robot. At the next higher level are manipulator-level languages which describe only the motion of the robot end effector in the Cartesian workspace. The user must specify robot motion and sensor interaction. These languages require personnel trained in the use of the specific languages. Manipulator-level programs are translated to joint-level programs through the use of kinematic and trajectory planners subject to the specific parameters of the robot.

The section demonstrates the effective use of a rule-based approach to solving the problem of formulating task-level assembly plans for general mechanical assemblies. Most current systems only allow assembly operations in directions parallel with the global x, y, and z coordinate system, which may not be possible for some mechanical assemblies. Also, most systems in existence employ simplified "part envelope" collision detection algorithms which may incorrectly detect component precedence constraints. One proposed system is implemented using the CLIPS (C Language Integrated Production System) expert system development shell and has successfully generated assembly plans including robot tool changes and subassembly reorientations. It exhibits superiority over existing systems in two areas: (1) it permits a multitude of various component assembly trajectories, and (2) it incorporates a robust part collision detection algorithm. Several examples illustrate the effectiveness of the proposed system.

System Overview

The major assumptions used during system design are summarized in this section.

(1) All parts are modeled as rigid polyhedral solids.
(2) Two types of fasteners may be used by an assembly: screw and nut/bolt.
(3) The assembly is built sequentially with a single component added one at a time (i.e., no parallel building of subassemblies).
(4) All components are assembled directly to their final positions with a single linear motion. Actions such as "insert and twist" are not allowed.
(5) No internal forces are present.
(6) Stability constraints are satisfied. The components stay in their assembled positions and remain fixed during subsequent operations.
(7) Workcell is composed of a single-armed robot and a work surface. Robot's end effector has flexible tooling capability to accommodate the following tool types: gripper, screwdriver, and nutdriver.
(8) Coordinate systems of the workcell and completed assembly are aligned. The assembly occupies space in the first octant of the coordinate system only.

Figure 12.8 illustrates the structure of the rule-based assembly planning system from a top-level, modular perspective. The system is supplied with the assembled product in a boundary representation (B-rep) format. These systems typically include an efficient user interface to facilitate the task of representing and manipulating assemblies and their components. The direct interface between a B-rep solid modeling system and this assembly planning system is very promising.

System Architecture

The *preprocessor* module performs topological and geometric data consistency checks of the assembly B-rep input data. If any inconsistencies from the input B-rep are detected, the system reports the error and halts execution.

The preprocessor module also converts fasteners (i.e., screw, nuts, and bolts) into a B-rep structure. To simplify creating the input data file from the graphics interface, the user is not required to specify the complete B-rep for all the fasteners. This conversion process is necessary to derive the geometric properties required to perform reasoning between the parts and the fasteners of the assembly. The preprocessor module also calculates the plane equation for each face in the assembly. This is an important piece of information used throughout the system because it includes the components of the outward face normal. The details of the plane equation and outward face normal will be described later. Finally, the preprocessor module determines candidate assembly directions for every component in the assembly. A part may be assembled in any direction parallel with any of its faces' normal vectors. Screws, nuts, and bolts may only be assembled monodirectionally, parallel with the part's centerline.

The *liaison detection module* determines any of three types of liaisons between any two parts. A liaison is loosely defined as a physical contact between parts. The types of liaisons detectable by this system are *insertion*, *attachment*, and *contact*. In essence, the output of this module defines the product graph. The graph represents the final assembly whose nodes are the components and the links corresponding to the physical liaisons between the components. Figure 12.9 shows the product graph of the container assembly as described in the example section. The output of this module will add physical liaisons between components detected to the CLIPS *fact list*.

The *obstruction detection module* employs a collision detection algorithm for every component in every candidate assembly direction. The objective is to determine the set of components that would obstruct the assembly operation if they were already in their final position. Or, similarly, consider the disassembling of the final product. Under the assumption that all components are rigid and there are no internal forces in the final assembly, the reverse of the disassembly sequence is a valid assembly sequence. This module will determine which components obstruct the removal of a particular component by "graphically" projecting the component in question onto a given plane. The projections of all other components on the same plane which have non-null intersections ascertain the component's obstructions. The output of this module is a list of obstructions which will dictate the precedence relationships of the assembly plan.

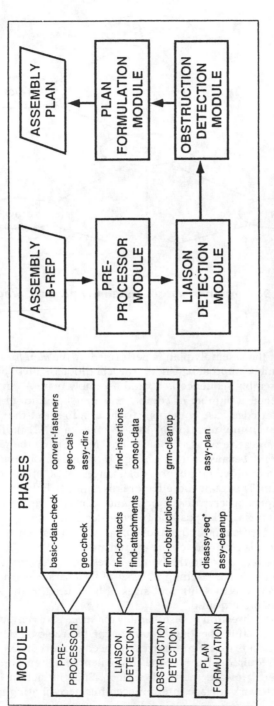

Fig. 12.8 System structure and control knowledge—phases of execution.

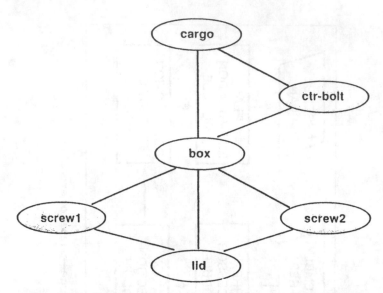

FIG. 12.9. Container sample assembly-product graph.

Construction of the assembly plan is performed by the *plan formulation module* via a disassembly approach. Under the conditions stated previously, the reverse of a disassembly sequence is a valid assembly plan. At any point in the disassembly sequence, a number of components may be removed from the subassembly. The knowledge base contains two criteria to select the "best" component for removal: (1) minimization of tool changes, and (2) uniformity in the directionality of successive disassembly actions. Minimizing the number of tool changes is important because a tool change is a time-consuming task for the robot to perform. A minimal number of tool changes saves time during execution of the assembly plan. The robot end-effector is assumed to hold one of three types of tools: a part gripper, a screwdriver, or a nutdriver. The gripper is required for moving parts from their initial position (part feeder or bin) to its final assembled position. A screwdriver is required to pick up and attach a screw to the assembly. Likewise, a nutdriver is required to pick up and attach a bolt to the assembly and to pick up and attach a nut onto the bolt. A variety of drivers are assumed to be required to match the corresponding number of fasteners used in the assembly. For instance, if there are two different sizes of bolts used in the assembly, two different nutdrivers are required.

Consistency in the direction of disassembly for successive removal is also used as a criterion in selecting the "best" component for removal. One reason for applying this criterion is that it minimizes the need to reorient the subassembly. A reorientation is required whenever the component to be removed may only be removed "downward" toward the work surface. Such an action is assumed to result in robot arm–work surface interference, thus necessitating rotation of the subassembly prior to the desired disassembly operation. A reorientation of the subassembly requires the part gripper. If the robot currently holds some other tool, a tool change is required adding at least one more step to the plan. Another reason for incorporating this type of criterion in the knowledge base is that it is simply "humanlike." That is, an individual will likely disassemble a product in an orderly fashion—removing as many parts as possible from one side of the product (i.e., in a consistent direction) before moving to another side. One can expect this criterion to simplify the fixturing requirements and decrease the amount of movement required by the robot arm.

The assembly plan follows directly from the derived disassembly sequence. Each step in the plan is asserted as a separate fact in the fact list and is numbered sequentially. The plan includes steps for tool changes and subassembly reorientations, as necessary. The system also collects statistics of the final assembly plan such as total number of steps, number of tool changes, and number of reorientations. This information is useful to the design engineer for comparing alternative product designs from an assemblability standpoint.

CLIPS

A rule-based approach to implementing an assembly planning system was undertaken using the C Language Integrated Production System (CLIPS) version 4.3. CLIPS is an expert system building tool created by the Artificial Intelligence Section of NASA/Johnson Space Center with support from the United States Air Force. CLIPS is being effectively used throughout the public and private sectors and is recognized as a powerful but low-cost tool for the development and implementation of rule-based systems.

CLIPS is a forward chaining rule-based language that has inferencing and representation capabilities similar to those of OPS5 (Brownston, 1985). As in most expert systems, it has three basic components: (1) the working memory fact list, (2) the knowledge base (rules), and (3) the inference engine. A program written in CLIPS consists of rules and facts. The inference engine decides which rules should be executed. Three defining constructs appear in CLIPS: deffacts, defrule, and deftemplate. The \fBdeffacts\fR construct is a convenient method whereby a set of initial facts (i.e., the initial knowledge) can be added to working memory.

Rules are defined using the *defrule* construct. Each rule has a name, a left-hand side (LHS), and a right-hand side (RHS). The symbol => separates the LHS and RHS. The LHS consists of one or more patterns or test conditions. The CLIPS inference engine attempts to match the LHS patterns against facts in the fact list. When all patterns and test conditions are satisfied, the rule fires and executes the actions of the RHS.

Groups of facts having the same relationship can be described by a template. Templates are created in CLIPS by using the *deftemplate* construct. Templates provide a means to abstract the structure of a fact by assigning names to each field found within the fact. CLIPS was designed with two kinds of integration in mind: (1) embedding CLIPS in other systems, and (2) calling external functions from the RHS or LHS of a CLIPS rule. Using CLIPS as an embedded application allows existing systems to use a rule-based subsystem to solve a portion of the overall problem as a subtask. In these situations, CLIPS can be called as a subroutine, and information may be passed to and from CLIPS. External or user-defined functions may be written in C or another language and linked to CLIPS. They can be called as predicate functions on the LHS of a rule to allow for specialized testing of conditions. On the RHS of a rule, they can be called for a number of reasons. User-defined functions allow CLIPS to be extended or customized in almost any way.

System Details

Notation and Terminology

Here, symbols contained in single-angle brackets, such as ⟨name⟩, represent a single field to be defined by the user or a generated output from graphical interface output. Symbols contained in double-angle brackets, such as ⟨⟨list⟩⟩, represent one or more fields to be defined by the user or a generated output from graphical interface output. Vertical bars indicate a choice among multiple parameters.

To clarify the terminology used throughout the text, every object in an assembly is called a *component*. Components are further defined to fall in one of two categories: *fastener* or *part*. The system currently handles two types of fasteners: screws and nut/bolts. *Parts* are components other than fasteners—usually the larger machined or cast components make up the bulk of the assembly. Figure 12.10 illustrates the hierarchy of these terms. Also note the term *subassembly* is normally used to refer to a *partially* assembled product.

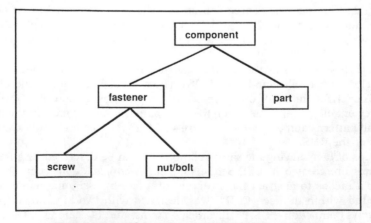

FIG. 12.10. Object terminology hierarchy.

Desired Assembly Specification

The system is integrated with a solid modeler to provide a more user-friendly input interface. The solid modeler also provides a graphical user interface to design and modify the assembly. The solid modeler that uses a B-rep data structure simply requires a translation facility to generate the geometric representation in the format of CLIPS facts. It also includes a simulation facility to graphically demonstrate the assembly plan steps.

Input generated from the solid modeler to the planning system is accomplished through the use of the CLIPS deffacts construct. There are four basic categories of input knowledge: system parameters, assembly facts, part facts, and fasteners facts. Four *system parameters* are required by the system. First, there is a trace option that allows the user to receive a detailed account of the system's execution. Pertinent facts are echoed to the screen as they are added to the fact list. The second is an allowable error margin used when comparing two values. The selected margin will depend on the units of measure. For assemblies using inches as the unit of measure, an error margin of 0.01 in. to 0.001 in. will suffice. Next is a parallelism error margin used when comparing the direction of vectors and opposing object faces. An allowable parallelism error margin is included to determine two vectors (faces) as parallel when they are within plus or minus $\langle \theta \rangle$ radians to one another. Last is a proximity constant specifying the maximum distance between two adjoining objects (faces). This constant will depend on the tolerances used in the assembly design.

The *assembly fact* is of the form (*assembly* (*name* ⟨*assy-name*⟩) (*components* ⟨⟨*list-of-component-names*⟩⟩)) where the assembly is given a name and its components are listed. The *part facts* specify the name of the part and a list of its faces and vertex in the part. An example of a fact that specifies a part and a list of its faces is (*part*(*name* ⟨*part-name*⟩)(*faces* ⟨⟨*list-of-face-names*⟩⟩)). There are currently two types of *fasteners* supported by the system: screw and nut/bolt. Each screw in the assembly is defined internally by a reference point, a reference vector, and a screw class. Similarly, each bolt is defined by a reference point, a reference vector, and a bolt class. The reference point is located on the plane parallel to the screw (bolt) head base and on the centerline of the screw (bolt). The reference vector coincides with the centerline of the screw (bolt) in the direction of insertion (see Fig. 12.11). This classification method is quite similar to the pure primitive instancing modeling representation scheme.

Preprocessor Module

The preprocessor module calculates the plane equation for each face in the assembly. The plane equation for each face in the assembly can be defined by the linear equation: $ax + by + cx + d = 0$. The vector (a, b, c) is termed the plane's normal vector and is orthogonal to the plane. The preprocessor calculates a face's plane equation (normalized) based on the Newell method (Wilson and Rit, 1990) using the vertices of its perimeter loop.

Another geometric property that the preprocessor module calculates is the candidate assembly directions for every component in the assembly. The system

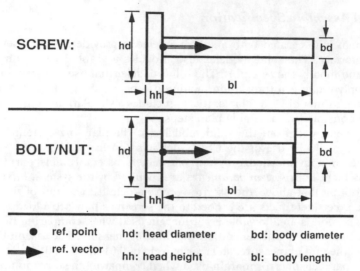

●	ref. point	hd: head diameter	bd: body diameter
➤	ref. vector	hh: head height	bl: body length

FIG. 12.11. Fastener convention.

determines the part's assembly in any direction parallel with any of its face's normal vectors. This is one aspect of the system that goes beyond any other systems which only allow parts to be assembled parallel to the coordinate axes and the fasteners only to be assembled monodirectionally parallel with their centerline. The following is a partial output format that lists the candidate assembly directions for the components.

= > assy-dir: handle (+/–) 0 0.5 0.866

= > assy-dir: handle (+/–) 0 –0.866 0.5

= > assy-dir: handle (+/–) 1 0 0

= > assy-dir: handle (+/–) 0 0.866 –0.5

= > assy-dir: handle (+/–) –1 0 0

= > assy-dir: handle (+/–) 0 –0.5 –0.866

= > assy-dir: set-screw 0 –1 0

= > assy-dir: handle-screw –1 0 0

= > assy-dir: base-bolt1 0 0 –1

= > assy-dir: base-bolt2 0 0 –1

= > assy-dir: base-bolt1@nut (–) 0 0 –1

= > assy-dir: base-bolt2@nut (–) 0 0 –1

Liaison Detection Module

A liaison is defined as a relationship between two components. A liaison exists if one component constrains the freedom of motion of the other by a mating condition. Here, three types of mating conditions are considered: contact, attachment, and insertion. The *contact* condition holds between planar faces of a pair of parts. Two faces, face A and face B, are said to contact one another if the following conditions hold:

(1) Their outward face normals oppose one another within the range of the parallelism error margin.
(2) The distance between the two face planes is less than or equal to the proximity constant.
(3) The intersection of the projections of face A and face B is non-null.

Figure 12.12 illustrates the contact condition. This condition plays a key role in determining the attachment liaisons because it is simply a refinement of the contact liaison. A rule for locating two faces of differing parts which lie on adjacent opposing planes is given in the following display.

RULE: adj-opposing-planes

PURPOSE: Locate two faces of differing parts which lie on adjacent opposing planes.

CONDITIONS: Two different faces from two parts, and their plane equations. The outward normal vectors of the two faces must oppose one another within the range of the parallelism error margin. The directed dis-

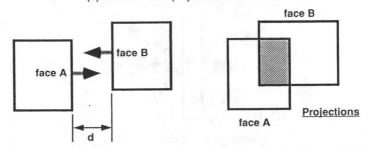

FIG. 12.12. Contact mating condition.

tance from the plane of the first face to a vertex on the second face must be positive and less than the proximity constant.

ACTIONS: Assert adjacent-opposing-planes fact specifying the two faces.

An *attachment* condition exists between two contacting parts if they are held together by a fastener. To determine if a part is connected by a fastener, a cross-section of the fastener's body is projected orthogonally "through" the assembly from the base of the fastener's head for a length equal to its body length. If this projection has a non-null intersection with any part's face, the fastener extends through the part. This is illustrated in Fig. 12.13. A rule that selects the coordinate plane with the greatest projection vector component is given in the following display.

RULE: sel-proj-pln-screw

PURPOSE: Select the best projection plane for each screw to test which part face the screw protrudes through.

CONDITIONS: A screw and its reference vector.

ACTIONS: Asserts proj-plane-screw fact specifying the coordinate plane (XY, YZ, or XZ) consistent with the largest component of the reference vector.

Part A is said to be *inserted* in part B if the following conditions exist:

(1) Part A has two contacts with part B (i.e., two pairs of faces are in contact).
(2) The two faces of part B are parallel and their outward normals are opposing.
(3) The two faces of part A lie "interior" to both of part B's faces.

Conditions (between two faces):

(1) Contact mating condition exists

(2) Bolt or Screw body "protrudes" through both faces

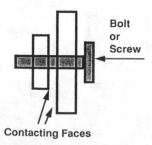

FIG. 12.13. Attachment mating condition.

Figure 12.14 illustrates the insertion mating condition. An insertion rule is listed in the following display.

RULE: insert

PURPOSE: Determine if one part is inserted in another.

CONDITIONS: Two parts with two pairs of contacting faces. The two faces of the one part (bounding part) are parallel and opposing. A vertex on either side of the other part (inserted part) must be on the "positive" side of both of the bounding parts' faces.

ACTIONS: Assert an insert fact that specifies that the first part is inserted into the second.

To summarize these relationships, the system detects the liaisons of the container assembly, for example, and adds them to the fact list in the following format:

(contact-part lid box)

(contact-part box cargo)

(insert cargo box)

(attach-screw screw1 lid box)

(attach-screw screw2 lid box)

(attach-bolt ctr-bolt cargo box)

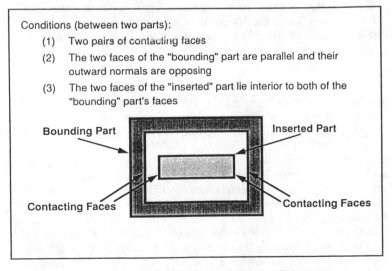

Conditions (between two parts):
   (1)   Two pairs of contacting faces
   (2)   The two faces of the "bounding" part are parallel and their outward normals are opposing
   (3)   The two faces of the "inserted" part lie interior to both of the "bounding" part's faces

Bounding Part   Inserted Part

Contacting Faces   Contacting Faces

FIG. 12.14. Insertion mating condition.

In nature, this module defines the product graph. The graph represents the final assembly whose nodes are the components, and the links correspond to the physical liaisons between the components. These liaisons are used during the formulation of the assembly plan. The plan will specify the tasks to be performed by the robot which will establish the existence of the liaisons.

Obstruction Detection Module

An obstruction is defined as a component that prevents the removal of a given component in a particular direction. Detection of all obstructions is performed by a collision detection algorithm that utilizes the reverse of all the candidate assembly directions (i.e., the disassembly directions). The purpose of this module is to determine the set of components which would obstruct the assembly operation if they were already in their final position. From a disassembly viewpoint, the components that physically hinder a component's removal must be determined.

The *collision detection* algorithm uses a "graphical" projection technique. The algorithm works as follows to determine the obstructions of component **A** in the direction of vector **N**. Component **B** is any other component in the assembly.

Collision Detection Algorithm:

For every face of **A** that faces "somewhat" in the same direction as **N** (call this face **O**):

(a) Select a face of component **G** that faces "somewhat" in the opposite direction of face **A** and lies in the direction of **N** (call this face **B**).
(b) Select one of the three coordinate planes as the plane of projection. The selection is based on the greatest vector component of **B**.
(c) Project face **O** and face **B** onto the projection plane.
(d) If the intersection of the two projections is non-null, ascertain that component **A** is obstructed by component **B** in the **B** direction.

The term "somewhat" is defined as follows and illustrated in Fig. 12.15. If θ is the angle between two vectors (in this case face normal vectors), then the vectors are considered to be "somewhat" opposing if θ is greater than 90 deg. ($\cos(\theta) < 0$). Likewise, they are "somewhat" in the same direction if the angle between the two vectors is less than 90 deg. ($\cos(\theta) > 0$).

Determination of the intersection in step (d) can be quite complex due to the number of possible cases. For instance, initially the perimeter loops of face **O** and face **B** are projected and a determination of their intersections is made. If the projection of face **O** is a proper subset of the face **B** projection (or vice versa), the intersection test continues to check if face **O** falls completely in a "hole" of face **B**. If face **O** falls in a "hole," then the intersection is null. Figure 12.16 illustrates the case. An obstruction rule that selects a part, a candidate assembly direction, and any face that faces somewhat in the same direction of disassembly is given in the following display.

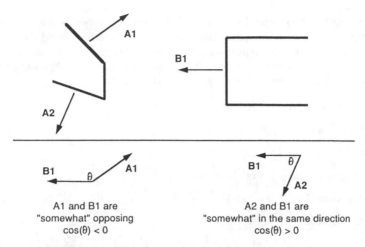

A1 and B1 are
"somewhat" opposing
$\cos(\theta) < 0$

A2 and B1 are
"somewhat" in the same direction
$\cos(\theta) > 0$

FIG. 12.15. "Somewhat" relationships.

RULE: candidate-blocking-faces

PURPOSE: Generate candidate blocking faces for each part in every disassembly direction.

CONDITIONS: A part, a disassembly direction, and any face of this part that faces "somewhat" in the same direction of the disassembly direction.

ACTIONS: Assert candidate-blocking-face fact which specifies a part, the direction of disassembly, and a face of this part that may block its removal.

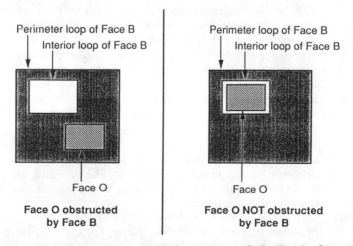

Face O obstructed
by Face B

Face O NOT obstructed
by Face B

FIG. 12.16. Obstruction detection—case of "hole" in face B.

The output of this module is a list of obstructions where each entry includes the component being obstructed, the direction of movement, and the component that restricts it. These obstructions prescribe the precedence relationships of the assembly plan. To summarize the obstruction concept, the obstructions for the lid of a container assembly are asserted in the fact list as

(obstruction lid 0 −1 0 block)

(obstruction lid 0 −1 0 box)

(obstruction lid 0 −1 0 ctr-bolt)

(obstruction lid 0 −1 0 ctr-bolt nut)

(obstruction lid 0 1 0 screw1)

(obstruction lid 0 1 0 screw2)

The three numeric fields reference the x, y, and z elements of the direction vector and the last field is the obstructing component.

Plan Formulation Module

The mechanical assembly is analyzed using a disassembly technique to formulate the assembly plan. Assuming all components are rigid and there are no internal forces in the final assembly (e.g., there are no "snap-together" parts), the reverse of the disassembly sequence is a valid assembly sequence. The rules used in this module will generate a "good" feasible assembly plan based on two criteria:

(1) *Minimization of tool changes.* Operations will be sequenced so that tasks with the same robot end-effector tooling requirements are grouped together. A minimal number of tool changes will save time during the execution of the assembly plan.

(2) *Uniformity in the directionality of successive assembly tasks.* It is preferred to insert all parts, as much as possible, from a single direction. This requires less robot motion, simplifies fixturing requirements, and avoids extra operations to reorient the subassembly. A savings of both set-up and run-time costs are realized under this criteria.

The criteria tend to generate an efficient assembly plan by reducing the amount of action required on behalf of the robot. The planning system's determination of the "best" component for removal is based on rules of thumb and not on theoretical optimization principles.

Beginning with the complete assembly located in its final position in the workcell, the system disassembles the assembly. During the disassembly process the following state information is maintained:

(1) A list of components remaining in the subassembly.
(2) The orientation of the subassembly with respect to the workcell coordinate system.
(3) The type of tool occupying the robot's end-effector.
(4) A list of the actions taken to arrive at the current state from the initial state.

The disassembly algorithm is given as follows:

Repeat until there is only one remaining component (i.e., the "base" part, if one has been specified):

Step (1) Generate a list of at least one candidate component for removal based on the following criteria. Each criterion is applied successively until at least one candidate has been nominated. A candidate component is one that is not obstructed in a specified direction by any of the other components in the current state.

(a) Any components that can be removed in the same direction as the previous disassembly direction (directly upward for the first repetition).
(b) Any components that can be removed in a direction within 45 deg. of directly upward.
(c) Any components that can be removed in a direction within 90 deg. of directly upward.

The system was developed with the positive y direction representing the "directly upward" direction. This may be easily changed if a different coordinate system is used.

Step (2) If there are no candidate components nominated, the subassembly must be reoriented. Update the state information to reflect the new orientation and go to step (1).

Step (3) Choose one of the candidate components such that a tool change will not be necessary. If not possible, select any candidate component and update the state information to reflect the required tool change. Update state information to reflect the removal of the chosen component.

Step (4) The final remaining component constitutes the last part to be "disassembled." Update the state information to reflect this knowledge.

The algorithm places a greater weight on the uniformity of assembly direction by generating the candidate components based on a "preferred" disassembly direction first. It then selects among the candidates to suppress a tool change if possible. This weighing approach forces the system to require a reorientation of the subassembly only when absolutely necessary (i.e., when removing any non-base component with any tool is not possible).

When a component cannot be removed in the same direction as the previous direction, three directional regions are checked successively until at least one candidate component is found. First, any components that can be removed in the upward vertical direction are nominated. If still no candidate components are found, any components that can be removed in a direction within 45 deg. of the upward vertical direction are nominated. If still no candidate components are found, any components that can be removed in a direction from 45 deg. to 90 deg. of the upward vertical direction are nominated. Progression through these direction "regions" is based on the assumption that the upward vertical direction requires the least amount of robot effort and is the "preferred" direction, of choice second only to the direction of the prior disassembly action.

A reorientation is assumed necessary whenever the component to be removed during the disassembly process can only be removed "downward" toward the work surface. Such an action would entail the component colliding with the work surface and/or exceeding the flexibility limits of the robot arm. The reorientation task is accomplished by rotating the subassembly around the x axis by a constant amount. Currently, this constant is set to 90 deg. through the "disassy-info" def-facts statement. The system was also successfully tested with this constant set to 180 deg. It may be altered according to the user's desire. The assembly operation is assumed to begin and end with the robot loaded with the part gripper tool. The generated assembly plan will always begin with the task of changing the tool to the part gripper. If necessary, the last task of the plan will be to change the tool to the part gripper. This is logical because the assembled product will likely be removed from the workcell to a pallet or bin on completion. The plan incorporates tasks to conduct all necessary tool changes to complete the assembly operation.

Assembly Plan Output Format

Each step in the plan is asserted in the fact list as a fact of the form (*step* ⟨*i*⟩⟨*task description*⟩⟩), where $i = 1, 2 \ldots, n$ and n is the total number of steps in the plan. The task description describes the robot action required. Note that the task descriptions are syntactically oriented more for human interpretation than for demonstration purposes. The rules may easily be modified to generate task descriptions more adaptable to machine interpretation. Some task descriptions include a direction represented by three numeric values. These values correspond respectively to the x, y, and z elements of the direction vector with respect to the workcell coordinate system.

Throughout the assembly sequence, stability constraints are assumed to be satisfied. An unstable condition exists when a component is free to move from its current position through the force of gravity. This condition may result from either of two situations. One, a task in the plan may specify that a component be assembled to the subassembly but there is no support provided from the work surface or another component of the subassembly. Second, a stable subassembly may become unstable as a result of a reorientation task. In order to fulfill this assumption, fixtures that hold the subassembly together during the assembly process may be required. The determination of the fixturing requirements (and their design) exceeds the scope of this chapter.

{   ..   }

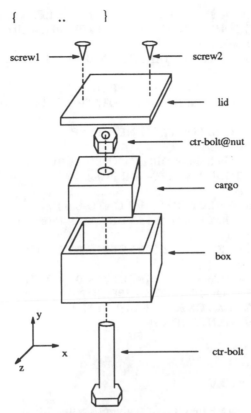

FIG. 12.17. Container sample assembly (adapted from [Lee and Gossard, 1985]).

An Example

An assembly example is given in this section to show the effectiveness of the proposed system. This assembly, adopted from Lee and Gossard (1985), is composed of three parts (*box*, *lid*, and *cargo*), two screws (*screw1* and *screw2*), and one nut/bolt (*ctl-bolt*). The assembly is illustrated in Fig. 12.17. The product graph of the assembly, as shown in Fig. 12.9, is effectively generated on execution of the liaison detection module. The assembly plan generated by the system follows.

ASSEMBLY PLAN FOR THE CONTAINER ASSEMBLY
(step 1   CHANGE TOOL TO PART-GRIPPER)
(step 2   GRASP box)
(step 3   PLACE box IN FINAL CONFIGURATION POSITION)
(step 4   ROTATE box 90 DEGREES AROUND X-AXIS)
(step 5   GRASP cargo)

(step 6   INSERT cargo DIRECTION 0 4.3711e-08-1 INTO box)
(step 7   CHANGE TOOL FOR FASTENER TYPE: long-bolt)
(step 8   GET ctr-bolt)
(step 9   INSERT BOLT ctr-bolt DIRECTION 0 −4.3711e-08 1 THRU PARTS:
      box cargo)
(step 10 CHANGE TOOL TO PART-GRIPPER)
(step 11 GRASP SUBASSEMBLY AND ROTATE MINUS 90 DEGREES
      AROUND X-XIS)
(step 12 CHANGE TOOL FOR FASTENER TYPE: long-bolt)
(step 13 GET ctr-bolt nut)
(step 14 ATTACH ctr-bolt)@nut DIRECTION 0 −1 0)
(step 15 CHANGE TOOL TO PART-GRIPPER)
(step 16 GRASP lid)
(step 17 PLACE lid DIRECTION 0 −1 0 ONTO box)
(step 18 CHANGE TOOL FOR FASTENER TYPE: three-inch-screw)
(step 19 GET screw2)
(step 20 INSERT SCREW screw2 DIRECTION 0 −1 0 THRU PARTS: box lid)
(step 21 GET screw1)
(step 22 INSERT SCREW screw1 DIRECTION 0 −1 0 THRU PARTS: box lid)
(step 23 CHANGE TOOL TO PART-GRIPPER)
(assy-complete * 7 COMPONENTS * 24 TOTAL STEPS * 7 TOOL CHANGES *
1 ASSEMBLY REORIENTATIONS)

12.4   CONCLUSION

This chapter has presented an intelligent system that generates assembly sequences and formulates task-level assembly plans utilizing the geometry of the assembly. A rule-based approach has been demonstrated to be an effective means for solving this type of planning problem. The purpose of intelligent assembly system is to aid the engineer and to enhance the design process by analyzing, optimizing, evaluating, and formulating the design. Furthermore, the manufacturing process of the given assembly design will also be automated. Although interaction with intelligent systems is secondary to the primary task of design and planning, a truly intelligent assembly system will be able to integrate with interfaces that are compatible with the goal. To provide intelligent systems with compatible interfaces, the following research directions need to be addressed. In addition to two criteria for determining the "best" assembly plan: tool changes and directionality, other criteria to consider include fixture complexity, manipulability (perform difficult operations with more easily handled parts), and locality (perform operations near each other consecutively). Clearly, the chosen criteria may contradict each other. Furthermore, a future assembly planning system can be improved by allowing the user to select which criteria to consider and to assign weights to each to indicate their relative importance. In addition, the design of assembly interface (Boothroyd and Dewherst, 1989) will increase the capability of the system. With these improvements, the problem-solving capability of the system will be increased significantly.

REFERENCES

Boothroyd, G., and Dewherst, P. 1989. *Product Design for Assembly.* 2nd ed. Wakefile, Rhode Island.

Bourjault, A. 1984. *Contribution a une Approach Methologique de l'Assemblage Automatise: Elaboration Automatique des Sequence Operatoires.* Thesis, Univ. of Franche-Comte, France, November.

Brownston, L. 1985. *Programming Expert Systems in OPS5: An Introduction to Rule-Based Programming.* Reading, Massachusetts: Addison-Wesley.

Chang, P. R., and Lee, C. S. G. Design of real-time assembly scheduler on massively parallel computing engines. Technical Report, *TR-ERC 88-25*, Purdue University, W. Lafayette, Indiana.

Chen, C. L. P. 1991. Automatic assembly sequences generation by pattern-matching. *IEEE Trans. on Systems, Man, and Cybernetics* 21 (2):376–389.

Chen, C. L. P., and Wichman, C. 1992. A CLIPS rule-based planning system for mechanical assembly. *Proc. of NSF Design and Manufacturing Systems Conf.*, pp. 833–836, January 8–10, 1992.

De Fazio T. L., and Whitney, D. E. 1987. Simplified generation of all mechanical assembly sequences. *IEEE Journal of Robotics and Auto*, 3 (6):640–658.

Delchambre, A. 1991. An automatic, systematic and user-friendly computer-aided planner for robotized assembly. *Proc. of IEEE Int'l Conf. on Robotics and Auto*, pp. 592–598.

Fu, K. S., Gonzalez, R. C., and Lee, C. S. G. 1987. *Robotics: Control, Sensing, Vision, and Intelligence.* McGraw-Hill.

Huang, Y. 1991. A knowledge-based approach to automatic generation of assembly plans. Ph.D. thesis, Purdue University, School of Electrical Engineering, May, 1991.

Homem de Mello, L. S. 1989. Task sequence planning for robotic assembly. Ph.D. thesis, Carnegie Mellon University, Department of Electrical and Computer Engineering, May, 1989.

Homem de Mello, L. S., and Sanderson, A. C. 1990. Evaluation and selection of assembly plans. *Proc. of IEEE Conf. on Robotics and Auto.*, pp. 1588–1593.

Jentsch, W., and Kaden, F. 1984. Automatic generation of assembly sequences. In *Artificial Intelligence and Information-Control Systems of Robots*, ed. I. Plander, 1977–200. North-Holland: Elsevier. 1984.

Lee, K., and Gossard, D. C. 1985. A hierarchical data structure for representing assemblies: Part 1. *Computer-Aided Design* 17 (1):15–19.

Mujtaba, M. S., Goldman, R. A., and Binford, T. 1982. The AL robot programming language. *Comput. Engr.* 2:77–86.

Nnaji, B. O., *et al.* 1988. A schema for CAD-based robot assembly task planning for CSG-modeled objects. *Journal of Manufacturing Systems*, 7 (2):131–145.

Popplestone, R. J., Ambler, A. P., and Bellos, I. 1978. PART: A language for describing assemblies. *The Industrial Robots* 5(3):131–137, Summer.

Wilson, R. H., and Rit, J. 1990. Maintaining geometric dependencies in an assembly planner. *Proc. of IEEE Int'l Conf. on Robotics and Auto.*, pp. 890–895.

Wolter, J. D. 1988. On the automatic generation of plans for mechanical assembly. Ph.D. thesis, University of Michigan, Department of Electrical Engineering and Computer Science, September.

Chapter 13

A Design Methodology for Automated Manufacture

Osama K. Eyada
Department of Industrial Engineering and Operations Research
Virginia Polytechnic Institute and State University
Blacksburg, Virginia

Edward C. De Meter
Department of Industrial and Management Systems Engineering
Pennsylvania State University
University Park, Pennsylvania

13.1 INTRODUCTION

Historically, when manufacturers were small businesses, a single individual or a small group of individuals would be responsible for the decisions made throughout the entire product life cycle. Being familiar with all tasks related to product realizations, these individuals could readily assess the interrelationships and tradeoffs that arise during the different decision stages. As these companies grew in size, division of labor and tasks across functional areas became necessary. Now, most individuals have become specialized in specific tasks and often do not have knowledge in the workings of other functional areas. Consequently, they may lack the insight to fully recognize the implications of their decisions on other activities downstream.

In particular, the separation of the design and manufacturing tasks resulted in products that are designed with little consideration given to the product fabrication. The products as designed may be unduly expensive or impossible to manufacture. Design changes can be costly and time consuming, especially when performed after production has begun. Such concerns are particularly significant in the design of new products, which may necessitate the implementation of new manufacturing processes or facilities. Table 13.1 shows the relative cost of engineering design changes at different stages of the product development cycle.

It has been reported that by the time a product has been designed, when only about 8% of the total product budget is spent, the design has determined 80% of the lifetime cost of the product (Bakerjian, 1992). Although the product functional requirement is the primary product design consideration, a different design fulfilling the same product function may result in substantial savings

Table 13.1. Cost of Engineering Changes (Bakerjian, 1992)

Time of Design Change	Cost ($)
During design:	1000
During design testing:	10,000
During process planning:	100,000
During test production:	1,000,000
During final production:	10,000,000

in product cost and other manufacturing resources. Consequently, an intelligent design is one which not only fulfills the product functional requirements, but also addresses its manufacturability.

With the trend toward the unmanned factory of the future, design for automated manufacture is increasingly important. Automation places more constraints on the product design because consideration has to be given to how machines and computers can perform the various steps in product processing with minimal manual supervision. The selection and implementation of automated manufacturing systems usually involve greater capital investment compared to traditional manufacturing practices. Trade-offs between product functionality and design considerations for automated processing, assembly, handling, and packaging must be made early in the design cycle to realize the full benefit of automation.

In designing for automated processing, knowledge of the available process capabilities and flexibilities are important. Supported product mix, allowable design changes, and batch size are typical factors which must be considered when choosing between design alternatives. The proper choice of materials for different parts can significantly reduce manufacturing costs, as well as improve product reliability and performance.

Two main tenets have emerged as the result of the extensive research in design for automated assembly: stacked design and parts minimization. With a stacked design, or single direction of assembly, and the minimum number of parts, problems of parts location, parts orientation, and assembly time are also minimized. However, forcing a single direction of assembly, and combining multiple components into one, may result in complex components which are difficult to manufacture. The best design integrates product functionality with minimization of parts and their complexities. An example of the reduction in the number of parts through product redesign is shown in Fig. 13.1.

Automated materials handling and packaging require design considerations for ease of feeding, orientation, and handling (Pham, 1982). Steps must be taken to prevent parts from tangling, nesting, or telescoping when placed in an automatic feeding device. Additional features may be added to the parts or the shape of the parts can be redesigned. Part orientation problems may be eliminated by improving on part symmetry and reversibility through the addition of features.

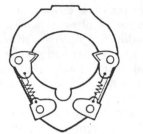 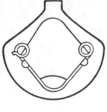

Before (13 parts)   After (2 parts)

FIG. 13.1. Redesign for minimizing number of parts
(Corbett *et al.*, 1991).

Considerations for ease of gripping and placement of components during handling and assembly should also be addressed.

Recently, considerable effort has been dedicated to modeling the design process in an attempt to synthesize more intelligent designs and higher quality, lower cost products. These efforts range from the use of hierarchical structures that can be described using combinatorial mathematics, to optimization techniques based on fuzzy set theory, and on up to the use of knowledge-based advisors. Guidelines and tools have been developed to bring manufacturing considerations into the product design stage.

This chapter presents a survey of proposed design models and tools, and offers a two-phase design methodology for design for automated manufacture. In the first phase, a preconceptual design analysis of desired product functions is performed with the objective of identifying redundancies and decomposing the overall product function into primary, secondary, and supporting functions. In the second phase, an iterative multistage design procedure enables the appropriate manufacturability trade-off analyses to be performed. The design methodology covers all stages of the product development. The applicability of the proposed design methodology is illustrated with an example.

13.2 SURVEY OF DESIGN MODELS AND TOOLS

Since the mid-1980s, the National Science Foundation has directed its efforts toward establishing an interdisciplinary design theory. Although several research works have been geared toward this goal, a commonly accepted theory of design has yet to be realized. This can be attributed to the fact that design is a process that is influenced by people and organizations (Dixon, 1989), and which requires gathering, maintaining, and matching knowledge (Waldron *et al.*, 1989). Nevertheless, the basic design process can be divided into four stages: (1) problem definition, (2) synthesis, (3) analysis and optimization, and (4) evaluation.

During problem definition, design requirements and constraints such as product function, performance characteristics, environmental considerations, expected market demand, available resources, physical constraints, and company tradition are identified. During conceptual design, alternative designs are synthesized based on the identified design requirements and subject to the design constraints. Design analysis and optimization are closely related to design synthesis and are performed iteratively to identify the best design. During design evaluation, the selected design is tested to determine if the functional requirements of the product have been successfully realized. Attempts to model the design process and to provide the necessary tools to automate or aid the different stages of the process will now be described.

Spillers and Newsome (1989) proposed the use of a hierarchical tree structure to define a design during the conceptual design stage. A design is defined by listing its associated properties, and the properties of these properties, and so forth. An example of the resultant hierarchical tree structure of a design is given in Fig. 13.2. Weights can be assigned to each of the branches to indicate their relative importance. Repeated properties are then combined to delineate better their function or influence on the design. The relationship between the properties, and their relative subproperties are then expressed using partially ordered sets. These partially ordered sets are then decomposed into independent chains, which play the role of subcomponents within the design. This representation facilitates the detailed analysis of the effect of a given component within a design. For instance, the impact of a component design change on the shape, performance, or reliability of the overall design can be observed.

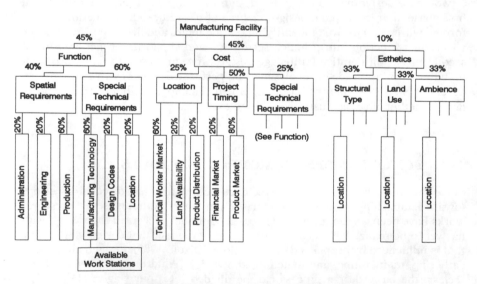

FIG. 13.2. Hierarchical description of a design (Spillers and Newsome, 1989).

Waldron *et al.* (1989) applied systemic theory to attempt a formal representation of functions in the conceptual design process. They observed that designers work in terms of functional units which are selected from a library of previous designs, from other sources, or created if necessary. To select from the available choices, designers rely on the use of heuristics and creative problem-solving techniques which they develop through their experience in designing. Two types of constraints, primary and subordinate, which direct and set the context of a design are identified. Conceptual design, then, is viewed as a process of elimination among the set of design alternatives. The systemic approach of design representation can accommodate the inclusion of compiled knowledge and of relatively high-level representations of previous designs in terms of their associated primary and subordinate constraints. This approach allows the design to be expressed as a classification hierarchy which can easily be translated into symbolic representation schemes. For instance, a design depository system can be used to suggest different design alternatives based on matching the primary and subordinate constraints associated with the design specifications to the available design alternatives. Problem-solving methodologies from artificial intelligence such as pattern matching and rule-based systems can be applied.

Serrano and Gossard (1988) proposed a framework for constraint management in conceptual design. Under this framework, the design process is viewed as the recognition, formulation, and satisfaction of constraints, which are iteratively added, deleted, and modified. A *constraint* is a relationship between a set of parameters defining some characteristics of the product. Constraints can either be geometrical or nongeometrical, and are formulated as piecewise continuous equalities or inequalities. A knowledge-based system, consisting of mechanical design tools that allow designers to experiment with different design alternatives, was developed using a graph theoretical approach. Techniques were also presented for evaluating and maintaining consistency in the systems of constraints.

Kim (1988) modeled the design process as a sequence of transitions from an initial knowledge base to a final design. The design problem is presented in terms of two sets, representing functions and constraints. From these two sets, a set of design criteria is formulated. The design process is characterized by mapping functional requirements onto a set of design components. The design components are a collection of form features that encapsulate specific functional characteristics. The form–function mapping procedure is repeated until all the design criteria have been satisfied. The procedure effectively transforms a null design (a design that has no features) to a design with form features satisfying all of the desired functional requirements.

Rinderle *et al.* (1989) proposed representing a mechanical device as a set of parameters related by constraints based on the devices form–function characteristics which arise from physical laws, spatial relationships, and material limitations. Each parameter describes some characteristic of the form or behavior of the device under consideration. The constraints relate to the parameters typically through equalities or inequalities. A collection of these constraints forms a network or a bipartite graph with each node representing either a constraint or a parameter. Collectively the constraints define the space of acceptable designs. Assigning values to some parameters such that none of the constraints are violated results in an instance of the design. The representation scheme aids the designer by providing a way to automatically identify relevant form–function relations. The specific requirements and objectives of a design can be used to further constrain the solution space and specify the criteria for identifying the best among all the design alternatives.

Agogino and Rege (1987) and Agogino *et al.* (1989) are currently examining the use of hierarchical influence diagrams as a decision analytic framework for the life cycle design and manufacture of mechanical products. Their intent is to create an influence diagram structure that will tie product design and manufacturing decisions to product quality, cost, and market risks. An influence diagram is a graphical/numerical means of representing complex decision problems involving uncertainty using nodes and directed arcs. Nodes represent state variables, decision variables, and value functions. State variables contain information regarding the current state of knowledge accumulated by an expert system. Decision variables represent decision rules. Value functions represent the goals or objectives of a decision maker. Directed arcs are influences, either probabilistic, fuzzy, informational, or causal, among the state variables, decision variables, and value functions. An expert system utilizing influence diagrams has been demonstrated by Agogino and Rege (1987).

Chang (1989) has specified the architecture of an automated design environment for the selection and design of electromechanical parts. His architecture consists of seven software modules (Fig. 13.3). The first module is an interactive user interface which uses a knowledge-based system to extract job specifications

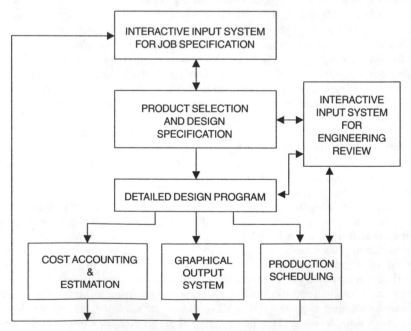

FIG. 13.3. VIDA system (Chang, 1989).

from customers. The second module is a knowledge-based product selection and design specification system. It uses either traditional heuristic search techniques or fuzzy set analysis to match customer job specifications to product classifications. The third module is a detailed design system that utilizes a knowledge base in conjunction with standard design algorithms to generate automatically detailed product designs. The fourth module uses a knowledge base to estimate product costs associated with labor, material, tooling, and overhead. The fifth module is a product planning system. It combines knowledge of existing production systems with scheduling heuristics to create a production schedule and to produce product drawings. The sixth module is a graphical output system. The seventh module is an interactive engineering review system which permits engineers to review and alter design decisions made by the previous modules.

The UMASS advisor developed by Boothroyd (Cobb, 1984) for the analysis of mechanical designs is composed of five independent, interactive software modules (see Fig. 13.4). The first, "Design for Automatic Assembly," accepts a Group Technology (GT) code for an assembly component and determines its physical size, shape envelope, geometric part relationship to insertion axis, its method of fastening, and its potential handling or feeding problems. In addition, this first software module also determines relative values for assembly time, equipment costs, design efficiency, and the theoretical minimum number of parts for the assembly.

The second module, "Assembly System Economics," uses mathematical models in conjunction with information obtained from the "Design for Automatic Assembly" module to determine the most economical assembly system. The third module, "Design for Automatic Handling," evaluates parts for automatic feeding and suggests methods for design improvement. The fourth module, "Design for Manual Assembly," is similar to the third module, but is geared toward manual material handling. The fifth module, "Assembly Machine Simulation," is used to evaluate the effects of machine cycle time, part quality, clearance time of faulty parts, and the number of service operators available on the assembly system performance.

Manivannan et al. (1989) have developed a knowledge-based system for the specification of ISO tolerances for rotational mating components with either interference, clearance, or transition fits. The system uses a knowledge base containing basic tolerancing rules established by the International Standards Organization (ISO). During execution, users are queried for desired nominal shaft/hole diameters, permitted deviations, tolerance bounds, and types of fit. This information is used in conjunction with the rule base to automatically specify the appropriate hole and shaft tolerances. The specification and analysis of tolerance for assemblies involving more than two components are not addressed.

A similar system (EX-TOLD) developed by Ahmad and MacDonald (1987) utilizes a knowledge base derived from expert designers. Design engineers were interviewed to establish how tolerances are used in industry. The expertise extracted from these designers were represented in a Prolog-based expert system shell called PROSE. A prototype of this knowledge-based system has been interfaced with a CAD system (MEDUSA).

An approach for automating the assembly packaging process utilizing a combination of optimization and solid modeling techniques was discovered by Kim

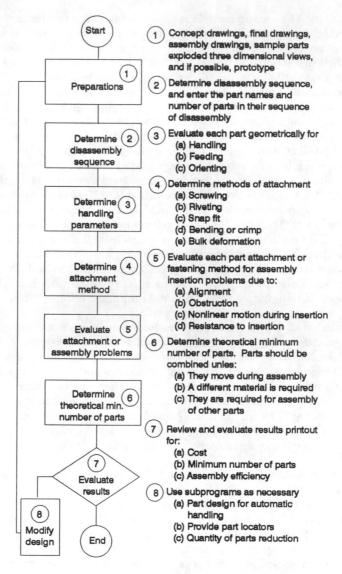

FIG. 13.4. UMASS procedure flowchart (Cobb, 1984).

and Gossard (1989). Here, the optimal location of the part components within the assembly is derived from the user-specified spatial relationships among the components. These spatial relationships are specifications of the desired relative location and orientation of one component with respect to other components in the assembly. These user-specified spatial relationships are formulated as inequality and equality constraints, which may express the physical, geometric, or kinematic relationships among the components, or express human factors and maintenance concerns. The equality constraints are used to infer the initial location of the components, and the inequality constraints are treated as penalties which are included in the objective functions to be optimized. An example of the objective function might be to minimize the volume of the product envelope. The developed approach can be used to allow the dimensions of the components to be redesigned during optimization if they can be expressed as a function of component location.

All the design models reviewed address only the conceptual design stage where the primary design intent is to satisfy the product functional requirements. The various analysis tools and knowledge-based advisors which attempt to address the manufacturability of the design are mainly intended for use as design analysis tools. In order to address the suggestions or results of the analysis, it may be necessary to make significant changes to the design. Conceivably, the extent of changes that may be suggested by the analysis packages and accommodated is constrained by the original design itself. To be fully effective, manufacturing considerations should be incorporated into the product design as early as possible, ideally in parallel with the functional requirement of the product.

13.3 DESIGN FOR AUTOMATED MANUFACTURE

For production in an automated manufacturing environment, the product design should be initiated by taking into consideration the following factors:

- Satisfaction of marketing (external) and organizational (internal) requirements
- Component minimization
- Material minimization
- Allowance for automated component manufacture
- Allowance for automated assembly
- Provision of features for automated inspection
- Allowance for automated material handling, packaging, and shipping
- Ease of maintenance and repair.

The following design methodology takes these objectives into account and covers all stages of product development. The design process is viewed as a sequence of design decisions made in a top-to-bottom fashion using logical iterations. This procedure is a guide rather than a set of rigid rules that could prohibit creativity and innovation. It takes a macro level view of the design process and addresses when and how the preceding objectives can be met. Consistent with the trend toward automation, many of the steps within this methodology are amenable to computerization.

To ensure the creation of optimal or near optimal designs, the proposed design methodology is divided into two phases: Phase I—Functional Analysis (product function packaging) and Phase II—Iterative Multistage Design. Without a thorough, preconceptual design analysis of product functions and their packaging, achieving an optimal design with respect to the preceding criteria is impossible. Steps taken during product function packaging are:

(1) Identification of primary product functions
(2) Packaging of primary functions
(3) Identification of subfunctions and support functions
(4) Packaging of subfunctions and support functions

Steps taken during multistage design include:

(1) Creation of preliminary designs for function volumes
(2) Evaluation of components for standardization
(3) Determination of critical dimensions and tolerances
(4) Examination of mating parts for ease of automated manufacture and assembly
(5) Evaluation of product functions and fabrication

Phase I: Functional Analysis

Identification of Primary Product Functions

The first step in product development is the creation of a list of marketing and organizational requirements. Marketing requirements are obtainable from a marketing group or consultant. Organizational requirements are influenced by product mix, product options, and long-term strategies. Elements within this list are then ordered with respect to their priority. Note that in many circumstances, trade-offs must be made between elements with the same priority. Once this list is complete, product primary functions which meet these requirements are identified.

For example, in the design of a printer, many marketing requirements need to be considered. Should the printer produce the highest quality print for a moderate price or print the fastest at an acceptable quality? Should the printer be tailored to specific applications or designed for general usage? Typical factors which influence the marketing requirements for a data-processing-system printer are listed in Table 13.2. Many of these factors are interrelated. For example, the print quality of a wire matrix printer is influenced by the types of fonts that it supports.

Table 13.3 provides a set of marketing requirements for the printer, listed in order of priority. From this list the primary printer functions are identified. They are (1) print, (2) printer control (microprocessor), (3) keyboard interface, and (4) computer interface. Note that in many cases, products will only provide a single primary function.

At this design stage, a distinction between product functions and component functions should be made. Product functions are those which directly meet marketing requirements, and thus should never be compromised. Component func-

Table 13.2. Typical Factors Considered in Printer Design

Print Technology:
- wire matrix
- daisy wheel
- ink jet nozzle
- others

Print Characteristics:
- quality
- speed
- size
- font
- colors
- others

Print Media:
- forms
- papers

Printer Size:

Interface Requirements:
- to PCs
- to a keyboard

Others (e.g., cost and logic complexity)

Table 13.3. Printer Requirement List

(1)   Printer size must be within specified limits
(2)   Printer should provide a keyboard interface
(3)   Printer should provide an RS-232 computer interface
(4)   Printer should use wire matrix print technology
(5)   Printer should provide four fonts selectable from computer or keyboard
(6)   Printer should provide multiple print format selectable from computer or keyboard
(7)   Print media is limited to a continuous form of 8.5 by 11.5 inches
(8)   Printer should use a form of friction feeding mechanism
(9)   Printer should operate within a normal office environment

tions support product functions and are negotiable. For example, a bolt holding two parts together serves a component function. If the two parts are made as a single component then the need for the bolt no longer exists.

Packaging Primary Functions

A product envelope is the volume within which all product components must fit. In the absence of a volume constraint, a three-dimensional, unconstrained envelope is used. Components delivering primary product functions occupy volumes within a product envelope. Packaging involves the placement of these functional volumes within a product envelope. When packaging, considerations for their interrelationships, maintainability, accessibility, and manufacturability must be taken into account. An optimal package is one which ultimately results in the least number of product components and which ensures ease of product manufacture, assembly, and maintenance. As a design progresses in detail, its packaging may be altered to meet new requirements. Nevertheless, good packaging in the beginning stages of design ultimately minimizes design costs and leads to better designs.

Figure 13.6 shows the primary function volumes of the printer composed of seven basic parts (Fig. 13.5) packaged within its envelope. To satisfy human interfacing requirements, the print volume is placed on top so that a user can observe printer operation while typing on a keyboard. In addition, its placement makes for ease of assembly and replacement. The computer interface volume is placed in the lower-back corner of the envelope to provide three surfaces for direct computer interface. The placement of this volume in another location, such as in the center, would require an additional connection to one side of the printer, thus resulting in extra components and additional manufacturing costs. The controller volume is placed close to the computer interface volume because of their close interrelationship, thus minimizing connection costs.

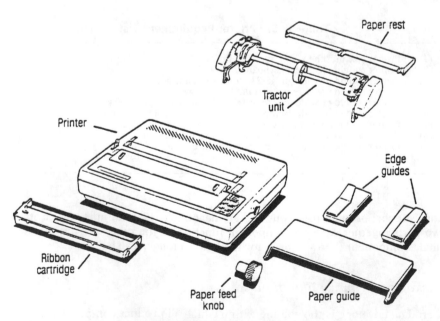

FIG. 13.5. Printer parts.

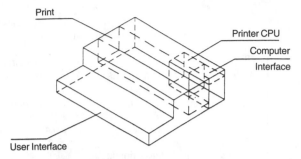

FIG. 13.6. Packaging of the primary printer function volumes.

Identification of Subfunctions and Support Functions

In this stage, each of the primary product functions are divided into subfunctions using the same approach employed in determining the primary functions. Additional decomposition is exercised until no further divisions are feasible. In addition, supportive functions, which enhance the primary functions, are identified. For example, a cooling fan may be required to support a microprocessor by keeping its temperature below a maximum limit.

By identifying subfunctions and support functions early in the design process, those which are common to multiple primary functions may be identified. As a result, efforts will not be wasted on the design of components satisfying the same functions. The result of a functional decomposition is a tree-structured, function hierarchy. Primary functions represent the roots of the tree, while subfunctions and support functions represent the branches.

Figure 13.7 shows a partial function hierarchy of the printer. The print function is composed of three subfunctions: (1) move print surface, (2) move print mechanism, and (3) move print pins. In total, these functions ensure the proper positioning and printing of characters. The move print pins subfunction is divided into two further subfunctions: (1) buffer digital instructions, and (2) convert instructions to pin movement. These subfunctions ensure that the proper character is printed at a given location.

The flexible printer control function is divided into four subfunctions: (1) control printing, (2) monitor switch requests (on-line/off-line, etc.), (3) communicate with keyboard, and (4) communicate with computer. These functions ensure that the input signals are properly converted into printed characters. The board interface function accepts a digital input from a keyboard and stores it into a buffer. The computer interface function accepts and translates an RS-232 formatted signal and stores it into a buffer. In addition to the subfunctions described, a power supply support function is included.

Packaging of Subfunctions and Support Functions

Once subfunctions and support functions are identified, their dependencies can be established and listed in a tabular format. Entries may be weighted to desig-

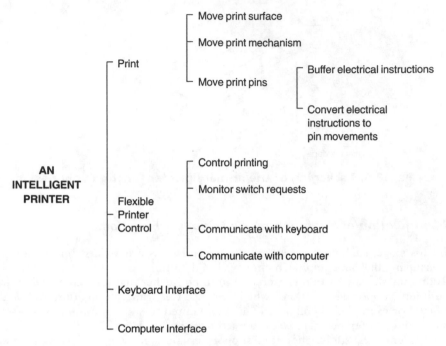

FIG. 13.7. Printer functional hierarchy.

nate their relative importance. An example of a nonweighted dependency table for the printer is supplied in Table 13.4.

At this stage, dependency table data can be used in packaging of subfunction and support function volumes with other design criteria such as reliability, maintainability, accessibility, manufacturability, and assemblability. Appropriate analysis modules utilizing either optimization or artificial intelligence techniques can be invoked for these purposes. Subfunction volumes are packaged into the volumes of their primary functions, whereas support function modules are packaged into the product envelope.

In some circumstances, packaging decisions are straightforward. For instance, function volumes with strong dependencies should always be placed together to avoid the addition of bridging components and materials. However, in general, most packaging decisions are quite complex and require designers to make tradeoffs between design criteria. For example, function volumes which are considered the most reliable should be placed near the center of the product envelope, whereas those that need to be accessible should be placed at the periphery. However, what should be done with volumes which are the most reliable and which require regular access?

Due to their complexity, packaging decisions are best computerized. However, automation is not a trivial task because of the mixture of qualitative and quantitative data which must be integrated into a decision. To tackle this problem, packaging techniques must be developed which integrate analytic, numeric,

Table 13.4. Dependency Between the Printer Function Modules

		1	2	3	4	5	6	7	8	9	10	11	12
Move print surface	1		x			x	x						
Print to media surface	2	x		x		x							
Convert Elec. to Mech.	3		x			x	x	x	x				
Control Panel	4					x		x	x		x	x	
Serve switches	5	x		x	x		x						
Drive motors	6	x	x	x								x	
Process users logic	7		x	x	x					x		x	
Communicate with comp.	8		x	x							x	x	
Provide typing	9									x			
Translate typing	10						x		x			x	
Computer interface	11			x			x						
Power supply	12			x		x	x	x		x			

and knowledge-base algorithms. An approach similar to the one reported by Kim and Gossard (1987) may be used. Regardless of problem complexity, packaging should always be applied to the location of subfunction and support function volumes in order to identify and address conflicts between design criteria early in the design process.

Phase II: Iterative, Multistage Design Process

Creation of Preliminary Designs for Function Volumes

Upon exiting the functional analysis phase, a product function hierarchy has been established and packaged. Over the next five stages, the product functions will be translated into detailed assembly designs in an iterative fashion. The first stage in this transition is the translation of subfunction and support function volumes into preliminary designs of subassemblies.

To specify optimal designs, a designer must: (1) create and evaluate numerous design alternatives at various levels of abstraction, and (2) choose parameter values for the design alternatives selected. Unfortunately, when performed manually, these processes are labor intensive, time-consuming, and expensive. Consequently, productivity during this iterative design stage can be enhanced dramatically through the use of design automation software.

A database approach similar to Group Technology could be utilized to facilitate the creation of design alternatives. Using this approach, relational databases which tie product functions to design alternatives at various levels of abstraction would serve as design storehouses. Design data would be stored using a standardized, CAD-based format. To extract design data, a user would request a database search against a specified product function. In this fashion, a user could access a broad spectrum of designs which perform a desired function. To promote quick evaluation, each design would also include data on performance, reliability, environmental restrictions, and manufacturability. Thus to eliminate some of the alternatives extracted from a database search, a user could specify a design search against a set of product constraints.

With respect to the printer example, a database search against the drive motor function could lead to a large listing of electric motors ranging from brushed DC motors to stepper motors. Constraints such as maximum torque, dynamic response, and commercial availability could reduce this list to a particular class of stepper motors.

To facilitate the parameterization of designs which are not commercially available, form–function charts such as the ones advocated by Rinderle *et al.* (1989) could be utilized. By using these charts, designers can easily determine the effects of parameter selection on total system performance. Automation of form–function charts can be accomplished through the use of spreadsheet algorithms. Integration with the design database previously described could be accomplished by having form–function charts stored in combination with design data.

Evaluation of Components for Standardization

After an assembly design has been initially specified, component parts within the assembly are evaluated with respect to standardization. Parts, such as fasteners and washers, which perform similar functions but utilize different shapes or materials may be subject to standardization in order to reduce design complexity and manufacturing costs. Likewise, parts that are commercially available are identified so that make versus buy evaluations may be conducted. Parts that are not commercially available may be redesigned so that commercial substitutes may be used. Finally, parts that are determined to have no commercial substitutes may be substituted with designs that have a history of production, thus eliminating the need for process plan development. To automate part identification and evaluation, feature-based recognition techniques can be used in combination with Group Technology concepts.

Determination of Critical Dimensions

On completion of standardization evaluation, subassembly parts which must be manufactured in-house have been identified. Those with no prior history of production are now evaluated with respect to critical dimensions and tolerances. Dimensions are considered critical if they influence contact between mating surfaces. Tolerances are applied to critical dimensions to ensure proper fits between mating surfaces.

For example, in order for the printer to type quality print, the distance between its movable print head and its print platen must remain relatively constant. Consequently, all dimensions that influence printer head to platen distance are considered critical. Examples include guide rail diameter, guide rail straightness, and guide bearing diameter.

Unfortunately, manufacturing processes are unable to produce the parts to exact size and form. To ensure the proper functioning of the part, tolerance information that specifies the allowable variation to the part geometry is specified. Tight tolerances can ensure that the product will have high quality, but this generally leads to a higher manufacturing cost resulting from the additional manufacturing operations required, inspection requirements, and increased processing time. New processsing equipment with higher degrees of accuracy may be required. Thus a design engineer should always be aware of the process capabilities of available equipment, as well as the relative costs of assigning tolerances. In general, a good design engineer will (1) minimize the number of critical dimensions within an assembly, (2) minimize the number of parts that contain critical dimensions, and (3) specify maximum tolerances to ensure proper fits.

The selection of critical dimensions and tolerances becomes quite difficult as assembly complexity increases. Fortunately, the analysis of assembly components for the selection of critical dimensions and tolerances lends itself to automation. Current efforts by Ahmad and MacDonald (1987) and Manivannan *et al.* (1989) have demonstrated the feasibility of using knowledge-base techniques for tolerance selection and allocation.

Examination of Mating Parts

On completion of the detailed design of all subassemblies, a final evaluation should be performed before the product is prototyped and manufactured within a pilot facility. This evaluation involves checking each set of mating parts within the product for ease of automated manufacture and assembly. Items which may be checked include:

(1) The ability of parts to be formed rather than machined
(2) The ease with which part geometry may be machined
(3) The ability of parts to be machined with the minimum number of reference surfaces
(4) The ability of parts to be machined with the minimum amount of repositioning
(5) The ability of component surfaces to be mated automatically
(6) The ability of components to be grasped mechanically or through some other automated means
(7) The ability of components to be mechanically fed
(8) The ability of components to be assembled in a single direction
(9) The ability of surfaces to be fastened automatically.

Much of the preceding evaluation procedure has been accumulated through the work of Dewhurst and Boothroyd (1984) and other researchers, as well as through the rules of thumb and heuristics developed by manufacturing engineers over the past 25 years. As a result, this evaluation process is amenable to automation through the application of knowledge-base, group technology, and feature-based recognition techniques.

Evaluation of Product Functions and Fabrication

The last stage in the iterative design sequence is product and manufacturing process prototyping. During this stage, the basic manufacturing process is checked to determine whether it is capable of producing the product within design specifications. Information gained from this stage may lead to modifications in the manufacturing process or in the design to improve its manufacturability. On successful completion of this stage, a prototype product is then thoroughly tested against its functional requirements to identify design deficiencies. Information gained from this testing may lead to further refinements of the product at one of the previous design stages.

13.4 CONCLUSION

It is generally recognized that the practice of designing products with manufacturing in mind can shorten the product development time, minimize development cost, improve product quality, and ensure a smooth transition into production. To fully exploit the cost and quality advantages of automation, a different design approach than the ones traditionally used must be employed. This chapter has provided a brief review of the available design models and tools, and has proposed a design methodology for automated manufacture. For the automation of the design process, considerable work is still needed to implement intelligent systems that can provide the necessary support tools. For example, tools should be developed for automatically examining technology alternatives for functions, and for automatic tolerance specification and analysis of complex assemblies. With the availability of these design automation tools, designers can direct more of their effort toward creative thinking to come up with better innovative designs.

REFERENCES

Ahmad, K., and Macdonald, A. 1987. An expert system on tolerances in mechanical design (ExTOLD). *Proc. of the ESD/SMI Expert Systems Conference and Exposition for Advanced Manufacturing Technology*, Dearborn, Michigan, pp. 309–326.

Agogino, A. M., Imanio, W., and Wang, S. S. 1989. Decision—Analytic methodology for life cycle design. *Design Theory '88*, pp. 313–314.

Agogino, A. M., and Rege, A. 1987. IDES: Influence diagram-based expert system. *Mathematical Modelling* 8:227–233.

Bakerjian, R., ed., 1992. *Tool and Manufacturing Engineers Handbook*. Vol. 6, *Design for Manufacturability*, 4th ed. Society of Manufacturing Engineers.

Chang, S. S. L. 1989. A fuzzy set algorithm for engineering design applications to the component parts industry. *Design Theory '88*, pp. 117–131.

Cobb, M. F. 1984. Design-for-assembly is the key to increased productivity. *RCA Engineer* 29:4–10.

Corbett, J., Dooner, M., and Pym, C. 1991. Design for Manufacture, Strategies. Principles and Techniques (New York: Addison Wesley).

Dewhurst, P., and Boothroyd, G. 1984. Design for assembly: Automatic assembly. *Machine Design* 56:87–92.

Dixon, J. R. 1989. On research methodology towards a scientific theory of engineering design. *Design Theory '88*, pp. 316–337.

Kim, J. J., and Gossard, D. C. 1989. Reasoning on the location of components for assembly packaging. *Proc. of the ASME Design Automation Conference*, Montreal, Canada, pp. 251–257.

Kim, S. H. 1988. A general model of design: Formalization and consequences. *Manufacturing Review* 1:109–116.

Manivannan, S., Lehtihet, A., and Egbelu, P. 1989. A knowledge-based system for the specification of manufacturing tolerances. *Journal of Manufacturing Systems* 8:153–160.

Pham, D. T. 1982. On designing components for automatic assembly. *Proc. of the 3rd International Conference*, Stuttgart, Germany, pp. 205–214.

Rinderle, J. R., Colburn, E. R., Hoover, S. P., Paz-Soldan, J. P., and Watton, J. D. 1989. Form–function characteristics of electromechanical designs. *Design Theory '88*, pp. 132–147.

Serrano, D., and Gossard, D. C. 1988. Constraint management in MCAE. *Proc. of the 3rd International Conference on Applications of AI in Engineering*, Stanford, California, pp. 1–14.

Spillers, W. R., and Newsome, S. 1989. Design theory: A model for conceptual design. *Design Theory '88*, pp. 198–215.

Waldron, M. D., Waldron, K. J., and Owen, D. H., 1989. Use of systemic theory to represent the conceptual mechanical design process. *Design Theory '88*, pp. 36–48.

PART III

Design in Manufacturing

The current product design process is often iterative where prototype products must be built and tested. Since product quality is increasingly becoming important for companies, there is a need to improve the design process to meet the quality goals. Process control has long been an area of study. The material discussed in Chapters 14 through 17 emphasizes the integrity of design and manufacturing.

Chapter 14 focuses on how intelligent process control can help maintain the integrity of product design. Three specific areas of product design are covered: testing of product quality issues, using neural networks for modeling during production to estimate product adherence to specifications based on process parameters, and using combined neural networks and expert systems in lieu of Shewhart control charts during production to detect undesirable shifts, trends, and cycles. These three areas aim at similar objectives. First, a product should be designed to attain the desired performance level. Second, the process, including raw materials, equipment conditions, and environmental factors, should be optimized with regard to product quality. Third, should shifts affecting quality occur, they should be detected in a timely and reliable fashion.

Chapter 15 discusses effective evaluation and redesign of circuit networks with signal integrity problems through (1) the evaluation and redesign to be performed in multiple levels of detail, and (2) the definition of knowledge about circuit part hierarchies, circuit component categories, and constraints for each level on which evaluation and redesign are performed. Furthermore, in order to redesign a faulty circuit in the smallest number of iterations one needs to define knowledge for selecting the most appropriate way of redesigning the faulty circuit. The knowledge has to be selected based on certain criteria discussed in the chapter.

The automatic acquisition of the new knowledge is facilitated when the acquisition component is integrated with a performance system. When doing so, the knowledge of the performance system, as well as any problem solving information generated, can be directly evaluated by the learning component. Furthermore, the quality and effect of the knowledge that is learned can be directly utilized by the performance system, and appropriate action can be taken accordingly by the learning component.

By compiling the redesign knowledge of only one plan into a knowledge source, including eligibility and operation control knowledge, the same results is accomplished as if replaying many plans. However, if more than one plan is compiled into a knowledge source, the generalization of the operators and the additional knowledge that is acquired, allows the performance system to form more plans and thus solve more problems than a system that is only replaying a single plan. In order for the latter system to be able to solve a variety of problems it has to utilize analogy, which may be difficult to identify in certain domains, including engineering design.

In Chapter 16, the implementation of fuzzy logic methodology to the design of the intelligent controller is discussed. A fuzzy logic based controller includes a set of heuristic rules to implement control actions. The need for heuristic logic has been recognized in industrial control due to safety considerations. Industrial process controllers often incorporate heuristic logic to deal with practical problems such as integrator windup, alarm conditions and switching between automatic and manual modes. Tuning a specific controller may also require heuristic logic. Typically, a control engineer applies a set of commonly accepted rules to tune the controller, however, it is also known that these rules are not comprehensive. Most often, an intuitive judgment and rules of thumb are also incorporated into the process.

Heuristic rules of a fuzzy controller determine the control action in terms of a set-point error and its derivative. The rules are normally written to mimic the actions of an experienced process operator. It is assumed that the process operator is willing to share his/her knowledge in terms of a set of production rules. However, by using automated knowledge acquisition techniques, one can extract production rules by observing the behavior of the process operator. Several industrial applicants of fuzzy controllers have been reported in the literature in the last ten years. One emerging feature of these controllers is that they appear to be robust even though they use a minimum amount of information about the process dynamics. Perhaps, the robustness is due to the generation of a single control action by combining the contributions of several control rules.

The performance of fuzzy controllers can be further enhanced by adaptively modifying the control rules. This is particularly important if the process and environment dynamics are changing in time. In Chapter 16, an approach is introduced in which the structure of a fuzzy controller is modified by observing the changes of process dynamics.

In Chapter 17, a hierarchial framework is discussed for analyzing specifications for a material handling system. Since handling and storage represent a major portion of the activities in manufacturing companies, "design for handling" should be considered, along with "design for manufacturability" and "design for assembly." When the major design variables have been determined, the second level of the hierarchy, equipment selection, becomes the primary focus. Interface issues are of particular importance in this problem. Equipment specifications occur after selection of the equipment type and those are addressed by vendors.

In each category of material handling problems, there is great potential for the development and application of knowledge-based systems. Vendors would be the most likely candidates to lead in the development and maintenance of knowledge-based systems for the detailed equipment specification problem. For the system specification and equipment selection problems, the potential sources of support are less certain. It is obvious, however, that there are significant savings to be obtained through better design decisions for material handling systems. Knowledge-based tools play a major role in making those decisions.

Chapter 14

Impact of Intelligent Process Control on Product Design

Alice E. Smith
Department of Industrial Engineering
University of Pittsburgh
Pittsburgh, Pennsylvania

14.1 OVERVIEW

This chapter focuses on how intelligent process control can help maintain the integrity of product design. There are three specific areas covered:

(1) The use of predictive neural networks during product design to test product quality issues
(2) The use of neural networks for modeling during production to estimate product adherence to specifications based on process parameters
(3) The use of combined neural networks and expert systems in lieu of Shewhart control charts during production to detect undesirable shifts, trends, and cycles.

These three areas have similar objectives. First, a product should be designed to attain the desired performance level. Second, the process, including raw materials, equipment conditions, and environmental factors, should be optimized with regard to product quality. Third, if shifts affecting quality occur, they should be detected in a timely and reliable fashion.

The current product design process is often iterative, where mock-up or prototype products must be built and tested for their performance on applicable quality measures prior to final design. Because product quality is increasingly becoming a competitive edge for companies, they need to circumvent this trial and error process without sacrificing quality. Thus process control has long been an important area of study. This chapter is concerned with statistical process control, which attempts to predict quality based on process parameters and to diagnose quality problems. The objective is to find an optimum combination of values for the process variables to maximize the probability of obtaining and maintaining acceptable quality. When products depart from quality standards, statistical process control can assist in determining which variables were the cause and what process adjustments are needed. Control charts, one facet of statistical process control, have been in place since the 1930s. They are constructed to provide robust detection of process changes which require investigation and correction.

This chapter covers the application of intelligent techniques, primarily neural computing, to the three areas of product design listed at the beginning.

14.2 USING NEURAL NETWORKS DURING DESIGN FOR QUALITY

The design process presents two interesting issues. First, products often have complex, irregular shapes with significant room for creative design and functional improvement. Second, the design process is time-consuming and fraught with uncertainty when it is based on iterative improvement. This design trial-and-error feedback loop needs to be tightened up by improving the analysis stage before manufacture (Suri and Shimizu, 1989). Predictive neural network models can relate multiple quantitative and qualitative design parameters to product performance. These models can allow product designers to iteratively and interactively test parameter changes and evaluate corresponding changes in product performance before a prototype product is actually built and tested. This "what if" modeling ability can speed and economize the design process, and result in better quality products. A neural model can also supplement controlled experiments during product testing to help ascertain the optimum design specifications and tolerances. A third use of neural computing in product design for quality is to act as an expert system, where rules are learned directly through product instances rather than defined through knowledge engineering.

Neural networks are good solutions because of their capability to simultaneously relate multiple quantitative and qualitative variables. Also, their ability to form models based solely on the data, rather than on assumptions of linearity or other static analytic relations, is especially useful. Because neural networks need training data, experimental results must be available. This, however, is usually a limited set. Unlike many neural network manufacturing applications (such as machine vision or quality control) copious amounts of data cannot easily be generated in product design. To obtain the best possible neural network models, and to validate results, strategies that maximize learning with sparse data must be adopted. One such method is the "leave-k-out" procedure for training (Lawrence, 1991). A small number of vectors, k, out of the training vectors, are held back each time for testing and networks are trained, changing the k hold-back vectors each time. Because the size of each network is usually modest for product design applications, and the number of training vectors is small, training proceeds rapidly and creating these multiple networks is not burdensome. Another method to make the most of sparse training data is to inject noise into the training set, creating multiple, noisy versions of each actual training vector.

Two studies have used neural networks for product design by training a multilayered perceptron to act as an expert system (Hung and Adeli, 1991; Zarefar and Goulding, 1992). Hung and Adeli: trained a network to select a steel beam design, whereas Zarefar and Goulding trained a network to design a gear box. Both efforts used documented design policies, heuristics, and calculations to construct a rule base (or decision table). The network was then trained on representative examples adhering to this rule base. This approach, like others that use neural networks in lieu of expert systems, is advantageous in that rules are learned directly through design examples rather than through tedious, and often problematic, knowledge acquisition. One disadvantage of a neural network acting as an expert system is that explaining and tracing through the reasoning process are impossible; the neural network acts essentially as a black box.

Previous work using neural networks for predictive modeling in manufacturing design include Chryssolouris et al. (1989), Liu and Liu (1990), Cariapa et al. (1991), and Schmerr et al. (1991). Chryssolouris et al. dealt with design of manufacturing systems using simulation augmented with neural network interpolation. Liu and Liu used backpropagation neural networks to interpolate between test points of a circuit. The tests related three circuit design parameters and two voltage conditions to one performance parameter—the variability of output current of the circuit. The objective was to find the design settings which yielded the smallest variation over all voltage conditions. The next two works focused on interpolating between Taguchi design points using a neural network so that a full factorial design could be simulated to search for optimal design parameter settings. These works used small subsets of whole products to test their approaches. Cariapa et al. (1991) looked at tool polishing operations with filamentary brushes, and Schmerr et al. (1991) tested fatigue cracking of a small structural member. The Taguchi approach is not appropriate for all products because many do not adhere to any known analytical description of performance.

Another approach used known quality tests on sanitary ware products to develop both predictive networks for quality and sensitivity studies of the effects of design parameter alteration on quality measures (Ben Brahim et al., 1992). After translating as many parameters as possible into continuously valued numeric measures so that products could be better compared, a leave-k-out training procedure was used to develop predictive networks for performance on each of the quality tests based on the design parameter specifications. A sensitivity model for each quality test neural network was built by changing each design parameter in small increments across its range, as shown in Fig. 14.1. These models can be used interactively by design engineers to test the effects of product design changes on the resulting product performance. In this way, designs can be optimized for performance given cost and manufacturability constraints before prototype models are built and tested.

14.3 NEURAL NETWORKS FOR STATISTICAL PROCESS CONTROL

Typical process control procedures include statistical analysis of periodic batch samples, control charts of sample mean or range, and trial and error. One of the anticipated technologies for intelligent process control is artificial neural networks, as instanced by this excerpt from the trade literature in plastics: "In injection molding [neural networks] will take real-time action as the process is running. It will be the biggest thing in the next ten years" (Plastics Technology, 1990).

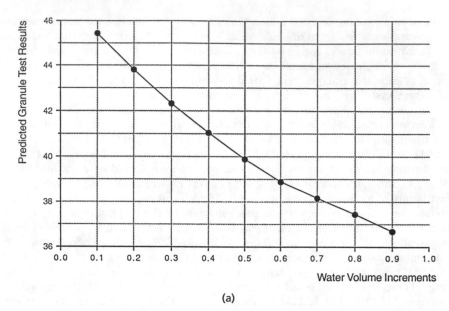

(a)

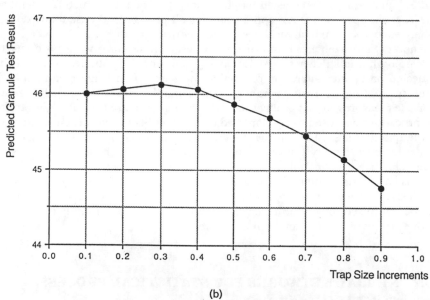

(b)

NOTE: to study the effects of design parameter alteration on quality measures. A sensitivity model for each quality test neural network was built by changing each design parameter in small increments across its range.

FIG. 14.1. Neural sensitivity model for design for quality (Ben Brahim *et al.*, 1992).

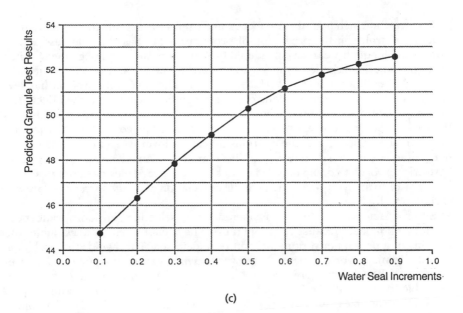

(c)

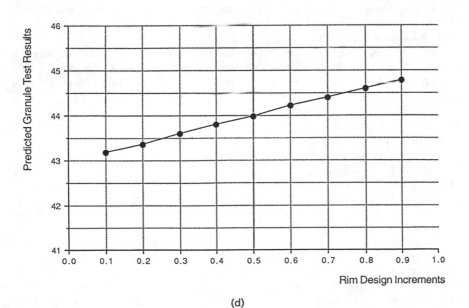

(d)

FIG. 14.1. *Continued*

One way in which neural networks can be useful for manufacturing statistical process control is in the prediction of product quality based on process conditions. Product quality can be considered both in absolute terms (e.g., mean outer diameter) and in variable terms (e.g., standard deviation and range of outer diameters). Creating a model that relates input variables to output product has several uses. First, an automatic control system can base actions on the effects the process conditions have on the product, and not just on the process conditions themselves. Second, process variables can be analyzed piecewise for their impact on the final product. Third, the relationship can be inverted so that desired product characteristics can dictate certain line conditions. An advantage of the neural network approach to data analysis is that significant variables need not be established prior to analysis—networks handle correlation and autocorrelation among variables well.

Several factors have to be considered when selecting an appropriate neural network model. Because most operations have calibrated data available, the training of a neural network model can be supervised. This avoids the problems of self-organizing, or competitive, networks which can be unstable and unpredictable. Although binary representations can be formed from data, it is often desirable to retain all the information in the form of analog input and output. Qualitative variables, such as smooth or hot, should be translated to an appropriate numeric scale, retaining as much information about the variable as possible. If the process has temporal aspects, either time itself or relative time, this should be accounted for in the network selected. Time can be translated into an input variable, a moving window of input data can be used, or a network which allows temporal handling in its architecture (e.g., a recurrent network) can be selected. Because the vector lengths and training set sizes are usually relatively small, training can be infrequent and off-line. This alleviates pressure to find quick, approximate methods for training.

In process control, work has been done to neurally relate input parameters to product variables in both an associative and a predictive model. Association tasks are usually diagnostics for use during manufacturing. Burke identified tool wear states during machining using a competitive learning network, a task normally done by human operators (Burke, 1989). A similar subject was pursued by Guillot and Ouafi (1991), who used a supervised network for use in untended machining to recognize tool breakage. A third neural model for monitoring during machining used the frequency of the vibration signals to classify if machine deterioration was taking place (Knapp and Wang, 1992). The plastics industry was studied for diagnostics and corrective action with a backpropagation correlation model of injection molding process parameters and product defects (Wu et al., 1991). The input vectors were the quality defects, whereas the output vectors contained recovery instructions.

Predictive models attempt to estimate product parameters based on process conditions before product manufacture. Andersen et al. (1990) used backpropagation networks to relate input parameters, arc current, arc voltage, travel speed, and wire speed, predictively to quality measures of a weld, bead width, penetration, reinforcement height, and cross-section area. Okafor et al. (1990) pursued a similar approach in milling for estimating surface roughness and bore tolerance using input variables of cutting force components, acoustic emission, and spindle vibration. They used a moving window of inputs of size five to estimate the trend in the process. Smith and Dagli (1991) related many input variables of a plastic extrusion process to a prediction of the lot quality with backpropagation. Smith used a similar approach for the injection molding of brake linings to predict product quality and its variability (Smith, 1993).

These works suggest that all processes can be diagnosed and modeled successfully by neural networks, although the results may not be necessarily superior to statistical or other analytical techniques. There is sustained interest, however, for reasons other than superiority of performance. One reason is the ability to learn about relationships through the data itself, rather than assuming probability distributions or explicitly coding an analytical model. The second reason is that training can handle multiple, related or nonrelated inputs and outputs simultaneously. The third reason is that a neural network can dynamically adjust to changing line conditions by continuous training or sporadic retraining. The last reason is that hardwired neural networks are expected to be readily available in the near future, which implies cost effective, real-time control.

14.4 NEURAL NETWORK CONTROL CHARTS

Overview of Control Charts and Their Implementation Problems

Control charts are commonly used in manufacturing environments to analyze process parameters to infer whether the process is within or out of control, and to diagnose process evolution through temporal characteristics. Some processes that benefit from control chart tracking are filtration, extraction, fermentation, distillation, refining, reaction, pressing, metal cutting, heat treatment, welding, casting, forging, extrusion, injection molding, spraying, and soldering (Miller and Walker, 1988).

W. A. Shewhart first proposed the use of control charts in 1931, which came to commonly bear his name as Shewhart control charts (Shewhart, 1931). Figure 14.2 shows a typical Shewhart control chart. Through the ensuing years many different formulations became known, such as moving average and range charts, proportion (P) charts, number of defectives (C) charts, cumulative sum charts, and control charts with warning limits (Gibra, 1975; Saniga and Shirland, 1977; Montgomery, 1980). However, most manufacturers use versions of the early control charts, which track sample mean (X-bar charts) and sample range (R charts), as checks on the process state and the process variability. One reason these two charts are relied upon is the difficulty of choosing the best control chart from the many available for a given situation.

A difficulty with control charts is the determination of whether a process is actually within control or not. Because sample points are subject to noise due to measurement, humans, and other factors, they form a nonspecified probabilistic distribution. An extreme point may come from a process which is, in fact, under control. Or a point within control boundaries may come from a process which has shifted to out of control. Misclassification of these overlapping sam-

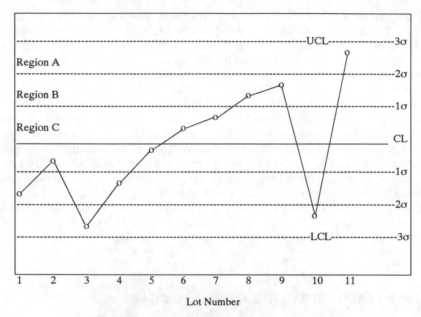

FIG. 14. 2. Typical Shewhart control chart.

ple points results in either (1) Type I or (2) Type II errors. Type I errors are false alarms, whereas Type II errors are the opposite, i.e., they miss an out of control signal. Besides control limits, there are certain patterns of sample points which indicate that the process is moving toward, or cycling through, out-of-control situations. Again, classifying these points correctly is stochastic and requires a certain expertise in the process and the concept of control.

Use of Expert Systems for Control Charts

Some earlier work has been done to relate intelligent computing to manufacturing control charts. Most of these have taken the form of using expert, or knowledge-based systems to select proper control methodologies and to advise on the analysis of the selected methodologies (Alexander and Jagannathan, 1986; Dybeck, 1987; Scott and ElGomayel, 1987; Evans and Lindsay, 1988; Hosni and Elshennawy, 1988; Eid and Losier, 1990; Willborn, 1990; Dagli and Smith, 1991). These systems do a good job where the problem involves analysis of relatively few alternatives and the analysis depends mostly or wholly on qualitative information. Thus, selection of the proper control chart or advice on corrective actions given a certain diagnosis are appropriate venues for the expert system approach. Where expert systems are clumsy and inadequate is in the analysis of voluminous, continuous, analytical data, which is what is usually available from line measurements.

Use of Neural Networks for Control Charts

A first use of neural networks for control charts is simply to have them act as barriers for signaling a point within control limits or beyond control limits. This was done by Yazici and Smith (1992) for a plastic extrusion process. A neural network acted as an X-bar control chart monitor for four process variables simultaneously with perfect results. Although performance was not better than analytical or human monitoring, the ability to simultaneously monitor multiple variables is an advantage, which would become particularly distinctive when using hardware neural network chips on the line for this purpose.

A few studies have used neural computing to detect location (usually mean) and variance (usually range) shifts. Pugh proposed using backpropagation networks to learn when mean shifts had occurred for a sample size of five (Pugh, 1989, 1991). He found that the neural networks produced average run length results about equal to a standard X-bar control chart with 2σ control limits, and improved significantly on Type II errors over X-bar charts. Guo and Dooley looked at positive shifts in both mean and variance using backpropagation neural networks compared to cumulative sum and moving sum charts (Guo and Dooley, 1990). They found their best network reduced errors in classification by about 40% from the control chart heuristics. Smith (1992) found that a backpropagation control chart could simultaneously act as both an X-bar chart and an R chart, and provide better detection than the traditional charts for processes that are slightly shifted in location or variance.

Instead of detecting shift and variance changes, two other studies examined neural pattern recognition to detect well-known control chart patterns symptomatic of special cause infestation. Hwarng and Hubele (1991) used a backpropagation classifier on six control patterns: trend, cycle, stratification, systematic, mixture, and sudden shift. They found that a neural classifier with binary input and output performed well enough to serve as a supplement to traditional control charts. Smith (1992) used a similar approach with continuous input vectors representing four patterns: trend, cycle, stratification, and over controlled. Future control chart points, out to five time periods, were predicted based on previous points to assist with pattern classification.

Composite Intelligent Systems for Control Charts

Besides control analysis, a knowledge-based system can select the control chart strategies most effective for the manufacturing domain. The system can also specify likely causes or select corrective actions given the diagnosis of the pure neural network or a combined neural/expert decision. This approach was tried in a prototype neural network/expert system quality monitoring and diagnostic system for plastic extrusion (Smith and Yazici, 1992). Figure 14.3 shows the schematic of the prototype system which uses neural predictions to assist with the rule-based diagnostics and corrective actions.

Analytic analysis is not the whole of control chart inference. There is often valuable information of a qualitative or intuitive nature to be considered. This

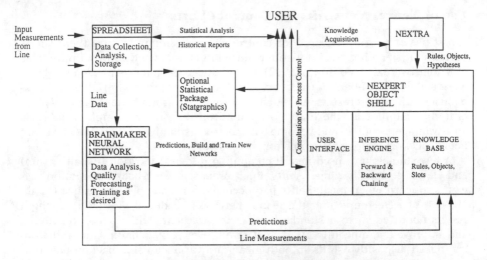

FIG. 14.3. Composite system for statistical process control (Smith and Yazici, 1992).

information may come from line conditions, product attributes, or knowledge of the line operators or other personnel. Melding this information, if it is present, with the output of a neural network will result in a robust system that considers all pertinent factors. This also alleviates the drawback to the user of the pure neural network approach being essentially a black box.

REFERENCES

Alexander, S. M., and Jagannathan, V. 1986. Advisory system for control chart. *Computers & Industrial Engineering*, 10:171–177.

Andersen, K., Cook, G. E., Karsai, G., and Ramaswamy, K. 1990. Artificial neural networks applied to arc welding process modeling and control. *IEEE Transactions on Industry Applications* 26:824–830.

Ben Brahim, S., Smith, A. E., and Bidanda, B. 1992. Estimating product performance and quality from design parameters via neural networks. *Proc. of the IIE Research Conference*, pp. 319–323.

Burke, L. I. 1989. Automated identification of tool wear states in machining processes: An application of self-organizing neural networks, Ph.D. thesis, University of California, Berkeley.

Cariapa, V., Akbay, S. A., and Rudraraju, R. 1991. Application of neural networks for compliant tool polishing operation. In *Computer-Aided Production Engineering*, ed. V. Venkatesh and J. McGeough, 271–280. Amsterdam: Elsevier.

Chryssolouris, G., Lee, M., Pierce, J., and Domroese, M. 1989. Use of neural networks for the design of manufacturing systems. *Proc. of the Winter Annual Meeting of the American Society of Mechanical Engineers*, 57–63.

Dagli, C. H., and Smith, A. E. 1991. A prototype quality control expert system integrated with an optimization module. *Proc. of the World Congress on Expert Systems*, pp. 1959–1966.

Dybeck, M. 1987. Taking process automation one step further: SPC. *Proc. of the Sixth Annual Control Engineering Conference*, 643–651.

Eid, M. S., and Losier, G. 1990. QCMS: A quality control management system. *Computers & Industrial Engineering* 19:495–499.

Evans, J. R., and Lindsay, W. M. 1988. A framework for expert system development in statistical quality control. *Computers & Industrial Engineering* 14:335–343.

Gibra, I. N. 1975. Recent developments in control chart techniques. *Journal of Quality Technology* 7:183–192.

Guillot, M., and El Ouafi, A. 1991. On-line identification of tool breakage in metal cutting processes by use of neural networks. In *Intelligent Engineering Systems Through Artificial Neural Networks*, ed. C. Dagli, S. Kumara, and Y. Shin, 701–709. New York: ASME Press.

Guo, Y., and Dooley, K. J. 1990. The application of neural networks to a diagnostic problem in quality control. In *Monitoring and Control for Manufacturing Processes*. New York: ASME, 111–122.

Hosni, Y. A., and Elshennawy, A. K. 1988. Knowledge-based quality control. *Computers & Industrial Engineering* 15:331–337.

Hung, S. L., and Adeli, H. 1991. A model of perceptron learning with a hidden layer for engineering design. *Neurocomputing* 3:3–14.

Hwarng, H. B., and Hubele, N. F. 1991. X-bar chart pattern recognition using neural nets. *ASQC Quality Congress Transactions*, 884–889.

Knapp, G. M., and Wang, H.-P. 1992. Machine fault classification: A neural network approach. *International Journal of Production Research* 30:811–823.

Lawrence, J. 1991. Data preparation for a neural network. *AI Expert* 6:34–41.

Liu, L., and Liu, G. H. 1990. Neural network computing applied in design for manufacturability. *Proc. of the IEEE/SEMI International Semiconductor Manufacturing Science Symposium*, 107–110.

Miller, R. K., and Walker, T. C. 1988. *Artificial Intelligence Applications in Manufacturing*. Madison, Georgia: SEAI Publications.

Montgomery, D. C. 1980. The economic design of control charts: A review and literature survey. *Journal of Quality Technology* 12:75–87.

Okafor, A. C., Marcus, M., and Tipirneni, R. 1990. Multiple sensor integration via neural networks for estimating surface roughness and bore tolerance in circular end milling. *1990 Transactions of NAMRI/SME*, 128–137.

Plastics Technology. 1990. Injection in the 90's: How high tech? April 1990, 78–86.

Pugh, G. A. 1989. Synthetic neural networks for process control. *Computers & Industrial Engineering* 17:24–26.

Pugh, G. A. 1991. A comparison of neural networks to SPC charts. *Computers & Industrial Engineering* 21:253–255.

Saniga, E. M., and Shirland, L. E. 1977. Quality control in practice: A survey. *Quality Progress* 10:30–33.

Schmerr, L. W., Nugen, S. M., and Forourachi, B. 1991. Planning robust design experiments using neural networks and Taguchi methods. In *Intelligent Engineering Systems Through Artificial Neural Networks*, ed. C. Dagli, S. Kumara, and Y. Shin, 829–834. New York: ASME Press.

Scott, L. L., and ElGomayel, J. I. 1987. Development of a rule-based system for statistical process control chart interpretation. *Quality: Design, Planning, and Control*, ed. R. E. DeVor and S. G. Kapoor, 73–91. New York: ASME Press.

Shewhart, W. A. 1931. *Economic Control of Quality of Manufactured Product*. Princeton: Van Nostrand Reinhold.

Smith, A. E. 1992. Control chart representation and analysis via backpropagation neural networks. *Proc. of the 1992 International Fuzzy Systems and Intelligent Control Conference,* 275–282.

Smith, A. E. 1993. Predicting product quality with backpropagation: A thermoplastic injection moldingcase study. *International Journal of Advanced Manufacturing Technology* 8:252–257.

Smith, A. E., and Dagli, C. H. 1991. Controlling industrial processes through supervised, feedforward neural networks. *Computers & Industrial Engineering* 21:247–251.

Smith, A. E., and Yazici, H. 1992. An intelligent composite system for statistical process control. *Engineering Applications of Artificial Intelligence,* 5:519–526.

Suri, R., and Shimizu, M. 1989. Design for analysis: A new strategy to improve the design process. *Research in Engineering Design* 1:105–120.

Willborn, W. W. O. 1990. Expert systems in support of quality management. *ASQC Quality Congress Transactions,* 758–763.

Wu, H.-J., Liou, C.-S., and Pi, H.-H. 1991. Fault diagnosis of processing damage in injection molding via neural network approach. In *Intelligent Engineering Systems Through Artificial Neural Networks,* ed. C. Dagli, S. Kumara, and Y. Shin, 645–650. New York: ASME Press.

Yazici, H. and Smith, A. E. 1992. A composite system approach for intelligent quality control. *Proc. of the IIE Research Conference,* 325–328.

Zarefar, H., and Goulding, J. R. 1992. Neural networks in design of products: A case study. In *Intelligent Design and Manufacturing,* ed. A. Kusiak, 179–201, New York: John Wiley & Sons.

Chapter 15

A Knowledge-Based Environment for Signal Integrity Problem Detection and Correction

Evangelos Simoudis
Lockheed AI Center
Palo Alto, California

15.1 INTRODUCTION

It is often the case that after a digital system is manufactured it does not work as its designers intended it to. The reason for such malfunction can usually be traced to problems on one or more of the printed circuit boards (pcb) that comprise the system. A printed circuit board contains circuit networks. These are structures that consist of drivers, essentially logic gate outputs, receivers, namely logic gate inputs, and terminators, namely resistors, and clamp diode networks. All the elements of a network are interconnected via transmission lines.

After the design of a digital system is complete, the database that contains the design information and design constraints is given to the manufacturing organization. One of the steps that has to be performed during the manufacturing process includes laying out onto printed circuit boards the circuit networks that comprise the digital system. This step is performed by a layout tool that utilizes information about company-specific manufacturing constraints. The designers are not always aware of the manufacturing constraints and, therefore, do not take them into account during the design phase. In the process of satisfying the manufacturing constraints, the layout tool will often violate the design constraints. For the system to be acceptable it must comply with both the design constraints and the manufacturing constraints.

The violation of one type of design constraint gives rise to *signal integrity problems*. The three most common signal integrity problems in digital systems include violations of

(1) The noise margins that are imposed by the designers on each logic device,
(2) The timing constraints the network has to obey, and
(3) Cross talk between circuits.

The faster logic device switching speeds, and the drive for higher densities of integrated circuits that are laid out on printed circuit boards, is causing more signal integrity problems to become visible now than in earlier years. The companies that design digital systems employ signal integrity engineers who carry, in addition to their electrical engineering knowledge, knowledge about the various pcb processes and technologies. These engineers correct signal integrity problems by considering the behavioral and structural characteristics of each component of every circuit network that is part of a specific pcb. In order to obtain the behavioral characteristics of the network, the engineers model each component, simulate the network, analyze the simulation results to find signal integrity problems, and try to diagnose the cause of each problem. When signal integrity problems are detected, the original circuit network is redesigned so that the problems can be eliminated. This time, however, the manufacturing constraints are taken into consideration.

Discovering and correcting signal integrity problems is difficult for four reasons:

(1) The character of the signal seen on a digital circuit network is often a combination of different signal integrity problems. The individual problems must be identified, and their possible interactions have to be known before attempting to solve each problem. Once the interactions are known, solving one problem can result in the automatic solution of some of the others.

(2) Sometimes there are no obvious solutions to signal integrity problems, whereas other times there is no unique solution to each problem.

(3) The changes made to the topology and the geometry of a faulty circuit as a result of redesigning are likely to affect the behavior of more than one component in the circuit.

(4) There is a lack of published material that specifically addresses this process even within a company. As a result, few well-trained signal integrity engineers exist who can deal with all the circuit designs that are generated today.

In order to deal with the preceding difficulties, a methodology has been developed, to be used by designers, for *evaluating* circuit networks in order to discover signal integrity problems, and for *redesigning* the faulty circuit networks. Evaluation consists of the following phases:

(1) Simulation—to obtain the circuit's behavior
(2) Analysis—to detect signal integrity problems

If signal integrity problems are detected, the methodology prescribes ways of diagnosing the causes of each of the problems detected and redesigning the circuit in order to solve the problems. Redesign involves the alteration of a circuit's structure.

The methodology addresses the majority of the signal integrity problems that are encountered in digital circuit designs. Signal integrity engineers are still expected to solve the problems that are encountered less frequently in a design. However, even the knowledge that is incorporated in the methodology changes over time. Such changes are inevitable as the various circuit technologies and manufacturing processes evolve. Furthermore, each design group may use its own criteria for deciding how to redesign a faulty system. The redesign knowledge seems to change most frequently. Therefore, to guarantee that the methodology does not become outdated, it was imperative to devise ways of incrementally acquiring redesign knowledge.

In order to effectively implement an environment that incorporates the methodology along with a redesign knowledge acquisition component, artificial intelligence techniques were used. An environment was implemented consisting of two major components: the Transmission Line Troubleshooting System (TLTS), which is used for the detection and correction of signal integrity problems, and REKL, a tool for automatically acquiring new redesign knowledge of the type used by the redesign components of TLTS. In particular the methodology used analysis and diagnosis knowledge-based systems, planning techniques for the implementation of the redesign function, and machine learning techniques for the implementation of REKL. The majority of the knowledge in the methodology is company proprietary. However, it is expected that other companies have similar proprietary evaluation and redesign knowledge which they can incorporate into a framework similar to the one described here.

This environment is being integrated into a printed circuit board *designer's suite of tools*. By using the environment, the designer can detect and correct the majority of signal integrity problems he or she is introducing in the design *before* the design is either prototyped or manufactured. This style of designing digital systems is much cheaper than the more traditional style in which signal integrity problems are detected and corrected after a board has been prototyped or, worse, after it has been manufactured. Furthermore, the methodology identifies the types of knowledge that need to be communicated between design and manufacturing.

15.2 PREMISES OF THE METHODOLOGY

In order to effectively deal with signal integrity problems, a methodology was developed for simulating circuit networks, analyzing the simulation results to find the problems, diagnosing the causes that have been identified through the analysis, and redesigning the faulty networks in order to solve the problems. The methodology is applicable to all circuit networks regardless of (1) the fabrication technologies of the drivers and the receivers, and (2) the topology of the networks. A description of the circuit analysis, diagnosis, and redesign knowledge that is used by the methodology is given later. The organization of knowledge within the methodology is based on two premises

(1) Circuit evaluation is facilitated if it is performed hierarchically.
(2) Because there may be many ways of redesigning a circuit to solve a signal integrity problem, selection criteria must be developed so that each time a circuit needs to be redesigned, the most appropriate way to redesign is chosen.

Hierarchical Evaluation

Because the character of the signal seen on a digital circuit network is often a combination of different signal integrity problems, evaluation can be facilitated if it is performed hierarchically. In this hierarchy, the most obvious signal integrity problems are identified first. Once these are solved, the circuit can be evaluated in a more detailed way so that any other, less obvious signal integrity problems are revealed and corrected. The most obvious signal integrity problems are the ones which are related to

(1) Violations of DC current/voltage levels
(2) Propagation delay violations

To identify these problems, the circuit is simulated using heuristic methods. Heuristic simulation helps the designer understand the device with which he or she is dealing, and creates a basis that can be used later for understanding the output of the simulation that is based on detailed behavioral models of this device. For example, assume that a designer wants the signal of a circuit's driver to reach the last receiver in the circuit within 10.5 ns. The propagation delay can be determined heuristically by using the length of the transmission lines between the driver and the receiver in question and the total capacitance of each circuit device and its package. Analysis of these results, the circuit's structure, and the user's specifications determines if a propagation delay problem exists. Diagnosis knowledge determines the cause of the problem. Rough redesign is then performed and solves the problem to the extent the first level of evaluation is concerned. The fact that the circuit has a propagation delay problem is propagated to the second level of evaluation.

The second level of evaluation is responsible for revealing problems which are related to violations of:

(1) The dynamic response of the circuit
(2) Noise margins

The problems at this level are revealed by simulating the detailed behavioral models of each circuit component and taking into account the problems that were revealed in the first level of evaluation. For example, if the analysis that follows the simulation reveals that a propagation delay problem still exists in the circuit, further redesign is performed. TLTS does not have to examine the possibility of the propagation delay being the side effect of some other signal integrity problem because of the conclusions that were established by the first level of evaluation. Therefore, the results of the detailed simulation are better utilized through the use of the two-level evaluation.

The lack of an evaluation hierarchy has been forcing designers to look directly into the detailed behavioral models of the faulty circuit. For example, in order for the designer to find the propagation delay problem without using the hierarchy:

(1) The detailed model of each device in the circuit has to be simulated.
(2) The simulation results have to be analyzed. If the designer's timing specification is not satisfied then a propagation problem exists. The

causes of the propagation delay problem have to be diagnosed, and the designer, utilizing a knowledge of signal integrity problem interactions, has to deduce that this problem is not the side effect of some other signal integrity problem.

(3) A way of redesigning the circuit to solve the propagation delay problem has to be identified and implemented.

(4) The circuit has to be resimulated to verify that the problem has been solved. If the problem is not solved, the preceding process has to be repeated. Due to the complexity of steps 2 and 3, circuit evaluation must be performed by well-trained engineers, thus delaying the time a pcb is ready for production.

Selecting the Appropriate Redesign Method

For each signal integrity problem that can be identified through evaluation, there are methods for redesigning a faulty circuit in order to solve the problem. Each method contains several modifications that can be made to a faulty circuit. To correct the problems that are revealed by the first level of evaluation, simple modifications are made to the circuit. These modifications consist of changing devices that belong to the circuit or adding devices to it. The modifications which are made in order to correct signal integrity problems that are revealed by the second level of evaluation are more detailed and affect other components of the circuit network such as transmission lines, packages, vias, and so on.

Because there may be many candidate methods for redesigning a faulty circuit, it was necessary to identify the criteria that needed to be considered while selecting the appropriate redesign method. A redesign method is appropriate if it has a high probability of solving a signal integrity problem. The selection criteria are partitioned into two classes. The criteria in the first class consider the performance requirements the user places on the circuit. They also express the restrictions placed by the technology specifications. In other words, they express the necessary and sufficient conditions that need to be satisfied in order for the design to be acceptable. The criteria in the second class capture preferences to manufacturing process, the cost of redesigning the circuit in a particular way, pc board space dependencies, and design process limits. Selection knowledge is expressed by using criteria either from the first class only or by using criteria from both classes. The same set of criteria is used in the selection knowledge responsible for choosing a redesign method to solve problems that are revealed by either level of evaluation.

For example, suppose that the driver of the network does not supply enough current to the receivers to put them in the high logic state, but it does supply enough current for the low logic state. Further suppose that (1) there is another, unused driver available on the driver's package, (2) minimum layout cost is required, and (3) no space on the pc board exists for additional integrated circuits. Under these specifications, the most appropriate way to redesign the circuit to solve the signal strength problem is to add to it another driver from the ones available in the existing driver's package. If minimum layout cost is not an issue, then replacing the circuit's driver, namely replacing the integrated circuit that contains the driver, with another whose specifications match the designer's requirements, could be considered as an alternative way of redesigning the faulty circuit. The criteria in the second class may vary between design groups or even between designers within the same design group.

15.3 THE ARCHITECTURE

The knowledge of the methodology was organized around a blackboard architecture. There is a separate blackboard system for each level of evaluation and redesign. Each system contains a blackboard, knowledge sources, and a control knowledge source. The *blackboard* contains the circuit that is being evaluated, the simulation results, the signal integrity problems associated with the circuit, the causes of each signal integrity problem, and redesign goals. Each of the simulation, analysis, and diagnosis modules, as well as each of the redesign methods, is represented as a *knowledge source*. REKL is also a separate knowledge source. The *control knowledge source* determines which of the knowledge sources that are eligible for operating on the blackboard will execute its actions. Details about each blackboard, the knowledge sources, and the control knowledge source are given in Simoudi (1989). The first blackboard, a number of the knowledge sources, and some of the data flow paths between the blackboard and the corresponding knowledge sources are shown in Fig. 15.1. The uses of a blackboard architecture are as follows:

- Supports modularity. A uniform interface between each knowledge source and the blackboard is established. The existence of such an interface allows the independent development of each knowledge source.
- Guarantees expandability. New knowledge sources may need to be created as the engineers' experience in solving signal integrity problems increases. The existence of a uniform interface between the knowledge sources and the blackboard ensures that new knowledge sources can be created and added into the architecture at any time. As long as each knowledge source has the same interface as all the other knowledge sources, its addition will not influence the operation of the entire system.

Furthermore, existing knowledge sources can be replaced. Knowledge sources may need to be replaced when a version of TLTS is tailored to the needs of a particular user group. For example, if it is decided in the future that the simulator SPICE should not be used by TLTS, a new simulator can be easily fitted in the blackboard architecture. In addition, knowledge sources may need to be modified because their use has shown that the knowledge they contain is incorrect.

- Provides flexibility by allowing the knowledge sources to function autonomously as well as cohesively. This means that (1) each knowledge source retains its own task-specific view of simulation, analysis,

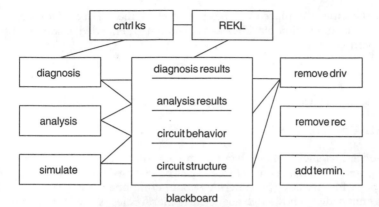

**FIG. 15.1. Data flow paths between blackboard
and corresponding knowledge sources.**

diagnosis, or redesign, and (2) the blackboard provides a communication medium common to all knowledge sources which allows knowledge sources to cooperate toward the solution of a problem.

The levels of each blackboard in TLTS are represented as instances of an object. Each knowledge source, including the control knowledge source, is also represented as an instance of an object. The object which represents a knowledge source has the following attributes: name, source level, destination level, action rules, eligibility rules, action-cs, and eligibility-cs.

Every knowledge source has a name, a source level, namely the blackboard level the knowledge source examines in order to determine if it can operate on the blackboard, and a destination level, the blackboard level where the knowledge source places the results of its operations. The names of the levels in the two blackboards are shown in Fig. 15.1. The data paths associated with each knowledge source show the source and destination levels of the knowledge source.

The eligibility-rules attribute contains the names of the rules that determine whether or not the knowledge source is eligible for operating on the blackboard given the blackboard's current contents. The action-rules attribute contains the operations that the knowledge source can perform on the blackboard. These operations are also given in rule-based format.

The attribute action-cs contains knowledge for resolving conflicts among rules which arise during the execution of the rules that belong to the action-rules attribute. The attribute eligibility-cs contains similar knowledge for the eligibility rules.

The knowledge of a control knowledge source is placed in the action-rules attribute. The other attributes of this particular knowledge source have no values. The user places the circuit on the first level (called the circuit structure) of the blackboard system which contains the knowledge of the first level of evaluation and redesign. When the processing of the first blackboard system is completed, the circuit is placed on the first level of the second blackboard with a message sent to the first blackboard by the control knowledge source of the first blackboard system.

15.4   KNOWLEDGE REPRESENTATION

Circuit Description Knowledge

Experience has shown that effective network simulation, analysis, problem diagnosis, and redesign require three types of circuit knowledge: (1) knowledge about parts hierarchies, (2) knowledge about component categories, and (3) constraint knowledge. Knowledge about parts hierarchies is used for specifying that a component is part of another component or of a circuit network. For example, a specific driver (call it driver1) is part of a particular circuit network (call it net1). Similarly, a transistor (call it tran1) is part of the driver driver1. The knowledge of parts hierarchies also contains the attributes of each component, the relation between the attributes, and connectivity information between the components. For example, the attributes of a transmission line are characteristic impedance, capacitance, inductance, length, and delay per unit length. Furthermore, the characteristic impedance Z_0, the inductance L, and the capacitance C of a transmission line are related by the equation:

$$Z_0 = \sqrt{} \qquad (1)$$

Therefore, if the inductance and capacitance are known, then the characteristic impedance can be derived from Eq. (1). Portions of the parts hierarchies knowledge of network net1 is shown in Fig. 15.2.

The knowledge about parts hierarchies is used by the simulation and diagnosis knowledge sources. The simulation knowledge sources use the knowledge of parts hierarchies to derive the behavior of a component and of the entire circuit network. For example, a portion of the parts hierarchy associated with driver1 is shown in Fig. 15.3. The following SPICE model is derived for driver1 out of the complete information contained in this hierarchy.

```
.SUBCKT STTLSPC 1 8
VCC100 0 5.0
R1 100 2 3500
R2 100 4 1125
R3 100 6 62.5
R4 7 0 4375
R5 5 10 312.5
R6 5 9 625
*
*
Q1 3 2 1 TR1
Q2 4 3 5 TR1
```

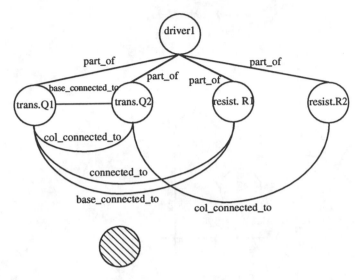

Fig. 15.3. Portion of parts hierarchy associated with driver1.

Q3 6 4 7 TR1
Q4 6 7 8 TR1
Q5 8 5 0 TR1 AREA=2
Q6 10 9 0 TR1
*
*
D1 2 3 D1
D2 3 4 D1
D3 4 6 D1
D5 5 8 D1
D6 9 10 D1
*
*
.MODEL TR1 NPN (BR=.1 IS=1E-16 RB=60 RC=10 RE=1 VA=200 VB=200
+ IK=10MA IKR=10MA TF=.1NS TR=10NS CCS=.5PF CJE=.5PF PE=.7 ME=.33)
*
*
.MODEL D1 D (IS=1E-10 RS=5 TT=.1NS CJO=.5PF EG=.69)
*
*
.ENDS STTLSPC

The knowledge about the parts hierarchies is also used by the redesign knowledge sources. The redesign knowledge sources remove components from a cir-

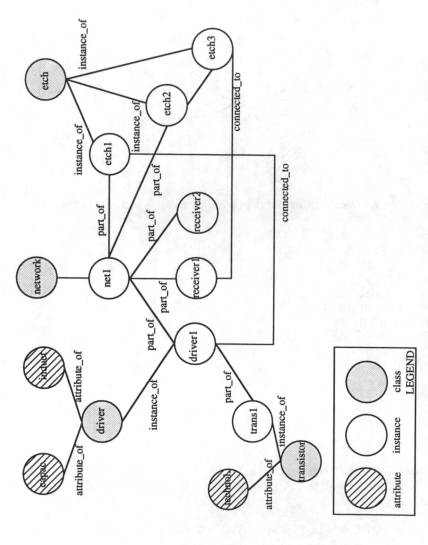

Fig. 15.2 Portions of the parts hierarchies knowledge of network net1.

cuit, add components to it, use circuit components to form new circuits, and change the values of the attributes that describe a component.

Knowledge about component hierarchies is needed for expressing categories of network and device components. For example, a circuit driver is a device. A receiver is also a device. The knowledge about component hierarchies used by TLTS is shown in Fig. 15.4.

By establishing the knowledge about component hierarchies, features and relations that are placed on members of the categories are propagated from the more abstract categories to more specific ones. Therefore, a driver inherits all the features of a generic device such as impedance, capacitance, function, and so on.

Constraint knowledge is used for placing time and signal strength restrictions on the network. For example, the excess current, namely the difference between the current that is sourced by the network's driver and the total current which is sunk by the network's receivers, cannot be less than zero. Therefore, the constraint on the value of the excess current I_{ez} is $I_{ez} \geq 0$.

The circuit knowledge is implemented using object-based programming. Object programming is used because it allows:

- The definition of hierarchies. In this way the knowledge on component hierarchies is defined.
- The definition of attributes, attribute relations, membership relations, and connectivity information. In this way the knowledge of the parts hierarchies is defined.
- The definition constraints.
- The propagation of attributes, and relations along the established hierarchies.

Each circuit network component is an object. Circuit networks are also objects. The part hierarchies knowledge of a specific network consists of pointers to the objects that represent its components. Similarly, the part hierarchies knowledge

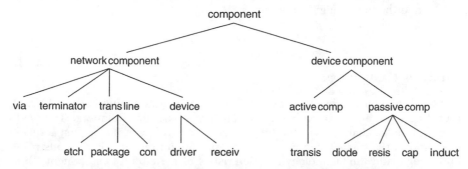

FIG. 15.4. Component hierarchies used by TLTS.

of driver or receiver objects contains pointers to the instances that represent the transistors, the resistors, and so forth that belong to the driver or receiver.

The relations of the attributes of each circuit component are implemented as procedural attachments on each attribute. Constraint knowledge is also implemented as procedural attachments in the form of *demons* on each attribute. When describing a circuit the user selects component descriptions from a database. The descriptions are used for obtaining the attribute values of the objects which belong to the circuit that is being evaluated. The user then describes how the created objects (devices) are connected. During this phase the user specifies the values of the attributes describing each piece of transmission line. Once the circuit is thus described, it is placed by the user on the first level of the blackboard in one of the two blackboard systems. This is done by sending a message to the object representing the level of the blackboard.

Simulation Knowledge

Derivation of the circuit's behavior for the purposes of the first level of evaluation is done through the use of simple equations. These equations use the parts hierarchies knowledge that describes the electrical and physical properties of each circuit component.

Derivation of the circuit's behavior for the purposes of the second level of evaluation is done by the simulator SPICE. TLTS uses the following:

(1) The knowledge of parts hierarchies that identifies the low-level components of a device (transistors, resistors, etc.) and their connectivity. From this information, the simulation knowledge source builds the subcircuits that will be used in the SPICE input file.

(2) The knowledge of parts hierarchies with connectivity between the components of the circuit network and the characteristics of the interconnecting transmission lines. From this information the SPICE input file is completed and the duration of the simulation is determined. A separate input file is created for the simulation of the high to low transition and the low to high transition.

Analysis Knowledge

The analysis phase consists of examining the network's simulation results and revealing signal integrity problems by detecting constraint violations. The analysis knowledge that is used for the detection of problems in the first level of evaluation uses rules which correlate the simulation results, circuit constraint knowledge, and the technology characteristics of the circuit's components. For example, *detect-prop-delays1*

IF the first receiver violates the timing constraints imposed by the user

AND at least one more receiver violates timing constraints imposed by the user

THEN deduce propagation delay problem

In order to detect problems in the second level of evaluation, the analysis component examines the information that is generated from the SPICE output data. Such information includes:

(1) The knee of each waveform.
(2) Nonmonotonicities which exist in the region of each waveform that lies between the two voltage values representing the fabrication technology's thresholds. For each such nonmonotonicity the following information is also derived:
   (a) The beginning and end points of a nonmonotonicity curve
   (b) The highest or lowest point of the curve
   (c) The energy under the curve
   (d) Whether the energy under the curve can be canceled out by the negative energy of a curve having opposite polarity
(3) Plateaux is the part of the waveform that lies between the two threshold voltages. The points which form each plateau are also saved.
(4) Reflections. After a device switches logic state, it is important that it remains in that state for the duration of the simulation. Every time a reflection is identified the following information is derived:
   (a) The beginning and end points of the reflection curve
   (b) The highest or lowest point of the curve
   (c) The energy under the curve
   (d) Whether the curve is the superposition of two other reflection curves

This information is then used by rules, where it is compared to the constraint knowledge in order for constraint violations, namely signal integrity problems, to be detected. For example,

detect-prop-delays2

IF the simulated propagation delay of the receiver is 10% higher than the constraint placed by the user

THEN deduce propagation delay problem

All the signal integrity problems in a network within a particular level of analysis are identified simultaneously. In case multiple signal integrity problems exist, TLTS prioritizes them in order to decide which problem to solve first. Prioritizing requires that knowledge about problem interactions is represented explicitly.

Diagnostic Knowledge

The TLTS has two diagnostic knowledge sources, one for each level of evaluation. The diagnostic knowledge sources take as input for determining causes of problems the signal integrity problem (constraint violation) that was identified through analysis and the parts hierarchies knowledge of the circuit being analyzed. During the diagnosis phase, TLTS uses constraint propagation to trace the source of the constraint violation. Each diagnostic knowledge source is rule based. An example of a diagnostic rule is the following:

diagnose-prop-delays1

IF a propagation delay problem has been deduced

AND the circuit has a cluster of receivers

THEN the cause of the problem is due to the capacitance of the cluster

The preceding rule accesses the parameters of the equation that is used for the calculation of the propagation delay (the constraint which was violated), determines that capacitance is one of the parameters in the equation, and then tries to determine if there exists in the network a cluster of receivers which includes the problem receiver.

All the causes for the signal integrity problem with the highest priority are identified simultaneously. If multiple causes are found, they are prioritized. In establishing priorities between the detected causes, TLTS uses knowledge about signal integrity problem interrelations. The cause with the highest priority is the one whose elimination will result in the solution of the signal integrity problem under consideration.

Redesign Knowledge

In order to redesign a faulty circuit network, TLTS uses the topology and geometry of the circuit, any user established constraints, the signal integrity problem with the highest priority, and the most probable cause of this problem. For each signal integrity problem that can be identified through evaluation, there exists knowledge sources which contain redesign knowledge, and whose application is aimed at solving the signal integrity problem.

Redesign Knowledge Sources

A redesign knowledge source contains:

(1) Knowledge for determining if the knowledge source is capable of solving a particular signal integrity problem,
(2) A set of redesign goals,
(3) A collection of *redesign operators* that achieve the goals, and
(4) Knowledge for controlling the execution of the operators.

Every knowledge source contains a set of production rules which determine if the knowledge source can operate on the blackboard. As was mentioned in section 15.3, these rules are called *eligibility demons*. The left-hand side (LHS) of each such rule specifies a set of conditions under which the knowledge source can operate on the blackboard. In the case of the redesign knowledge sources, these conditions take into account the analysis and diagnosis results, as well as any constraints the user has imposed on the circuit. For example, the production rule called *remove-receivers-eligible1* specifies one set of conditions under which the knowledge source called *remove receivers* can operate on the blackboard:

remove-receivers-eligible1

 IF a propagation delay problem has been detected

 AND the cause is due to the capacitance of a cluster of receivers

 THEN the knowledge source *remove receivers* is eligible

Rather than having a separate rule for each set of eligibility conditions, the knowledge source could have had a single production rule with a disfunction of sets of conditions in its LHS. Such an implementation would have resulted in a smaller rule base. However, it would have been difficult to debug, maintain, and augment such rules due to the complexity of their LHS. The process of how to select which of the eligible knowledge sources to invoke is described later in the chapter.

When a redesign knowledge source is invoked, a plan for redesigning the faulty circuit has to be formed out of the operators that belong to the knowledge source. The first step in this process is for all the goals that the knowledge source contains to be posted on the blackboard. This does not imply that all of the goals need to be achieved in every plan which is formed out of the operators. It does imply however that at least some of the goals will need to be achieved. For example, removing a receiver from a circuit involves two steps: (1) removing the receiver, and (2) removing the circuit element that connects the receiver to the rest of the circuit. Such an element may be a connector, a piece of etch, or a via.

The knowledge source called *remove receivers* that is considered every time a cluster of receivers in the circuit are responsible for a propagation delay problem, has the following goals: remove a receiver, remove an etch, remove a via, and remove a connector. Assume that receivers *re3* and *re4* that belong to the circuit shown in Fig. 15.5 are responsible for the propagation problem that was detected. In a plan to eliminate these receivers from the circuit, the goal remove an etch will be achievable, whereas the goals remove a via and remove a connector cannot be achieved.

A plan consists of instantiations of the redesign operators that belong to the knowledge source that has been invoked. Each redesign operator is represented as a production rule. The LHS of each operator describes the conditions under which a redesign operation may be performed. These conditions express circuit topology characteristics and constraints placed by the user/designer on the circuit element on which the operator is applied. The knowledge expressed in the LHS of the eligibility rules allows the LHS of the redesign operators to remain

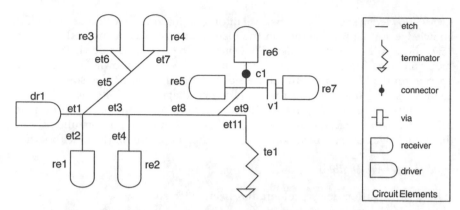

FIG. 15.5. Circuit and circuit elements; receivers re3 and re4 are responsible for propagation problem.

simple. If eligibility rules did not exist, the knowledge currently expressed in the LHS of such rules would have had to be included in the LHS of the redesign operators. As a result of the simplicity of each operator's LHS, every redesign operator can belong to several knowledge sources. For example, the operator called *remove etches* is part of the knowledge sources called *remove receivers* and *remove branches*.

Associated with each operator is the redesign goal that the operator can achieve. When the conditions in the LHS and the goal the operator can satisfy match against the contents of the blackboard, the operator is considered for inclusion in the redesign plan being formed. If the conditions of a particular operator are not satisfied and no other operators exist that can substitute for the failing operator, the plan formation process is abandoned. At this time if there exists other redesign knowledge sources which are eligible for operating on the blackboard then one is selected. Otherwise control is returned to the user.

The right-hand side (RHS) of a redesign operator describes the operation and takes care of the side effects that result from the operation. For example, if a receiver is removed from the circuit then all the circuit elements that were connected to it have to be informed of this change. This is done by sending messages to the object instances that represent these circuit elements. An operator, called *remove-etches*, which can remove a piece of etch from the circuit is shown. A piece of etch is removed whenever only one of its two ends is connected to another circuit element.

remove-etch

IF no network element is connected to the one end of an etch

AND the user has specified that the piece of etch can be removed

THEN remove this etch from the network

GOAL remove an etch

It is not always possible to guarantee that the collection of operators a knowledge source contains is complete. Operators may not be included in a knowledge source because it is assumed they will not be used within a particular redesign context. By making explicit the redesign goals that are part of each redesign knowledge source and the goal that each operator can satisfy, the user of TLTS can identify missing goals and, consequently, missing operators.

During the plan formation process, depending on the topology of the faulty circuit, some operators may be used in the plan more than once, whereas others may not be used at all. For example, the knowledge source called *remove receivers* has operators with the following names: *remove-receiver, remove-etch, remove-connector, remove-via, move-terminator, retrieve-device, place-device, place-etch*, and *place-connector*. If receivers *re3* and *re4* need to be removed from the network in Fig. 15.5, the following actions are involved: (1) removing receivers *re3* and *re4* (performed by the operator *remove-receiver* which will need to be included in the plan twice), (2) removing etches *et5, et6*, and *et7* (performed by the operator *remove-etch* which will need to be included in the plan three times). These network elements once removed will have to be placed on a new network that will have a driver identical to the driver of the original circuit. This requires: (3) retrieving a driver from a component database (performed by the operator *retrieve-device*), (4) placing and connecting etches that are identical to *et1, et5, et6* and *et7* from the network of Fig. 15.5 (the operator *place-etch* will need to be included in the plan four times), and (5) connecting receivers *re3* and *re4* to this new network (performed by the operator *place-device*).

Determining the sequence in which the redesign operators will be executed in a plan is very important. Inappropriate sequencing will lead to interactions which may prevent a redesign plan from succeeding. For this reason it is necessary to associate operator control knowledge with each redesign knowledge source. The control knowledge is in the form of rules. The rule for resolving the conflict between the operators *remove-receiver* and *remove-etch* that was encountered in step (2) of this example is the following:

sched-rule11

    IF the operator *remove-etch* is eligible

    AND the operator *remove-receiver* is eligible

    THEN prefer the operator *remove-receiver*

These rules are invoked at each step of the redesign plan formation process. They accept all the redesign operators that can be applied during a redesign step and decide which operators should be applied during the step. They also decide how many instantiations of a particular operator will be applied during a redesign step. For example, the operator called *remove-receivers* is instantiated twice in the course of redesigning the circuit in Fig. 15.5. Both instantiations can be applied during the same step or they can be applied during separate steps.

Once the sequencing of the operators in a plan is determined, the plan is executed on the circuit being redesigned. The plan for removing receivers *re3* and *re4* is the following: (1) remove receiver *re3*, (2) remove receiver *re4*, (3) remove etch *et6*, (4) remove etch *et7*, (5) remove etch *et5*, (6) retrieve driver, (7) place driver, (8) place copy of etch *et1*, (9) place etch *et5*, (10) place etch *et6*, (11) place etch *et7*, (12) place receiver *re3*, and (13) place receiver *re4*.

The execution of a plan does not guarantee that the signal integrity problem is eliminated from the faulty circuit. Evaluation follows the redesign phase. If the evaluation reveals that signal integrity problems are still present, the diagnosis and redesign phases are repeated. The capability of TLTS to interleave evaluation and redesign allows the tool to determine how to proceed during the next pass through the evaluation-redesign loop. In the domain of TLTS, if the signal integrity problem with the highest priority is not solved within three evaluation-redesign iterations, the redesign path that was initially taken by the tool is abandoned. The user's help is then sought. In particular, the user needs to instruct TLTS where to backtrack so that a different redesign path can be pursued in order to attempt to solve the same signal integrity problem. When the backtracking point is decided, TLTS establishes on the blackboard the appropriate faulty circuit and starts the redesign phase. Other options that the user has on backtracking are

(1) Relax the constraints placed on the original circuit and instruct TLTS to attempt to solve the same signal integrity problem.
(2) Instruct TLTS to attempt to solve a different signal integrity problem, if one exists.

Control Knowledge Source

Selecting which of the eligible knowledge sources will operate on the blackboard is particularly important in the case of redesign knowledge sources. An inappropriate or random choice of redesign knowledge source may delay or make impossible the attainment of a problem-free circuit. It may also lead to signal integrity problem interactions. Namely, while trying to solve one signal integrity problem others may be created or future modifications of the circuit may be impossible because of the redesign knowledge source chosen.

As was mentioned earlier, criteriahas been developed for selecting the most appropriate way of redesigning a faulty circuit, given a set of user specifications. These criteria are combined in a special type of rule in TLTS, which play the role of *meta-rules*. Each meta-rule accepts a set of eligible knowledge sources and determines which knowledge source will operate on the blackboard. The meta-rules form the knowledge of the control knowledge source of a blackboard system. An example of a meta-rule is the following:

meta-rule12

IF a signal propagation delay problem has been detected

AND the problem is attributed to a cluster of receivers

AND space exists on the pc board

AND the knowledge source *remove receivers* is eligible

AND the knowledge source *shorten etch lengths* is eligible

THEN select the knowledge source *remove receivers*

This selection is made because the knowledge in the knowledge source *remove receivers* removes receivers from a circuit and forms a different circuit with them. Because there is space on the board, this new circuit will be able to be laid out. Hence the selection of the knowledge source *remove receivers*.

When a plan cannot be formed out of the operators that are included in the redesign knowledge source which was selected by the control knowledge source, another knowledge source has to be selected. In this case, the redesign knowledge source selected is the one that was considered when the failing knowledge source was selected. If a situation like this arises in the preceding example, then the knowledge source called *shorten etch lengths* will be invoked.

The knowledge in the meta-rules can also be incomplete. Due to incomplete knowledge it is not always possible to solve a signal integrity problem within three iterations through the evaluation-redesign loop because the most appropriate redesign knowledge source may not be invoked. In these cases, the backtracking strategy of TLTS is utilized.

During the testing of the detailed simulation–analysis–diagnosis–redesign loop in this study, an interesting discovery was made. It was observed that the meta-rules used during the redesign phase vary between different groups of circuit designers and signal integrity engineers. A learning component was designed and implemented that allows TLTS to acquire new meta-rules from each of its users, should these be different from the ones the tool already has.

For cases when the meta-rules cannot identify only one knowledge source to take control of the blackboard, TLTS has the capability of concurrently invoking all the chosen redesign knowledge sources. Each invoked knowledge source creates its own copy of the faulty circuit network. When all the invoked knowledge sources finish executing, the user selects which of the redesigned circuits will be evaluated. Because of this selection, the redesign space is evaluated in depth first. Therefore, when TLTS decides to backtrack because it has not been able to solve a signal integrity problem within three evaluation–redesign iterations, it needs to be instructed by the user if it should follow one of the unexplored branches of the redesign space, in an attempt to solve the same signal integrity problem, or if it should attempt to solve a different signal integrity problem.

15.5 A DETAILED EXAMPLE

Assume the designer has created the circuit shown in Fig. 15.6. The devices in this circuit are implemented in TTL technology. Assume that the designer wants the driver's signal to reach the first receiver in the circuit in 6.2 ns and the second receiver in 7.3 ns. The design places the circuit in the first level (circuit structure) of the first blackboard system so that the circuit can be evaluated.

The first step in the evaluation process is the simulation of the circuit's behavior. The simulation knowledge source places the simulation results of the circuit

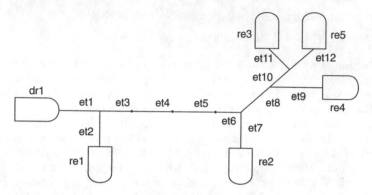

FIG. 15.6. Example circuit.

for the transition from the high state to the low state on the second level of the blackboard. These results are shown in Fig. 15.7.

The analysis knowledge source examines the simulation results and reveals that the driver's signal reaches the first receiver in 10.3 ns and the second receiver in 7.5 ns. The rule called *detect-prop-delay1*, which belongs to the analysis knowledge source of the first blackboard based system and whose definition was given in the section that describes the analysis knowledge of TLTS, executes because

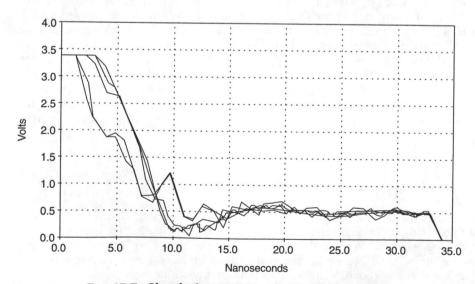

FIG. 15.7. Simulation results of the circuit for the transition from the high state to the low state.

its conditions are satisfied. This rule places its conclusion, namely that a propagation delay problem exists in the circuit, on the third level of the blackboard. It is assumed that no other rules from this knowledge source are executed.

The diagnosis knowledge source is then invoked in order to determine the cause of the detected propagation delay problem. The rule called *diagnose-prop-delays1* from this knowledge source is executed and determines that the propagation delay is due to the capacitance of the cluster of receivers *re3*, *re4*, and *re5*. This result is placed on the fourth level of the blackboard. The redesign knowledge sources examine the analysis and diagnosis results to determine which knowledge source will be eligible for redesigning the faulty circuit. The eligibility rule called *remove-receivers-eligible1* which belongs to the knowledge source *remove receivers* will execute. The execution of this rule informs the control knowledge source of the first blackboard system that the knowledge source *remove receivers* is eligible for redesigning the faulty circuit and will attempt to solve the detected signal integrity problem. It is assumed that the knowledge source called *shorten etch lengths* is also eligible for redesigning the circuit. This implies that an eligibility rule similar to *remove- receivers-eligible1* was executed and informed the control knowledge source that the knowledge source *shorten etch lengths* is eligible to solve the propagation delay problem.

Once all the appropriate eligibility rules are executed, the control knowledge source has to determine which knowledge source will operate on the faulty circuit because two knowledge sources are candidates for doing so. In order to make such a determination, the meta-rules which belong to this control knowledge source will be invoked. The meta-rule called *meta-rule12*, whose definition was given earlier, will execute because the two knowledge sources that are described in the LHS of this rule are eligible and the use has not placed any constraints on the available pc board space. As a result, the redesign knowledge source called *remove receivers* is selected to be invoked.

The knowledge source will form a plan to redesign the faulty circuit out of the operators which it contains. This plan will be similar to the one presented in the section describing the redesign knowledge of TLTS. The plan is the following: (1) remove receiver *re3*, (2) remove receiver *re5*, (3) remove receiver *re4*, (4) remove etch *et11*, (5) remove etch *et12*, (6) remove etch *10*, (7) remove etch *et9*, (8) remove etch *8*, (9) retrieve driver, (10) place driver, (11) place copy of etch *et1*, (12) place copy of etch *et3*, (13) place copy of etch *et4*, (14) place copy of etch *et5*, (15) place copy of etch *et6*, (16) place etch *et8*, (17) place etch *et9*, (18) place etch *et10*, (19) place etch *et12*, (20) place etch *et11*, (21) place receiver *re4*, (22) place receiver *re5*, (23) place receiver *re3*. The resulting circuits are shown in Fig. 15.8.

The circuit that contains the two receivers *re1* and *re2* is placed on the first level of the blackboard in order to be reevaluated. For this reason, the circuit is first simulated. The simulation results, which are placed on the second level of the blackboard, are shown in Fig. 15.9.

The propagation delay of the signal from the driver to the receiver *re1* is 6 ns and the propagation delay to the second receiver *re2* is 7.2 ns. Because both of these propagation delays satisfy the designer's constraints, none of the rules in the analysis knowledge source will execute. This signals the control knowledge source that the processing in the first blackboard system has completed. The con-

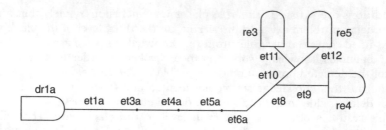

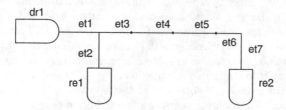

FIG. 15.8. Results of plan to redesign faulty circuit.

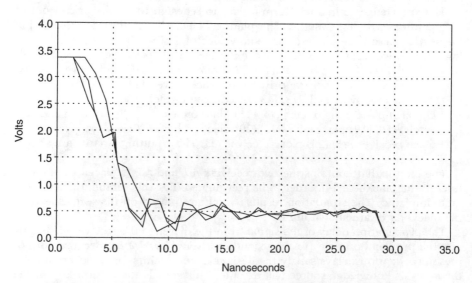

FIG. 15.9. Simulation results from second blackboard level.

trol knowledge source proceeds by sending a message to the second blackboard system, which places the redesigned circuit on the first level of the blackboard of the second blackboard system. For the purposes of this example, it is assumed that the evaluation of the circuits has revealed no more signal integrity problems. At this point the processing stops and the user is given the two circuits which now meet the design constraints.

15.6 LEARNING REDESIGN KNOWLEDGE

The use of TLTS by pcb design groups helped identify two reasons why the tool is not always adequate.

(1) TLTS does not have knowledge for redesigning a circuit in a way that is acceptable by the designers using the tool. New ways to redesign a faulty circuit are created:
    (a) In order for design groups to better deal with their design constraints, and
    (b) As new product lines, new manufacturing processes, and so on, are established.
(2) The choices made by TLTS on how to redesign a faulty circuit are different from those that would have been made by a designer in a particular design group. This occurs because each design group uses its own constraints when deciding how to redesign a faulty circuit. These constraints express preference to a design style, the layout cost of implementing the redesign, the manufacturing process, and so forth.

To address these issues and thus increase the utility of the tool, a component called REKL was designed and implemented. REKL is able to acquire new redesign knowledge and incorporate it into TLTS. This learning component acquires four types of redesign knowledge: redesign operators, operator scheduling rules, eligibility demons, and meta-rules.

REKL acquires redesign knowledge by interacting with TLTS, the performance system, and the user. The first three types of redesign knowledge are extracted from redesign plans that the user forms in cooperation with TLTS. Rather than forming a macro rule that contains the knowledge in a plan and then incorporating the macro rule into the performance system, or storing entire plans and then redesigning a faulty circuit by trying to replay a stored plan, the learning component extracts each type of knowledge, generalizes it, and expresses it using the appropriate representation. As a result, the acquired knowledge is organized into knowledge sources, which can then be used for the redesign of a *variety* of faulty circuits rather than circuits that are identical to the circuit for which the plan was created, as would be the case if the plans could only be replayed. Finally, because the acquired knowledge is expressed using the programming constructs of TLTS, it is easier to inspect, maintain, and modify whenever the need arises.

15.7 FORMING NEW REDESIGN KNOWLEDGE SOURCES

In order to form a new redesign knowledge source, REKL needs to acquire the low-level redesign goals that the operators in the knowledge source will be able to achieve, the redesign operators that will achieve these goals, the knowledge for controlling the sequencing of these operators, and the eligibility demons. This knowledge is acquired by having REKL observe the problem-solving activity that is followed by TLTS in cooperation with the user in various situations and contexts. REKL then acquires the appropriate knowledge by examining the problem-solving information that was created and compiling redesign knowledge from it. In particular, REKL follows a four-step process to form a new redesign knowledge source. These steps are:

(1) REKL records the performance specifications and the secondary constraints placed on the circuit by the user and the evaluation results (analysis and diagnosis) generated by the corresponding knowledge sources.
(2) The user cooperates interactively with TLTS and dynamically creates plans for redesigning a faulty circuit.
(3) The plans are saved by the learning component.
(4) After a number of plans have been captured (the number is determined by the user), the user issues a command and the learning component:
   (a) Identifies (marks) the redesign knowledge (goals, operators, and scheduling rules) contained in these plans. This knowledge forms the action part of the new redesign knowledge source.
   (b) Uses the evaluation results that are associated with each plan to form the eligibility demons of the new redesign knowledge source.

Throughout the rest of the chapter, to demonstrate how a new redesign knowledge source is formed, examples are used that are appropriate for the acquisition of the redesign knowledge source called *break branch*.

Recording Evaluation Results

In addition to the given circuit, the user of performance specifications, and the secondary constraints, REKL records:

(1) The analysis knowledge that is used for the identification of the signal integrity problem.
(2) The diagnosis knowledge used for the detection of the cause of a signal integrity problem, if such a problem exists.

For the example, assume that the evaluation of the circuit shown in Fig. 15.5 has revealed two signal integrity problems: a signal strength problem and a propagation delay problem. The rule called *detect-signal-strength1*, whose definition was previously given, reveals the signal strength problem. The rule called *detect-prop-delays1*, whose definition is given reveals the propagation delay problem.

detect-prop-delays1

IF the first receiver violates the timing constraints imposed by the user

AND at least one more receiver violates timing constraints imposed by the user

THEN deduce propagation delay problem

The diagnostic rule called *diagnose-prop-delay1* identifies the cause of the propagation delay problem as impedance discontinuity in the circuit.

diagnose-prop-delays2

IF propagation delay problem has been deduced

AND there exists an impedance discontinuity in the transmission lines of the circuit

THEN the cause of the problem is due to the impedance discontinuity

The learning component keeps track of the instantiations of the analysis and diagnosis rules that are created. Through a backchaining process it determines the inferencing sequence that links the instances of the analysis and the diagnosis rules that identified each signal integrity problem and its corresponding cause. One such sequence links instantiations of the rules *detect-signal-strength1* and *diagnose-signal-strength1*. Another links the instantiations of the rules *detect-prop-delay1* and *diagnose-prop-delay1*. The user selects which problem he or she will try to solve through redesign. The rule sequence that has identified this problem is marked so that the redesign plan to be created later is associated with it.

Creating Redesign Plans

To create a plan for redesigning the faulty circuit, the user interactively selects goals from a catalog of predetermined goals and posts them on the blackboard. TLTS also maintains a catalog of redesign operators that can achieve these goals. As soon as the goals are posted on the blackboard all the redesign operators examine the blackboard. The operators that can satisfy the posted goals become eligible for execution. The user instructs TLTS to apply one of the eligible operators. After the operator is executed the cycle repeats, namely the user chooses another operator and so on until all of the user's goals have been achieved.

In this mode of operation two fundamental assumptions are made:

(1) The redesign operators used in the plans must already exist in the TLTS catalog. This is not an unreasonable assumption in the domain of pc board redesign because the set of redesign transformations that can be performed on pc boards is small and does not change as new pc board technologies are created. In other domains, such as VLSI circuit redesign, the number of possible transformations is large and con-

stantly changing as new technologies are being developed, thus making difficult the creation of a catalog, which can be reused over time, of all the possible transformations.

(2) If a redesign operator is missing, the user can define it and incorporate it into the catalog. This may not be a realistic assumption because it expects the user to learn the syntax of the operators and define the operation in terms of the programming language used in the system.

The plan formation process is illustrated in the following example. Suppose TLTS is trying to solve the propagation delay problem that has been revealed in the circuit of Fig. 15.5. For this reason, assume that an impedance discontinuity exists on etch *et3*. Further assume that the user would like to create a redesign knowledge source, which will be called *break branch*. This knowledge source will have knowledge for breaking a branch, forming a new branch out of the removed receivers, and attaching this branch to the transmission line that connects the circuit's driver to the rest of the circuit. For the purposes of this example, only the part of the plan which achieves the breaking of the branch will be shown.

Suppose the goal catalog has the following goals: (1) remove-a-driver, (2) remove-a-receiver, (3) remove-a-piece-of-etch, (4) remove-a-connector, (5) remove-a-via. Also, the user would like to remove receivers *re5* and *re6* from the circuit. The user first marks the two receivers that will be removed and then selects the goals remove-a-receiver, remove-a-connector, and remove-a-piece-of-etch. The operator *remove-receiver* is instantiated. The user instructs TLTS to apply the operator and receiver *re5* is removed. Once this receiver is removed, the operator *remove-etch* is instantiated. The operator *remove-receiver* is also instantiated. The user instructs TLTS to apply the operator *remove-receiver* removing receiver *re6*. After this step, the operator *remove-connector* is instantiated. So next the user has to choose between the instantiations of the operators *remove-etch* and *remove-connector*. He chooses the operator *remove-etch*, which is then applied, removing etch *et10* followed by the selection and application of the operator *remove-connector* that causes the connector *c1* to be removed. At this point, it is assumed that the plan has been completed and has to be stored by the learning component. The plan consists of the following actions: remove receiver *re5*, remove receiver *re6*, remove etch *et10*, and remove connector *c1*. Actions that belong to the plan but are not shown in this example are place etch *et10* and connect it to etch *et1*, place connector *c1* and connect it to etch *et1*, place receiver *re5*, and place receiver *re6*.

Storing Redesign Plans

In order to compile the knowledge of a set of redesign plans into a knowledge source, the context of each plan needs to be stored along with the plan itself. The context of a plan consists of the following:

(1) The operators the plan contains.
(2) The signal integrity problem present in the circuit being redesigned (*saved during the evaluation phase*).

(3) The cause of the signal integrity problem (*saved during the evaluation phase*).

(4) Any operators that were eligible for execution during each cycle of the plan creation process, in addition to the operator that was selected for execution.

(5) The structure of the circuit after each redesign operator is applied.

Each plan and the structure of the redesign circuit are linked with the evaluation results. The plans that are created for the solution of the same signal integrity problem having the same cause are organized into a set. The set is given the name of the knowledge source that will be formed by compiling the knowledge in the plans. The name is provided by the user. This name is also used by REKL for accessing the set.

Compiling Redesign Knowledge

The learning component compiles the redesign knowledge which is contained in a set of plans into a new knowledge source. The name of the knowledge source is the one used to organize the plans. In particular, REKL identifies the goals that were achieved in each plan. It then includes in the knowledge source being formed the union of the identified goals. As a second step, REKL generalizes the operators that are contained in the plan and includes in the knowledge source the union of the generalized operators. For example, assume there are two plans in the set that is indexed under the name *break branch*. The first plan is the one created for the redesign of the circuit in Fig. 15.5. The second plan is used for the removal of receivers *re3* and *re5* from the branch formed by receivers *re3*, *re4*, and *re5* in the circuit of Fig. 15.10. The plan is the following: (1) remove receiver *re3*, (2) remove receiver *re5*, (3) remove etch *et11*, (4) remove etch *et12*, and (5) remove etch *et10*.

The low-level redesign goals that will be included in the new knowledge source are remove-a-receiver, remove-a-piece-of-etch, and remove-a-connector, because

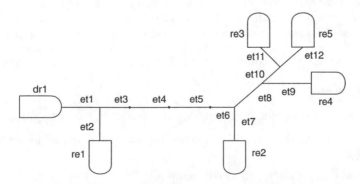

FIG. 15.10. Circuit where receivers *re3* and *re5* will be removed from branch formed by *re3*,*re4*, and *re5*.

these are the only three goals that were achieved in the two plans. The operators that will be included in the new knowledge source are *remove-receiver*, *remove-etch*, and *remove-connector*, because the first plan uses the operators *remove-receiver, remove-etch*, and *remove-connector*, whereas the second plan uses the operators *remove-receiver* and *remove-etch*; their union being the operators *remove-receiver, remove-etch*, and *remove-connector*.

Out of the operator precedence relations, as these were established by the sequence of application of each operator in a particular plan, the learning component forms the scheduling rules that are associated with the operators. A scheduling rule which is formed from the operations in the first plan is the following:

new-sched-rule0

IF the operator *remove-etch* is eligible for execution

AND the operator *remove-connector* is eligible for execution

THEN prefer the operator *remove-etch*

Many of the redesign knowledge sources that TLTS contains include scheduling rules that use domain-specific knowledge. In the current implementation of the learning component, these types of control knowledge cannot be captured, explicitly. It has to be noted, however, that the precedence relations implicitly contain domain-specific knowledge.

In order to form the eligibility rules (demons) that correspond to the knowledge source that is being formed, REKL utilizes parts of the captured information about the context of each plan. As was mentioned earlier, the learning component stores the inferencing chain of the analysis and diagnosis rule instantiations that detected each signal integrity problem and its cause. The LHSs of the rules in the chain that is associated with the problem being solved are used as the LHS of an eligibility rule. Therefore, an eligibility rule is formed out of each plan in the set. If more than one analysis rule and more than one diagnosis rule belong to a particular inferencing chain, then the LHS predicates of all the rules are used in the LHS of the formed rule, rather than the predicates of only the first analysis and the first diagnosis rule because each predicate represents one of two facts: (1) a constraint violation, or (2) the cause of a particular violation. The RHS of every such rule contains the consequent: (is-eligible *knowledge-source-name*). For example, one eligibility rule which can be formed from the context of the two plans that are being compiled into a knowledge source is the following:

new-eligibility-rule4

IF the first receiver violates the timing constraints imposed by the user

AND at least one more receiver violates the timing constraints imposed by the user

AND there exists an impedance discontinuity

THEN the knowledge source *break branch* is eligible

A new redesign knowledge source is developed incrementally. Even after a set of plans are compiled, the user may still have to create plans dynamically because the knowledge source could be missing redesign operators. For example, assume that the user would like to use the knowledge source that was created out of the two preceding plans. Only this time, the user would like to relocate the branch that includes receivers *re6* and *re7* from the circuit of Fig. 15.5 in order to attempt to solve the propagation delay problem. It is apparent that removing receiver *re7* will also require removing via *v1*. Unfortunately, the redesign knowledge source called *break branch* does not have an operator for removing vias because such an operator was not used in any of the plans that were utilized while forming the new knowledge source. In this case, the user will have to create a plan dynamically in order to deal with this situation. After capturing this plan, the user issues the appropriate command to REKL so that the knowledge of the plan will be compiled into the knowledge source *break branch*. The learning component takes the union of the operators that have already been incorporated into the knowledge source with the operators in the plan being compiled, thus updating the set of redesign operators which the knowledge source contains.

15.8 LEARNING METAKNOWLEDGE

There are two instances when metaknowledge needs to be acquired. The first instance is after a redesign knowledge source is created. At this time, the user of REKL has to instruct the performance system when to select this new knowledge source in relation to the other existing redesign knowledge sources. The second instance occurs when a design group uses different criteria for choosing among the sets of redesign knowledge sources which are already part of TLTS. In both instances, REKL uses the same process for capturing new metaknowledge. In particular, given a faulty circuit, REKL:

(1) Records the user's design specifications, the secondary constraints placed by the user such as type of manufacturing process, layout cost, and so on, and the problem-solving (evaluation and redesign) information that is generated by the performance system.
(2) Forms meta-rules.
(3) Refines meta-rules that have been previously formed, as needed.

Recording Information

REKL records the design specifications and the secondary constraints posted on the blackboard by the user only after the circuit is found to be faulty by an analysis knowledge source. It also keeps track of the instantiations of the analysis and diagnosis rules and creates the inferencing chains that link each analysis with the corresponding diagnosis rule instantiations, in a way similar to the one previously described. During the redesign phase, and while metaknowledge is being acquired, the user is required to decide which knowledge source will operate on the blackboard, even if there already exists a meta-rule that expresses the user's choice. REKL first records the user's choice, and then it determines if any of the meta-rules that are already included in the control knowledge source fired. If the meta-rules fired, then REKL examines if the user's choice was included in any of the fired meta-rules. If the control knowledge source is empty, or if the user's choice was not identical to the consequent of one of the meta-rules that fired, then the choice is saved for future use. The learning component also records the names of the redesign knowledge sources that are eligible for operating on the faulty circuit but which were not chosen by the user.

Once the chosen redesign knowledge source operates on the blackboard, and the circuit is redesigned, REKL forms meta-rules that capture the user's choices during that cycle through the evaluation–redesign loop. It also records the evaluation results on the redesigned circuit. When no analysis rules are executed, then it is assumed that the circuit has no signal integrity problems. At this point, REKL operationalizes the meta-rules which it has already formed.

Forming Meta-Rules

In order to form the LHS of a new meta-rule, the learning component uses the results of analysis rules, the results of diagnosis rules, the secondary constraints that were established by the user, and the names of the knowledge sources that were eligible for execution at the time the user made a choice on how to redesign the faulty circuit. The RHS of the meta-rule contains the name of the redesign knowledge source that was selected by the user and ultimately invoked. The method of forming meta-rules can be considered as *macro formation*. In this respect, it is similar to the *production compilation* method used in the system ACT* (Anderson, 1983).

For example, assume that after the evaluation of the circuit shown in Fig. 15.5, the user has decided to solve the signal strength problem. In addition, the user has determined that there is no available space on the pc board. Further suppose that the following two redesign knowledge sources have expressed eligibility for operating on the blackboard, *change circuit's driver*, and *add another driver* in parallel to the existing one. Finally, assume that the user chooses the first redesign knowledge source. It has to be mentioned here that the system has no means of determining if the user is making a correct design decision when selecting a particular redesign knowledge source at the time the decision is made. For this reason, the meta-rules which are formed are not immediately operationalized. The meta-rule, called *new-meta-rule1*, that was formed from the example above is

new-meta-rule1

    IF a signal strength problem is detected

    AND the cause of the problem is attributed to the driver

    AND space constraints exist on the pc board

AND the knowledge source called *change circuit's driver* is eligible

AND the knowledge source called *add another driver* is eligible

THEN select the knowledge source called *change circuit's driver*

In order for this meta-rule to be later selected and applied by TLTS, the conditions of a new problem situation (signal integrity problem, cause of the problem, secondary user constraints, and eligible knowledge sources) will have to match exactly those in the LHS of the rule. This is not always possible, especially because the secondary constraints may vary between designs and design processes. For this reason, the learning component also creates an abstracted version of each meta-rule whenever the user imposes secondary constraints. The LHS of every abstracted rule consists of the LHS of the analysis and diagnosis rules that detected the signal integrity problem and its cause. Namely, it does not contain the secondary user constraints. The learning component has knowledge about these secondary user constraints and can thus automatically omit them from the LHS of an abstracted meta-rule. For example, the condition "no additional space exists on the pc board" is one such secondary user constraint which will be omitted from the abstracted version of *new-meta- rule1*. The LHS of the abstracted meta-rule also contains the names of the redesign knowledge sources that were eligible for operating on the blackboard. The RHS of the abstracted meta-rule contains the name of the redesign knowledge source that was selected by the user. The definition of the abstracted rule, called *new-meta-rule2*, that corresponds to rule *new-meta-rule1* is

new-meta-rule2

IF a signal strength problem is detected

AND the cause of the problem is attributed to the driver

AND the knowledge source called *change circuit's driver* is eligible

AND the knowledge source called *add another driver* is eligible

THEN select the knowledge source called *change circuit's driver*

As was already mentioned, the two formed meta-rules are not operationalized as soon as they are created. Instead, they are attached to the data structure that contains the information that was used in creating the two meta-rules. Meta-rules are operationalized and incorporated into the control knowledge source when the problem-solving activity of the user and TLTS results in a problem-free circuit. If the application of the selected redesign knowledge source has not resulted in a problem-free circuit, the process just described is repeated (namely, the user selects the signal integrity problem he or she wishes to solve, if more than one is present on the circuit, REKL forms the inferencing chain of the rules that detected the problem and its cause, the user selects the eligible redesign knowledge source of his or her choice, etc.), and another pair of meta-rules is created. If the problem is still not solved, and the same redesign knowledge sources express eligibility again for operating on the blackboard, the user has to backtrack to some previous version of the circuit and follow a new redesign strategy. In such instances, all the meta-rules associated with versions of the circuit that were created after the circuit to which the user decides to backtrack are eliminated. As shown in Fig. 15.11, if the user wants to backtrack to circuit c1, then the meta-rules that are associated with circuit c1, circuit c1.1, and circuit c1.2 are eliminated. Currently, this is the only way that the user can recover from making inappropriate redesign decisions, and, as a result, placing incorrect meta-knowledge in the control knowledge source. Once a circuit has been redesigned successfully, the meta-rules that are formed during the problem-solving session are operationalized and stored in the control knowledge source.

Because REKL creates two versions of each meta-rule, it is conceivable that under certain conditions both meta-rules will match against the contents of the blackboard and will be eligible to fire. To avoid this problem, a meta-rule control strategy is associated with the rules in the control knowledge source. This strategy selects the most specific of the meta-rules which match against the contents of the blackboard. Therefore, in a situation when both *new-meta-rule1* and *new-meta-rule2* match against the contents of the blackboard and are eligible for execution, *new-meta-rule1* will be preferred by the control strategy.

Refining Meta-Rules

It is often the case that, once operationalized, the meta-rules may need to be refined. For example, suppose that after *new-meta-rule1* and *new-meta-rule2* are operationalized, TLTS evaluates a circuit which will be laid on a pc board with no space or cost constraints. Further suppose that the analysis and diagnosis knowledge sources of TLTS reveal that there is a signal strength problem which is attributed to the current sourcing capabilities of the circuit's driver. For the

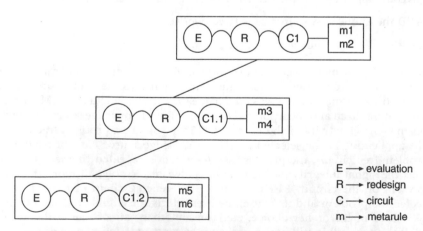

E ⟶ evaluation
R ⟶ redesign
C ⟶ circuit
m⟶ metarule

FIG. 15.11. When user backtracks to circuit c1, the metarules associated with circuits c1, c1.1, and c1.2 are eliminated.

reasons presented in the previous example, the same two redesign knowledge sources will be eligible for operating on the blackboard. However, only *new-meta-rule2* will be instantiated by the matcher because its conditions (analysis and diagnosis results) match against the current contents of the blackboard; *new-meta-rule1* will not match because one of its conditions (the one corresponding to pc board space constraints) does not match against the contents of the blackboard; *new-meta-rule2* is then applied, and it is suggested to the user to select the redesign knowledge source called *change circuit's driver.*

Assume the user knows that because there are no pc board space constraints it is *better* to add another driver to the circuit in order to solve the signal strength problem, rather than replacing the existing driver. This means that the suggestion made by the meta-rule *new-meta-rule2* is correct but not optimal. The inappropriate suggestion is the result of missing knowledge. In particular, the piece of knowledge which specifies that *if there is no space constraint then it is better to add another driver* needs to be incorporated into the appropriate meta-rules. In other words, the meta-rule *new-meta-rule2* needs to be refined (in this case, specialized).

To select a redesign knowledge source that is more appropriate than the one that was suggested by the meta-rule which fired, the user requests from TLTS a list of the other redesign knowledge sources that were eligible for execution at the time *meta-rule2* fired. The user is then informed that the only other eligible knowledge source is called *add another driver.* Assume that after the user chooses this redesign knowledge source, and the knowledge source is applied on the faulty circuit, the signal strength problem is eliminated. In this case, a new meta-rule needs to be created capturing the problem solving context. Furthermore, a meta-rule with a LHS which is identical to that of *new-meta-rule2* and with a RHS which expresses the user's choice needs to be created.

The first of the new meta-rules, which is created in a way similar to the one just described is

new-meta-rule3

    IF a signal strength problem is detected

    AND the cause of the problem is attributed to the driver

    AND no space constraints exist on the pc board

    AND no constraints on the cost of redesign exist

    AND the knowledge source called *change circuit's driver* is eligible

    AND the knowledge source called *add another driver* is eligible

    THEN select the knowledge source called *add another driver*

The new abstracted meta-rule is

new-meta-rule4

    IF a signal strength problem is detected

AND the cause of the problem is attributed to the driver

AND the knowledge source called *change circuit's driver* is eligible

AND the knowledge source called *add another driver* is eligible

THEN select the knowledge source *add another driver*

When new meta-rules are operationalized, the learning component does not check if the new rules introduce inconsistencies in conjunction with the meta-rules—*new-meta-rule2* and *new-meta-rule4* appear to be conflicting because for the same set of conditions (LHS), they select two different redesign knowledge sources. The conflict resolution strategy that is associated with the control knowledge source will allow both of these meta-rules to fire.

The problem of not being able to discriminate between the meta-rules with different RHSs does not only occur with abstracted meta-rules but with specific ones as well. In particular, it may be the case that two meta-rules have the same analysis and diagnosis results incorporated in their LHS, but different secondary constraints. For example, the following two meta-rules are such a pair:

new-meta-rule1

IF a signal strength problem is detected

AND the cause of the problem is attributed to the driver

AND pc board space constraint exists

AND the knowledge source called *change circuits's driver* is eligible

AND the knowledge source called *add another driver* is eligible

THEN select the knowledge source called *change circuit's driver*

new-meta-rule5

IF a signal strength problem is detected

AND the cause of the problem is attributed to the driver

AND no constraints on the cost of redesign exist

AND the knowledge source called *change circuit's driver* is eligible

AND the knowledge source called *add another driver* is eligible

THEN select the knowledge source called *add another driver*

Resolving Conflicts Between Meta-Rules

If the user has established that pc board space constraints exist, and that no redesign constraints exist, then both *new-meta-rule1* and *new-meta-rule5* will be eligible for execution. Furthermore, because they have the same number of conditions, the control strategy which is associated with the rules in the control knowledge source will not be able to select the one meta-rule over the other. In addition, two meta-rules may have the same conditions in their LHS and different RHS. This is the case with *new-meta-rule2* and *new-meta-rule4*. In order to address these two issues, i.e., nonoptimal knowledge and inability to discriminate between eligible meta-rules, the conflict resolution strategy of the control knowledge source allows all rules which it cannot filter out to fire in parallel. This results in the parallel invocation and execution of redesign knowledge sources. At the end of the redesign phase the user has to select which of the created circuits will be pursued further.

15.9 IMPLEMENTATION

TLTS is implemented in the expert system language ORBS (Fikas, 1985). Many of ORBS' features were created to address issues faced by tools involved in design. ORBS has been previously used for the development of knowledge-based VLSI circuit design environments (Simoudis and Fickas, 1985). The language supports forward chaining rule-based, procedural, and objected-based modes of computation.

The user of ORBS can define strategies for controlling the execution of the production rules. A strategy is composed of one or more *scheduling rules*, a construct provided by ORBS. A scheduling rule incorporates general and domain specific knowledge. The control knowledge that is associated with each set of eligibility and action rules was defined using scheduling rules. These rules were combined to form strategies. The strategies represent the body of knowledge which is the value to the attribute action-cs and eligibility-cs of each knowledge source. The rules in the control knowledge source were implemented as *meta-rules*, another construct provided by ORBS.

The prototype of TLTS is implemented on a μVAXII under the Ultrix operating system. It consists of 100 production rules which are used for analysis and diagnosis tasks, 50 production rules which are used as redesign operators, 26 meta-rules, 30 scheduling rules, 19 object classes, and procedures.

TLTS has effectively dealt with networks having up to 12 receivers. The networks had a variety of topologies. The use of a simulation–analysis–diagnosis–redesign loop with multiple abstraction levels has helped in better utilization of simulation results, and in avoiding unnecessary simulation runs. In particular, designers often overlook certain aspects of the circuit networks they design. For example, they may forget to terminate certain transmission lines. Such oversights, which cause signal integrity problems, can usually be detected through heuristic simulation and analysis.

REKL has not yet been tested as thoroughly as TLTS, which is already a 3-year-old-system. It is expected that as TLTS is more widely used, the testing of the learning component will become more extensive and thorough. REKL was first used for the acquisition of two new redesign knowledge sources. During this time, no new redesign operators were added to the TLTS catalog. These knowledge sources were added by a printed circuit board design group in order for

TLTS to be able to deal more effectively with some of the constraints imposed by this group while correcting signal integrity problems.

The first knowledge source, which is called *break branch* and which is used in examples throughout this chapter, consists of seven redesign operators. Even though the knowledge in this knowledge source was compiled out of four plans, it has to be noted that a prediction cannot be made as to how many plans will have to be created and compiled before the knowledge of a redesign knowledge source is considered complete. The knowledge source has two eligibility rules and three scheduling rules.

After this knowledge source was created it was integrated with two other knowledge sources that the system had for correcting propagation delay problems due to an impedance discontinuity in the circuit, namely *reduce receivers* and *shorten etch lengths*. Integration here means that REKL captured the meta-rules that allowed the new knowledge source to be appropriately selected by TLTS. The learning component captured eight meta-rules. These meta-rules proved useful because after they were created they allowed the designers to redesign a circuit with a propagation delay problem due to impedance discontinuity if the cost of the board's layout must be taken into account. In particular, if the layout cost should not be taken into account and space exists on the pc board, then the knowledge source called *remove receivers* is appropriate. However, when the cost of the layout has to be taken into consideration in order to implement the redesign, then it is better to break the target branch and move it next to the circuit's driver, rather than try to remove receivers from the circuit and form a new circuit with them. Once again it has to be stressed here that the reason the appropriate meta-rules are learned is because REKL coupled with TLTS.

To evaluate the benefit of incorporating an additional redesign knowledge source to TLTS, 10 circuits were chosen from a pc board having a propagation delay problem due to impedance discontinuity. Constraints were also specified that have to be satisfied when the circuits are redesigned. These faulty circuits were then presented to a signal integrity engineer who was asked to use TLTS and eliminate the signal integrity problem, while observing the necessary constraints, both when the tool did not have the redesign knowledge source called *break branch* and after it had acquired it. The designer was able to correct eight of the faulty circuits using the two redesign knowledge sources that TLTS already had. After the new redesign knowledge source was incorporated, the designer was able to correct only one of the remaining two faulty circuits. The correction of the final circuit would have required the acquisition of yet another knowledge source. This result shows that the returns from acquiring a redesign knowledge source may not always be as high as anticipated. However, because each design group could have its own ways of redesigning circuits, it may be more effective to distribute TLTS without any redesign knowledge sources and have the designers of each user group first input their redesign knowledge using REKL, and then start using TLTS. Such a mode of operation provides an even stronger justification for incorporating into TLTS a learning component similar to the one which was presented here.

The second acquired knowledge source is called *add terminator*. It is used for eliminating signal strength problems that are due to the sinking capabilities of the circuit's receivers. This knowledge source has four redesign operators, three scheduling rules, and three eligibility rules. Three plans were needed to capture the appropriate redesign operators. Six meta-rules were captured in conjunction with this knowledge source. Interestingly, the feature that allows the selection of this knowledge source over the two other knowledge sources that can be used for the solution of this signal integrity problem (namely the knowledge source called *change circuit's driver* and the knowledge source *add another driver*) is the cost of the layout. In particular, it is cheaper to add a terminator to a circuit if it does not have one, than to add another driver or to change the circuit's driver. Furthermore, it usually takes less area to add a terminator than to add another driver to a circuit. This characteristic allows the system to determine when to invoke the knowledge source *add terminator* and when to invoke the knowledge source *add another driver*.

In order to check again the effectiveness of this redesign knowledge source in conjunction with the two that were already present in TLTS, 10 circuits were identified from a printed circuit board that had signal strength problems, and constraints were obtained that had to be maintained while the circuits were being redesigned. A designer was asked to use TLTS to redesign each circuit—first, before the new knowledge source was incorporated into the tool, and second, after the knowledge source was incorporated. It was observed that the designer utilized suggestions from TLTS four times which resulted in the tool correcting the problem in four of the ten faulty circuits. When the redesign knowledge source called *add terminator* was added to the system, the designer chose it three times, which resulted in TLTS correcting seven of the ten faulty circuits. The results from this experiment came closer to what was originally expected from incorporating REKL and TLTS.

The addition of new knowledge sources does not significanly affect the performance of TLTS. In particular, every type of rule in the system (operator, eligibility, scheduling, and meta) is matched separately during the operation cycle of TLTS. Therefore, the meta-rules and the operators in the knowledge sources are not considered by the pattern matcher during the match–execute cycle for the eligibility rules. The largest group of rules which is ever considered by the matcher is the group of meta-rules. For example, when the control knowledge source contained 26 meta-rules, the match phase of the match–execute cycle took 1.73 sec. In this case, each meta-rule had an average of 4.9 condition elements in its LHS. When the control knowledge source had 40 meta-rules, the matching phase took 2.65 sec, an increase of 53.7%. Each of the 14 new meta-rules had an average of 4.7 condition elements in its LHS. As a reminder, all the meta-rules that match against the blackboard are executed.

In terms of storage requirements, the following was observed:

- Each receiver of the circuit shown in Fig. 5 requires 1k bytes of storage.
- A problem-solving sequence which includes the evaluation results of the input circuit, a redesign plan, and the evaluation results on the redesigned circuit requires 60K bytes of storage. This implies that storing a problem-solving sequence that succeeds in eliminating all constraint violations with one redesign, along with the two circuits (faulty and corrected), requires 80K bytes of storage. As mentioned in Steinberg (1984), if the signal integrity problems in a circuit are not eliminated within

three iterations through the evaluation and redesign loop, the user is advised to backtrack and follow a different path in the redesign space. This means that the maximum storage requirement for a problem-solving sequence is 480K bytes plus the storage requirements for the four circuits (the faulty one and the three versions that result from the redesign phase) that are involved in the sequence.

15.10 RELATED WORK

Redesign

Not many tools exist in the area of signal integrity problem detection and correction. Most of the existing tools can only address the analysis phase (VLSI System Design Staff, 1986; Poltz and Wexler, 1986). However, because of the implicit assumptions these tools make they can deal only with a limited number of fabrication technologies and network models. Furthermore, such tools expect the user to decide how to perform the analysis and to decide which parts of the results are important.

A number of knowledge-based tools have appeared over the last three years that automatically design and/or redesign artifacts (Brown and Chandrasekaran, 1986; Mittal *et al.*, 1986; Dixon *et al.*; Steinberg, 1984). AIR-CYL, the system described in Brown and Chandrasekaran (1986), automates the process of routine design. Routine design consists of accepting a set of specifications and then using a set of predefined plans to create an artifact that meets the specifications. The knowledge-based component of AIR-CYL uses meta-rules to choose which plan to execute, and then applies the steps that are included in the plan in a procedural way. AIR-CYL's meta-rules are similar to those of TLTS. The design steps that are included in a plan consist of changing the values of various predefined parameters in the artifact that is being designed. In contrast, during the redesign phase, TLTS dynamically creates a plan to redesign a circuit by deciding which operators will be used and how many times they will be applied, and then applies the plan. However, a TLTS redesign knowledge source can be used in the same way as a routine design plan by providing all the operators that will be used in the plan and specifying the order of execution of these operators by defining the appropriate operator control knowledge. Furthermore, the steps of the plan do not just consist of changing values of parameters but actually changes the topology of the circuit by adding new elements whenever appropriate.

Similar to AIR-CYL, PRIDE, described in Mittal, *et al.* (1986), has design knowledge stored in predefined plans. The steps in these plans also change the values of predefined parameters that describe the artifact, in this case paper paths of photocopy machines. PRIDE also has meta-rules that allow the system to determine which plan to apply. It is able to concurrently pursue all the plans that apply to a particular situation in a way similar to TLTS. Furthermore, PRIDE uses a backtracking mechanism which utilizes domain knowledge when it suggests how to fix constraint violations in the artifact that is being redesigned. Dominic (Dixon *et al.*, 1989) differs from TLTS as well as from AIR-CYL and PRIDE in that it uses little expert redesign knowledge and does not decompose design problems into subproblems. It also differs from TLTS in the way it evaluates the produced designs. Furthermore, as is the case with AIR-CYL and PRIDE, design in Dominic is defined as the filling of values of a set of predefined parameters that characterize the artifact which is being designed. Dominic uses meta-knowledge to select which parameter needs to be affected in order for a design goal to be satisfied. The meta-knowledge is given in the form of a *dependency table*. Dominic cannot simultaneously search multiple paths of the design space. Because design consists of altering the value of only one parameter at a time, Dominic is able to use constraint propagation and evaluate the effects of a design step before taking it. In this respect its operation is similar to that of AIR-CYL and PRIDE.

The REDESIGN system (Steinberg *et al.*, 1984) uses knowledge-based techniques to change a pc board design in order to meet a set of new design specifications. It differs from TLTS in that (1) it needs the plan that was used for the design of the original circuit, (2) it uses a different method than TLTS for the generation of redesign options, and (3) it cannot implement the redesign options that it generates. Because REDESIGN needs the original design plan to be able to redesign the circuit, it has to deal with the problem of establishing a correspondence between the steps that were taken in the original design and the steps that need to be taken for the modification of the design. These steps do not only involve design decomposition actions but they also involve circuit component modification actions. In particular, REDESIGN may have to decide how to map a simple step of the original plan to a complicated one in order to satisfy the user's specifications. The mapping has to be done in such a way so as to preserve the correctness of the circuit under construction. Because TLTS generates plans dynamically, it does not have to deal with the preceding problem.

The way REDESIGN generates redesign options cannot guarantee that any of the options will be implementable. In particular, REDESIGN uses its constraint propagator to identify which parts of the original circuit will need to be modified for the user specifications to be met. The knowledge that is incorporated in the constraint propagator is such that it only identifies which parts of the circuit will need to be changed. However, it has no design knowledge of how any of the proposed changes can be implemented, or if any of them make enough sense to be suggested to the user. The lack of such knowledge makes it necessary to require this knowledge from the user to implement a redesign option. The meta-knowledge in TLTS allows the system to determine the redesign method that will be followed. Furthermore, the knowledge within each redesign knowledge source allows TLTS to implement the proposed changes. Finally, the capability of TLTS to interleave evaluation and redesign (planning) allows the tool to determine how to proceed during the redesign phase and is thus more effective in solving the signal integrity problem at hand.

Learning

The first body of related work comes from the area of replay and derivational analogy. Two systems that capture design/redesign knowledge and then replay it are Bogart, which is described in Mostow and Barley (1987), and ARGO, which is described in Acosta *et al.* (1986).

The Bogart system can acquire new redesign plans; however, Borgart provides no means for grouping related plans. The captured plans can be reused only if the plan can be replayed. Bogart lacks a component that can adapt portions of or entire existing plans and apply them by analogy to different situations. In Bogart, either the user chooses which part of a plan to replay, or a plan is replayed as much as possible. This, in conjunction with the fact that related plans are not grouped together, implies that the user has to search a potentially large number of plans, understand the context under which they were created, and then decide if he or she would like to manually retrieve any of them. On the other hand, the learning component described in this chapter captures separately the goals that are specified by the user, the generalizations of the operators used to achieve these goals, and preferences in the execution sequence of the operators. From the captured knowledge, new plans are created every time a circuit needs to be redesigned. As a result, the user does not have to deal with the plan retrieval problem. The fact that the created plans perform local changes in a faulty circuit means that the size of the plans, and consequently the size of the planning process, does not make replanning prohibitive. Furthermore, because plans are created from scratch, deciding when to replay a portion of a plan, a process which requires analogical reasoning (Carbonell, 1983a, 1983b) is not needed.

Because the knowledge in the individual plans is not compiled as the number of captured plans increases, Bogart does not become more autonomous. The redesign capabilities of the learning component presented here increase as the knowledge of more plans is compiled in the knowledge source, provided that the plans contain new knowledge. Therefore, the capabilities of each new redesign knowledge source are dependent on the quality of the examples (plans) that are provided by the user.

Bogart does not distinguish any type of knowledge, except for redesign operators, which may play a role in performance. As a result, Bogart does not acquire any type of control knowledge. Consequently, even though other types of knowledge exist in the captured plans, such knowledge cannot be extracted and utilized under Bogart's current knowledge representation scheme.

The ARGO system learns both meta-rules and design implementation knowledge. However, ARGO is not able to distinguish between the two types of knowledge due to the limited capabilities of the knowledge representation language on which it is built. As a result, in order to apply a plan under two different conditions, two separate rules have to be formed, with different LHS but identical RHS. This representation method imposes large space requirements, once a large number of such rules and plans are accumulated by the system. As a result, ARGO is not expected to scale up. The knowledge that REKL incorporates into TLTS consists of generalizations of the operators that were used in the collection of related plans and not the plans themselves. More specifically, redesign plans are not stored after the knowledge they contain is compiled into a knowledge source. Consequently, REKL need only acquire the conditions under which an entire knowledge source is applicable, and not the conditions under which each specific plan is applicable.

After a design plan is formed, ARGO transforms the micro rules (operators) in the plan into a macro operator. However, when one of the micro rules changes as a result of an optimization or correction action performed by the rule base's developer, the knowledge representation of ARGO does not allow for the changes to be automatically reflected in all the plans that use the modified micro rule. Therefore, all the captured plans need to be examined, and the ones affected by the modifications to the micro rule need to be reimplemented. By generalizing the operators that were used in a collection of redesign plans, and by compiling the knowledge in the plans into a redesign knowledge source, modifications to a redesign operator do not imply that previous redesigned plans will have to be reexamined. Furthermore, because the modification is localized to the redesign operator level, the eligibility demons of the knowledge source to which the modified operator belongs will not have to be reexamined.

The second body of related work involves systems which integrate learning and problem solving. In this context, four systems are examined: SOAR (Laird *et al.*, 1987), PRODIGY (Minton, *et al.*, 1988), LEAP (Mitchell *et al.*, 1985), and CGEN (Birmingham and Siewiorek, 1988).

SOAR uses method similar to the ones presented in this chapter. In particular, SOAR captures problem-solving plans by compiling (chunking) a sequence of rules into a single one called a chunk. The LHS of a chunk consists of the union of the LHS predicates which exist in the rules which were executed, whereas the RHS of a chunk consists of the last predicate that resulted in the achievement of a problem-solving goal.

SOAR distinguishes between two types of knowledge: *search control* and *task implementation*. Each type of knowledge can be partitioned into *problem spaces*, *goals*, and *operators* for achieving the goals in each space. In this respect the knowledge organization of SOAR is very similar to that of TLTS, with spaces corresponding to the knowledge sources. The notation of the goals is the same in both systems and the operators correspond to either redesign operators or analysis and diagnosis rules. Just as in the case of SOAR, TLTS uses two types of knowledge: control (meta-rules, eligibility demons, and scheduling rules), and implementation (analysis rules, diagnosis rules, and redesign operators). Each of the types of control knowledge in TLTS can be thought of as belonging to a different space.

The notation of forming new problem-solving spaces using operators that are defined in existing spaces is not present in SOAR. The chunks that are being formed represent a piece of a problem-solving activity, but no further compilation of the knowledge in the chunks takes place. Because of the form the chunks take, the systems produced using SOAR may be hard to inspect, modify, and maintain. The developers of SOAR claim that updating or modifying the knowledge base is done by learning new chunks.

The PRODIGY system is also similar to TLTS in that it integrates a performance system and a learning component and it separates the search control from the domain or implementation knowledge. The learning component of PRODIGY is used for the acquisition of various types of control knowledge, not implementation knowledge. In this respect the learning component of PRODIGY is different from the learning component of TLTS. However, in the area of learning control rules, the learning component of PRODIGY learns both rejection and selection rules whereas the learning component of TLTS learns only selection rules.

The LEAP system was used for the acquisition of design refinement operators. Refinement operators can be likened to the plans that are produced by TLTS. Therefore, LEAP only learns one of the two types of knowledge that is acquired by the learning component presented in this chapter. Control knowledge has to be acquired by a different component, which is not part of LEAP. Because LEAP's rules are of the same granularity as the TLTS plans, there is no need to separately acquire scheduling rules similar to those used by the redesign component of TLTS. LEAP does not require the existence of a catalog of design operators, as does REKL. However, it does require another form of domain-specific knowledge in order to be able to verify the validity and generalization of a design operator composed by the user.

The CGEN system is integrated with the knowledge-based design toll M1. CGEN can capture both implementation and control knowledge, both of which are then utilized by M1. However, due to the fact that all domain knowledge is expressed in OPS5 rules, the knowledge base created by CGEN may be hard to inspect, maintain, and modify. Furthermore, CGEN, in a way similar to ARGO, creates a design rule (template) out of each training example that is provided by the user. For this reason, it is expected that the knowledge base which CGEN creates for M1, will have the same problems as the knowledge base created by ARGO. Because each of the rules captured by CGEN include both control and implementation knowledge, it is correctly pointed out by Birmingham (Birmingham and Siewiorek, 1988) that it is necessary to create abstractions of these rules. CGEN relies on the knowledge engineer to perform a major part of the work required for these abstractions. In contrast, through the proper partitioning of the redesign knowledge and the definitions of the appropriate implementation constructs, REKL needs to abstract only the meta-knowledge it captures, and it does so automatically. The eligibility demons and redesign operators are also generalized automatically as they are inserted into the knowledge sources which REKL forms.

The third body of related work concerns the area of knowledge compilation. The system KBSDE (Tong and Liew, 1987) is a knowledge compiler that generates design systems. KBSDE separates the knowledge compilation process into two components: representation and control. Representation has three levels itself: the knowledge level, the function level, and the program level. In REKL, the circuit component categories, the circuit parts hierarchies, and the developed redesign model correspond to the knowledge level of KBSDE. In the system presented here, the knowledge level is provided by the systems's developer. System architecture constructs such as knowledge sources, redesign operators, and eligibility rules correspond to the function level. The programming constructs (production rules, scheduling rules, objects, and Lisp functions) correspond to the program level. The learning component accepts input in the function level and maps it to the program level. The mapping produces knowledge sources which can form a range of plans each of which corresponds to what Tong terms a *candidate solution*. Based on this comparison, one can realize that KSBDE is a more general knowledge acquisition tool, whereas REKL is tailored to work with and utilize the knowledge of the performance system TLTS.

The final body of related work involves the field of automatic knowledge acquisition (KA). The SALT system (Marcus, 1988) uses KA techniques to capture design knowledge. It is similar to REKL because it relies on a problem-solving model which is incorporated into a performance system. However, contrary to REKL, it does not capture design/redesign by transforming a body of existing knowledge, instead, it elicits new knowledge from its user. The assumption that is made in SALT is that its user will only input knowledge of a specific granularity so that it can be successfully utilized by the performance program. However, such an assumption will be hard to maintain for a system whose knowledge base has to be developed by many experts.

The user of SALT is not allowed to partition a redesign (fixing) method in a way such that its parts can be shared by other bodies of redesign knowledge. For specific domains this limitation will result in large knowledge bases, which may prohibit a system similar to the performance system of SALT from scaling up. SALT is able to acquire multiple ways for fixing a particular constraint violation. For this reason it uses a form of meta-knowledge. However, this type of knowledge has to be predefined. Once this is done, the user specifies which piece of meta-knowledge has to be taken into consideration during the operation of the performance system. In contrast, REKL is able to create automatically meta-rules based on the specific problem-solving situation TLTS is trying to address.

15.11 CONCLUSION

In the process of trying to satisfy the manufacturing constraints for a digital system, design constraints are often violated. The violation of certain design constraints gives rise to signal integrity problems. The knowledge-based system TLTS was developed to help novice engineers identify and eliminate such problems. REKL, the learning component of TLTS, is used to acquire automatically new redesign knowledge from the interactions between TLTS and its users.

Effective evaluation and redesign of circuit networks that have signal integrity problems requires that evaluation and redesign be performed in multiple levels of detail. Also required are definitions of knowledge about circuit parts hierarchies, circuit component categories, and constraints for each level that evaluation and redesign are performed. Furthermore, in order to redesign a faulty circuit in the smallest number of iterations through the evaluation-redesign loop, one needs to define knowledge for selecting the most appropriate way of redesigning the faulty circuit. This selection knowledge needs to be based on certain criteria.

Redesign is facilitated by the definition of various types of relevant knowledge, including operator knowledge and control knowledge. The versatility and power of the TLTS redesign knowledge organization makes the redesign method used in TLTS applicable both in domains where routine design takes place and in areas where the redesign plans have to be created dynamically. Furthermore, the capability of TLTS to interleave evaluation and redesign allows the tool to determine how to proceed during the redesign phase.

The automatic acquisition of the new knowledge is facilitated when the acquisition component is integrated with a performance system. When doing so, the knowledge that the performance system contains, as well as any generated problem-solving information, can be directly evaluated by the learning component. Furthermore, the quality and effect of the knowledge that is learned can be directly utilized by the performance system, and appropriate action can be taken by the learning component.

The model that underlies REKL allows incremental acquisition of redesign knowledge. Furthermore, the techniques described are similar to the ones that are used by designers when they are determining new ways of modifying faulty circuits.

By compiling the redesign knowledge of only one plan into a knowledge source, including eligibility and operator control knowledge, one achieves the same results as replaying the plans. However, if more than one plan is compiled into a knowledge source, the generalization of the operators and the other knowledge that is acquired, gives to the TLTS performance system the capability to form more plans and thus solve more problems than a system which can only solve a problem by replaying a plan. In order for the latter system to be able to solve a variety of problems, it will have to utilize analogy, which may be difficult to identify in certain domains, including design.

REFERENCES

Acosta, R. D., Huhns. M. N., and Liuh, S.-L. 1986. Analogical reasoning for digital systems synthesis. *Proc. of IEEE ICCAD*, pp. 173–176, November 1986, Santa Clara, California.

Anderson, J. R. 1983. *The Architecture of Cognition*. Cambridge Massachusetts: Harvard University Press.

Birmingham, W. P., and Siewiorek, D. P. 1988. Automated knowledge acquisition of a computer hardware synthesis system. *Proceedings KAW88*, pp. 2-1-2-21, November 1988, Banff, Alberta, Canada.

Brown, D. C., and Chandrasekaran, B. 1986. Knowledge and control for a mechanical design expert system. *IEEE Computer* 19(7):92–100.

Carbonell, J. 1983a. Learning by analogy: Formulating and generalizing plans from past experience. In *Machine Learning*. ed. R.S. Michalski, J. Carbonell, and T. Mitchell, 137–161. Palo Alto, California: Tioga Publishing Company.

Carbonell, J. 1983b. Derivational analogy and its role in problem solving. *Proceedings AAAI-83*, pp. 64–69, 1983, Washington, D.C.

Dixon, J. R., Howe, A. E., Cohen, P. R., and Simmons, M. K. 1989. Dominic: A domain-independent program for mechanical engineering design. *International Journal for AI in Engineering* 1(1):23–28.

Fickas, S. 1985. Design issues in a rule-based system. In *ACM Symposium on Programming Languages and Programming Environments*, Seattle.

Laird, J. E., Newell, A., and Rosenbloom, P. S. 1987. Soar: An architecture for general intelligence. *Artificial Intelligence* 33(1):1–64.

Marcus, S. 1988. Understanding subtasks from a piecemeal collection of knowledge. *Proceedings KAW88* pp. 19-1-19-22, November 1988, Banff, Alberta, Canada.

Minton, S. 1988. Qualitative results concerning the utility of explanation-based learning. *Proceedings AAAI-88*, pp. 564–569, August 1988, Saint Paul, Minnesota.

Mitchell, T. A., Mahadevan, S., and Steinberg, L. I. 1985. LEAP: A learning apprentice for VLSI design. In *Proceedings IJCAI-85*, August 1985, Los Angeles, California, pp. 573–580.

Mittal, S., Dym, C. l., *et al*. Pride: An expert system for the design of paper handling systems. *IEEE Computer*, July 1986, pp. 102–114.

Mostow, J., and Barley, M. 1987. Automated reuse of design plans. *Proceedings ICED'87*, August 1987, pp. 632–647, Boston, Massachusetts.

Petrie, C. P., Russinoff, D. M., and Steiner, D. D. 1986. Proteus: A default reasoning perspective. *Proc. of the 5th Generation Conference*, National Institute for Software, October 1986, Washington, D.C.

Poltz, J., and Wexler, A. 1986. Transmission-line analysis of PC boards. In *VLSI Systems Design* 7(3):38–43.

Simoudis, E. 1989. A knowledge-based system for the evaluation and redesign of digital circuit networks. *IEEE Transactions in CAD* 8(3):302-315.

Simoudis, E., and Fickas, S. 1985. The application of knowledge-based design techniques to circuit design. In *Proc. IEEE ICCAD*, Santa Clara, California, November.

Steinberg, L. I., and Mitchel, T. M. "A knowledge-based approach to VLSI CAD: The redesign system. In *21st Design Automation Conference*, Albuquerque, New Mexico, June 1984.

Tong, C., and Liew, C. 1987. Knowledge compilation: A prototype system and a conceptual framework. *AI/VLSI Project Working Paper No 47*, February 1987, Rutgers University, New Brunswick, New Jersey.

VLSI Systems Design Staff. 1986. Survey of Circuit Board CAD Systems. In *VLSI Systems Design* 7(3):62–77.

Chapter 16

Fuzzy Knowledge Based Controller Design

C. Batur and V. Kasparian
Department of Mechanical Engineering
University of Akron
Akron, Ohio

16.1 INTRODUCTION

Controller intelligence is defined here as a methodology that will construct a robust controller from the input/output data of a complicated process for which constitutive equations are partially known. The need for controller intelligence is apparent in applications such as controlling kiln plants, autofocusing in cameras, and controlling autonomous vehicles. The subject of this chapter is the application of fuzzy logic methodology to the design of intelligent controllers.

Fuzzy logic based controllers consist of a set of heuristic rules to implement control actions. The need for heuristic logic has been recognized in industrial control for safety considerations. Industrial process controllers often incorporate heuristic logic to deal with practical problems such as integrator windup, alarm conditions, and switching between automatic and manual modes. Tuning a specific controller may also require heuristic logic. Typically, a control engineer applies a set of commonly accepted rules to tune the controller such as the Ziegler-Nichols tuning equations (Ziegler and Nichols, 1942). However, it is also known that these rules are not comprehensive. Most often, intuitive judgments and rules of thumb are also incorporated into the process. Commercial products are now available for the application of these heuristic/deterministic tuning procedures (Kraus and Myron, 1987).

Heuristic rules of a fuzzy controller determine the control action in terms of set-point error and its derivative. These rules are normally written to mimic the actions of an experienced process operator. It is assumed that the process operator is willing to share his or her knowledge in terms of a set of production rules. However, by using automated knowledge acquisition techniques, one can extract production rules by observing the behavior of the process operator (Batur *et al.*, 1991; Quinlann, 1989). Several industrial applications of fuzzy controllers have been reported within the last 10 years, for example Pedrycz (1989), Ray and Majumder (1985), Norman and Naveed (1985), Batur and Kasparian (1991a, 1991b), and Procyk and Mamdani (1979). One emerging feature of these controllers is that they seem to be robust even though they use a minimum amount of information about the process dynamics. Perhaps, the robustness is due to the generation of a single control action by combining the contributions of several control rules.

The performance of fuzzy controllers can be further enhanced by adaptively modifying the control rules. This is particularly important if the process and environment dynamics are changing over time. In this chapter an approach is introduced in which the structure of the fuzzy controller is modified by observing the changes of process dynamics.

16.2 FUZZY VARIABLES, MEMBERSHIP FUNCTIONS, AND FUZZY RULES

The first step in the design of a fuzzy controller is the fuzzification of the measured and the observed outputs of a given process. Most commonly, the observed process variable readily available is the process time response $y(k)$. Given $y(k)$, one can measure the rate of change $\dot{y}(k)$ of the process output. Because the objective of the controller is to generate a control action such that the process time response follows a desired trajectory, the fuzzy variables used in the controller rules are written in terms of the set point error $e(k)$ and the rate of change of the set point error $\dot{e}(k)$.

$$e(k) = r(k) - y(k) \tag{1}$$

where $r(k)$ is the setpoint. The second variable $\dot{e}(k)$ can be approximated by

$$\dot{e}(k) = e(k - 1) - e(k) \tag{2}$$

where T is the sampling period.

A typical control rule in terms of the process variables is *If error is small positive (SPE) and if rate of change of error is medium positive (MPDE), then apply small positive control action (SPC)*. One way to define "small positive" for the error term, "medium positive" for the rate of change of error term, and the "small positive control action" term is to use threshold values such as

If $e < e_1$, then error is small positive (SPE) and $\mu_{SPE}(e) = 1$

If $\Delta e_1 < \Delta e < \Delta e_2$, then change in error is medium positive (MPDE) and $\mu_{MPDE}(\Delta e) = 1$

If $u < u_1$, then control is small positive (SPC) and $\mu_{SPC}(u) = 1$

where $\mu(\cdot)$ is an arbitrary function (membership function) that takes the value of 1 if the threshold inequalities are satisfied, otherwise, it is 0. These functions are shown in Fig. 16.1. The same variables can be defined as fuzzy variables by modifying their membership functions as shown in Fig. 16.2. The modified membership curves are continuous smooth functions that assume values between 0 and 1. In this case, any value of an error signal can be small positive (SPE); however,

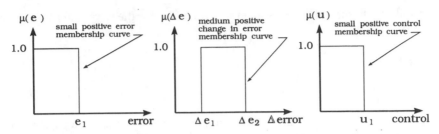

FIG. 16.1. Example of crisp membership functions.

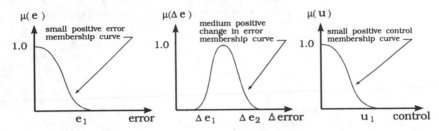

FIG. 16.2. Example of continuous membership curves.

if the error value is actually small, then the small membership curve will result in a membership value close to 1. On the contrary, if the error value was large, the resulting membership value generated from the small membership curve will be close to 0.

The following linguistic fuzzy variables and their membership functions are defined for the controller design introduced in this chapter:

Small Negative Error (SNE)	Small Negative Change in Error (SNDE)
Medium Negative Error (MNE)	Medium Negative Change in Error (MNDE)
Large Negative Error (LNE)	Large Negative Change in Error (LNDE)
Small Positive Error (SPE)	Small Positive Change in Error (SPDE)
Medium Positive Error (MPE)	Medium Positive Change in Error (MPDE)
Large Positive Error (LPE)	Large Positive Change in Error (LPDE)

Similarly, fuzzy linguistic variables for the control actions are defined as follows:

Small Negative Control (SNC)
Medium Negative Control (MNC)
Large Negative Control (LNC)
Small Positive Control (SPC)
Medium Positive Control (MPC)
Large Positive Control (LPC)

Small, medium, and large membership functions for the error and the changes in error are defined as

$$\mu(z) = e^{-\beta_1 z^2} \qquad \text{for small}$$
$$\mu(z) = 1.0 - e^{-\beta_2 z^2} \qquad \text{for large}$$
$$\mu(z) = e^{-\beta_3 (x+y)^2} \qquad \text{for medium}$$

where z could either be the error or the change in error signal, v is a parameter to offset the membership curve, and β_1, β_2, and β_3 are the parameters to shape the membership curves. Figures 16.3 and 16.4 show the membership curves for the error and the changes in error, respectively. The control action generated by the linguistic rules is an incremental action, i.e., the overall control signal applied to the process is $u(k) = u(k-1) + \Delta u(k)$, where $\Delta u(k)$ denotes the incremental action. The membership curves for the incremental control is given by the following equation,

$$\mu(\Delta u) = \frac{\Delta u}{C_{max}} \tag{3}$$

where small, medium, and large membership functions are generated by using different choices of C_{max}. Figure 16.5 shows the membership functions for the incremental control actions.

Usually, the shape of the membership functions is rather subjective in fuzzy controllers. For example, Kickert and Lemke (1976) and Lea (1988) have used nonlinear functions with adjustable parameters. The reasoning behind the bell

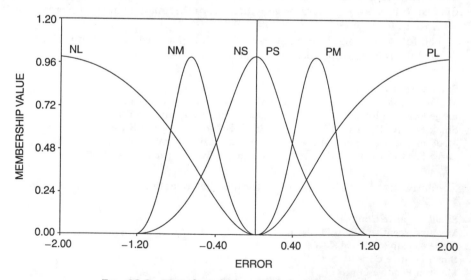

FIG. 16.3. Membership curves for the error.

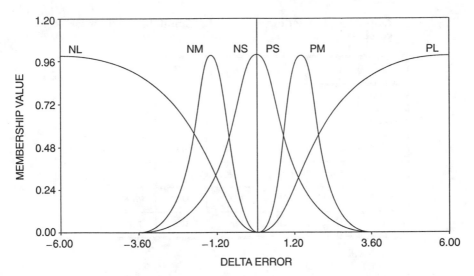

Fig. 16.4. Membership functions of the changes in error.

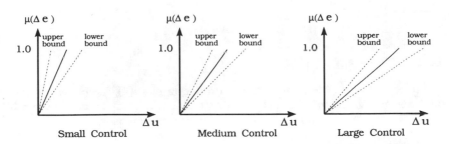

Fig. 16.5. Membership curves for the incremental control action.

shaped exponential membership function used in this chapter is to convey a typical human operator's judgment on these linguistic variables. Furthermore, the membership curves for the controller given by Eq. (3) are simplified so that the fuzzy controller can be tuned by changing the C_{max} parameter. Further discussion on the adjustability of the controller curve is presented in section 16.4.

Different controller rules are introduced for different systems. Table 16.1 shows the typical linguistic fuzzy rules that can be written in terms of the fuzzy variables introduced earlier. Fuzzy rules are derived from Table 16.1 in the following manner. Looking at row number one and column number one, Table 16.1 states the following rule: *If error is large negative (LNE) and the change of error is large and positive (LPDE), then apply large negative control action (LNC).* Thirty-

TABLE 16.1. Fuzzy Control Rules for Simulated First-Order
System

	LNE	MNE	SNE	SPE	MPE	LPE
LNDE	LNC	MNC	SNC	MPC	LPC	LPC
MNDE	LNC	MNC	SNC	MPC	LPC	LPC
SNDE	LNC	MNC	SNC	SPC	MPC	LPC
SPDE	LNC	MNC	SNC	SPC	MPC	LPC
MPDE	LNC	LNC	MNC	SPC	MPC	LPC
LPDE	LNC	LNC	MNC	SPC	MPC	LPC

five similar rules can be derived using the remaining rows and columns in the
table. Similar rules are used extensively by (Daley and Gill, 1986, 1987). In industrial applications, these rules would typically be written by the human operator
based on intuition concerning the response of the system to be controlled.

16.3 INFERENCE ENGINE

The inference engine determines the controller output u(k), given measurements
on the error e(k) and the change in error $\Delta e(k)$. If $\Delta e(k)$ is not directly measurable,
it can be calculated by a finite difference approximation as

$$\Delta e(k) = e(k) - e(k - 1) \tag{4}$$

To demonstrate the principle behind the inference mechanism, consider the
following rule: *If error is small positive (SPE) then apply small positive control
(SPC)*. It is assumed that SPE and SPC are defined by their membership functions as shown in Fig. 16.3 and Fig. 16.5, respectively. This simple knowledge
base consists of only one rule which defines some relationship between the two
linguistic variables SPE and SPC. This relationship is described as

$$R(u, e) = |\mu(u), \mu(e)|_t \tag{5}$$

where $|\cdot, \cdot|_t$ denotes the t-norm (Pedrycz, 1989). Denoting two arbitrary member-
ship functions as x and y, typical choices for the t-norm are

$$|x,y|_t = \min(x,y) \tag{6}$$

$$|x,y|_t = x \cdot y \tag{7}$$

$$|x,y|_t = \log\left[1 + \frac{(w^x - 1)(w^y - 1)}{(w - 1)}\right] \qquad 0 < w < \infty, w \neq 1 \tag{8}$$

$$|x,y|_t = \frac{xy}{w + (1 - w)(x + y - xy)} \tag{9}$$

It is not entirely known yet which form of the *t*-norm works best for real-life problems (Thole *et al.*, 1979). However, common choices are the (min) and the product (.) operators, perhaps due to their simplicity. The product operator is much more intuitive because the contribution of each argument is proportional to its magnitude, a feature that does not exist in the (min) operator. If it is decided to use the (min) operator, the one rule-based knowledge base can be expressed as

$$R(u,e) = \min(\mu_{SPC}(u), \mu_{SPE}(e)) \tag{10}$$

Figure 16.6 is a graphical representation of this relation. Before a specific error value $e(t)$ is considered as input to this relation, the problem is generalized and it is assumed that an arbitrary membership function is input to the relation $R(u,e)$. This arbitrary membership function may correspond to a linguistic variable such as "somewhat smaller error." The new membership function is also shown on the $\mu(e)$ plane of Fig. 16.6. If $\mu(e)$ is considered as input to the relation $R(u,e)$, the output from the relation can be found by the compositional rule of the inference

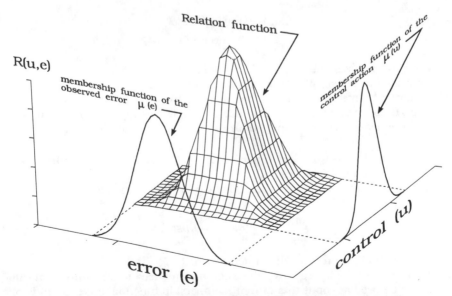

FIG. 16.6. Graphical representation of the relation $R(u,e)$.

operator of Zadeh (1975):

$$\mu(u) = R(u,e) * \mu(e)$$
$$= \max_e \min\left(R(u,e), \mu(e)\right) \tag{11}$$

This operation can be visualized by the following steps.

(1) A line is drawn parallel to (R, u) plane, from each point $(e, \mu(e))$ on the $(e, \mu(e))$ plane. The cluster of these lines defines a shell $S(u,e)$ for which the cross-section in e direction is in the form of $\mu(e)$.

(2) The intersection between the shell $S(u,e)$ and the relation $R(u,e)$ is determined. To obtain the intersection, evaluate $R(u^*, e^*)$ and $S(u^*, e^*)$ for a given location (u^*, e^*) and pick the minimum value. This step is the implementation of the (min) operator of Eq. (11). Obviously, instead of the (min) operator, any version of the t-norm can be used.

(3) The final step of the composition is the projection of this intersection on the (R, u) plane. The (max) operator of Eq. (11) projects the peaks of the intersection on the (R, u) plane. The resulting curve, $\mu(u)$ is the output of the inference engine to the fuzzy input $\mu(e)$.

In fuzzy controllers, inputs to the inference engine are not fuzzy variables, but are measured numerical quantities such as $e(t)$ and $\Delta e(t)$. If these values are to be used as inputs to the inference engine, they have to be fuzzified. One way to fuzzify a nonfuzzy variable is to define a fuzzy membership function that is nonzero only at the numerically observed value of this variable, i.e.,

$$\mu(e) = 1 \quad \text{if } e(k) = e^*$$
$$= 0 \quad \text{otherwise} \tag{12}$$

where e^* is the observed value of the error signal.

Returning to the simple knowledge base, the basic steps (a–c) of the compositional rule of inference can now be implemented for the fuzzified error signal $e(k) = e^*$. Because there is only one nonzero point for the input membership function, the previous steps can now be further simplified as the following:

(1) Given the membership function of SPE, evaluate this membership function for $e(k) = e^*$ to find $\mu(e^*)$.

(2) The output of the inference engine can be determined as

$$\mu_{SPC}^0 = \min_u(\mu_{SPE}(e^*), \mu_{SPC}(u)) \tag{13}$$

Steps (1) and (2) are further illustrated in Fig. 16.7.

The output of the inference engine should be reduced to one numerical value if it is to be used as input to a output membership function curve, $\mu^0(u)$ is one common way to defuzzify the membership function. By considering $\mu^0(u)$ as a

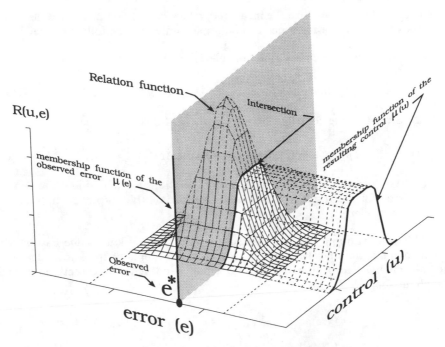

FIG. 16.7. Graphical representation of the simplified relation $R(u,e)$.

distributed load on the u axis, the centroid can be determined as

$$u^* = \frac{\displaystyle\int u\mu_{SPC}(u)\,du}{\displaystyle\int \mu_{SPC}^0(u)\,du} \tag{14}$$

Other approaches are also proposed for the defuzzification of membership functions. For example, picking μ^* as the maximum of $\mu^0(u)$ is another choice to defuzzify the membership function.

So far, a knowledge base consisting of only one rule and one input, $e(k)$, has been considered. Extension of the compositional rule of inference to more than one rule and one input is straightforward. To illustrate, consider a two-rule-based knowledge base that assumes $e(k)$ and $\Delta e(k)$ as inputs, The rules are

Rule 1. IF SPE and MPDE then SPC.

Rule 2. If MPE and SPDE then MPC.

Assume that e^* and Δe^* are the measured values of $e(k)$ and $\Delta e(k)$ at time t. The compositional rule of inference can be implemented by the following steps.

(1) Determine the contribution of rule 1, $\mu^0_{SPC}(u)$ as

$$\mu^0_{SPC}(u) = \min(\min(\mu_{PSE}(e^*), \mu_{MPDE}(\Delta e^*)), \mu_{SPC}(u)) \qquad (15)$$

(2) Similarly, the contribution of rule 2, $\mu^0_{MPC}(u)$ is determined as

$$\mu^0_{MPC} = \min(\min(\mu_{MPE}(e^*), \mu_{SPDE}(\Delta e^*)), \mu_{MPC}(u)) \qquad (16)$$

(3) As illustrated in Fig. 16.8, these contributions are added and the centroid of the resulting curve is determined as the output of the fuzzy controller μ^*.

This brief summary on the inference engine and the knowledge base shows that to create an adaptive fuzzy controller, the contents of the knowledge base can be changed according to some performance index. The next section presents such an adaptive scheme.

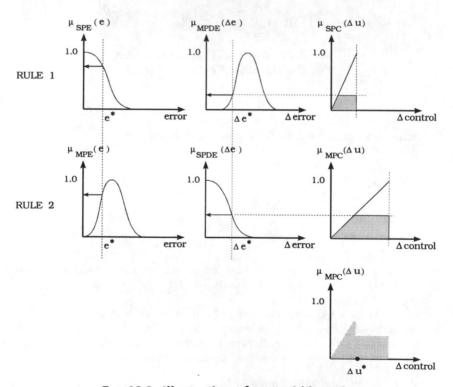

FIG. 16.8. Illustration of centroid-based compositional rule of inference.

CONTROLLER

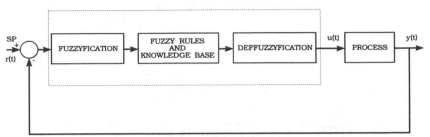

FIG. 16.9. Structure of fuzzy controller.

16.4 ADAPTATION OF THE FUZZY CONTROLLER

Figure 16.9 shows a structure for a typical fuzzy control system. The observed and the measured outputs of the process are compared to some reference value to generate a setpoint error. The fuzzification process assigns linguistic variables to these values with corresponding membership values. These linguistic variables are used in the controller rules to generate linguistic or fuzzy control actions. In the last stage, the linguistic control actions are defuzzified to generate the actual control action that will drive the process.

For a controller to be robust, it should perform reliably under changing conditions of the plant and the environment. Robustness can be achieved by having the controller adapt to the changes in the system. In fuzzy controllers, one way to have an adaptive controller is to start with a set of basic control rules and then add, modify, or eliminate rules in the knowledge base in response to the performance of the controller. In such schemes, the initial control rules provided by the human operator may not be preserved. The adaptive fuzzy controllers of Daley and Gill (1986, 1987), Procyk and Mamdani (1979), and Van Der et al. (1990) fall into this category. Another method to obtain an adaptive fuzzy controller is to have a fixed number of rules in the knowledge base and modify the membership functions. The adjustment of the membership curves in this case are made in response to some function of the control error. The work of Hirota et al. (1985), Kickert and Mamdani (1987), Porter et al. (1987), and Baraae and Rutherford, (1979) fall into this category.

The adaptation of the fuzzy controller discussed in this chapter is in the second category, i.e., the controller rules are fixed but their membership curves are modified, specifically, the membership curves of the controller output. Furthermore, these modifications are made based on the prediction of the error signal, i.e., $\hat{e}(k + 1)$ instead of the error signal $e(k)$. This provides a faster adaptation of the controller. Figure 16.10 shows the proposed structure of the predictive fuzzy controller. The controller membership curves are modified based on one of the following two performance indices. The first performance measure is the observation of the maximum absolute error magnitude within a prespecified window, i.e.,

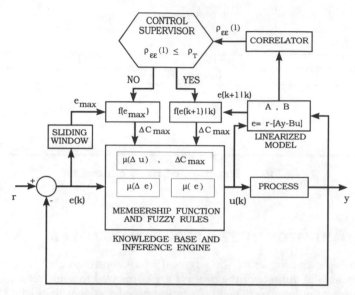

FIG. 16.10. Structure of the proposed predictive fuzzy controller.

$$e_{max} = \max(r(i) - y(i)) \qquad i = k, k - 1, \cdots, k - m + 1 \qquad (17)$$

where $r(i)$ is the set-point and m determines the length of the window. The second performance measure is the one-step-ahead prediction of the process error. The prediction error is defined as

$$\hat{e}(k + 1) = r(k + 1) - \hat{y}(k + 1) \qquad (18)$$

where $\hat{y}(k + 1)$ is the one-step-ahead prediction of the process output obtained from the on-line least squares estimates of the process parameters. A control supervisor is used to decide which performance measure is to be used at a given instance. This decision is made based on whether the prediction model obtained from the least squares model is reliable or not. If the model is reliable, then the one-step-ahead predictor of the error is used for the controller membership adaptation, otherwise the maximum absolute error criterion is used for modifying the controller membership curves. The reliability of the process model is measured using the normalized autocorrelation function

$$\rho_\alpha(j) = \frac{\displaystyle\sum_{k=1}^{N} \epsilon(k)\epsilon(k-j)}{\displaystyle\sum_{k=1}^{N} \epsilon^2(k)} \qquad j = 0, 1, 2, \cdots \quad 0 \le \rho_\alpha(j) \le 1 \qquad (19)$$

where $\epsilon(k)$ is the equation error, which can be calculated as follows

$$\epsilon(k) = y(k) - \hat{y}(k)$$
$$= y(k) - \left(\sum_{i=1}^{n} \hat{a}_i y(k - i) + \sum_{i=1}^{n} \hat{b}_i u(k - i - 1) \right) \qquad (20)$$

where $(\hat{a}, \hat{b})$ are the model parameters obtained by the least squares algorithm. As the equation error given by Eq. (20) goes to zero, the normalized autocorrelation function tends to zero. Hence, the decision of the control supervisor for the method of the adaptation of controller membership curves is based on whether the autocorrelation function is above or below some prespecified threshold value ρ_T, i.e.,

$\rho_\alpha(1) \leq \rho_T \rightarrow$ use $\hat{e}(k + 1)$ *for modifying controller membership curves*
$\rho_\alpha(1) \geq \rho_T \rightarrow$ use $e_{\max}$ *for modifying controller membership curves*

Figure 16.11 shows the method by which the controller membership curves are modified. Step changes in the $C_{\max}$ parameter of Eq. (7) are made which will effectively modify the shape of the controller membership functions. Figure 16.11 describes the functional relationship between $C_{\max}$ and $\hat{e}(k + 1)$ or $e_{\max}$. If $\hat{e}(k + 1)$ or $e_{\max}$ is large, then $C_{\max}$ is reduced; on the contrary, if $\hat{e}(k + 1)$ or $e_{\max}$ is large, then $C_{\max}$ is increased. This controller tuning methodology creates a "cautious" controller that will avoid oscillations following a process upset. Note that changes in the $C_{\max}$ controller parameter has the same effect as changing the gain in a conventional controller. Furthermore, to avoid drifts in the controller parameters, hard bounds are incorporated for each $C_{\max}$.

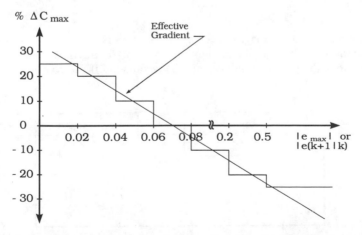

FIG. 16.11. Tuning procedure of the controller membership curves.

16.5 STABILITY OF FUZZY CONTROLLERS

Fuzzy controllers are inherently nonlinear. Furthermore, the self-tuning property of the fuzzy controller discussed in this chapter makes the controller nonstationary. This controller can be represented by the following functional relationship,

$$\Delta u(k) = f(e(k), \Delta e(k), \mu(e(k), \mu(\Delta e(k), \mu(\Delta u(k), C_{max}) \qquad (21)$$

In Eq. 21, $\mu(\Delta u(k))$ and C_{max} vary with time and therefore, the controller becomes nonstationary.

The stability of such systems can be analyzed if an appropriate Lyapunov function can be found. If the model of the process is known *a priori*. Chen (1987) has proposed an "Expert Lyapunov Function" to analyze the stability of such systems. Based on the process model and the expert-generated Lyapunov function, conditions can be imposed on the controller to guarantee the stability of the overall system.

If the process to be controlled is linear based on its input/output data, then an alternative method to analyze the stability of the overall system is by the Popov's or the Circle Stability Criterion. This method is a frequency domain criterion that provides sufficient conditions for asymptotic stability for certain classes of nonlinear systems as seen in Fig. 16.12 (Cook, 1986; Ray and Majumder, 1984). To demonstrate the application of this methodology for the analysis of fuzzy controllers, consider a rational, strictly proper and asymptotically stable plant G(s). For a given fuzzy controller with a stationary or nonstationary knowledge base and membership functions, if

$$\lambda_{min} < f(e, \Delta e, \mu(e), \mu(\Delta e), \mu(\Delta u), C_{max}) < \lambda_{max} \qquad (22)$$

and if

$$\frac{\lambda_{max} G(s) + 1}{\lambda_{min} G(s) + 1} = F(s) \qquad (23)$$

is positive real, then the origin of the closed system is stable. λ_{min} and λ_{max} are sections that bound the nonlinear element, in this case the fuzzy controller. It can be shown that the positive realness of $F(s)$ is satisfied if the Nyquist plot of the

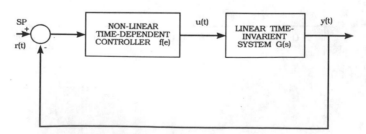

FIG. 16.12. Linear plant with nonlinear control element.

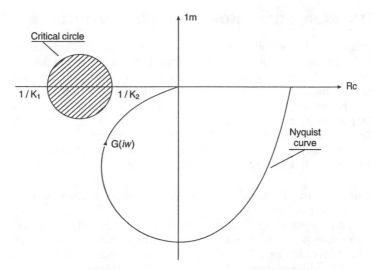

FIG. 16.13. Graphical representation of the Circle stability criterion for a linear plant.

plant $G(jw)$ misses a circle that passes through the points $-1/\lambda_{min}$ and $-1/\lambda_{max}$ on the real axis. Graphical representation of this can be seen in Fig. 16.13. To obtain the sectors that bound the nonlinearities, the controller is operated off-line by introducing all possible values of $e(k)$ and plotting the resulting control actions $\Delta u(k)$, as seen in Fig. 16.14.

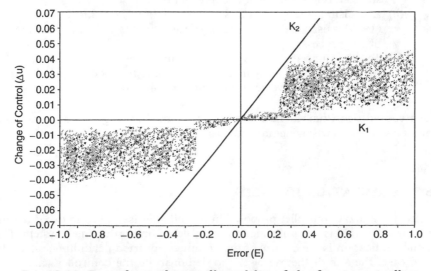

FIG. 16.14. Bounds on the nonlinearities of the fuzzy controller.

16.6 INVERSE FUZZY MODEL BASED CONTROLLERS

Conventional fuzzy controllers use a minimum amount of information about the process dynamics. This information is contained in $\{e(t), \dot{e}(t)\}$ which can also be expressed in terms of $\{y, \dot{y}\}$, respectively. In this chapter, one methodology to increase the amount of information available to a fuzzy controller is explored. However, the resulting controller is still a fuzzified Proportional plus Derivative (PD) controller which uses a partial knowledge $\{y(t), \dot{y}(t)\}$ about the process dynamics. What is more desirable, however, is to determine a fuzzy model of the process dynamics and to design a fuzzy controller that uses this fuzzy model. The rationale behind this approach is the following:

(1) The amount of information about the process dynamics to the controller is increased.

(2) If the process is nonlinear, it can be conjectured that a fuzzy model is a more powerful predictor than a simple linear model. For example, it has also been shown that predictive models are as powerful as the conventional time series models (Tong, 1978; Pedrycz, 1984; Tagaki and Sugeno, 1985; Xu and Lu, 1987).

(3) If a fuzzy model is available, one can design a predictive fuzzy controller instead of a fuzzified PD controller. Here, the reference value $r(t)$, is considered as the output of the fuzzy model and the compositional rule of inference operator is applied backward to determine the controller output. This controller can be viewed as a fuzzified deadbeat controller, or alternatively, an inverse model-based controller. This methodology is being currently investigated within the following framework (Srinivasan et al., 1992):

(a) Process input/output data $u(t), y(t)$ are quantized in terms of preselected reference membership functions.

(b) A decision tree generator, such as the ID3 algorithm of Quinlan (1989) is used to determine a set of rules that describe the dynamics of the process.

(c) To determine the controller output, interpret the set-point $r(t)$ as the output of the fuzzy model and evaluate the model input that if applied would have generated the set-point $r(t)$.

The proposed algorithm can be implemented on-line by using an incremental version of the decision tree generator such as the LEM33 algorithm of Chan (1991).

16.7 SIMULATION RESULTS

The adaptive fuzzy controller proposed in this chapter is applied to two different problems. The first is an application to a simulated first-order linear system. The second application is the control of the nonlinear inverted pendulum system. In either case, the aim of the exercise is to demonstrate the controller's ability to result in a satisfactory response by tuning the initial knowledge base.

The simulated first-order system in its discrete form is given as

$$y(k) = 0.47y(k - 1) + 1.8u(k - 1) + \epsilon(k) \qquad (24)$$

where $\epsilon(k)$ is the noise term at instance k. To illustrate the action of the supervisory control, the dynamics of the noise term is changed from uncorrelated to correlated noise during the simulation process. The noise correlation is given in the following form,

$$\epsilon(k) = 0.9\epsilon(k - 1) + \xi(k) \qquad (25)$$

where $\xi(k)$ is uncorrelated noise. The knowledge base or the governing control rules for the control of this simulated system is given in Table 16.1. Figure 16.15 shows the estimates of the process parameters obtained from the recursive least squares algorithm. On the same figure, the control supervisor response can be seen on the top part of the graph. The upper level indicates that the e_{max} criterion is used to update the controller membership curves, whereas the lower level indicates that $\hat{e}(k + 1)$, obtained from the process model, is used to tune the controller membership curves. The threshold value for the autocorrelation of the equation error is set to $\rho_T = 0.2$. The response of the system to step changes in the set-point $r(k)$ is shown in Fig. 16.16.

The second example is designed to illustrate the performance of the fuzzy controller in a situation for which it is not designed. The process is the nonlinear

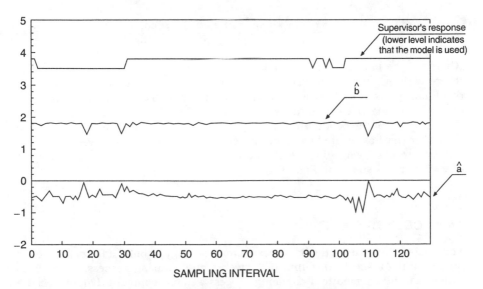

FIG. 16.15. Estimated system parameters obtained from least squares algorithm.

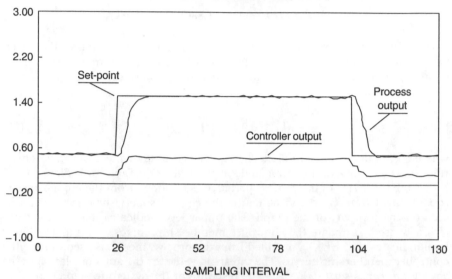

FIG. 16.16. Set-point response of the first-order simulated system.

inverted pendulum given by the following continuous model,

$$\ddot{y} = \frac{mgl \sin y - ml^2 \dot{y} \sin y \cos y - ul \cos y}{ml^2(1 + \sin^2 y)} \tag{26}$$

where u is the horizontal force applied to the system; $y, \dot{y}$, and $\ddot{y}$ are the angle of the pendulum, the angular velocity, and the acceleration, respectively; m is the pendulum mass; g is the gravitational constant; and l is the length of the pendulum. The objective of the fuzzy controller is to apply horizontal force u such that the angle of the pendulum is at some desired position. Table 16.2 shows the controller rules associated with this system. A schematic of the inverted pendulum system is shown in Fig. 16.17 and the response of the system for set-point of $y = 0.0$ deg. is shown in Fig. 16.18.

16.8 CONCLUSION

This chapter introduced the basic design methodology to build a fuzzy controller for regulating a specified output of a given manufacturing process. Fuzzy controllers can be adapted to a changing process and environment dynamic. If the performance of the fuzzy controller is not satisfactory, the knowledge base can be modified. Change in the structure is accomplished by modifying the controller

TABLE 16.2. Fuzzy Control Rules for Inverted Pendulum System

	LNE	MNE	SNE	SPE	MPE	LPE
LNDE	LPC	MPC	SPC	MNC	LNC	LNC
MNDE	LPC	MPC	SPC	MNC	LNC	LNC
SNDE	LPC	MPC	SPC	SNC	MNC	LNC
SPDE	LPC	MPC	SPC	SNC	MNC	LNC
MPDE	LPC	LPC	MPC	SNC	MNC	LNC
LPDE	LPC	LPC	MPC	SNC	MNC	LNC

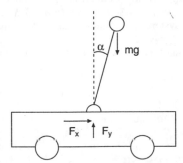

FIG. 16.17. Schematic of the inverted pendulum system.

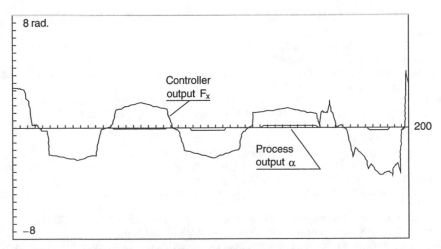

**FIG. 16.18. Response of the inverted pendulum
system for zero degree set-point value.**

output membership function in relation to the error between the set-point and the predicted process output. The circle criterion can be used to check the stability of the feedback system operating under the fuzzy controller.

REFERENCES

Baraae M., Rutherford D. 1979. Theoretical and linguistic aspect of fuzzy logic controller. *Automatica* 15:533–577.

Batur, C., Kasparian V. 1991a. Adaptive expert control. *Int. Journal of Control* 54(4):867–881.

Batur C., Kasparian V. 1991b. Predictive fuzzy expert controllers. *Computers Ind. Engng.* 20(2):199–209.

Batur C., Srinivasan A., Chan, C.-C. 1991. Automated rule base model generation for uncertain complex dynamic systems. *Eng. Applic. of Artificial Intelligence* Vol. 4, No. 4.

Chan, C.-C. 1991. Incremental learning production rules from examples under uncertainty: A rough set approach. *Int. Journ. of Software and Knowledge Eng.* Vol. 1, No. 4.

Chen-Wei, Xu. 1989. Fuzzy system identification. *IEEE Proceedings* Vol. 136, Pt. D, No. 4, July, pp. 146–149.

Chen, Y. Y. 1987. Stability analysis of fuzzy control: A Lyapunov approach. CH 2503-187, 1027-1031, IEEE.

Cook, P. A. 1986. *Nonlinear Dynamical Systems*. Prentice Hall.

Daley, S., and Gill, K. F. 1986. A design study of self-monitoring fuzzy logic controller. *Proc. Inst. Mech. Eng.* Part C, 200, C1 56–69.

Daley, S., Gill, K. F. 1987. Attitude control of spacecraft using an extended self-organizing fuzzy logic controller. *Proc. Inst. Mech. Eng.* 201, C1.

Hirota, K. Arari, Y., and Pedrycz W. 1985. Robot control based on membership and vagueness. In *Approx. Reasoning in Expert Systems*, eds. M. M. Gupta, A. Kandel, and J. B. Kiszka, pp. 621–635. Amsterdam: Elsevier.

Kickert, W. J. M., and Mamdani, E. H. 1987. Analysis of fuzzy logic controller. *Fuzzy Sets and Systems* 1:29–44.

Kickert, W. J. M., and Van Lauto Lemke, H. R. 1976. Application of a fuzzy controller in a warm water plant. *Automatica* 12:301–308.

Kraus T. W., and Myron, J. 1987. Self-tuning PID controller uses pattern recognition approach. *Control Engineering* 12:62–64.

Lea, N. R. 1988. Applications of fuzzy sets to data monitoring and process control. ISA Proc. Paper No. 88-1610.

Norman, P., and Naveed S. 1985. An expert system supervisor for a rotary cement kiln. IEEE Symp. on Expert Systems in Process Control, University of Salford, *Digest* 107.

Pedrycz, W. 1984. An identification algorithm in fuzzy relational systems. *Fuzzy Set and Systems* 13:153–167.

Pedrycz, W. 1989. *Fuzzy Control and Fuzzy Systems*. R.S.P. and John Wiley.

Porter, B., Jones, A. H., and McKeown, C. B. 1987. Real-time expert tuners for PI controllers. *IEEE Proc.* Vol. 134. Pt. D, No. 4, pp. 260–263, July.

Procyk T. J., and Mamdani, E. H. 1979. A Linguistic self-organizing controller. *Automatica* 15:15–30.

Quinlan, J. R. 1987. Simplifying decision trees. *Int. J. Man-Machine Studies* 27:221–234.

Quinlan, J. R. 1989. Induction of decision trees. *Machine Learning* 1:81–106.

Ray, K. S., and Majumder, D. 1984. Application of circle criteria for stability analysis of linear SISO and MIMO systems associated with fuzzy logic controller. *IEEE Trans. on Systems, Man and Cybernetics*, SMC-14, No. 2.

Ray, K. S., and Majumder, D. 1985. Fuzzy logic control of nonlinear multivariable steam generating unit using decoupling theory. *IEEE Trans. on Systems, Man and Cybernetics*, SMC-15, No. 4, July/August.

Srinivasan, A., Batur, C., and Chan, C.-C. 1993. Using inductive learning to determine fuzzy rules for dynamic systems. *Journal of Engineering Applications of Artificial Intelligence* 6(3):257–265.

Tagaki, T., and Sugeno, M. 1985. Fuzzy identification of systems and its applications to modeling and control. *IEEE Trans. on System, Man, and Cybernetics*, SMC-15.

Thole U., Zimmermann, H. J., and Zysno, P. 1979. The suitability of minimum and product operators for the intersection of fuzzy sets. *Fuzzy Sets and Systems* 2:167–180.

Tong, R. M. 1978. Synthesis of fuzzy models for industrial processes. *International Journal of Generating Systems* 4:143–162.

Van Der, R. F., Lemke, H. R. V. N., and Dukman, J. G. 1990. Knowledge-based fuzzy control system. *IEEE Trans*. AC. 35(2):148–155.

Xu, H.-W., and Lu, Y.-Z. 1987. Fuzzy model identification and self-learning for dynamic systems. *IEEE Trans. on Systems, Man, and Cybernetics*, Vol. SMC-17, No. 4.

Zadeh, K. L. 1975. The concept of linguistic variable and its application to approximate reasoning. *Information Sciences* 8:199–249; 301–375; 9:47–80.

Ziegler, G. J., and Nichols, N. B. 1942. Optimum settings for automatic controllers. *Trans. ASME* 64:759–768.

Chapter 17

Knowledge-Based Approaches for Material Handling System Design

Jessica O. Matson
Associate Professor of Industrial Engineering
University of Alabama
Tuscaloosa, Alabama

Joseph M. Mellichamp
Board of Visitors Research Professor of Management Science
University of Alabama
Tuscaloosa, Alabama

Sundar R. Swaminathan
Senior Consultant
American Airlines Decision Technologies
Dallas/Ft. Worth Airport, Texas

17.1 INTRODUCTION

A major step in the planning of a manufacturing facility, whether it is a new or existing facility, is the design and selection of the material handling system. The material handling function includes all aspects of handling, storing, and controlling the material (Tompkins and White, 1984). The handling system serves as the physical integrator within the manufacturing facility (White and Apple, 1985). In addition, it is estimated that handling activities account for 20% to 70% of the cost of production. Thus, well-designed handling systems are essential for reduced costs and efficient operations.

The material handling system design problem is generally considered to be interdependent with the facility layout problem. Although the two problems should ideally be considered simultaneously, an iterative approach is usually used in practice, with consideration of the handling system following the development of an initial layout. Tompkins and White (1984) suggest "that a number of alternative handling systems be developed and the appropriate layout be designed for each." Because of the computational effort in the development and analysis of layouts, a number of computer-based tools, e.g., CRAFT (Armour and Buffa, 1963), CORELAP (Lee and Moore, 1967), and ALDEP (Seehof and Evans, 1967), have been designed to assist in the development, evaluation, and/or improvement of a layout. Kusiak and Heragu (1987) provide a review of algorithms designed to assist in the layout problem.

There have been fewer tools developed specifically to assist with the design of the handling system. COFAD (Tompkins and Reed, 1976) permits consideration of alternative handling methods in conjunction with the improvement of an initial layout. SHAPE (Hassan, 1983) was designed as a research tool for considering both the layout and material handling equipment selection problem. Tools which focus only on the material handling system have typically been for special-purpose applications, as discussed in a later section. There is a need for computer-based tools to assist with general handling design problems. One approach for developing such tools is through the application of expert systems methodologies.

Potential of Expert Systems

In assessing the potential for applying expert systems methodologies to a particular decision domain, one must consider the likely payoff and the nature of the expertise involved in making the decision. In the case of material handling system design, it appears that expert systems approaches are clearly justified.

As has been mentioned, many such decisions are made on an ongoing basis by organizations of every size and orientation. The dollar amounts represented by these decisions are significant, in many instances amounting to millions of dollars. Thus, there is considerable financial incentive for development of objective methods for ensuring that efficient system designs are obtained.

From the perspective of expertise, it is clear that few organizations have engineering personnel devoted exclusively to material handling systems design decisions; thus, it may be stated that this type of expertise is scarce for most firms. There is also a sense in which the kind of expertise required for these design decisions tends to be centralized (as in the case of corporate engineering staffs or research centers) as opposed to being located at the point of use, i.e., at operational sites. Thus, expert systems approaches to the design problem could allow organizations to acquire specialized knowledge, located at the point of use.

Objective

The objective of this chapter is to examine the issues related to the application of knowledge-based systems for the material handling system design problem. Three categories of material handling design problems are identified: (1) system specification, (2) equipment type selection, and (3) detailed equipment specification. The design issues that are critical in the development of a knowledge-based system are investigated for each of the three categories, and a prototype knowledge-based system for equipment type selection is described.

17.2 MATERIAL HANDLING SYSTEM DESIGN

To determine the applicability of a knowledge-based approach, it is necessary to define the material handling system design problem. One might ask the following questions:

- What types of activities are involved in material handling system design?
- What knowledge is required?
- Who typically does material handling system design?
- What tools are available to assist in the design of a material handling system?

Material Handling Design Activities

Material handling system design generally follows the six-step engineering design process: recognition of need and problem definition, analysis of the problem, generation of alternatives, evaluation of alternatives, selection of the preferred alternative, and implementation. However, the specific activities can vary greatly depending on the nature of the problem. Activities and effort are directly tied to the layout of the facility. For example, the activities and knowledge that would be required for determining the handling system for a new facility would be quite different from the activities and knowledge that would be required for determining the handling system for a new process within a single department in an existing layout. Thus, it is necessary to define categories for the types of material handling problems that exist.

There are a number of different approaches that could be used to classify the handling design problem. Malmborg, Simons, and Agee (1986) suggested a three-level hierarchy for organizing a knowledge base for material handling equipment selection. The top level of the hierarchy contains knowledge required for the selection of a general category of equipment, such as conveyors or industrial trucks. The middle level contains the knowledge required to select a specific equipment type, such as a belt conveyor or a powered roller conveyor. The bottom level of the hierarchy includes the information needed to select a commercially available product. The three levels of the hierarchy would be used to select the commercial product to solve the handling problem.

Rather than focusing on the specification of a commercially available product as the ultimate solution to the handling problem, it is proposed that there are actually three related but different design problems, requiring different types of knowledge and effort. The three problems are (1) system specification, (2) equipment type selection, and (3) detailed equipment specification. The emphasis here is on the activities and knowledge that would be required for each of the three categories and the applicability of a knowledge-based approach for each.

The system specification problem concerns the design of a handling system for a new facility or a major addition to or relayout of an existing facility. This category represents situations where many moves with possibly diverse characteristics are required. In the design of such a facility, the handling system may be designed simultaneously with the design of the layout for the facility. The design problem is constrained primarily by cost and the nature of the material to be handled; a fixed layout does not exist. Data collection activities represent a significant portion of the effort because many of the statistics related to the operation of the facility may not be available. The end product of the system specification problem is a set of detailed requirements for a handling system without the specification of a particular device or equipment option. Alternatively, the system specification might result in the selection of a general equipment category (similar to the top level of the hierarchy of Malmborg, Simons, and Agee) that is deemed best for solving the handling problems.

On the other hand, many material handling problems often involve only single moves with fixed characteristics and can be addressed as an equipment type selection problem. It has been estimated that between 250,000 and 500,000 decisions involving selection of minor material handling equipment are made annually by plant engineers (Schultz, 1980). Such decisions might be required, for example, when a change in the product or process necessitates a change in the handling system within an existing fixed area. The constraints in such a problem may include not only cost and material type but also move path, equipment interfaces, and height restrictions, among others. The number and variety of constraints greatly limit the number of feasible equipment alternatives.

A third type of design problem involves the development of detailed equipment specifications for a selected equipment type. Situations do exist where the appropriate equipment type is obvious, e.g., when only a belt conveyor should be considered. The design activities for such a problem include developing the necessary detailed specifications to ensure that an efficient and cost-effective model is selected.

Types of Knowledge for Material Handling Design

Fisher (1986) identifies four types of knowledge that are necessary for factory design.

- Product-specific knowledge—related to the item produced in the factory
- Organizational knowledge—related to company policies
- Industry-specific knowledge—related to all products within the same industry
- Generic knowledge—general design knowledge

Using similar terminology but different definitions, the knowledge required for solving material handling design problems can also be categorized. Like Fisher's list, one type of knowledge would be generic design knowledge. The facility planner or material handling analyst must be knowledgeable of and competent in the application of general design principles, algorithms, and rules of thumb for layout and material handling. The knowledge in this category may cross over several disciplines. A second category of knowledge could be categorized as organizational knowledge. More broadly defined than in Fisher's list, the organizational knowledge for material handling system design includes not only organizational policies but also knowledge related to the material characteristics, move requirements, and facility constraints. A third type of knowledge would be product–specific knowledge. However, the product of interest is the material handling device that is being considered for application. The material handling analyst must be knowledgeable of the capabilities of a wide range of material handling products.

The three categories of knowledge are required in varying degrees for the three types of material handling design problems. The system specification problem typically requires a high degree of generic design knowledge and a low degree of product-specific knowledge. Organizational knowledge, although needed, may not be well documented. In the equipment type selection problem, however, the organizational knowledge is of primary concern, along with product-specific knowledge of appropriate material handling equipment options. For detailed equipment specification, the focus is again on product-specific and organizational knowledge.

Material Handling Analysts

The knowledge needed for the different types of material handling design problems provides an opportunity for different types of analysts to participate in the design process. Typically, material handling system design is done by consultants, vendors, or company engineers. Each type of analyst brings different skills, perspectives, and biases to the problem. Consultants are often called in for system specification problems because of their range of experience with large, complex problems. However, consultants must undergo a learning process related to the organizational knowledge that the company's engineers already have. In addition, consultants are not inexpensive. Vendors have the highest degree of product-specific knowledge for the specific products that they sell. This knowledge may provide an advantage if the vendor's product line includes the best solution to the handling problem. The vendor also may be somewhat more accountable to the firm for the operation of the recommended equipment. However, vendors may not be knowledgeable of some types of products and might be expected to have some biases. Unless the company is large, the company engineer may not be assigned as a full-time material handling analyst; hence, her generic design skills and knowledge may require updating, and she will not be as knowledgeable as a vendor regarding the vendor's product.

17.3 COMPUTER-BASED TOOLS FOR MATERIAL HANDLING SYSTEM DESIGN

The equipment type selection problem has traditionally been approached using checklists, principles, and handbooks. A 1966 article in *Modern Materials Handling* posed the question: "Can You Computerize Equipment Selection?" The article described a pilot study at the Georgia Institute of Technology to develop a computer program to provide the appropriate equipment recommendation for any handling task. It was suggested that the program would "end one of the most tedious and onerous jobs that a materials handling engineer must perform." Although there has been continued interest in the application of the computer for material handling equipment selection, there have been few computer-based tools designed for generalized equipment selection. Those that have been designed have not achieved widespread use. However, a number of more "focused" computer-based tools have been developed and would be applicable for the detailed equipment specification problem. For example, when the equipment options are limited to robots, a decision support system has been developed for selecting the model which has the appropriate features for the handling task (Jones et al., 1985); a similar approach has been described for selecting automated guided vehicles (Shelton and Jones, 1987). Another example is a system which helps the material handling analyst select the appropriate storage and retrieval system for tote-sized loads (Dunkin, 1988). In addition, the computer has been used to support the data analysis activities that are required in all categories of material handling problems. Techniques such as simulation and waiting line analysis are widely applied in material handling design.

Suitability of Expert Systems Methodology

Several distinguishing characteristics of the material handling system design problem indicate the appropriateness of applying expert systems methods. First of all, the problem is fairly well understood. The detailed equipment specification problem is perhaps more clearly comprehended by analysts than the system specification problem, but on the whole it can be concluded that the problem is grasped by analysts. Second, the problem is of moderate difficulty. If it were trivial, it would be of little concern; if it were exceedingly difficult, it would probably be addressed with task forces or committees.

A third characteristic is that genuine experts exist. It is expected that an experienced design engineer would consistently produce better designs than a novice and also that experts would agree on what constitutes a "good" design vis-à-vis a "bad" design. Finally, the design problem generally requires heuristic rather than algorithmic reasoning. It is true that elements of the problem can be reduced to objective procedures, but, on balance, these problems are solved by trial and error approaches which incorporate a great deal of experientially acquired knowledge.

Material Handling System Design Expert Systems

Only a few expert systems dealing with material handling system design decisions have been described in the literature. This section will briefly overview seven such systems, focusing on what part of the systems design problem each addresses.

MAHDE

MAHDE is a knowledge-based design aid developed by Gabbert and Brown (1989) to assist facility planners in the design of material handling systems for a facility. MAHDE considers manual handling, fork trucks, conveyors, transporters, monorails, AGV's, and flow racks; conveyors and monorails are further specified at a second level of detail. The system obtains from the user inputs describing the material to be moved and the environment in which the move is to occur. After initial inputs are made, MAHDE generates an initial system design. The user is next asked for preferences for various attributes including: level of investment, average uptime, flexibility, and mean time to repair. The system then generates a suitable design based on the user's preference structure. MAHDE appears to be a useful tool for exploring different material handling system scenarios for a facility and is aimed at the system specification problem.

IMHSS

Eom and Trevino (1992) describe IMHSS (Intelligent Material Handling and Storage Systems) as a framework for the selection, design, control, and justification of material handling and storage systems for electronics assembly. Their approach is based on the development of an object-oriented, knowledge-based model consisting of three subsystems. The material handling selection subsystem generates all feasible alternatives for the material handling and storage system, and the material handling design expert system applies analytical techniques for the alternatives generated by the selection expert system. A third expert system is for material handling control. Their approach is aimed at developing solutions which bridge the system specification and the equipment selection problems.

MATHES

Developed by Farber and Fisher (1985), MATHES is a rule-based expert system in the equipment type selection category. It aids designers in the selection of material handling equipment for interdepartmental unitized moves. MATHES considers 18 different material handling alternatives including conveyors, cranes, automated guided vehicles, industrial trucks, and manual handling. Four main parameters are considered in generating a recommendation: path, volume of flow, size of unit, and interdepartmental distance. The system's knowledge base includes 172 rules acquired through interviews with a material handling expert.

SEMH

SEMH (Selection of Equipment for Material Handling) is a system that incorporates both conventional analysis capabilities and expert system methods (Tabibzadeh, 1985). The expert system mode of SEMH aids the user in selecting the equipment type selection problem, equipment for a specific move. SEMH incorporates knowledge from textbooks and handbooks on equipment selection; the knowledge is structured in the form of rules. The system uses two major categories of attributes in defining the movement problem: material characteristics and move characteristics. These attributes are further subdivided into variables such as speed, frequency, and distance.

INSIMAS

The Interactive SImulation of MAterial flow System (INSIMAS) was described as an expert system being developed to aid in the design of automated handling systems such as AGV and monorail systems (Grosseschallau and Kusiak, 1985). The completed system was to incorporate an AI approach based heavily on mathematical programming techniques to generate solutions for vehicle routing and sequencing problems. This expert system represents an effort to develop a tool to refine the equipment type selection decision.

ROBOSPEC

ROBOSPEC is a specialized expert system developed to aid designers in the selection of industrial robots (Fisher and Maimon, 1987). The system embeds knowledge about the application of robots in the areas of handling, manufacturing, and assembly. ROBOSPEC utilizes a rule representation scheme for its knowledge and acquires relevant application inputs from the user to reach appropriate conclusions. The end result of a session with ROBOSPEC is the detailed specification of the selected industrial robot.

EXIT

EXIT is a PC-based expert system for industrial truck selection (Malmborg et al., 1989). The system contains knowledge about seventeen different types of industrial trucks, classifying trucks into five functional categories including: dock operations, unit load storage, order picking, in-process handling, and yard operations. Five different attributes are used in the truck selection decision: material type, material weight, load/unload level, load/unload method, utilization, physical restrictions, and operation. The primary knowledge representation scheme used in EXIT is rules; the inference mechanism is goal directed.

What is immediately apparent from an assessment of the published literature describing expert systems for material handling system design is that

- Researchers are just beginning to explore the usefulness of expert systems in this applications area.
- Attention to date has focused on very specific design decisions, e.g., specification of a particular robot for a given application, specialization of an AGV route in a facility, or recommendation of an appropriate type of equipment for a specific move.

It seems reasonable to conclude that as progress is made in this area, applications will move from the specific to the general. It should not be too long before expert systems with general/global design capabilities emerge.

In the following sections, some of the issues will be explored which must be addressed if knowledge-based systems which truly support material handling system design are to be developed.

17.4 SYSTEM SPECIFICATION ISSUES

One of the current themes in manufacturing system design research is that material handling considerations need to be integrated into the concurrent engineering process. Mullens and Swart (1992) cite several studies in which authors have criticized the existing practice of designing the material handling system after the product, process, layout, and schedule designs have been completed. The obvious conclusion is that these design tasks should be executed simultaneously—not sequentially.

A number of approaches have been proposed and are, in fact, being used to facilitate concurrent engineering. These include:

- Quality Function Deployment
- Axiomatic Design
- Design for Manufacturing
- Design Science
- Design for Manufacturing and Assembly
- The Taguchi Method
- Group Technology
- Failure Mode and Effects Analysis
- Value Engineering

Unfortunately, as Mullens and Swart point out, the only one that directly addresses material handling considerations is Design for Manufacturing and Assembly, which considers workplace handling issues. The other material handling issues (i.e., material transport, storage, containerization, and control) are not addressed in any of the proposed concurrent engineering approaches.

Mullens and Swart make several recommendations for including the full scope of material handling in the concurrent engineering process. The most significant of their proposals is that more effective material handling system design guidelines need to be developed and integrated into existing concurrent engineering methods. It is clear that this must be done; how it will be done remains to be determined.

There appear to be several ways of addressing this problem with knowledge-based methods. Three possibilities are embedding expert systems in existing concurrent engineering approaches, developing specialized expert systems that treat process and material handling system design simultaneously, and developing generic expert systems that attempt to integrate design issues.

Embedded Expert Systems

A number of the concurrent engineering approaches have been or are being computerized. It may be possible to develop expert systems that address material handling issues which can be embedded in these design packages. Mellichamp, Miller, and Wang (1989, p. 44) describe how such an approach has been integrated in a computer-based machine qualification program.

Specialized Expert Systems

Another possibility is to develop knowledge-based systems that simultaneously treat process and material handling design for specialized manufacturing systems. Flexible manufacturing and group technology systems offer potential for this type of development. Mellichamp, Kwon, and Wahab (1990) describe an expert system which operates in conjunction with simulation to generate an effective design for a flexible manufacturing system. The expert system described in this study treats both workplace handling and material transport issues.

Generic Expert Systems

Ultimately, generic expert systems will be developed that simultaneously address the full range of design issues for any type of manufacturing system. Such systems may evolve from existing concurrent engineering methods or they may be developed from scratch. Mellichamp et al. (1991) have proposed integrating Quality Function Deployment and Design for Manufacturability as a way of avoiding some of the problems of sequential design. Future efforts along these lines should lead to actual systems which treat material handling design along with other design tasks.

17.5 EXPERT SYSTEM DEVELOPMENT ISSUES

In developing expert systems to support material handling systems design, it is important to recognize that the nature of the expert system depends on whether the design decision deals with system specification, equipment selection, or equipment specification. Figure 17.1 shows how various decision issues, expert system architecture issues, and expert system interface issues map over the three categories of material handling system design problems. The following paragraphs will describe the implications of these key issues on expert systems development.

KNOWLEDGE-BASED SYSTEMS FOR MATERIAL HANDLING SYSTEM DESIGN	MATERIAL HANDLING DESIGN DECISIONS		
DEVELOPMENT ISSUES:	EQUIPMENT SPECIFICATION	EQUIPMENT SELECTION	SYSTEM SPECIFICATION
DECISION ISSUES:			
KNOWLEDGE	SPECIFIC . . . . GENERAL		
UNCERTAINTY	LOW . . . . HIGH		
COMPLEXITY	SIMPLE . . . . COMPLEX		
EXPERT SYSTEM ARCHITECTURE ISSUES:			
KNOWLEDGE STRUCTURES	SIMPLE . . . . COMPLEX		
INFERENCE	SIMPLE . . . . COMPLEX		
MODELS	NOT REQUIRED . . . . EMBEDDED		
EXPERT SYSTEM INTERFACE ISSUES:			
DATA BASES	NOT REQUIRED . . . . REQUIRED		
EXPLANATION	SIMPLE . . . . COMPLEX		
LEARNING	ROTE . . . . PRINCIPLES		
MAINTENANCE	DYNAMIC . . . . STATIC		

FIG. 17.1. Expert system development issues.

Decision Issues

The type of knowledge needed to build an expert system is certainly a function of the materials handling system design task which is to be addressed. The equipment specification task requires facts about specific makes and models of equipment—prices, cost data, speeds, operational capabilities, and so on. Much of the kind of knowledge needed for such a system would come from equipment vendors. At the other extreme, the system specification decision requires facts that are almost exclusively related to design principles—how material handling equipment interfaces with manufacturing processes or with shipping and receiving. In between, the equipment type selection task calls for knowledge that treats equipment options in a more or less generic sense. Thus, the knowledge requirement ranges from very specific to very general depending on the design task.

Uncertainty also tends to vary with the design task. The system specification task is generally compounded by uncertainty. Part of this is simply due to the complexity of such decisions, but there are other reasons. This task is often done while the facility design is emerging; thus, uncertainty is inevitable. Future expectations are important to the system specification process, introducing another element of uncertainty. By the time the planning process has reached the point of selecting a particular fork truck or industrial robot, most of the uncertainty has been filtered out of the decision. Expert systems developed for the system specification task, then, should be able to contend with uncertainty either in a probabilistic sense or in allowing the user to rapidly assess numerous scenarios. Systems developed for equipment specification or selection would not have to be as robust in this regard.

From a size or complexity perspective, it is clear that the equipment specification decision is relatively simple as compared to the system specification decision. This is true both in terms of the number of options or combinations that must be considered and the magnitude and depth of knowledge which must be accessed to generate a design. The implication of the size issue for expert system development relates to the hardware (and software) options available to developers. More memory and faster cycle times will be required, in general, in moving from the equipment specification to the system specification task.

Expert System Architecture Issues

Possibly the most influential factor affecting the architecture of expert systems is the knowledge representation scheme employed in the system. Most expert system development "shells" and languages are selected on the basis of knowledge representation capability. Of the expert systems already developed to treat material handling system design problems, most use simple rule structures as the primary knowledge representation scheme. This is because the existing expert systems predominantly treat the equipment specification or selection problem. As systems which treat the system specification problem emerge, it is expected that more complex knowledge representation schemes such as frames and objects will be required.

What has been said about knowledge representation is also true of inference. Rule-based systems typically utilize some type of forward or backward chaining mechanism to process through the rules. Existing systems use chaining almost exclusively as an inferencing mechanism. In order to address the system specification problem, more complex inferencing procedures will be required—expectations, message passing, and mixed strategies will be required. This will limit the software options (development tools) which will be available to developers and, in fact, may result in such systems being primarily developed from scratch using languages like C++, LISP, and Prolog.

A final architectural issue has to do with the requirement to access or embed conventional computing capabilities in material handling system design expert systems. There is virtually no need for such capabilities other than some basic mathematical facility for the equipment specification decision. For equipment selection decisions, some routing capability (network analysis or mathematical programming) or various assignment techniques are important. The system design problem, in general, requires a robust suite of computational options including routing, assignment, simulation, queueing, CAD, and similar capabilities. Thus, expert systems for material handling system design may or may not require embedded modeling capability depending on the specific design task addressed.

Expert System Interface Issues

A related issue has to do with the need for material handling design expert systems to interface with external databases. Equipment specification expert systems will be fact intensive in the sense that most of the knowledge in such systems is parameter data for the various equipment options included. However, little other data is necessary for these systems and it is unlikely that external databases would be incorporated to store such information. On the other hand, system specification expert systems will require much data of the kind likely to be maintained in external databases—manufacturing data, cost data, vendor information, and the like. Thus, there is a real requirement for an external database interface capability for material handling system design expert systems—this requirement decreases as the design decision becomes more specific.

Explanation capability is another interface issue which varies with the system design task. *Explanation* refers to the ability of an expert system to describe or relate the reasoning process involved in reaching a particular decision. Rule-based systems typically explain by showing the rule or sequence of rules invoked in arriving at a decision. Such a procedure is relatively simple involving little more than displaying text files of relevant individual rules. As knowledge representation structures become more complex and inferencing schemes more varied, explanation becomes more complicated. A system which reasons from principles, as a system specification expert system must ultimately do, will require an elegant explanation capability which may itself be guided by a complex inference process. Explanation, then, is a mixed bag in material handling system design expert systems ranging from a relatively simple to a very difficult task.

Learning poses an interesting challenge for developers of material handling system design expert systems. "Rote" learning has been implemented in equipment specification systems in the sense that the system maintains a file of previously made decisions and has the capability of comparing the current decision to the file. If a match is found (i.e., the same decision has been made), the system simply produces the historical recommendation without having to go through the decision logic. Obviously, for the much more complex system specification decision, such a simple approach will not work—the likelihood of duplicate decisions is virtually nil. It can be concluded that learning for complex systems design expert systems is a difficult challenge.

A final design issue that is interface-related has to do with the ease with which this class of expert systems may be maintained or kept current. Interestingly, the more specific the decision, the more dynamic the knowledge is likely to be and the more effort is required to maintain the system. For equipment specification, every time a vendor changes a design parameter, a price, or even a color, the knowledge base will need to be updated. The kind of knowledge required for the system specification design task is relatively stable and would require little updating over time; there is surely a relationship with learning in this connection.

To summarize, it is extremely important that developers recognize how various design, architecture, and interface issues will influence the requirements for material handling system design expert systems. Not to do so might result in trying to move a shovel full of dirt with a bulldozer or trying to move a mountain of dirt with a teaspoon.

17.6 OVERVIEW OF EXCITE

EXCITE (EXpert Consultant for In-plant Transportation Equipment) is a knowledge-based prototype developed to assist in the equipment type selection problem (Swaminathan, 1990). The system was designed to be used by engineers who are involved only part-time or infrequently in material handling design problems. A major effort in the system development was the compilation of the knowledge base through an extensive review of published guidelines, tables, and handbooks.

Features

A rule-based system, EXCITE uses forward chaining as its inference mechanism. It is coded in OPS83, a PC-based version of OPS5, and currently has 340 rules in its knowledge base. To make an equipment recommendation, the EXCITE system queries the user about the attributes of the handling problem. Because the system was developed with the objective of minimizing the number of attributes required to make a decision, the number of questions which the user must answer is minimized. Up to 28 attributes are considered in making a recommendation from the set of 35 alternatives; typically, user input is required for no more than 15 attributes. Tables 17.1 and 17.2 provide a list of the attributes and equipment alternatives, respectively. It should be noted that manual handling is considered as an option, but equipment used primarily for storage and warehousing is not considered.

One of the important features of the system is the consideration of equipment interfaces at each end of a move. EXCITE defines a move by its source and destination. The limits for a move consist of the farthest set of points for which the material type, e.g., pallet load, package, or unit, does not change. The material itself may change, but the material type cannot. Source and destination interface requirements are specifically considered in the equipment recommendation. For example, the positional accuracy requirements for the equipment would be different if the handling equipment for the move under consideration must interface with a robot versus a human operator.

EXCITE considers user preferences for flexibility, maintainability, and cost.

Table 17.1. Attributes Considered by EXCITE

1.	Accumulation capability (required or not)
2.	Aisle size (width)
3.	Area (fixed or variable)
4.	Automation (required or not)
5.	Bidirectional flow (required or not)
6.	Cross traffic (present or absent)
7.	Incline (exceed ten degrees or not)
8.	Interface (equipment interface requirements at source and destination)
9.	Load handled (uniform or variable)
10.	Loading/unloading (self-loading/unloading required or not)
11.	Material nature (sturdy or fragile)
12.	Material size (cubic volume)
13.	Material surface (flat rigid bottom or not)
14.	Material throughput (expected percent utilization of handling equipment)
15.	Material type (barstock, package, pallet load, unit)
16.	Material weight (pounds)
17.	Move course (straight or curved)
18.	Move distance (feet, from source to destination)
19.	Move flow (controlled movement required or not)
20.	Move frequency (regular/continuous or intermittent)
21.	Move path (fixed or variable)
22.	Move plane (change in level required or not)
23.	Move route (fixed or variable)
24.	Move type (machine loading/unloading, conveying, or transportation)
25.	Nature of loading (single or multiple loads per move)
26.	Positional accuracy (inches)
27.	Slope (decline, incline, or both)
28.	Truss height (feet)

The equipment recommendation includes a preference score, which indicates the degree to which the recommendation satisfies the user's preferences. For some situations, multiple recommendations are given (each with a preference score). The multiple recommendations are built into the rule base and are not determined by backtracking. A limited explanation capability is also available, and the use of certainty factors has been investigated.

Table 17.2. Equipment Options Considered in EXCITE

NONE			
1.	Manual		

POSITIONING DEVICES			
2.	Hoist	4.	Mechanized manipulator
3.	Robot	5.	Non-powered manipulator

MONORAILS			
6.	Heavy-duty powered monorail	8.	Hand-pushed monorail
7.	Light-duty powered monorail		

CRANES			
9.	Jib	11.	Gantry
10.	Bridge		

INDUSTRIAL TRUCKS			
12.	Pallet truck	16.	Tractor trailer
13.	Platform truck	17.	Side loader
14.	Hand truck	18.	Counterbalanced lift truck
15.	Walkie lift truck	19.	Narrow-aisle truck

AUTOMATED GUIDED VEHICLES			
20.	Tractor train	22.	Fork AGV
21.	Unit load carrier	23.	Light-duty AGV

CONVEYORS			
24.	Gravity roller	30.	Powered roller
25.	Gravity wheel	31.	Chain
26.	Gravity chute	32.	Inverted power and free
27.	Power and free	33.	Car on track
28.	Trolley	34.	Slat
29.	Belt	35.	In-floor towline

The present configuration of EXCITE is shown in Fig. 17.2. The system currently has

(1) An OPS83 interpreter
(2) Ten knowledge modules that incorporate rules
(3) An executive module that controls the overall system
(4) Two modules with rules for the query system
(5) A module with procedures for displaying equipment characteristics
(6) A module with initial procedures and attribute specifications

The program can be run on IBM PC-XTs.

Because of the consideration of the interface requirements, the analyst could potentially use the system in an iterative manner to select equipment types for a series of adjoining moves. However, it is recommended that EXCITE not be used in this manner without considering the combined performance of the linked moves. Selecting the best equipment type for individual moves does not guarantee the best solution for the combination of moves.

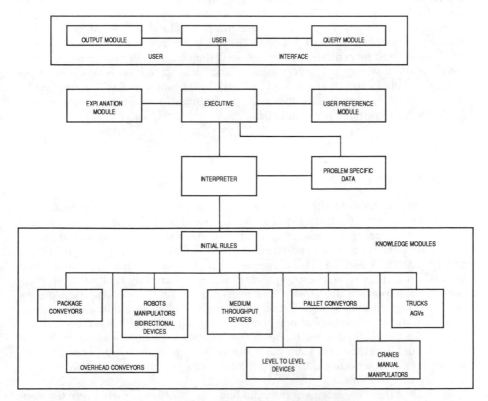

FIG. 17.2. Organization of EXCITE.

Example

As an illustration of a typical application of EXCITE, consider a situation requiring handling at a packing station where several different products are to be packed in corrugated cartons. Some of the cartons are to be immediately palletized for shipment. Other cartons are to be stored on shelves in a holding area prior to shipment. Carton sizes vary (based on the products to be packed) from $12'' \times 12'' \times 6''$ to $24'' \times 18'' \times 18''$. Carton weights range from 20 lb to 180 lb when packed. The packing is accomplished manually on a ball transfer table. The pallet is located adjacent to the packing station (a distance of 5 ft) and is on a lift table. Shelves for temporary storage are located 15 ft to 25 ft from the packing station. The peak handling requirement is 12 moves per hour, with an average requirement of 6 moves per hour. No obstacles exist in the movement path. In this situation, what handling device or devices would be appropriate?

In determining the equipment recommendations for this handling situation, EXCITE first asks the user the type of move (material transfer or maneuvering/transportation) and preferences for flexibility, maintainability, and cost. Next, the system examines the interface requirements at the beginning and end of the move. Here, the interface at the beginning of the move would be manual handling and/or the ball transfer table, and the interfaces at the end of the move include both the pallet and the shelves. Throughput is the next consideration, and the load requirements here might be classified as low or medium, based on the definition given by EXCITE. The move area might also be considered either fixed or variable, and the move distance is small. The material size is small, and the weight is low to medium. The recommendations based on these inputs include hoist, jib crane, and industrial manipulator. Each recommendation is scored on the basis of the user's preferences for the relative importance of flexibility, maintainability, and cost.

17.7 CONCLUSION

An effective material handling system is cirital to the efficient and productive operation of a manufacturing system. As discussed in this chapter, a hierarchial framework is appropriate for analyzing the scope of the material handling problem to be solved. For new products and manufacturing systems, the problem is one of material handling system specification. This effort should be integrated into the concurrent engineering process. Because handling and storage represent a major portion of the activities in the manufacturing enterprise, "design for handling" should be considered along with "design for manufacturability" and "design for assembly." When the major design variables have been determined, the second level of the hierarchy—equipment selection—becomes the primary focus. Interface issues are particularly important in this problem. Equipment specification occurs after selection of the equipment type and is most easily addressed by vendors.

In each of these categories of material handling problems, there is great potential for the development and application of knowledge-based systems. Current systems represent an initial step; there are many additional issues and opportunities that should attract researchers interested in material handling. However, the level of research activity will likely be influenced by the availability of funding for such efforts. Vendors would be the most likely candidates to lead in the development and maintenance of knowledge-based systems for the detailed equipment specification problem. For the system specification and equipment selection problems, the potential sources of support are less certain. It is certain, however, that there are significant savings to be obtained through better design decisions for material handling systems; knowledge-based tools can play a major role in making those decisions better.

REFERENCES

Armour, G. C., and Buffa, E. S. 1963. A heuristic algorithm and simulation approach to relative location of facilities. *Management Science* 9:294–309.

Dunkin, A. E. 1988. Analysis and design of storage and retrieval systems for tote-sized loads. Master's thesis, Georgia Institute of Technology, Atlanta, Goergia.

Eom, J. K., and Trevino, J. 1992. Hierarchical design of material handling and storage systems for electronics assembly. *Proc. of the 1992 International Material Handling Research Colloquium*, Milwaukee, Wisconsin, pp. 447–470.

Farber, J. B., and Fisher, E. L. 1985. MATHES: Material handling equipment selection expert system. NCSU-IE Technical Report #85-2, Department of Industrial Engineering, North Carolina State University.

Fisher, E. L. 1986. An AI-based methodology for factory design. *AI Magazine*, Fall, 72–85.

Fisher, E. L., and Maimon, O. Z. 1987. Integer and rule programming models for the specification and selection of robots. In *Artificial Intelligence: Implications for Computer Integrated Manufacture*, ed. A. Kusiak. Kempston, Bedford, U.K.: IFS (Publications) Ltd. and New York: Springer-Verlag.

Gabbert, P., and Brown, D. E. 1989. Knowledge-based computer-aided design of materials handling systems. *IEEE Transactions on Systems, Man, and Cybernetics* 19:188–196.

Grosseschallau, W., and Kusiak, A. 1985. An expert system for design of automated material handling systems (INSIMAS). *Material Flow* 2:157–166.

Hassan, M. M. D. 1983. A computerized model for the selection of materials handling equipment and area placement evaluation (SHAPE). Doctoral dissertation, Texas A&M University.

Jones, M. S., Malmborg, C. J., and Agee, M. H. 1985. Decision support system used for robot selection. *Industrial Engineering* 17:66–73.

Kusiak, A., and Heragu, S. S. 1987. The facility layout problem. *European Journal of Operational Research*, 29:229–251.

Lee, R. C., and Moore, J. M. 1967. CORELAP—Computerized relationship layout planning. *Journal of Industrial Engineering* 18:194–200.

Malmborg, C. J., Simons, G. R., and Agee, M. H. 1986. Knowledge engineering approaches to material handling equipment specification. *1986 Fall Industrial Engineering Conference Proceedings*, pp. 148–151.

Malmborg, C. J., Krishnakumar, B., Simons, G. R., and Agee, M. H. 1989. EXIT: A PC-based expert system for industrial truck selection. *International Journal of Production Research* 27:927–941.

Mellichamp, J. M., . Dixon, W. L., Jr., Sen, B., and Venkatachalam, A. R. 1991. An integrated approach to product/process design using knowledge-based methods. *Proc. 4th*

International Conference on Industrial Engineering Applications of Artificial Intelligence and Expert Systems, Kauai, Hawaii.

Mellichamp, J. M., Kwon, O.-J, and Wahab, A. 1990. FMS designer: An expert system for flexible manufacturing system design. *International Journal of Production Research* 28:2013–2024.

Mellichamp, J. M., Miller, D. M., and Wang, J. 1989. Computer-aided machine qualification. *International Journal of Quality and Reliability* 6:41–58.

Modern Materials Handling. 1966. Can you computerize equipment selection? 21:46–50.

Mullens, M. A., and Swart, W. W. 1992. Design synergy: Incorporating material handling considerations into concurrent engineering. *Proc. of the 1992 International Material Handling Research Colloquium*, Milwaukee, Wisconsin, pp. 354–359.

Schultz, G. A. 1980. Basic conveyor selection guidelines. *Plant Engineering Library*, pp. 1–63.

Seehof, J. M., and Evans, W. O. 1967. Automated layout design program. *Journal of Industrial Engineering* 12:690–695.

Shelton, D., and Jones, M. S. 1987. A selection method for automated guided vehicles. *Material Flow* 4:97–107.

Swaminathan, S. R. 1990. Development of a knowledge-based system for material handling equipment selection. Master's thesis, University of Alabama.

Tabibzadeh, K. 1985. An expert system approach to materials handling problems. Unpublished Doctoral dissertation, University of Houston.

Tompkins, J. A., and Reed, R., Jr. 1976. An applied model for the facilities design problem. *International Journal of Production Research* 14:583–595.

Tompkins, J. A., and White, J. A. 1984. *Facilities Planning.* New York: John Wiley and Sons.

White, J. A., and Apple, J. M., Jr. 1985. Material handling requirements are altered dramatically by CIM information links. *Industrial Engineering* 17:36–41.

INDEX

About the Editors

Cihan H. Dagli is an Associate Professor in the Department of Engineering Management at the University of Missouri—Rolla. His research interests are in intelligent manufacturing with special emphasis on artificial neural network applications. Dr. Dagli has authored and edited numerous other books and articles, has been British Council Research Fellow, and presently serves as lead editor of the ASME Press series on *Intelligent Engineering Systems through Artificial Neural Networks*.

Andrew Kusiak is Professor and Chair of the Department of Industrial and Management Engineering at the University of Iowa. Interested in applications of artificial intelligence and optimization in engineering design and manufacturing, Dr. Kusiak is the author and editor of numerous other books and articles in the field of intelligent manufacturing. He is also a frequent speaker at international meetings, professional seminars, and as a consultant to industrial corporations such as Motorola, John Deere, and Rockwell International.